To my patient and
understanding husband
Truman Nelson Helber

FOREWORD

Publication of a new textbook is an event of great importance, particularly for a field that represents a low prevalence group of children. The first books dealing with the education of blind children (Valentin Haüy, 1786, and Johann Wilhelm Klein, 1819) described the pioneering efforts and experiences in educating blind children. After these documentations of early attempts, other books appeared from time to time, written for those who were seeking information on the current state of the art and its scientific foundations, as well as the most advanced thinking in this field.

Textbooks in the narrower sense, that means texts especially written for academic teaching, became needed when teacher education outgrew the "apprenticeship" period and was taken over by institutions of higher education. The first of these textbooks was exclusively designed for teachers in residential schools. The few more recent ones were more public school oriented and thus followed the radical changes that took place beginning with the 1950s. Up to that time, less than 20 percent of all blind children attended public schools and more than 80 percent went to residential schools. Now, the enrollment is almost exactly reversed and about 80 percent attend public schools and 20 percent, residential schools. Credit for this reversal must go largely to the parents of blind and visually handicapped children on the one side, and to school boards, administrators, and teachers in public schools on the other side. The former knew and made known their children's needs and the latter responded by increasingly providing services on the local level.

There are two points of agreement among almost all textbooks: 1) No single kind of provision, may it be the residential school or any of the public school arrangements, will meet the needs of all blind and visually handicapped children. All have their advantages and deficiencies that must be weighed judiciously with every child's placement. Each one, if it provides quality education, can be the best environment for some but not for all, for some of their schooling time but not necessarily for all of it. Therefore, each has its function and should be available for those pupils who can best thrive in it. 2) Teachers of blind and visually handicapped children must be specifically, that is categorically, prepared for their profession in order to do justice to the very special needs of this group of children. Psychological and educational research show the many areas of development and functions in which lack or impairment of vision affects cognitive, emotional, social, and other aspects of life. No "generalist" can possibly meet these special needs.

I am certain that I have the consensus of all my professional friends and colleagues when I express to Geraldine Scholl our profound thanks for having undertaken the time, and even more importantly, the ego-consuming task of editing this volume and coordinating the contributions of so many select authors. To her and to all of them we are most grateful.

May this book fulfill their and our expectations and contribute to making life and the pursuit of happiness easier and more equal for blind and visually handicapped children and youth.

Berthold Lowenfeld, Ph.D.
Oakland, California
March 1986

TABLE OF CONTENTS

Study questions and Additional readings:
at the end of each chapter.

Education of the Visually Handicapped: A Selective Timeline:
Inside front and back covers
Geraldine T. Scholl, Mary Ellen Mulholland, Alberta Lonergan

LIST OF CHARTS, TABLES, and FIGURES

CHARTS

PREFACE

The 1960s and the 1970s witnessed a tremendous expansion in the number of teacher preparation programs in all areas of special education due largely to the infusion of federal financial assistance under P.L. 94-142, the Education of All Handicapped Children Act of 1975, and its predecessors, P.L. 85-926 of 1958 which initiated support for the preparation of professional personnel in the education of the mentally retarded and Section 301 of P.L. 88-164 of 1963, which expanded the preceding legislation to include all types of handicapped children. As a result, programs for the preparation of professional personnel in the education of visually handicapped pupils grew dramatically. Frances A. Koestler, in her 1976 study *The Unseen Minority: A Social History of Blindness in the United States*, could report only seven teacher preparation programs in as many states, three of which were full time, prior to P.L. 88-164. In April 1984 the *Alliance News*, a publication of the then Association for Education of the Visually Handicapped and the American Association of Workers for the Blind, included in their annual listing 43 teacher preparation programs in 25 states and Puerto Rico.

This increase in the number of teacher education programs was accompanied by a similar increase in the range of courses required to prepare all prospective teachers to meet the challenges and mandates of P.L. 94-142, specifically to be able to work in a variety of settings employing a variety of approaches based on the individual needs of all pupils. Concurrently with this expansion of programs, research demonstrated the positive results from visual efficiency training for pupils with severe visual impairments. Finally, there was increasing recognition that only small numbers of pupils are totally without usable vision. These factors spurred the trend toward preparing teachers to work with a broad range of pupils with diverse educational characteristics and degrees of visual impairment.

The evolution of available college texts during this period reflects these developments. *Education and Health of the Partially Seeing Child*, written by Winifred Hathaway of the National Society for the Prevention of Blindness (NSPB), now the National Society to Prevent Blindness, first published in 1943 by the Columbia University Press, became a standard text for colleges and universities preparing teachers of the partially seeing as well as a reference for school administrators, nurses, and other professionals concerned with the education of children with partial sight in special classes within the public schools. The book was subsequently revised in 1947 and again in 1954 by Mrs. Hathaway. After her death in 1954, a fourth edition was published in 1959, revised under the direction of Franklin M. Foote, then executive director of NSPB; Dorothy Bryan, assistant to the director, Division for Exceptional Children in the Illinois State Department of Public Instruction; and Helen Gibbons, consultant in education at NSPB.

No further revisions were made of the Hathaway book, because attitudes and practices were changing from a conservation or sight saving approach to one of making efficient use of limited vision. There were no comparable texts during this period devoted to educating children who were considered "blind" since most of these children were educated in residential schools where teachers were typically prepared through an apprenticeship system.

In the early 1970s, the Education Committee of NSPB and an ad hoc committee appointed by American Foundation for the Blind (AFB) met to draw up an outline and determine a time schedule for the publication of a college level textbook which would describe the specialized needs of visually handicapped children, both those considered as partially seeing and those classified as blind, and to describe techniques for their educational programs. These efforts culminated in the publication in 1973 by John Day Company of *The Visually Handicapped Child in School* edited by Berthold Lowenfeld and with contributions from a wide range of educators and researchers. This became the standard text and reference in most teacher education programs for the visually handicapped.

Although some of the material contained in *The Visually Handicapped Child in School* is still current, a number of events make it out of date, the most significant being the passage of P.L. 94-142, The Education of All Handicapped Children Act in 1975. In addition, research in education and special education as well as new developments in medicine and technology created the need for a new text. Under the initiative of AFB in 1981, work began on the planning and writing of *Foundations of Education for Blind and Visually Handicapped Children and Youth: Theory and Practice.*

The purpose of *Foundations of Education for Blind and Visually Handicapped Children and Youth: Theory and Practice* is to provide an overview of issues in educational theory and practice. It draws together current information about the nature and educational needs of blind and visually handicapped children and youth from birth to 21 years and details current best practice in their education. The authors of the chapters, all outstanding leaders in their respective fields, draw on current research and scholarly writing in each topical area. Chapters include extensive references to the work of others in the field and list supplementary resources for additional information.

Foundations of Education for Blind and Visually Handicapped Children and Youth: Theory and Practice is a basic resource on visually handicapped pupils and their educational program needs, including those with other impairments, and makes a contribution which should stimulate ongoing research and development in the field. The book is designed for students who are preparing to be special education teachers and for practicing teachers who wish to update their knowledge concerning visually handicapped pupils. It provides much useful information and discussion material for orientation and mobility instructors and for pre- and in-service special education teachers of other categorical groups who may need to know about the nature and special requirements of pupils who have a visual impairment in addition to other mental, physical, emotional/social, or learning problems. It is structured to serve as a basic reference tool for administrative and supervisory personnel and for support or ancillary service providers who have contact with pupils who have visual impairments. Such support personnel may, in our experience, include school psychologists, social workers, nurses, physical and occupational therapists, speech and language teachers, and regular teachers who have visually handicapped children enrolled in their classrooms. Finally, it is a source of information and analysis of current options for parents of visually handicapped children who now have greater involvement and rights in making decisions about their child's education under P.L. 94-142.

The content of *Foundation of Education for Blind and Visually Handicapped Children and Youth: Theory and Practice* is based on the assumption that readers are familiar with concepts of normal growth and development, with the educational needs and characteristics of all children, and with the curriculum, methods, and materials used in regular schools. The intent of certain chapters, e.g., 3, 9, 11, and 19, is to present an overview of the topic that should be covered in greater depth in other specific courses in the teacher preparation program.

Foundations of Education for Blind and Visually Handicapped Children and Youth: Theory and Practice begins with an historical background of the education of the visually handicapped. The rest of the book is divided into three sections. Part I provides a nine-chapter overview of basic information about visually handicapped children and youth essential for both pre- and in-service teachers who will be working with these pupils in an educational setting:

background information on definitions and terminology, numbers, and demographic characteristics

anatomy and physiology of the visual system

the impact of a visual impairment on growth and development

sensory/perceptual development including the use of other sensory systems in the educational process

increasing visual efficiency through the use of optical and nonoptical aids

the educational needs of infants and young children and their parents

needs of visually handicapped children and youth with other exceptionalities

special needs of children and youth with severe multiple handicaps

multicultural considerations in the educational program

Part II discusses in seven chapters the components that are basic to any educational program for visually handicapped children and youth:

assessment of educational needs through formal and informal procedures
development of the individualized education program
description of the various educational settings that are available for placement
the role and function of the teacher
working with parents in a cooperative relationship
the team approach to advocacy
educational resources necessary to implement the individualized education plan

Part III presents in four chapters special concerns related to the school curriulum:

materials and methods necessary for teaching oral and written communication skills
orientation and mobility
social and daily living skills
modifications required for teaching social studies, mathematics, science, foreign languages, creative arts, and physical education
The final chapter discusses the transition from school to adult life, the culmination of the educational program.

Foundations of Education for Blind and Visually Handicapped Children and Youth: Theory and Practice would not have been possible without the assistance of many professionals in the field. We thank the authors of the various chapters for their acceptance of our decisions to move materials they had written to other chapters in order to eliminate duplication and overlap. To Sally Mangold of the University of California at San Francisco, Rivka Greenberg, doctoral student at the University of Michigan, and Virginia Sowell of Texas Tech University, we are indebted for careful reviews and constructive comments on the entire manuscript. We are especially grateful to Marjorie Ward of The Ohio State University for her contribution to and editorial consultation on the entire manuscript, to Debra Budick and Bruce Rosenthal for their contributions to Chapter 3, and to Ken Stuckey for assistance with the timeline. For reviews of selected chapters, we thank Eva Friedlander, Doris Helge, Emilie M. Kief, Charles Moody, Michael Orlansky, Lee Robinson, Sally Rogow, Burton Voss, and William Winkley. Finally we are grateful to staff members, authors and nonauthors, of the American Foundation for the Blind for ideas and reviews of selected chapters.

This book would not have been possible without the encouragement and very able assistance of Mary Ellen Mulholland, director, Publications and Information Services Department at AFB, and staff members who worked on this book: Catherine Brooks, Beatrice Jacinto, Sauna Trenkle, Alberta Lonergan, Griffin Smith, Ann LaFargue-Peckham, Aleksander Christou, and others. I am grateful for their help and encouragement. Finally, special thanks to my husband for tolerating my numerous lengthy periods away from home and for sacrificing vacations, weekends, and evenings without my company while I was working on the book both at home and in New York. Without the help of these persons, this book would not have been possible.

Geraldine T. Scholl
Ann Arbor, Michigan
March 1986

CHAPTER **1**

Education for the Visually Handicapped: A Social and Educational History

Ferne K. Roberts

This chapter summarizes the significant developments in the education of blind and visually handicapped pupils in the United States over the last 150 years. The history of education of visually handicapped children and of professional preparation of their teachers, the development of residential schools in the United States, the establishment of day school programs for blind and partially sighted children, and the evolution of tactile reading and writing are traced. The genesis of the field's national professional agencies and organizations is also discussed.

Throughout history there have been stories told about remarkable and talented blind people who managed, often with insightful assistance, to educate themselves and to make significant contributions to their societies. Homer is perhaps the first name that comes to mind: the *Iliad* and the *Odyssey* were known before 700 B.C. More recent illustrious blind persons are Nicholas Saunderson (1682-1739), a noted professor of mathematics at Cambridge University, whose sponsor was Isaac Newton; Francois Huber (1750-1831), a Swiss naturalist who studied the life of bees; and Maria Theresia von Paradis (1759-1824), a Viennese pianist and music teacher for whom Mozart wrote the Concerto for Piano and Orchestra in B-Flat. However, until the mid-eighteenth century none of the scattered attempts to educate blind children provided the impetus for the development of systematic programs. This chapter presents the highlights of the social and educational history of formal education for visually handicapped children from that point.

France was the cradle of new attitudes toward blindness and of the first school for blind children. The philosophical groundwork was laid by Diderot, physician to King Louis XV and a great Enlightenment philosopher. In 1749 he published *Letter on the Blind for the Use of Those Who See.* Much of this essay was based on Diderot's contacts with two of the outstanding blind people mentioned above: Nicholas Saunderson and Maria Theresia von Paradis. The competence

of these two people convinced him that blind people could lead normal lives and that they could be intellectually competent (Diderot, 1749).

Diderot and his contemporaries, including Paine, Jefferson, and Franklin in the United States, espoused the needs, rights, value, and obligations of the individual. How fortunate it is for us that he extended his philosophy to include blind individuals!

The next giant step was taken in Paris in 1784 by Valentin Haüy when he established the *Institution des Jeunes Aveugles* (Institution for Blind Youth). He attributed his interest in educating blind children to two experiences. One night in a cafe he saw a troupe of blind men in grotesque costumes performing a skit which elicited pity and ridicule from the audience; his revulsion made him resolve to teach blind people to read so that they could earn their living in more dignified ways. Several years later he attended a concert given by Maria Theresia von Paradis. After the concert, Haüy was intrigued to learn about her ability to read and write using pin-pricked letters (Koestler, 1976; Lowenfeld, 1975).

Haüy immediately set about fulfilling his earlier pledge to educate blind children. His first student, Francois Lesueur, was a bright adolescent who had been supporting his widowed mother and siblings by begging. Francois agreed to study half the day and to continue begging the other half; eventually Haüy subsidized his education so that he could give up begging entirely. The Institution's enrollment grew rapidly, partially as a result of demonstrations of student accomplishments given wherever Haüy could find audi-

Author's note: Deep appreciation goes to Marguerite Levine, Archivist at the American Foundation for the Blind, 1960-1985, for help in locating primary sources and checking facts and dates.

ences. He believed that all students should study music and acquire vocational skills, and it was his students' ability to read and write, to perform music, and to carry out everyday activities that he showed off. Admiration for their competence, not pity for their blindness, was what he hoped to engender for

Valentin Haüy, producer of first embossed type for touch reading (1745–1822).

his students. In 1786 King Louis XVI requested Haüy to take about 30 of his pupils to Versailles for six days during the Christmas season so that he could see the effects of their education. Haüy hoped that the King would take the Institution under his protection but no such help was offered (Illingworth, 1910).

During the French Revolution the Institution did operate under state protection, but in 1799 Napoleon abruptly ordered the pupils to a home for blind adults which had a limited educational program, causing Haüy to accept requests from several other European countries, including Russia, to help establish residential schools.

In spite of political upheavals in France and in the life of his school, Haüy's contribution was a lasting one. He founded the first school for blind children, which became a model; he emphasized reading and fostered the development of embossed print; and he believed in the vocational potential of blind people and instituted vocational training at his school.

The third great contribution to the advancement of education for blind children was made by Louis Braille in the early 1800s. The genesis of the embossed dot code and Braille's adaptation of it are discussed in the section on embossed writing later in this chapter. The significance of Braille's contribution is critical: without a system of effective communication through reading and writing, the education of blind children would undoubtedly have remained as it had been through the Middle Ages (Lowenfeld, 1975).

DEVELOPMENT OF EDUCATIONAL PROGRAMS IN THE UNITED STATES

It was over half a century after the foundation of Haüy's Institution that the first schools for blind children were opened in the United States. Three private schools were then founded almost simultaneously. In 1829 the New England Asylum for the Blind, subsequently named Perkins Institution and Massachusetts Asylum for the Blind, and now called Perkins School for the Blind, was incorporated. It opened its doors to students in Boston in July 1832, under the direction of Samuel Gridley Howe who had visited several European schools the year before. He would undoubtedly have been the first to open the school's doors had he not become involved in an effort to free Polish refugees who were interned in Prussia and been imprisoned as an "emissary." Lafayette was one of those who intervened on his behalf before he could return home (Richards, 1909).

In New York City, the New York Institution for the Blind, now called the New York Institute for the Blind, was incorporated in 1831 and opened in March 1832 with Dr. John Dennison Russ as director.

The third school, the Pennsylvania Institution for the Instruction of the Blind, was founded under the aegis of prominent Quakers and opened in 1833 in

Louis Braille (1809–1852)

Philadelphia with Julius R. Friedlander as principal. In 1899 the school moved to another section of Philadelphia, Overbrook, and was renamed Overbrook School for the Blind. The move to Overbrook had been preceded by the construction of a campus with cottage-style living, modern classrooms, and landscaped grounds. The head of the school at the time, Edward E. Allen, a former teacher from Perkins, so impressed the field that he was asked to return to Perkins as director in 1906 (Koestler, 1976).

The first three and several subsequent schools were privately financed and were inspired by men who were acquainted with the Institute for Blind Youth in Paris and other newly founded residential schools in Europe. The European residential school model and

Samuel Gridley Howe (1801–1876)

the fact that in the early nineteenth century it was fashionable for the well-to-do to send their children to boarding schools made it seem logical and desirable to establish residential schools for blind children in the United States (Irwin, 1955). In 1837 the first state-supported school was opened in Ohio in response to the view that children, including blind children, were entitled to a free, public education. Between 1832 and 1875 thirty public and private schools were established. The majority of the 49 presently existing residential schools were established before 1900, often just after statehood was achieved. Since 1900 several residential schools have been established to serve multiply handicapped children. Nine states have never had residential schools: Alaska, Delaware, Maine, Nevada, New Hampshire, New Jersey, Rhode Island, Vermont, and Wyoming (Bledsoe, 1971). These states have traditionally paid tuition to send blind children who prefer or require residential school placement to schools in neighboring states.

Residential school education of black children who were blind tended to follow the segregation or integration patterns of their various geographical areas. Before the Civil War and the Emancipation Proclamation, it is doubtful whether any black blind children were educated in the South, since education was largely denied to their sighted siblings. Slowly,

southern residential schools began to open separate facilities for these children. In 1931 there were 10 separate departments in residential schools and five independently administered schools for black children (Koestler, 1976). Generally the programs for these children were inferior to those for white children. One of the reasons for this was the poor quality of equipment and educational materials which were often hand-me-downs from the departments for white children with the frequently disastrous result that the dots in braille books were so worn down that they were impossible to read. Another reason was that black teachers were often unable to attend the limited number of segregated training facilities or to afford the cost of travel to nonsegregated facilities in other parts of the country (Koestler, 1976).

Throughout the nineteenth century residential schools were usually the sole resources for the education of visually handicapped children. However, the segregated residential concept came under attack when the first schools were founded. Howe himself, although he helped found or dedicate several residential schools, was an outspoken advocate of public day school education. As early as his visit to European schools in 1831, he summed up his impressions by saying that they should serve "as beacons to warn rather than lights to guide" (Richards, 1909, p. 147). On the positive side, Howe seems to have come home with three convictions that helped him shape the

Edward E. Allen (1861–1950)

educational program of his school: each blind child must be considered as an individual and be educated according to his interests and abilities; the curriculum of the residential school should conform as closely as possible to that of the public day schools, with added stress on music and crafts; blind students must be trained to take their places in the social and economic life of their communities (Lowenfeld, 1973).

Chart 1.1   Founding dates of residential schools in the United States

Name of School	Date of Founding
Perkins School for the Blind	1832
New York Institute for the Education of the Blind	1832
Overbrook School for the Blind (Pennsylvania)	1833
Ohio State School for the Blind	1837
Virginia School for the Deaf and the Blind	1839
Kentucky School for the Blind	1842
Tennessee School for the Blind	1844
Governor Morehead School (North Carolina)	1845
Indiana School for the Blind	1847
Mississippi School for the Blind	1848
Wisconsin School for the Visually Handicapped	1848
South Carolina School for the Deaf and the Blind	1849
Illinois Braille and Sight-Saving School	1849
Missouri School for the Blind	1850
Louisiana State School for the Blind	1852
Georgia Academy for the Blind	1852
Maryland School for the Blind	1853
Iowa Braille and Sight Saving School	1853
Texas School for the Blind	1856
Alabama Institute for the Deaf and the Blind	1858
Arkansas School for the Blind	1859
Michigan School for the Blind	1865
Minnesota Braille and Sight Saving School	1866
Kansas School for the Visually Handicapped	1867
California School for the Blind	1867
New York State School for the Blind	1868
West Virginia School for the Deaf and the Blind	1870
Oregon State School for the Blind	1873
Colorado School for the Deaf and the Blind	1874
Nebraska School for the Visually Handicapped	1875
Florida School for the Deaf and the Blind	1885
Washington State School for the Blind	1886
Western Pennsylvania School for Blind Children	1890
Montana School for the Deaf and the Blind	1893
Connecticut Institute for the Blind	1893
Utah School for the Blind	1896
South Dakota School for the Blind	1900
New Mexico School for the Visually Handicapped	1903
Lavelle School for the Blind (New York)	1904
Virginia School at Hampton	1906
Idaho State School for the Deaf and the Blind	1906
Oklahoma School for the Blind	1907
North Dakota School for the Blind	1908
Arizona State School for the Deaf and the Blind	1912
Hawaii School for the Deaf and the Blind	1914
Royer-Greaves School for the Blind (Pennsylvania)	1921
Instituto Loiza Cordero Para Ninos Ciegos (Puerto Rico)	1921
Louisiana State School for Blind at Southern University	1922
Hope School for Blind Multiple Handicapped Children	1957

Source: C.W. Bledsoe, The family of residential schools, *Blindness*, (1971), pp. 25-26.

In his annual report of 1850, Howe voiced concern for some of the negative aspects of segregated education:

> Now when a hundred of these children are brought together in an institution formed for training and instructing them in common, it is manifest that different moral influences begin to bear upon them, and to mould them into new shapes, or rather to stamp deeper certain original peculiarities which the teacher would fain efface. With all the advantages for intellectual culture, there mingle certain influences which we find to be unfavorable. (Howe, 1851, p. 14–15)

One of Howe's most memorable and frequently quoted statements was made in 1866 when he delivered an address at the laying of the cornerstone of the New York State School for the Blind at Batavia.

> All great establishments in the nature of boarding schools, where sexes must be separated; where there must be boarding in common, and sleeping in congregate dormitories; where there must be routine and formality, and restraint, and repression of individuality; where the charms and refining influences of the true family relationship cannot be had—all such institutions are unnatural, undesirable, and very liable to abuse. We should have as few of them as possible, and those few should be kept as small as possible. (Howe, 1866, p. 38)

In 1871, at the convention of the American Association of Instructors of the Blind (AAIB)—later called the Association for the Education of the Visually Handicapped—Howe deplored the social sequestration of residential schools and advocated public day school education in all subjects not requiring visible illustration (Howe, 1871). He also described a cottage system which he had recently instituted at Perkins as an alternative to large dormitories. There were strong objections to this idea from several residential school superintendents, notably Wiggins (1873) of the Ontario School and Loomis (1873) of the Illinois school. Both felt that children must be educated for society, and not for family life, and that the cottage plan would foster an unhealthy attachment to family-style living in adulthood (Frampton & Kearney, 1953)—an argument difficult to understand in the light of twentieth-century beliefs regarding child development.

The cottage system was nevertheless adopted in 1911 by John Bledsoe, superintendent of the Maryland School for the Blind. He was committed to the notion that blind children could be perfectly normal and that small living units would foster normalcy. His was the first totally cottage-family plan residential school (Bledsoe, 1971).

Another of Howe's innovations, the education of a deaf-blind girl, was greeted with national and international praise and astonishment. Undoubtedly it was his conviction that each child's course of study should be based on interest and ability, which led to his enthusiastic admission of Laura Bridgman to Perkins in 1837. Laura had contracted scarlet fever at the age of 18 months. Two sisters and a brother died of the disease and Laura was left deaf and blind. Howe heard about her, found her family, and convinced her parents that she could be educated at Perkins. As it turned out, Laura lived the rest of her life there.

Howe himself provided much of Laura's instruction. She learned to read raised letters, at first associating words with objects by rote. Howe was with her when

*Laura Bridgman (R) with Oliver Caswell at Perkins
(1829-1889)*

her breakthrough in understanding the meaning of language came about: "At once the countenance lighted up with a human expression—it was an immortal spirit, eagerly seizing upon a new link of union with other spirits" (Howe, 1840, p. 26). Laura was the chief attraction at Perkins on exhibition days and many famous people, including Charles Dickens (1907) in 1842, went to see her.

In 1841 Oliver Caswell, left deaf and blind from scarlet fever at age three, was admitted to Perkins and he and Laura were educated together. Howe described Laura as brighter and more inquisitive and Oliver as jollier and friendlier (Schwartz, 1956).

Helen Keller was, of course, a later notable deaf-blind person to be associated with Perkins. Surely her life would have been vastly different if Howe had not involved himself directly in the education of deaf-blind children. When Howe died in 1876 his son-in-law, Michael Anagnos, succeeded him as director of Perkins. Anne Sullivan had just graduated from Perkins when, in 1887, Anagnos heard from Helen Keller's parents. Helen's mother had read Dickens' *American Notes*, in which he referred to Howe and Laura Bridgman. Anagnos recommended Anne, gave her access to Howe's extensive notes on his methods of instructing Laura and Oliver, and lent his moral support to her efforts. He later arranged for Helen and Anne to live at Perkins as guests for three years (Koestler, 1976).

Day School Classes for Blind Children

The first sustained attempt to place children in a public day school setting began in Scotland. In 1872 the Scottish Education Act included provisions for educating blind children among sighted children in public schools. This was most likely the first legislation which officially called for integrated education of blind pupils with their nonhandicapped peers (Lowenfeld, 1975).

In the late 1890s in Chicago, parents tried to persuade the Board of Education to set up an institution for blind children so that they could go to school near their homes. Frank H. Hall, then superintendent of the Illinois School for the Blind, went to Chicago several times to convince the educational authorities

Helen Keller (L) with Anne Sullivan

not to set up a special institution but rather to enroll the children in the regular classes making only the special provisions necessary to enable them to complete their work. He believed that contacts and competition with their sighted peers with whom they would live and work in the future was preferable to segregation during the school years (Irwin, 1955). In September 1900, Hall released one of his teachers, John Curtis, to carry out an experimental program in Chicago. Four years later Curtis reported that there were 24 blind pupils in grade school and five in high school. He felt that teaching blind children in public schools had limitations and would not be advisable for all children but that the plan justified strong consideration (Koestler, 1976). Curtis initiated a plan which was to be widely copied. He divided the city of Chicago into geographical grids and established a special room in one conveniently located school within each grid. Blind children spent most of their time in the regular classes. Special teachers were employed to teach braille and typing, and to help the blind students achieve full participation in the schools (Abel, 1957; Irwin, 1955).

The Chicago program's effect was pervasive. In 1905 Cincinnati established day classes in a special school building, but in 1913 the classes were reorganized so that blind children could spend some time in regular classes. In 1907 a teacher from the Chicago program went to Milwaukee to set up classes in the public school system there. The Board of Education in New York City, during its deliberations regarding the

Frank H. Hall (1841–1911)

establishment of public day school classes in 1909, invited Hall from Illinois to confer with them. At that meeting he made an impassioned plea for the education of blind with sighted children:

> Three cities have inaugurated the wise plan of teaching blind children in classes in the public school. I think the method of segregating the blind, keeping them not with the class with whom they will live after they leave school, cutting them off from society, is the greatest mistake that was ever made. The public school is the place to educate a blind boy, associating him with the people with whom he will associate when he leaves school. (Irwin, 1955, p. 149)

New York followed Hall's advice and in 1909 set up a program modeled after the Chicago grid system. Cleveland set up a similar program in the same year and other cities around the country opened classes in the next five years. In 1920, Seattle opened an integrated program but then changed it into a segregated system which caused many parents to send their children to the state residential school at Vancouver where there was better equipment (Irwin, 1955).

Personal interviews with some of the early teachers and their students in New Jersey, Ohio, and Minnesota indicate that the initial programs in these states were truly integrated (Taylor, 1978). Students were enrolled in the regular classes and went to the special teacher only for specialized instruction, with only the youngest students spending prolonged periods in the special room.

Education of Partially Sighted Children

Until the beginning of this century there were no concerted efforts to provide special educational programs for children with limited but useful vision. Some partially sighted children, particularly those who had high myopia, attended residential schools for blind children, where, even as late as the 1960s, they were taught to read braille, sometimes being blindfolded so they would not read with their eyes. As long as it was believed that children with low vision would harm their eyes by using them for close work, this practice was viewed as humanitarian rather than restrictive. In Chapter 6, "Low Vision and Visual Efficiency," the use of vision will be fully discussed.

In England at the beginning of the century, a new type of educational program which had far-reaching influence was initiated. Dr. James Kerr, the first medical director of the London School Board, initiated a school health program in which one of the first undertakings was a survey of the vision of all children. In connection with this survey, Dr. Bishop Harman, an ophthalmologist, was appointed to take charge of ophthalmological services in London schools for blind children. He found many who were not blind but had high myopia, a visual impairment that required special educational programs. In 1907 Kerr prepared a report of these findings for the Second International Congress of School Hygiene, stating that these low vision children were not blind and should not be in schools for the blind, but should be given an education adapted to their needs. A member of the education committee of the London County Council heard the report and subsequently requested the approval of the Council for a program based on Kerr's ideas. Thus in 1908, a class, the first in the world devoted specifically to the education of partially sighted children, was opened. The class, housed in a building on the playground of an elementary school, was called the "Myope School" to distinguish it from the school for blind children (Hathaway, 1959). The pupils went to the elementary school for all oral and some other work because Kerr felt that partially sighted children should not be entirely separated from sighted children. A sign over the door of the school read "Reading and Writing Shall Not Enter Here," in accordance with the prevailing opinion that to use residual vision was to further reduce it (Hathaway, 1959). After some experience, however, large letters on chalkboards and large rubber-stamp letters were allowed (Hathaway, 1959).

Dr. Edward E. Allen, director of the Perkins Institution, attended a conference in London, heard of the Myope School and visited classes there. Allen had already recognized the educational and psychological problems of the partially sighted students in his school, and he felt that children with some vision were apt to develop a superior attitude that was almost certain to be devastatingly deflated when they returned to their own communities. These pupils were also annoyed with regulations which were necessary for the safety of the students who were blind. Blind children often asked the partially sighted students to serve as guides, which caused overwork and fatigue. Many of the partially sighted students in his school, accordingly, left school before graduation, having found the setting burdensome (Hathaway, 1959).

With these problems in mind, Allen encouraged the School Committee of Boston to open the first class in the United States for partially sighted pupils in April, 1913 in Roxbury. He also espoused the inclusion of children whose lowered vision resulted from various causes in addition to myopia, in contrast with the London program. This class, called the "Defective Eye-Sight Class" was housed in a small, unused school building so the children were inevitably segregated from classes with sighted children. Allen received approval to use funds from Perkins to purchase materials for the new class (Hathaway, 1959; Merry, 1933).

The second class was started in September, 1913, by Robert Irwin, director of the program for visually handicapped children in Cleveland. He placed blind and partially sighted students in separate classes and

Robert B. Irwin (1883–1951)

saw to it that each group had materials suited to students' needs. The children in this program spent part of each day in the regular classes (Hathaway, 1959; Merry, 1933).

Robert Irwin also pioneered the earliest known efforts to encourage partially sighted children to read print. In 1914 he did research to discover what type size and style would be easiest to read. He had the first large print books printed in 36 point, clearface type which was especially developed for the purpose.

In 1919 Irwin conducted further tests to determine the relative legibility of certain standard type faces. It was determined that 24 point Caslon Boldface was the best and it was widely used for many years (Hathaway, 1959).

Irwin was influential in securing the passage by his state legislature of a law that subsidized public school classes for blind and partially sighted children. He was appointed to the position of statewide supervisor for visually handicapped children, the first in the country (Koestler, 1976).

The Beginning of the Second Century of Education of Visually Handicapped Children

A century after the first residential schools were established in the United States, the nature of educational programs for visually handicapped students was being reconsidered. Factors which influenced the growing uncertainty ranged from John Dewey's educational philosophy which focused on individual children and their learning styles and needs to the individualized rehabilitation of war-blinded veterans who subsequently demonstrated their ability to carry on as responsible workers, husbands, fathers, and citizens. Also, research on child growth and development indicated that children grew best in their own families. Parents and professionals alike began to demand local school programs which would allow school placement decisions to be based on children's needs and parents' preferences.

Not the least of the factors which shook the field of education for visually handicapped students was a book by Thomas Cutsforth, *The Blind in School and Society*, first published in 1933. Cutsforth was blind from the age of 11 and had attended a residential school for seven years. As a doctoral candidate he conducted research in several residential schools which led him to condemn the "establishment" in his book. In addition, he included chapters on topics which were then considered unorthodox: The Phantasy Life of the Blind; Sex Behavior of the Blind; Personality Problems in Institutions for the Blind; and Verbalism—Words versus Reality.

However, until the mid-nineteen forties the ideas of Cutforth and others who wanted to change the philosophy of education of visually handicapped children had limited effect on actual practice for one straightforward reason: a number of medical advances, such as the use of silver nitrate in the eyes of newborns to prevent ophthalmia neonatorum and the widespread use of immunizations for diphtheria, measles, scarlet fever, and smallpox, had effectively reduced the incidence of visual handicaps. Thus there was adequate space in residential schools and limited pressure on public day schools to establish programs.

Then, within a period of fifteen years, the incidence of visual handicaps shot up as a result of two disastrous epidemics. Retinopathy of Prematurity (ROP), formerly retrolental fibroplasia (RLF), which primarily affected premature infants of low birth weight, came first. It was estimated that between 1949 and 1956 the population of visually handicapped children increased by 39 percent as a result of ROP (Spungin, 1977). Second, the rubella epidemics of 1964-66 left in their wake about 30,000 handicapped children, 15 to 20 percent of whom had serious eye defects (Koestler, 1976; Lowenfeld, 1975).

From the mid-forties on, in America, the need for educational programs, residential and day school alike, outstripped the establishment's capacity to develop and expand programs and to prepare teachers, houseparents, and support personnel. The two national professional agencies in the field of the visually handicapped, The American Foundation for the Blind and The National Society for the Prevention of Blindness, sponsored conferences, work sessions, inservice and preservice programs and provided funds for scholarships to prospective teachers in an effort to meet the need for teachers.

Both residential and day schools were beleaguered by parents and professionals alike to admit this new generation of visually handicapped children. The need was particularly difficult to meet because many of the children from these epidemics were multiply handicapped. Since the leaders of most residential schools had fostered the image of the elite boarding school, they were reluctant to enroll students who did not appear to fit into the academic curriculum. Local public schools, many of which had never had programs for visually handicapped students, did not have qualified teachers or support personnel, and they had long histories of referring all legally blind children to the residential schools. Under these pressured circumstances it is easy to understand why the old debates about residential versus day school programs arose with renewed vigor.

In the mid-fifties, the American Foundation for the Blind introduced a list of preferred educational options to give a framework to the debates:
1. Education in a public or private school for the blind;
2. Education with sighted students in public or private schools, together with a resource or special class teacher available during the entire school day;
3. Education with sighted students in public or private schools with itinerant teaching services available at regular or needed intervals (Lowenfeld, 1956, p. 138).

In the end, both residential and day schools initiated, modified or expanded programs. The two most significant results were that 1) many residential schools redefined their missions and set up facilities for multiply handicapped children, and 2) many day schools in-

itiated or expanded programs, with the result that while in 1948 less than 10 percent of legally blind children were in day schools, more than 80 percent were there in 1980. Later chapters in this book will provide details about program changes which were designed to meet the needs of these new populations.

Tactile Reading and Writing

The education of blind children did not truly begin until a methodology—a workable system of reading and writing—was devised. Early efforts to resolve this problem included a system of knots on a length of twine, writing on wax tablets, and the use of carved-wood Roman letters (Illingworth, 1910; Lowenfeld, 1971). None of these gave rise to an enduring, workable system.

Valentin Haüy and his first student noticed that the reverse sides of printed pages had tactually legible characters. At that time printers routinely used wet paper for printing; thus the paper itself took on the forms of letters to some extent. Haüy had letters cast in reverse so that when printed on wet paper they left tactile impressions in correct position and order. Subsequently he modified the letters somewhat to make them easier to read. For writing, his students used a metal pen with a rounded tip to produce raised letters in reverse on the back of heavy paper (Illingworth, 1910; Lowenfeld, 1973). This system for reading and writing was used at the residential school in Paris until 1854, and in all the other early schools in Europe and America.

The Beginnings of Braille

Louis Braille, born in 1809 near Paris, was blinded at the age of three while playing with one of his father's harness-making tools. At first he attended his local village school but at age 10 he was admitted to the Royal Institution for Blind Youth in Paris. That school emphasized music as a vocational goal for many of its students and Louis subsequently became a church organist. At the age of 19, he was asked to join the teaching staff at the school and it was there in 1829, at age 20, that he published an explanation of his embossed dot code which he believed would be superior to the embossed letters which Haüy employed as a means of reading. By 1834 he had perfected the code for literary braille and was at work on a code for music notation. The officials at the Institution were not easily convinced that Braille's dot system was more effective than the embossed letter system which Haüy had first developed. The teachers did not like the system because they had to memorize a new code and the administrators felt that the dot code set blind people apart. However, the students to whom Braille had taught his system preferred it and finally, in 1844, when a new building was being dedicated, Guadet, the vice-principal of the Institution, described the raised-dot system and paid tribute to Braille (Roblin, 1960).

Braille's point system was based on the work of an army artillery officer, Charles Barbier, who in 1821 devised a raised dot code which could be read by touch during night maneuvers. "Ecriture Nocturne" had a 14-dot cell, seven vertical dots in two rows. Barbier also devised a slate and stylus, very similar to present-day equipment, for writing messages to fellow officers. Barbier's code was demonstrated at the Paris school and it was then that Braille began work on his codes (Roblin, 1960). He soon realized that the seven-dot-high cell was impossible for children to cover with their finger tips. Hence he developed the cell of three vertical dots in two rows. His code did not employ the fewest dots for the most frequently used letters in the alphabet and this fact was one of several reasons why other systems were devised and the War of the Dots, as it came to be called, was waged in the United States and Britain for almost 80 years (Irwin, 1955; Koestler, 1976).

Braille died of pulmonary consumption in 1852 and was buried in his home town, Coupvray (Roblin, 1960). On the centennial of his death, his body was removed to the Pantheon in Paris. This proposed removal so incensed the citizens of Coupvray that the government authorities finally made one concession: the bones from Braille's hands still lie in an urn at his original grave site.

Tactile Reading and Writing in United States Schools

When the first three residential schools for blind children were established in the United States in the early 1830s, they depended heavily on equipment from Europe. Thus, they adopted the embossed Roman letter system used by Haüy. Braille had published an article about his proposed dot code in 1829 but few people paid any attention to it. Educators felt that embossed letters had the advantage of being easily read by teachers and of not setting blind people apart from sighted readers (Irwin, 1955).

Samuel G. Howe, director of the Perkins Institution, developed an embossed letter type, Boston Line Type, which was an angular modification of Roman letters. In 1853 and for the next fifty years, books were embossed in this type at Perkins. Howe remained adamantly opposed to braille throughout his life, referring to it as "Choctaw" (Irwin, 1955).

In the early 1860s, Dr. Simon Pollak, a board member of the Missouri School for the Blind, observed the use of braille in schools in Europe. As a result of his enthusiastic description, his school officially adopted braille. At about the same time William Bell Wait, teacher and later superintendent of the New York Institution for the Blind, tried to get the schools in Boston and Philadelphia to join him in adopting braille. When they refused, he set to work on a system of his own—New York Point, which resembled a braille character turned on its side. Capital letters were modified by the removal of one to three dots to create

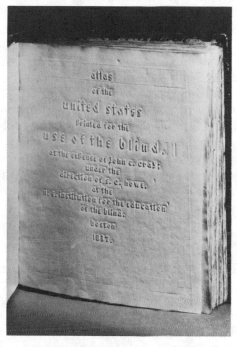

Boston Line Type developed by Howe

lower case letters. At a meeting of AAIB in 1871, New York Point was endorsed and recommended for use in the schools for blind children (Wait, 1871).

After 1900, Boston Line Type began to disappear and almost equal numbers of American schools used New York Point and American Braille, which was an adaptation of braille developed by Joel W. Smith, a teacher at Perkins, after Howe's death. American braille provided for capitalization by a dot prefix and for the use of fewer dots for the letters occuring most frequently in the English language (Lowenfeld, 1973; Irwin, 1955).

This is but a brief overview of the "War of the Dots." In 1909 Helen Keller, in pleading for the adoption of braille by the New York City day school classes, dramatized the issue when she indicated that she had to read four different embossed codes in order to have adequate access to the available publications (Lowenfeld, 1973). Finally in 1932, American and British committees signed an agreement to adopt Standard English Braille as the uniform type, a century after Louis Braille presented his code.

The feasibility of a blind student's writing an embossed code seems to have commanded relatively little attention amidst the reading controversies. We can only assume that nineteenth century scholarship for blind children was less based on ability to write; that the battles over embossed systems obscured the writing problem; or that educators accepted as fact that slow and labored writing was the fate of blind children. However, in 1892, Frank H. Hall, superintendent of the Illinois residential school, effectively solved a large part of the writing problem. His Hall Braille Writer was basically an adaptation of the typewriter, with a moveable carriage and six keys separated in the middle by a space bar. Although educators believed that young pupils could not operate the Hall Writer and that anyhow, children should first learn to use the slate and stylus, the mechanical writer greatly enhanced educational opportunities for blind students. In the 1940s, the American Foundation for the Blind produced its own braillewriter which, however, was not successful. In 1950 the Howe Press at Perkins School for the Blind produced the Perkins Brailler, an easier-to-use adaptation of Hall's machine.

CONCEPTS REGARDING USE OF VISION

As we have seen, the earliest history of education of children with partial vision was based on the premise that to use residual vision was to lose it. "Sight conservation" and "sight-saving" were terms used to identify special educational programs for these children and the chief role of their teachers was to provide an education which entailed little or no reading or other visual tasks. Hathaway (1959) recommended that "the special teacher is to check the program in order to see that . . . periods of close eye work are not scheduled so that one immediately follows another. . ." (p.99). In fact, teachers spent many hours reading to pupils. Sometime in the 1930s, ophthalmologists began to reverse this prevailing belief and to suggest that use of vision did not reduce it and that, on the contrary, children could learn to use their remaining vision to greater advantage through practice (Barraga, 1973; Faye, 1970). Needless to say, this opinion was viewed with skepticism and it is probable that even today many people are secretly half afraid that the "new" theory is wrong. Slowly, it gained acceptance as evidenced by the changes in names of programs, in roles of teachers, and in production of educational materials. The first step toward susbstantial acceptance of print reading for partially sighted children was marked by the decision of the American Printing House for the Blind, in 1947, to provide large print books and by the establishment of Stanwix House, a publisher of large type texts at about the same time.

One factor which slowed the trend toward use of residual vision and toward basing mode of reading on visual function rather than on medical diagnosis was related to a lack of educational definitions of visual handicaps. The definition of legal blindness, which was adopted in 1934 by the American Medical Association and was subsequently included in the Aid to the Blind Title of the Social Security Act of 1935, has been used for over four decades as the eligibility criterion for receipt of benefits and, by default, as the basis for educational decisions. This definition calls all who have central (distance) visual acuity of 20/200 or less in the better eye, after correction, or who have certain visual field deficits, legally blind. In a trend which defied logic, many children who fit within this definition were labeled, thought of, and educated as blind persons and their education often took place in residential schools. Unthinking acceptance of this definition and the taboo against use of vision literally locked children with useful vision into a world of confusion. They knew they could see certain things, yet at school and often at home they were refused the use of books with regular type and pictures. They were taught braille. In fact, they were sometimes blindfolded so that they would not be tempted to read braille by sight and they were subject to reprimand for trying to do so.

The attitude of educators of visually handicapped children of the 1930s was expressed by Merry (1933):

> Reading should be reduced to a minimum in a sight-saving class. It is important for the teacher to bear in mind that her pupils will not have ready access to Clear Type books when they leave school and if they have formed reading habits they may make use of books, newspapers, and magazines at the expense of their vision. Although this restriction of reading habits undoubtedly deprives children of an outstanding educational, social, and recreational advantage, the conservation of their sight is of greater importance and an attempt must be made to substitute other activities for reading. (p. 90)

At last in 1963 the last barriers to use of vision were breached when Barraga, then a doctoral student at George Peabody College, completed her dissertation based on a research study in which very low vision children were given specialized instruction with appropriate materials in attempts to increase their visual *efficiency* (Barraga, 1964). Efficiency is the key word here. The purpose of the study was to find out whether visual *behavior* could be improved through training. Barraga devised a scale for the assessment of visual efficiency and a set of learning activities and materials appropriate to various components of visual function. At the beginning of her study, 60 percent of legally blind students registered with the American Printing House for the Blind were reported to have remaining vision in excess of light perception. Her research population was drawn from that group. The study reported unqualified success in improving the visual behavior of the research group (Barraga, 1964).

The significance of this landmark study lay in its demonstration that visual efficiency is a process, not a static entity. One of the first effects of the study was that residential and day schools began to allow low vision children to use whatever size print they preferred. Until that time many teachers felt that unless they used special materials with visually handicapped children, they were derelict in their duty and that somehow their roles as special teachers were diminished. Of course the primary benefit of the study was the change of focus from "how much visual loss" to "how much useful vision." This led to the use of multiple reading modes for some children—braille, print, and recordings. Up to that time, incredible as it now sounds, there were heated arguments about selection of one reading mode to the exclusion of others. Also, since medical assessment of near vision is usually dependent on ability to read print, ophthalmologists and optometrists were rarely able to describe the near visual acuity of young, multiply handicapped or other visually handicapped children who did not read print. The *Barraga Visual Efficiency Scale* (Barraga, 1970) was the educator's first systematic approach to assessment of visual efficiency on near-vision tasks.

The First Federal Law to Support Education of the Handicapped

From the day the first residential school for blind children opened its doors, the problems of a suitable reading mode and adequate quantities of books were ever-present. Shortly after the Perkins Institution was opened, funds were raised for a facility to emboss books, the first of its kind. After Howe's death, the facility was called the Howe Memorial Press and it is still in operation (Best, 1934). Perhaps its best-known product is the Perkins Brailler but it also produces other educational material and equipment. However, this press produced a limited quantity of books in Boston Line Type, primarily for Perkins students.

In 1853, 21 years after the first school was opened in the United States, the superintendents of residential schools met in New York to discuss approaching Congress to request a grant for the embossing of books for blind students (Merry, 1933). This meeting seems not to have reached consensus. However, in 1858 a printing house, later to become the American Printing House for the Blind, was set up as a Kentucky corporation, to be maintained by a special tax imposed by the state's legislature. The annual allotment was five dollars for each blind resident of the state. Again, as with the Howe Press, this new press met the needs of a limited number of blind students.

However, several state legislatures appropriated funds to contribute to the development of this Kentucky venture and some private donations were received. The Civil War made joint state action increasingly difficult and delayed the development of a nationwide effort to establish a national printery.

Finally in 1879, as a consequence of a petition by the American Association of Instructors of the Blind (AAIB), Congress passed an Act to Promote the Education of the Blind (Best, 1934; Irwin, 1955; Koestler, 1976; Nolan, 1983). This Act was "the first law enacted in the long history of federal legislative efforts to support the education of the handicapped" (Nolan, 1983, p. 1).

The new Act established the American Printing House for the Blind (APH) as a national resource and stipulated that: articles it distributed must be manufactured in part or totally by APH; federally appropriated funds must be spent on production of equipment and materials, not on buildings; and that in addition to the seven Louisville citizens who were trustees, the superintendents of every public institution for the blind would be ex-officio trustees (Irwin, 1955; Nolan, 1983).

In 1956 an amendment to the Act extended eligibility to all blind children enrolled in public day school programs and the APH charter was amended to include as ex-officio trustees all "chief state school officers" or their designees. In 1970 eligibility was again extended to include children in nonprofit private institutions such as multi-service agencies for the blind which offer educational programs for multiply handicapped blind children (Nolan, 1983).

The "War of the Dots" had a profound effect on the activities of the newly founded APH. Until about 1920 APH concentrated on production of embossed books. This was a difficult period because residential schools were by no means unanimous in their decisions regarding choice of books in New York Point, Modified Braille, or Boston Line Type. In 1879 embossed texts were produced in Boston Line Type and New York Point and music in New York Point. In 1882, by vote of the trustees, 50 percent of textbooks were to be published in New York Point. Very slowly braille grew in popularity and in 1893, eight books were published in Modified Braille, using plates from the Missouri School for the Blind. In 1900 the first books in American Braille were published with plates from the schools in St. Louis, Philadelphia, and Lansing and in 1910 the trustees agreed that 40 percent of the textbooks would be printed in that code. The Board of Trustees and other groups of and for the blind passed a resolution in favor of one uniform type and in 1918 Revised Braille, Grade 1 1/2 was adopted for all textbooks. Standard English braille Grade 2 was adopted in 1932, but for about ten years some educators insisted on Grade 1 1/2 for books for the first six grades (Nolan, 1983). Once the obligation to emboss and inventory textbooks in more than one code was removed, APH began to produce other educational materials. By 1921 tangible apparatus such as maps, braille writers, and arithmetic slates, were available and the 1936 catalogue listed recordings for the first time. The first experimental Large Type books were printed in 1947 and computerized braille was initiated in 1964 (Illingworth, 1910; Koestler, 1976; Nolan, 1983). A full discussion of resources, media, and technology is found in Chapter 17.

PERSONNEL PREPARATION

During the first eighty-five years of the history of residential schools for visually handicapped children, teachers and houseparents acquired their specialized skills through apprenticeship. This was the system which had been developed in Europe and it, along with the whole residential school concept, was adopted in the United States. In fact, many school superintendents of the time preferred this pattern and resisted the idea of university-based teacher preparation because they wanted to foster their own ideas and techniques among their teachers.

Most of the teachers in the early residential schools had had no previous teaching experience. Many had only high school degrees, and many were graduates of the schools in which they were employed (Koestler, 1976). As late as 1949-50 when Robert Irwin was writing material that was posthumously published in *As I Saw It* (1955), he said, "The great majority of teachers in the schools for the blind have not been especially trained for their work. During the first twenty-five years of the century superintendents seemed to feel that almost anyone could teach blind children" (p. 135).

Since many partially sighted children were enrolled in residential schools for blind children, their teachers faced the same situation. When Allen in Boston and Irwin in Cleveland pioneered day school classes for the partially sighted, and the idea began to spread, the acuteness of the teacher preparation problem was evident. The teachers in day school programs did not even have the advantage of apprenticeship under experienced teachers because there were none. Hathaway said of this period:

> For some years after the first educational facilities were made available to partially sighted children in 1913, there was no established precedent for teachers to follow, and no opportunity for them to prepare for this very specialized work. Each teacher had, therefore, to try to solve through the trial and error method the problems that were constantly arising, thus experimenting to a certain extent, with children who had difficulties enough of their own to meet. (1959, p. 64)

University-Based Preparation

The first university-based teacher preparation course was offered at the University of California in 1918 (Best, 1934). However, the first enduring sequences of training courses were established in Boston and Nashville in the early 1920s. In 1921, Allen, superintendent of the Perkins Institution, took a giant step toward professionalization of his own and other residential school faculties when he approached the Harvard Graduate School of Education with a proposal to initiate a six-month training program to be operated in cooperation with Perkins. The program was established as the Harvard Course on Education of the Blind. By 1925 the need for supervised practicum was recognized and a second six-month sequence was developed. This portion of the program, called the Special Methods Course, was given under the direction of a Perkins faculty member and included a residential apprenticeship of lectures, observations, and student teaching. The total sequence offered graduate credits toward a master's degree. Thus, a new, high standard was set for teachers of visually handicapped children—advanced training at the graduate level (Koestler, 1976). The program was subsequently moved to Boston University and then to Boston College but it has been in continuous operation since its inception.

Also in 1925, Wampler, superintendent of the Tennessee School for the Blind, initiated a six-week summer course in cooperation with George Peabody College for Teachers. The trainees lived at the Tennessee school and attended classes at Peabody which were taught by Wampler and visiting faculty. This course was discontinued in 1928 for financial reasons but it was revived in 1931 at a cost to students of $7.00 a week for board, room, and laundry, and $4.00 per credit hour. Even these costs were prohibitive during the depression and the program lapsed again until 1935 when the American Foundation for the Blind gave Peabody College a one-year grant which enabled it to start up again (Koestler, 1976).

Obviously the two new sequences attracted different populations: the Perkins-Harvard program was designed for teachers who had just graduated from colleges or normal schools. The Tennessee School-Peabody summer sessions were best suited to teachers who were already teaching but who wanted to upgrade their knowledge and skills or who wished to enter the field of the visually handicapped. These two patterns have persisted throughout the country with the summer sessions in the ascendance during the 1950s when the sudden rise in the number of visually handicapped due to the post-war baby boom and the advent of ROP created an unprecedented need for teachers. In the 1960s and 1970s, full-time graduate preparation became the predominant pattern as a result of federal funding and the rising concern for teacher competencies.

Irwin and some of his teachers from Cleveland offered the first summer training program for teachers of partially sighted children at Teachers College, Columbia University, in 1922. A small demonstration class of partially sighted children was in session each day for observation and practice teaching. In the next three summers, George Peabody College also held summer sessions for teachers of partially sighted children. The 1925 session marked the first time that courses for teachers of blind children and of partially sighted children were offered at the same university (Hathaway, 1959).

Beginning in the late 1940s, there was a surge of interest in special education and several universities established teacher preparation sequences in various areas of exceptionality. Four factors appear to have influenced the renewal of interest in preparing teachers for visually handicapped children. First, the rapid expansion of both day and residential school programs to meet the demand for placements for children handicapped by ROP. Second, the philosophical shift toward education of visually handicapped children in their home communities was leading to a differentiation of teaching roles for various types of schools and programs. Third, the shift from the "sight conservation" concept ended the era in which protection of sight was the primary role of the teacher; new teaching skills were required. Fourth, techniques for teaching daily living skills and independent mobility, systematized and demonstrated by the Veterans Administration program for blinded veterans of World War II, were perceived to be adaptable for use with children, in which case, teacher training was required (Roberts, 1973). One of the first of this new wave of training centers was the Department of Special Education at San Francisco State College. In 1948, this graduate level department was opened with a full-time faculty position in each of eight major areas of special education, including the area of visual impairment. Florence Henderson was in charge of developing and directing this major area and many in a whole generation of leaders in the education of visually handicapped children received their inspiration and preparation from her (Abel, 1967).

In 1957, Dr. Samuel Ashcroft, at that time the only educator in the country to hold an earned doctorate in the field of the visually handicapped, was employed by George Peabody College to develop and direct a year-round graduate teacher preparation program.

Professional Qualifications of Teachers

Within a decade after the first university-based teacher preparation courses were instituted, the field was actively working on descriptions of the qualifications of teachers of visually handicapped children. At that time state departments of education did not have criteria or procedures for certification of teachers of handicapped children, so there was no guidance from that direction. In an effort to upgrade the quality of their teaching staffs, residential schools, in particular, were searching for standards. In answer to this need,

the American Association of Instructors of the Blind appointed a committee in 1932 and charged it with responsibility to formulate recommendations regarding qualifications for teachers of blind children. Certification was to be based upon completion of university-based preservice or inservice courses and on demonstrated ability to read and write braille. There was a grandfather clause which allowed substitution of successful teaching experience for some of the formal course work. The certification system was adopted at AAIB's 1938 convention and the first awards were made in 1940. As late as 1985 some schools still relied on this certification system because their states had inadequate or no certification procedures for teachers of visually handicapped children. The Association for Education and Rehabilitation of the Blind and Visually Impaired, which represents the merger of AEVH and AAWB, still administers the teacher certification program.

In 1954 the United States Office of Education stepped into the breach and published a status report, *College and University Programs for the Preparation of Teachers of Exceptional Children* (Mackie & Dunn, 1954) and in the next few years it issued consensus reports on studies of the competencies of teachers in various areas of exceptionality, including *Teachers of Children Who Are Blind* (Mackie & Dunn, 1955) and *Teachers of Children Who Are Partially Seeing* (Mackie & Cohoe, 1956). In each study, 100 teachers identified and evaluated the competencies which were important in their work. Subsequently, special education supervisors, specialists in state departments of education, and nationally recognized leaders grouped and evaluated the competencies. The consensus of the two studies in the area of the visually handicapped was that the optimum teacher preparation model should include an undergraduate major in elementary education, two or more years of successful teaching in the regular classroom, and graduate training in education of blind or partially sighted children, including 50-250 clock hours of practice teaching.

In response to the field's concern about professional preparation the American Foundation for the Blind published *Training Facilities for the Preparation of Teachers of Blind Children in the United States* in 1953. This report was formulated at a symposium of nine different institutions which offered courses for teachers of blind children and it presented descriptive materials about their training curricula (Abel, 1962). Then in 1957 AFB appointed a Teacher Education Advisory Committee to work with its staff to formulate standards for the preparation of teachers of blind children. Two national work sessions were convened by that Committee in 1958 and 1959 to develop program objectives for a teacher education sequence.

The resulting document, *A Teacher Education Program for Those Who Serve Blind Children and Youth* (AFB, 1961) proposed a broader view of the range of competencies required for the adequate education of visually handicapped children than that of earlier publications. The Committee felt that teachers must have competencies in an area not previously stressed— enlistment of assistance from specialists within and outside of the school to meet the personal, social, and learning needs of these children and youth.

Concurrently, the National Society for the Prevention of Blindness was developing guidelines for a basic teacher preparation program for teachers of partially sighted children. A minimum schedule of courses had been presented in 1925 but a review was needed and in 1957 an advisory committee was appointed to assist in the fourth revision of Hathaway's book, *Education and Health of the Partially Seeing Child* (1959). At that time it was estimated that 70,000 partially sighted children were in school but that only 8,000 were being served by qualified teachers. The recommendation was made that a basic 120 clock hour sequence which would prepare teachers to work in cooperative, resource room, or itinerant programs, should include at least 30 clock hours in each of the following areas: organization and administration of facilities for educating partially sighted children; procedures for conducting work in elementary, junior and senior high schools; observation and practice teaching with children in all three program models; and anatomy, physiology, and hygiene of the eye (Hathaway, 1959; NSPB, 1956).

Another step in the specification of qualifications for teachers of handicapped children was taken by the Council for Exceptional Children (CEC) in the 1960s. The Professional Standards Committee of the Council, with the help of funding from many agencies including AFB and NSPB, organized a massive Project on Professional Standards. Over a period of two years, approximately 700 special educators participated in the formulation of standards for preparation of personnel for special education administration and supervision and for preparation of teachers in seven areas of exceptionality, including the visually handicapped. It was, in fact, at one of these work sessions that the term *visually handicapped* was finally adopted by leaders in the fields of blindness and partial vision, to cover the continuum of visual impairments. The standards for preparation of personnel for the education of visually handicapped children included basic preparation in general education, an overview of all areas of exceptionality, and specific preparation in the area of visual impairment (CEC, 1966).

The National Accreditation Council for Agencies Serving the Blind and Visually Handicapped (NAC) was founded in 1967. While its primary mission, as far as education was concerned, was to provide a process for the accreditation of residential schools for blind children, the standards and criteria for evaluation of the professional staff inevitably affected schools' recruitment policies. Along with the CEC Professional Standards Project, the NAC standards for teacher qualifications sounded the death knell for the jeering old adage about teachers who failed at everything else finding a safe niche in schools and classes for visually handicapped children.

Preparation of Black Teachers

The preparation of black teachers of visually handicapped children lagged far behind that of white teachers. Prior to passage of desegregation laws, "Racial segregation not only kept black children in separate schools staffed by black teachers, but prevented those teachers from attending courses given at white southern colleges such as Peabody" (Koestler, 1976, p. 425-426). Most of the black teachers did not earn enough to be able to attend northern colleges. In 1937 the American Foundation for the Blind conducted a survey of the Negro schools for the blind. The report revealed such a desire on the part of the teachers for special training that AFB piloted a summer training program at West Virginia State College, a Negro school, in 1939. In 1942 the program was moved to The Hampton Institute where credits could be applied toward a graduate degree. These two programs were so well attended that they continued for 14 years (Koestler, 1976). The desegregation laws and the advent of federal funding for teacher preparation opened up opportunities for all qualified candidates to enroll in colleges of their choice.

Preparation of Orientation and Mobility Instructors

One of the greatest tragedies in the history of education of blind children was the almost total lack of systematic training for safe, independent mobility until after World War II. Until this problem was resolved, a blind student's independent action and personal responsibility were seriously curtailed. For several centuries there were scattered tales of dogs or geese serving as guides to blind persons but these appear to have been either apocryphal or reports of serendipitous encounters with unusual animals (Koestler, 1976). One of the first published analyses of the mobility needs of blind persons appeared in 1872 in London. A blind man who had been active in establishing home handicraft industries and workshops for the blind in Britain, wrote a treatise which included a chapter "On the Blind Walking Alone, and of Guides." In it he said,

The importance to every blind man of acquiring the power of walking in the streets without a guide can scarcely be exaggerated. Loss of sight is in itself a great privation, and when to it is added the want of power of locomotion, the sufferer more nearly approaches the condition of a vegetable than that of a member of the human family. (Koestler, 1976, p. 302)

After World War I some work was done in France and Germany on training German Shepherd dogs to guide blinded veterans. In 1923 at the AAWB convention, a German dog trainer spoke and gave a demonstration and in 1927 the *Saturday Evening Post* published an article by an American woman, Dorothy Harrison Eustis, who owned an estate in Switzerland where she bred and trained dogs for police work, guard duty, and army communications. She had also seen guide dogs being trained in Germany and was ready to undertake such a project in the United States. After several months she succeeded in enlisting the interest of a small group who incorporated The Seeing Eye in Nashville, Tennessee in 1929. Thus began the first approach in the United States to the solution of an age-old problem. This development did very little to change the lives and education of blind children because dog guides are not usually recommended for young children. But it did help adults and it laid the ground-work for a change in philosophy regarding the potential for a high degree of independence for blind persons.

Thirty years later, in 1959, the first formal step was taken to establish university programs for the systematic training of orientation and mobility instructors who would teach youth and adults orientation to their environments and independent travel using a long cane. In June of that year, the American Foundation for the Blind called a conference on Orientation and Mobility to consider the professional preparation of instructors. Topics discussed at this meeting included criteria for selection of orientation and mobility personnel, training curriculum, length and academic level of training courses, and appropriate sponsorship of training programs. It was evident that the basic curriculum would be based on that of the Veterans Administration which had been developed to assist in the rehabilitation of blinded World War II veterans. One year later, 1960, the first university-based graduate level course for orientation and mobility specialists was inaugurated at Boston College under the name Peripatology Program. In 1961 the second master's level course was opened at Western Michigan University as the Orientation and Mobility Specialists Program.

In 1966 the U.S. Office of Education granted funds to San Francisco State College and Florida State University to start orientation and mobility training programs with a special emphasis on personnel who were prepared to work with visually handicapped children and youth in residential and day schools. The Florida program was the first to provide orientation and mobility training at the undergraduate level, in conjunction with a teacher preparation program. Since educators increasingly realized that very young children required early help in developing concepts and orientation to their environments and that most secondary students were ready to learn independent travel skills, the two new programs seemed to be a dream coming true. By 1971 orientation and mobility training for children and youth was seen as so valuable that about 45 percent of graduates of all orientation and mobility training programs were employed in residential and day schools (Blasch, 1971). Chapter 19 of *Foundations of Orientation and Mobility* (1980), covers present training and employment data.

PROFESSIONAL ORGANIZATIONS AND ASSOCIATIONS

A number of organizations and associations which have had significant effects on the course of education of visually handicapped children have been referred to earlier in this chapter. Each was founded because large numbers of professionals, parents, and consumers felt the need for services not otherwise available. The following brief histories describe the establishment of the American Association of Instructors of the Blind (AAIB), the American Association of Workers for the Blind (AAWB), the American Foundation for the Blind (AFB), the National Society to Prevent Blindness (NSPB), The Division for the Visually Handicapped (DVH), and the National Accreditation Council (NAC).

Formation of Two Membership Associations

In 1853 there were 18 public and private residential schools for blind children in the United States. The original three privately endowed and financed schools in Boston, New York, and Philadelphia had been in existence for 20 years and they had taken the lead in helping to establish new schools, to identify common problems and advocate exemplary practices.

At that point they felt that greater cohesiveness was needed and that some universal problems, such as production of embossed reading materials, could best be addressed by a united voice. The New York Institution for the Blind hosted a three day meeting out of which came the idea for a membership association that was to become the Americn Association of Instructors of the Blind (AAIB). Samuel Howe was elected president of the as-yet-unnamed association (Frampton & Kearney, 1953; Abel, 1967; Koestler, 1976). Although the Civil War undoubtedly interfered with the cooperative action needed to nurture the fledgling, it was also felt that Howe was not committed to the goal of the organization and that he felt that his long-time leadership role was being threatened (Koestler, 1976). Thus it was not until 1871, 18 years after the first meeting in New York, that other leaders called a second meeting at which a constitution was adopted, a name selected, and a date set for the next annual meeting.

During the late 1940s, there was pressure from within AAIB to give the organization more influence and visibility in the field of education. Thus, in 1951, the *International Journal for the Education of the Blind* was founded and in 1952 the constitution was revised. The goal of this revision was to open the organization to more people who were interested in education of blind children and to democratize the structure so that each member had a vote. There was a push to get public day school teachers, residential school house-parents, guidance counselors, and other school personnel to join. The membership increased rapidly and many day school teachers joined, but it was not until 1974 that a nonresidential school person was elected president of the organization. In 1968, in recognition of the growing trend toward utilization of low vision for even the most severely visually handicapped children and toward individualization of instruction based on visual function, the board of directors voted to change the name of the organization to Association for Education of the Visually Handicapped (AEVH) and the name of the journal to *Education of the Visually Handicapped*.

In the last decade of the nineteenth century, another group became interested in educational opportunities at the post-secondary level. This group first met in 1895 as a society of blind persons. In 1896 they enlarged their membership and adopted the name American Blind People's Higher Education and General Improvement Association. For several years this group met occasionally to consider ways to help visually handicapped people to more fully participate in the lives of their communities. They advocated a special college for the blind, government scholarships, and nonsegregated admission to colleges and universities. These goals were not generally supported and by 1905 the members admitted defeat in that direction and decided to address other problems of adult blind persons. They renamed their organization the American Association of Workers for the Blind (AAWB) and opened membership to all categories of personnel in agencies serving blind people as well as to interested lay people (Best, 1984; Koestler, 1976; Merry, 1933).

These two membership associations continued side by side, holding their biennial conventions in alternate years. There were always some professionals who belonged to both associations and as time went on there was increasing sentiment to combine them. In June, 1984, several years of preparation culminated in a merger under the name Association for Education and Rehabilitation of the Blind and Visually Impaired (AER).

Formation of the American Foundation for the Blind

In 1920 and 1921, at their respective biennial conferences the AAIB and AAWB Boards of Directors passed resolutions which led to the establishment of the American Foundation for the Blind (AFB), a national nonprofit professional organization. Leaders of the two membership organizations had seen a need for a full-time, professionally directed, national body which could provide sustained support for legislation, coordinate research and disseminate information to the field.

On June 28, 1921, at the close of the AAWB conference three incorporators were named and a Board of Trustees was elected. The enabling resolution authorized "a properly constituted organization to

M.C. Migel and Helen Keller at the laying of the cornerstone of AFB, at 15 West 16 Street, New York (1934).

cooperate with all existing agencies in work for the blind and the partially blind, and to do such other things as are not or cannot be done by the existing agencies" (Koestler; 1976, p. 23).

The National Society to Prevent Blindness

Wide-spread concern for the prevention of blindness, particularly ophthalmia neonatorum which had recently proven to be preventable by the simple expedience of placing drops of silver nitrate in newborns' eyes, led to the founding, in 1915, of the National Society for the Prevention of Blindness (NSPB) (changed in 1978 to National Society to Prevent Blindness). In cooperation with AFB, NSPB also pioneered the standardization of eye report forms and a standard classification of causes of blindness (Koestler, 1976). On the educational scene NSPB emphasized the special learning problems of partially sighted children, particularly as they differed from the learning modes of blind children.

Winifred Hathaway, associate director of the new organization, visited states and localities to alert them to the educational needs of partially sighted children, to stimulate passage of legislation which would assure program development, and to conduct teacher preparation courses. In an effort to come up with suitable descriptive titles for the early classes for partially sighted pupils, a word used often by Theodore Roosevelt was taken over—conservation. He was concerned with conservation of resources and since the goal of the early programs for partially sighted students was to limit the use of and thus conserve vision, the concept seemed ideal. About 1918, Boston changed the name of its class from "defective eyesight class" to "classes for conservation of eyesight." Cleveland used the term "conservation of vision classes," and New York used "sight conservation classes" and the term "sight-saving" was adopted in some areas (Hathaway, 1959).

Council for Exceptional Children, Division for the Visually Handicapped

In 1922 the Council for Exceptional Children (CEC) was founded as a professional membership organization to promote awareness and understanding of the needs of exceptional children and to bring professionals closer together to share knowledge and stimulate professional growth. Teachers and other professionals who worked in educational programs for all handicapped children joined CEC. While teachers of blind children could belong to CEC, as a matter of fact most of them belonged to AAIB. Teachers of partially sighted children could belong to either or both organizations.

In 1948 a continuously growing sense of identity of a field apart from blindness led teachers of partially sighted children to establish a membership group, Council for the Education of the Partially Seeing, and to seek divisional status in CEC. This was the first request ever made by a group of CEC members to establish a division-type relationship. By 1952 this Council adopted its own constitution which spelled out the terms of the affiliation with CEC. The present constitution was adopted in 1967 and the name changed to Division for the Visually Handicapped (DVH) (Council for Exceptional Children, 1982).

The National Accreditation Council

An historical development which has significantly influenced the residential schools, as well as agencies for the visually handicapped, was the establishment, in 1967, of the National Accreditation Council for Agencies Serving the Blind and Visually Handicapped (NAC). This organization, the first to establish standards and set criteria for both self and peer on-site evaluation of schools and agencies for the visually handicapped, developed standards and procedures for the accreditation of residential schools. (While these standards may be used informally as guidelines by day school programs, there is no mechanism for

their accreditation by NAC). NAC's standards cover all aspects of residential school administration, plant management, health services, curriculum, and dormitory living. A revision of the residential school standards in the late 1970s made provisions for evaluation of preschool programs and units for multiply handicapped children. The two aspects of the accreditation process which have done the most to effect school improvement are, first, the self-study which each school seeking accreditation must complete and second, the opportunity for selected school personnel to serve on NAC's on-site review teams at other schools.

About half of the country's residential schools have received accreditation and since 1973 the U.S. Department of Education has officially recognized NAC as the responsible agency for accrediting residential schools for blind children.

All of these associations and organizations have given the field of service to the visually handicapped cohesiveness, a mechanism for program improvement, and a sense of identity for teachers in a low-prevalence disability category.

CONCLUSION

In the same year, 1749, that Diderot wrote his "*Lettre sur les aveugles a l'usage de ceux qui voient*," Rodriquez Pereire invented sign language for the deaf. Clearly the Enlightenment and its focus on the individual's rights, needs, and obligations was fostering the birth of ideas about the worth and educability of handicapped persons. While it was 35 years before Haüy opened the first school for the blind, the Institution des Jeunes Aveugles, never again has there been a period when new programs, equipment, and curricula were not being developed. The beginnings were experimental and some times wrong-headed, as are some practices today, but formal education of visually handicapped persons was underway and here to stay.

The field has tended to focus on the initiation of programs and the development of suitable curricula for visually handicapped children. Important as these are and will always be, perhaps the most significant events of the century and a half since the first residential schools were opened in the United States relate to the increasing professionalization of education in general and of education for visually handicapped children in particular. Even here, Samuel G. Howe was a man ahead of his time. Among his many "causes" was his support of Horace Mann's first normal schools, as teacher preparation schools were then called. In 1840 the Massachusetts legislature went on record as opposed to these schools as seedbeds of free thought (Schwartz, 1956).

However, neither Howe nor any other of the pioneer residential school superintendents felt the need for their teachers to receive professional training—the education of visually handicapped children was considered to be so specialized that teachers could only be prepared on the job, often under the tutelage of the superintendent himself. Many teachers were graduates of the schools in which they taught and were assumed to need very little further training. The notion that teachers of visually handicapped children should first of all be qualified regular classroom teachers arose in the first quarter of the twentieth century (Roberts, 1973).

With this country's current concern for the improvement of education and the focus on evaluation of teachers and identification of master teachers, the further professionalization of education is likely. An additional burden rests on the shoulders of special education teachers—in times of change and reduced financing for schools, the pressure to excel as teachers increases. If programs for visually handicapped students are misunderstood or perceived to be inadequately staffed, they are curtailed. Thus, competent, courageous, and committed teachers are needed now as surely as any time in the history of education for children who are visually handicapped.

Study questions

1. Using Robert Irwin's actions as described in this chapter, outline what you believe to have been his philosophy of education for visually handicapped children.

2. With four classmates, role play Samuel G. Howe, Simon Pollack, William Wait, Joel W. Smith, and Helen Keller discussing the advantages and disadvantages of the various line and point systems.

3. Discuss the significant effects of Barraga's studies on visual efficiency on the education of visually handicapped children.

4. What reasons did some educators of visually handicapped children give for opposing residential school education? Cite names and their major tenets.

5. Cite at least three reasons for the century-long delay in establishing professional preservice preparation for teachers of visually handicapped children.

6. Why did early leaders in the education of partially sighted children feel that they should not be educated with blind children?

7. Do you believe it is important for personnel who work with visually handicapped children to belong to professional organizations and/or associations? Why?

8. Why did it take so long after Louis Braille completed his six-dot code for tactile reading and writing in 1834, for the field to adopt braille?

9. What were Haüy's three main contributions to the history of education of blind children?

10. Describe Samuel Gridley Howe's professional dilemma in the light of his stated philosophy of education for blind children.

Additional readings

Abel, G.L. (1959). *Concerning the education of blind children*. New York, N.Y.: American Foundation for the Blind, Inc.

American Foundation for the Blind. (1957). *Itinerant teaching service for blind children: Proceedings of a national work session*. New York, N.Y.: Author.

American Foundation for the Blind. (1954). *The Pine Brook Report: National work session on the education of the blind with the sighted*. New York, N.Y.: Author.

Cutsforth, T.D. (1951). *The blind in school and society: A psychological study*. New York, N.Y.: American Foundation for the Blind, Inc.

Jones, J.W. (1969). *The visually handicapped child at home and school*. Washington, D.C.: U.S. Department of Health, Education and Welfare.

Koestler, F. (1976). *The unseen minority: A social history of blindness in the United States*. New York, N.Y.: David McKay Co.

Lowenfeld, B. (1981). *Berthold Lowenfeld on blindness and blind people*. New York, N.Y.: American Foundation for the Blind, Inc.

Lowenfeld, B. (1975). *The changing status of the blind: From separation to integration*. Springfield, Ill: Charles C Thomas.

Schwartz, H. (1956). *Samuel Gridley Howe*. Cambridge, Mass.: Harvard University Press.

Spungin, S.J. (1977). *Competency-based curriculum for teachers of the visually handicapped: A national study*. New York, N.Y.: American Foundation for the Blind, Inc.

PART 1

DEFINITIONS, DEVELOPMENT, AND THEORY

INTRODUCTION

An understanding of the needs and characteristics of all children is basic to understanding the needs and characteristics of children who have visual impairments. The chapters in this section build on this basic knowledge. The nine chapters in this section describe the unique needs of visually handicapped children and youth and how they may be expected to differ from children and youth with normal vision. This knowledge and understanding is essential to the assessment process from which the educational program is developed and implemented, topics included in Parts 2 and 3.

Chapter 2 describes the population known as "visually handicapped children and youth." It includes a review of the meaning of blindness, various definitions of blindness and visual impairment, commonly used terminology, prevalence/incidence data, and known demographic characteristics.

Chapter 3 presents an overview and background information about the visual system: a summary of the process of seeing including the anatomy and physiology of the eye, a description of the various pathologies or visual impairments found among the school age population, the medical assessment of visual impairments, and suggestions for the teacher on interpreting an eye examination report.

Chapter 4 summarizes normal growth and development in the physical/motor; mental/cognitive; and social/emotional areas. Research findings related to similarities and differences in the growth and development of children and youth with visual impairments are reviewed. Chapter 5 discusses the visual perceptual process and the development of visual behavior. The role of the visual perceptual process in cognitive development is included and the contribution of other sensory systems to learning and development is described.

Chapter 6 examines procedures for assessing visual functioning and for assisting pupils to increase their visual efficiency through the appropriate selection and training in use of optical and nonoptical low vision aids.

The preceding chapters reviewed characteristics and needs that in general apply to all visually handicapped children and youth. The next four chapters in this section examine variations that may have an impact on educational programming for some visually handicapped children and youth.

Chapter 7 describes the special needs of children prior to school age. The long history of programs and services to parents and their visually handicapped infants and young children is summarized and research studies related to the efficacy of early intervention programs for both normal and handicapped young children are examined in the final part of this chapter.

Some visually handicapped children and youth have other combinations of educational disabilities that must be considered when developing and implementing an adequate educational program for them. These include visually handicapped children and youth who are also gifted, or emotionally disturbed, or educable mentally retarded, or learning disabled. These combinations are examined in Chapter 8.

The special programming needs for visually handicapped children and youth with major disabilities, those who are described as severely multiply handicapped, are discussed in Chapter 9. Appropriate assessment instruments, procedures for instruction, curricular modifications, variations in the special service delivery models, and alternative living arrangements necessary for this population are examined.

Visually handicapped children and youth have the same racial, ethnic, and religious background as normal children and may live in rural and remote areas. These variations also have an impact on educational programming. Chapter 10 examines the impact of minority status on program planning and modifications necessary for those pupils who live in rural areas.

CHAPTER 2

What Does It Mean to Be Blind? Definitions, Terminology, and Prevalence

Geraldine T. Scholl

This chapter describes the visually handicapped children and youth who are the subject of this book. Background information about what it means to be blind or visually handicapped is summarized. Definitions, including their historical evolution and the currently accepted functional definitions, are discussed. Terms that have been and are currently used to describe this population are defined. Prevalence and incidence data about blindness and visual impairments and known demographic characteristics on the population are summarized.

What is it like to be blind? Is the world totally dark to a blind person? Aren't all blind people good musicians? Why do some blind people wear thick glasses? How can a blind child learn in a regular classroom?

These questions are among those which are frequently asked by people who have little knowledge or experience with persons who have severe visual impairments. This chapter summarizes background information about the children and youth who are the focus of this book. It is divided into four parts. The first briefly considers questions similar to those raised at the beginning of this chapter, namely, what blind people are like and what it feels like to be blind. The second part discusses the various definitions of blindness and visual impairment, their historical evolution, and the currently accepted educational definition. The third reviews the various terms used to describe blind and visually handicapped pupils. The fourth presents incidence/prevalence information about the population and summarizes known demographic information.

THE MEANING OF BLINDNESS AND VISUAL IMPAIRMENT

What "blindness" means to people is frequently related to their experiences, attitudes, and beliefs which in turn influence their relationships with persons who are blind. These relationships are further influenced by the experiences, attitudes, and beliefs of blind persons toward persons with sight, toward their blindness, and toward themselves. This part discusses these topics.

What Blindness Means

Many people assume that individuals who are 'blind' have no vision and thus live in a world of total darkness (Schulz, 1980). Their experiences in the dark with groping for articles or tumbling over furniture lead them to assume that blind persons live in a similar world. In reality, only about 10 percent of all persons labeled as blind are totally without sight (Kahn & Moorhead, 1973) and only about 20 percent of school-age children labeled as visually handicapped (Hatfield, 1975). Most persons considered blind do respond to some visual stimulation, e.g., light and dark; or shadows; or moving objects; and do not live in a world of total darkness.

Another erroneous belief is that a visual impairment is punishment for sins, either one's own or one's ancestors. This view was frequently found in ancient times but persists, sadly, even among some persons in present-day society. Instances of this point of view can be found in both classical and modern literature (Monbeck, 1973). There is of course no evidence for this negative and profoundly harmful attitude.

A related myth holds that blindness is the result of venereal disease. Some venereal disease can result in visual impairment, but with modern medicine, such cases are relatively rare (Vaughan, Cook & Asbury, 1980).

Why are misconceptions about blindness important to understand? Because they are usually related to how the person who holds them views and relates to individuals who are blind.

Beliefs About Blind People

Society assigns a deviant role to its handicapped population and bases expectations of behavior it deems appropriate for handicapped persons on beliefs or myths, generalizations, and attitudes about the particular condition (Gliedman & Roth, 1980). There are numerous beliefs about persons who are blind or visually handicapped, such as they are musical; they are dependent and helpless; they are beggars.

Some of these beliefs originate in our cultural heritage; others are related to limited experience with persons who have visual impairments which tends to emphasize the unknown and sometimes mysterious aspects of the impairment (Monbeck, 1973). None of these nor other similar beliefs describe accurately the population known as blind and visually handicapped.

Some are musical but many are not. Some are dependent but most are independent, earn a living at some productive employment, and are leaders in their communities. Some are beggars but so are some nonhandicapped persons. Persons with visual impairments are a diverse group in society. They are thin and fat; tall and short; fun-loving and grouchy; they have all the characteristics found in any group of people. *They possess no characteristics specific to themselves as blind persons* (Lowenfeld, 1981), and *they show no typical reaction to being blind* (Schulz, 1980). Like all persons, they are the product of their own unique heredity and environment and are individuals. Thus, it is not possible to generalize about any common characteristics of persons with visual impairments.

Attitudes toward the handicapped, including those with visual handicaps tend to be negative (Kirtley, 1975; Livneh, 1984; Monbeck, 1973; Siller, 1984; Tuttle, 1984) and to focus on what the person cannot do rather than what he can do. Coping with negative attitudes is frequently a greater challenge to the blind person than coping with the impairment (Rusalem, 1972; Schulz, 1980; Smith, 1984; Tuttle, 1984). Teachers of visually handicapped pupils must help their students learn to cope with negative attitudes and must assist others, such as teachers, other school personnel, students, parents, the community, to develop positive attitudes toward persons with visual impairments. Attitude change is a complex process and involves assisting persons to change their own attitudes (Monbeck, 1973). This process must include

providing information to counteract myths, generalizations, and other false beliefs as well as active participation in activities, such as role playing, counterattitudinal advocacy, and value confrontations designed to contribute to behavior change (Watts, 1984).

Paradoxically, unrealistically positive attitudes may also be an important consideration (Kirtley, 1975). In ancient times blind persons were sometimes viewed and revered as prophets, as interpreters of dreams, and as wise sages (Kirtley, 1975). Today many persons believe that the lack of vision endows an individual with supernatural abilities, such as in hearing and touch, or in some artistic ability, usually music. There is, however, no evidence that blind persons have greater abilities in these areas (Hayes, 1941). These attitudes too may work to the disadvantage of persons with a visual impairment when they cannot meet the unrealistic expectations that are assigned to them by some persons.

Beliefs of Blind People

Blind and visually handicapped persons also hold varying beliefs about persons with normal vision, about their own impairments, and about themselves.

The attitude of handicapped persons toward normal people is a largely unexplored area. Rusalem (1972) reviews several studies and concludes that envy of the

normal, impatience with others in understanding their situation, and demands for special considerations found in some visually handicapped persons are most effectively modified through interaction with normal persons at all levels and through assisting visually handicapped persons to develop more realistic self-concepts. The integration of today's visually handicapped children and youth in regular school programs and activities should help both sighted and visually handicapped persons develop more positive attitudes toward each other.

The attitudes of blind persons toward the effects of their impairment represent variations of two opposing views: that blindness is a disaster and that it is a nuisance or practical inconvenience (Kirtley, 1975;

Lowenfeld, 1981). Both views appear to present extremes but might be reconciled through an understanding of the interpretation of the individual components in each view.

Proponents of variations of the disaster view, Carroll (1961), Cholden (1958) and Cutsforth (1951), recognize blindness as a severely limiting impairment that requires a reorganization in all aspects of the individual's functioning. This reorganization is essential in the process of adjustment to the reality of the limitations imposed by the impairment.

Proponents of the nuisance view attribute social prejudice and discrimination as basic to the adjustment process and that it is not the visually handicapped person who must adjust, but rather the sighted society. They suggest that with acceptance visually handicapped persons can achieve "successful levels of personal, social, and economic adjustment when given the necessary opportunities for doing so" (Kirtley, 1975, p. 137).

Berthold Lowenfeld, a noted educator of blind and visually handicapped pupils, presents a moderate position. He says that blindness "imposes three basic limitations on the individual:
1. In the range and variety of experiences.
2. In the ability to get about.
3. In the control of the environment and the self in relation to it" (Lowenfeld, 1981, p. 68).

These three restrictions Lowenfeld views as "the objective effects of blindness" (p. 79). The way in which an individual behaves or learns to adjust to the impairment is dependent on several subjective variables: personality, additional handicaps, and factors related to the visual impairment including degree of vision, cause of the impairment, age and type of onset, and present condition. This recognition of the critical nature of the impairment, with accompanying options for adjusting to it seem to reconcile the seemingly opposing views of the two extremes.

Minority status and discrimination are a reality for the handicapped (Gliedman & Roth, 1980), but a reality that requires concerted efforts on the part of all persons to eliminate. With equal opportunities to develop their capacities, society and visually handicapped persons may come to view their impairment more as a nuisance than a disaster.

Blind persons, like most people, tend to absorb the attitudes of those about them regarding their value and self-worth (Rusalem, 1972). They live up to the expectation and behavior that significant others ascribe to them. When negative attitudes and expectations prevail, the visually handicapped person will become socialized into a role that is consistent with those attitudes and expectations (Scott, 1969). When significant persons in the environment view visually

handicapped people as being inferior and having a low status, they begin to think of themselves in a similar manner, namely, dependent and abnormal. The goal of education should be directed toward fostering positive self-esteem and independence (Tuttle, 1984).

Concluding Comments

The content in the preceding part might best be summarized by defining three terms that are of increasing importance in the field of rehabilitation (Sigelman, Vengroff, & Spanhel, 1984) and that have implications for education as well. These are impairment, disability, and handicap.

An impairment refers to an identifiable defect in the basic functions of an organ or any part of the bodily system (Sigelman et al. 1984). For example, a person who cannot see, or cannot hear, or cannot move a limb because of some injury or defect in the organ or limb has an impairment. The medical profession typically identifies and defines impairment.

A disability is the limitation, restriction, or disadvantage imposed on an individual's functioning as a result of the impairment. Earlier in this part, Lowenfeld's three major restrictions that blindness imposes on an individual were described. These are disabilities imposed on an individual by the visual impairment. Sigelman et al. (1984) identify five life function areas where an impairment can contribute to a disability: health, social-attitudinal, mobility, cognitive-intellectual, and communication.

Sometimes the disabling effects of an impairment can be alleviated through some medical or nonmedical intervention. For example, a person may be visually impaired because he has astigmatism but wears glasses to correct this impairment; his functioning in his environment is not necessarily hindered and he is not disabled. The role of the educator is critical to insure that children and youth with visual impairments have the educational disabling effects of the visual impairment reduced to the greatest possible extent through the modifications in their school programs which are described in Part 3.

A handicap results when an individual is placed at an actual or perceived disadvantage in the performance of normal life functions because of personal and societal expectations and attitudes toward the impairment. For example, if all jobs required reading fine print, all persons with visual impairments would be handicapped. All jobs do not require normal visual functioning but sometimes persons with visual impairments are not even allowed opportunities to demonstrate their competence. When this happens, they are handicapped because of societal attitudes. Disabilities do not necessarily become handicaps. Individuals with low vision who need educational or rehabilitation services are disabled; however, when appropriate services are secured to reduce their visual disabilities through use of low vision aids and visual efficiency training and when their visual performance meets required standards for a particular activity, they are no longer handicapped. Handicaps may also result from limitations imposed by someone else. For example, if a blind child has learned sufficient orientation and mobility skills

to enable him to travel safely to the neighborhood grocery store but his parents are afraid to permit him to travel alone, the child is handicapped by the parental restriction. Handicaps may also be self-imposed. For example, if a blind child refuses to help herself and waits for classmates to get her books and materials when she could secure them herself, then she is imposing restrictions or handicaps on herself by fostering in her classmates the attitudes and beliefs that she is helpless.

Parents and teachers should identify situations and behaviors in the life space or ecology of visually handicapped children and youth that may be potentially handicapping. Furthermore, they should encourage independent functioning from the earliest years and should structure an environment that builds self-esteem.

DEFINITIONS

Definitions of blindness and visual impairment vary depending on the discipline or agency providing services (Rusalem, 1972). This part presents a summary of the most commonly used definitions.

Although relatively few persons are "blind," as noted in the previous part, the term does have a specific definition developed for legal and social purposes, usually referred to as "legal blindness." Classification for legal blindness requires a clinical measurement of the amount of vision, called a refraction, such as that obtained by use of the Snellen Charts. (Procedures for obtaining clinical measurements, or refractions, are described in Chapter 3.) This clinical measurement must fall within the specific parameters which were adopted in 1934 by the American Medical Association.

Central visual acuity of 20/200 or less in the better eye with corrective glasses or central visual acuity of more than 20/200 if there is a visual field defect in which the peripheral field is contracted to such an extent that the widest diameter of the visual field subtends an angular distance no greater than 20 degrees in the better eye. (Koestler, 1976, p. 45)

This definition became part of the Aid to the Blind Act of 1935 and hence, part of the federal law. It should be noted that the definition for blindness in other nations may differ from this accepted legal definition in the United States (Goldstein, 1980).

Persons who have a measured visual acuity of 20/200 can see at 20 feet what persons with "normal" vision see at 200 feet. Individuals who have the use of only one eye are not considered legally blind if the vision in their better eye, with correction, is better than 20/200 and their visual field is wider than 20 degrees. Because the definition refers to corrected vision, an individual whose uncorrected vision falls within the parameters of the legal definition but whose corrected vision is above those parameters is not considered legally blind.

This definition of blindness does not take into account variations in visual functioning: individuals who may experience fluctuations in vision, or who have pathologies which cause them to have difficulty functioning under certain environmental conditions, or who have visual acuities better than 20/200 but who are inefficient in the use of their vision, or who have a deteriorating eye condition. In addition, when measuring visual acuities for a determination

of legal blindness, only distance vision is measured. Although there is often a relationship between near and distance visual acuities, all persons perform tasks in their specific settings which have varied visual requirements so that at times near vision may be the more critical variable in the performance of certain tasks. For example, near vision is more important for the performance of visual tasks within arm's reach, e.g., reading. Most school tasks require good near vision and teachers must know what modifications and compensatory aids can be used to assist the child with a visual impairment to participate effectively in these school tasks. Chapter 6 describes various techniques and aids for increasing the use of near vision; the chapters in Part 3 describe remedial techniques and methods that can be employed in the school curriculum to compensate for the lack of good near visual acuity.

Good distance visual acuity is important in moving about in the environment. To maximize the use of distance vision and to compensate for its limitations, skills in orientation and mobility must be developed. (See Chapter 19.) To plan a good educational program for a child with a visual impairment, the teacher must

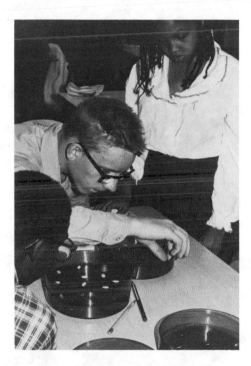

know which school tasks require good near vision and which require good distance vision and to know techniques, methods, and compensatory procedures that will assist the child to make the maximum use of both near and distance vision in the educational program. How to interpret this information from an eye examination report is discussed in Chapter 3.

The definition for legal blindness is currently used by the federal and state governments and some private agencies serving the blind and visually handicapped for determining eligibility, e.g., income tax deductions and special state and federal services and financial aid. The definition is also used by the American Printing House for the Blind (APH), which provides educational materials to legally blind school-age children, through funds from the federal government. Many of these materials are visual but can be used by those legally blind pupils who have some vision. The resources and procedures for obtaining materials from APH are described in detail in Chapter 17.

Educators have long struggled with the problem of definition (Jones 1962). Prior to the 1960s, children whose vision classified them as legally blind were typically educated in residential schools or special classes for the blind, often called braille classes, where tactile materials were used in their educational programs. Children whose corrected vision fell between 20/200 and 20/70 in the better eye were called partially seeing and were typically educated in settings where special visual materials were used. These classes were called sight-saving or sight-conservation classes because the educational practice at that time discouraged the use of vision on the assumption that vision could become over-used and harmed by use (Jones, 1962).

Following the demonstration by Barraga (1964) that through a systematic program of instruction, children with even very limited vision could learn to utilize their visual abilities more efficiently, the terms "blind," "legally blind," and "partially seeing" became inappropriate especially in determining eligibility for educational programs and services. At the same time, since similar visual materials could be used effectively in the education of children labeled as "blind" and those labeled as "partially seeing," educational programs in separate classes gradually disappeared so that today children with the full range of visual abilities are educated in the same classes or programs and are usually labeled "visually handicapped." In such classes, there will be some children

who are blind and must rely totally on tactile materials; some who have very low vision which can often be used more efficiently through training but who may use some tactile materials to supplement visual materials; and some who have limited vision that can be used effectively in their educational programs.

As educators began to view total reliance on measured visual acuity as less meaningful in planning appropriate educational programs, they developed more functional definitions of blindness and visual impairment for placement in educational settings and eligibility for programs and services. The definition

Table 2.1   Definitions of visual impairments

Legal		Educational (Visually Handicapped)			Office of Rehabilitation Services (Visually Impaired RSA Code)			World Health Organization (Colenbrander, 1977)			
								Low Vision		Blind	
Blind	Partially Seeing	Blind	Low Vision	Limited Vision	100-109	110-119	120-124	Severe	Profound	Near Blind	Blind
Visual acuity of 20/200 or less in the better eye with correction or restriction in the visual field of less than 20 degrees (Koestler, 1976, p. 45)	Visual acuity better than 20/200 but less than 20/70 in the better eye with correction (Hathaway, 1979, p.17)	Learns through tactile or auditory materials (Caton, 1981, p. 219)	Severely visually impaired after correction but can increase visual functions (Corn, 1980, p. 3)	Use of vision limited under average circumstances (Barraga, 1983, p.23)	Blindness, both eyes, no light perception	Blindness, both eyes (with correction not more than 20/200 in better eye or limitation of field less than 20 degrees)	Blindness, one eye, other eye defective (better eye with correction less than 20/60, but better than 20/200 or corresponding loss in visual field)	Performs visual tasks at a reduced level	Difficulty with gross visual tasks	Vision unreliable	Totally without sight

included in the Education for All Handicapped Children Act (P.L. 94-142) illustrates this trend. Visually handicapped children are defined as having "a visual impairment which even with correction, adversely affects a child's educational performance. The term includes both partially seeing and blind children" (DHEW, 1977, 121a.5, b, 11). Thus, instead of referring to pupils as "legally blind" or "partially seeing," teachers usually refer to the students whom they serve as "visually handicapped," the designation used in the federal and most state laws.

For purposes of eligibility for rehabilitation services, five gradations of visual impairment are recognized: total blindness; legal blindness; vision between 20/200 and 20/60; blindness in one eye; and other visual limitations (DE-OSERS, 1975). The last two are not usually considered severe impairments under the usual circumstances of daily living. Familiarity with these definitions is important when teachers refer students for rehabilitation services as they prepare for the transition from school to the adult world. (See Chapter 22.)

The World Health Organization definition divides blind into two groups: "near blind" and "blind"; and low vision into "severe" and "profound."

The above definitions are summarized in Table 2.1.

The term visually handicapped describes the target population about whom this book is written and includes those pupils who have a visual impairment of sufficient severity that it interferes with their ability to learn through the usual visual sensory channels, and who may or may not have accompanying physical, mental, cognitive, or social/emotional problems. The 'label' assigned to these children varies according to the program and the state.

Because a large number of pupils with other disabilities also have a visual impairment, two other definitions from P.L. 94-142 are included here. Specialized educational programs often required for these children are described in Chapter 9.

Children who have both a visual and a hearing impairment are frequently labeled "deaf-blind" although they usually have some vision and/or hearing. P.L. 94-142 defines this group as having "concomitant hearing and visual impairments, the combination of which causes such severe communication and other developmental and educational problems that they cannot be accommodated in special programs solely for deaf or blind children" (DHEW, 1977, 121a.5, b, 1). Children who have two or more other disabilities that interfere with their educational program are defined under P.L. 94-142 as those having "concomitant impairments (such as mentally retarded-blind, mentally retarded-orthopedically impaired, etc.), the combination of which causes such severe educational problems that they cannot be accommodated in special education pro-

grams solely for one of the impairments. The term does not include deaf-blind children" (DHEW, 1977, 121a.5, b, 5). It should be noted that not all children labeled as "multiply handicapped" have a visual impairment. The educational needs of children who have a visual impairment and another severe disability, including deafness, are discussed in Chapter 9; those with other exceptionalities, including giftedness, in combination with a visual impairment are discussed in Chapter 8.

TERMINOLOGY

Students identified as visually handicapped represent a wide range of visual abilities. However, they share one common characteristic—a visual restriction of sufficient severity that it interferes with normal progress in a regular educational program without some modifications. Different terms are used in the educational literature to describe this population. As noted in the preceding part, the term "blind" has limited applicability; the term "partially seeing" is rapidly disappearing from the literature (Barraga, 1983); and, as noted in a previous part, the term "visually impaired" may refer to a condition that is not necessarily handicapping to the child. Since this book is concerned with children who have visual impairments that do handicap them educationally, the terms "visually handicapped" as applied to individuals and "children with visual impairments" will be used to encompass the broad range of children who require special education programs and services because of their visual limitations. The term "low vision" or "children with limited vision" will be used to denote those who can usually be educated to varying degrees through their visual sense. The term "blind" will be used for those who must be educated through tactile and sensory channels other than vision. For those children who have additional disabilities, the term "multiply handicapped" will be used for those with mild and moderate conditions (see Chapter 8) and "severely multiply handicapped" for those who must usually be educated with different methods and materials in separate settings (see Chapter 9).

The various terms applied to classes, programs, and schools are presented in Chapter 13.

INCIDENCE/PREVALENCE

Data on numbers and demographic characteristics of blind and visually handicapped persons are difficult to obtain for a variety of reasons. The lack of consensus on the definition for blindness and visual impairment noted in the preceding part compounds the difficulties in data collection; there is no central registry for handicapped persons in the U.S.; drawing comparisons from the available data sources is difficult because of the varying definitions and age ranges adopted for data collection; each data source has its own weaknesses.

The content of this part must therefore be interpreted in light of these problems.

The sources of data for this part are as follows:

American Printing House for the Blind (APH)

The American Printing House for the Blind maintains a registry of legally blind school age children and youth in order to determine a school or state's entitlement to the Quota Account. (See Chapter 17.) APH data include all visually handicapped children classified as legally blind regardless of where they are being educated but do not include those who, while not legally blind, require special education programs and services because of their visual limitations, that is, visual acuity better than that defined for legal blindness.

Model Reporting Area (MRA)

MRA was a voluntary data collection project involving 16 states which agreed to collect uniform data on blind persons of all ages. It was in existence from 1962 to 1971. During its brief life it gathered much valuable information on the legally blind population. However, it is not known how representative the participating states were of the entire U.S. population nor how representative the legally blind population included in the data are of all blind persons since data collection sources were primarily schools and agencies.

National Center for Health Statistics: Health Interview Survey (NCHS-HIS)

Health Interview Survey data are collected on the noninstitutionalized civilian population through interviews on a representative sample of the population. Information about visual impairments is based on self-reports, defining a visual impairment as inability to read newspaper print even with glasses.

National Society to Prevent Blindness (NSPB)

The NSPB relies on several sources, including APH, the Model Reporting Area, and the National Center for Health Statistics Health Interview Survey for making estimates about the visually impaired population (NSPB, 1980). Thus, weaknesses of these data bases are inherent in any of their estimates.

U.S. Department of Education (USDE)

P.L. 89-313, an amendment to the Elementary and Secondary Education Act, entitled "The Aid to Education of Handicapped Children in State-Operated Institutions Act" and P.L. 94-142, "The Education for All Handicapped Children Act" require the collection of data from states on the numbers of children being served under the provisions of these two pieces of legislation for reimbursement purposes. Each state uses its own definition of "visual impairment" for this purpose, provided it falls within the parameters of the federal def-

inition. Thus, different states may use slightly different definitions. In addition, a child may be counted only once, which means if a visually handicapped child is enrolled in another program, he is counted in that disability category, even though he may also be receiving services from a teacher of the visually handicapped. For more information on these sources, see Kirchner (1985).

Statistics on numbers of persons with visual impairments are usually reported for incidence and prevalence. Incidence refers to the number of new cases of a condition within a given period of time; prevalence refers to the number of persons with a particular condition living at any one time (NSPB, 1980).

Reliable data concerning the number of new cases of visual impairment occurring during any year are difficult to obtain partly because there is no national registry system in the United States. Children, particularly those with limited vision, are not usually reported to any data collection agency until they reach school age. In 1977 an estimated 884,000 new cases of visual impairment were reported with about 10 percent in the severe category, that is, unable to read a newspaper even with glasses and approximately 46,600 were legally blind; 6.1 percent were under the age of 17 years and more than half were 65 years and over (NSPB, 1980).

In 1977 there were about 1.4 million persons in the United States with severe visual impairments; of these approximately 500,000 were classified as legally blind; almost half were age 65 and over; and 5.9 percent were age 17 and under (NSPB, 1980). In the school age population there are an estimated 39 legally blind children per 100,000 school population or one in 2,500 (Hatfield, 1975). NSPB (1980) estimates that one child in 500 has a visual impairment that interferes with the educational process but most of these are refractive errors which are correctable with glasses.

In summary, both incidence and prevalence data show that visual impairments are more common among the population age 65 and over with a relatively small proportion of children in the population of those classified as severely visually impaired.

Table 2.2 reports P.L. 94-142 and P.L. 89-313 child count data for visually handicapped, deaf-blind, and multiply handicapped. The number of children being served under the label of "Visually handicapped" declined in 1978-79 following the addition of separate categories for "Deaf-blind" and "Multiply handicapped." Since many visually handicapped children tend to have additional handicapping conditions (See Chapters 8 & 9), it is difficult to determine whether children formerly served under the label of "visually handicapped" are now included in one of the other two categories. In addition, the number of children with visual impairments being served in programs for other categorical goups, such as those for mentally retarded or emotionally disturbed, cannot be ascertained.

The proportion of visually handicapped children among the total population of those receiving special education programs and services is small, less than one percent even when the deaf-blind are included.

Data from the American Printing House for the Blind are reported in Table 2.3. The count is somewhat higher. These data include all school age children who are legally blind regardless of their educational setting and the presence of additional handicaps.

The problem of securing accurate data on the numbers of visually handicapped with and without other impairments is critical because such information is necessary to determine the number of teachers and programs needed in order to plan adequately for the pupils. It is also used for both state and federal reimbursement. The regulation of the Department of Education regarding duplicate counting works to a particular disadvantage to leadership personnel and more importantly to the pupils themselves. Administrators of small districts with few visually handicapped children may place them in other programs if they qualify for another category because operating a program for a small number of children is not financially feasible; teachers without preparation in educational programming for their visual impairments may be at a loss to accommodate such children; and pupils may not receive the specialized educational program to which they are entitled under P.L. 94-142. In addition, teacher educators cannot plan effectively for the future number of teachers who will be required to serve visually handicapped children. The increasing numbers of children placed in programs for multiply handicapped (Table 2.2), raises the question whether this category has become an "umbrella" wherein children with diverse handicapping conditions are placed in the same program, but where they may or may not be served fully for all their educational needs.

Responsible decisions cannot be made unless accurate data are available but securing such data remains a continuing challenge to the field (DHEW, 1976; Goldstein, 1980; Jones, 1962; Kahn & Moorhead, 1973; Kirchner, 1983, 1985; Koestler, 1976; NSPB, 1980; OSTI, 1971; Scholl & Vaughan, 1980).

Demographic Data
Since accurate data on numbers of pupils with visual impairments are lacking, information concerning their demographic characteristics is also limited.

Sex Distribution
Table 2.4 reports distribution by sex from various data sources. In general, there are slightly more males than females in the school age population (ages 5-19) who are classified as legally blind. The proportion by sex

tends to be reversed in the 65 and over age group, partly because the life expectancy of females is greater than that of males (NSPB, 1980).

Geographical Distribution
There are some variations among states and regions regarding the prevalence of persons with severe visual impairments. In 1978 the estimated prevalence rate of legal blindness for the U.S. was 225.1 per 100,000; by state the rate per 100,000 ranged from a low of 139.3 for the state of Hawaii to a high of 370.1 for the District of Columbia (NSPB, 1980). The NSPB report estimates prevalence and incidence rates for each state on three factors assumed to contribute to the prevalence of visual impairments: the proportion of the nonwhite population, the proportion 65 years of age and over, and the infant mortality rate. In the absence of hard data, these estimates must suffice.

Nonwhite Composition
Data concerning the racial or ethnic composition of the visually handicapped population are very limited and where available, group all minorities together under the term "nonwhite." Neither Hatfield (1975) nor NSPB (1980) report such information. The Model Reporting Area study (Kahn & Moorhead, 1973) reported 36 percent nonwhite among the 99,347 persons registered in 1970; with 12.8 percent nonwhite in the 0-19 population of 9,671. However, data for more than one-third in each group were missing and the 16 states involved in the data collection are not nationally representative (Kirchner & Peterson, 1985). Kahn and Moorhead (1973) conclude that the rates for nonwhites appear to be higher than for whites; however, since the data for the Model Reporting Area are obtained primarily from registers of state and private agencies serving the visually handicapped, there may be a bias since the nonwhite population tends to come to the attention of such agencies because of their greater need for services and financial aid (Kahn & Moorhead, 1973).

In summary, little is known either about the actual numbers of visually handicapped children or about their demographic characteristics, partly because definitions vary among agencies collecting data and partly because there are problems encountered in securing data. This may be a continuing problem until joint efforts are made among the reporting agencies to reach consensus about definition and reporting procedures that will result in the collection of more accurate data.

Table 2.2   Handicapped children ages 3-21 receiving special education and related services under P.L. 94-142 and P.L. 89-313

	1977-78		1978-79		1979-80		1980-81		1981-82		1982-83		1983-1984	
	N	%	N	%	N	%	N	%	N	%	N	%	N	%
Total	3,777,286	100.00	3,911,888	100.00	4,028,262	100.00	4,173,059	100.00	4,228,050	100.00	4,291,942	100.00	4,333,558	100.00
Visually Handicapped	35,471	0.94	32,519	0.83	32,605	0.81	32,904	0.79	30,995	0.73	31,067	0.72	31,531	0.73
Deaf-Blind	—	—	2,330	0.06	2,537	0.06	2,855	0.07	2,622	0.06	2,538	0.06	2,492	0.06
Multiply Handicapped	—	—	50526	1.29	61,489	1.53	69,981	1.67	73,622	1.74	65,241	1.52	67,189	1.55

Table 2.3   School aged children registered with the American Printing House for the Blind

	1977-78	1978-79	1979-80	1980-81	1981-82	1982-83	1983-84
Legally Blind	27,772	29,361	30,580	31,907	32,885	34,557	44,313
Deaf Blind	1,631	1,735	1,893	2,013	2,054	2,089	—
Total	29,403	31,096	32,473	33,920	34,939	36,646	44,313

Table 2.4   Percent of legally blind by sex from three data sources

	NSPB (1980) Under Age 20	Hatfield (1975) Under Age 19	MRA (Kahn and Moorhead, 1973) Under Age 19
School-Age			
Males	55.7	54.2	55.7
Females	44.3	45.8	44.3
Aged 65 and over			
Males	41.8	—	41.0
Females	58.2	—	59.0

Study questions

1. Interview a blind or visually handicapped adult about the limitations imposed by the visual impairment, school experiences, discrimination in employment, housing, access to community facilities, etc. Compare with the content included in the first part of this chapter.

2. Discuss limitations of the definition of legal blindness for educators as applied to identification, assessment, placement, and educational programming for visually handicapped youngsters.

3. Discuss the advantages and disadvantages of your state's definition of visually handicapped pupils for educational placement and planning.

4. Define what is meant by a visual acuity of 20/200; 20/60; 20/20. Compare your visual acuity, corrected and uncorrected, with that of some of your classmates.

5. Describe how a child with a visual impairment would be handicapped in the performance of five typical school tasks at any grade/age level you choose.

6. Describe how a child with a visual impairment would not be handicapped in the performance of five typical school tasks at any grade/age level you choose.

7. Discuss with classmates the problem of securing accurate data on numbers of visually handicapped pupils and propose a procedure for more accurate data collection.

8. Identify demographic data that you think are necessary for appropriate educational program planning. Present your rationale.

9. Read two books written about or by visually handicapped persons. Relate the contents to any aspect of the content in this chapter. For suggested books see those listed in "Additional readings."

10. Compare information about the visually handicapped population in another country of your choice regarding the definition of blindness, numbers, age distribution, and causes of visual impairments.

Additional readings

Hartman, D. and Asbell, B. (1978). *White coat, white cane.* Chicago, Ill.: Playboy Press.

Jones, R.L., ed. *Attitudes and attitude change in special education: Theory and practice.* Reston, Va.: Council for Exceptional Children.

Kirchner, C. (1985). *Data on blindness and visual impairment in the U.S.: A resource manual on characteristics, education, employment, and service delivery.* New York, N.Y.: American Foundation for the Blind, Inc.

Krentz, H. (1972). *To race the wind.* New York, N.Y.: Putnam.

Schulz, P. (1980). *How does it feel to be blind?* Van Nuys, Calif.: Muse-Ed.

Smith, M.M. (1984). *If blindness strikes: Don't strike out-A lively look at living with a visual impairment.* Springfield, Ill.: Charles C Thomas.

Sullivan, T. and Gill, L.T. (1975). *If you could see what I hear.* New York, N.Y.: Harper & Row.

Tuttle, D. (1984). *Self-esteem and adjusting with blindness.* Springfied, Ill.: Charles C Thomas.

Ulrich, S. (1972). *Elizabeth.* Ann Arbor, Mich.: University of Michigan Press.

Zook, D. (1974). *Debby.* Scottdale, Penn.: Herald Press.

CHAPTER **3**

The Visual System

Marjorie E. Ward

This chapter presents a basic explanation of the structures of the eye, their relationship to each other, and their functions in the visual system to establish an introductory framework for this text. However, it should not be considered as providing sufficient information for a course on the eye. The first section contains a brief explanation of the anatomy and physiology of the eye, information about some of the causes of visual impairment in school-age children, a review of the kinds of information in clinical eye reports and an illustration of how a teacher might draw out information important for daily instruction and educational goals from these reports.

How do we get the outside world "inside" of us? What makes it possible for us to know what surrounds us and who is near us? Why do we recognize some places and people and not others? What makes it possible for us to distinguish colors and sounds and textures?

The responses to these and similar questions lead to a consideration of the sensory channels that human beings have available—the senses of hearing, seeing, and smelling that bring us information about both distant and nearby environments and those of tasting and touching that help reveal what is actually making physical contact with us. The sense of vision for most people plays the mediator role to help organize and negotiate the environment and put objects, sounds, aromas, tactual impressions, and people in perspective. This sense of sight and the vision of our world we gain from it involves a very complex and intricate system that incorporates electromagnetic, chemical, and electrical energy and requires precise muscle coordination to control the movements of the exquisitely sensitive structure that we call the eye.

The purpose of this chapter is to provide basic information about the eye, an overview of the visual system and what can happen if components of this visual system do not function as they should. The first section contains an elementary discussion of anatomy and physiology of the eye with emphasis on what is necessary to understand a child's general growth and develop-

ment as explained in Chapter 4, sensory perceptual development as presented in Chapter 5, and aids and adaptations to enhance vision as outlined in Chapter 6. The second section contains information about visual impairments, some of their causes, and how they can affect functional vision. The final section illustrates how clinical information obtained from eye specialists can be interpreted by teachers of visually handicapped children and youth and be used for educational purposes to develop long-range goals as well as to plan daily instructional activities, select materials, and arrange classroom conditions for learning.

THE EYE AND ITS FUNCTION

The study of the eye will focus first on the anatomy of the eye, that is, the structures of the eye and their relationship to each other. A basic knowledge of the anatomy will establish the framework for considering the physiology of the eye, how these structures function alone and together to contribute to the efficiency of the visual system. An initial examination of the structures of the eye, their relationship to each other, and their function within the visual system reveals a very small, usually just less than one inch on the horizontal axis, intricately designed, compact organ.

Orbit and Eyelids

The eye lies in a pear-shaped bony orbital cavity or eye socket, the front of which can be closed off by the eyelids. The fat and connective tissues that surround

Author's note: Deep appreciation goes to Dr. Gary L. Rogers and Rae Fellows from the Columbus Children's Hospital for reviewing this chapter.

the eyeball in the orbit provide protection for the eye, the optic nerve which exits from the back of the eyeball or globe and the six extrinsic muscles that attach to the globe and to the walls of the orbit. The six muscles in each eye are innervated by cranial nerves in the central nervous system. These pairs of muscles enable the two eyes to move together in the directions of gaze or to converge to see a visual target clearly at close range. Figure 3.1 shows the location of the extraocular muscles, and Figure 3.2 illustrates how the six pairs of muscles are coordinated in normally functioning eyes to move the two eyes in the six cardinal directions of gaze. In Chart 3.1, the eye muscles are listed along with their primary function in moving the eyeball, the central nerve (CN) that innervates them, and a description of what can happen if a muscle does not function properly.

Besides the eyeball, muscles, protective fat, and connective tissue, the orbit contains blood vessels, nerves, and the lacrimal gland. The lacrimal gland is situated in the forward upper outer portion of the orbit. It secretes tears that flow down over the surface of the globe into the fold below the margin of the lower eyelid and finally drain out through the lacrimal sac that empties into the nose and nasopharynx. (See Figure 3.3.)

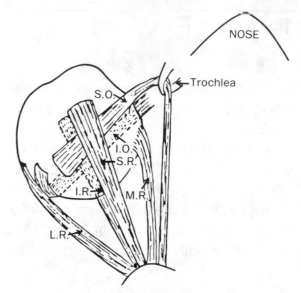

Figure 3.1   The extraocular muscles, viewed from above
I.O., inferior oblique;
I.R., inferior rectus;
L.R., lateral rectus;
M.R., medial rectus;
S.O., superior oblique;
S.R., superior rectus.

Source: S. Goldberg, *Ophthalmology made ridiculously simple* (Miami, Fla.: Medmasters, 1982), p. 7.

Helping protect the orbit and its contents are the eyebrows, lashes and lids. The lids contain additional glands that secrete oils and substances to help lubricate the cornea and prevent the evaporation of the tears (Vaughan & Asbury, 1980). Opening and closing the eyelids aids the flow of tears across the eye. The brows, lashes, and lids together with the bony tissue of the eye socket provide a cushion against bumps and strikes, and a shield against dirt, perspiration, and bright lights.

The conjunctiva, a transparent mucous membrane, covers the posterior surface of the eyelids and the white front portion of the eyeball. The most common eye disease in western countries is conjunctivitis or inflammation of this very thin protective covering.

Globe

The eyeball itself can be thought of as having three layers: the outer protective layer, the middle vascular layer, and the inner nerve layer where light rays should come to a point of focus. Information from the

Chart 3.1		Extrinsic eye muscles	
Eye Muscle	Nerve	Primary Function	Deficit
Medial rectus	Oculomotor (CN3)	Moves eye nasally	Eye cannot look temporally.
Lateral rectus	Abducens (CN6)	Moves eye temporally	Weakness of upward gaze.
Superior rectus	Oculomotor (CN3)	Moves eye up	Weakness of downward gaze.
Inferior rectus	Oculomotor (CN3)	Moves eye down	Vertical diplopia head tilt (compensation for imbalance of rotation).
Superior oblique	Trochlear (CN4)	1) Moves eye down when eye is already looking nasally. 2) Rotates eye when eye is already looking temporally. 3) Moves eye down and out when eye is in straight ahead position.	
Inferior oblique	Oculomotor (CN3)	1) Moves eye up when eye is already looking nasally. 2) Rotates eye when eye is already looking temporally. 3) Moves eye up and out when eye is in straight ahead position.	

Source: S. Goldberg, *Ophthalmology made ridiculously simple.* (Miami, Fla.: Medmasters, 1982), p. 6.

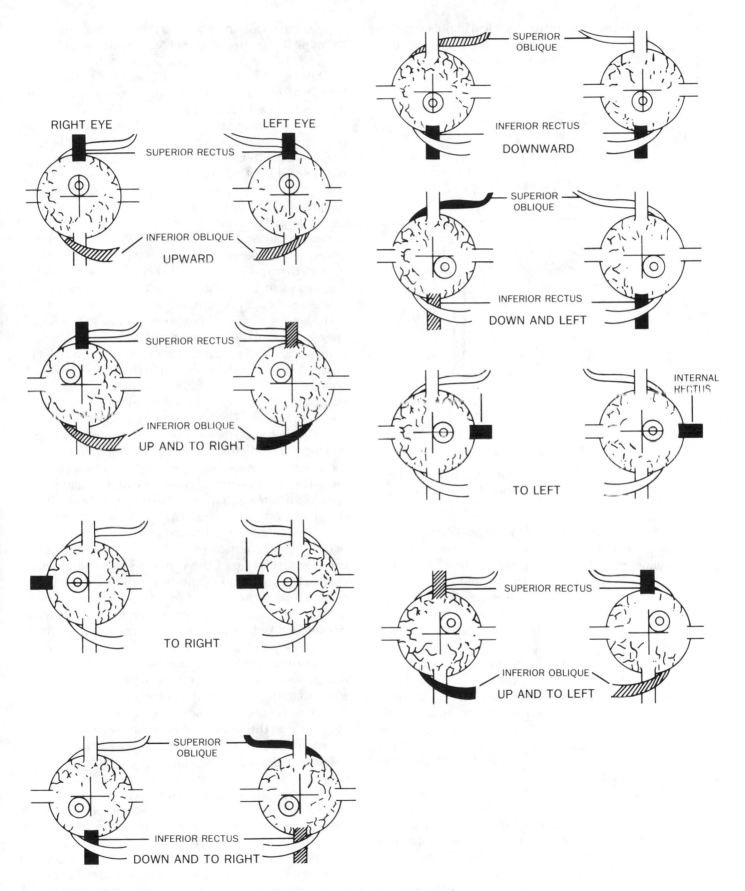

Figure 3.2 Primary and secondary action of extrinsic eye muscles.

Source: American Optical.

nerve layer is transmitted as electrical impulses to the occipital lobe of the brain where that information is interpreted and processed for storage and retrieval. (See Figure 3.4.)

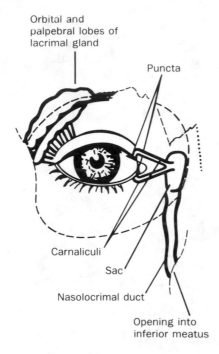

Figure 3.3   Lacrimal apparatus

Source: F.W. Newell & J.T. Ernest, *Ophthalmology: Principles and concepts* (St. Louis, Mo.: C.V. Mosby Co.), p. 43.

The *outer layer* consists of the tough, fibrous white part of the eye called the sclera and the transparent, avascular cornea. While only approximately 1 mm thick at the periphery in the mature eye and about .8 mm in the center, the cornea has five clearly defined layers of cells, membranes, and fibers. The cornea must remain avascular and in a state of relative dehydration (deturgescence) to retain its transparency. Injury or infection can upset the delicate balance and introduce germs that can lead to corneal scarring.

The *middle layer* of the eyeball, the *uveal tract*, consists of the choroid, the iris, and the ciliary body. The choroid is rich in blood supply and lies between the sclera and the inner retinal layer. Its function is to provide nutrients to the retina. A portion of the ciliary body is the ciliary muscle which helps control the thickness of the lens by contracting and relaxing the fibers that regulate the tension on the lens of the eye. The lens lies behind the pupil, the hole through which light rays enter the back of the eye. Changes in the tension of these fibers, zonules of Zinn, allow the transparent lens to vary its refractive power or power to bend light rays and accommodate to preserve clear focus for near as well as for distance objects. Another part of the ciliary body, the ciliary process,

secretes aqueous humor, a liquid that circulates through the pupil from the posterior chamber into the anterior chamber in the front part of the eyeball.

While not actually a part of the middle layer, the lens is affected by the action of the suspensory ligaments, or zonules of Zinn, that the ciliary muscle controls, as was mentioned above. The *lens* is the only refractive medium or light-bending structure in the eye that can alter its curvature. The lens is thus responsible for the fine-tuning of light rays so they form clear images where they strike the inner retinal layer. As an individual grows older, however, the elasticity of the lens decreases. Reading glasses usually are necessary around the age of 45 when the loss of adjusting or accommodative power is significantly great enough to make seeing detail at close range difficult. The loss of accommodation due to the natural aging process is called presbyopia.

The lens for a variety of reasons may lose its transparency and lead to the formation of a cataract. A cataract is an opacity or clouding of part or all of the lens which prevents light from traveling on to the back of the eye. A cataract at the present time cannot be "cured," but the opaque lens can be removed when the eye no longer has useful vision. Once the natural lens of the eye is removed, however, the optical system is out of balance and light rays will not be focused on the retina unless there is some compensation for the power of the natural lens. The most common compensation is glasses or spectacle lenses. The substitute spectacle lens frequently produces excess magnification in relation to the unoperated eye, limited peripheral vision, and poor depth perception (NSPB, 1982). A contact lens can alleviate some of the problems associated with spectacle lenses and is another way to compensate for the loss of the natural lens. Most older cataract patients are good candidates for an intraocular lens implant (IOL) which is placed inside the eye at the time the cataract lens is removed. The IOL, positioned in the approximate site of the natural lens, has a predetermined dioptric power to bend light rays that pass through to the retina in the posterior of the eye. The IOL, however, cannot accommodate or adjust its curvature as the healthy, young natural lens can; so a spectacle lens is frequently necessary for close work.

The nerve layer formed from retina is the *inner layer* of the eyeball. The retina is made up of 9 distinct cell layers and approximately 125 million rod and cone cells (Newell & Ernest, 1974). The thinnest area of the retina, the macula, is the point of clearest vision. The fovea centralis, the central portion of the macula, contains only cone cells that are responsible for day vision and give us our sense of detail and color. Cones predominate in the macular area while the 120 million rods are more dispersed through the retina and predominate in the peripheral regions. Rods are sensitive to motion and

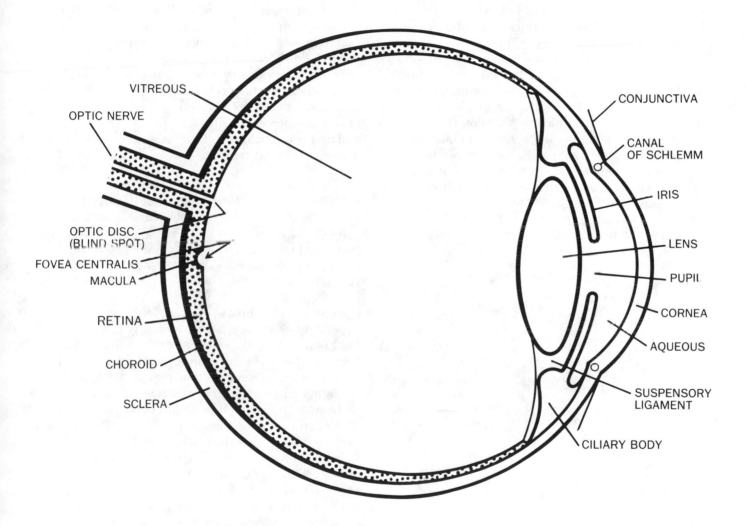

Figure 3.4   Structures of the eye.

Source: National Society to Prevent Blindness.

the presence of light and thus are essential for night vision. A healthy retinal layer is critical to the efficient process of vision. Degenerative diseases of the retina that damage the macular region can cause losses in central vision, a common occurrence in the older adult population over age 60. Other conditions can affect the rod cells, for example, retinitis pigmentosa, and lead to decreased night vision. Color vision becomes vulnerable if the cone cells are compromised.

There are three chambers in the globe which are important to both eye health and function. The *anterior chamber* lies behind the posterior surface of the cornea and the anterior surface of the iris. The *posterior chamber* lies behind the iris and pupil and in front of the anterior surface of the lens. Both of these chambers are filled with aqueous humor, the clear watery liquid secreted by the ciliary process. The aqueous humor should drain out through the canal of Schlemm. If the drainage process is impeded for some reason, pressure can build up in the eye. This pressure increase is called *glaucoma* and is a leading cause of blindness across all age groups in the United States, although more common among the adult population over age 40 (NSBP, 1980).

A third chamber in the eye is the large *vitreous cavity* filled with vitreous, a transparent physiological

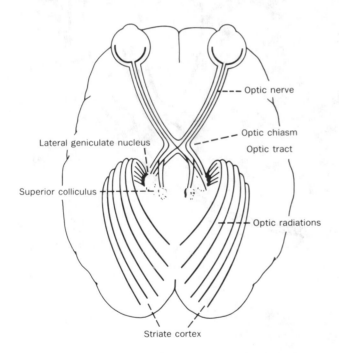

Figure 3.5   Diagram of visual pathways.

Source: A. Blakeslee, Recent advances in vision-loss research, *SSR*, **53** (1984), p. 8.

gel that is 99 percent water and that makes up about two-thirds of the volume of the eyeball and three-fourths of the weight. If the vitreous escapes or is extracted without replacement, the eyeball will collapse. The vitreous gel may become stained by

blood if there are hemorrhages in the back of the eye as may happen in cases of diabetic retinopathy discussed later in this chapter.

The rods and cones of the retina when stimulated by light rays send their messages on to the brain via the one million fibers of the optic nerves. The optic nerves are actually an extension of the second cranial nerve (CN 2) and, if damaged, cannot regenerate or be repaired. The fibers of each optic nerve divide, and some fibers from each eye decussate or cross over to the opposite side at the optic chiasm as illustrated in Figures 3.5 and 3.6. The result is that some information from each eye in the normal visual system arrives on each side of the brain. Damage to various parts of the optic pathways can be localized in some instances by determining what portions of an individual's visual field is restricted. In Figure 3.6, there are examples of how injuries at specific sites along the optic nerves and pathway would affect the receipt of stimuli from regions of the visual field.

Problems of Structure That Affect Function

In the normal and healthy eye, rays of light travel through the transparent cornea, the major refractive surface of the eye, through the aqueous to the lens where fine adjustments are made so the rays can pass through the vitreous and land on the retina in focus. (See Figure 3.7.)

Many people, however, have refractive errors depending on where light rays come to a point of focus. That point is slightly in front of the retina in myopia because the eyeball is longer than normal on the horizontal axis. It is slightly (and hypothetically) behind the retina in hyperopia or at different points in relation to the retina in astigmatism usually because the surface of the cornea is not spherical but oblong. This results in blurred vision along meridians. (See Figure 3.8.) Most refractive errors can be corrected with lenses. Some ophthalmologists are using surgical techniques now to alleviate low to moderate degrees of myopia, but the procedures are still undergoing refinements.

Concave spherical (divergent or minus) lenses are used to correct for myopia while convex spherical (convergent or plus) lenses are used to correct for hyperopia. For astigmatism, cylindrical lenses are prescribed that have different refractive powers along specific meridians to provide what the eye requires in convergent or divergent power to bring light rays to a point of focus. (See Figure 3.9.)

Another problem in eye structure that can lead to possible difficulties with visual function is muscle imbalance. The paired or yoked muscles work together to produce conjugate eye movements in the six cardinal directions of gaze. (See Figure 3.2.) If these muscles are not innervated equally, if muscle strength is unequal, or if there is any muscle paralysis, then the eyes may not appear straight and, in fact, may not achieve good, clear, binocular vision. Binocular vision refers to the ability of the two eyes to focus on one object and to fuse the two images into one single image. The term *strabismus* refers to the condition where an eye deviates from the horizontal or vertical axis. If there is a tendency for the eye to turn, the turn is referred to as a *-phoria*. If the turn is constant, the term used is *-tropia*. The turn may be in toward the nose (*eso-*), or toward the temple (*exo-*), or up (*hyper-*) or down (*hypo-*) in relation to the horizontal axis. A person whose right eye has a tendency to turn in, for example when the person is tired or has done a lot of close eye work, is said to have a right esophoria. If the turn were constant, it would be a right esotropia.

If a child has strabismus, there is danger of diplopia, double vision, because the image the eye picks up does not fall on the retina at a point corresponding to the place it reaches in the second eye. Because this double image can be very confusing and intolerable, at some point along the visual pathways or in the brain, the bothersome image is suppressed and ignored. This suppression can lead to amblyopia, poor vision through lack of use rather than due to organic disease.

Options for the treatment of strabismus include the correction of any refractive errors; patching or occlusion of the good eye for carefully prescribed periods of time each day to stimulate use of the weaker eye and equalize the visual acuities; orthoptic exercises in selected cases; medication, again to force use of

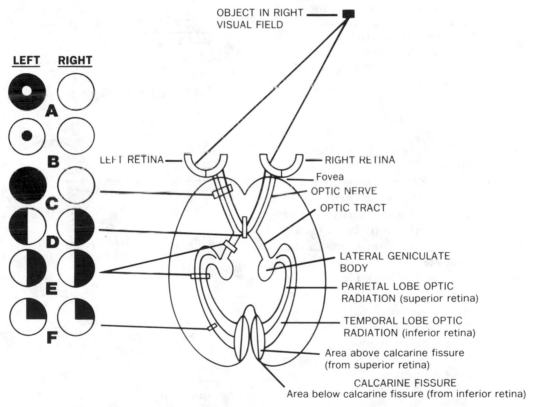

Figure 3.6   **The visual pathways as seen from above the brain. Letters A-F refer to visual field defects following lesions in the corresponding brain areas. Circles indicate what the left and right eyes see (the left and right visual fields). Black areas represent visual field defects. A. Constricted field left eye (e.g., end-stage glaucoma). When constricted fields are bilateral. It sometimes signifies hysteria. B. Central scotoma (e.g., optic neuritis in multiple sclerosis). C. Total blindness of the left eye. D. Bitemporal hemianopia (e.g., pituitary gland tumor). F. Right homonymous hemianopia (e.g., stroke). F. Right superior quadrantopia.**

Source: S. Goldberg, *Clinical neuroanatomy made ridiculously simple* (Miami, Fla.: Medmasters, 1979), p. 38.

the weaker eye; and surgery. The major goals in the treatment of strabismus are clear vision (acuity), cosmetically straight eyes, and binocular vision (fusion). In many cases, only the first two goals are achieved (Vaughan & Asbury, 1980).

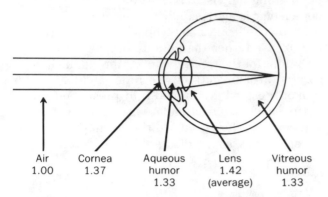

Air   Cornea   Aqueous   Lens   Vitreous
1.00   1.37   humor   1.42   humor
                    1.33   (average)   1.33

Figure 3.7   The passage of light rays through the eye structures to the point of focus on the retina in the normal eye. Numbers indicate the index of refraction for each refractive surface relative to the passage of light through air.

While refractive errors and muscle imbalance do contribute to the population of children and adults who have impaired vision, these conditions are not considered major causes of blindness or visual impairment. Most refractive errors can be corrected with lenses, and those that cannot be corrected to within the normal range of visual acuity do not account for a large percentage of individuals considered to be visually impaired. Strabismus can be found in about 1½ to 3 percent of children (Vaughan & Asbury, 1980). If not diagnosed and treated while the child is still young or at least before age five or six, then the effects on the crossed or turned eye can be quite serious. But in the absence of disease or defect, the second eye usually retains good functional vision. The major causes of limited or loss of vision are described in the next section.

CAUSES OF BLINDNESS AND VISUAL IMPAIRMENT

Many conditions can contribute to the impairment of eye structures and tissue. Whether or not the impairment actually leads to limitations in visual function, however, depends upon such factors as the site and severity of the tissue damage as well as the age of the individual at the time the problem occurred. Some conditions originate during the prenatal period, others can stem from events that occur during the birth process, and still others may develop as the individual matures. Conditions that are not hereditary

and that are acquired or caused by accident after birth are called adventitious. Some hereditary conditions actually do not become manifest or obvious until adolescence or the adult years, while other hereditary conditions may be congenital. Remember that congenital means present at birth and it is possible that an inherited condition may not appear until some

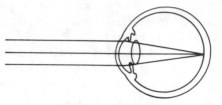

Emmetropia (normal) eye

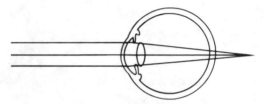

Hyperopia (farsightedness)

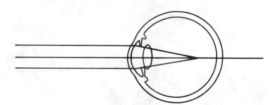

Myopia (nearsightedness)

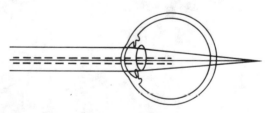

Astigmatism (mixed)

Figure 3.8   Refractive errors

months or years later. In other words, not all hereditary conditions are congenital, and not all congenital conditions are hereditary. Some hereditary and other later-developing conditions, for example, retinitis pigmentosa and Usher's Syndrome, may be diagnosed prior to their clinical appearance with the aid of sophisticated diagnostic procedures.

In this section, major causes of visual impairment and blindness will be discussed, and some of the diagnostic procedures will be described.

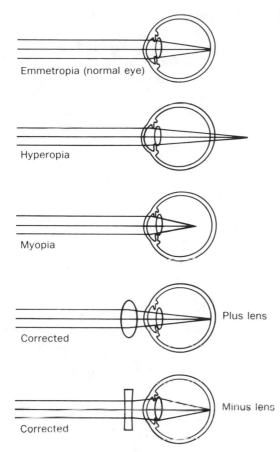

Figure 3.9   **Refraction of light rays in emmetropic eye and in ametropic eye both with and without corrective lens.**

Major Causes

The major causes of blindness and impaired visual function can be described according to their site, type, and etiology. (See Appendix A.) Site refers to location within the orbit or globe, type indicates the diagnosis, and etiology refers to the underlying cause of eye affection. In Table 3.1, the distribution of the total cases of blindness, based on the definition of 20/200 or less in the better eye after correction, is presented for all age groups and for each sex. The figures for Table 3.1 and for those that follow in this section come from an analysis of data carried out by The National Society to Prevent Blindness (NSPB, 1980) that examined data pools collected in 1970 from a 16-state region that included approximately 31 percent of the population of the United States in that year. While there are many questions regarding the accuracy and representativeness of this information, according to the NSPB and researchers at the National Eye Institute, these estimates for 1978 based on data from 1970 are "the best and most comprehensive that have ever been available for such a large segment of the population in this country" (NSPB, 1980, p. 3).

Across all age groups, the leading causes of blindness are glaucoma, macular degeneration, senile cataract, optic nerve atrophy, and diabetic retinopathy. In Table 3.2, the leading causes are identified for all ages and for the three age groups that contain the school age population. The leading known causes of blindness among those under age 20 are congenital cataracts, optic nerve atrophy, and retinopathy of prematurity (ROP). Causes of visual impairment are presented according to etiology in Table 3.3. Overall, among the three age groups into which school children fit, prenatal influences account for the largest percentage of cases. Common prenatal conditions are congenital anomalies and absence of part or all of an eye structure (such as coloboma of the iris), cataracts, glaucoma, and albinism.

Injuries and poisonings account for many known instances of blindness among the school age groups. Actually, injuries are not considered a *major* cause of blindness among children or adults since technically both eyes would have to be severely affected; but injuries are a leading cause of *preventable* blindness, at least monocular blindness. Data on the major causes of eye injuries were collected by The National Center for Health Statistics (NCHS) via the Health Interview Survey in 1971 and again in 1977. The most common eye injuries were wounds, contusions, foreign bodies, and burns (NSPB, 1980). As for product-related injuries, Table 3.4 gives the number and percentages by age groups of the most hazardous products to the eyes. These products are not meant to be viewed in a cause-effect relationship with eye injuries; rather, these items are frequently involved in eye accidents because of damage to a component part or to improper use, care or placement. Fortunately, not all eye injuries lead to blindness in the injured eye.

As for poisonings, the administration of high concentrations of oxygen for extended periods of time to newborn infants of low birth weight led to many cases of what is now usually called retinopathy of prematurity (ROP), formerly referred to as retrolental fibroplasia (RLF). Oxygen, necessary in many instances to preserve the life of the infant, triggered changes in the retinal blood vessels and in some cases proliferation of vessels into the vitreous with risk of retinal detachment. For many babies the net result was functional blindness and for others partial vision. When the relationship between low birth weight and high concentrations of oxygen over time was discovered in the early 1950s and monitoring procedures introduced, the incidence of ROP decreased dramatically. Note the changes in figures for ROP across ages in Tables 3.1, 3.2, and 3.3. Today there are still some cases of ROP in infants whose birth weights are very low, even though the amount of oxygen and the length of time it is administered are carefully controlled and monitored.

Infectious diseases in Table 3.3 again account for a large number of cases of impaired vision in children. This category includes rubella, also called German measles, a disease which, if contracted by the mother during her first trimester of pregnancy, can cause damage to the eyes, ears, heart, and central nervous system of the developing fetus. These systems and structures are especially vulnerable to infection during the early weeks after conception. Rubella may not even be noticed by the pregnant mother, but the virus can apparently interfere with the transcription of genetic information in the cells of the developing

Table 3.1   Percentage distribution of total cases of legal blindness by age and sex according to site and type of affection: U.S. 1978.

Site & Type of Affection	Age								Sex	
	Total	0-5	5-19	20-44	45-64	65-74	75-84	85+	Males	Females
TOTAL	100.0	100.0	100.0	100.0	100.0	100.0	100.0	100.0	100.0	100.0
Eyeball	22.8	24.8	26.6	20.8	22.1	25.6	23.6	18.8	23.7	21.9
Glaucoma	13.5	6.2	4.2	4.6	11.9	18.3	19.4	16.5	12.8	14.2
Congenital	1.0	6.2	3.7	2.6	0.7	0.2	0.2	0.1	1.4	0.7
Other	12.5	—	0.5	2.0	11.2	18.1	19.2	16.4	11.4	13.5
Myopia	4.0	0.8	6.5	4.9	4.9	4.4	2.9	1.5	4.3	3.7
Albinism	1.4	1.5	7.1	3.7	0.8	0.3	0.0	0.1	1.6	1.1
Anophthalmos & Microphthalmus	0.6	6.2	1.7	1.4	0.5	0.3	0.1	0.0	0.7	0.5
Other	3.3	10.1	7.1	6.2	4.0	2.3	1.2	0.4	4.3	2.3
Cornea and Sclera	5.0	1.6	2.0	4.9	7.0	5.9	4.5	3.0	5.0	4.9
Keratitis	2.0	0.8	0.6	1.6	3.2	2.5	1.6	1.0	1.6	2.2
Other	3.0	0.8	1.4	3.3	3.8	3.4	2.9	2.0	3.3	2.7
Lens	14.4	17.0	17.3	10.4	11.2	12.5	15.4	23.7	12.7	15.9
Cataract	13.8	17.0	15.8	9.5	10.3	12.0	15.2	23.5	12.2	15.2
Prenatal	2.6	16.3	12.9	5.4	2.0	0.8	0.3	0.1	3.3	2.0
Senile	8.3	—	—	0.5	5.4	9.0	12.4	20.6	6.0	10.5
Other	2.9	0.7	2.9	3.6	2.9	2.2	2.5	2.8	2.9	2.7
Other	0.6	0.0	1.5	0.9	0.9	0.5	0.2	0.2	0.5	0.7
Uveal Tract	6.1	4.7	5.8	8.2	8.7	6.1	4.1	2.8	6.5	5.7
Uveitis	2.3	0.8	0.9	2.7	3.4	3.1	1.7	1.0	2.2	2.5
Chorioretinitis	2.7	1.6	2.6	3.7	3.8	2.3	1.9	1.3	2.9	2.4
Other	1.1	2.3	2.3	1.8	1.5	0.7	0.5	0.5	1.4	0.8
Retina	30.9	17.1	19.6	31.8	28.8	30.5	34.6	35.0	29.1	32.5
Retinopathy of Prematurity	2.5	9.3	8.5	10.8	0.1	—	—	—	3.0	2.1
Detachment of retina	1.7	0.8	0.7	1.6	2.3	2.2	1.5	0.8	2.1	1.2
Macular degeneration	11.7	0.8	3.3	4.4	5.0	8.7	20.8	27.8	9.1	14.2
Retinitis pigmentosa	4.7	0.8	2.4	7.5	8.8	4.4	1.9	0.6	6.2	3.2
Diabetic retinopathy	6.6	—	0.1	4.2	9.8	11.7	6.0	1.8	5.3	7.7
Other retinopathy	1.7	0.8	0.3	0.4	1.3	2.0	2.9	2.8	1.4	2.0
Other	2.0	4.6	4.3	2.9	1.5	1.5	1.5	2.0	2.0	2.0
Optic Nerve & Optic Pathway	11.4	27.9	23.0	18.7	13.8	9.4	5.4	3.0	14.8	8.2
Optic nerve atrophy	7.0	12.4	12.2	10.3	8.6	6.5	2.8	2.2	8.9	5.1
Optic neuritis	1.6	1.6	1.0	2.9	2.6	1.5	0.8	0.4	2.2	1.1
Nystagmus	1.3	2.3	5.5	3.5	1.2	0.3	0.1	0.0	1.9	0.8
Other	1.5	11.6	4.3	2.0	1.4	1.1	0.7	0.4	1.8	1.2
Vitreous	0.2	0.7	0.1	0.2	0.4	0.4	0.2	0.1	0.3	0.2
Multiple Affections	5.4	—	0.4	1.0	3.8	6.2	8.7	10.0	3.6	7.0
Undetermined and Not Specific	3.8	6.2	5.2	4.0	4.2	3.4	3.5	3.6	4.2	3.6

Adapted from: NSPB, *Vision problems in the U.S.: Data analysis*, (New York, N.Y.: Author, 1980), p. 9.

Table 3.2   Leading causes of legal blindness for selected ages: U.S. 1978.

Causes	All ages N[1]	Rate[1]	Under 5 N[1]	Rate[1]	5-19 N[1]	Rate[1]	20-44 N[1]	Rate[1]
Glaucoma, except congenital	62,100	28.1						
Macular degeneration	58,250	26.3					3,650	4.7
Senile cataract	41,500	18.7						
Prenatal cataract			1,050	6.8	4,500	8.0	4,450	5.7
Optic nerve atrophy	34,500	15.6	800	5.2	4,250	7.5	8,550	10.9
Diabetic retinopathy	32,650	4.8					3,500	4.5
Retinitis pigmentosa	23,250	10.5					6,200	7.9
Myopic	19,850	8.9			2,250	4.0	4,050	5.2
Retinopathy of prematurity			600	3.9	2,950	5.2	8,950	11.4
Anophthalmos, microphthalmus, glaucoma, congenital			400	2.6				
Retinoblastoma			250	1.6				
Albinism					2,500	4.4		
Nystagmus					1,900	3.4		
All other	225,900	102.1	2,700	17.6	16,400	29.0	43.450	55.5
TOTAL	498,000	225.1	6,450	42.0	34,750	61.6	82,800	105.7

[1]Per 100,000 population each age group. Ratios are based on population estimates in (000s) as of July 1, 1978. Adapted from: NSPB, *Vision problems in the U.S.: Data analysis*, (New York, N.Y.: Author, 1980), p. 11.

structures. The result can mean hearing loss, cardiac malformation, cataracts, and mental retardation in the child. Vaccine to immunize individuals against the disease is available and, while of no value to those who have already had rubella or been affected by it, it can decrease the number of persons who might contract the disease and transmit it to any pregnant woman not innoculated against it.

Other infectious diseases besides rubella can result in damage to eyes, either before birth or after. These include the venereal diseases, toxoplasmosis, tuberculosis, and trachoma. The latter is a leading cause of preventable blindness in Africa, Asia, and the Middle East. Trachoma is an infection of the conjunctiva and cornea that can lead to corneal scarring if not treated. Trachoma is preventable through the use of antibiotics. An estimated 400 million people in the world have trachoma and could sustain significant visual loss (Vaughan & Asbury, 1980).

Neoplasms are tumors. Tumors can cause damage to eye structures and possibly even necessitate the removal of the affected eye. Retinoblastoma, a life-threatening malignant tumor that in approximately 30 percent of the cases occurs bilaterally, usually appears before the child reaches the third birthday. At present, the treatment of choice is enucleation. In selected cases when the tumor is small, radiation and cryosurgery are options. Tumors affecting vision can occur in the brain, exterior to the eye in the orbit, in the pituitary gland, or in the eyeball itself.

Many general systemic diseases that affect the vascular and metabolic systems put the eyes at risk. Diabetes is a prime example of a metabolic disorder that can result in diabetic retinopathy with changes in the retinal blood vessels, hemorrhages, and proliferation of blood vessels. The occurrence of diabetic retinopathy seems to be more closely related to the duration and control rather than to the severity of the diabetes. At greatest risk are those individuals who have been diabetic for twenty years or more (Vaughan & Asbury, 1980). Although children who have diabetes may not experience eye difficulties, as they grow older, the possibility of eye problems increases. Note in Table 3.3 the increase in the percentage of cases through age 74.

Multiple sclerosis, thyroid gland disorders, certain vitamin deficiencies, and other systemic diseases can lead to eye problems with vision loss. While the total numbers of children affected may be relatively small, some cases do occur and are of extreme significance to the individuals affected.

As with many attempts to identify the causes of blindness and limited vision among the general population and attempts by the NSPB to uncover major causes specifically among school age children (Hatfield, 1975), a concern is the large number of cases of blindness reported as cause "undetermined" or "not specified." This designation along with the large number for which the cause is at present "unknown to science" accounts for over 23 percent of the cases reported. The glaucomas, except for those secondary to disease or trauma, fall under this category as in most cases the reason for the increase in pressure within the eye is not clearly understood.

A condition that frequently is found in children and adults whose vision has been impaired since birth or shortly thereafter is nystagmus. Nystagmus is an involuntary, rhythmical oscillating movement of one or both eyes from side to side, up and down, in a rotary pattern, or in some combination. The movement can be pendular and regular or jerky with a comparatively slow move in one direction and a rapid return. Nystagmus may accompany other eye conditions, usually those that have existed for an extended period of time. It can also be congenital or originate during the first two or three years of life. Treatment is directed at the primary condition if the nystagmus accompanies another condition. Nystagmus alone is usually asymptomatic (Faye, 1984), but some children and adults may turn or tilt the head in an effort to decrease the speed, amplitude, or duration of the eye movements. The mechanism for nystagmus is not fully understood (Vaughan & Asbury, 1980). Under certain circumstances nystagmus can be elicited in individuals with normal vision, for example by looking as far to the side as possible for a period of time or by watching a rotating drum marked with alternating dark and light bands or looking at railroad cars moving along the tracks.

Table 3.3   Percentage distribution of total cases of legal blindness by age and sex according to etiology: U.S. 1978.

Etiology†	Total	Age							Sex	
		0-5	5-19	20-44	45-64	65-74	75-84	85+	Males	Females
TOTAL	100.0	100.0	100.0	100.0	100.0	100.0	100.0	100.0	100.0	100.0
Infectious Disease	4.6	14.0	6.7	5.1	6.1	5.2	2.8	1.3	4.8	4.4
Rubella	0.5	10.8	4.0	0.2	0.0	—	—	—	0.5	0.4
Syphilis	1.7	0.0	0.1	1.3	2.9	2.7	1.1	0.4	2.1	1.3
Toxoplasmosis	0.3	1.6	1.3	0.9	0.2	0.1	0.0	—	0.4	0.3
Trachoma	0.2	—	0.0	0.0	0.1	0.3	0.4	0.3	0.2	0.2
Tuberculosis	0.1	0.0	0.1	0.2	0.3	0.2	0.1	0.0	0.1	0.2
Other	1.8	1.6	1.2	2.5	2.6	1.9	1.2	0.6	1.5	2.0
Injuries/Poisonings	6.4	9.3	10.8	18.5	6.5	3.4	1.6	0.7	8.6	4.3
Excess oxygen (ROP)	2.5	9.3	8.5	10.8	0.1	—	—	—	1.9	3.1
Other	3.9	—	2.3	7.7	6.4	3.4	1.6	0.7	6.7	1.2
Neoplasms	1.1	5.4	3.5	2.2	1.4	0.5	0.2	—	1.2	1.0
Retinoblastoma	0.2	3.9	1.4	0.5	0.1	—	—	—	0.3	0.2
Other	0.9	1.5	2.1	1.7	1.3	0.5	0.2	—	0.9	0.8
General Diseases	31.8	3.1	3.2	8.9	23.8	36.9	47.8	58.7	23.7	39.4
Diabetes	7.9	—	0.0	4.8	11.3	14.5	7.5	2.6	6.1	9.7
Senile degeneration	20.1	—	—	0.3	8.5	18.8	36.0	53.0	14.0	25.8
Vascular disease	2.0	—	0.3	0.5	1.9	1.9	3.5	2.7	2.0	1.9
Other	1.8	3.1	2.9	3.3	2.1	1.8	0.8	0.4	1.6	2.0
Prenatal Influence	19.5	55.0	52.2	44.2	21.8	9.9	4.5	1.7	24.9	14.4
Hereditary	14.7	37.2	40.1	31.8	17.1	7.8	3.6	1.5	18.6	11.1
Other congenital	4.8	17.8	12.1	12.4	4.7	2.1	0.9	0.2	6.3	3.3
Unknown to Science	13.2	0.0	2.6	4.9	12.8	17.5	18.8	16.1	12.5	13.8
Multiple Etiologies††	3.1	—	0.1	0.4	2.3	3.8	5.4	4.9	2.2	3.9
Undetermined and Not Specified	20.3	13.2	20.9	15.9	25.3	22.8	18.9	16.6	22.0	18.7

†Estimated distribution according to etiology by National Society to Prevent Blindness based on unpublished Model Reporting Area register data as of December 31, 1970.

††Includes: Senile degeneration and diabetes (5%), Senile degeneration and other etiology except diabetes (65%), Diabetes and other etiology except senile degeneration (6%), and all other combinations (24%).

Adapted from: NSPB, *Vision problems in the U.S.: Data analysis*, (New York, N.Y.: Author, 1980), p. 8.

Table 3.4   Most hazardous products, all ages and each age group: U.S., 1977.

Product	Number of Eye Injuries[1]	% of Total in Age group
All ages:		
1. Metal pieces, nos[2]	24,609	9.4
2. Contact lenses	17,559	6.7
3. Motor vehicles, except two wheeled	8,294	3.2
4. Other chemicals	6,950	2.7
5. Baseball	6,918	2.6
6. Glass, unknown origin	6,240	2.4
Total	262,112	100.0
Under 5 years of age:		
1. Cigarettes, cigars, pipes	2,278	9.3
2. Clothes hangers, all types	771	3.1
3. Beds, nos[2]	720	2.9
4. Toys, nos[2]	648	2.6
5. Tables, cocktail	625	2.5
6. Motor vehicles, except two wheeled	584	2.4
Total in age group	24,616	100.0
5-14 years of age:		
1. Baseball	2,799	6.0
2. Pencils, nos[2]	1,767	3.8
3. Metal pieces, nos[2]	1,759	3.8
4. Glass, unknown origin	1,649	3.6
Total in age group	46,269	100.0
15-24 years of age:		
1. Contact lenses	10,797	13.4
2. Metal pieces, nos[2]	8,544	10.6
3. Sun lamps	3,299	4.1
4. Motor vehicles, except two wheeled	3,131	3.9
5. Welding equipment, nos3/4[2]	2,219	2.7
6. Batteries, nos[2]	2,166	2.7
Total in age group	80,856	100.0
25-64 years of age:		
1. Metal pieces, nos[2]	13,900	13.2
2. Contact lenses	6,093	5.8
3. Motor vehicles, except two wheeled	4,179	3.9
4. Other chemicals	3,324	3.1
5. Batteries, wet cell	3,061	2.9
Total in age group	105,694	100.0

[1] Estimates from the U.S. Consumer Product Safety Commission, unpublished data. Those for the 65 and over age group omitted because numbers are too small for reliability.
[2] not otherwise specified

Adapted from: NSPB, *Vision Problems in the U.S.: Data analysis* (New York, N.Y.: Author, 1980), p. 30.

Diagnosis of Visual Impairments

Parents and teachers may be the first to suspect that something is wrong with a child's eyes. Various eye specialists are trained in the use of diagnostic procedures to determine specific causes or rule out any problem with the child's eyes. Teachers and parents may find themselves conferring with ophthalmologists, optometrists, orthoptists, and opticians as they seek eye care. An *ophthalmologist* is a medical eye specialist or physician who concentrates on the diagnosis and treatment of defects and diseases of the eye by prescribing lenses, performing surgery, using drugs and other forms of medical treatment. An *optometrist* is a trained and licensed nonmedical eye specialist who measures refractive errors and muscle disturbances and prescribes and fits lenses. Some optometrists, and also some ophthalmologists, specialize in the evaluation of patients for possible use of low vision aids. (See Chapter 6.) In some low vision clinics both of these eye specialists are on the staff. Working in conjunction with some eye specialists is the *orthoptist* who is trained to give eye exercises in cases of muscle imbalance and suppression of foveal stimulation. An *optician* is a technician trained to grind lenses according to prescription, fit contact and spectacle lenses, and adjust spectacle frames to the wearer.

Eye specialists use a wide variety of diagnostic procedures and tests in their assessment of the integrity, health, and function of the eye and the optic pathways that lead to the back of the brain. Among the more common procedures are the following ones, but the eye specialist will decide which of these or other more sophisticated procedures are called for in a given situation.

1. Notation of symptoms patient may exhibit—pain, double vision, tearing, dryness, blind spots, halos around lights, floaters, photophobia (light sensitivity), poor night vision, blurriness, difficulty reading, etc. In combination with a careful and detailed history, this information is a rich source and will help determine the type and extent of further testing.

2. Check appearance of eyes—attention to size, shape, position, color, presence of discharge, inflammation, etc.

3. Visual acuity—Typically visual acuity is checked with the Snellen Letter or E Chart, the latter preferred for children and any others who cannot accurately identify letters. Acuities are taken for both distance and near vision.

4. Field of vision—The normal field of vision, illustrated in Figure 3.10, covers approximately 150 degrees on the nasal to temporal axis and approximately 120 degrees on the superior to inferior axis (Jose, 1983). A number of different confrontation techniques using grids and screens can be used to determine defects in the central field and the peripheral field of vision in each eye. The eye specialist will select the one most appropriate to the specific situation.

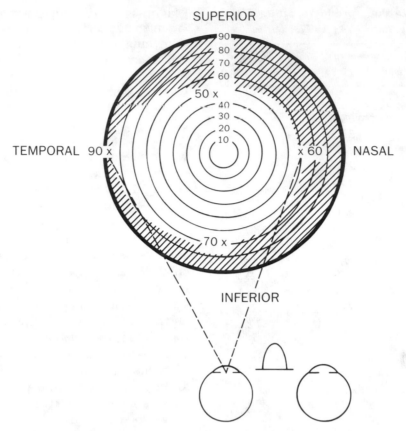

Figure 3.10   The normal full visual field for the left eye.

Source: R. Jose, *Understanding low vision* (New York, N.Y.: American Foundation for the Blind, Inc., 1983), p. 98.

5. Biomicroscopy—Use of a slit lamp with high power magnification and illumination provides the eye specialist with a more detailed view of the eyelids and eyeball.

6. Tonometry—Intraocular pressure may be measured by several techniques. Tonometers require the use of a local anesthetic solution in the eye. Most glaucoma screening programs use a technique that does not involve touching the eye with anything except a puff of air. This type of screening procedure is quite satisfactory for initial screening purposes, but indentation and applanation tonometry are considered more precise for clinical purposes.

7. Ophthalmoscopic examination—The ophthalmoscope provides a good view of the retina and the internal structures of the eye. The ophthalmologist routinely instills a mydriatic, a drug that dilates the pupil but does not affect accommodation, so as to obtain access to the peripheral retina and regions of the fundus. The ophthalmoscope is considered indispensable in the study of eye diseases (Vaughan & Asbury, 1980).

8. Gonioscopy—Particularly in suspected cases of glaucoma, gonioscopy is done to examine by direct visualization the anterior chamber angle. Local anesthetic, special lighting, a special microscope, and a goniolens are required for the examination.

9. Corneal staining—To reveal corneal abrasions and irregularities, or to help locate foreign bodies in the eye, a dye may be instilled in the eye. Fluorescein dye is frequently selected.

10. Color perception—Tests for color perception require that the patient identify patterns, often numbers, made up of colored dots on a background of dots of a different color. The colors are selected so patterns are not discernible to persons with color perception defects in the frequencies of those colors. Red-green confusion is the most common problem in both males (8 percent) and females (0.4 percent) while blue-yellow is quite rare in both sexes (Vaughan & Asbury, 1980). Problems with color vision are almost always sex-linked and transmitted through the mother to the male offspring.

11. Amsler Grid—To detect blind spots or scotomas in the visual field, a patient may be asked to focus on a dot on a grid chart and then indicate any area of distortion on the grid or absence of grid pattern. Blind spots in the field can indicate where on the retina or in other structures there may be damage.

Sometimes for a variety of reasons, children, and even adults, will try to fake poor vision. Using prisms and special lenses and mirrors, eye specialists can catch attempts to feign poor vision or blindness.

While the previous list of assessment procedures and techniques contains those frequently encountered during an eye examination, there are many other more sophisticated noninvasive procedures as well. Some of these techniques that may be helpful in the diagnosis and treatment of eye problems found in low vision and blind children and youth are described in Appendix A.

One of the skills needed by teachers of visually handicapped youngsters is the ability to interpret information reported by eye specialists to determine what is relevant for instructional purposes and what signs school personnel should watch for that might suggest significant deterioration, or improvement, in a child's eye condition. The next section contains a description of the information frequently contained in reports completed for school programs by eye specialists. (See Chart 3.2 for other diagnostic procedures.)

INTERPRETING EYE REPORTS

In most programs for visually handicapped school aged children, an eye examination report completed by an eye specialist, either an ophthalmologist or an optometrist, is required annually for each child in the program or for each child referred to the program. Many school districts, intermediate units, counties, and administrative units have adopted the form developed by the NSPB or have designed one similar to it for this annual report. A current report is retained in the permanent record folder for each child in the program.

The information on the annual eye report is clinical in nature and may not be directly useful in determining instructional objectives and teaching strategies. There is, nevertheless, much information that is valuable to the teacher of both low vision and blind students. A review of the types of information requested on the NSPB form should illustrate the importance of the data for the astute teacher. Refer to Figure 3.11 and Chart 3.3 as you read the following sections. Each section will describe one type of information to be reported on the NSPB Eye Report Form.

Identifying Information

A record of the child's name, age, address, and school placement identifies for the eye specialist the child for whom the report is requested. While in some cases the parent may take the form to the eye specialist who can then complete it at the time of the child's eye exam, in most cases, the report form will be mailed to the eye specialist along with a cover letter that explains why the report is needed. Rather than expect the eye specialist to fill in the identifying information,

Chart 3.2   Specialized diagnostic procedures

Visually-Evoked Potential (VEP) - an objective measure mainly of macular function as measured with scalp electrodes placed over the occipital cortex. The VEP can be used to detect lesions in the optic nerve and pathways to the brain (Faye, 1983).

Electroretinopathy (ERG) - the "best single objective test of overall retinal function" (Faye, 1983, p. 223). The ERG measures electrical responses from the retina when flashing light is presented to both the light- and dark-adapted eye. It is particularly useful in the diagnosis of retinitis pigmentosa, even before the presence of symptoms or visible fundus lesions (Faye, 1983, p. 226).

Electro-oculography (EOG) - test of the function of retinal pigment epithelium. The EOG requires that the patient be able to cooperate during the testing time by changing fixation from one visual target to another. Skin electrodes pick up shifts in corneal-retinal electrical potential as the gaze switches, and changes in potential are considered indicative of problems in the retinal pigment epithelium, one of the nine layers of the retina. Faye (1983) reports that the ERG is perhaps a better test of overall retinal function than the EOG which is not widely used in clinical practice.

Ultrasonography - provides a measure of the structural integrity of the eye by using the reflection of extremely high-frequency waves to determine shape, size, thickness, position, and density of soft tissue in the orbit and the eyeball. Ultrasonography and echography are helpful in locating tumors and foreign bodies, and in detecting detached retinas.

Computer-assisted tomography (CT) - a primary procedure for X-ray diagnosis of orbit and brain lesions (Vaughan & Asbury, 1980). By taking many readings in the transverse axial plane and using a computer to reconstruct a picture from the readings in any specific plane, the specialist can obtain 3-dimensional representations of orbital structures, fatty tissue, sinuses, muscles, and areas adjacent to the globe and orbit. CT scans are relatively fast, safe, and noninvasive which makes them a very valuable diagnostic procedure.

Contrast sensitivity (CS) - a subjective measure of an individual's ability to detect and discriminate objects and fine detail under conditions of reduced or low contrast (Ginsburg et al, 1984; Faye, 1983). CS curves indicate how a person can see large targets (low spatial frequency) of poor contrast as well as small targets (high spatial frequency) such as letters or planes or road signs of poor contrast. Faye (1983) has noted that CS curves may help explain why, even when Snellen acuities are within the normal range, functional vision for the visual tasks during the course of a normal day may present problems. CS tests can be quite useful in the evaluation of patients with cataracts, multiple sclerosis, early glaucoma, and amblyopia (Faye, 1983; Ginsburg, 1981).

CONFIDENTIAL   EYE REPORT FOR CHILDREN WITH VISUAL PROBLEMS   **R L B**

NAME OF PUPIL_____ SEX_____ RACE_____
(Type or print)   (First)   (Middle)   (Last)

ADDRESS_____ DATE OF BIRTH_____
(No. and street)   (City or town)   (County)   (State)   (Month) (Day) (Year)

GRADE_____ SCHOOL_____ ADDRESS_____

I. HISTORY

A. Probable age at onset of vision impairment. Right eye (O.D.)_____ Left eye (O.S.)_____

B. Severe ocular infections, injuries, operations, if any, with age at time of occurrence _____
_____

C. Has pupil's ocular condition occurred in any blood relative(s)? _____ If so, what relationship(s)?_____

II. MEASUREMENTS (See back of form for preferred notation for recording visual acuity and table of approximate equivalents.)

A. VISUAL ACUITY

	DISTANT VISION			NEAR VISION			PRESCRIPTION		
	Without correction	With best correction*	With low vision aid	Without correction	With best correction*	With low vision aid	Sph.	Cyl.	Axis
Right eye (O.D.)	_____	_____	_____	_____	_____	_____	_____	_____	_____
Left eye (O.S.)	_____	_____	_____	_____	_____	_____	_____	_____	_____
Both eyes (O.U.)	_____	_____	_____	_____	_____	_____	Date_____		

B. If glasses are to be worn, were safety lenses prescribed in: Plastic_____ Tempered glass_____ *with ordinary lenses

C. If low vision aid is prescribed, specify type and recommendations for use. _____
_____

D. FIELD OF VISION: Is there a limitation? _____ If so, record results of test on chart on back of form.

What is the widest diameter (in degrees) of remaining visual field? O.D._____ O.S._____

E. Is there impaired color perception? _____ If so, for what color(s)?_____

III. CAUSE OF BLINDNESS OR VISION IMPAIRMENT

A. Present ocular condition(s) responsible for vision impairment. (If more than one, specify all but underline the one which probably first caused severe vision impairment.)

O.D. _____

O.S. _____

B. Preceding ocular condition, if any, which led to present condition, or the underlined condition, specified in A.

O.D. _____

O.S. _____

C. Etiology (underlying cause) of ocular condition primarily responsible for vision impairment. (e.g., specific disease, injury, poisoning, heredity or other prenatal influence.)

O.D. _____

O.S. _____

D. If etiology is injury or poisoning, indicate circumstances and kind of object or poison involved. _____
_____

IV. PROGNOSIS AND RECOMMENDATIONS

A. Is pupil's vision impairment considered to be: Stable_____ Deteriorating_____ Capable of improvement_____ Uncertain_____

B. What treatment is recommended, if any?_____

C. When is reexamination recommended?_____

D. Glasses: Not needed_____ To be worn constantly_____ For close work only_____ Other (specify)_____

E. Lighting requirements: Average_____ Better than average_____ Less than average_____

F. Use of eyes: Unlimited_____ Limited, as follows:_____

G. Physical activity: Unrestricted_____ Restricted, as follows:_____

TO BE FORWARDED BY EXAMINER TO:

Date of examination_____

Signature of examiner _____ Degree_____

Address _____

If clinic case: Number_____ Name of clinic_____

Figure 3.11   **Eye report for children with visual problems**

PREFERRED VISUAL ACUITY NOTATIONS

DISTANT VISION. Use Snellen notation with test distance of 20 feet. (Examples: 20/100, 20/60). For acuities less than 20/200 record distance at which 200 foot letter can be recognized as numerator of fraction and 200 as denominator. (Examples: 10/200, 3/200). If the 200 foot letter is not recognized at 1 foot record abbreviation for best distant vision as follows:

HM	HAND MOVEMENTS
PLL	PERCEIVES AND LOCALIZES LIGHT IN ONE OR MORE QUADRANTS
LP	PERCEIVES BUT DOES NOT LOCALIZE LIGHT
No LP	NO LIGHT PERCEPTION

NEAR VISION. Use standard A.M.A. notation and specify best distance at which pupil can read. (Example: 14/70 at 5 in.)

TABLE OF APPROXIMATE EQUIVALENT VISUAL ACUITY NOTATIONS

These notations serve only as an indication of the approximate relationship between recordings of distant and near vision and point type sizes. The teacher will find in practice that the pupil's reading performance may vary considerably from the equivalents shown.

Distant Snellen	Near A.M.A.	Near Jaeger	Near Metric	% Central Visual Efficiency for Near	Point	Usual Type Text Size
20/20 (ft.)	14/14 (in.)	1	0.37 (M.)	100	3	Mail order catalogue
20/30	14/21	2	0.50	95	5	Want ads
20/40	14/28	4	0.75	90	6	Telephone directory
20/50	14/35	6	0.87	50	8	Newspaper text
20/60	14/42	8	1.00	40	9	Adult text books
20/80	14/56	10	1.50	20	12	Children's books 9-12 yrs
20/100	14/70	11	1.75	15	14	Children's books 8-9 yrs.
20/120	14/84	12	2.00	10	18 }	
20/200	14/140	17	3.50	2	24 }	Large type text
12.5/200	14/224	19	6.00	1.5		
8/200	14/336	20	8.00	1		
5/200	14/560					
3/200	14/900					

FIELD OF VISION. Record results on chart below.

Type of test used:_____   Illumination in ft. candles:_____

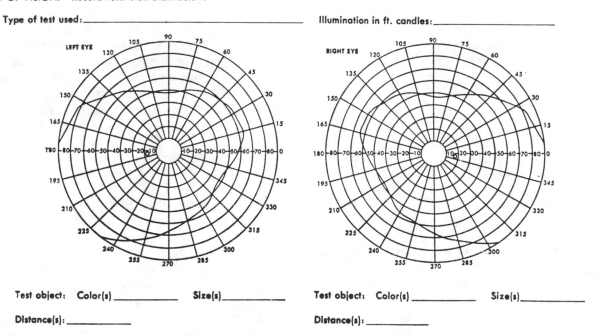

Test object: Color(s)_____   Size(s)_____   Test object: Color(s)_____   Size(s)_____

Distance(s):_____   Distance(s):_____

Stat 4 Rev/869/10M National Society to Prevent Blindness, 79 Madison Avenue, New York, NY 10016

Figure 3.11   Eye report for children with visual problems

it should be supplied whether the form is mailed or is hand-carried by the child or the parent. In a few situations, the teacher may accompany the child and parent to the examination and can present the form with the request that the information for the other sections be reported at the completion of the examination.

The information on the eye report should be considered confidential in nature, as is indicated on the form itself, just as are any other records pertaining to the child's achievement, performance, health, behavior, and potential. Teachers, guidance counselors, and administrators who legitimately have access to the child's records must respect this confidentiality. Chart 3.3 presents abbreviations frequently used in eye reports.

History

Obtaining a complete and accurate history of previous health problems, treatments, and habits is considered to be one of the most critical components of any type of physical examination. Certain elements of the health history are particularly important for the teacher of visually handicapped youngsters to know about, not only for what they might contribute to a better understanding of the present condition of the child being examined but also for what they might suggest regarding the child's record of past eye care and parent follow-through and possible dangers for other family members.

O.D.	ocular dexter (right eye)
O.S.	ocular sinister (left eye)
O.U.	oculi unitas (both eyes)
△	prism diopter
+	plus or convex lens
−	minus or concave lens
C.F.	count fingers
H.M.	hand movements
L.P.	light perception
N.L.P.	no light perception

Chart 3.3   Abbreviations frequently encountered in eye reports.

One of the first questions asked during the collection of the health history pertains to the probable age of onset of the eye problem. A preschool youngster who has had little or no functional vision since birth brings to school that first day a very different repertoire of experiences in terms of both quantity and quality from those of the child who has enjoyed normal vision since birth. (See Chapters 4 and 7.) Children learn much by just watching what others are doing, by visually exploring their surroundings, and by combining their visual examination with tactual investigations of objects

they grasp and even mouth. Later chapters in this text explain the development of vision and vision perception and its impact on cognitive, psychomotor, and psychosocial development. (See Chapters 4, 5, and 6.) For purposes of this discussion, it is sufficient to point out that the congenitally visually handicapped child, the child whose visual impairment and subsequent limitations in functional vision have existed since birth or shortly thereafter, generally has learning characteristics and instructional needs that are significantly different from the adventitiously visually handicapped child, the child whose limitations in visual function developed after the age of three or four years (Lowenfeld, 1981). The instructional needs of both children in school may call for modifications in the regular school program in order for these children to receive an appropriate education.

Other aspects of the health history are also important: previous eye problems that have required medical treatment and the age at which those occurred, immediate or extended family members who have the same eye condition as the child, or other eye problems that may be hereditary. The teacher of visually handicapped children will, at some point, want to discuss with the parents whether or not other family members have been examined to determine if signs of any hereditary eye problems are evident.

Measurements

Visual Acuity

Clinical measurements of vision include distance and near visual acuities with and without correction, a report of what correction has been prescribed for spectacle or contact lenses, a record of the field of vision for each eye, and information about any problem with color vision. Distance visual acuity is perhaps the measurement that many teachers will check first, but all of the other measurements and especially near vision are also important for what they can suggest about functional vision that should be explored in the classroom setting.

As mentioned in Chapter 2, determination of eligibility for services because of limited vision is frequently made on the basis of severe field loss or limited distance visual acuity—20/200 or less in the better eye after or with the best correction, the definition of blindness for legal purposes. On the eye report, distance acuity can be reported with and without correction. Many times children who wear corrective lenses are checked only while wearing their lenses. For some people no correction with lenses is possible; consequently, no acuity would be reported in that column on the report form.

For school-aged youngsters, near vision acuity is extremely important. Acuity is reported with and without correction for near vision. When a child has been fitted with a low vision aid, either some type of telebinocular or monocular aid for distance or a magnifying aid for near work, acuity is reported for vision when using that aid. (See Chapter 6.) As will be explained in later chapters, visual acuity measures taken in a clinical setting that may be strange, perhaps even anxiety-producing and certainly quite different from the typical work setting at home or school, can give a good idea of visual function in that setting; but they will not necessarily reveal how efficiently a given child will use his vision at school or home. It is imperative that the teacher of visually handicapped children determine how the child uses whatever vision he has at school, under what conditions he can work best, and what modifications in the task, time limits, materials, setting, and/or lighting might increase that child's visual function. That information in summary form should be made available to the eye specialist for review before the child's examination.

At times, there may to be a discrepancy between the acuity demonstrated in the clinical setting, at school, or at home. Many factors can contribute to this discrepancy, not the least of which is anxiety. The astute teacher will consider other possibilities as well. For example, a five year-old child was referred to a school program because the eye specialist found her visual acuity to be 20/200 O.U. and he was concerned about her school performance. The teacher of visually handicapped who received the referral note talked with the child's kindergarten teacher, with the school nurse who knew the family, and then spent time watching the little girl draw, color, and do her reading readiness activities.

It was clear that, while she could copy shapes and letters accurately, she did not know the names of the shapes or letters. She appeared to have no problem seeing details or color, and she worked with materials at the normal distance from her eyes. During the teacher's conversation with the eye specialist, mention was made of the fact that the child did not yet know the names of the alphabet letters. When the eye report form was returned to the school several weeks later, the child's visual acuity was reported to be well within the normal range for a child five years old. The child's acuity had first been checked with the Snellen Letter Chart and her performance was, of course, poor because she had not yet learned the letter names and could not match them to the letter shapes. When checked with the Snellen E Chart in several weeks, her performance improved dramatically. Teachers need to be alert to possible reasons for poor performance in one setting and not in others.

A word needs to be said about reports of the distance from the visual target at which visual acuities are taken. For distance vision, the usual distance is twenty feet or the simulation of twenty feet. Sometimes a visually handicapped person will be able to see the largest visual target on the test chart only at some distance closer than twenty feet. The examiner may then report an acuity such as 10/400, which means that the individual recognized at a distance of ten feet what a person with normal acuity, or 20/20, could recognize at a distance of 400 feet. While such information is helpful for some purposes, such as for the determination of eligibility for services, it does not reveal much useful information regarding visual efficiency and performance in the nonclinical setting.

Measurements of near visual acuity are generally given in terms of inches, meters, or Jaeger chart numbers that pertain to type size. The NSPB form has a conversion chart that can be helpful in deciphering the specialist's notation if it is not in the anticipated figures. Check the back side of the form for a table of approximate equivalent notations.

Lenses

Knowing how to read a child's prescription can provide information about the strength or power of the lenses the child is to wear and suggest factors the teacher of visually handicapped and the regular class teacher should keep in mind. While understanding the intricacies of prescription lenses is well beyond the scope of this text, certain basic information is not.

Prescriptions for corrective lenses are reported in terms of the refractive or bending power of the lenses. The unit of bending power of an optical lense is measured in diopters. For a convex lens, one that converges light rays as would be necessary to sharpen vision in the hyperopic eye, the shorter the focal distance, the more powerful the lens. (See Figure 3.12.) A convex or plus lens of 10D would have more bending power than a 2D lens. The same is true for a concave or minus lens that diverges light rays, as would be necessary for the myopic eye; the shorter the focal length the more bending, in this case spreading, power the lens has. A −10D lens would be more powerful or stronger than a −2D lens.

Corrective lenses can be spherical or cylindrical. A spherical lens has the same refractive power on all axes, while a cylindrical lens has more power along one axis than along others. Spherical lenses are prescribed for simple refractive errors and cylindrical lenses are used to correct for astigmatism. The NSPB Eye Report Form provides space for recording the power of the spherical lens prescribed for each eye, any cylindrical lens, and the axis or direction in which the cylindrical power is to be set. If an individual has been given a bifocal lens, then that will usually be reported as OU− add +3D (both lenses will have an added power of +3D for near vision, probably fixed for a comfortable reading distance).

What, then, is important for the teacher of visually handicapped children to note when examining the

CONVEX (CONVERGING) LENSES

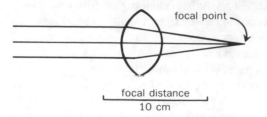

A. +10 D lens

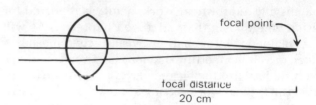

B. +5 D lens

CONCAVE (DIVERGING) LENSES

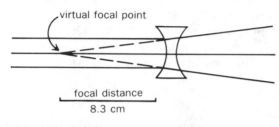

C. −12 D lens

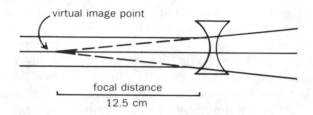

D. −8 D lens

Figure 3.12   Power of lenses

prescription portion of a child's eye report? A number of items should stand out:

Power of the lens: The more power, generally the poorer the individual's vision is without correction and the more important it is for the lenses to be worn all the time. The exception to this would be for some nearsighted children who might remove their glasses for near vision tasks since their natural near vision may be sufficient.

Presence of astigmatism: With astigmatism, it becomes even more important for the child not only to keep his spectacles on but also to keep them adjusted on his face properly so the power of the corrective lenses matches up accurately with the power of the child's eye on the various meridians.

Power of a lens greater than +12D: This could suggest that the child's own lens had been removed. That could be confirmed or rejected by checking other parts of the report to see if the child is aphakic or has had cataract surgery. It could also mean that the child is extremely farsighted. In extreme cases, even distance vision after correction may not be very good.

Very strong minus lens: a −6D to −8D or stronger lens will probably mean the wearer is quite nearsighted.

Disparity between strength of correction in one eye compared to that of the other eye: When the difference between the powers of the two lenses is large, as in the case of a child who is extremely farsighted in one eye and nearsighted in the other (anisometropia), the child may tend to favor one eye for some tasks, like reading, over the other. The reason is related to the difference in the size of the image received on the retina of each eye; a plus lens that converges light rays tends to increase the size of the image. A difference in size, if noticeable to the individual, may be resolved by some youngsters by favoring one eye over the other for tasks requiring near vision.

Safety lenses: Ideally, all people who wear spectacle lenses should have safety lenses that are shatter resistant. Spectacle frames should be fire resistant as well. Some tragic accidents have been reported to the NSPB as a result of lenses shattering, cutting the eyelids, and/or penetrating the cornea or deeper structures of the eye. The NSPB-sponsored Wise Owl Club and Wise Owl Jr. Club members give ample testimony to the advantages of wearing safety lenses or safety goggles in laboratories and workshops. Each year new members are added to the clubs by having their eyesight saved in industrial or school laboratory accidents as a result of wearing safety lenses or goggles.

Low vision aids: In Chapter 6, much more will be said about the various types of head-borne, hand-held, and stand-type low vision aids. If an aid has been prescribed or a recommendation has been made that the child be evaluated at a low vision clinic to determine whether or not an aid might be helpful, then the teacher of visually handicapped pupils needs to be certain either that the child has the aid and knows how and when to use it or that the appointment is made and kept for the low vision evaluation.

Field of Vision

Some youngsters have very good central visual acuity but limited field or peripheral vision. The field loss may be in one or both eyes and may or may not be in the same location in each field. Children with impaired central vision may have patches or islands of useful vision of varying sizes which will require that they learn to redirect their gaze in order to permit rays of light entering the eye to stimulate that portion of their retina that is actually activated by light. Children whose visual acuity in the better eye exceeds 20/200 may be eligible for services for visually handicapped youngsters if their field of vision in the better eye is reduced to 20 degrees or less.

Usually the eye report for a child with a field loss will contain an illustration to indicate where the child's fields are restricted and to what degree. Such information can be helpful to the child and the teacher to confirm where areas of functional field are and to suggest directions of gaze that might collect more stimuli than a direct gaze could, especially if the child's central vision is not clear or sharp. (Note the Field of Vision charts on Figures 3.11 and 3.13.)

Several types of tests can determine the extent of any field loss. The purpose of all of them is to identify where in the visual field for each eye the individual can see the test objects or light points. The results are generally used to make inferences about what portions of the retina of each eye are sensitive to light stimulation. If for some other reason the field is restricted, as might be the case after retinal hemorrhage or optic nerve damage, the test results indicate from where in the field light rays can actually pass unimpeded through the various media of the eye to the retina.

Children with extensive field losses need to be alert to auditory and other cues that warn of people and/or objects present or approaching from the area where visual cues are absent. They also must learn to move the head and eyes to scan their environment with the part of the vision that is still functional.

Color Perception

Problems with discriminating color are much more common in males than in females (Vaughan & Asbury, 1980). Complete absence of color vision (achromatopsia) is quite rare, .3 per 100,000 in males and lower in females (Jose, 1983), and most people who do have difficulty interpreting color have normal visual acuity (Vaughan & Asbury, 1980). Children and adults may confuse colors because their retinal cone receptors lack the pigment necessary or else their cones are less sensitive in general to light waves and levels of light intensity and do not detect red-orange, yellow-green, or blue light wave lengths when light waves strike them.

Usually, there are no serious learning problems when teachers are aware that a child has difficulty distin-guishing various colors and hues. But for beginning readers, for example, whose activities may include "reading" picture stories or drawing their own pictures to illustrate stories they make up or hear, appropriate use of colors and color words may pose a problem and result in unusual combinations. Another area of concern is the recognition of color in traffic lights when a child must cross light-controlled intersections. The child who cannot clearly distinguish red from green can learn which color appears where on the traffic signal and what is correct behavior for the red, the green, and the yellow positions. One bright second grader who had learned that he was to cross when the bottom (on a vertical sign) or right (on a horizontal signal) green traffic light was on, asked his teacher what he should do when the middle light switched on. That same child had taught himself to read the names of the colors printed on his crayons so he could color his pictures according to the teacher's instructions. He had difficulties, however, when no instructions were given and when the teacher based the questions asked during reading class on color aspects of the pictures—"What is the boy in the red shirt doing?"

If problems with color perception are suspected, the teacher should consider this when selecting instruc-tional materials or discussing strategies with the child's regular teacher. Color deficiency can be a serious problem when trying to follow color-coded directions or seeking employment in occupations which require the best possible perception of all colors. Problems with color perception for school-age children usually do not create major difficulties so long as the teacher under-stands the possible limitations.

Some individuals have only one eye or normal vision in one eye but limited vision in the second eye. A child who has poor or no vision in one eye may need assis-tance to develop compensatory skills but not require even minor modifications in the instructional program. For example, a child with a temporal peripheral field loss may need to learn to be alert for sound cues that people or objects are approaching from that side and to turn his head in that direction to pick up visual cues. A child with poor central vision in one eye will want to determine where to hold reading materials so he can read with comfort and efficiency with his good eye. A child with useful vision in only one eye will need to be particularly alert for auditory signals from his blind side and will want to develop strategies to make up for the absence of depth perception. These might include looking for shadows and intervening objects and using knowledge of distance perspective to help determine the space between objects or the space between the viewer and other stationary or moving objects. Knowing specific situations in which judgment of distance is particularly difficult is also important: situations like running on a playground at recess, reaching for objects on a desk or shelf or items in the cafeteria line, or drivng behind a pickup truck from which boards or poles are extending.

Causes of Blindness and Visual Impairment

Most eye report forms provide space for the eye specialist to report what condition is affecting the eyes at that time and what previous conditions— diseases, injuries, infections, etc.—may have led up to the present condition. For example, a child may be extremely nearsighted and at high risk for retinal detachment or even secondary glaucoma because of degenerative myopia. The degree of degeneration as determined by clinical examination of the sclera, optic disk, choroid, retina, and vitreous may actually have little relationship to the severity of the myopia as measured by the strength of the correction, that is, the dioptic power, needed to bring visual acuity as close to 20/20 as possible (Vaughan & Asbury, 1980). While functional vision is a prime concern for instructional purposes, the degree of degeneration is a major focus in the clinical examination and in the determination of any restriction on physical activities. The teacher of visually handicapped pupils needs to be cognizant of the implications of eye conditions and should examine carefully any information on etiology.

Frequently, the eye specialist will indicate if the condition is hereditary and what implications there might be for other family members. If the genetic patterns of transmission (autosomal dominant, autosomal recessive, or sex-linked) are known, the eye specialist may explain what they are. The teacher of visually handicapped youngsters can use this information in discussing with the family the importance of examinations for other family members who may be a risk either because they manifest clinical signs of the condition or because they may be carriers but not affected. In addition, there comes a time when the adolescent raises questions about his eye condition and whether or not that eye condition can be passed on to offspring. The teacher of visually handicapped adolescents may be the one whom the visually handicapped youngster approaches with questions. Though certainly not likely to be trained in genetics or an expert on patterns of genetic transmission of hereditary eye conditions, frequency of pentrance, degree of expression, or determination of pedigree, the teacher will want to know enough to respond to basic questions about dominant, recessive, and sex-linked patterns of transmission and to recognize when additional sources of information or referrals to genetic counseling clinics may be necessary and helpful. Teachers of blind and low vision children are often called upon to explain just what certain diagnoses mean, how the eye is affected, or what the educational implications of a particular disease or defect or hereditary condition are.

If the condition has been caused by injury or poisoning that occurred under circumstances at school that could have perhaps been avoided had adequate precautions been taken or supervision provided, certainly the teacher of visually handicapped pupils will want to do what is possible to prevent any similar event from happening in the future. The NSPB estimates that about 90 percent of all eye accidents might have been prevented had precautions been taken. Teachers may be able to prevent needless eye injury and possible loss of vision by anticipating thoughtless actions on the playground, noting where dangerous equipment or supplies are kept, recognizing improper use or placement of sports, shop and laboratory equipment, and insisting that protective goggles and safety lenses be used for risky instructional and athletic events.

Many times the etiology of a child's eye condition is simply not known (NSPB, 1980). Sometimes a condition can be given a name and clearly identified as, for example, glaucoma or congenital cataracts, but the reason the condition exists in the first place may not be known to science at this time. Additional research into cause and treatment and more information about the effects of disease, infection, environmental pollution, nutrition, and lifestyle on the human body should eventually lead to the identification of ways to prevent or at least reduce the incidence of visual impairment among both the school-age and adult population.

Prognosis and Recommendations

The eye specialist should note for the child's file any information regarding the stability of the child's eye condition. If the condition may deteriorate, the teacher needs to know what signs the child might exhibit in school that could indicate a significant change. For example, a child with Marfans syndrome might complain of blurry vision, a possible indication of a dislocated lens. The presence of significant signs calls for immediate contact with the child's family to arrange for examination by the child's eye specialist. It is better to err on the conservative side than to allow complaints that could indicate serious trouble to go unheeded.

The eye specialist will usually report what treatment has been recommended and when the child's next examination should be scheduled. The teacher should note this information and follow up with the parents to make certain recommendations are carried out. If medication is to be administered during the school hours, then the teacher can help obtain the permissions that the school district requires for school personnel to give the pills or eye drops that the child requires. Some medications have side effects that can affect school performance; therefore, the time that a child takes medication should be scheduled to the extent possible so as not to disrupt school activities.

Teachers should be alerted to any side effects such as drowsiness or blurred vision that might affect the child's energy level or work quality and report these observations to the child's eye specialist.

Some eye conditons such as degenerative myopia call for a restriction on certain types of physical activity, primarily that which has a high probability of hard physical contact with other players, e.g. football, field hockey, diving, or with playing equipment like in dodgeball or volleyball. If limits on physical activity or impact are advisable, then such information must be communicated to the student's teachers, especially the physical education teacher. But just because physical contact sports are restricted or ruled out does not mean that the visually handicapped student cannot participate in other types of physical activities and athletic events. This message also needs to be conveyed to the child's teachers as well as to the child.

Eye specialists may offer recommendations for classroom lighting requirements, seating for classroom work, type or mode of reading to be taught, and even school placement. These recommendations can be very helpful but must be considered in light of the context in which they are determined—the clinical environment which generally bears little resemblance to the child's school facilities.

While they may serve as a starting point for discussion, the teacher of visually handicapped students together with the particular child will need to determine the most comfortable ambiance and task lighting levels for classwork, the placement of the desk or table and chair for efficient use of functional vision, and the best working distance from task or visual target to the eyes. As for the determination of the reading mode and school placement, many factors enter into these decisions which can be made only after consideration of all the special education needs of the particular child (Faye, 1970), and the design of the program to meet those needs as laid out in the child's Individualized Education Plan (discussed in Chapter 12). Any recommendations for instructional planning, programming, and placement made by eye specialists must be evaluated along with other information collected during the required multifactored assessment that is carried out for each visually handicapped child.

Additional Information to Aid Interpretation

Eye report forms frequently will provide space for the eye specialist to report additional information about the eye condition or visual functioning of the patient and also may include information for the reader of the report regarding terminology and measurement notations used in the report. The NSPB report form contains both on the backside of the form.

First is information explaining the notations commonly found in reports for distance vision and near

vision. While Snellen acuities in the United States are generally based on a 20-foot test distance (Faye, 1984, p. 31) and reported as 20/20, 20/40, . . . 20/200, the metric equivalent, 6 meters, is also used and acuities may be noted as 6/6, 6/12, . . . 6/60. For some patients who are not able to see the test objects at the usual distance, other notations are sometimes given. Faye (1984) has defined these in decreasing levels as:
Hand movements: ". . . gross object and motion perception without detail discrimination. The farthest distance at which the patient can see hand motion should be noted" (p. 32).
Light projection: "Ability to locate the direction of light; should be checked in at least 8 quadrants (Faye, 1984, p. 32). Light projection awareness is useful for orientation within the environment and localization of the self and other persons or objects in that environment."
Light perception: "Ability to tell whether it is light or dark; generalized rather than localized perception of light (p. 33)."
Blind or no light perception (NLP): No awareness of exogenous or external light.

For near visual acuities, notations may be given in standard American Medical Association (A.M.A) notation based on inches from the test card, as, for example, 14/42 at 10 inches. Sometimes the metric notation (1M) is used. While examiners may also indicate the Jaeger size of type that the patient has been able to read at the time of the examination, Faye (1984, p. 45) considers Jaeger notation to be outmoded. The NSPB report form shows the approximate equivalents for Snellen distance; A.M.A., Jaeger, and metric near; percentage of near visual efficiency; and type sizes.

A chart showing the normal field of vision for each eye is also provided on the NSPB report form. The examiner can shade in the portion of the field that is constricted and the areas of the central field where scotomas exist or macular degeneration has resulted in reduced visual acuity. The completed chart can give the reader a good idea of where the patient may find "islands" of vision that may be useful for certain tasks or in specific situations. These field drawings can also help explain why a particular student might turn his head slightly when attempting to see an object or person directly in front of him. Information about field defects is very important to note and to interpret for the student, the parents, and any instructional personnel.

As should be clear from this discussion, much information of significance for educational and instructional purposes can be gleaned from a clinical eye report by the teacher who is knowledgeable about basic anatomy and physiology of the eye, conditions that can interfere with how the eye functions and with the process of seeing, and implications of eye disorders in school-aged children and youth. To illustrate the importance of translating clinical test results to implications for use of functional vision under typical everyday conditions of light and contrast, we can look at the relationship between visual acuity and preferred reading mode.

Relationship Between Visual Acuity and Preferred Reading Mode

The relationship between visual acuity or degree of vision and reading medium has been of particular interest to teachers as well as to researchers at the American Printing House for the Blind (APH) where decisions must be made annually regarding what textbooks to publish in braille and/or in large print and recorded form. Studies conducted by APH personnel in 1960, 1963, 1966, 1969, 1972, 1976, and 1979 have been based on the Federal Quota registration figures of children considered blind for legal and administrative purposes for each of those six years. In Table 3.5, the nine categories of degree of vision as they were used in these APH studies are shown along with the 1979 proportions of students in each category. Only about twenty percent of those students registered fit into the Category IX—totally blind. In Table 3.6 are the proportions of the group who were reported to be using each of the reading modes: braille, large print, recorded materials, regular print, or some combination of modes. These proportions reflect usage in residential school, local school district, and commission programs for visually handicapped students.

What seems striking is the fact that for 1979 only approximately 16 percent of these students with a best visual acuity of 20/200 or less in the better eye after correction read braille. Another 3 percent used both braille and large print. In all categories of vision, especially the three lower (VII-IX), the use of aural materials has increased since earlier studies (Willis, 1979). Analysis of these data and those from the earlier studies also reveals a constant decrease in the proportionate number of students who use braille as their chief reading mode. In 1958, approximately 58 percent of the students registered used braille while in 1979, the number was about 16 percent.

It is apparent that, even among those school-age individuals whose visual acuity for administrative purposes puts them in the category of "blind," a relatively small number use braille as a main reading medium while a large number use print materials including regular print, and a significant number rely on their listening skills to acquire information. In light of these data and figures from more recent Federal Quota registrations by grade and reading media that show increases in the numbers of non-readers as well as regular print readers, it seems that the skills necessary for teachers of visually handicapped students become more numerous and complex as the characteristics of the students, school programs, the social context, and times change.

Table 3.5   Categories of degree of vision with total and proportion of 1979 students in each category

Visual Category	Visual acuity or other designation	Proportion of Total	Number of students
I	20/200-18/200	.39	11,769
II	17/200 13/200	.03	1,003
III	12/200-8/200	.11	3,305
IV	7/200-3/200	.01	824
V	2.5/200-.4/200	.03	229
VI	Count fingers	.04	1,311
VII	Hand movements	.06	1,780
VIII	Light projection and/or perception	.14	4,215
IX	Totally blind	.20	6,124
			30,560

Source: D.H. Willis, Relationship between visual acuity, reading mode, and school systems for blind children. A 1979 replication (unpublished paper), 1979.

CASE STUDY

An eye report for ten year old Fran Manning, a new student in the fifth grade in Spruce Elementary School, appears in Figure 3.13. Her report was completed by Dr. Jenkins approximately six weeks after school had started. No school records had yet been received from Fran's former school district in another state.

Here is a set of questions Fran's itinerant teacher asked herself as she examined the report. As you read the report, see how you would respond to the questions and what other questions you might ask.

History

1. Since what age has Fran had impaired vision? What, if anything, might that suggest about her overall development?
2. Has anyone else in Fran's family shown signs of a similar condition? Could the condition, in Fran's case congenital cataracts (OU) and glaucoma (OS), be inherited? Are the parents aware of this? If they are not, what should the teacher do or say?
3. Has Fran previously received services from any program for visually handicapped children? Are records available yet? Where? What do her parents report about the strengths and weaknesses of that program? What does Fran say? Did she have an Individualized Education Program (IEP)? (See Chapter 12.) What will be important to look for in the school records when they finally arrive?

Measurements

1. What improvement in distance vision do Fran's spectacles give her, according to her visual acuities with and without correction? What about her corrected near visual acuity? Does the school report say

CONFIDENTIAL   EYE REPORT FOR CHILDREN WITH VISUAL PROBLEMS   R L B

NAME OF PUPIL _Fran_   _L._   _Manning_   SEX _F_   RACE _W_
(Type or print)   (First)   (Middle)   (Last)

ADDRESS _60 Willow Lane, Treesdale (Highland)_   DATE OF BIRTH _2_/_17_/_75_
(No. and street)   (City or town)   (County)   (State)   (Month) (Day) (Year)

GRADE _5_   SCHOOL _Spruce Ele._   ADDRESS _____

I. HISTORY

A. Probable age at onset of vision impairment. Right eye (O.D.) _birth_   Left eye (O.S.) _birth_

B. Severe ocular infections, injuries, operations, if any, with age at time of occurrence _none known_

C. Has pupil's ocular condition occurred in any blood relative(s)? _Yes_   If so, what relationship(s)? _father_

II. MEASUREMENTS
(See back of form for preferred notation for recording visual acuity and table of approximate equivalents.)

A. VISUAL ACUITY

	DISTANT VISION			NEAR VISION			PRESCRIPTION		
	Without correction	With best correction*	With low vision aid	Without correction	With best correction*	With low vision aid	Sph.	Cyl.	Axis
Right eye (O.D.)	1/200	20/200		J12			+12.50	+1.50	x 120
Left eye (O.S.)	1/200	20/200		J20			+12.50	+2.00	x 105
Both eyes (O.U.)							Date O.U. +.300 add		

B. If glasses are to be worn, were safety lenses prescribed in: Plastic _X_   Tempered glass _____   *with ordinary lenses

C. If low vision aid is prescribed, specify type and recommendations for use. _____

D. FIELD OF VISION: Is there a limitation? _Yes_   If so, record results of test on chart on back of form

What is the widest diameter (in degrees) of remaining visual field?   O.D. _____   O.S. _____   _aphakic field OU._

E. Is there impaired color perception? _No_   If so, for what color(s)? _____

III. CAUSE OF BLINDNESS OR VISION IMPAIRMENT

A. Present ocular condition(s) responsible for vision impairment. (If more than one, specify all but underline the one which probably first caused severe vision impairment.)
O.D. _cong. cataracts – ou_
O.S. _cong. nystagmus – ou_
not known

B. Preceding ocular condition, if any, which led to present condition, or the underlined condition, specified in A.
O.D. _____
O.S. _____

C. Etiology (underlying cause) of ocular condition primarily responsible for vision impairment. (e.g., specific disease, injury, poisoning, heredity or other prenatal influence.)
O.D. _____
O.S. _____

D. If etiology is injury or poisoning, indicate circumstances and kind of object or poison involved. _____

IV. PROGNOSIS AND RECOMMENDATIONS

A. Is pupil's vision impairment considered to be: Stable _OO_   Deteriorating _OS_   Capable of improvement _____   Uncertain _____

B. What treatment is recommended, if any? _surgery – OS – glaucoma_

C. When is reexamination recommended? _monthly_

D. Glasses: Not needed _____   To be worn constantly _X_   For close work only _____   Other (specify) _____

E. Lighting requirements: Average _X_   Better than average _____   Less than average _____

F. Use of eyes: Unlimited _X_   Limited, as follows: _____

G. Physical activity: Unrestricted _____   Restricted, as follows: _no physical contact sports_

TO BE FORWARDED BY EXAMINER TO:

Date of examination _10/22/84_
Signature of examiner _W.S. Jakem_   Degree _MD_
Address _3600 Ivy Blvd., Cirque, Pa._
Name

If clinic case: Number _____   of clinic _____

Figure 3.13   Fran Manning's eye report.

PREFERRED VISUAL ACUITY NOTATIONS

DISTANT VISION. Use Snellen notation with test distance of 20 feet. (Examples: 20/100, 20/60). For acuities less than 20/200 record distance at which 200 foot letter can be recognized as numerator of fraction and 200 as denominator. (Examples: 10/200, 3/200). If the 200 foot letter is not recognized at 1 foot record abbreviation for best distant vision as follows:

HM	HAND MOVEMENTS
PLL	PERCEIVES AND LOCALIZES LIGHT IN ONE OR MORE QUADRANTS
LP	PERCEIVES BUT DOES NOT LOCALIZE LIGHT
No LP	NO LIGHT PERCEPTION

NEAR VISION.   Use standard A.M.A. notation and specify best distance at which pupil can read. (Example: 14/70 at 5 in.)

TABLE OF APPROXIMATE EQUIVALENT VISUAL ACUITY NOTATIONS

These notations serve only as an indication of the approximate relationship between re-cordings of distant and near vision and point type sizes. The teacher will find in practice that the pupil's reading performance may vary considerably from the equivalents shown.

Distant Snellen	Near A.M.A.	Jaeger	Metric	% Central Visual Efficiency for Near	Point	Usual Type Text Size
20/20 (ft.)	14/14 (in.)	1	0.37 (M.)	100	3	Mail order catalogue
20/30	14/21	2	0.50	95	5	Want ads
20/40	14/28	4	0.75	90	6	Telephone directory
20/50	14/35	6	0.87	50	8	Newspaper text
20/60	14/42	8	1.00	40	9	Adult text books
20/80	14/56	10	1.50	20	12	Children's books 9-12 yrs
20/100	14/70	11	1.75	15	14	Children's books 8-9 yrs.
20/120	14/84	12	2.00	10	18 }	Large type text
20/200	14/140	17	3.50	2	24 }	
12.5/200	14/224	19	6.00	1.5		
8/200	14/336	20	8.00	1		
5/200	14/560					
3/200	14/900					

FIELD OF VISION.   Record results on chart below.

Type of test used:_____   Illumination in ft. candles:_____

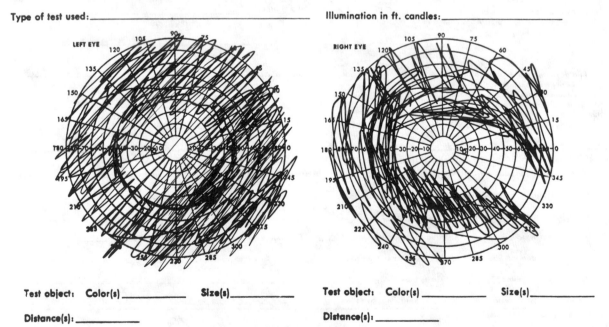

Test object: Color(s)_____   Size(s)_____   Test object: Color(s)_____   Size(s)_____

Distance(s): _____   Distance(s): _____

Figure 3.13   Fran Manning's eye report.

Table 3.6   Comparison of distributions of mode of reading by visual categories: 1979 APH data.

Reading Mode	Visual Categories									Proportion of Total	Total N
	I	II	III	IV	V	VI	VII	VIII	IX		
Braille	0.2	0.3	0.6	.15	.27	.21	.16	.35	.37	16	5,009
Large Type	.43	.50	.43	.40	.33	.39	.17	.05	.01	28	8,501
Braille and large type	.02	.04	.06	.08	.11	.09	.04	.02	.01	3	884
Large type and regular print	.23	.25	.20	.13	.08	.10	.03	.01	.00	13	4,004
Regular print	.14	.11	.08	.05	.03	.05	.01	.00	.00	7	2,207
Aural	.15	.07	.16	.18	.19	.16	.60	.56	.61	32	9,901
Not given	.00	.00	.00	.00	.00	.00	.00	.00	.00	0	57
											30,563

Source: D.H. Willis, Relationship between visual acuity, reading mode, and school systems for blind children: A 1979 replication (unpublished paper), 1979.

anything about her level of visual function in the classroom? Does her performance in school resemble her performance in the clinical setting? If not, what factors may be influencing her performance?

2. Are her lenses plastic safety lenses, tempered glass, shatter-resistant?

3. Has Fran been evaluated for low vision aids? Should she be?

4. According to her prescription, what type of refractive error must Fran have? Does she have any astigmatism? What about the strength or dioptic power of her correction? Does she have a bifocal or aid for reading? What are the implications for tasks requiring use of near vision?

5. Given her prescription and reading aid, are her glasses adjusted properly so they are comfortable and stay positioned properly on her nose?

6. Does Fran have any limits in her field of vision in either eye? If so, where? What will she need to learn or remember to help her compensate for her restricted peripheral vision, especially in her left eye? What problems might she have in reading? scanning? examining pictures? searching for environment landmarks? finding objects dropped on the floor?

7. The report shows Fran to be aphakic. What does that mean? Does her prescription reflect that? What should Fran's teacher be told so she will understand Fran's need for glasses at all times?

Causes of Blindness

1. What is the probable reason that Fran has impaired vision? What treatment has she had? What about her degree of nystagmus—does it increase or decrease under certain conditions? Does her teacher know about this and understand why?

2. What caused Fran's cataracts? Do other family members have cataracts or glaucoma?

Prognosis and Recommendations

1. Since the glaucoma in Fran's left eye is reported to be "deteriorating," what signs or problems should we watch for in school and report to her parents? Is Fran aware of these signs?

2. According to the report, Fran may need surgery on her left eye because of the glaucoma. What is her reaction to this? What should or can her teacher do, say, or explain to alleviate any fears, answer her questions, and generally help her to understand and cope with the physical and emotional aspects of surgery? When the time comes, what should be said to her teacher and classmates and by whom?

3. When is she to return to see her eye specialist? Has the appointment been made?

4. Has the eye specialist made any recommendation for Fran's school program, placement, or physical arrangements in the classroom? Have these been considered during the preparation of her IEP? Has her eye specialist been kept informed of her progress in school and the conditions under which she uses her vision most efficiently (lighting levels, task demands, contrast, types of materials, etc.)?

5. Are there to be any limits on Fran's physical activity in school? If so, do Fran and her teacher(s) know what they are and why they are necessary? Do they also understand that these restrictions do not preclude all physical activity? In what activities can she participate without danger of bumps or bangs to her head or high probability of being knocked down?

6. Is the eye report signed and dated?

7. Has a report been made for the school files of Fran's eye specialist, the address to which report forms should be sent, the date of her last report, and her distant visual acuity for purposes of APH registration?

8. Has a copy of this eye report been placed in Fran's school file and reviewed with the school nurse?

Other questions about Fran's visual status may be generated after checking her performance in the classroom, playground, cafeteria, gym, hallways, and school bus and after talking with her parents and, in some cases, the eye specialist. If there is a discrepancy between what they report and what is observed in school, then the teacher will certainly want to confer with the parents and eye specialist. But a teacher who can respond to the questions outlined here is well along the way to an understanding of the implications of Fran's visual impairment for purposes of instruction and long-range planning.

GLOSSARY OF TERMS RELATED TO THE EYE

Although the eye is a small structure, it is extremely complex and contains an immense network of nerves, blood vessels, cells and specialized tissues. To understand how the eye operates, it is necessary to know the names and functions of some of its parts.

Aqueous (a'kwe-s). Watery liquid which flows between the lens and the cornea, nourishing them.

Choroid (ko'roid). Blood vessel-rich tissue behind the retina which is responsible for its nourishment.

Cornea (kor'ne-ah). Transparent covering at the front of the eye which is part of the eye's focusing system.

Iris (i'ris). Colored, circular membrane, suspended behind the cornea and immediately in front of the lens which regulates the amount of light entering the eye by adjusting the size of the pupil.

Lens (lenz). Transparent tissue behind the iris which bends light rays and focuses them on the retina.

Macula (mak'u-lah). Pigmented central area, or "yellow spot," of the retina devoid of blood vessels; it is the most sensitive area of the retina and is responsible for fine or reading vision.

Optic Nerve (op'tik nurv). The nerve at the back of the eye which carries visual impulses from the retina to the brain. The area at which the optic nerve connects with the retina is known as the optic disc.

Pupil (pu'p'l). The adjustable opening at the center of the iris that allows light to enter the eye.

Retina (ret'i-nah). Light sensitive tissue at the back of the eye that transmits visual impulses via the optic nerve to the brain.

Schlemm's Canal (shlemz ke'nal). A passageway for the aqueous fluid to leave the eye.

Sclera (skle'rah). The tough, white, protective coat of the eye. The portion of the sclera that surrounds the cornea is covered by the conjunctiva.

Vitreous Body (vit're-us). Transparent, colorless mass of soft, gelatinous material filling the center of the eye behind the lens.

Equipment and Techniques

Cataract surgery (kat'ah-rakt). various techniques can be used to improve a cataract, depending on the type of cataract, the condition of the patient, and the preference of the surgeon. In general, cataract surgery is one of the most successful operations performed with 90 to 95 percent of patients regaining useful vision.

Cryosurgery (kri'o-sur'jer-e). Surgical technique employing the use of extreme cold for such purposes as reattaching a detached retina and removing cataracts, as well as for other purposes.

Electoretinogram (ERG) (e-lek'tro-ret'i no-gram). Instrument for measuring the electrical response of the retina to light; used as an aid in the diagnosis of certain retinal diseases.

Fluorescin Angiography (floor-es'e-in an'je-ograh-fee). Technique to locate damaged blood vessels in the eye by injecting fluorescent dye in the bloodstream at the arm and recording its progress through the ocular vessels with photography.

Ophthalmoscope (op-thal'ma-skop). Instrument with perforated mirror and light used in viewing the interior of the eye, especially the retina and choroid.

Perimeter (pe-rim'e-ter). Used to measure visual field; usually consists of a metal arc of a circle, marked off in degrees with a light source attached which rotates with the arc.

Photocoagulation (fo'to-ko-ag'u-la shun). Use of heat or light, such as that produced by a laser, to weld hemorrhaging blood vessels occurring in such diseases as diabetic retinopathy, and as an adjunct in the treatment of other retinal disorders, such as retinal detachment.

Slit Lamp Biomicroscope. Diagnostic instrument which provides a narrow beam of strong light and is useful for examination of the front portion of the eye.

Snellen Chart (snel'en). Chart consisting of lines of letters in graded size. Each is labeled with the distance at which it can be read by the normal eye. Most often used for testing visual acuity at 20 feet; thus the state of vision classified as 20/20 refers to the ability of a person with normal vision to read a particular line on the chart at 20 feet.

Tonography (to-nog'rah-fee). Recording of changes in intraocular pressure by applying a weighted instrument to the surface of the eye for a short period of time. Used to help confirm diagnosis of glaucoma.

Tonometry (to-nom'e-tree). Momentary measurement of pressure in the eye. Used to screen for glaucoma.

Mechanics of Sight

Although the mechanics of sight are complex, research has provided a great deal of information about the visual system. Such information is valuable not only for understanding how the eye functions in health, but also for studying certain disease processes.

Accommodation—Ability of the eye to adjust its focus for near and distant vision.

Cones—Specialized visual (photoreceptor) cells in the

retina, responsible for sharpness of vision and color vision (see "Rods").

Dark Adaptation—Biochemical and neurologic process by which the eye becomes more sensitive to light in the dark.

Distance Vision—Ability to perceive objects distinctly at a distance, usually measured at 20 feet.

Near Vision—Ability to perceive distinctly objects at normal reading distance, or about 14 inches from the eyes.

Peripheral Vision—Ability to perceive the presence, motion, or color of objects outside the direct line of vision.

Refraction—Bending the light rays when passing from one transparent medium into another of different density; in vision, refraction by the cornea and lens brings images to sharp focus on the retina.

Rhodopsin—Light-sensitive pigment of the rods; bleaches in the light, and regenerates in the dark. It plays a key step in the transformation of light energy into visual perception.

Rods—Straight, thin cells in the retina containing light-sensitive pigments; responsible for night vision (see "Cones").

Visual Acuity—Expression of acuteness of vision, ability to discriminate fine details of objects. Normal visual acuity is measured as 20/20 which is an arbitrary designation usually based on the ability to read a line of letters or symbols of a given thickness and size from a distance of 20 feet.

Visual Field—Entire area which can be seen without the shifting position of the eyes.

Eye Disorders

Diseases of the eye can cause visual disability ranging from minor impairment to total blindness. Some forms of visual disability can be prevented through prompt attention, and others may be cured. But, unfortunately, there are other eye conditions that cannot be prevented or treated. Research supported and conducted by the National Eye Institute, a component of the Institutes of Health, aimed at improved prevention, diagnosis, and treatment of visual disorders. Through such research, a great deal of knowledge has already been gained about the eye and the diseases which threatens its normal function.

Cataract (kat'ah-rakt). One of the leading causes of blindness in the country, cataract is clouding of the lens which obstructs the passage of light to the retina. Almost all cataracts can be successfully removed by surgery with resulting restoration of useful vision. There are four main types of cataract: senile—the most common form, associated with aging; congenital—occurring at birth; secondary—following another eye disease; and traumatic—following an injury.

Corneal Disease (kor'neal). Diseases of the cornea may scar this transparent tissue causing visual disability. Causes of corneal disease include injury, infection, and allergic reactions. Corneal diseases can frequently be successfully treated by drugs or surgery. In some cases corneal transplants can restore vision to people who have suffered corneal scarring.

Diabetic Retinopathy (di'ah-be'tik ret'inop'ah-tee). Disorder of the blood vessels in the retina stemming from diabetes. It is one of the leading causes of blindness. If detected early, the most common form of the disease usually can be controlled with drugs. In other cases, surgery may be necessary.

Macular Degeneration (mak'u-lar di-jen'er-a'shen). Irreversible and progressive damage to the macula portion of the retina resulting in a gradual loss of fine or reading vision. It is a leading cause of blindness in this country and is usually associated with aging.

Retinal Detachment (ret'n-el de-tach'ment). Separation of the inner layer of the retina from the outer layer. If detected early and treated promptly with surgery, retinal detachment can often be repaired and vision restored.

Study questions

1. Describe the path of light rays from the environment through the eye to the retina. What medium does most of the refracting? What structure can alter its curvature and thus alter its refractive power? Why is this desirable?
2. What protection does the eyeball have?
3. What are three major layers of the globe? What is the primary function of each?
4. Describe three types of refractive error and explain how each might be corrected.
5. What are the major causes of blindness among the general population in the United States? among school-age children?
6. Define these terms:

ophthalmologist	visual acuity
optometrist	field of vision
accommodation	contrast sensitivity
suppression	power of a lens
presbyopia	fovea centralis

7. Describe the types of information typically included in an eye specialist's report of an examination of a visually handicapped child. What are important contributions each type can make to a teacher's better understanding of how that child might function visually?

Additional readings

Faye, E.E., ed. (1984). *Clinical low vision.* (2nd Edition). Boston, Mass.: Little, Brown & Company.

Faye, E.E., ed. (1970). *The low vision patient.* New York, N.Y.: American Foundation for the Blind, Inc..

Harley, R.K. and Lawrence, F.A. (1977). *Visual impairment in the schools.* Springfield, Ill.: Charles C Thomas.

Jan, J.E., Freeman, R.D. and Scott, E.D. (1977). *Visual impairment in children and adolescents.* New York, N.Y.: Grune Stratton.

Jose, R.T., ed. (1983). *Understanding low vision.* New York, N.Y.: American Foundation for the Blind, Inc..

National Society to Prevent Blindness (1980). *Vision problems in the U.S.: A statistical analysis prepared by Operational Research Department, NSPB.* New York, N.Y.: Author.

Newell, F.W. and Ernest, J.T. (1974). *Ophthalmology: Principles and concepts.* St. Louis, Mo.: C.V. Mosby Company.

Vaughan, D. and Asbury, T. (1980). *General ophthalmology.* Los Altos, Calif.: Lange Medical Publications.

CHAPTER 4

Growth and Development

Geraldine T. Scholl

This chapter summarizes the stages in normal or typical growth and development in the psychomotor, cognitive, and affective areas. Research findings related to these areas in the growth and development of children and youth with visual impairments are examined and influences that might account for differences found in children with visual impairments compared with the normal are discussed. Guidelines and principles for planning educational programs that can assist in meeting the special developmental needs and minimizing hazards that a visual impairment might impose are summarized.

An understanding of normal growth and development is essential to an understanding of the growth and development of children with visual impairments. Growth is typically defined as an increase in size, a quantitative change; development is an increase in complexity, a qualitative change (Olson, 1959). The terms are usually used together since quantitative and qualitative changes are intertwined and a clear distinction between them is often difficult to determine.

The process of growth and development is at the same time similar for all children and unique for each child (Mussen, Conger, & Kagan, 1979). It is similar in that there are identifiable stages through which all children progress; it is unique in that the rate of progression differs for each child. This principle applies to children with visual impairments as well and in general their growth and development tends to be more alike than different from that of nonhandicapped children. Variations in their growth and development can usually be attributed to influences related to the visual impairment either directly or indirectly. Direct influences are those which result from the visual impairment, e.g., as restrictions in the acquisition of certain cognitive concepts that require the use of vision, such as color or three dimensions. Indirect influences are those found in the ecology or environment in which the child lives which can restrict and deprive him of opportunities and experiences because of attitudinal factors and lack of knowledge about the nature of the visual impairment. This chapter focuses on both types of influences of the visual impairment on psychomotor, cognitive, and affective develop-

ment. Although these areas are discussed as though they can be isolated, they are interrelated and exert a mutual influence upon each other.

The chapter is divided into four parts. The first part discusses general characteristics of growth and development including the role of heredity and environment, the sequential nature of development, the stability of the organism as it proceeds through the stages of growth and development, the influence of selected characteristics of the visual impairment on the process, and a summary of approaches to development. The next three parts review "normal" growth and development in the psychomotor, cognitive, and affective areas. Each part summarizes normal growth and development; reviews research findings related to blind and visually handicapped children; and presents guidelines for meeting special developmental needs. Each of the preceding three parts briefly examine the role of education, specifically the school curriculum, in meeting developmental needs.

GENERAL CHARACTERISTICS OF GROWTH AND DEVELOPMENT

Several factors related to growth and development are basic to an understanding of the process in both normal and visually handicapped children. These include: the issue of heredity vs. environment; the sequential nature of development; the tendency of the organism to maintain stability; some characteristics of the visual impairment that exert an influence on the process; and different approaches to growth and development.

Role of Heredity and Environment

The interrelationship of heredity and environment or nature/nurture has been a subject for study among developmental psychologists for many years without agreement concerning the respective contribution and importance each plays in the process (Weisfeld, 1982). There is general agreement that each human being is endowed at conception with an inherited potential and that the degree to which that potential is achieved is dependent on the environment and the opportunities it provides (Mussen et al, 1979). Both exert a critical influence on the developmental process. There is evidence that certain physical characteristics, such as color of hair (Fein, 1978; Mussen et al., 1979) and physical height (Bloom, 1964), are determined by heredity. There is considerable controversy concerning the inheritance of intelligence (see Dobzhansky, 1973; Fein, 1978; Jensen, 1973; Mussen et al., 1979) and relatively little is known about the inheritance of emotional and personality characteristics (Mussen et al., 1979).

The absence of strong evidence concerning the role of heredity particularly in the cognitive and affective areas has led to a recognition of the importance of the environment. In addition, it is possible and more hopeful to modify the environment than it is to change the biological and genetic make-up of an individual. It is important to note that the influence of the environment on the immature organism begins not at birth but rather at conception. For example, risk factors during pregnancy, such as malnutrition, use of drugs, and smoking, exert a negative impact on the growth and development of the fetus and may have an impact on the achievement of one's physical height and growth (Bloom, 1964) and early cognitive development (Mussen et al., 1979; Stechler & Halton, 1982).

Motor skills develop and are refined in an enriched environment that provides opportunities for practice through physical activity (Krogman, 1972). Correlations of intelligence between identical twins reared apart compared with those for identical twins reared together provide evidence that the environment can be a factor in the development of intelligence (Bloom, 1964). Affective development begins with the mother-child attachment at birth and disturbances in this process may result in later problems (Joffe & Vaughn, 1982). It would appear that emotional, social, and personality characteristics are shaped by the environment throughout the life span rather than by heredity (Hodapp & Mueller, 1982; Mussen et al., 1979). In summary, environmental factors exert an important influence on the achievement of potential.

A "perfect" environment remains an illusive ideal and the amount of environmental stimulation exists on a continuum with some degree of deprivation present for most persons. Fortunately, an enriched environment can compensate for many of the inevitable "mistakes" in handling and child rearing, deprivations in experience, and restricted opportunities for developmental stimulation (Brim & Kagan, 1980; Kagan, 1984). When environmental deficiencies are excessive and occur at an early age, however, difficulties may arise in achieving maximum potential (Bloom, 1964).

The above brief discussion of environmental factors has implications for teachers and parents of children who are blind and visually handicapped. The critical importance of environmental stimulation on the development of psychomotor and cognitive skills points to the need for parents to receive early intervention and professional assistance to help them provide an enriched environment for their infants and young children to stimulate growth in these areas. Further, the affective growth of the child is critical from the beginning of life. Thus, intervention programs for parents and their infants are essential. The special needs in growth and development during early childhood are described in Chapter 7.

Sequential Nature of Development

In most instances, the developmental process occurs in a sequence with definable stages through which all children pass. For example, the child must be able to chew and swallow before he can speak; he must be able to sit up without support before he can walk; he must acquire skill in oral or expressive language before written language can be introduced; he must relate to and find his place within the family constellation before he can be successful in relating to peers and others outside the family. Each skill or task must be mastered before the child can move on to a skill or task at the next higher level.

Knowledge and understanding of this sequential nature of growth and development will assist parents and teachers of blind and visually handicapped children and youth in planning and implementing appropriate intervention strategies. Because of the inhibiting nature of the visual impairment, enriched experiences and direct teaching are often necessary to help the child master a particular skill at one level in order to facilitate movement to the next higher level. The mastery of a skill cannot be expected until its antecedent steps in the sequence have been mastered. Readiness for any aspect of learning can be most effectively assessed when the stages in the developmental process are recognized and experiences for learning are provided at the optimal time.

Stability of the Organism

Although it would appear that the process of growth and development is a smooth curve and proceeds upward gradually, this is not usually true. Spurts in growth tend to be followed by periods when gains are consolidated and when there may appear to be no progress (Gesell & Ilg, 1946; Olson, 1959). When a new skill is being learned or is just beginning to emerge, there may be a forward and backward movement until it becomes incorporated into the child's functioning. Temporary regression, particularly in emotional development, may appear prior to movement to a higher integrative level or when some event disturbs the equilibrium, such as the birth of a sibling. These periods of seeming plateaus or regression have been described as an adaptive way of dealing with growth (Noam, Higgins & Goethals, 1982).

Parents and teachers need to recognize that these temporary periods of disorganization or disequilibrium are to be expected. Patience and understanding are needed to help the child over rough periods. Periods of regression are particularly evident in infants and very young children and in severely multiply handicapped children. (See Chapters 7 & 9.)

Characteristics of the Visual Impairment

Several characteristics of the visual impairment have relevance for the developmental process: age of onset, etiology, type and degree of vision, and prognosis. These are usually reported on the form completed by the ophthalmologist or optometrist following an eye examination as described in the preceding chapter. Some implications of these variables on growth and development are noted here briefly.

Children who lose their vision before the age of five years are usually considered as congenitally visually handicapped for educational purposes because they retain relatively little visual imagery and memory for color (Lowenfeld, 1980). This early onset group constitutes the majority of visually handicapped children in school. Children who lose their vision after the age of five years may have greater difficulty becoming tactile rather than visual learners and may also evidence accompanying emotional reactions to their loss of vision particularly when the loss occurs as late as adolescence (Lowenfeld, 1980). Teachers and parents must be sensitive to potential educational and emotional effects that the time of onset might have on development and behavior.

Knowing the cause of the visual impairment is important because some eye conditions are accompanied by pain, or photophobia, or brain damage. An hereditary eye condition may precipitate problems during adolescence when the young person begins to think of marriage and a family. In addition, stress on parents may accompany hereditary eye conditions and may suggest the possibility of emotional problems between the parents, particularly if one blames the other for the child's eye condition. Thus it is important for teachers to know the diagnosis of the child's visual impairment and its potential accompanying impact on behavior and learning. Chapter 3 discusses some of the implications of various eye conditions for the teacher.

It may seem that even a small amount of vision would be advantageous; however, limited vision may yield imperfect sensations, which in turn yield imperfect perceptions that become vague impressions which might be confusing in the educational process. (See Chapter 5.) In addition, parents, teachers, and the community tend to expect more from children who have partial vision, thus placing more stress and pressure on them to perform as a person with normal vision. Finally, the child with limited vision may view himself as belonging to neither the sighted nor the visually handicapped world, which may result in a reduced self-concept or emotional problems. As noted in the preceding chapter, the medical assessment of residual vision frequently does not provide meaningful information for educational purposes; parents and teachers must often rely on observation in order to know how much to expect of the child visually. Patience is often necessary to help the child accept the limitations of his visual impairment.

Prognosis, the future of the eye condition, frequently has implications. Parents and teachers need to be aware of potentially deteriorating vision in order to help the child adjust to and prepare for the eventual visual loss. Adolescents, as they look toward future careers and life style, may need to consider this possibility in their planning.

Ways of Looking at Growth and Development

A number of theories of growth and development have evolved based on the varying emphases placed on the basic nature of the human being, the qualitative/quantitative issue, the heredity/environment or nature/ nurture controversy, and what it is that develops (Miller, 1983). It should be noted that no one theory presents a view of the total child; each has its strengths and weaknesses; and each asks different questions about development. This part summarizes very briefly some of the more popular theories that will form a background for the remainder of the chapter. References are provided for additional information. For a general description of several theories, Miller (1983) is recommended.

Chart 4.1 includes five theories that focus on stages in the developmental process. It should be noted that ages are approximate. Three theories, Erikson, Havighurst, and Kohlberg, extend their stages into adulthood. The stages beyond adolescence are not included here.

Psychosexual

The focus in the psychosexual developmental perspective is on the dynamic interaction of three structures: the id, innate drives; the ego, the reality mediator; and the superego, the conscience (Miller, 1983; Noam et al., 1982).

Chart 4.1   Selected theories of child development

Ages	Psychosexual: Freud (Hall, 1954)	Psychosocial: Erikson (1963)	Developmental Tasks: Havighurst (1972)	Cognitive Development: Piaget (Miller, 1983)	Moral Development Kohlberg (1981)
0	*Oral stage* Successful feeding leads to security	*Basic trust vs. basic mistrust* Dependence on caregivers	*Stage 1* Learning to take solid foods Learning to walk Learning to talk	*Early sensorimotor stage* Modification of reflexes Primary circular reactions Secondary circular reactions Coordination of secondary schemes	*Completely egocentric* No moral concepts Fear of punishment
1	*Anal stage* Toilet training leads to conflicts about compliance with external demands	*Autonomy vs. shame, doubt* Need to adjust to socialization demands		*Later sensorimotor stage* Tertiary circular reactions Invention of new meanings through mental combinations	
2			*Stage 2* Learning to control the elimination of body wastes Learning sex differences sexual modesty Forming concepts and learning language to describe social and physical reality Getting ready to read Learning to distinguish right and wrong and beginning to develop a conscience	*Preoperational period* Semantic function (using signifiers, i.e, symbols and signs Egocentrism Rigidity of thought Semilogical reasoning	
3	*Phallic stage* Pride in body and skills Oedipal conflict	*Initiative vs. guilt* Need to adjust to rules Desire to explore Developing sense of right and wrong			
4					*Preconventional* Punishment and obedience orientation Instrumental relativist orientation

Ages	Latency stage	Industry vs inferiority	Concrete operational period	Stage 3	Conventional level
5	Repression of childhood sexuality Free to concentrate on developmental tasks of childhood	Facing and meeting expectations of others Coping with frustration and failure			
6			Concept of conservation Relations Temporal-spatial representations	Learning physical skills necessary for ordinary games Building wholesome attitudes towards oneself as a growing organism Learning to get along with age-mates	
7					
8				Learning an appropriate masculine or feminine role Developing fundamental skills of reading, writing, and calculating Developing concepts necessary for everyday living	
9				Developing conscience, morality, and a scale of values Achieving personal independence Developing attitudes toward social groups and institutions	
10					Interpersonal concordance or "Good Boy-Nice Girl" orientation
11					Society system and conscience maintenance

Ages	Psychosexual: Freud (Hall, 1954)	Psychosocial: Erikson (1963)	Developmental Tasks: Havighurst (1972)	Cognitive Development: Piaget (Miller, 1983)	Moral Development: Kohlberg (1981)
12+	*Genital stage* New more mature personality begins to develop	*Identity vs. role diffusion* Need to question old values, to achieve mature sense of identity	*Stage 4* Achieving new and more mature relations with age-mates of both sexes	*Formal operational period* Advanced logical and mathematical schema Comprehension of abstract or symbolic content Reduced need for objects for thinking	
13	More mature sexual and intimacy relationships		Achieving a masculine or feminine social role		
14			Accepting one's physique and using the body effectively		
15			Achieving emotional independence of parents and other adults Preparing for marriage and family life Preparing for an economic career Acquiring a set of values and an ethical system as a guide to behavior Desiring and achieving socially responsible behavior		*Postconventional* Autonomous or principled level Social contract orientation Universal ethical principle orientation

Freud used a stage approach to describe the interplay and relative importance in development of these structures during each stage and their contribution to personality development.

It should be noted that Freud developed his theories from work with patients, most of whom had varying degrees of neurotic behavior. His treatment was historical, that is, he helped the patient to return to the origin of the problem, which was typically during infancy and early childhood, through analysis of dreams, early memories, and drawings; he then assisted his patient to resolve the problem at that level. His analysis of the origin of patients' problems led to the development of his theories. His contributions lie in his abilities as a meticulous observer and an original thinker (Miller, 1983) and in his focus on individual differences (Noam et al., 1982). See Hall (1954) and Thompson (1950) for introductory material on Freud's theories.

Erikson

Erikson, one of the neo-Freudians, moved away from Freud's biological approach and expanded into the influence of social factors on development (Miller, 1983; Noam et al., 1982). He focused on the development of identity, his concept for the ego, in eight psychosocial stages through the entire life span. His contribution lies in his emphasis on the social influences on development, based on his studies of various social settings and cultures and on his emphasis on life as a quest for identity (Miller, 1983). His own writings (Erikson, 1950; 1968; and 1978) provide material for further exploration into his theories.

Havighurst

Havighurst was influenced by Erikson and his theory of psychosocial development. He evolved a concept of developmental tasks that provide a middle ground between the needs of an individual and society's demands (Havighurst, 1972). He viewed nature as providing the possibilities for human development which are realized through learning within the culture. The achievement of the developmental tasks leads to happiness and to later success whereas failure leads to unhappiness in the individual and disapproval by society, which can then cause difficulty in achieving later tasks. In two of his works, Havighurst (1953; 1972) provides suggestions for educators to assist pupils in achieving developmental tasks within the school setting.

Piaget

Piaget's theory of cognitive development is perhaps the most widely known. The stages will not be reviewed here because they are discussed in the later section on cognitive development. Elkind and Flavell (1969), Flavell (1963), Furth (1969), Ginsburg and Opper (1969), Miller (1983), Piaget (1970), and Pulaski (1980) provide good summaries of Piaget's theories as they are related to education.

Kohlberg

Kohlberg and his associates elaborated on Piaget's work on moral development and focused on the evolution of morals and values within the individual (Carroll & Rest, 1982). Kohlberg believes that, although they may be unaware of it, teachers are moral educators and the moral climate in the classroom is the hidden curriculum (Kohlberg, 1981). He based his work on studies of American adolescents who were presented with moral dilemmas. On the basis of these results and additional studies, he defined three levels of moral thinking, each with two related stages. The child prior to the age of four, is viewed as egocentric with no moral concepts. Kohlberg (1981) provides detailed rationale and descriptions for his moral stages with special emphasis on the role of education in moral development.

Social Learning Theory

The preceding theories included in Chart 4.1 defined growth and development in stages; each evolved at the initiative of a "great man." Social learning theory came from a number of researchers on learning theory and has been evolving over a long period of time (Miller, 1983). The roots of present day social learning theory are found in the work of Watson on behaviorism; of Hull and Spence on discrimination learning; of Skinner on operant conditioning; and of a group of young scholars who combined the traditions of Freud and Hull, namely Mowrer, Miller, Dollard, Sears, Doob and Whiting (Miller, 1983). Early social learning theory was based on the belief that personality is learned and that socialization, the process by which society teaches its children to behave, is learned through imitation.

The most influential current version of social learning theory is that of Bandura (Miller, 1983). Modern social learning theory focuses on social behavior and the social context of behavior. The context includes the characteristics of the person, the person's behavior, and the environment. Observational learning includes more than mimicking. According to Bandura, modern social learning theory includes the following principles: a new behavior, even a complex form, can be symbolically contructed through listening to another person or through reading; observations can be sources of information that assist in developing new behaviors; behavior change comes about through three sources of influence: the person, his behavior, and the environment (Miller, 1983). The major developmental variables include physical maturation, which is of importance only to the degree that the child has sufficient physical maturity to reproduce what he sees; experience with the social world; and cognitive development.

Social learning theory is an integrative theory which includes operant conditioning, reinforcement, and socialization processes. It provides a way to conceptualize why behavior varies in different situations and it focuses on the context within which the behavior occurs (Miller, 1983). As an evolving theory, it has some weaknesses but because it builds on the strengths of many related theories, it holds promise of resolving them.

Additional information may be found in Bandura (1973; 1977); Miller (1983); Rosenthal and Zimmerman (1978).

The following three parts of this chapter describe more fully these general considerations as they relate to the stages and sequences in the three areas of growth and development.

PSYCHOMOTOR DEVELOPMENT

During the first few years of life, physical growth and development take precedence and lay the foundation for later cognitive and affective development. Knowledge and understanding of the stages in normal psychomotor growth and development are basic to understanding the special problems that may be encountered in working with blind and visually handicapped infants and young children.

Normal Physical Growth and Development

Beginning with conception and continuing during the first few years of life, physical growth predominates. In the forty weeks between conception and birth, the fetus increases in weight 65 billion percent; during the first year, the infant increases in length by 50 percent and in weight by 200 percent (Krogman, 1972). After the first year this rapid rate of growth tapers off with a minor spurt at puberty, when for a brief period, girls tend to be taller and heavier than boys. (See Figures 4.1 & 4.2.) Physical growth and development proceed in a head-to-foot direction, called the cephalocaudal sequence (Olson, 1959); from body trunk to extremities, i.e., arms and legs; and from large muscle to small muscle control (Krogman, 1972). At sixteen weeks of age, the normal infant will follow a moving object with his eyes and may even attempt to reach for it (Ilg & Ames, 1955). This early visual tracking of an object marks the beginning of learning to control arms, hands, and finally fingers. Good hand coordination evolves from early experiences and experimentation by the infant with eye-hand movement and reaching for objects.

The infant prepares for walking through a sequence of steps in gaining control of his body. He first holds up his head and looks at his world in an eyes-front position; this provides exercise in gaining muscular control of the neck and upper trunk muscles. He then learns to sit without support. As the object world outside the immediate reach of his arms becomes more interesting, he propels himself in the direction of a desired object, usually through crawling or creeping.

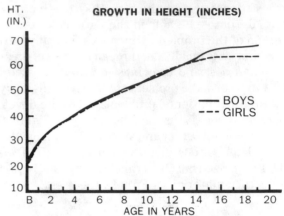

Figure 4.1   Growth in Height, Birth to Adulthood (22 Years)

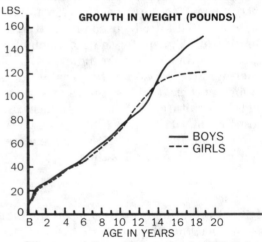

Figure 4.2   Growth in Weight, Birth to Adulthood (22 Years)

Source: W.M. Krogman, *Child growth* (Ann Arbor, Mich.: University of Michigan Press, 1972), p. 32.

He begins to pull himself to a standing position and later stands without support. Finally, after some walking by following furniture or holding the hand of an adult, he walks without support. By 15 months of age the child is walking and exploring his world on his own. Once he is in an upright position and has achieved balance to propel himself forward, he is soon running, jumping, and by age 5-6 years, skipping. Later physical development is largely an expansion and refinement of these early skills.

The normal child is stimulated to move about spontaneously in order to obtain a better grasp of his environment. Preschool and early elementary school age children are in constant motion and teachers plan their programs to channel this need for activity into acceptable forms that provide opportunities for satisfying this basic need for movement.

The growth spurt during adolescence completes the general physical growth and development of the individual and for a period of time may cause the adolescent problems in managing and coordinating a rapidly growing body. During this period, puberty, the attainment of sexual maturity, also occurs (Chumlea, 1982).

Variations in Children with Visual Impairments

The visual impairment in and of itself does not retard physical growth and development. In fact, the motor development of the child with a visual impairment during the first few months of life is not markedly different than that of the nonhandicapped child (Warren, 1984). In later motor development, however, there are indirect influences which can and often do have an impact on the process. These are related to characteristics of the visual impairment; lack of visual stimulation; inability to make use of imitative learning; and environmental factors.

Characteristics of the visual impairment. The etiology of the visual impairment may also cause other disabilities, which can retard physical and motor development, such as brain damage, severe mental retardation, and cerebral palsy. Some of these factors, their resulting disabling effects, and remedial techniques are described in Chapters 8 and 9.

The age of onset is also important. Griffin (1980) concluded in his study that lack of vision from birth has a detrimental effect on motor development and delays the acquisition of early motor skills. Some congenitally blind children prefer the prone position which affords them greater security and stability (Garry & Ascarelli, 1960). Long periods in the prone position, however, may delay walking. The older the child when the onset of the visual impairment occurs, the more likely he is to have acquired basic psychomotor skills through visual channels and thus may evidence less retardation in skill development.

Finally, the degree of vision, that is, the visual acuity, is a factor. The greater the degree of vision and the greater the skill of the child in using that vision, the more likely he will learn through visual channels. For example, even very limited visual ability to see persons standing erect provides a needed model and motivation to also stand erect and eventually walk. Imitative learning may also be facilitated when the child has sufficient vision to observe what others in his environment are doing.

Knowledge of the child's visual impairment, as discussed in Chapter 3, and of the sensory-perceptual processes as discussed in the following chapter, are essential to understanding and assessing the child's present level of development so that effective programs of intervention for the acquisition of psychomotor skills can be implemented.

Lack of visual stimulation. A brief observation of the activities of the normal infant leads to an appreciation of the role that vision plays in stimulating psychomotor development. For example, early visual tracking, as noted above, motivates the infant to reach and grasp. Lack of vision deprives the infant of this critical motivation and frequently causes a delay in the acquisition of physical skills particularly in using the body, in hand coordination, and in development of the fine muscles. The normal infant is stimulated to hold his head up in order to enjoy the object world. Lacking this motivation, the infant and young child with a visual impairment will often not develop good muscular control of the head, neck, and trunk muscles.

Walking may be delayed and sometimes will be awkward because the muscles necessary for walking are not well developed. The nonhandicapped toddler spends much time picking up small bits of paper or other minute objects from the floor, thereby improving his fine hand coordination. The toddler with a visual impairment lacks this type of exercise. The absence of motivation to secure an interesting object in the environment through creeping or crawling encourages physical inactivity and may result in a delay in walking. The lack of visual stimulation, therefore, may result in a lack of motivation to move about and use muscles that are essential to gain good control of the body as well as to explore the environment.

Lack of imitative learning. Much of early learning is through imitation, primarily visual imitation (Miller, 1983). The child with any degree of visual impairment has a more limited access to this mode of learning. All persons learn much from watching and imitating adults and peers throughout their lives. The early parallel and imitative play of preschool youngsters leads to diad play, and ultimately to the refinement of skills in games and other physical activities of the adolescent. This valuable experience of learning through watching others is lacking for the visually handicapped child and deprives him of valuable opportunities to develop physical skills.

Environmental factors. Many children with visual impairments are retarded in their physical growth and development because of environmental factors, particularly the early environment of the home. Parents may overprotect and fail to provide opportunities to learn because they misunderstand the infant's and young child's need for many structured opportunities to learn to use his body effectively in exploring his world. Work with parents in early intervention programs is essential in order to help them facilitate their child's psychomotor development.

Summary. The development of good gross and fine motor skills is an important prerequisite for developing and refining reading and writing skills as discussed in Chapter 18 and for formal orientation and mobility training as discussed in Chapter 19. Important milestones in psychomotor development are included in Table 19.2 in that chapter and provide the parent and teacher with guidance on when to introduce direct teaching of a particular skill where there appears to be a developmental lag that may be attributed to one or more of the factors described above.

Meeting Developmental Needs

The role of the parent and teacher in the developmental process is critical. Early intervention is essential if the child is to develop as near normally as possible. (See Chapter 7.) Delays in the acquisition of psychomotor skills beyond the stage of readiness may result not only in below-average performance of a skill but also may have an impact on later cognitive and affective development.

Intervention must begin in early infancy with providing substitutes for visual tracking. For the blind child, knowledge of the object world comes primarily through tactile and only secondarily through auditory channels. Thus, to make use of sound as a motivation for reaching and grasping, the child must first have attached a meaning to that sound and be interested in the object with the sound (Fraiberg, Smith & Adelson, 1969). The hands, mouth, feet—all parts of the body—should be used to explore and learn about the object world. Touching of people and objects should be encouraged. Activities that require the use of fine hand coordination, such as manipulating small blocks and beads, are essential if the child is to be successful in those school tasks that require that skill, such as braille reading and writing.

Intervention during the early school years should include activities that continue to develop fine hand coordination, ability to move about in the environment with freedom and ease, and direct teaching of skills that are usually acquired through imitative learning. The child with a visual impairment must

often be taught the necessary skills to keep him up with his peers and to satisfy his desire for movement. Parents and teachers should observe the activities of the peer group and if the child is not able to learn these skills through imitation, he should be taught them directly so that he can acquire proficiency in motor skills on the level of his peers. Early work in these areas will facilitate the later work of the orientation and mobility instructor (Chapter 19) and in the development of social skills (Chapter 20).

Stereotypic Behaviors

Opportunities to satisfy the basic need for movement and activity must be provided from earliest infancy, otherwise the child with a severe visual impairment will seek to satisfy the need within himself rather than outside himself and gain his satisfaction from seemingly aimless physical activities, or stereotypic behaviors, sometimes referred to as 'blindisms.' This latter term is a misnomer because most of these behaviors have been observed in other handicapped, particularly autistic, developmentally delayed, and emotionally disturbed, and in some nonhandicapped children (Burlingham, 1965; Warren, 1984). Stereotypic behaviors include body rocking, head swaying, and eye rubbing. They are characterized as being repetitive and not directed toward the attainment of any specific goal (Eichel, 1978).

There are many speculative theories concerning the cause of stereotypic behaviors. They have been attributed to lack of adequate sensory stimulation so the child uses his own body for stimulation and activity (see Burlingham, 1967; Cutsforth, 1951; Guess, 1966; Knight, 1972; Scott, 1969; Warren, 1984); restricted locomotion and limited motor and physical activity so the child cannot easily change his environment by moving to another place to maintain and satisfy the need for physical activity (see Burlingham, 1965; Guess, 1966; Hoshmand, 1975; Merry, 1933; Tait, 1972); social deprivation resulting from long periods of hospitalization wherein there is limited interaction

with others (see Berkson, 1973; Smith, Chethik & Adelson, 1969); inadequate primary caregiver-child relationships that do not provide opportunities and encouragement for the child to engage in a variety of behaviors (see Hoshman, 1975; Knight, 1972; Tait, 1972); lack of ability to imitate others in the environment and learn a variety of socially acceptable behaviors (see Smith et al., 1969). Teachers and parents should attempt to determine which of these causes is most relevant for the child and then modify the environment to eliminate the need to engage in the stereotypic behavior. Prevention through keeping the child busy, physically active, interested in his environment, and moving about as much as possible is the most effective prevention for many of these mannerisms. Additional suggestions for dealing with these behaviors are included in Chapter 20.

COGNITIVE DEVELOPMENT

Early psychomotor development leads to the development of cognition and the expanding mental abilities in the child. The early sensory exploration by the infant and toddler of the object world leads to his perceptual development and later to the formation of concepts upon which the knowledge of the abstract world can be based. Concepts grow out of the perceptual process and become enriched as the child develops language. The breadth of perceptual experiences deter-

mines in large measure the breadth of conceptual development. To be meaningful, concepts must be based on sensory experiences. (See the following chapter.)

Of the several theories on the development of cognition, the stages of intellectual development of Piaget will be outlined here. See Flavell (1963), Ginsburg and Opper (1969), and Pulaski (1980) for more details.

Normal Cognitive Development

Piaget describes the first two years of life as the sensorimotor stage during which time the infant progresses from reflex activity to more systematic and organized behavior. He learns that he has control over the object world and will visually search for a toy he has lost. He will reach for and grasp his toys. He learns that objects are independent of himself. He learns to imitate and to respond to people through imitative behavior. Finally, he takes the first steps toward establishing verbal communication. The acquisition of speech begins with the cooing of the infant at about 16 weeks; babbling at about 28 weeks; and putting sounds together at about 40 weeks. Language development proceeds in a similar sequential fashion. At 28 weeks the infant attends to voices and by 40 weeks responds to simple commands. By 15 months he says single words to express ideas and by 2 years he puts words together to form simple sentences (Bloom & Lahey, 1978; Molfese, Molfese & Carrell, 1982; Ulrey, 1982; Whitehurst, 1982; Wilkinson & Saywitz, 1982).

At approximately 2 years of age, the child enters the symbolic or preconceptual phase when the imitative behavior of the previous period becomes internal imitation (accommodation) and provides the child with symbols which acquire meaning through assimilation. He applies his symbols in a playful make-believe fashion to other situations as he tests out their appropriateness. He begins to use language for objects and events that may not be present at the moment.

At about 4 years of age, the child enters the phase of intuitive thought. This stage and the preceding preconceptual phase are sometimes called the preoperational stage. Language, which now becomes repetition, monologue, and collective monologue, is described by Piaget as egocentric, in that the child is neither concerned with nor interested in what another is saying. By contrast, communication is based on interaction with others and has as a purpose the relaying or sharing of information. During this period the child employs imitation more or less consciously in a preidentification fashion. Further, he broadens his social horizons and interest in the world about him.

The child passes through the stage of concrete operations from approximately 7 to 11 years of age. He acquires the ability to order and to relate experiences into a gestalt or organized whole. He establishes systems of classification and moves from inductive to deductive thinking. Although language is now a tool of communication, he still employs symbolic speech without true understanding of meanings. He now looks beyond the family for models to imitate.

At about age 12, the child enters the stage of formal operations, Piaget's final period of intellectual development. During this stage, the adolescent moves from the concrete to the abstract. He enters the world of ideas; formulates hypotheses concerning various results of an action and considers what might occur; he utilizes language as a means of communicating thoughts and ideas; he reaches an understanding of his world and where he fits into that world.

It should be noted that the ages attached to the stages are approximate and that development through the stages may not proceed evenly on all fronts. (See Chart 4.1.)

Variations in Children with Visual Impairments

A visual impairment places a child at a disadvantage in cognitive development particularly in the areas of sensory stimulation, concept development, and communication. Lowenfeld (1981) lists three restrictions of blindness on cognitive development: on the range and variety of experiences, on the ability to move about, and on the control of the environment. The child is deprived of a valuable source of sensory input with the result that development may take place more slowly and be uneven across specific intellectual abilities, although definitive research evidence is limited in this area (Warren, 1984).

Blind infants may not be significantly delayed during the first part of the sensorimotor stage (Warren, 1984). However, at about four months of age when hand-watching becomes a preoccupation with the nonhandicapped child, the blind child is at a disadvantage causing a delay in directing his attention to the outside world (Sandler, 1963). Although tactile and auditory schemas unite to provide organization to the blind child's world (Fraiberg, Siegel, & Gibson, 1966), these do not perform the same unifying function that vision does for the normal child (Warren, 1984). Furthermore, the child encounters difficulty in distinguishing between the self and nonself. The implications of this deficiency will be discussed in the following section. Language development would appear to be similar to that of nonhandicapped children during the sensorimotor period (Adelson, 1983).

There is limited research about the impact of the visual impairment on cognitive development during the preschool years. It might be assumed that the child would have difficulties with assimilation and accommodation during the preconceptual stage because of limited experience with the environment; less direct access to objects, particularly those too large and those too minute to explore tactually; and more restricted opportunities to expand language abilities

because of his experiential background. However, this period appears to be neglected in the literature.

There is more known about the abilities of visually handicapped children in the stage of concrete operations. In classification of objects and events, one of the basic abilities in cognition, lags have been identified to varying degrees with greater lags for chidren who are congenitally blind (Hatwell, 1985; Higgins, 1973; Stephens and Simpkins, 1974). Similar lags were found for conservation of substance, liquid volume, and weight and length (Gottesman, 1973; Stephens & Simpkins, 1974; Tobin, 1972). Following his extensive review of the literature, Warren (1984) cautions that, although there appear to be significant lags in the cognitive development of blind chidren compared with sighted children, such conclusions may be premature because comparisons of blind with sighted children may not be valid. He suggests that research on the cognitive development of blind children should be studied by comparing blind subjects.

In summary, because concepts grow out of the perceptual process and because the visual sensory input is lacking or limited, concept development may also be restricted. The child may never grasp some concepts such as color; he may have difficulty acquiring concepts of distance and time without many and varied meaningful experiences from other sources of sensory information; he may require more direct instruction to compensate for the lack of imitative learning. Thus, he may encounter difficulty moving beyond the stage of concrete operations.

Oral and written communication provide a mechanism for sharing ideas and concepts with others. This is accomplished through speech and language. The process of acquiring speech and language appears to be the same for children with visual impairments as it is with normal children but the slower physical development, more restricted range of experiences, and lack of visual stimulation may cause the child to be slower in language development (Mills, 1983). In addition, he may require a longer time to attach meanings to certain words. Concepts for objects which cannot be perceived by touch because they are too large, such as the moon, or too minute, such as an insect, must be developed through use of models and descriptions provided by others. Too heavy reliance on such secondary sources, however, may result in meaningless verbalism (Burlingham, 1965; Harley, 1963).

The use of nonverbal communication represents an area where little is known. As early as 16 weeks of age the normal infant smiles in response to a smile, a nonverbal reply. During the first year, she often expresses wants nonverbally, as with a frown, and in turn responds to looks of others. As she grows through childhood, she continues to respond to others with various forms of nonverbal communication. Since most nonverbal communication is largely dependent on visual stimuli, the child with a severe visual impairment is unable to utilize it to communicate thoughts and feelings. Research is needed to determine what forms of nonverbal communication can be employed by persons with severe visual impairments and more importantly whether skill in nonverbal communication can be taught (Warren, 1984).

Meeting Developmental Needs

Bloom (1964) postulates that an enriched environment is most effective in producing positive change in human characteristics when they are in their period of most rapid growth. Negative environmental influences, once considered to have a lasting influence on development, are now considered amenable to change and modification (Brin & Kagan, 1980; Kagan, 1984). Ideally, education can play a significant role in this process. Compensation for the limiting influences of the visual impairment on cognitive development should begin in the preschool years. (See Chapter 7.) A rich background of experiences will help the child with a visual impairment achieve more normal cognitive development. Thus programs for parent and early childhood education are essential in order to reduce the disadvantages imposed by the visual impairment.

It would appear that the depth of experiences through other sources of sensory input may make up in part for the lack of breadth across the total sensory base. Many concrete experiences are needed especially during the sensorimotor stage to enable the child to develop knowledge about the object world. Other sources of sensory input must be exploited to the maximum. (See Chapter 5.) All available sensory cues should be utilized in order to make up for the deficiencies caused by the visual impairment. In addition, the child should be encouraged to make maximum use of any residual vision. (See Chapter 6.)

AFFECTIVE DEVELOPMENT

It is difficult to separate cognitive from affective development since they are interrelated and exert mutual influences on each other (Joffe & Vaughn, 1982). Piaget (1981) suggests that the cognitive area be viewed as development of "behaviors related to objects" and the affective as "behaviors related to people" (p. 74). Hence, cognitive and affective development must be viewed as parallel aspects in the total process of growth and development. In addition, there is overlap among emotional, social, personality, and moral development. Since it is difficult to separate these aspects, they are considered under the more general term of "affective" in this part.

The visual impairment has little direct influence on affective development but indirect influences can exert a significant impact.

Normal Affective Development

Affective development begins when the mother holds her newborn infant in her arms for the first time immediately after birth. This closeness initiates bonding and the beginning of a long period of affective development that should culminate ultimately in an independent, self-confident adult. This maternal fondling and cuddling mark the beginning of learning to love and to be loved. Bonding provides a base of security for the movement of the infant into the external world (Joffe & Vaughn, 1982).

As the infant grows older, eye contact with the parents initiates a social relationship first with mother and father. Visual contact seems to be an essential element in this early process of building relationships (Burlingham, 1964).

During this time, the child is also developing his self-concept, that is his perception of self relative to that which is not-self in the physical and social environment (Wylie, 1961). The development of the self-concept begins in infancy and continues throughout the life-span, undergoing constant modification in response to the environment (Lerner & Shea, 1982).

Vision provides the infant with his first experiences in recognizing himself as distinct from his environment. As he observes his mother moving away from and toward him, he begins to learn that she is an object separate from him. Through visual exploration, he discovers his fingers and hands, toes and feet, spending hours visually exploring their relationship to him while he gradually learns that they are a part of him, unlike other people and his toys, which can be separated from his body (Wylie, 1961). This process of developing a body image, an aspect of self-concept, continues through visual exploration of other parts of the body, through mimicry play with parents and siblings, and later through observation and study of himself in a mirror.

After his parents, the infant expands his world to include other family members, including siblings. From the security gained through meaningful family attachments and relationships and with increased physical maturation to move about more freely in the environment, the child reaches out to others outside the family and builds social and emotional relationships with them. Acceptance comes from compatibility and correspondence with peer group norms. Again, visual contacts with others supply the necessary feedback for the child to initiate relationships and to know when he is acceptable and accepted. Through vision he learns which behaviors are accepted in particular settings and imitates those which will make him acceptable.

The recognition of self as an individual is facilitated by parents and family. In the home, love and acceptance, opportunities to move from a protected to a semiprotected position outside the family, and expectations of success communicated to him help the child develop a positive view of himself. Later, in school the teacher continues the process by encouraging him to meet challenges within the school setting, to recognize his capacities and limitations realistically, and to expect from him a level of performance consistent with his abilities. The self-concept continues to evolve throughout childhood as the environment provides experiences with success and failure that form the basis for evaluation of one's self and what one can and cannot do. The peer group provides further feedback and reinforcement necessary to learn about one's self, giving approval or disapproval, encouragement or discouragement to actions and behavior. This give and take is often nonverbal in nature, such as frowns or approving smiles (Chandler & Boyes, 1982; Hodapp & Mueller, 1982).

During adolescence the socialization process moves to the peer group, which becomes the base of security that the family has previously provided. Peer groups provide adolescents with an oppportunity to define themselves as group members, to gain an understanding of relationships, to interact with their equals, and to realize that they are of value to others (Newman, 1982; Siegel, 1982). Difficulties may arise when peer group norms are in conflict with family norms. At this point the adolescent must develop his own set of behavioral norms drawing from peers and family.

During adolescence, the concept of one's self as male or female emerges on the basis of prior experiences in the life-span (Lerner & Shea, 1982). These include opportunities for identifying with an appropriate sex model and imitation of dress, mannerisms, and behavior of that model. Puberty, the onset of the ability to procreate, presents adolescents with a dilemma: bodies that are sufficiently physically mature to reproduce but a society that views them as too immature to meet the consequences of their procreative efforts (Dreyer, 1982).

A system of values becomes incorporated into the self during this period based primarily on family and peer relationships and experiences. This moral development is the core component of human adaptation and the key to survival in our society (Lerner & Shea, 1982; McKinney & Morse, 1982). The formation of a personal value system has been cited as a criterion marking the end of adolescence (Siegel, 1982).

The acceptance of self as a person of worth and contributing member of society is the ultimate objective of adolescence. Unlike certain human characteristics such as physcial height, the self-concept is responsive to the environment throughout the life-span and changes constantly in response to environmental changes (Brim & Kagan, 1980; Kagan, 1984).

Preparation for a vocation is another task of adolescence (Havighurst, 1953; 1972). Assuming productive employment is a valued aspect of American society and adolescents spend time during the secondary school years engaging in career exploration, discussions with family, peers, and school personnel about vocational possibilities, and finally arriving at a decision of the most appropriate vocational goal for themselves as they prepare to move into adulthood. (See Chapter 22.)

Variations in Children with Visual Impairments

From the preceding summary it is clear that a severe visual impairment may impose limitations on attaining optimal affective development. Some of these are reviewed in this part.

A severe visual impairment frequently places the infant at a disadvantage beginning at birth. Some visually handicapped infants do not have close physical contact with their mothers or other family members for some months following birth due to their delicate physical condition which may require long periods of hospitalization. When released from the hospital, the infant may not like to be touched and will resist touching or cuddling. Parents, after the long period of separation, may need time to readjust to the new baby and must be patient in helping the infant learn to enjoy being cuddled.

Teachers of young blind children often need to provide them with more physical contact than is typical for children with vision. The greater need for being close to an adult may be due in part to the delay in being handled and in part to a desire to obtain the security and acceptance that the child with vision receives from eye contact. Teachers must be aware of the individual child's needs but must also recognize that there is a point beyond which close contact with another person becomes socially unacceptable. For example, it is appropriate for the primary teacher to hold a child on her lap when the child needs comforting but such behavior on the part of the teacher would be considered inappropriate with an adolescent.

The lack of early eye contact can retard the bonding that is necessary between mother and infant (Fraiberg,

Smith & Adelson, 1964). Some parents may react negatively to the lack of eye contact, thereby setting up a cycle of reinforcement that retards the development of an adequate and meaningful relationship between parent and child. Relationships with siblings may be affected because the infant with a visual impairment may require more of the parents' attention and also because the visually handicapped sibling does not meet their expectations of being a companion.

The absence of vision deprives the infant of observing the back and forth movement of family members from his presence, thereby slowing down the process of learning to distinguish between self and not-self. In addition, the visually handicapped infant is slower to learn about his body parts through exploration, later through mirror play, and still later through comparison of himself with his peers.

The move of the child from family into peer groups may be hindered because the child cannot see to imitate his peers or to utilize nonverbal communication skills in order to know when he is acceptable; if he is not acceptable, he cannot initiate the necessary behaviors to secure acceptance. His lack of vision may prevent him from learning what is accepted by the peer group. In general, the social development of visually handicapped pupils does seem to differ from that of the nonhandicapped (Warren, 1984). McGuinness (1970) found that visually handicapped pupils in integrated settings had more age appropriate behaviors than those in segregated settings. He suggested that this finding may be related to greater contact with nonhandicapped children in the former setting. Any degree of vision has also been found to result in a higher level of social development (Bauman, 1973; Lairy & Harrison-Covello, 1973).

Adolescence may be a particularly difficult time because any degree of visual impairment will set the child apart and peer group desire for conformity will segregate the adolescent who realistically cannot be 'like' his peers in all respects. Because they cannot see the latest fads in clothing, mannerisms, expres-

sions, and other aspects of adolescent life, girls, in particular, are at a disadvantage and may be set apart from the peer group because they are not like members of the group.

Adolescents with visual impairments may have difficulties in accepting themselves as being handicapped with certain capacities and limitations as defined by the impairment. Cholden (1958) postulates that the adolescent must first accept himself as a person before he can accept himself as a visually handicapped person. Since acceptance of one's disability is considered an important step in the adjustment process (Wright, 1960), it is necessary that the foundation be laid during childhood and adolescence for an adequate and realistic self-concept, so that acceptance of one's self as a handicapped person may evolve.

While relatively few persons might be considered as totally independent, adolescence is a time when independence is highly valued. The dependent nature of a visual impairment tends to prolong the period of dependence and make the normal degree of independence of adulthood somewhat more unattainable than for the nonhandicapped person. Many of the rites of passage into adulthood, such as driving a car, traveling alone to distant places, earning money, are unavailable to many visually handicapped adolescents, sometimes because of overprotective parents.

A visual impairment thus has a profound influence on affective development. How these influences may be alleviated is discussed in the next part.

Meeting Developmental Needs

Early intervention programs are essential to assist parents in their adjustment to the advent of a visually handicapped infant into the family. The ultimate adjustment of the person with a visual handicap is dependent in large measure on the attitudes of parents, their own adjustment, and their adjustment to the child and to the visual impairment (see Cholden, 1958; Cowen, Underberg, Verillo, & Benham, 1961; Endress, 1968; Hallenbeck, 1954; Sommers, 1944). Thus parents should be helped to develop positive attitudes within the family toward the child and toward the visual impairment.

As the child moves into the peer group culture, parents and at times when appropriate, siblings, may need to help the child initiate efforts to enlarge his circle of relevant others. Demonstrating the abilities of the youngster to his peers may assist in bridging the gap. Because the child cannot learn from visual imitation, parents, and later teachers, should help the child acquire the skills that may help him become part of the group.

The more limited range of peers and peer experiences may have a retarding effect on the development of the self-concept. Often parents attempt to protect the child from negative feedback concerning appearance and behavior which may result in his developing an unrealistic view of himself. School experience may further reinforce these feelings when teachers are not realistic in their expectations and make special concessions and excuses because of the visual impairment (Scott, 1969). While success experiences are necessary to develop an adequate self-concept, some experiences with failure may provide the necessary ingredient for developing a realistic self-concept.

Vision plays an important role in developing an identity with one's own sex. Blind adolescents lack the opportunity to imitate the dress, manners, and behavior of a model and thus may encounter problems in achieving their sex role identification. Boys are at a particular disadvantage because they tend to remain within the home under maternal influence, and they may lack the opportunity to engage in the rough play of male adolescents which leads to learning the conventional male role. During adolescence, parents, siblings, and teachers may need to work together to identify the social deficiencies of the adolescent compared with his peers and help him overcome these deficiencies. For example, information concerning current fads in dress and stimulating interest in his appearance and how to 'look like' the peers might help him be more acceptable.

Another problem area for some visually handicapped adolescents is accepting the need to be dependent. The goal of maturity is to become independent, but total independence in all areas is neither a desirable nor an attainable goal. The nature of the visual impairment tends to prolong the period of dependence and this should not be viewed by the adolescent as necessarily negative (Warren, 1984). Parents and teachers must therefore help the adolescent know when independence is appropriate within the limitations of the impairment and when dependence is acceptable and necessary.

The visually handicapped adolescent has a particularly challenging time choosing an appropriate vocation. Limited experiences with part-time work during secondary school years will inhibit the needed work experiences often requested by prospective employers. Chapter 22 describes ways in which the school can facilitate career development.

Finally, throughout his life, the person with a visual impairment needs to obtain from family and friends the feedback that he misses from the mirror in order to look and behave in socially acceptable and age-appropriate ways. The foundation described in Chapter 20 on training in social skills should be emphasized throughout the school years and continued into adulthood by the relevant others in the person's life.

Basically the educational needs of visually handicapped children are similar to those of all children. The school curriculum for all should be directed toward helping each child attain maximum potential and realize personal objectives. In order to take advantage of the school curriculum, however, children with visual impairments need some specialized curricular content that will meet their unique psychomotor, cognitive, and affective developmental needs. The chapters in Part III are directed toward providing such information for teachers.

Study questions

1. List ways in which your environment has had an influence on your development. How do your siblings differ from you in physical characteristics, ability, and personality? How do you and your siblings differ from your parents? Can the differences be attributed to heredity or to environment? In what ways?

2. Observe a normal infant under the age of 2 years. Describe his present level of psychomotor, cognitive, and affective development. If possible, list skills in each area that are emerging at the time of your observation.

3. Observe a child with a visual impairment and a child of approximately the same age who does not have a visual impairment. How do they differ in their psychomotor development? Can you account for the differences from information in the school records?

4. Teach a child with a visual impairment some physical skill such as skipping; teach the same skill to a child with normal vision. How did your approach to teaching and their learning differ?

5. Select some game, such as checkers, Chinese Checkers, or chess. Teach it to a child with a visual impairment and one with normal vision. How did your teaching techniques and their learning styles differ?

6. Select a specific age group. Make a list of ways in which a child at that age with no vision and a child the same age with visual acuity of around 20/70 might differ in their psychomotor, cognitive, and affective development.

7. Select two children with different eye conditions. Compare their developmental level. What differences might be attributed to characteristics of their vision problem?

8. Select two visually handicapped children. Prepare a case history for each including information from the school records, interviews with teachers and parents if possible, and your own observations. List differences in their family background and environment that might account for their psychomotor, cognitive, and affective developmental levels.

9. Observe a blind child or adult interacting with a peer group. What nonverbal communication did you observe being used by those with vision? How could

information from the nonverbal communication be explained to the blind child or adult?

10. Interview a visually handicapped adolescent about his hopes and plans for the future, vocationally and socially. From the school records, interviews with the teacher and parents (if possible), and your own observations, how realistic are these expectations? Give a rationale for your position.

11. Select one theoretical approach to development. Find out all you can about it from the references listed in the chapter. Prepare a report for your classmates.

12. Which of the theoretical approaches to development is most consistent with your philosophy of educating visually handicapped pupils? Provide a rationale.

Nadelman, L. (1982). *Research manual in child development.* New York, N.Y.: Harper & Row.

Scott, R.A. (1969). *The making of blind men.* New York, N.Y.: Russell Sage Foundation.

Smart, M.S. and Smart, R.C. (1977). *Children: Development and relationships.* (3rd ed.) New York, N.Y.: Macmillan Publishing Co., Inc.

Warren, D.H. (1984). *Blindness and early childhood development* (2nd ed. Rev.) New York, N.Y.: American Foundation for the Blind, Inc.

Additional readings

Cratty, B. and Sams, T. (1968). *The body image of blind children.* New York, N.Y.: American Foundation for the Blind, Inc.

Cutsforth, T. (1951). *The blind in school and society.* New York, N.Y.: American Foundation for the Blind, Inc.

Fein, G.G. (1978). *Child development.* Englewood Cliffs, N.J.: Prentice-Hall.

Fraiberg, S. (1977). *Insights from the blind.* New York, N.Y.: Basic Books.

Gardner, H. (1982). *Developmental psychology: An introduction.* (2nd ed.) Boston, Mass.: Little, Brown & Company.

Hatwell, Y. (1985). *Piagetian reasoning and the blind.* New York, N.Y.: American Foundation for the Blind, Inc.

Higgins, L. (1973). *Classification in congenitally blind children: An examination of Inhelder and Piaget's theory.* New York, N.Y.: American Foundation for the Blind, Inc.

Lowenfeld, B. (1981). *Berthold Lowenfeld on blindness and blind people.* New York, N.Y.: American Foundation for the Blind, Inc.

Lydon, W.T. and McGraw, L. (1973). *Concept development for visually handicapped children: A resource guide for teachers and other professionals working in educational settings.* New York, N.Y.: American Foundation for the Blind, Inc.

Mills, A.E. (1983). *Language acquisition in the blind child: Normal and deficient.* San Diego: College-Hill Press.

Mussen, P.H., Conger, J.J., and Kagan, J. (1979). *Child development and personality* (5th ed.) New York, N.Y.: Harper & Row.

CHAPTER **5**

Sensory Perceptual Development

Natalie C. Barraga

This chapter addresses the roles of the three major senses in the learning process: how the hearing, skin, and visual senses receive and process information. The relation of sensory perceptual systems to motor and cognitive development is applied specifically to children and youth with visual impairments. Mental mapping as an aspect of cognitive organization for the information of more stable concepts is reviewed as a means of understanding cognitive styles of visually handicapped pupils.

As a basis for understanding the sensory perceptual abilities and limitations of visually handicapped children and youth, some discussion of the process by which all children experience and interact with the world seems imperative. With his first breath at the moment of birth an infant has the capacity to become a receiving, participating, interacting human being who enjoys a reciprocally satisfying relationship with his immediate environment, and eventually a fulfilling involvement with an ever-expanding world. The central nervous system of the human organism is so constituted that it experiences a continuing hunger for stimulation through the sense organs in order to establish contact between the body and external surroundings. Physical energy within the human being or stimuli from the outside excite the sensory receptors and upset the body's state of equilibrium creating a need for some satisfying "input" to return the organism to a peaceful or restful state.

The senses are stimulated by the sights, sounds, touches, tastes, and smells that surround every infant and young child. As the sensory nerves send messages to the central nervous system, and specifically the brain, these are gradually given meaning as perception begins. Eventually, perceptions of the world begin to group themselves in patterns which can be remembered, and learning for each child assumes an emergent style.

Most sensory systems consist of the sensory organ, receptor cells in or near the organ itself, and neurons or transmitting nerves which are in turn connected to the cell body in the cortex of the brain. Visual and auditory stimulations are specific and direct and received in identified areas of the brain in an approx-

imate representation of the environmental source of stimulation. The tactile or haptic sense provides less discrete information because touch, temperature and texture, and internal muscle movement are all involved in what is being perceived through this system. Similarly, the olfactory and gustatory sensory systems accept stimulations from many sources and there is no direct sensory nerve to separate and define either of them (McBurney & Collings, 1977).

OVERVIEW

The Senses and Learning

The learning process in most children is so automatic and spontaneous that little consideration is given to all of the factors involved, especially to the importance of the sensory systems and their relationship to the brain. Combining the fragmentary bits of sensory stimulation into meaningful perceptions, then into stable concepts generates the functional knowledge for thinking and communicating abstract ideas. All this sorting, coding, and organizing of perceptions and concepts to make them fit together for individual learning and behavior is a complex mental task even when all sensory systems and the brain are intact and operating at maximal efficiency. Regardless, the process is learned in a unique style by each child and is later characterized as "learning style" (Piaget, 1973).

Some theorists suggest that a child's learning style is well established by the age of three years, and is less amenable to alteration after that, although changes may be accomplished up to the adult years with orderly consistent teaching of different styles. The long term effects of such attempts at modification of learning styles has not yet been determined (Furth, 1969; Keogh, 1973). Cognitive development and organization will be discussed in greater depth later in this chapter. Suffice it to say at this point that what a child receives through the senses, interprets in the brain, internalizes into the central nervous system, and acts upon through the motor system becomes that child's model of her total world.

Sensory Perceptual Terminology

Because so many terms which have different meanings to educators, psychologists, and others are used in discussing sensory perceptual development and learning, a few of them will be defined to help the reader know the meaning given to them in this chapter. *Sensations* are "energies that stimulate or activate nerve cells" (Ayres, 1981) and involve sensory organs and the peripheral nervous system, but all are

not necessarily received and interpreted as having any meaning. Whether or not information is provided through sensations depends on the receptivity of the transmitting channels, the efficiency of the receptor centers in the brain, the connecting links or pathways among the various sensory channels, and the ability of the coding and processing centers to give meaningful interpretation. The strength of the sensations through various senses cannot be measured, although differences in sensations can be determined.

When a baby or child becomes aware of the differences or likenesses between sights, sounds, smells, tastes, and touches, then she is *discriminating*. Discriminations are extremely gross in the baby as she attends to a very small portion of the available features at any point, but they become increasingly refined as subtle differences and a greater number of features are given attention at the same time.

Recognition occurs when the child knows that what is seen, heard, touched, tasted, or smelled is familiar and has been experienced previously. At this point, it is obvious that memories of certain sensations and

discriminations are being stored and recalled, which is one of the first evidences that learning is taking place.

A long term process of mediation and integration of sensations, discriminations, and recognitions permits differentiation and specification of sensory input into usable information as *perceptions* (Bower, 1977; 1979; Bruner & Anglin, 1973). As learning continues and constant elaboration of the percepts occur, changes take place in the perceptual system itself. Although it is believed that the sensory and perceptual systems are coordinated rather than differentiated in the early months of life (Bower, 1977), both systems begin to register modality specifics after perceptions begin forming. The child then has the capacity to seek and accept stimulation of one specific sense to the exclusion of other sensory stimulations. Sensory learning is then determined to a great extent by the experiences, interests, and available stimulations in the unique world of each child.

Sensitivities and Acuities of the Systems

Each sensory system seems to need a minimum level of stimulation before the nerve impulses can cross the synaptic junctions and move along to the appropriate receiving station in the brain. Receptor cells in various organs have affinity or disposition to external stimuli designed specifically for that sense (Ludel, 1978); for example, only cells in the retina of the eye are sensitive to light rays; receptor cells in the inner ear are totally indifferent to light rays, but are acutely sensitive to sound waves which arouse no activity in retinal cells.

Laboratory studies center around determination of thresholds for the different sensory systems. Considerable information has been acquired regarding visual and auditory thresholds, but much less is known about tactile thresholds since they vary widely for different parts of the body; virtually nothing is known about thresholds for smell and taste senses. The intensity of the stimulation is not necessarily related to the sensation received in the brain; myelination of nerve fibers, especially the optic and auditory nerves, helps to determine the speed and strength of the transmission along the nerve fiber. Nonmyelinated fibers conduct impulses very slowly, whereas myelinated fibers conduct impulses quite rapidly (Fernandez, 1983; Geldard, 1972). (See Chapter 3.)

Physiological maturation seems to affect sensory reception and that can occur only when the sensory system receives continuing stimulation through messages flowing consistently along the nerve fibers. This fact is related to the difficulty in determining acuity levels for the various sensory systems, and the fallacy that acuity measurements give accurate information about the usefulness of a sensory organ for learning. Even when thresholds and acuities can be measured, those measurements do not measure what is being received in the brain, how it is integrated with previous stimulation, and the interpretation given to it by the unique individual. Acuities do indicate whether or not enough neural energy has reached the particular sense organ to exceed the minimum threshold of stimulation.

Visual acuity is limited by the intensity of the discrimination between the stimulus target and the light surrounding it, the distance from the visible target, the accommodation needed to bring the object to focus, and the time needed to respond to the information received, considerations of critical importance when thinking about persons with impairments in the visual system (Gregory, 1974). Hearing acuity is related to the vibration of receptor cells in the cochlea caused by the intensity of the sound waves traveling through air and fluid, the frequency (rate) of vibrations, and the masking effects of the environment. So there can be no fixed unchanging level of sensitivity of the auditory system to any one sound or groups of sounds (Ludel, 1978).

Measurement of acuities of the skin senses is an almost impossible task; touch sensitivity varies over the body surface because different parts of the body have lesser or greater numbers of receptors. There is no way to separate kinesthetic information from touch information. About the only type of tactile acuity that can be determined is to measure the amount of pressure or weight necessary to produce feeling in a specific part of the body. No one really understands the properties of chemical stimuli that produce sensations in the taste and smell senses so that thresholds and acuities cannot be estimated at the present time.

The overriding consideration for teachers is not the sensitivity or acuity of various sensory systems, but whether the child can respond to sensory stimulation, and how he can receive and interpret it for learning and functioning.

Relation of Senses to Cognitive Development.

Bower (1977; 1979) believes that the senses are coordinated, but not differentiated at birth; he purports a "primitive unity" of senses such that auditory stimulation specifies something to see and touch, visual stimulation signals something to touch, and tactile stimulation indicates something to see.

The infant, prior to the ability to differentiate, may not know whether he is seeing something or hearing something simply on the basis of sensory stimulation, but becomes increasingly sensitive to which sensory modality is registering a specific stimulation in the early weeks of life. The environment in the early weeks and months is a critical determinant of sensory awareness and use, thereby influencing sensory preferences very early in life. For example, if the sensory environment is rich in visual stimulation and contrast but virtually void of stimulating sounds, then the auditory system is used less, and later on the child may show less sensitivity to useful and meaningful sounds. On the other hand, if there is an environment full of constant noise, never changing lighting conditions, and probing, touching, and moving of the infant, there is little chance for differentiation of the senses. This is a major concern of neonatologists and others when preterm infants live the first two or three months of their lives in the unchanging environment of the neonatal units. The environment is "sterile" and void of useful sensory stimulation (Schaeffer, Hatcher, & Barglow, 1980; Touwen, 1980; Rose, Schmidt, Riese, & Bridger, 1980).

The patterns of sensory reception established by the infant and young child become a vital part of the child's learning style and perceptual cognitive development in the early years. The child is mediator between the external world of sensory stimulation and her own pattern of sensory awareness, selectiveness, and organizing of information into a series of interactive interpretations (Liepmann, 1973). Perceptual cognitive development seems to follow a more stable pattern when children use all of their available senses during the preschool years. Use of all sensory systems to their optimal capacity helps each child to reach his maximum learning potentiality. Some theorists even suggest that a child's pattern for cognitive development is becoming established by three years of age, but may be modified or even changed for many years.

Motor Integration

Just as sensory stimulation and interpretation are food for the brain to grow and develop, digestion of that food is achieved through motor integration of the sensory information. Motor integration can occur only when the infant and young child use the motor system in responding to the sensory stimulation. At birth, there are innumerable rhythmic involuntary movements which contribute to the development of motor patterns as they are gradually brought under control in order to reach what is seen or to touch what is heard. Movement enables the body to receive tactual stimulation, encounter the voids of space and to make contact with people and objects. Movement helps the infant to define the capabilities and limitations of the body in relation to space and to begin to feel the position of body parts and the muscle power needed to perform certain movements. Putting all these perceptions together in relation to purposeful movements in order to accomplish a desired goal constitutes what Piaget (1973) termed internalization.

The relationship between movement and the various senses is not at all clear and many questions are still being asked; did the infant look because there was movement or did she move because she saw something, or did the head turn because a sound was heard or was the infant turning the head in order to look? Whether sensory stimulation promotes movement or whether movement provides more desired sensory stimulation is still a matter of speculation. Nevertheless, there are many indications that the sensory and motor systems are intertwined and that sensorimotor development proceeds with greater rapidity when the reciprocal action between the sensory and motor systems is optimal. Children who lag in development in any of the sensory or motor systems seem to progress less rapidly in perceptual cognitive areas as well. Bruner and Anglin (1973) refer to integration as a grouping of percepts so that there is congruity between what we see, feel, smell, hear, and taste. A "traffic jam" happens in the brain when this organizing and grouping cannot bring the different sensory and motor perceptions together compatibly (Ayres, 1981).

Perceptual cognitive learning seems to be closely related to the development of language since object and action words form a part of the communication system as concepts are learned. At first, the young child seems to use language to speak to himself primarily, secondarily to communicate with others, and only later understands the use of language as a social and emotional means of interaction and communication. If, as some suggest, inner language is the internal representation of sensory motor learning, then receptive language challenges the child to modify and adjust her own internal perceptions to those expressed through the language of others. The resolution of conflicts of differences between the personal perceptions and the expressed perceptions of others contributes to the refinement of concepts, as what is thought can be communicated through language. This interchange of language with playmates, parents, and teachers, is a factor in the development of unique thoughts which we often refer to as intelligence (Furth, 1969). The child's chief avenue for use of language and confirmation of beginning concepts is through play with peers and adults. Through play a child reveals his range and variety of experiences as well as his motoric flexibility and shares these through expressed language for social communication.

The discussion of the sensory and motor systems, language, and the establishment of patterns of learning leads to one final conclusion. The human organism uses all its capacities to bring together a unified intake and output of information that is meaningful and useful to it for the purpose of developing, learning, and functioning in concert with its surroundings. The process is similar for all, but the uniqueness and individuality may become evident as each sensory system is discussed in depth in relation to each other and to the motor and perceptual cognitive systems. The impact of impairments on development of the systems, and learning and functioning of children with impairments will constitute the major thrust of the next sections.

THE VISUAL SYSTEM

A greater quantity of information is gained in a shorter period of time through use of the visual system than through any other single sense organ. The eye provides the brain with the sensations for the interpretation of color, the dimensional quality of objects, the impression of distance, and the ability to follow an experienced movement while the body remains stationary. Often called the primary sensory channel for extension of the human being beyond her own body, vision is the mediator for other sensory impressions and acts as a stabilizer between the person and the external world. More incidental learning occurs through looking than through use of any other sense. The system involves many other body systems, and the process of looking and seeing is a complex one which can best be understood by clarifying some terms and discussing the component parts of the system and the process and progression of development in relation to learning.

Educational Terminology

An in-depth discussion of the physiology of the eye and the structural and disease conditions found in children was presented in Chapter 3, but there are some other terms which are relevant to this particular discussion. Educationally, there is a general consensus of words which are most appropriate for use with children and youth but may not be used as widely in legal, clinical, and rehabilitation settings. For

Chart 5.1   Educational characteristics of low vision students

Levels of Visual Disability	Performance Capability
Moderate visual disability	With use of special aids and lighting may perform visual tasks almost like students with normal vision
Severe visual disability	In performance of visual tasks, may require more time, take more energy, and be less accurate even with aids and other modifications
Profound visual disability	Performance of even gross visual tasks may be very difficult and detailed tasks cannot be handled visually at all

Adapted from: A. Colenbrander, Dimensions of visual performance, *Archives of American Academy of Ophthalmology*, **83**, p. 335.

example, instead of referring to students as "legally blind," a generic term, teachers are more likely to refer to all students whom they serve as *visually handicapped*, the designation included in federal and most state laws. The word blind applies only to those who have no vision or only light perception; the condition may exist from birth or shortly thereafter or the person may be blinded by accident or disease at any time. The impact on development and learning will be determined by the age of onset along with numerous other factors in the home and family life, the cultural conditions, and the intervention services available to the parents and child as early as possible. Educationally, the blind student learns through braille and auditory material without use of the visual sense (Caton, 1981).

Levels of vision were defined by Colenbrander (1977), and focus on function as normal, low vision, and blind. Chart 5.1 identifies the educational characteristics of low vision students.

As can be seen, low vision students are a very heterogeneous group, a topic discussed at greater length in the following chapter.

Components of the System
The sense organ, the eye, is a physical structure which is an outgrowth of the optic nerve. The eye itself has many parts and functions which have been described in detail in the Chapter 3. The intactness and structural alignment of the parts will influence the functioning of each part of the eye and of the entire system. The amount and kind of light received by the eye affects the stimulation of retinal cells to generate energy to transmit to the brain. The neurological system is involved once the retinal cells have sent bursts of electrical energy along the optic nerve, the connecting link to the brain and the perceptual cognitive system. Each aspect of this complicated system must work in synchrony for visual development and processing of visual information to be a vital part of learning. When the systems are all working normally, the visual skills such as fixation, tracking, focus, accommodation, and convergence are achieved through looking in day-to-day activities in the early weeks and months. Things to see provide for storage of visual images in the brain very early and these images are elaborated, modified, and refined as learning and perceptual development continues.

Visual Perceptual Development
The brain drives the eye according to Haith and Campos (1977), and studying fixation patterns of infants and young children may lead to inferences of what the brain is trying to do. Learning seems to begin when infants actually seek out visual input by choosing when to look and at what to look. Studies indicate that infants

do the following: 1) open the eyes if awake and alert; 2) maintain an intense vigilant search even if there is no light; 3) continue to search even if they find light but no edges; 4) scan back and forth across contour when they locate it; and 5) maintain a narrow scanning range if the located contour is in the vicinity of other contours, but a broader range if the pattern density is low (Dubowitz, Dubowitz, Morante, & Verghote, 1980; Fantz, Fagan, & Miranda, 1975; Hubel & Wiesel, 1979).

Haith and Campos (1977) postulate that infants behave as they do visually so as to maintain visual cortical firing activity at a maximal level and to steadily increase the rate of firing. Active visual searching and scanning are necessary if cortical stimulation is to be maintained. If so, this need may be revealed in findings regarding selective attention and habituation to certain stimuli by infants (Fantz, 1974; Friedman, 1972) suggesting that infants will attend to visual stimuli as long as they are receiving visual information and they stop looking when there is no new information to be gained.

Visual perception involves examining an object, distinguishing the essential features, understanding the relationship between the elements, and integrating the information into a meaningful whole, further evidence of the integral relationship between the motor, perceptual, and cognitive systems. Because of the vast knowledge of visual perception created by recent research, it is now possible to define the functions and skills of the visual system, combine it with what is known of perceptual cognitive development, and estimate the "visual age" of a child by his responses to visual stimuli. This is the only sensory system that has been studied sufficiently to do this. Development of the system is related to the stimulation provided by looking and by integrating movement patterns precipitated by the looking (Barraga, Collins, & Hollis, 1977). As can be observed in the Chart 5.2, visual development stimulates response of the motor system as early as five to six months of age; the perceptual system (visual imagery and object constancy) by six to seven months of age; and the cognitive system by one year of age when matching and imitating behavior indicate memory of visual input (Barraga, 1983).

Visual Impairment and Learning
The extent to which impairment in one or more parts of the visual system affects visual development or exactly how the progession may be altered is not known at this time. Obviously, when there is structural defect or disease in the eye itself, visual skills will be developed with greater difficulty, and more slowly. Miranda and Hack (1979) found that "extreme central nervous system damage precluded visual orienting responses in the newborn." Hoyt (1983), an ophthalmologist, advocates surgery within eight to sixteen weeks after birth for

Chart 5.2   Sequence of visual development

Developmental Age	Visual Responses and Capabilities
0-1 month	Attends to light and possible forms; weak ciliary muscles and limited fixation ability.
1-2 months	Follows moving objects and lights; attends to novelty and complex patterns; stares at faces; begins binocular coordination.
2-3 months	Eyes fixate, converge, and focus; discriminates faces and yellow, orange, and red color waves.
3-4 months	Eye movements smoother and acuity improving; manipulates and looks at objects.
4-5 months	Eyes shift focus from objects to body parts; attempts to reach for and move to objects; visually explores environment; recognizes familiar faces and objects; tracks objects across entire field of vision.
5-6 months	Reaches and grasps objects indicating eye-hand coordination.
6-7 months	Shifts visual attention from object to object; reaches and rescues dropped objects; fluid eye movements.
7-8 months	Manipulates objects looking at results; watches movements and scribbling.
9-10 months	Visual acuity very good, accommodation smooth; looks for hidden objects even around corners; imitates facial expressions; plays looking games.
11 months to 1½ years	All optical skills refined and acuity sharp; fits objects together and marks spontaneously.
1½ to 2 years	Matches objects, points to objects in book; imitates strokes and actions.
2 to 2½ years	Visually inspects objects in distance; imitates movements of others; matches colors and like forms; increased visual memory span; orders objects by color; regards and reaches.
2½ to 3 years	Matches geometric forms; draws crude circle; inserts circle, square and triangle; puts pegs in holes and two puzzle pieces together.
3-4 years	Matches identical shaped objects by size; good depth perception; discriminates line lengths; copies cross, discriminates most basic forms.
4-5 years	Refined eye-hand coordination; colors, cuts, and pastes; draws square; perceives detail in objects and pictures.
5-6 years	Perceives relationships in pictures, abstract figures, and symbols; copies symbols; matches letters and words.
6-7 years	Identifies and reproduces abstract symbols; perceives constancy of letter/word styles; associates words with pictures; reads words on sight.

Source: N. Barraga, *Visual handicaps and learning*, (rev. ed), (Austin, Tex.: Exceptional Resources, 1983), pp. 79-80.

children born with severe cataracts. He says that without such swift action the children almost always grow up with very poor vision. Because cataracts block stimulation to visual portions of the brain, the pathways develop imperfectly. Use of soft contact lenses provides sharp visual images so crucial to full development of the brain's visual center from the very beginning.

Changes in visual behavior and movement have been found when intensive visual stimulation and visual learning activities have been provided for infants and young children who were diagnosed as having visual impairments (Ashcroft, Halliday, & Barraga, 1965; Barraga, 1964; Holmes, 1967; O'Brien, 1976; Wilson, McVeigh, McMahon, Bauer, & Richardson, 1976; Miranda & Hack, 1979; Ferrell, 1980).

Even though evidence shows that some visual development can continue as long as light can enter the eye(s), the nature and severity of the impairment may make it difficult to control eye muscles, focus on the visual object, and form a meaningful image from blurred and/or distorted visual information. Because most impairments limit the distance at which a person can see objects, there is likely to be a reduction in spontaneous acquisition of visual knowledge about the world, and, of equal importance, there is no visual clarity to act as mediator between distant sounds and smells. This stabilizing and integrating of sensory information is especially critical in the early months and years. Disproportionate features in space, position in space, depth perception, and merging of forms because of lack of sufficient contrast present difficulty in visual motor integration of low vision children (Kraetsch-Heller, 1976).

Young children are very adaptable and flexible in the use of their bodies and sense organs. They see what they see and have no knowledge of what or how they *should* see the world; they may be totally unaware of limitations in their visual capacities or efficiency in visual functioning. They think the world looks to everyone else just as it does to them. Eye specialists and educators alike stress that all children with low vision suffer from lack of spontaneous visual stimulation and may need to be taught to develop their visual perceptual abilities in order to achieve their potential visual efficiency. The congenitally severely visually impaired child at any age is like a baby as far as visual development is concerned unless he is carefully stimulated and taught how to look, to note visual cues and make visual comparisons. Complete visual maturity takes about sixteen years. To reach a state of full visual perceptual integration may take even longer (Valvo, 1971).

Low vision students may receive many visual impressions which they are unable to organize and interpret accurately unless there is a sequential learning program that helps them to differentiate between important cues and "visual noise" and guides them in seeking the highest level of visual efficiency possible. A program to address the unique considerations for low vision learners (Barraga & Morris, 1980) is available.

Teacher's Role

Teachers working with students with impaired but useful vision need to be sensitive to a number of personal and environmental factors which may affect their functioning. The attitudes of clinical personnel and family may have influenced whether they think of themselves as "seeing" persons or as "blind" persons. If the term "legally blind" was used in the diagnosis and the family has treated the child as not being able to see, then that child will be underdeveloped visually and literally have to learn to see just like an infant. Generally, this happens less and less frequently, but may still occur in some areas of the world. A person who has not used the impaired vision may actually have to learn how to look before he can begin to use the vision for functioning. In the older child, this will probably take much longer especially if there has been little encouragement or motivation to do so previously. A new way of sensing the environment takes time to internalize into behavior.

The teacher's role and attitude are important in modifying or changing the student's attitude about herself in approaching and attempting to accomplish visual tasks. If stress is placed on speed of performance rather than quality of learning through all the senses, then less time may be spent on teaching how to look and how to see. An emphasis on learning to use impaired vision may not be for the purpose of visual reading exclusively, but for increasing flexibility in functioning in a variety of situations and under a multitude of environmental conditions. In fact, many severe and profound low vision students will do very little visual reading.

Students are individuals also and one may function quite well visually in a particular setting but may be far less visually efficient in another setting because of the numerous personal variables related to visual functioning. For example, visibility is one of the important considerations. Light refers to the quantity of illumination on the task whereas lighting involves the quality and brightness of the entire visual environment. The combination of light and lighting determines the degree to which something can be seen and constitutes what is called the visibility factor. Some persons require more light but less brightness, while others need less light but greater brightness in the total surrounding area. The following chapter addresses illumination in greater depth.

Other factors which influence visibility include: contrast between the object/task and the immediate area; the absence or presence of glare; and the type of artificial lighting used. Since there is little a person can do to control lighting out of doors, many persons with low vision find that they function more efficiently when there is less direct sunlight; others find there is more visual clarity on bright sunshiny days. Making generalizations is difficult since the type of impairment, the sensitivity of the individual, and the nature of the task make visual functioning unique for each person.

Whatever the individual characteristics of low vision students, each needs the opportunity to learn to use impaired vision either as a primary learning sense or as a supportive sense in every possible situation and to feel comfortable and confident in doing so. Some may never read the newspaper, but learn to read enough to monitor signs in the environment or to read a menu or the directory in an office building. Equally important for them is to use visual cues for orientation in unfamiliar areas or to seek visual landmarks when traveling in less familiar surroundings. All of these visual skills enhance self concept and feelings of independence.

Students who lose their sight suddenly, or begin to lose vision gradually because of disease conditions may pose a host of questions for teachers. When should he stop trying to use the deteriorating vision and rely on other senses? The answers are not simple nor are they the same for each individual. Many persons rely on visual imagery and visual memory to continue to function visually long past the point anyone would expect, while others quit using their vision when they no longer see objects with sharpness and clarity. Many psychological, physiological, and intellectual factors interact to affect the motivation of the person to continue to function visually. The general suggestion to teachers is to support the student in continued use of reduced vision by helping to recall visual imagery and memories as he gradually transfers more and more reliance on other senses when needed, a topic to be continued in the following paragraphs.

When the visual sense is functioning with a high degree of efficiency, the intake of information through vision is such that it is used as the fundamental sense for understanding and expanding one's environment. Sensory data from other channels provide additional supplementary knowledge. Children who are visually handicapped (including those who are totally blind) find the world less accessible to them through the visual sense and may need to rely primarily on other senses while developing the visual sense as supplementary to others.

Children who are totally blind need to involve their whole bodies in searching for and receiving information about themselves and the objects available to them in their environment. By exploration with hands, feet, and the entire body, infants and young children can be actively engaged in bringing knowledge of the world to themselves instead of having their senses "acted upon" (Fraiberg, 1969).

THE TACTUAL KINESTHETIC SYSTEM

The interrelationship between the tactual and kinesthetic senses in seeking and conveying information to the brain for coding, association, and interpretation is such that these two systems will be discussed simultaneously. "For successively progressing impressions and their connections, movement is indispensible" (Révész, 1950, p. 97) suggests that clear impressions can be gained tactually only when touching involves movement.

Often referred to as the "skin senses" the tactual and kinesthetic system involves touch, movement, and body position in space. These senses assume paramount importance in development in relation to reduction in visual ability, and are the primary learning avenues for children who are blind. Although the information is less precise than visual information, may be transitory and often inconsistent, and at times difficult to integrate, great emphasis needs to be given to stimulation of this system in all visually handicapped children. In infancy, the body is constantly handled and moved with little opportunity for involvement except passive resistance. However, the touch and tender handling of the nurturing persons

helps to bind the infant to the world beyond himself. Fraiberg (1977) found that the most reliable stimulus for evoking a smile in blind infants was gross kinesthetic stimulation, suggesting that establishing an early relationship between tactual kinesthetic awareness within the child and external influences may be a strong factor in development.

Passive movement of the arms, legs, head and neck, and trunk may be considered a counterpart to illumination for visual development in stimulation of the tactual kinesthetic system. Even though passive stimulation may be received at the unconscious perceptual level, storage of motor patterns may contribute to later cognitive learning. As the infant initiates more and more movement, the hands touch, grasp, push, and lift, providing a basis for active exploratory and manipulative use of the muscles. This movement stimulates receptor systems in the muscles, tendons, and joints providing an interface between touch and movement (Schiff & Foulke, 1982). Touch has been referred to as the "reality sense" (Taylor, Lederman, & Gibson, 1973), meaning perhaps that body contact gives more stable information than the distance senses of vision and hearing. The lips and hands have large concentrations of tactile receptors and are the most sensitive transmitters of tactile information to the cortex, a fact to be considered when observing blind babies mouthing objects longer than is thought appropriate (Ludel, 1978).

Gradually, the muscular system is strengthened to the point where voluntary control over movements can be exercised. Lacking the sense of vision to guide movements and to coordinate the use of hands to explore and seek out information, development and learning in the blind child is dependent on planned stimulation to enable him to progress in the handling of his body, and to begin to note the differences among the things he touches and that touch him. Prior to using his hands to explore, the infant gains a wider variety of information through the mouth and so needs many opportunities to suck and mouth foods of different consistencies and any objects he finds pleasing and which are safe.

Encounters with a variety of soft textures in stuffed animals of similar contour are desirable. Textural preference appears to develop very early in life and may have some relationship to accuracy of tactile discrimination at a later time (Griffin & Gerber, 1982; Hanninen, 1976). Just becoming accustomed to many different textures may be an arousing stimulus for the tactile kinesthetic sensory system.

Tactual Kinesthetic Perceptual Development

Little evidence is available upon which to define clearly the progressive sequence (if such occurs) of tactual kinesthetic perception in unimpaired children. Even less is known about visually handicapped children. Some basic principles have emerged from comparisons with sighted children, but the inability to differentiate the effects of vision in supplementing tactual kinesthetic reception necessitates many assumptions for which no verification can be offered.

Five distinguishable activities in cutaneous reception offered by Juurmaa (1967) seem to be related to perception: 1) a receptor is moved along various surfaces (differentiation is most often in the rough-smooth dimension); 2) estimation of the distance between two receptors located opposite to each other, with an object in between (estimation of the thickness of an object); 3) estimation of the distance between two points on the skin (two-point discrimination); 4) observation of differences in degree of static pressure; and 5) observation of differences in movable weights.

Révész (1950) distinguished between visual form recognition and tactual structure recognition; form is primary in visual perception as an immediate impression, whereas structure predominates in tactual perception and is an analysis of the relationship of parts. Distinction in tactual perceptual performances

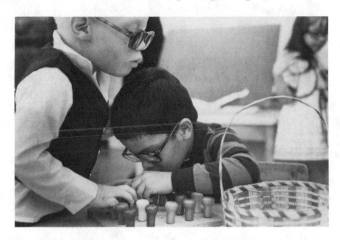

is that of simultaneous general impressions (stationary hand) for global perspective and successive tactile perceptions (moving or grasping hand) for detailed analytic information (Fieandt, 1966).

The sequence of discrimination capabilities, the tasks performed, and the perceptual aspects of tactual kinesthetic perceptual development have been addressed by several writers from whom inferences can be drawn (Barraga, 1983; Griffin & Gerber, 1982; Kershman, 1976; Simpkins, 1979; Warren, 1984). The perceptual development in this sensory system seems to follow a pattern similar to the following:

Awareness and attention to differences in textures, temperatures, vibrating surfaces, and materials of varied consistencies.

Structure and shape can be perceived when the hands grasp and manipulate objects of many shapes and different sizes. Early handling and exploring helps to isolate distinctive components of objects for future recognition.

The relation of parts to the whole can be understood when play provides for taking apart and putting together blocks, toys, and household objects. At this time, concepts of mental space and grouping of objects can be perceived also.

Graphic representations in two dimensional form are a high level of tactual perception and the representations may have little resemblance to the three dimensional object previously handled and now presented in a flat perspective. Recognition and association can be fostered by beginning with simple structural patterns such as geometric forms and gradually increasing to more complex drawings.

Braille symbology requires a level of tactual kinesthetic perception comparable to that of print letter and word recognition. Symbol recognition through touch is a complex, abstract level of perceptual cognitive association.

Along with consideration for the perceptual aspects of tactual learning, attention must be given to the development of such mechanical skills as hand movement, finger positions and dexterity, wrist flexibility, and light touch, all of which have been identified as necessary for efficient braille reading (Mangold, 1977; 1978; Olson, 1981). Careful assessment of tactual kinesthetic development through the preschool years is necessary as a guide to appropriate intervention and tactual stimulation activities which help assure that blind children have the readiness preparation required for using touch as the primary learning sense.

A high level of tactual perceptual development is essential for the derivation of meaning from braille symbology; the association of words and experiences with objects permits the child to relate dynamic real-life experiences to stories. The development of tactual kinesthetic perceptions is never complete; unfortunately, there is a tendency to reduce the emphasis on tactual learning as the child progresses in school work and to replace it with verbal skills "about the world." There is need to continue practice in coding, organizing, and responding to tactually perceived information. For example, using graphic representations and teaching students to make their own tactual pictures has a direct relationship to learning to read charts and maps by touch, a skill given too little attention in educational programs (Bentzen, 1982; Lederman, 1982).

The fact that there is still little consensus about how to represent many things in graphic form and the symbology to use in displays for tactual perception may be a factor in the limited use of embossed maps and other types of raised-line drawings. Studies need to be designed to increase tactual perceptual efficiency in blind children through a planned sequence of activities and to determine whether or not such an approach could result in more effective use of touch in map reading and other forms of tactual displays.

Up to this point, discussion of the tactual kinesthetic sense has dealt with hand movement with the body in stationary position. Use of the body in orientation and movement within space is another important aspect of this system. "Space is a feeling that can be imagined even without vision, and spatial concepts are internalized based on actions" (Simpkins, 1979, p. 86). Mental space is actually constructed as movements and actions are coordinated and internalized when exploratory and movement opportunities are provided consistently, and spatial perceptions seem to increase with age and experience (Warren, 1984). Spatial perceptions can be confirmed by mental mapping of position of objects encountered along certain routes, and by using touch as a guiding support to movement in confined areas, a principle utilized early on by orientation and mobility instructors when they teach trailing. (See Chapter 19.)

Students with low vision will need to have the same stimulating tactual and kinesthetic experiences so as to use these systems as support for reduced visual capability, and rely on these senses rather than vision in certain environments and under some circumstances when visibility is a problem. Without exception, all visually handicapped students need to have greater attention given to development and use of the tactual and kinesthetic senses to enhance their efficiency in learning and functioning in school and throughout life.

THE AUDITORY SYSTEM

Nerve endings for the auditory sense are encased in bone within the inner ear and the reception area is deep in the center of the brain. Consequently, the infant makes little use of this sense in the early weeks and months, and babies seem to be completely insensitive to ordinary sounds around them. Probably, they begin to use sound information about the fifth or sixth month, and often then only when accompanied by either visual or touch stimuli. Discrimination of sound in relation to observed objects may be noticed before the end of the child's first year, but object sound association, except for the human voice, is not evident until after the first birthday (Fraiberg, Smith, & Adelson, 1969). Sound stimuli to which the infant responds in the first year are the human voice and soft rhythmic music. After the first year or two, the auditory sense becomes a major activating sense for the blind child and is a supporting sense for the child with low vision. Some have suggested that the ears of a blind person are comparable to the eyes of a sighted person, but accepting this idea without qualification could give a false impression. The blind person could develop a high level of auditory acuity for particularly appealing sounds but have little, if any, relationship to auditory perception of meaningful sounds.

Because of the consistent uncontrollable emission of sounds into the environment, human beings have little control over auditory input until they can learn to mask sounds by selective listening and perception, a skill not easily learned without adult supervision and guidance in calling attention to useful and meaningful sounds. To be able to determine which sounds have meaning is a difficult task without vision, and even more complicated when there is no body contact with the sound producing object.

Components of the System

The auditory nerve connects the hair-like follicles (nerve endings) in the cochlea with the brain by transmitting neural energy generated by vibrations through air, bone, and fluid. The conducting mechanisms are separated from the nerve cells (inner ear), and examination of both of them is more complex than examination of the eye. The outer ear (Pinna) catches and directs the sound to the middle ear. The middle ear consists of three bones which send vibrations into the inner ear where nerve fibers are stimulated. Any malformation or limitation in these conducting mechanisms limits the strength of the vibrations entering the inner ear and causes a conductive hearing loss. If the conducting elements are functioning properly, but there is structural damage in the nerve tissues in the cochlea or in the auditory nerve itself, or in the reception area in the brain, there is a nerve or neural loss of hearing. Problems in the conducting system can usually be pinpointed and many can be medically or surgically treated to correct or minimize the effects on conduction. If there are intact and functioning conducting mechanisms, the assumption is made that the difficulty lies either in the inner ear or in the brain itself. The latter is considered a central nervous system (CNS) loss. The infant who hears begins to respond to sound by babbling around the fifth month, and by imitating self-produced and external sound stimuli shortly thereafter. Less definitive information about auditory perception is available than about visual perception, but the progression in development is probably similar to that of vision.

Auditory Perceptual Development

The auditory processing system is very complex; in fact, there are many systems, but there seems to have been little interest in investigating how the system works when hearing is normal. Most studies have dealt with deafness, so a great deal of speculation is involved when trying to discuss a normal sequence of auditory perceptual development (Eisenberg, 1976).

Sounds are constant in the environment, and although some are loud enough to startle the infant, few have meaning until they are repeated consistently and are paired with visual or tactual stimuli. Even then, adult guidance is necessary to get the baby to attend to the desired sound. The sequence of learning to understand and give meaning to sounds seems to follow a pattern similar to the following (Barraga, 1983):

Awareness and attention to sounds may be manifest first by a stilling (listening) in the baby, then increased anticipatory body action when the sound is stimulating. Pleasing and comforting sounds of the human voice or soft music seem to produce a soothing effect which often leads to sleep. Placing sound-producing objects on or near the infant's body heightens aware-

ness especially when the movement of a body part produces the sound (bell on shoe, and baby raises leg).

Response to specific sounds may begin by four to five months of age and are usually indicated by a form of smiling, a turn of the head, or intent listening behavior which Piaget (1973) termed "listening to hear." At this point, ear-hand coordination (similar to eye-hand coordination) is beginning, an important skill for the low vision or blind child. As more and more sounds are recognized, there is a tendency for increased manipulation of objects simply to hear the sounds produced. Vocalizations may become spontaneous and approximate the sound heard.

Sound discrimination and recognition are indications that learning and memory are progressing rapidly. The baby is noting the difference between human voice, household sounds, musical tones, and distinct noises in the out-of-doors. Attending to these sounds fosters localization of the sound as coming from a particular direction or promotes searching behavior to see or touch the sound source. This is an appropriate time for adults to talk about the sounds, give names to sound sources, and engage in vocal imitation with the infant. Using sound to organize movement and to make associations between voices, footsteps, and objects is an especially critical point in learning of a low vision or blind child. Differentiating sound sources when they cannot be readily seen encourages freedom of movement toward the sound in order to encounter the object with the body, an important experience for the visually handicapped child.

Recognition of words and interpretation of connected speech is the next step in auditory development. Just as objects have words associated with them, actions also have words to describe them and learning what the body is doing is related to body image and to organizing purposeful movements upon direction of another person. The child who sees makes the association of actions and words readily, but when vision is impaired or totally absent, it is not so easy. Adults need to talk to the child about movements and actions to be sure that the child's words are appropriate to the action. There is some suggestion that imitative speech develops more rapidly in blind children than in sighted children simply because of the constant reliance on sound and listening to maintain contact with the environment and people around them. Passive auditory stimulation by radio and television without meaningful conversation about what is heard often results in echolalic speech or verbalizations that are simply repetitious and without real meaning. Playing word and rhyming games with visually handicapped children is helpful in strengthening recognition and association.

Clarification of auditory perceptions comes through others listening to her responses and answering her questions about herself and the environment. Permitting her to engage in meaningless auditory self-stimulation or nonsense vocalization without interjection of thought-provoking conversation makes no contribution to her perceptual development.

Selective listening to verbal instructions is a rather high level of auditory perception; selecting from all the sounds those which are important at the moment requires cognitive concentration. Adults need to encourage and expect verbal acknowledgment of directions by the child, or at least some indication that they have listened to the instructions and understood them. Simply repeating what an adult has said is not necessarily an indication that what is expected of the child is perceived accurately. Unless a child can translate the words heard into representative movements and actions, there is no reason to believe that the auditory input is contributing to cognitive development. The child without vision or with reduced acuity forms action images just as the child who sees forms mental images of what is observed. These images are associated with spoken language and create a basis for association and recall as language increases in abstraction. When the child pairs an action with a word, the movement or action is internalized and responses can become automatic when instructions are given verbally.

Auditory processing and listening for learning is the ultimate level of auditory perceptual development, and is a skill essential for academic progress and continued cognitive development of visually handicapped students. Listening will be a primary learning mode for blind students for the rest of their lives, and will be a strong supportive medium for low vision students. Reading aurally is a very different perceptual task from reading visually. The acoustical display to be coded and processed is controlled by the rate of input of the reading medium and not by the reader (Cobb, 1977). The only information available to the aural reader, in one time dimension, is the singular word presented in sequence; once the sound has passed, it cannot be recalled for consideration. Unless the words are remembered, processed, and coded as heard, the resultant perception may be inaccurate, distorted, or totally without meaning. Although aural reading offers many advantages for the blind student, far more attention should be given to listening for the most efficient organization of word sequences into chunks of information to be associated with previous and subsequent learning. The idea is not just to teach listening skills, but to teach aural study habits so that students learn to listen to *something* in order to relate it to something previously learned (Cobb, 1977).

Far beyond the skills of selective listening for instructions and conversation, auditory perception is of great importance to the visually handicapped student in movement, orientation, and eventually independent travel. Sounds are reflected off large objects which permit low vision and blind travelers to locate halls, corners, alleys, and such without making physical contact. Perception of sounds suggesting danger is critical for safety and survival. Mobility instructors place great emphasis on training in sound perception while moving about in the environment for both safety and orientation cues (Weiner, 1980). (See Chapter 19.)

OTHER PERCEPTUAL SYSTEMS

Little is known about the process of perception in the taste and smell senses, and they seem to be less critical in learning and cognitive development; nevertheless they have importance to visually handicapped persons. Extensive use of the senses of smell and taste becomes socially unacceptable as human beings increase in age, but utilization of them has significance to the person without good vision. Because of their close physiological proximity, these two systems work in unison with each other. As a person tastes, he also smells the object or food; indeed the smell often determines or influences the taste. This phenomenon provides a measure of guidance and safety to the growing infant. Some things with pleasant odors are not equally appealing to the taste, nor is an unpleasant smell always indicative of displeasing taste or of something to be avoided. The opportunity to explore the environment through the use of these senses provides valuable information to be processed and utilized with other sensory data in perceptual development.

Potent or pleasant odors may arouse curiosity especially when not experienced previously. Rather than being alarmed when a child tastes clay or paste or even less edible substances, teachers may help the child substitute touch and verbal interchange to eliminate some of the need to taste undesirable materials in order to gain information. Some children actually enjoy smelling printers ink, and ask many questions about why some books smell different from others. Overall, the olfactory sensitivity can be useful in making desirable distinctions between environmental and school materials. Detection of odors can be helpful as orientation cues for the child learning to move about within the home and school, and as signals of proximity for independent travelers in the community. For these reasons, attention should be given to assisting the child in her use of smell and taste, explaining to her and directing her movements so that cues serve as a means of supplementing her knowledge of the environment. The association of perceptions through the various senses enhances the development of "processing strategies" for utilization of all senses, and possible cross modal integration, a topic discussed in the next section.

INTEGRATION OF SENSORY INFORMATION

The innateness of coordination and unity of the senses at birth is a point of view taken by some (Bower, 1979); the other point of view advocated by others is that experience is responsible for coordination of the senses (Bushnell, 1981). At first thought these two views seem to be incompatible, but may not be if one considers that both processes must occur before one's understanding of reality is the *same as* the reality. If information through each sensory channel is coded in specific form, how do they get integrated? Is there some sort of rule that determines the crossmodal transfer? What is the integration like? Is there some sort of hierarchial order for specific types of information? Answers to these questions raised by Walk and Pick (1981) are not readily available. There is, however, considerable theorizing by several authors which deserves consideration.

Bushnell (1981) considers the senses as active instruments which seek and explore, providing performing knowledge before conscious knowledge. Intersensory behaviors seem to be supported by some sort of conceptual awareness of sensory inputs. When infants reach to touch what they see and look to see what they have touched, vision and touch are coordinated and integrated for location. These crossmodal or supramodal abilities seem to be developing throughout the early years of life in all babies. Not enough evidence is available to define sequences of development or attach ages to certain abilities at this time. When this crossmodal knowledge is complete, there is differentiation in addition to integration, and according to Bushnell (1981) "the ontogeny of intermodal relations is not a simple, unitary process but is instead a many faceted one, the developement of which is gradual, complex, and interdependent with experiences and with developments on other fronts" (p. 33).

When infants examine toys and objects, they discover the correlations between visual size and tactual size, visual shape and tactual shape and can integrate perceptual features of vision and touch as they look and grasp. Butterworth (1981) suggests that auditory and visual information become associated with each other through their common links with the tactual kinesthetic systems. He says that "the role of active movement in development is to refine the innate coordination by establishing feedback control" (p. 56). Abravanel (1981) discussed integration of information from the eyes and the hands and concluded that perceptual exploration that is either visual or haptic gives common characteristics. There seem to be changes in perceptual processing with age and much of the improvement seems to be related to general development in perceptions and knowledge across all the sensory systems. Memory and imagery representation, strategies for coding and processing information, and retrieval patterns may all have importance in aiding the process of intersensory transfer. Millar (1981) concluded that sense modalities are neither separate nor unitary—they are complementary and convergent, a thought to be considered when discussing integration of sensory information when one or more sensory systems is impaired or lacking.

When the visual system is impaired or completely nonfunctional, reliance on the other sensory systems increases in direct proportion to the degree of visual impairment. Just how this affects the transfer and integration of information for perceptual and cognitive development is not fully understood. Absence of active interaction is more detrimental than deprivation of vision in constructing sensorimotor schema according to Millar (1981). Perhaps blind persons rely on a completely different spatial organization of tactual kinesthetic information as well as auditory information. Whether or not any deficits experienced by blind students can be remedied by alternative sources is not at all clear, although it is known that spatial organization is less easily achieved by touch since appropriate reference cues are often lacking.

Having low vision or having had prior visual experiences seems to make some difference. Although vision, touch, and movement all contribute to sensory integration, they each emphasize different aspects of information about the world; these aspects may only affect the manner and means of coding and not the integration itself.

Anater (1980) says that loss of vision requires a shift to auditory and haptic systems which may provide contradictory information when individuals are trying to rely on stored visual images. In studying blind students while attempting to determine the effect of auditory interference on processing of information derived from the haptic modality, he found that haptic information was processed independently of auditory interference. The conclusion was that haptic information did not have to be converted to an auditory format as suggested by some previous studies. For blinded adults, sensory training exercises seemed to increase muscle relaxation, and to enhance the use of all other senses. Perhaps the sensory systems develop and function differently in congenitally blind persons, but if so, the process and pattern is yet to be determined. What really matters is that there seems to be the same potential for perceptual cognitive development in children with visual impairments as there is for children with all sensory systems intact and functioning. What may need to be considered is that the coding process may be unique to each individual, and that the perceptions may be different because they are based on nonvisual information intake which is likely to affect the integrating process.

COGNITIVE ORGANIZATION
AND MENTAL MAPPING

Reference was made previously to the relationship between the use of the senses, the coding and organizing of perceptions, and the eventual formations of concepts. Concepts are achieved through a process of associating numerous perceptions developed from all sensory data, and from the processed information, formulating ideas about the world. Concepts may range from functional to abstract, depending on the quantity and quality of information upon which the ideas are based. Concepts serve human beings in adapting to the environment and are never static, unchanging units, but are formed, reformed and interrelated continually.

The manner in which the brain groups or codes and relates incoming data to previously received information may be considered a constructive process resulting in the formation of individualized "cognitive structures" in the higher brain centers which lead to "cognitive patterning" or to the development of a "cognitive style" of learning. Simpkins (1978) says that cognitive organization (mental development) is a continuous construction similar to the erection of a large building that becomes more stable with each addition. Cognitive development seems to be affected by such factors as organic growth and maturation, social and emotional reciprocation with others, concrete experiences, and language interaction to modify, adapt, and coordinate the process.

Numerous speculations have been offered relative to the possible effect of visual impairments on cognitive development and functioning and whether or not conceptual organization is in fact different in totally blind persons, but as yet no definitive conclusions are possible. Mental images of congenitally visually handicapped persons are likely to be fewer in number and possibly less accurate than those stored by individuals with normal sight. Since the referents for imagery are different for blind persons and for some low vision ones, the forms of mental images may also differ from those of sighted people (Hall, 1981). Several investigators have studied various areas of cognitive functioning and reasoning abilities in blind children and youth, but none has been reported on low vision students to date. Rubin (1964) compared abstract functioning among congenitally blind, adventitiously blinded, and sighted persons, and found that the blind persons performed less well than both the other groups on a series of tests of abstraction.

Witkin and his associates (1968) conducted a study on cognitive patterning in congenitally totally blind children and said that to form impressions of objects as discrete and as structured through senses other than vision was possible but much more difficult. On a series of tasks involving analytic abilities in perception and problem solving, body concepts, and verbal performance on Wechsler scales, they found a consistency among individual blind children in tactile performance and body concepts; marked differences were evident in the extent to which cognitive functioning was articulated: analytic and structured or relatively global. As a group, blind children had less developed articulation than did a matched group of sighted children, but the difference was not as great as might have been expected. Some blind children showed highly developed abilities to analyze and structure their thinking suggesting that blindness may serve as an "impetus to the development of differentiation."

A subsequent study by Witkin and other associates (1971) concluded that lack of vision slows the pace in the usual progression in cognitive development from global to articulated, but not greatly. Congenitally totally blind children were equivalent to sighted children in verbal comprehension ability but superior in tasks requiring prolonged auditory attention.

Concept Formation

To gather information about the development of scientific thinking in blind children and adolescents, Boldt (1969) presented some interesting views in regard to the way blind pupils develop abstract thought patterns. Ten different modes of concept formation were identified and explained: 1) sensory associative; 2) magical; 3) anthropomorphic; 4) purposive; 5) substantive; 6) dynamic; 7) uncritical functional; 8) analogical; 9) critical functional; and 10) causal. At ten years of age, blind children were two years behind sighted children in concept development, but had progressed to a level comparable to sighted children by 15 years of age. He concluded that the development of concepts in blind children could be understood as a process of progressive disassociation of subject and object, and only toward the end of this disassociation is real conceptualization attained. No doubt cognitive development and organization in blind children is more related to learning opportunities, range in variety of life experiences, and attention given to explanation and clarification of the environment than to the fact that information is unattainable through the visual sense. In a large group, however, blind children seem to find it more difficult to determine when they have sufficient knowledge for perceptual closure and for the formation of complete concepts.

A more recent study of classification in blind children (Higgins, 1973) found they did not exhibit a significant developmental lag in the attainment of classificatory logic indicating "that the condition of total congenital blindness per se is not sufficient to produce a delay in the formation of the intellectual structures underlying classification" (p. 40).

Comparing stage development (as defined by Piaget) between blind and sighted children, Gottesman (1976) concluded that vision and visual imagery are not necessary for performance on Piagetian tasks of haptic perception but that there did not seem to be a sequential development of age and stages as suggested by Piaget. Looking at the development of Piagetian reasoning in congenitally blind children, Stephens and Grube (1982) found a lag of as much as eight years between them and a matched group of sighted students at three different age levels. Such tasks as conservation, classification, logic, mental imagery, spatial relationships, and formal operations were adapted for blind students. Concrete reasoning was about the same but logical thought requiring mental imagery or spatial perspective was decidedly below that of sighted children of the same age. In a second phase of the study, they designed and administered a remedial program to determine if individual children could remove their deficits in reasoning when given an appropriate set of reasoning activities. The remediation was definitely successful in that the experimental group was superior to the control group on 17 of the 26 variables, and that they showed marked improvement from pre-test to post-test on 22 of the 26 variables. The two areas where no improvement was noted were mental imagery and classification; abstract relationships between numbers and properties of objects were especially difficult.

The majority of studies on cognitive development in blind children find that some concepts are learned at the symbolic level only and that it is difficult to use them in problem-solving situations; concrete reasoning appears to be no different than in sighted individuals; and mental images need to be formed by direct experience (Hall, 1981; Miller, 1982; Stephens & Grube, 1982).

Some of the above studies have reflected difficulty in mental mapping (analytic and articulation tasks), an ability directly related to independent travel. Finding one's way is mediated by mental processes; a traveler learns a spatial layout, updates his own position relative to surroundings, and applies general spatial concepts to other travel situations (Rieser, Guth, & Hill, 1982). Congenitally blind and early blind students were very poor in spatial updating compared to late blinded students, leading to the conclusion that two years of vision is not sufficient for full development of spatial perceptual capacity, but having vision for eight years is. Fletcher (1980; 1981) studied spatial representation in blind children and found that a systematic pattern of exploration seemed to help in remembering spatial relationships whether looking at a map or examining representation of an actual route. General intellectual ability seemed to correlate positively with performance and the ability to form cognitive maps. She found also, that children with even light or movement

perception were more likely to form cognitive maps than were totally blind children.

The process through which concepts are formed and cognitive styles (thought patterns) are developed by children with severe visual impairments is still not clear. There may be differences in the early years related primarily to the time required to store enough mental images for processing and coding. Perceptual closure and stability in the formation of abstract concepts seem to require more time for those who have no vision. There is no evidence, however, to indicate that the nature and quality of cognitive organization, once achieved, is significantly different from that of sighted children. Providing a range and variety of concrete experiences in the early preschool years, presenting classification and reasoning tasks throughout the school years, and presenting problem solving situations during adolescence and early adult years are of vital importance. Marked attention should be given to language interaction with meaningful vocabulary in discussion of thoughts and ideas to enhance the organization of thinking patterns in visually handicapped children.

TECHNOLOGY AND SENSORY PERCEPTUAL FACTORS

The explosion of electronic and other technological devices in recent years presents problems as well as possible blessings for visually handicapped individuals. At this time, little effort has been made to examine critically the relationships between the sensory perceptual characteristics of learners and the usefulness of machines or equipment to a specific person. More time seems to have been spent on promoting the technology than in conducting well designed research into who can make most effective use of it. Unfortunately there are still no objective criteria available to assess performance when making use of any of the technical equipment.

There are three pieces of equipment available that have been studied at least to a limited degree: the Optacon, the Sonicguide™ and the Kurzweil reading machine. Studies with the Optacon (Bliss & Moore, 1974; Koenig & Rex, 1983; Moore, 1973; Terzieff, Stagg, & Ashcroft, 1982) indicate that a number of variables are primary determinants of the effectiveness of the Optacon as a reading device such as: a high level of intellectual functioning, long periods of training and consistent use, and a high degree of motivation needed to expend the time and energy necessary for efficiency. There is still need for a formal means of measuring achievement in Optacon reading especially with younger children over a long period of time in order to make comparisons with other means of learning to read.

Use of the Sonicguide™ as a spatial sensing system and as a stimulus for movement in young blind children has been explored sporadically, but not with the same children over several years time, so that no conclusions are possible at this time. Foulke (1981) suggests that early experience is of particular importance in programming the central nervous system and developing learning sequences. After the preschool years, the nervous system is less pliable and responsive to the tactile and auditory stimulations provided by the equipment. He stresses also that greater emphasis should be placed on the users than on the tools themselves, remembering that equipment and tools do not teach or perform, but can only assist the user in performing more effectively and efficiently.

The limited studies of the Kurzweil reading machine have dealt primarily with adults, so very little is known about the capacity or disposition of school age learners to decode, organize, and store in memory the sounds produced by synthetic speech. Probably, this piece of equipment will be a supportive device during the more advanced school years, rather than a useful tool in the earlier years.

The important thing is for teachers neither to accept nor reject any device or piece of technical equipment without careful evaluation of its characteristics, consideration of how it can facilitate the accomplishment of objectives for individual students, and to develop software and programs designed to further educational goals. Educators are the persons who can make the best suggestions for refinement of equipment by working in concert with the designers and technicians. No piece of equipment or machine is of value in and of itself; the value lies in how well it permits the user to achieve her objectives by use of technology. If the available technology can be utilized while keeping in mind the sensory perceptual characteristics of visually handicapped individuals discussed throughout this chapter, the future may hold great promise for learners with sensory impairments.

Study questions

1. Explain the process of perceptual development as it relates to learning through the senses.
2. What does sensory acuity mean? Discuss some of the ways sensory acuities can be measured in the various senses.
3. Discuss the relationship between sensory learning and cognitive development.
4. Outline the components of the visual system.
5. Trace the major factors of critical points in the sequence of visual development from birth to six years of age.
6. Explain the interaction between the sensory

systems (vision in particular) and the motor systems during development.
7. What do you consider to be the greatest difficulties of the low vision student in trying to use impaired vision most efficiently?
8. What is the role of the tactual-kinesthetic and auditory systems in supporting the impaired visual system for maximum learning?
9. What are some of the ways mental organization and cognitive mapping may be affected in low vision persons?
10. On the basis of the information in this chapter, outline the content of a program for a one year old child with low vision to provide maximum stimulation of the senses as a base for future learning.

Additional readings

Ayres, J. A. (1981). *Sensory integration and the child.* Los Angeles, Calif.: Western Psychological Services.

Barraga, N.C. (1964). *Increased visual behavior in low vision children.* New York, N.Y.: American Foundation for the Blind, Inc.

Barraga, N.C. (1983). *Visual handicaps and learning.* Austin, Tex.: Exceptional Resources.

Faye, E.E. (1984). *Clinical low vision.* Boston, Mass.: Little, Brown and Company.

Hatwell, Y. (1985). *Piagetian reasoning and the blind.* New York, N.Y.: American Foundation for the Blind, Inc.

Juurmaa, J. (1967). *Ability structure and loss of vision.* New York, N.Y.: American Foundation for the Blind, Inc.

Liepmann, L. (1973). *Your child's sensory world.* New York, N.Y.: Dial Press.

Ludel, J. (1978). *Introduction to sensory processes.* San Francisco, Calif.: W.H. Freeman.

Lydon, W.T., and McGrew, L. (1973). *Concept development for visually handicapped children: A resource guide for teachers and other professionals in educational settings.* New York, N.Y.: American Foundation for the Blind, Inc.

McBurney, D.H., and Collings, V.B. (1977). *Introduction to sensation/perception.* Englewood Cliffs, N.J.: Prentice Hall.

Schiff, W., and Foulke, E. (eds.). (1982). *Tactual perception: A sourcebook.* New York, N.Y.: Cambridge University Press.

Walk, R. D., and Pick, H.L., Jr. (1981). *Intersensory perception and sensory integration.* New York, N.Y.: Plenum Press.

Warren, D.H. (1984). *Blindness and early childhood development.* (Rev. 2nd ed.) New York: American Foundation for the Blind, Inc.

CHAPTER 6

Low Vision and Visual Efficiency

Anne L. Corn

Students with low vision may learn to maximize their use of vision through a variety of approaches and instructional systems. This chapter takes the reader from the functional vision assessment through the application of results to instructional programming and offers suggestions for the use of environmental cues, optical aids, and techniques to make efficient use of vision. The use of alternative approaches to task performance is stressed so the educator can increase the repertoire of strategies for the use of vision.

It seems appropriate that a chapter on visual functioning and visual efficiency be included in a text on education of visually handicapped pupils. This would not have been the case had this text been written twenty years ago. Prior to that time a misconception about the use of "impaired vision" existed in the schools. Children with low vision were "protected from" using their eyes in an effort to retain their eyesight for as long a period as possible. As noted in Chapter 1, programs were referred to as "Sight Saving" or "Sight Conservation." For a time period after this misconception was realized, programs retained these labels and, although children were encouraged to use their eyes for educational purposes, little was done to help them to improve their abilities to use existing vision.

In the early 1960s Barraga (1964) demonstrated through her studies of residential school children that "visual efficiency" could be significantly increased with a systematic program of instruction. Since that time, advances in research, optics, and technology have resulted in curricular development for the purpose of assisting children with low vision to utilize their available vision.

FACTORS RELATED TO VISUAL EFFICIENCY

Visual efficiency has been defined by Barraga (1983) as "the most inclusive of all terms. . .visual acuity at a distance and at near range, control of eye movements, accommodative and adaptive capabilities of the visual mechanism, speed and filtering abilities of the transmitting channels, and speed and quality of the processing ability of the brain are all related to visual efficiency. Visual efficiency is unique to each

child and cannot be measured or predicted clinically with any accuracy by medical, psychological, or educational personnel" (p. 24-25).

In other words, multiple physiological and psychological factors are taken into account when there is a discussion of visual efficiency. Functional vision refers to the ability to use vision to perform desired tasks. For example, two individuals with similar clinical measurements may be able to use a standard ruler with an optical aid to measure the edge of a table. Both would have "functional" use of their vision and this information would be helpful to regular and special teachers, rehabilitation counselors, and family members. However, with this information, one could not state whether the two individuals have the same level of "visual efficiency." One of these individuals may consider this to be a very difficult visual task while the other may find it easy to perform.

A three dimensional model which attempts to address the many factors needed for visual function has been proposed (Corn, 1983). (See Figure 6.1.) Although the dimensions of the model may vary for different individuals, minimum volume levels are needed to perform specific visual tasks. Visual efficiency may, in some way, be related to the minimum volumes required for comfort in sustaining visual function.

Belliveau (1980) states that ". . .the teacher/trainer has to be thoroughly familiar with the functional implications of all the variables and be competent in adapting basic training principles to the always new combination of variables and needs."

Increasing one's ability to use vision and therefore increasing one's visual efficiency may be considered the goal of instructional programs in the use of low vision. Prior to establishing such a program, however, a functional vision assessment is needed.

The ophthalmological and/or optometric reports, as well as observations of the child, are taken into consideration when determining which formal or informal functional vision assessments should be used. The educator or rehabilitation professional should have

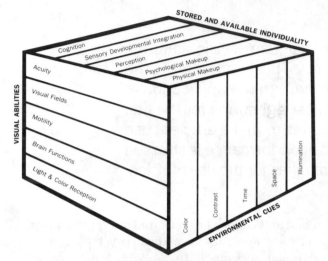

Figure 6.1   Corn's model of visual functioning

Source: A. Corn, Visual function: A model for individuals with low vision, *JVIB*, **77**(8), p. 374.

a working understanding of the pathological condition, its treatment, and its prognosis in order to plan an individualized approach to assessment and instruction in the functional use of vision. The functional vision assessment is used to determine how the individual functions with vision in daily activities and/or under specific conditions. "Any level of vision can be assessed. Children who have the acuity to see hand movements, for example, would be assessed functionally in terms of their use of shapes, colors, contrast and light cues. This information will have a number of educational implications—for indoor and outdoor mobility, social interactions, living skills and so forth" (Roessing, 1982, p. 35). Criterion-referenced checklists, observation reporting forms, and other formalized instruments have been developed to guide functional vision assessments for different populations and different levels of visual functioning. Informal procedures or a "bag of tricks" can also be used to assess the use of vision in children who appear to be untestable with formalized approaches, or when assessing an individual with specific outcomes in mind, e.g., to determine whether a child can see (and sustain) a new reading series which has been introduced in a regular class. While some assessment procedures are task specific (e.g., Can the child reach on visual cue?), others include items which ad-

dress the "integrity" of the visual abilities when an external stimulus is introduced (e.g., Can the child track with her eyes to follow a moving target?).

The following are vision assessment procedures: *Teacher's Guide for Evaluating Visual Function* (Efron and Duboff, 1975): This assessment was developed for deaf-blind children; it may also be a valuable tool for working with other multiply handicapped children who are low functioning. It has three parts: Sensation, Visual Motor, and Visual Perception. Techniques and materials for improving visual functioning are offered which can be readily blended into all areas of the instructional program.

Program to Develop Efficiency in Visual Functioning (Barraga, 1980): This program includes two packages. The first package includes the *Diagnostic Assessment Procedure (DAP)* and the *Low Vision Observation Check List*. The DAP is used to assess visual functioning in low vision persons and the check list provides information about the use of vision in a variety of settings. The second package contains the *Design for Instruction*. Based on the assessment procedures, the instructor uses an Instructional Planning Index to determine where in the instructional program, her student should begin. *The Source Book on Low Vision* also accompanies the second package. It provides background and practical suggestions for working with low vision learners. It is available on quota account funds through the American Printing House for the Blind (APH). This program was designed for individuals with a mental age of at least three years.

Functional Vision Inventory for the Multiply and Severely Handicapped (Langley, 1980): The Functional Vision Screening Test and the Functional Vision Inventory Profile were both developed through the Peabody Model Vision Project and are contained in one document. "The screening test is used to discriminate children who exhibit vision problems so severe that they interfere with the child's learning process. . . If a severe visual problem does exist, the Functional Vision Inventory should be administered to determine the type and degree of vision that the child functionally uses" (Langley, 1980, p. 38). The Functional Vision Inventory includes the following six sections: Structural Defects/Behavioral Abnormalities, Reflexive Reactions, Eye Movements, Near Vision, Distance Vision, and Visual Field Preference.

The Functional Vision Checklist Summary Sheet (Roessing, 1982): This checklist is geared to academic instruction for children who are members of regular classes. It covers the following areas: a summary sheet of clinical information and classroom modifications, checklists for academics, assessment forms for mobility, physical education, and living skills.

Sloan Reading Cards: Although usually considered to be part of the clinical evaluation, these near vision cards are helpful in determining a comfortable print reading size. They include short excerpts of texts including the imperfections of everyday reading materials.

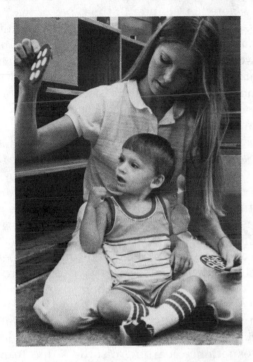

Informal approaches to vision assessment procedures are called for when: 1) in spite of an "untestable" or "blind" label, a teacher or parent feels that the child has vision; 2) the teacher needs to document specific visual behaviors related to classroom-based tasks; 3) the teacher is assisting students in determining optimal visual environments; or 4) when a child has experienced a change in visual function.

The first of these situations is probably the most difficult in terms of procedures and emotional impact. Children who are multiply handicapped and who are unable to respond to standard methods for obtaining clinical measurements are at risk of being labeled blind when in fact some vision is present. It is recommended that the educator systematically address each of the environmental cues to be sure that all possible combinations of stimuli are presented in an effort to elicit visual behaviors. Choosing tasks which motivate the child is also essential. For example, a child who does not have head or limb control may systematically open her mouth when food is presented within six inches of her face. If this child also responds to an inedible bead (without food odor), then the size of the target and the distance may be used for a judgment regarding the child's use of vision. Another child may exhibit

specific autistic tendencies. He may not attend to penlights or traditional stimuli. However, this child may follow a rhythmically moved dot or pattern which is presented on a closed circuit television. By gradually reducing the size of the target, judgements may be made regarding the child's use of vision.

Electrodiagnostic approaches may be used to determine whether light is entering the visual system. While these procedures may be performed for medical purposes, they are outside the realm of the educator or rehabilitation professional. Information obtained by medical and/or optometric personnel should be shared with educational team members; acquired information should be considered in the planning or discontinuance of instructional programs. For further information about these tests, the reader is referred to Chapter 3.

INSTRUCTIONAL APPROACHES IN THE USE OF VISION

When an assessment of visual function indicates that an instructional program is appropriate, three distinct approaches may be employed to assist individuals in the use of low vision. These approaches are Vision Stimulation, Visual Efficiency, and Vision Utilization Instruction. The age of the individual, the type of visual impairment (e.g., lowered visual acuity, field restrictions, and previous visual experiences) are essential factors in choosing the appropriate instructional approach. Some individuals will begin with a vision stimulation program and progress through instruction for vision utilization; others will begin with visual efficiency training and not proceed past this type of instruction. The three programs overlap to some degree and should not be considered as separate entities.

Vision stimulation programs are primarily used with individuals who have a minimal amount of vision and/or have not, to any great extent, used their vision for visually oriented behaviors or for incidental learning. Some individuals may have vision but have never learned to interpret that which is being viewed into concepts which can be useful. Smith and Cote (1982) state:

> The area of the brain which is responsible for vision will remain underdeveloped unless stimulation and visual experiences are provided. How efficiently the child functions visually is a direct result of the quality of the sequential presentation of visual stimulation experiences. For visually impaired children, vision is not an automatically learned process. (p. 11)

In vision stimulation programs and throughout visual efficiency training and vision utilization instruction, a developmental approach is stressed. (See Chapter 5 for a review of this developmental sequence.) The extent to which children with low vision follow the sequence is not known. Extraordinary approaches may be utilized which do not follow the patterns of normal development. For example, one individual may never learn to sustain tracking objects with his eyes. Rather, this individual will use head movements which may be more efficient when considering his visual impairment. To date, educators have applied to the visually handicapped population what is known about "normal" visual development.

Vision stimulation programs may include such sequences as learning to determine whether a light is on, attending to an object, following a moving object with head and/or eye movements, and reaching for objects which are perceived through the sense of sight. Often, pairing of stimuli will be used to gain the visual attention of children who do not appear to independently react to visual stimuli. Adults may also benefit from vision stimulation programs; they may find that "new found" vision can be helpful in certain circumstances. *Look At Me* (Smith & Cote, 1982) is a resource manual for the development of residual vision in multiply impaired children. It includes activities for instruction and a functional vision assessment. In addition, the book covers information on such topics as basic anatomy of the eye, common disorders and diseases, and sensory integration training.

Visual efficiency training may be viewed as the next program in the sequence of visual instruction. This form of instruction takes into account the perceptual factors which are included in the development of functional vision. At this level, those with low vision learn to distinguish patterns of visual stimuli, differentiate outlines and inner detail of objects, and transfer this learning into two dimensional pictures and symbols. The term, *visual efficiency training*, should not be confused with the definition offered by Barraga (1983) at the beginning of this section. Visual efficiency training has come to be concerned with tasks with two and three dimensional objects in near space. Overall efficiency, as defined, refers to both near and distant tasks with both static and moving objects. *Program to Develop Efficiency in Visual Function*, the design for instruction mentioned above, is an instructional procedure for the development of visual efficiency.

Vision utilization instruction involves such areas as environmental modifications, the use of optical and nonoptical aids, and techniques to maximize the use of vision. While some curricula have been suggested for instruction in the use of optical aids (Weiner and Vopata, 1980), programs do not currently exist which have been used on a wide scale.

Among the roles and responsibilities of the certified teacher of the visually handicapped, "the use of residual vision is one of the most important aspects of the curriculum" (Spungin, 1984, p. 32). Orientation and mobility instructors also work with low vision in-

dividuals in the use of visual abilities; they work with distance vision with and without optical aids. They may also teach such near tasks as map reading and reading timetables. In agencies which work with adults, professionals with a variety of job titles are designated as instructors in the use of low vision. In addition, several low vision clinics maintain staff who provide instruction in the use of optical aids.

Except for the instruction offered in the use of optical aids, as noted in Chapter 3, the types of instruction discussed in this chapter differ from "visual training" programs offered by eye specialists. For example, orthoptists, working under the direction of ophthalmologists, are interested in helping individuals use both eyes together to obtain binocular vision. This type of training deals with the physiological aspects of the visual system. The form of vision habilitation which is being addressed here assumes that the individual has undergone whatever "treatment" is available for the improvement of organic visual functions. In other words, these programs help individuals to function with the visual abilities which they possess rather than assisting them to improve the physiological or organic system.

Although teachers of the visually handicapped may be dealing with individuals who have visual-perceptual impairments in addition to their visual handicaps, vision stimulation, visual efficiency training, and vision utilization instruction are not intended to remediate visual-perceptual disabilities. Should a child experience learning disorders due to neurological problems which are not the result of an impairment of the organic visual system, an educational specialist in learning disabilities should become part of a multidisciplinary educational team.

During assessment and instructional procedures, several issues may need to be addressed. The emphasis and value placed on the use of vision in an overall educational program must be determined for individual students. For some children with severe and profound handicaps, given certain time constraints, there may be more essential life skills which need to be taught for the child to reach his ultimate level of functioning. For others, intensive instruction in the use of vision may enhance learning potential. (See Chapter 9.)

None of the programs mentioned above should be considered as subjects to be taught only in block periods of time. Rather, visual functioning should be considered as a part of each segment of the curriculum. For example, if a student is learning to reach for objects using vision, she should be provided with reaching experiences during activities of daily living. Those who are learning to use optical aids should be provided with opportunities to use them in math class as well. Children in regular classes should become adept in the use of new techniques prior to the time when they are expected to use them in the classroom. In this way, they will not be expected to learn a visual skill like copying from a chalkboard along with new material which is being presented in the class.

Instructional Considerations

For students who use vision as a mode for learning, adult and peer expectations sometimes interfere with the acquisition of new visual skills. For example, a child may fear that he will not be allowed to use nonvisual strategies which have been comfortable and which have helped him function in educational and home settings. At first, the use of vision may seem inefficient, and the child will prefer to function as blind, e.g., reading braille at 50 words per minute rather than using print which seems laborious. Individuals who have low vision may need to exert more effort to use their vision than those with "normal" vision. Fatigue factors need to be considered. Nonetheless, children and adults should be provided with opportunities to use their vision. Instruction in the use of vision should become part of the Individualized Educational Program.

Students should not be encouraged to "look sighted" at all costs or to always expect themselves to function as sighted individuals. Depending upon the level of visual functioning, the use of vision may or may not prove to be the most efficient or preferred method to approach a task. For example, it may be easier to use nonvisual methods for locating a keyhole or for pouring salt over one's food. Combining visual and nonvisual methods may lead to heightened efficiency. Ultimately, it is the student who will decide the extent to which learning and functioning with vision will be added to his or her repertoire of coping strategies. These decisions should be respected as long as the student assumes responsibility for obtaining visual information, e.g., homework assignments.

Independent of an individual's level of visual functioning, there will be times when the needs of a low vision individual will be the same as those of a functionally blind individual. An example is transportation. Neither the functionally blind person nor the sighted person with low vision will be able to read street signs from a moving bus. In an unfamiliar area of a city without familiar landmarks, both individuals will need "sighted assistance." However, the individual with low vision may not receive assistance as readily because his needs are not always evident. In this and other similar situations, the individual with low vision will need to explain his needs.

On the other hand, "passing," or appearing to be fully sighted, does have many advantages. For example, it eliminates a barrier which may affect initial interactions when one is being introduced to someone. However, it also "costs" the individual; by not explaining

her needs, she may miss visual information and fear being "found out." Reluctance to use certain aids or techniques, e.g., a monocular telescope, may result from a desire to remain inconspicuous. The technique or aid, in effect, labels the individual as one who is disabled or "handicapped."

Those with low vision derive great pleasure as well as information from their visual abilities. Some individuals with low vision may be visually oriented learners. Some will enjoy visual activities such as painting, photography, and sports. The aesthetic experiences of an individual with low vision may be different from those of a fully sighted individual; those with experiences should not, however, be valued in relation to "normal" visual experiences. A red gingham dress may appear at a distance of two feet to be a lovely pink, which may be seen as more attractive in an artistic sense than the true print.

Low vision need not interfere with all of one's life activities. Sufficient, if not abundant cues, may be present for an individual to perform specific tasks. Entering a dimly lit restaurant may present a difficult visual situation for one individual who may decide to use a sighted guide to negotiate steps and to avoid bumping into chairs. Another person with low vision, will find that vision does not cause any problems since the chairs have a distinct upholstery pattern which provides "visual boundaries" in the room, and a companion has walked in front of him. By watching his companion's motions, he may easily locate any steps which might be present. It is important for the professional to understand the function of cues which might be "unnoticed" by normally seeing adults.

LOW VISION AIDS

In 1270 Marco Polo visited China and recorded the fact that convex (magnifying) glasses were used by the aged to read fine print. Roger Bacon, the English Franciscan monk, is credited with being the first "to recognize the value of convex lenses for those who were old or who had weak sight" (Stein and Slatt, 1983, p. 235). It is also known that in 1784 Benjamin Franklin invented bifocal lenses. Koestler (1976) reported that at the 1924 meeting of the American Medical Association, a paper was presented on the use of telescopic lenses. It was stated that Anne Sullivan Macy had been fitted with these lenses and that she had written to the Illinois Society for the Prevention of Blindness: "You may be as enthusiastic as you please for me in endorsing the telescopic lenses—I never knew there was so much in the world to see."

The ophthalmologist who is credited with being the father of low vision therapy is Dr. Alfred Kestenbaum. In his practice in Vienna, a patient, who had macular degeneration, told him that he was reading a letter from a friend from London. As those with this pathology were not expected to be able to read regular print, he was challenged as to his methods for reading. The patient had used a linen tester which provided the needed magnification. Fleeing from the Nazis, Dr. Kestenbaum came to the United States where he pursued the use of magnification lenses for low vision patients (Safir, 1980).

However, owing to the erroneous misconceptions which surrounded the use of impaired vision in educational practice, it wasn't until the second half of the twentieth century that lenses were used with the low vision population to any great extent. Today, the provision of optical aids is not, and should not be considered to be an educational luxury. Rather, they are individualized educational tools which provide access to regular print for those who can benefit from them. They may be likened to hearing aids which give hearing impaired persons access to the auditory environment. Like hearing aids, optical aids do not "cure" the sensory impairment; they do not create a situation which allows the individual to function "as if" he is fully sighted.

Along with the advantages of altering retinal spread so that the individual can make sense of the physical attributes of an object, optical aids bring with them optical and physical disadvantages and limitations. This should not, however, deter anyone who is interested in learning to use optical aids. Many individuals use such aids with ease and comfort, acquiring normal reading speeds and information needed for efficient use of distance vision.

Low vision aids may be divided into two groups: optical and nonoptical. Optical aids are made up of lenses placed between the eye and the object to be viewed. Optical aids alter the spread of the "image" on the retina of the eye. The retina does not receive a permanent "photographic impression." Rather, the retina is made up of millions of photoreceptive cells which are activated by light; these cells transmit signals to the brain via the optic nerve. (See Chapter 3.) Tinted lenses are also optical aids when they are used to enhance functional vision. Electronic aids (e.g., closed circuit television, the Coloreader, aids which use fiberoptics, and the Viewscan), are also optical aids in that they utilize lenses to alter the retinal spread.

Nonoptical aids do not involve lenses. Rather, they are devices which alter environmental cues, i.e. illumination, contrast, space, time and spatial relation (see Figure 6.1). These will be discussed later in relation to environmental modifications.

There has been controversy surrounding the prescription and distribution of optical aids. Some distributors of optical aids require that a prescription be secured from an ophthalmologist or optometrist. This assures the individual that the most appropriate aid is being provided and that magnification is not being used to "mask" a condition which could be treated

with optometric or medical attention. Others believe that "nonprescription" aids, those which provide magnification without individualized prescriptions for astigmatism, prisms, etc., should be made available through the general marketplace. Hand magnifiers and binoculars are among these devices which can be purchased directly from manufacturers or from opticians. When dealing with children and youth, it is strongly recommended that clinical low vision evaluations be provided and that prescriptions for optical aids be secured from low vision specialists who are ophthalmologists or optometrists. Obtaining the correct power of an aid is crucial to the effectiveness of the aid. These low vision specialists may be found in low vision clinics or in private practice. The *Directory of Agencies Serving the Visually Handicapped in the U. S.* (AFB, 1986) lists low vision clinics which are located in most states.

It is also strongly recommended that teachers of the visually handicapped make recommendations to the prescribing eye specialist regarding the mounting system(s) of aids. With a knowledge of the advantages and disadvantages of specific mounting systems and their relationship to classroom and home based tasks, the teacher is able to offer valuable information for deciding on the mounting system for a particular aid. Older students should be consulted regarding the mount which will be more comfortable and efficient for them.

The type and extent of visual impairment will determine the type of optical aid which will be prescribed. Magnification is usually given to those individuals who have low vision acuities and/or central scotomas (area of diminished or no vision). Minification systems (minus lenses and reversed telescopes) and fresnel prisms are sometimes beneficial to those with restricted visual fields. If an individual with a field restriction is given magnification, it provides a visual experience similar to trying to look at a photographic enlargement on the same size page as the original. When an individual has a combination of these types of visual impairments (e.g., low visual acuity and a field restriction), decisions are made regarding the need to increase size and/or the amount of information presented in the visual field. It should be noted that an individual with scotomas or peripheral field restrictions will have eye and head movements which will help diminish (to some extent) the significance of these restrictions. If an individual has multiple scotomas and potential for binocular vision, visual field charts are needed to determine the overall effect of the scotomas.

Increasing the overall area of the "image" on the retina is known as magnification. This can be achieved in three ways. First, the low vision individual can reduce the distance between his eye and the object to be viewed. In other words, by getting closer to the object, a greater area of the retina is used for a particular object. The second method of increasing the retinal spread is by enlarging the actual object. An example of this approach is the provision of large-type materials. The third approach is the use of lenses to create an "apparent" increase in the size of the object. Optical aids use this third approach.

Closed circuit television systems (CCTVs) and the Viewscan are available for those individuals who can benefit from high powers of magnification. At one time these devices were seen as a last resort. Two reasons for this include cost and a lack of portability for CCTVs. The Viewscan was developed as a portable aid and several manufacturers of CCTVs have worked to reduce the size and weight of their products. Although only a percentage of those with low vision will need these devices, they should be viewed as alternative visual systems which may complement other optical and nonoptical methods.

The microcomputer may also be seen as a magnification aid. By altering the size of the print on the cathode ray tube (CRT) screen, using special software and within the limits of the monitor, the operator can view what she has typed into the computer. In this way typed material is enlarged or magnified prior to printing a hard copy of the work. Some microcomputers may also be connected to closed circuit televisions as well as to the Viewscan; in this way the size of the letters is increased beyond that which is available on a 40-column CRT screen. In addition, using a CCTV eliminates the dot matrix type of characters. Monochromatic CRT screens can also be obtained in such colors as white, green, or amber with black backgrounds. Printers connected to microcomputers are available to print regular as well as large type "hardcopies." The educational field for the visually handicapped is only beginning to see the far reaching benefits of microcomputers for the low vision population.

Understanding Lenses

There are two basic theories which answer the question, "What is light?" One theory is the corpuscular theory (light is made up of a stream of invisible particles) and the other is the electromagnetic theory. The electromagnetic theory is commonly used in optics. In this theory, light is made up of waves which travel outward from a source. These waves travel in groups and are known as light rays. For a more thorough discussion of the theories of light, the reader is referred to a series of programmed instruction texts prepared by the American Optical (1976).

Light originates from a luminous body (e.g. the sun, a light bulb, a flame), and its rays strike any and all objects which are not blocked by other objects. Each object whether luminous or nonluminous, has an infinite number of object points from which light is emitted or reflected. For every object point on an object, divergent light rays are reflected in all directions.

When light rays travel from objects from a twenty foot distance, they are believed to be so close together that they are said to be traveling parallel to each other. Object points which are closer than twenty feet have light rays which are considered divergent to each other.

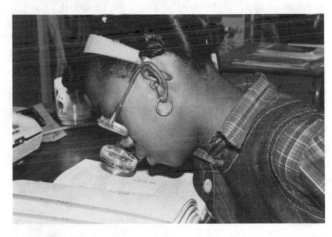

In order to "see" an object clearly, an "image" of each object point must ultimately excite a specific number of photoreceptor cells on the retina. This correspondence will occur if the light rays are bent or turned to converge them from their parallel or divergent lines of direction. Herein lies a mechanical problem: how to bend rays from object points so they will meet as image points on the retina.

As stated before, magnification is the spreading of the image over a greater area of the retina. For a person with low vision, the use of magnification does not "clear up" the blurred image as one would adjust a television screen. Rather, the blurred image is spread so that the image points are exciting more photoreceptor cells which are spread over a greater part of the retina. Detail of objects becomes "apparent." All the letters are blurred. While maintaining the same amount of contrast and illumination on the page, the larger letters can be read; the detail is spread over a larger area. For some individuals, the same task of reading the letters may be accomplished by altering such environmental cues as illumination, color, contrast, and/or the time of presentation rather than, or in addition to, using magnification.

This principle of magnification also holds true for the low acuity individual who is employing distance vision. Since objects in the distance appear to be small (occupy a small area of the retina), the use of magnification, either by walking closer or using a magnification aid (telescopic system), will spread the image. The person will then be able to determine that the "blur" in the distance is made up of individual objects (e.g., trees), or that objects are made up of individual parts (e.g., leaves on trees, parts of an airplane).

Magnification also helps those who are experiencing central scotomas. The spreading of an image over the normal retina will diminish the significance of the scotoma. The size of the scotoma is not altered; rather, the details of the letters are positioned so as not to be blocked out by the scotoma. Here too, the individual with a central scotoma will want objects in the distance to be brought closer or enlarged. The amount of illumination for this individual may also

be a crucial factor in the use of vision. Instruction in the use of a technique called *eccentric fixation* may also be used with some who have central scotomas. With this approach the individual is taught to use a different part of the retina (outside the macular region) for the central viewing (Goodrich & Quillman, 1977).

When an individual experiences peripheral field loss (without acuity loss), any magnification will create a smaller field than the individual actually has. Also, if there is no acuity loss, there is no need for enlargement. Those with peripheral loss are more apt to enjoy objects at a distance or those which may be minified. Head and eye movements are recommended which will help individuals with peripheral limitations to systematically gain information from the environment.

Plus Lenses

The power of a lens may be determined by using a measurement system developed for optics. A "diopter" is the unit of measure which is used for lenses. When one reads a prescription for standard corrective lenses or for near vision optical aids, measurements are usually listed in diopters and the notation is "D." A plus lens will have a rating of +D. It has also been established that four diopters is equal to one "X" power of magnification. Therefore, in order to determine the "X" power, the number of diopters is divided by four. For example, a +16D lens is the same as a 4X lens and a +20D lens is the same as a 5X lens. Thickness alone does not determine the strength of a lens; checking the dioptic power of a lens is the best way to determine its strength.

It is now possible to determine the focal length of a lens by knowing the "dioptic power" of the lens. The reciprocal of 1/D in meters indicates the focal length. If a lens was rated as a +20D lens, then the focal length would be 1/20 meters.

Since the stronger lens will have a smaller focal length (as the number of diopters increases, the focal length decreases), the individual using the lens will need to keep the lens closer to the object he is viewing. Generally, when working with magnifying lenses, the stronger the lens the smaller will be the diameter of the lens. In this way, the thickness and the weight of the lens will be kept to a minimum. As a result of the short lens to object distances, some individuals may experience illumination problems which may be alleviated by repositioning the material and/or adding illumination.

When magnifying lenses are placed in spectacle frames, the diameter and weight of these lenses are reduced by creating *lenticular* lenses. These lenses are generally surrounded by a nonprescription lens which is called the *carrier* lens. Often, these lenses will be placed on only one side of the pair of glasses. This also relates to the focal length of lenses. These high powered lenses have very short lens-to-object distances. If both lenses have high powers, then the minimal distance needed between the eyes and the object will not be available for convergence to take place. Convergence occurs when one looks at an object at a near range. Both eyes turn toward each other so that the same image of an object is *situated* on the maculas of both eyes. When the individual has potential for binocular vision, prisms may also be added to high plus lenses which *redirect* the images and allow for fusion of the two images to take place.

The central portion of a lens is known as the optical center. It is through this area from which one should view an object. When the periphery of a lens is used, distortions of the lens become apparent. The stronger the lens the more distortions seem to occur. When individuals first obtain bifocal lenses, they may need to learn how to locate the optical center of the *add* or additional lens. Some children receive a higher line of demarcation between the two lenses in order to facilitate their use. The executive bifocal (with a straight horizontal line of demarcation) may also be used with those children who have difficulty maintaining their focus through the typically shaped (half circle) section.

The dioptic powers of lenses are additive. In one hand-held container, often called a doublet lens, two lenses are assembled. If one lens is rated +16D and the other is rated +12D, a lens of +28D is created.

Minus lenses

Minus lenses have concave edge(s) and are also rated in dioptic powers. Its powers are also additive. For example, a −6D lens and a −8D lens (without air space between them) will create a −14D lens. Minus lenses effectively minify objects so that the objects appear smaller than their true size; the field of view, however, appears to increase as more objects may be seen through the lens. Rather than converge light rays, the minus lens causes rays to emerge more divergent than they were upon entering. The focal length is determined by extending the divergent light rays back through the lens until they meet. The same approach is used with plus lenses; the focal length is the reciprocal of the dioptic power in meters.

Reading Standard Prescriptions

An understanding of standard prescriptive lenses will be helpful in understanding prescriptions for low vision aids. Hyperopia, myopia, and astigmatism are generally *corrected* by use of plus, minus, and cylindrical lenses, respectively. The *add* is the additional lens which is placed in a spectacle frame to form a bifocal lens.

A prescription, therefore may look like that shown in Figure 6.2. This individual will be receiving a prescription for hyperopia and will have a bifocal lens and a correction for astigmatism.

Mounting Systems

Optical aids for near and distance tasks may be placed in three basic mounting systems. These include hand held, stand (including stand-based), and spectacle borne aids. Each mounting system has advantages and disadvantages which are related to user preferences for cosmetic, handling, cost, types of prescriptions to be included in the aid, and the relationship which is established between the lens and the demands of the visual task. This latter factor appears to be very important in educational settings. Some individuals will also obtain their prescription in more than one mounting system in order to perform all desired visual tasks.

Advantages and disadvantages of different mounting systems are presented in Chart 6.1.

Telephone

Name _____   Date _____

Address _____

		SPH.	CYL.	AXIS	PRISM	BASE
Distance	((R	+4.75	+1.75	80		
	((					
	((L	+4.00	+2.50	95		
Reading	((R	+2.50		Multifocal ◻ ◻ Yes No	Color ◻ ◻ Yes No	Pupillary Distance
Addition	((L	+2.50				

Figure 6.2   Sample standard prescription

Chart 6.1   Near vision lenses

Hand-Held Lenses

Advantages

The eye-to-lens distance is variable.
> This affects field of view, posture and head movements.

The angle of the lens to object is variable.
> The lens may be placed at angles which allow the user to perform such tasks as using a card file.

Hand held lenses can be placed at a distance from the eye.
> In order to read some instrumentation, the reader can maintain a more comfortable posture.

The cost of hand held lenses is low in comparison to other mounting systems.
> Replacement or spare lenses may be less costly than spectacle lenses.

By firmly positioning one's hand on an object, the hand held lens may be used as a stand magnifier.

Some individuals consider a hand held lens to be cosmetically acceptable.
> Hand held lenses are seen in daily work situations (e.g. stamp collectors, biologists) and may be understood by the public.

Handling and care of hand held lenses are facilitated by their size and compactness.
> These aids may be easily carried and retrieved from pocket or purse.

Change of focus from near to distance is easily achieved.
> The user can look up from his work without needing to remove glasses.

The magnifier can be positioned on the last word(s) read when taking notes.
> It is often difficult for an individual with low vision to scan a page and locate the last word(s) read.

Hand held lenses can be placed directly on a mirror so the user can view his eyes.
> This is helpful for such tasks as applying make-up, tweezing brows or viewing one's eyes.

Hand held lenses allow for variations in eye, lens, head and/or object movments.
> Some individuals prefer to hold head and reading material steady while moving the lens while others prefer a "fluid field" in which the head and lens are steady while the object moves. The former may be done with a hand held lens, while the latter may be accomplished with a hand held or spectacle lens.

Hand held lenses are advisable when an individual cannot place her head close to an object.
> An example of such tasks is using a photographic enlarger.

More than one power of magnification may be placed in the same carrying case.
> A "doublet" lens may contain two different lenses which, when placed together, create a third power.

Disadvantages

Glare and reflections from the top surface of the lens are bothersome to some individuals.
> This can be reduced somewhat by bringing the eye closer to the lens and, hence, using the head to block direct light sources.

High powers of hand held lenses have small diameters and hence, small fields and require that the user position his head very close to the lens. This also reduces the amount of illumination falling on the page.

Prescriptions for astigmatism cannot be placed in a hand held lens.
> Those requiring a corrective lens for astigmatism will need a spectacle mount.

Both hands cannot be used simultaneously while using a hand held aid.
> In educational programs this does not often present a problem. However, when painting pottery, hand sewing, or assembling a model, it may cause some problems. On the other hand, threading a needle and other tasks which may be considered "two-handed tasks" may be accomplished with appropriate positioning of the hand held lens.

Stand Mounted Lenses

Advantages	Disadvantages

Stand magnifiers have a fixed lens-to-object distance. The user does not have to maintain the focal length of the lens by holding it a specific distance from the object.

Stand magnifiers may incorporate light gathering properties, or have built-in illumination sources.
Some lenses are made so that light is "concentrated" on the object. Recent advances in fiberoptics are also available in stand magnifiers.

The user can vary the angle at which he aligns the eye and the lens when using certain "dome type" magnifiers.
Generally, stand magnifiers require that the user position his eye perpendicular to the surface of the lens.

Some stand magnifiers include a built-in additional lens.
Two separate powers of magnification are available within one lens.

Some stand magnifiers come in "focusable" forms.
By screwing a focusable lens into a housing, the lens to object distance is adjusted. By varying the distance between the eye and the lens, the user can vary the power of the optical system.

Stand-based magnifiers (those with a "goose neck" or other extension between the lens and the object) allow users to position objects at a distance from their eyes and to simultaneously use both hands.
These lenses may be helpful for such tasks as making jewelry or inspecting insects. The greater working distances which can be achieved may also be beneficial when working with vibrating machinery.

Bar magnifiers generally cover one line of print.
Although bar magnifiers do not usually come in high powers of magnification, they are helpful for those who have difficulty keeping their eyes on one line of print or for those who like to use the bar as a placeholder. In addition, this type of magnifier allows for scanning an entire line without needing to move a hand held lens.

Some stand and stand-based magnifiers contain their own light source.
For those who require additional illumination, or for those who are bothered by glare and reflections, illuminated magnifiers are helpful.

The inside edges of thick books are difficult to read with stand magnifiers.

For several stand magnifiers, the eye must be positioned perpendicular to the surface of the lens.

When stand-based magnifiers have large diameters, they are generally low powered aids.
Children with good accommodative abilities may prefer to move their eyes closer to the object rather than use a low powered lens.

Stand based magnifiers, particularly those with large diameters, are cumbersome and difficult to move around classrooms.

Hand-Held Monoculars

Advantages	Disadvantages
These aids may appear less conspicuous than spectacle mounted lenses (often referred to as "bioptic lenses").	One hand is needed to hold and focus the aid.
Some monoculars are placed on rings while others are less than a few inches in length.	For extended periods of viewing, hand held aids may cause arm fatigue. In addition, some tasks require the use of both hands as in playing a musical instrument or driving a car (with a special license for driving with a telescope).
Hand held lenses require fewer head movements than bioptic lenses.	Hand held monoculars do not generally come with wide angle or "camera" lenses in which the power of the lens is variable.
The hand held aid may be moved by hand movements in order to scan a chalkboard or view a play.	Some hand held monoculars do, however, include lenses which allow for two powers, e.g.: 6X and 8X.
There is less care required of a hand held monocular than for a bioptic.	Some individuals using hand held lenses require instruction in such areas as maintaining stability of the aid, one handed focusing, and placement of the ocular lens when prisms are part of the aid.
There are fewer breakable parts.	Some of these instructional techniques are not needed with bioptics.
Hand held monoculars are less expensive than bioptics.	In order to bring the hand held aid close to the eye (for maximum field), the user will need to remove a standard correction.
The ocular lens may be brought close to the eye.	The user will need to replace a standard correction for and near work following the use of a monocular. This may be time consuming.
This allows for the widest field of view; as the lens is brought further away from the eye, the field of view is decreased.	
Either eye or hand may be used with a hand held lens.	
Hand held aids do not require the user to bear the weight of a telescope while wearing glasses.	
Some hand held monoculars contain a clip which may be used to attach the monocular to a pair a glasses.	
The user will be able to use the aid as a hand held device and then mount it on spectacles to perform such tasks as typing and viewing television.	
Hand held aids are often more efficient in the time it takes to retrieve and spot an object.	
Some individuals begin to focus the aid before it is brought to the eye.	
Hand held monoculars may be aligned to view objects placed at an angle to the observer.	
This approach is used for looking directly into display cases in a museum or department store.	

Spectacle Mounted Lenses

Advantages	Disadvantages

Spectacle mounts allow for both hands to be used simultaneously.

> Some tasks require that both hands be used (e.g. typing from a printed page or sewing). This also allows the user to hold the object with both hands and utilize a "fluid field" (eye and lens remain steady while the object is moved).

Coordination is not needed to move a hand held lens.

The lens is always fixed close to the eye.

> This allows for a wide field of view.

For those who are able to use binocular vision, spectacle lenses may be used.

Prescriptions which have high powers of magnification, may include prisms.

Half frame lenses are available for those who wish to switch from a near task to a distance task without removing their glasses.

Some consider spectacle mounts to be more cosmetically acceptable than a hand held aid.

> Unusual glasses may be considered more acceptable than an additional aid, particularly if the user will be using a standard correction in addition to an optical aid.

More than one type of correction may be placed in the spectacle.

> Astigmatism corrections may be placed in the spectacle in addition to a power of magnification.

The weight of high plus lenses in spectacles can be reduced by creating lenticular lenses.

> The diameter of the high plus lens is decreased and a "carrier" lens is used to fill up the space within the frame.

Spectacle lenses require somewhat more care than hand held lenses.

The cost of spectacle lenses is higher than the cost of hand held lenses.

Spectacle lenses with high powers of magnification require short working distances.

> Since the focal length is fixed by the power of the lens and the lens is placed a specific distance from the eye, the working distance is short.
>
> This requires additional head movements to accommodate the length of lines on a printed page. This close working distance may cause fatigue over a period of time.
>
> In addition, lenses which are positioned in the "line of vison" need to be removed in order to change focus from a near to a distance task.

Spectacles with high powers (and without prisms) do not allow for sufficient working distances for convergence to take place.

> When this occurs, lenses are placed in only one lens. This may cause problems if the user has binocular vision and one lens may need to be occluded.

Bioptic Lenses

Advantages	Disadvantages

Both hands are available for tasks which require them. Playing a musical instrument or driving may not be accomplished with a hand held monocular.

Bioptics may be less fatiguing when observing a play or sporting event over a period of time.

The user can have a near and distance prescription in the same aid without removing or retrieving his glasses.

These lenses are not cosmetically appealing to many school-age children or adults.

The weight of the telescopic portion may be a factor in acceptance of the aid.

The cost of bioptic lenses is higher than that of hand held lenses.

Bioptic lenses require more care.

> There are more parts which are breakable.

Because the telescopic portion is in a fixed position, head movements are needed for scanning (stationary) or panning (moving) objects.

Only a distance prescription may be contained in a hand held aid whereas a bioptic allows for placement of the telescopic portion as well as a standard correction in the carrier lens.

One should keep in mind, however, that that which is an advantage for one individual may be considered a disadvantage to another. Although some tasks may be accomplished with more than one mounting system, some activities may be facilitated by one mounting system over another.

Telescopic Lenses

Telescopic lenses are used for visual tasks which are a distance from the user's eyes. The simplest of telescopic systems is made up of a minus lens (ocular lens), a barrel, and a plus lens (objective lens). The ocular lens is placed nearest the eye while the objective lens is placed nearest the object to be viewed. The power of the lenses and the length of the barrel, or the distance between the two lenses, affects the distance at which the observer can focus on an object. When the lenses are closer together, objects in

the distance are in focus; when the lenses are at a greater distance from each other, the telescope may be focused on objects at closer ranges. While some telescopes have fixed focal ranges and are called "afocal" telescopes, many of the telescopes which are prescribed for school age students are focusable aids. Each student must learn her particular aid's characteristics and learn to focus it accordingly. A further discussion on focusing telescopes will be offered in the section covering instructional techniques.

While most people are familiar with binoculars, hand held telescopes for those with low vision are often prescribed for use with one eye and are called "monoculars." Binoculars, however, should not be ig-

nored as an appropriate aid for some individuals with low vision (Genensky, 1974).

The minimal distance at which specific telescopic aids can maintain focus is determined by the telescopic system in use. Some "short focus" telescopes can be used for near-vision tasks while others cannot focus on objects which are closer than a few feet from the observer. Some telescopic systems can accept a "reading cap." This is a plus lens which is placed on the aid which provides a focus at an intermediate distance, approximately fourteen to eighteen inches from the observer's eyes. This is helpful for such tasks as reading music on a music stand when one's instrument creates a distance between the musician and the page, or sewing on a sewing machine where it is unsafe to place one's face close to the machinery.

INSTRUCTIONAL IMPLICATIONS

Instructional techniques include the specifics of optical aid manipulation, the introduction of nonoptical aids into the task, and problem solving skills for matching the task to the optical aid. While some individuals with low vision are able to take their prescribed optical aids from the eye specialist and can immediately benefit from their use, others will require an individualized instructional approach to receive maximum benefit from them. Sloan and Habel (1973) found that "as a rule, children adapt well to reading aids in spectacle form" (p. 1026). This facility in children may be due to their ability to view objects at near ranges and to maintain good motor control. In addition, they have not as yet established more "normal" reading distances. Some suggestions have already been offered for use with specific types of mounting systems. Faye (1975) cautioned that too much time spent in initial training can lead to boredom and fatigue. "Introductory training in the use of the aid should be practical and direct" (p. 246).

Near-Vision Lenses

Resting one's hand on the page and maintaining a view through the optical center of a lens are helpful suggestions for smooth, coordinated movements of a hand held lens. At times the user should be encouraged to increase the speed with which she is reading.

For map reading it is sometimes advisable that the user take a look at the whole map with an unaided eye to obtain a general idea of the major shapes, roads, etc. If a route is being planned, finding the destination first and resting one's finger on it will help the user find a direction for the magnifier to follow.

Whether a student is using a hand held or spectacle lens, placing a finger at the beginning of a new line will help maintain one's position on a page. With practice this may not be necessary.

Distance Aids

At times the user may wish to magnify an object in the distance which is seen, e.g., a clock on a wall. At other times, he will need to enlarge an object which is outside his range of vision, e.g., a bird on a branch. In either case, the user will need to align the object, the lenses of the telescope, and his eye. Some suggestions are offered for efficient spotting of objects.

When choosing which hand and eye will be used with a monocular, several factors need to be considered. Some users prefer their dominant hand and/or their dominant eye. Others will prefer to work with the nondominant hand so that a writing instrument is placed in the dominant hand. If the user has only one eye, she will generally choose to work with the hand which is on the same side of the body if her same side hand can comfortably manipulate the aid. To take greatest advantage of the visual field of an aid, glasses should be removed when using a telescope.

One handed manipulation of hand held monoculars helps to reduce the time needed to spot a stationary or moving object; in this way the ocular lens is not shifted by the hand which turns the barrel. If the object cannot be seen with the unaided eye, the user will need to coordinate a hand movement with a sound or verbal direction.

When lifting a hand held monocular to the eye, the user should brace his hand against a part of his face. This stabilizes the aid. If the user is wearing glasses, it is advisable that she remove them so that the ocular lens is placed close to the eye. This allows for a maximum field of view. If the aid contains prisms, it is advisable that the user lift the aid with the same hand position each time, e.g., placing the thumb on one end. This will help position the ocular lens.

Any slight movement of the ocular lens will give an apparent movement to objects in the visual field of the aid. With stronger telescopes, this apparent movement seems exaggerated and objects will seem to pass through the field at a faster rate.

Once a user is knowledgeable about a particular aid, it becomes possible to begin focusing the aid before it comes in contact with the eye. Once it is aligned with the eye, refinements may be made in the focus. This skill calls for an estimation of the distance of the object from the eye. If a student has not worked with focusing an aid, the instructor may explain the process by beginning with a slide projector. The student may be asked to manipulate the focus knob so the projected image is focused. In this way, the instructor can simultaneously view that which the student considers to be in focus on a large screen. One should note, however, that individuals with low vision may not be bothered by a scene which is "imperfect" by normal standards.

The depth of focus is the area in the distance which will remain in focus with a specific position of the ocular and objective lenses of the telescope. Two objects may be placed two feet from each other and be positioned two and four feet from the observer. In order to obtain a focus on both objects, the user may need to refocus the aid from one object to another. However, if the same two objects were two feet from one another and positioned ten and twelve feet from the observer, both objects would remain in focus and the telescopic aid would not need to be refocused. An application of this situation may be seen in seating a student in the classroom. The telescopic aid may provide students with more seating choices. Those who do not want to continuously refocus do not have to sit in the first row. On the other hand, those who find focusing and refocusing an aid quite simple need not be concerned about where they sit.

Scanning is the skill needed to observe a stationary object in a systematic manner. For example, one would scan a chalkboard in order to read words which have been written on it. Another use of scanning occurs when one has attempted to spot an object which is too small to be seen with the unaided eye. The user can first locate and spot a larger nearby object and knowing its position in relation to the smaller object, can scan along an imaginary line to the desired object. Another example of scanning is used in locating street signs or traffic signals. The user may attempt to locate the actual sign and "miss" by aligning the aid with the sky. Since he may be unable to determine the direction to the sign, excess time may be used. Instead, the user may first scan the horizon in order to locate the pole of the street sign and then scan up the pole until contact is made with the sign.

Panning is a term which is often used in photography to assist a photographer to shoot a fast moving object. It is appropriate to use this term for following a moving object with a telescopic aid. Some activities might include watching cars travel along a bridge, following boats going under the bridge, or following an airplane in the sky. Locating an airplane in the sky is perhaps one of the more difficult skills. By locating a land-based object, e.g., a housetop, above which the airplane appears and then moving upward on an imaginary line, the user will be able to locate the airplane. If two objects are traveling at the same speed, the object in the distance will appear to move at a slower speed through the visual field. Without the cues of daylight, an experienced telescopic aid user may accept the challenge of spotting the moon or bright stars in the sky.

For those individuals who receive bioptic lenses, instruction may include such skills as tilting their head in order to align the lenses with objects of regard and learning to take special care of the lenses. Some bioptics are referred to as "camera" lenses. These lenses provide for variations in magnifying power.

There may also be a desire to be able to spot objects while the user is in motion. Spotting street signs, stores, animals and other objects as a passenger on a moving vehicle is an important skill. It should also be pointed out that some individuals with low vision have obtained driver's licenses with bioptic lenses. There is great controversy regarding the use of these lenses for driving; states have the prerogative whether such licensure will be allowed within their state. The role(s) of the teacher of the visually handicapped, counselor, and orientation and mobility instructor have yet to be determined when such a prescription has been written for school-age visually handicapped students.

There are many problems which may be encountered in the use of optical aids in the classroom. Above all, the student must see the value of the aid. As Friedman (1976) stated,

> High in the ranking of potential problems is the appropriateness of the prescription—or of not prescribing. When its effectiveness is not apparent to the child, the prescription of a low vision aid, even if functional, may show as poor judgement as does prescription of the wrong or inappropriate aid. (p. 376)

If a prescribing eye specialist has a goal of a more powerful aid, or a different aid, this information should be shared with school personnel. Problem solving skills will be developed as low vision individuals attempt to use prescribed aids for a variety of tasks. For example, one individual may wish to use a standard bathroom scale. A telescopic aid may be helpful. Another student may be working with a keypunch machine. Although hand held and spectacle borne magnifying lenses can be used to accomplish this task, a distance aid seems to be more helpful for efficient keypunching.

Closed Circuit Televisions

These devices electronically enlarge printed material and flat objects. With adjustments of lenses, the user can magnify images at any power within the ranges of the aid. The enlargement is seen on a television screen which the user can adjust for brightness and contrast. In addition, the user can switch the polarity, from black print on a white background to white print on a black background. Some models of closed circuit televisions also allow the user to block off part of the screen so that one or a few lines are observable at one time. Closed circuit televisions are also used as writing devices as the user is able to write under the camera and the writing is enlarged on the screen. Additional attachments are available which allow the user to view what is being typed on selected typewriters or on a chalkboard on the television screen. As mentioned previously, some computers which can be connected to closed circuit televisions have been developed and the television screen takes the place of a computer screen.

Instructional techniques include learning the mechanics of the machine as well as determining a comfortable working distance and print size. These will be determined, in part, by the reading approach used. For example, the user may work with a fluid field by keeping his head and eyes steady (it is understood that one's eyes will move to a certain extent in the process of reading) while the reading material is passed through the visual field. In this case, the print size will need to be seen within the field which will be used. If, however, the user chooses to maintain a steady head and move his eyes, the print will need to be of such a size that it can be seen at both ends of the screen; at the edges, the distance from the eyes is greater than at the center. When the user employs head and eye movements, the print size may be adjusted accordingly. Some users will also prefer to sit very close to the screen while others will enjoy looking at the screen from a distance.

Some creative teachers have developed activities with the closed circuit television for instruction in the use of vision. Enlarging photographs of familiar scenes or people will provide an opportunity to see details which are not apparent without enlargement. Class activities are also made interesting when small objects, insects and the like, are presented on the television screen.

The Coloreader is an optical enlarger which will enlarge 8.5× or 25× the size of the original. This device enlarges color and projects some flat, three dimensional objects, e.g., rings.

The Viewscan is a portable print enlarger which produces a magnified picture on a television tube. It uses square dots of "soft view orange light" to create letters. It is also possible to use a microcomputer with the Viewscan. Instructional techniques would include manipulation of a small camera which is used to track print on the original page while the user reads the screen.

Psychosocial Aspects of Optical Aids

Some school-age students may appear self-conscious and reluctant to use optical aids in the classroom. At certain ages, such as during adolescence, this may be heightened. Educators can ease the situation by providing an accepting atmosphere in which the student is to use the aid.

When optical aids are introduced to children at early ages, they are more apt to become part of the child's repertoire of coping strategies. Although educators are not prescribers of optical aids, they can bring games into the regular or special class which involve optics. Playing sea captain, detective, photographer, stamp collector, and jeweler are among the games through which young children may be introduced to toys which use optics as tools. Children are often fascinated by the magnifying powers of clear glass marbles; children's books in which optical aids are employed may be read to young children. Older students may benefit from lessons which are incorporated into the school curriculum about lenses, e.g., photography.

Some students may find talking with older students or adults who have used aids helpful. Allowing time for classmates to look through optical aids may alleviate the effects of an aid with an unusual appearance. To illustrate, Corn (1977) included a day at the circus with a new aid (Mac) in a children's book. After sharing his aid with a girl sitting next to him, Billy says, "She could see the lion's tongue with Mac!" (Corn, 1977, p. 25).

Role playing potentially negative experiences with optical aids and finding motivating materials, e.g., record album covers, comic books, and menus at fast food restaurants will stimulate interest in the use of optical aids.

At times the student will be confronted with conflicting information regarding the use of optical aids. Some parents and other significant adults in the child's life may find it difficult to observe a child using aids and may inadvertently discourage usage. Others may feel that the prescribed aid should be used at all times which, in fact, may be contraindicated by the prescription.

The use of optical aids is but one of the many options available to the student with low vision. So long as the student becomes responsible for obtaining visual information, the choice of options should be respected. Nonetheless, the teacher of the visually handicapped should present situations in which optical aids will benefit a low vision student and be sure that the student is efficient with the aid(s).

Environmental Modifications

Environmental cues are physical attributes of objects in the environment which allow an individual to know that the objects exist through the sense of vision. These cues, seen in Figure 6.1, are: color, illumination, contrast, spatial relations and time. Although time is not a physical attribute in the same sense as color and space, it is imperative that viewing time is available for objects to be seen by the viewer.

Color has three components: hue, intensity, and value. Hue refers to the actual color of objects (e.g., red, green, blue). Many low vision individuals prefer yellow. Intensity of colors refers to the brightness of the color while the value refers to the placement of the color along a black-white continuum (e.g., pink would have a different value than red).

Illumination refers to the amount and type (incandescent, fluorescent) of light and the reflectance of the object on which it falls. The distance of the light source to the object and the distance of the object to the viewer's eyes are also important factors. In addition, glare and distracting reflections should be taken into consideration when choosing a type of illumination and the position of its source in relation to the viewer. At various times during the day, the amount and type of light may vary from person to person and those with specific pathologies (e.g., albinism and children with aniridia) may be prone to photophobia, preferring lower light levels. On the other hand, there are individuals with conditions such as retinitis pigmentosa who may prefer higher levels of light. When working with multiply handicapped children who may be positioned on the floor or in certain reclining positions, the instructor should position himself to see what illumination is facing the child with whom he is working.

Contrast is determined by colors or black and white which are placed next to each other or by different light levels which fall on the same object of regard.

Spatial relations include the size and shape of objects, the complexity of inner and outer detail of objects, the distance objects are to the observer, the patterns which are created by objects and parts of objects, and clutter which is in the visual field.

Time factors include the duration of exposure (including frequencies of flickering lights) and the speed through which objects pass the visual field. For example, one may give a child with low vision extra time to view an object. The frequency of a timed presentation may be seen in the use of an emergency vehicle's blinking lights. These lights are used to attract attention. At times, some children with low vision will attend to blinking or quivering lights when they will not react to stationary lights. Caution is suggested, however if medical conditions require that a child refrain from seeing such presentations.

All people have thresholds for specific environmental cues below and above which they will not be able to function with vision. For example, too little or too much light will cause visual function to cease; those with photophobia would have different thresholds than those without photophobia.

The use of one cue may be more effective than another for a specific task. Increasing contrast for some individuals may be more beneficial than increasing the size of the objects involved in the task. Combinations of cues may also be considered for efficient visual function. For example, one may benefit from magnification of print. However, for an individual who requires additional light, adding illumination to magnification will be beneficial.

One cannot ignore the psychological, physical, sensory, cognitive, and perceptual factors which are involved in visual function. For example, physical stamina and motor coordination would be needed in order to benefit from very high powers of magnification for purposes of reading.

It is advisable for all individuals who have low vision to determine which of the cues and combinations of cues provide optimal environments for visual function. This can be done through a systematic approach to observing the cues and preferences in a variety of settings. For example, one individual may discover that he is able to read in bright sunlight (for short periods of time) that which he cannot read indoors under household lights.

Once it is known which cues create favorable visual environments, it is possible to maximize visual functioning by making modifications in the environment. Two examples of such modifications are:
1. By placing tape at the top and bottom of a flight of stairs, a contrast is created where a patterned floor prevents the low vision individual from detecting the first step.
2. Rather than needing to see numbers on an oven dial, the low vision individual may choose to place colored strips of tape at key temperatures (e.g., red at 350 degrees and blue at 400 degrees).

Since those with low vision do not live and work in environments which can always be modified, it is essential that children and adults with low vision learn to "read" the cues which exist in the community. Examples include:
1. Looking at the same flight of stairs, as in the above example, one may learn to become aware of the steps by observing shadows which are created by step patterns.
2. Reflections may be helpful in locating a plexiglass barrier to a salad bar (primarily when there is no visible frame surrounding the perimeter of the plexiglass).

Shadows and other cues may be helpful under certain environmental conditions. On the other hand, shadows may be detrimental to visual function in other situations.

At times, the low vision individual will encounter a situation where he will be able to maximize visual function by altering his body position. Two examples of this type of situation follow:
1. While approaching a store which has an address listed on glass, backlighting may prevent easy viewing of the numbers. However, by approaching the number at an angle to the glass, the effect of the backlighting is diminished.
2. When the sun is behind a street sign, the letters appear to blend into the background color. If the viewer were to move to the other side of the sign, the sunlight may be used to illuminate the sign and hence, the letters appear to be more prominent.

When individuals with low vision miscue (think that one object is another), additional information is gathered regarding visual function. For example, if a crack in a white porcelain sink appears to be an insect, the individual with low vision has not seen the detail which is contained in the crack.

Techniques may also be used to facilitate visual function without altering environmental cues.
1. An individual who has nystagmus may use a head tilt to obtain a position so that print may "appear" to spread.
2. Those with cataracts may shield their eyes so that more direct light rays enter their pupils.

When a task cannot be accomplished through the use of optical aids, environmental modifications or techniques, altering the task may be needed. For example, reading a mercury thermometer is not possible for some individuals with low vision. Rather than choosing a thermometer with an embossed dial or with a spoken output, the low vision individual may choose to use a digital thermometer with a magnifier.

Problem solving skills are essential for low vision individuals who will encounter new visual demands of classroom and home tasks. In recreation, as well, applications will be made for improved visual function. It should be remembered that nonvisual approaches to tasks are preferable in some circumstances and for some individuals. Examples of combining visual and nonvisual approaches include:
1. Locating a keyhole with vision and then using a tactual method for placing the key in the keyhole.
2. Listening to recorded texts while using vision to observe charts and graphs and to highlight parts of the printed page.

The low vision population has, in the past, been the recipient of inappropriate services. Through new definitions, instructional programs, and the use of technology, those who have low vision can learn to use and derive pleasure from their visual abilities.

Individuals who have low vision benefit from specific instructional procedures which have been developed to help them to maximize visual function. These procedures begin with an assessment of visual function and incorporate programs for vision stimulation, visual efficiency training, and vision utilization instruction. The educator has a responsibility to assure low vision individuals every opportunity to learn to use and maximize vision. The unique needs of individuals must be taken into consideration as one plans and executes programs of instruction. Nonvisual approaches and combinations of visual and nonvisual approaches are often useful for comfortable and efficient task completion.

Study questions
1. What is visual efficiency?
2. What is the difference between a clinical evaluation and a functional vision assessment?
3. What are the three approaches to instruction in the use of available vision? How are they different?
4. What are some of the issues facing educators who provide instruction in the use of low vision?
5. What are some of the psycho/social aspects related to the use of vision which are encountered by the individual?
6. What are optical aids and how might a child receive an appropriate prescription?
7. What advances have been made in recent years in technology for those with low vision?
8. What are some of the advantages and disadvantages of each of the mounting systems for optical aids?
9. What are some "helpful hints" in learning to use a hand-held monocular?
10. What are some approaches a teacher may use to help a child feel comfortable in the use of his or her optical aids?
11. What are environmental cues and how may they be used in an educational program?

Additional readings
American Academy of Ophthalmology. (1982). *Low vision services—Policy statement*. San Francisco, Calif.: Author.

American Optical. (1976). *Basic optical concepts: A course in programmed instruction*. Southbridge, Mass.: Author.

American Optical. (1976). *The human eye: a course in programmed instruction*. Southbridge, Mass.: Author.

American Optical. (1976). *Lenses, prisms and mirrors: A course in programmed instruction*. Southbridge, Mass.: Author.

American Optical. (1976). *Normal and abnormal vision: A course in programmed instruction*. Southbridge, Mass.: Author.

Cockerham, P. (1984). *Low vision: Questions and answers*. New York, N.Y.: American Foundation for the Blind, Inc.

Gardner, L. and Corn, A.L. (1984). Low vision: Topics of concern. In Scholl, G.T. (ed.) *Quality services for blind and visually handicapped learners: Statements of position*. Reston, Va.: Council for Exceptional Children, pp. 48-50.

CHAPTER 7

Infancy and Early Childhood

Kay Alicyn Ferrell

Historical and social factors leading to the provision of early education for visually handicapped infants and preschoolers are reviewed in the larger context of research and legislation involving all young handicapped children. Issues surrounding the growth and development of young visually handicapped children are examined, and strategies are provided for meeting their unique developmental and learning needs.

Early childhood education for blind and visually handicapped children has a long and proud history. During a time when most parents and professionals believed that infants were nothing more than a blank tablet, ready to be inscribed with the meanings and learnings of life, visually handicapped infants and their parents were receiving home counseling services. Today, the emphasis is focused less on the counseling needs of parents than it is on facilitating the blind child's developmental progress through an organized and systematic plan of intervention. Parents and families are now involved in all phases of assessment and training within a transdisciplinary, mutual participation model of service delivery (Powell, 1981).

The first programs for blind infants began primarily as homes for neglected children in the late 1800s (Koestler, 1976). The determination of neglect was not made in a court of law, however, but was assumed solely on the basis of the child's blindness. Parents could not provide an adequate home environment when their child was blind, and it was felt that blind infants would receive a better education with professionals in a residential program. Such programs existed as recently as 1938, when the Arthur Sunshine Home and Kindergarten for Blind Babies, in Summit, New Jersey, closed its residential program. Fortunately, however, the Arthur Home continued its home counseling and training functions and established a standard of service to blind children and their families that endured for many years.

The post-war baby boom and advances in medical technology combined to produce a virtual epidemic of blind infants in the late 1940s and early 1950s. Physicians were able to keep preterm, low birthweight infants alive, but they were unable to control the occurrence of retinopathy of prematurity (ROP), the abnormal growth of capillaries behind the lens of the eye, which caused increased intraocular pressure and often resulted in detached retinas. The numbers of children began to make residential placements less feasible and day programs were established, where visually handicapped infants and young children remained at home with their parents but attended special programs at residential schools and other agencies for the visually handicapped. The focus of these programs remained on the parents, but the assumption that parents were unable to meet their children's needs gradually gave way to the principle that parents could be taught to provide the stimulation and nurturing that would promote the blind child's optimal growth and development.

This change in approach paralleled other social and educational developments in the twentieth century. Intelligence was viewed as a fixed part of an individual in the early 1900s—something that the individual was born with and that could not be changed. One study published in the early 1900s reported on several generations of one family, the Kallikaks, to demonstrate that intelligence (in this case, mental retardation) was hereditary, passed on to one's children and one's children's children, without possibility of change or improvement (Goddard, 1912). Given that atmosphere, methods of measuring intelligence were developed to sort out those who would most benefit from public education (which was becoming more universal at this time) from those who were least likely to benefit. The Great Depression began to cast doubt on these traditional notions of intelligence, however, when supposedly bright individuals suddenly found themselves without work, money, or a future. The game rules had changed.

Against this background, some educators began to look again at the concept of intelligence, and in particular at infants in institutions. One first such study (Skeels & Dye, 1939) looked at infants who had been placed in institutions for the mentally retarded. One group of babies was left on the regular ward, receiving the standard type and amount of care. A second group was placed with a group of older mentally retarded women in the institution, who were encouraged to care for the babies by feeding, holding, and playing with them. At the age of 18 months, the measured intelligence quotient of the babies who had received the extra care had increased by an average of 28 points, while the control group IQ had decreased an average of 26 points (Skeels, 1941). When a follow-up study was conducted 30 years later, the babies who had received the augmented care program had become independent adults with higher educational achievement than the standard care infants, many of whom were still institutionalized (Skeels, 1966).

In 1958, Kirk demonstrated that 3-6-year-old mentally retarded children could also benefit from an enriched educational experience. Seventy percent of the subjects in the experimental group had a 10-30 point increase on intelligence tests, while the control group IQ had actually declined. Hunt (1961) and Bloom (1964) followed with theories on the plasticity of the brain, advancing the belief that learning was both easier and faster in the early years. Bloom even stated that one-half of everything to be learned was learned before the age of five. No longer was intelligence considered to be static; rather, it could be changed by changing the environment, and the best time to do so was in early childhood.

FEDERAL INVOLVEMENT IN EARLY EDUCATION

Two primary factors affected the federal government's interest in early education: the election of a president whose sister was mentally retarded and the growth of the civil rights movement. President John F. Kennedy's first-hand knowledge of mental retardation publicly exposed one family's experience and helped to focus national attention on the needs of handicapped individuals. Coupled with Kennedy's emphasis on space exploration, and his belief that the youth of America was its future, federal involvement in education generally became the means of equalizing educational quality in a widely disparate state and local educational system. Furthermore, it was clear that discrimination had its effects long before children attained mandatory school age; desegregating schools and passing equal opportunity laws would do nothing to change the status quo if minority children entered school with a social and cognitive disadvantage. The Head Start Program was established in 1965 to give minority and disadvantaged preschoolers a chance to prepare for kindergarten and perhaps to get a step ahead of their classmates. For all its high aims, Head Start did not initially produce the desired effects—graduates of Head Start programs did not maintain initial gains on intelligence and achievement tests (Karnes & Teska, 1975; Westinghouse Learning Corporation, 1969). Nevertheless, the underlying principle of early intervention continued to receive widespread support, and later studies have in fact shown that Head Start graduates perform better during their school years (Lazar, Hubbell, Murray, Bosche, & Boyce, 1972).

Individual rights and equal opportunity for handicapped individuals was a natural outgrowth of the black civil rights movement; if early intervention could be helpful for minority children, it could also be helpful for handicapped children. In 1968, with the passage of P.L. 90-538, Congress created the Handicapped Children's Early Education Program (HCEEP). HCEEP was designed to develop demonstration programs for handicapped preschoolers with financial support for the first three years, after which state or local educational agencies were expected to take over and provide continuing financial support. Eighty percent of the 280 projects funded by HCEEP which completed their three-year funding period prior to 1981 continued to serve children independent of HCEEP funding (Roy Littlejohn Associates, 1982). The success of the HCEEP program and its impact on early education in general is demonstrated not only by this high percentage of continuation programs, but also by documentation that for every child and family directly served by an HCEEP-funded program (some 21,000), 6.4 children have "received services through continuation of demonstration projects and through replication of projects" (p. 146). In 1973, Head Start programs were required to serve handicapped chidlren as 10 percent of their total enrollment (P.L. 93-644). In 1982-83, the percentage of handicapped children enrolled was 11.9 percent (Administration for Children, Youth and Families, 1984).

Efficacy of Early Education

Follow-up Studies of HCEEP Graduates

Follow-up studies of graduates of HCEEP-funded programs have been more promising than the initial Head Start results. Research has consistently shown that about one-third of HCEEP graduates enroll in elementary special education programs and about one-third in regular classrooms with special education support services (DeWeerd & Cole, 1976; Hayden, Morris, & Bailey, 1977; Lazar, Hubbell, Murray, Bosche, & Boyce, 1972; Stock, Newborg, Wnek, Schneck, Gabel, Spurgeon, & Ray, 1976). One recent study found that 55 percent of HCEEP graduates were placed in integrated settings with nonhandicapped children, while 67 percent performed in the average or above-average range when compared to their peers (Roy Littlejohn Associates, 1982). Furthermore, a follow-up study of nine- to eleven-year-olds currently enrolled in programs for the trainable mentally retarded indicated that the number of years of preschool education may affect later performance: Those children who had received two or more years of early education demonstrated higher skill acquisition when compared to the control group (Moore, Fredericks, & Baldwin, 1981). Twenty-one HCEEP projects have been certified by the Joint Dissemination and Review Panel (JDRP) in Washington, D.C., as providing evidence of significant child gains and overall cost effectiveness (Roy Littlejohn Associates, 1982; White, Mastropieri, & Casto, 1984).

The 21 programs approved by JDRP served emotionally disturbed, deaf and hearing impaired, developmentally delayed, multiply handicapped, physically handicapped, Down Syndrome, communicatively disordered, and "mixed handicap" children between the ages of birth and 8 years. It is reasonable to assume that visually handicapped children were among those served, and that they made as much progress as the group as a whole. Categorical programs

exclusively for visually handicapped infants and preschoolers have not demonstrated the efficacy of early education because of several methodological problems: (1) The programs generally have a small enrollment, due to the low prevalence of visual impairment in the general population, and the early childhood program may be only an ancillary part of a larger program for school-age children; (2) the population is so heterogeneous that comparisons between and among subjects is difficult; (3) standardized instruments that have traditionally been used to document child progress are not valid for use with a visually handicapped population and penalize the visually handicapped child rather than measure actual performance; (4) the criterion-referenced tests and curricula commonly used with visually handicapped infants are not meant to be used for comparison purposes; and (5) teaching methodology has not been data-based, so that record keeping is often anecdotal and not subject to stringent evaluation.

Other aspects of efficacy research have focused exclusively on the cost effectiveness, or cost benefits, issue. Wood (1980) calculated the cost of providing special education at various age levels, concluding that the cumulative cost is lower the earlier the child becomes part of an educational program. Special education services begun at birth cost less than those begun at age two, which in turn cost less than special education services begun at school age. Schweinhart and Weikart (1980) reported on one project where preschool graduates were followed through to adolescence; the benefits resulting from parents' released time (because the child was in preschool and under someone else's care) and the projected lifetime earnings for the child were also calculated to demonstrate even greater cost benefits. Cost effectiveness of early education programs for visually handicapped infants and preschoolers has not been studied.

Efficacy studies in general, however, while they present convincing arguments in support of early education, are based on data that "*mostly* show weak and transient effects" (Strain, 1984, p. 4). Furthermore, all of the JDRP-approved projects suffer from serious threats to internal validity (White et al., 1984). As Strain (1984) suggests, however, studies of the efficacy of early intervention may themselves no longer be efficacious. There is no way of knowing, for example, that babies who appear handicapped at 12 months of age will actually be handicapped at 6 years; therefore, to state that the early education program made the difference in a school-age child's need for special education services ignores the effects of a series of other events occurring in that child's life. The fallacy of such studies can be seen if the records of all 6-year-old special education students are examined to determine how many had any form of preschool program—most of them probably would have received some form of early education; but examining the records of all *nonspecial* education 6-year-old students would undoubtedly turn up just as many who had received early intervention. In the first instance, early education does not appear to make a difference; in the second, a 6-year-old without special educational needs may or may not be a beneficiary of early education. A logical question then is: Does the early identification of children as handicapped and subsequent provision of services predispose a child to later labeling as handicapped? And were the nonhandicapped 6-year-olds who received early intervention actually misdiagnosed in the first place?

There are other reasons to end the debate over early education for visually handicapped children. First, as Strain (1984) points out, much of early intervention is based on the "innoculation" theory—i.e., that educational intervention in the early years will prevent the need for special education later. But, in most cases, a baby who is visually impaired at 12 months will still be visually impaired at 6 years. Regardless of the amount or type of early education received, some form of special education and/or related services will still be needed at school age. Viewed in this context, early education can provide young visually handicapped children with learning experiences that are unavailable because of the limitations imposed by the visual impairment, but it cannot prevent the need for special education later. It may affect the amount and type of support services required, but the option to withhold special education services simply does not exist.

Second, real intervention effects are almost impossible to determine (Strain, 1984). Young visually handicapped children cannot be assessed accurately by standardized instruments and "progress" is therefore subjective and ambiguous. Developmental tests are not normed on visually handicapped children; many items are visual in nature and thus impossible to achieve; the children are not reinforced for good test-taking behavior when they are unable to accomplish test items; and changing the test in any way, including adapting the test procedures or providing feedback to the child, invalidates the test and renders the results useless. As Strain states, "For many groups of preschool handicapped children, the bias created by nonmotivated testing is likely to be substantial" (p. 5), particularly in programs that utilize extensive feedback and reinforcement techniques. Norm-referenced tests also assume that the child has been exposed to traditional family living environments, toys, animals, and household items (Duncan, Sbardellati, Maheady, & Sainato, 1981). But it is the lack of exposure—of access to every day, incidental information—that places the visually handicapped child most at risk. To test a child on this basis is more a measure of the home environment than it is of the child's ability.

Third, cost effectiveness becomes a moot issue when

visually handicapped children will most likely always require special services and equipment just to obtain the same access to information that costs sighted individuals nothing. When compared to the expense of computer access and electronic braille, early education may actually be the smallest portion of a visually handicapped child's total educational expense and will probably bear little relation to how much is spent later. Of far more concern, however, is that the issue of cost effectiveness can backfire: the argument can always be made to defer expenditures until school age, when benefits to the child are far more tangible.

For all of these reasons, it is no longer reasonable to discuss whether or not early intervention works. It makes far more sense to discuss whether early intervention is necessary to enable visually handicapped chidren to benefit from a free appropriate public education during their school years.

Rationale for Early Education of Visually Handicapped Children

Early education for visually handicapped children continues to be premised on a belief that a visual impairment is primarily a problem of access to information that affects how something is learned, not what is learned. By providing opportunities to learn in ways that circumvent the visual impairment as early as possible, there is no limit to what can be learned.

Neonatal Competency

Access to information is critical in the early life of a blind or visually handicapped child. A growing body of infant research literature, for example, points to the sophisticated abilities of infants when only a few days old. Newborns can follow a moving object with their eyes, turn to the source of sound, console themselves, and screen out competing stimuli (Brazelton, 1973); stick out their tongues in imitation (Friedrich, 1983); respond selectively to sweet and salty tastes (Crook, 1978; Friedrich, 1983; Hart, 1980; Pick, 1961); and distinguish the odor of their mother's breast pad from those of other women (Macfarlane, 1975). Where infants were once thought to have blurred vision, 6-month-olds are now believed to have the visual acuity of adults (Cohen, DeLoache, & Strauss, 1979) and have demonstrated cross-modal transfer (an ability to take information obtained through one sensory modality and utilize it in another sensory modality) (Rose, 1981). Three-month-olds can discriminate very minute changes in color (Bornstein, 1976), and 5-month-olds can recognize black-and-white line drawings of their mother's faces (DeLoache, Strauss, & Maynard, 1979). The relative stability of neonatal visual-perceptual abilities has led some researchers to suggest the use of visual fixation, tracking, and preference responses in infancy as indicators of high-risk status in childhood (Miranda & Hack, 1979). Rosenblith (1974) has found that newborns who have poor fixation and tracking responses fail visual memory tests at 8 months of age, and eventually perform poorly on gross motor scales at 4 years (Miranda & Hack, 1979). As research techniques improve, the complex, interdependent nature of the infant's sensory motor and cognitive processes becomes more evident—and the risks for the visually handicapped child become more glaring.

The sensorimotor theories of Piaget (see, for example, Piaget & Inhelder, 1969) illustrate the importance of vision for the developing infant. According to Piaget, vision motivates, guides, and verifies an infant's interactions with the environment, and thus acts as a stimulus for developing motor patterns and later for forming cognitive relationships. As new skills are learned, they are assimilated by the infant—literally added to the infant's information bank—and are accommodated into the infant's repertoire of knowledge and action—i.e., learned, processed, and applied to new situations. For the first 18 months, the infant acts on this sensorimotor foundation. An infant with limited visual abilities is clearly at risk during this period if motivation and sensory feedback is not readily available.

It has been estimated that development in the first three years of life determines the future competence of all children. White (1975) believes that what happens during these first years sets the stage for all future learning and can make the difference between a socially and cognitively adaptable 6-year-old and one who is unable to make the transition to school. Kagan (1972), however, believes that even one-year-olds are able to think—to process information, solve problems, and resolve discrepancies. He even suggests that the reactions of one-year-olds to discrepant stimuli (in this case, novel auditory or visual stimuli to which the child has not been exposed) can be used to assess developmental status. In view of Ferrell's (1983/1984) research, where visually handicapped infants between the ages of 6 and 24 months did not exhibit cross-modal transfer (which is based on response to novel stimuli), the risk to infants born with a visual impairment is even more apparent. If a primary information source—vision—is interrupted or eliminated altogether, and a secondary sensory information source—touch—is ineffectual, how is the infant to develop the sophisticated cognitive processes that permit him to learn and gradually expand his world?

Critical Periods

Moreover, it has been suggested that infants go through critical periods in their development—optimum times for learning specific skills because the appropriate motor and sensory inputs are crystallizing at just the right moment (Hunt, 1961; Langley, 1980; see also Clarke & Clarke, 1976). If these critical periods are missed, the skills might never be learned, or, if they are learned out of sequence, higher level skills may rest on a faulty foundation (Langley, 1980; Moore, 1984; Scott, 1962). For example, visually handicapped children who skip the crawling stage have not had an opportunity to practice weight shift, reciprocal balance, and hip and trunk rotation. Often, their manner of walking lacks fluidity and grace of movement, and they may walk stiff-legged, shifting weight from one leg to the other, with feet spread wide apart (Ferrell, 1985). While older children can be given a compensatory program to attack this problem, there is always a loss of time and energy, and the child is placed in the position of "catching up."

Research in support of the notion of critical periods is based either on ex post facto research or on animal studies. For example, older children with reading difficulties were examined for common threads in their early experience, and were found to be noncrawlers. The difficulty with this reasoning, however, is that there is no way of knowing if all infants who did not crawl eventually become problem readers. In order to establish such a cause-effect relationship, children who do not crawl would need to be followed for years to see how many of them are actually problem readers when they attain school age. There are undoubtedly just as many good readers who skipped crawling as there are problem readers.

Much of the animal research dates back to the pioneering work of Hubel and Weisel (1963), who identified the existence of a critical period during which kittens were particularly susceptible to permanent visual loss as a result of visual deprivation. Since the neurological system of human infants closely resembles that of both kittens and rats (Rose, 1981), studies which tend to establish a critical period in animals have been used to support the theory of a critical developmental period in human infants.

Whether or not a critical period exists, however, a visual impairment still interferes with when and how an infant obtains information. If acquiring a certain skill takes longer, acquiring higher level skills based on that first skill will take longer yet, and the risk of developmental delay becomes more and more a certainty.

Prevention of Secondary Handicaps

The prevention of secondary handicaps may make the strongest case for early education for visually handicapped infants. For most infants, the primary mode of obtaining information about the world is through the visual channel. If vision is limited, the amount of information is also limited. Fraiberg (1977), for example, claims that blind infants are delayed in locomotion because they are not able to reach to sound until late in the first year after birth. This inability to achieve ear-hand coordination at approximately the same age that sighted infants achieve eye-hand coordination not only prevents the child from achieving further motor milestones, but affects the ability to develop cognitive relationships as well. Infants who do not form attachments to significant others may eventually exhibit emotional pathologies (Lewis, 1983). Inadequate language stimulation often results in delayed expressive language; failure to attain concepts of object permanence may result in apparent mental retardation. All of these secondary handicaps are preventable; they occur because there has not been sufficient instruction to the child. To some extent, these secondary handicaps can be ameliorated later, but it is then a question of reteaching rather than teaching in a natural, sequential, supportive environment.

DEVELOPMENTAL NORMS FOR VISUALLY HANDICAPPED CHILDREN

Developmental Lags and Self-Fulfilling Prophecies

While the field of early intervention for the visually handicapped has been active for many years, it has been markedly deficient in the amount of information it has produced on the development of blind and visually handicapped children (Warren, 1984). It has been characterized by case studies and anecdotal reports lacking in empirical support, or by narrow investigations that are either unrelated to prior research or fail to account for the variability of the population. While several good articles have been written highlighting the problems that visually handicapped infants and their families face, and many books have been written suggesting common-sense approaches for parents (see additional readings at the end of this chapter), there is little hard evidence that the rate and sequence of development of visually handicapped infants are any different from those of sighted infants. It is even legitimate to question whether the knowledge of risk actually causes, rather than ameliorates, the problems that have been documented in some children.

Warren (1984) presents an excellent critique of the research literature and calls for a longitudinal, broad-based study incorporating the many environmental and demographic variables which may affect the development of visually handicapped children. Until such normative data are available, and until educational intervention programs have been evaluated for the effectiveness of their techniques, it cannot be stated definitively that there are lags, or that they are caused solely by the visual impairment. It is just as likely that a developmental lag occurs in an individual child because the adults around the child *expect* it to occur. If blind infants are not expected to reach until late in the first year, for example, parents and teachers

may not start looking for the child to reach until then, in effect decreasing the child's chances to learn to reach prior to that time simply because the opportunity has never been provided.

Use of a Sighted Standard

In spite of the weaknesses inherent in the data available, it is generally believed that blind and visually handicapped children are delayed in locomotor, cognitive, and social development when compared to nonhandicapped children. The problem, however, may rest in the comparison itself: it assumes that the experiences of visually handicapped children are similar to those of nonhandicapped children when in fact they may be totally different. Does the feel and smell of a banana, for example, produce the same concept in a child's mind as the sight and taste of one? Is the sound of an object as motivating to reach out to as the sight of it?

The nature of many of the developmental scales utilized in early educational programs assumes that vision is the predominant source of sensory input. The differences seen in visually handicapped children may be nothing more than artifacts of a testing procedure refined and standardized on children who quite literally perceive the world differently. It may be that blind children lag behind sighted children in some developmental phases because it is necessary for them to do so. More must be understood about the rate, sequence, and interaction of development in visually handicapped children before lags or deficits—based on a sighted standard—can be interpreted.

Developmental Studies

There have been four major efforts to produce what might be considered as age norms for the development of visually handicapped children: *Blindness in Children* (Norris, Spaulding, & Brodie, 1957); standardization of a Social Maturity Scale for Blind Preschool Children (Maxfield & Buchholz, 1957); the ten years of study by Selma Fraiberg and her colleagues in the Child Development Project at The University of Michigan Medical Center (Fraiberg, 1977); and the assessment scales created in England by Jean Reynell and Pamela Zinkin at the Royal National Institute for the Blind (Reynell, 1983). All have produced different results. Some clearly indicate differences in the development of visually handicapped children, while others attribute apparent differences to lack of experience.

Chart 7.1 lists the ages at which various skills were attained by subjects in these four studies, compared to age norms for nonhandicapped children as given in the Bayley Scales of Infant Development (Bayley, 1969). Any comparison should be done with caution, however; even the Bayley norms are fifteen years old. Note that: (a) all four report their findings in different ways, so that pooling the data from all studies in order to obtain a broader perspective on the population is virtually impossible; (b) where ranges are given, the visually handicapped range overlaps the Bayley range at least one-half month, and often overlaps for more than half of the given range; (c) where median ages are given or have been extrapolated, the greatest differences between visually handicapped and nonhandicapped children can be seen; and (d) the most complete data are given for the study with the smallest sample size. A cursory examination of Chart 7.1 thus leads to ambivalent conclusions: Differences between visually handicapped and nonhandicapped children could be great, or they could be minimal. A closer look at the studies themselves is therefore warranted.

Norris, Spaulding, and Brodie (1957) This is the only study that sought to establish developmental norms; 66 children born between 1945 and 1952 comprised the intensive group. The youngest child was seen at 15 months; the oldest, at 6 years of age. They had no handicaps other than blindness, although 85 percent were born prematurely and subsequently developed ROP. Approximately two-thirds of the subjects were females.

Administration of the Cattell Infant Intelligence Scale (Cattell, 1940) did indeed show that blind children took longer to achieve certain milestones, particularly in the motor area, but Norris et al. accurately suggest that many of the test items reflected the amount of experience required rather than the amount of skill achieved. The development of children in the intensive group was approximately equal to that of sighted children, except for those items requiring prior experience. The study concluded that there were no special developmental problems directly attributable to blindness itself. Each child's functioning was actually more closely related to the opportunities that had been provided for learning experiences and was closely related to the child's current level of development. The investigators further concluded that lags in development increased geometrically; the greater the time that elapsed between when the child was ready to learn and when the opportunity to learn was actually provided, the greater the time delay before the child actually acquired the skill.

Social Maturity Scale for Blind Preschool Children (Maxfield & Buchholz, 1957) Popularly known as the Maxfield-Buchholz Scale, this study was not designed as a developmental study, but was an effort to inventory the "social competence of the young blind child, with the level of expectancy based on the performance of other blind children in the same age range" (p. 3). The 1957 scale revised the Maxfield-Fjeld (1942) adaptation of the Vineland Social Maturity Scale (Doll, 1953) and was standardized on a group of 398 children ranging in age from 5 months to 5 years 11 months. Sixty percent of this group was born prematurely with subsequent ROP; cataracts and optic atrophy were seen in the next largest numbers of children. Most subjects (64 percent of the ROP children and 48 percent of the non-ROP children) had more than light perception, while 19 percent had light perception or less. The degree of vision of almost one-fourth of the sample was unknown. The placement of items on the scale was based on the percent of children passing at that year level. Reliability and validity studies were not attempted. All subjects were involved in some sort of service program, but the extent of intervention was not given.

Child Development Project (Fraiberg, 1977) Fraiberg's study of blind children over a 10-year period has been widely cited in and out of the field of vision, although results were available for only 10 children, none of whom had other handicaps or central nervous system damage. Only 3 infants were preterms with subsequent ROP (compared to 85 percent in Norris et al. and 60 percent in Maxfield & Buchholz). They were first seen between the ages of 1 and 11 months and were followed in a "home-based education and guidance program" (p. 272) until the age of 2-1/2 years. Fraiberg concluded,

> Under these optimal conditions for study, the effects of blindness per se could be examined, and inferences regarding the function of vision in sensorimotor organization could be made through the study of the effects of the deficit. Blindness as an impediment to adaptation was clearly discerned in each of the areas of development in this study, even when we employed our knowledge to facilitate development and helped the child and his parents find adaptive solutions. (p. 272)

Fraiberg frequently states that the results should not be generalized to the entire population of blind infants.

The Reynell Zinkin Scales (Reynell, 1983) Only the mental development portion of these scales had been published by late 1984. They were intended as an assessment tool to guide the intervention process. Age level equivalents were provided largely to compare the child being assessed with the larger group of visually handicapped children. Severely multihandicapped children were excluded from the study, although the sample of 109 children did include 17 with mild cerebral palsy and 8 with hearing impairment. No data were given on sex of the subjects, causes of blindness, or age at onset of blindness, but subjects were divided into partially seeing and blind groups based on the presence or absence of visually-directed reaching. Unfortunately, the size of each group is not given; the reader is told how many recordings were obtained for each group (approximately equal numbers), but almost 60 percent of the children

Chart 7.1 Comparison of age of acquisition of selected developmental skills by visually handicapped and nonhandicapped children

Skill	Visually Handicapped				Sighted
	Norris, Spaulding & Brodie (1957) n=66	Maxfield & Buchholz (1957) n=398	Fraiberg (1977) n=10	Reynell (1983) n=109[a]	Bayley (1969)
Smiles to familiar voice		Year 0–I	1.0–3.0 mos.	2–4 mos. B/PS	.7–6 mos. med=2.1 mos.
Stranger avoidance			7.0–15.0 mos. med=12.5 mos.	9–11 mos. B/PS	3–8 mos. med=4.8 mos.
Separation protest			11.0–21.0 mos. med=11.5 mos.		
Midline reach and attainment on sound cue only	50% at 9 mos. 75% at 12 mos.		6:18–11:1 mos. med=8:27 mos.	4–8 mos. B/PS[b] 8–9 mos. B/PS[d]	4–8 mos.[c] med=5.4 mos.
Elevates self by arms, prone	75% at 6 mos.		4.5–9.5 mos. med=8.75 mos.		.7–5.0 mos. med=2.1 mos.
Sits alone momentarily	25% at 9 mos. 75% at 12 mos.		5.0–8.5 mos. med=6.75 mos.		4.0–8.0 mos. med=5.3 mos.
Rolls from back to stomach	50% at 9 mos. 75% at 12 mos.	Year 0–I	4.5–9.5 mos. med=7.25 mos.		4.0–10.0 mos. med=6.4 mos.
Sits alone steadily	25% at 9 mos. 75% at 12 mos.	Year 0–I	6.5–9.5 mos. med=8.0 mos.		5.0–9.0 mos. med=6.6 mos.
Raises self to sitting position		Year 0–I med=13–24 mos.	9.5–15.5 mos. med=11.0 mos.		6.0–11.0 mos. med=8.3 mos.
Stands up by furniture (pulls up to stand)	50% at 15 mos. 75% at 18 mos.	Year I–II	9.5–15.0 mos. med=13.0 mos.		6.0–12.0 mos. med=8.6 mos.
Stepping movements (walks, hands held)	50% at 12 mos. 50% at 15 mos. 75% at 18 mos.	Year I–II med=25–36 mos.	8.0–11.5 mos. med=10.75 mos.		6.0–12.0 mos. med=8.8 mos.
Stands alone	50% at 18 mos. 50% at 21 mos. 75% at 24 mos.	Year I–II med=25–36 mos.	9.0–15.5 mos. med=13.0 mos.		9.0–16.0 mos. med=11.0 mos.

Milestone				
Walks alone, 3 steps	50% at 21 mos. 50% at 24 mos. 50% at 27 mos. 75% at 30 mos.	11.5–19.0 mos. med=15.25mos. Year II–III med=25–36 mos.		9.0–17.0 mos. med=11.7 mos.
Walks alone, across room	50% at 24 mos. 50% at 27 mos. 50% at 30 mos. 50% at 33 mos. 75% at 36 mos.	12.0–20.5 mos. med=19.25mos. Year II–III med=25–36 mos.		11.3–14.3 mos.[e] med=12.1 mos.
Listens selectively to familiar words		6.6–11.5 mos. med=8.6 mos. Year I–II	10–12 mos. B/PS	5.0–14.0 mos. med=7.9 mos.
Responds to verbal requests		6.6–13.5 mos. med=9.8 mos.	14–19 mos. B / 14–18 mos. PS	6.0–14.0 mos. med=9.1 mos.
Jabbers expressively		6.9–16.0 mos. med=9.4 mos. Year 0–I	8–10 mos. B / 10–12 mos. PS	9.0–18.0 mos. med=12.0 mos.
Imitates words		8.9–17.5 mos. med=10.3 mos.		9.0–18.0 mos. med=12.5 mos.
Says two words		12.7–32.0 mos. med=18.5 mos. Year I–II med=25–36 mos.	19–22 mos. B / 22–24 mos. PS	10.0–23.0 mos. med=14.2 mos.
Uses two words to make wants known		13.2–26.9 mos. med=20.6 mos. Year I–II med=25–36 mos.		14.0–27.0 mos. med=18.8 mos.
Sentence of two words		17.9–37.3 mos. med=26.3 mos. Year II–III med=37–48 mos.	29–31 mos. B / 27–29 mos. PS	16.0–30.0 mos. med=20.6 mos.

[a] B=blind; PS=partially sighted.
[b] Reach to sound, not necessarily secured.
[c] Visually-directed reaching.
[d] Localized reach to sound, not necessarily secured.
[e] Norms taken from Denver Developmental Screening Test (Frankenburg & Dodds, 1967).

were assessed only once, which could imply unrepresentative and unbalanced scales for both groups. If 60 percent were observed only once, the quality and duration of the intervention program is also in question.

The Reynell Zinkin Scales are further confounded by the manner in which the age level equivalents were obtained. Apparently, raw scores were converted to age scores on the Maxfield-Buchholz, then converted through the use of scattergram plots and means to age level equivalents for each item on each subscale. No reliability or validity studies were conducted.

Weaknesses of Past Studies

While the technical inadequacies of the Reynell Zinkin Scales are obvious, the application of any of the developmental studies to the current population of visually handicapped infants and young children would be both misleading and frustrating for the following reasons:

Etiology of Eye Conditions Causes of visual impairment have changed over the years. The Norris et al. study included a sample of over 85 percent children who were born prematurely and subsequently developed retinopathy of prematurity. By the time Fraiberg's study concluded, only 30 percent of the sample was preterm with ROP. The most recent study on the causes of blindness in young children indicated that prenatal influences and ROP were the most frequent diagnoses (Hatfield, 1975). Today's figures simply cannot be predicted without adequate surveys of the population; it is even possible that recent medical advances are resulting in an increase in the incidence of various eye conditions. Factors affecting etiology in the 1980s include: (a) survival of preterm infants at increasingly lower birth weights; (b) identification of environmental influences, such as toxic waste dumps, nuclear radioactivity, and industrial

pollution, as the cause of numerous birth defects and anomalies; and (c) aging of the parent population, as more couples delay childbirth until careers are established, thus making both parents higher risks for pregnancy and birth complications.

Small Sample Sizes The relatively small size of the samples involved in the four major studies make generalization to the larger population of visually handicapped young children extremely difficult. None of the studies provide any information on measures of central tendency or variability around the mean, other than a median (sometimes) and/or a range. Probability has not been computed against the nonhandicapped ages—that is, no effort was made to determine the likelihood of the differences between blind and sighted samples occurring by chance. The 398-child sample used in the standardization of the Maxfield-Buchholz would yield more convincing generalizations if the sample were more representative of today's population, but a largely singly-handicapped ROP sample clearly bears little resemblance to the children involved in early education in the 1980s. (For a discussion of incidence and etiology factors, see Chapters 2 and 3.)

Early Education Programs Special education for visually handicapped infants and preschoolers is more widespread today than it was in the 1950s or 1960s. All four studies included some type of intervention, but the earlier ones probably focused on the parents more than on the direct teaching of the child. Fraiberg, too, used a parent counseling approach. The intervention style utilized with the Reynell Zinkin Scales is unknown. With the passage of mandatory special education for visually handicapped infants in 12 states and the success of the Handicapped Children's Early Education Program, services are more often delivered by educators today than by social workers or rehabilitation teachers, and attention is placed on changing child behavior, although parent training is a large part of the intervention plan. The effects of an educational, behavior-oriented approach may affect the rate of development of visually handicapped children, and differences documented in past years may be either more obvious or less obvious.

Implications

The inconclusiveness of these four major developmental studies does not suggest that early education for blind and visually handicapped children is an unproven

science. In fact, as Barraga (1983) and Warren (1984) illustrate, the blind or visually handicapped child encounters numerous obstacles in the early years that may be overcome by specific intervention techniques or that simply might be, or ought to be, considered normal for visually handicapped children. Still, every teacher has known at least one blind child who "breaks all the rules"—who achieves developmental milestones at the same age as sighted children, and who appears "normal," in the sighted sense, in every conceivable way. What is not known is what makes for individual differences among blind children, or among children with varying degrees of visual impairment. It is no longer sufficient to state that blind and visually handicapped children are so heterogeneous that cause-effect relationships

Chart 7.2   Curricular concerns for visually impaired children

Sensory Development:
Kinesthetic modality
Tactual
Auditory
Olfactory
Gustatory
Vision

Gross Motor Development:
Reaching
Transferring
Midline Skills
Throwing
Head Control
Crawling and Creeping
Walking

Fine Motor Development:
Grasping
Locating Objects
Body Sensitivity to Objects
Handcrafts
Spatial Orientation
Cutting
Touch Identification
Marking and Drawing
Tracing
Reproduction
Sequencing
Pre-Braille

Social Development:
Emotional Responses
Separation
Fear of Strangers
Parental Influences
Development of Independence

Receptive Language Development:
Attending to Sound
Localization of Sound
Discrimination of Sounds
Sound-Symbol Association
Vocabulary Comprehension
Laterality
Directionality
Listening for Sequences
Auditory Overload

Expressive Language:
Expressions of Feeling
Babbling
Vocabulary Building
Self-Image
Concept Statements

Cognitive Development:
Causality
Means-End
Object Permanence
Problem Solving
Classification
Environmental Structure
Reasoning
Concept Development
Generalization
Conservation

Self-Care Development:
Eating
Dressing
Toileting
Grooming
Peer Interaction
Understanding the Body
Self-Concept
Helping Others

SOURCE: R.F. DuBose, Working with sensorily impaired children: Part I: Visual impairments, S.G. Garwood (ed.), *Educating young handicapped children: A developmental approach* (Germantown, Md.: Aspen Systems Corporation, 1979), pp. 323-359.

cannot be identified, or that developmental studies cannot be undertaken. They must be initiated.

In the interim, the role of the teacher of the visually handicapped is clear: (a) know the risks—know where developmental problems have been documented and understand why they might occur; (b) provide every possible learning opportunity to minimize those risks; and (c) set expectations for performance that are based on what is possible. What is known about blind and visually handicapped infants is neither definitive nor complete, but by providing as many opportunities to learn a skill as possible, the teacher can feel assured that at least the child's chances for learning are greater than they would have been without the opportunities. To limit the opportunities—to expect a blind infant not to like lying on her tummy, for example—is to reduce her chances for development. If a blind infant is excused from lying on her tummy because "it's not an interesting position for her" or "she has no reason to lift her head because she can't see," that infant will have little opportunity to learn head and neck control, trunk stability, or weight-bearing on the hands. That in turn will reduce the infant's chances of learning how to sit, crawl, and walk. In short, neither parents not teachers can take any aspect of the visually handicapped child's experience for granted.

UNIQUE DEVELOPMENTAL NEEDS OF VISUALLY HANDICAPPED CHILDREN

DuBose (1979) has identified some 62 curricular concerns for visually impaired children (see Chart 7.2). A discussion of these concerns can be found also in DuBose (1976), Warren (1984), and in other chapters of this text. The unique needs set out below highlight some of these areas.

Locomotion

Considerable attention has been placed on the delayed locomotor abilities of visually handicapped infants, including creeping, crawling, and walking. Fraiberg (1977) attributed the delays to a failure to establish object permanence and, consequently, later development of directed reaching. In short, visually handicapped infants do not begin to move around on their own until they understand that objects and people exist even when not in direct contact with the infant's sensory experience. Until that time, the infant lives in a fantasy world under the influence of what might be called the "Good Fairy syndrome"—where objects appear and disappear into a void (L. Harrell, personal communication, May 1983). The infant must realize, first, that the toy (or bottle, or mommy) is somewhere out there. Secondly, he must have the motivation or desire to secure that object. And third, he must realize that he can influence whether or not he actually does

secure it—that the choice is his, and his actions or lack of action will produce a result one way or another.

Obviously, there is more involved in locomotion than object permanence and reach to sound. Motivation, purpose, and cause-effect relationships are equally as important. While a child may be taught to reach to sound through stimulus-response or conditioning techniques, and while he may or may not understand that food and toys arrive from somewhere, he has no way of learning his own ability to get those toys or that food if they appear out of thin air. Adults, teachers and parents alike, frequently anticipate the visually handicapped child's needs without giving him a chance to indicate what he wants. By doing so, they eliminate the child's choice and control of the situation, and they foster his dependence. Independence training begins in infancy, not at age 2, 6, or when college is imminent.

Locomotion as a unique developmental need of visually handicapped children illustrates the interactive nature of development. Teaching an infant to crawl by concentrating on manipulation alone—that is, putting the child through the movements of crawling—is insufficient for developing purposeful locomotion. Every skill taught must be taught in the context of every other goal for that child. Locomotion is not an isolated experience.

Rotation of Body Parts

Rotation of body parts is prerequisite for good locomotor ability (Ferrell, 1985; Hart, 1983). It is also frequently undeveloped or missing altogether in young visually handicapped children because the visual impairment limits the opportunites available to practice it.

All motor development proceeds from head to toe, and rotation is no exception. It is the head which first rotates in the infant, either to follow a visual target, as neonates do; or in a reflexive manner, as with the asymmetrical tonic neck reflex; or later in response to moving objects again. As the infant gains head and neck balance, the turning of the head comes more and more under his control, and the emergence of the symmetrical tonic neck reflex signals the ability of one body part to turn independently of all other body parts.

Vision continues to play a role in rotation, however, as the infant grows. A baby lying on his stomach, who catches sight of something moving in the corner of his eye, will turn toward it with his head and possibly the shoulders and part of the trunk. In a sitting position, he sees something beside him, slightly out of reach, and he turns toward it, extending one arm to support himself, and then perhaps bringing the other arm around to reach for it, thus causing trunk rotation. This places him in a position that is preliminary to a crawling position. When he finally does crawl, he is practicing both trunk and hip rotation and weight shifts—all integral skills involved in walking.

The child with little or no vision, however, does not receive all these opportunities to practice rotation. The reflexive head turn occurs, and sound localization gradually develops so that the infant is able to achieve some voluntary rotation, but the natural, incidental, and frequent occurrence of head turning, trunk rotation, and reaching across the midline simply does not occur without vision acting as a mediary. Opportunities to practice rotation must be provided by creating situations where sound and voice can stimulate curiosity and movement (see, for example, Ferrell, 1985). It seems possible that the delays documented in locomotion could just as easily be attributable to inadequate practice of rotation as much as to an instability to reach out to sound. Quite literally, the blind infant may not know how to move his body to achieve locomotion unless he is specifically taught how to do it.

Fine Motor Skills

It is often expected that fine motor and tactual development is more highly developed in blind children because they are forced to rely on these senses for information; but as Cutsforth (1951) has pointed out, such skills must be specifically taught. Frequently overlooked, however, is the importance of differentiation of the index finger.

An infant's grasp develops from a reflexive grasp onto anything placed in the palm of the hand, to the highly refined pincer grasp, which allows the child to pick up tiny items such as raisins or pieces of cereal. The pincer grasp also signifies the readiness of the child to obtain information through the fingers. Up to that point, one finger is indistinguishable from another: the infant experiences any object placed in the hand as a whole object. As infants take more weight on their hands—for example, pushing up on their tummies while in a prone position, and crawling—the grasp gradually changes from reflexive to palmar, where all fingers are utilized; to a scissors grasp, where thumb and index finger are moved laterally toward one another; to the pincer, where tips of thumb and forefinger are directly opposed. Prior to acquiring a true pincer grasp, the infant will begin to use the index finger for pointing, and for exploring parts of objects (particularly recesses). At the same time, infants begin to take a more active role in their own feeding, by holding and eating foods, using a utensil, and picking up small pieces of food.

Visually handicapped children may be at a disadvantage, however, if they have not received opportunities to bear weight on hands. If expectations are such that the infant does not spend time in the prone position, or if crawling is delayed because of a lack of opportunity or motivation or both, similar delays may be seen in tactual development. This will have

reverberating effects on the infant's self-feeding, manipulatory, and exploratory behavior. The literature is replete with descriptions of blind infants not able to feed themselves until age 3, or of their haphazard throwing of objects without evidence of voluntary release; but the relationship of opportunities for weight bearing and development of grasp is rarely discussed. It is entirely possible that the motor restrictions placed on visually handicapped children in early infancy—either by lack of vision or lack of opportunity and experience—may have greater impact on overall development than the blindness itself.

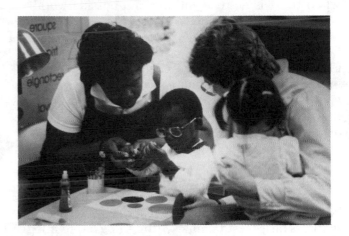

Object Concept

Fraiberg (1977) frequently discussed the importance of the object concept. Simply, the object concept is the knowledge that something exists when it is out of immediate contact with the individual. For the young infant, this may mean the realization that mother and father will always return; but it also means that the toy played with yesterday will be sought out today. A child with vision is able to make this connection more easily than the visually handicapped child, because vision gives both immediate feedback and verification to the object. Substituting sound or tactual qualities may not be sufficient for the blind child, however.

Squeeze toys, for example, are usually interesting for infants because of their manipulative, auditory, and visual characteristics. When a sighted child plays with a squeeze toy, he is receiving all three sensory inputs simultaneously. If the same toy is held out to him by an adult, with or without noise, it has the same visual characteristics as it had when the baby was handling it himself. The child with limited vision, however, may only experience the tactual and auditory qualities of the squeeze toy. When an adult holds the toy out to him, without noise, there are no clues present as to what is being offered. If the adult squeezes the toy, it may or may not sound the same as it did when the infant was holding and squeezing it himself. The amount of information available to the child has decreased. Consistent exposure to the toy in various situations will help the visually handicapped child learn that it is the same object regardless of who is holding it. The larger concept—the existence of a world of people, objects, and new experiences—may not be so easy. It is a big jump from concrete objects to abstract thinking about an environment not immediately accessible.

Aquisition of the object concept signals that the blind child is entering a new phase, where he is perhaps capable of using verbal symbols (i.e., talking) and can lose some of the self-centeredness that results when there is no recognition of an outside world.

Classification

Classification is a higher level of abstract thought which indicates that new information is being processed and applied to previously learned information, such that new ideas or new categories of information are developed. In children, classification usually develops first by identifying commonalities based on physical attributes—such as labeling by size, shape, and color. During this stage, a child reared in the city may see a horse or cow on a trip to the country and promptly label it a "dog," because he is observing the common features he is most familiar with. A dog has four legs and a tail; so does a cow and a horse. This "city kid" has a set of characteristics in mind which signal "dog"—and the farm animals fit directly into this set.

Later, classification occurs by groups (such as all animals or all fruits), then by function (such as all eating utensils or all clothing), and later by association (such as things for fishing, or items associated with housecleaning—apron, broom, cleanser, etc.). The risk for visually handicapped children is that much of this process of classification rests on observation and trial-and-error. The sighted child watches what others do, and practices it. Some relationships are pointed out, but most are formed independently. The visually handicapped youngster does not have that luxury and may not know that aprons are worn while cooking or cleaning unless someone specifically tells him, or unless he is permitted to help out in the kitchen and is given his own apron to wear. Without continuous opportunities to learn and put all of these concepts into some logical order of classification, the visually handicapped child only has pieces of the puzzle.

Social Interaction

Fraiberg (1977), Als, Tronick, and Brazelton (1980), and Warren (1984) have devoted considerable attention to social interaction and the attachment process; thus, a discussion of the adaptive communication necessary between parents and very young infants will not be repeated here. The visually handicapped child misses many of the nuances of social interaction, however, which might explain and help interpret the responses of both peers and adults.

A great deal of interpersonal communication depends on nonverbal communication, such as body language, facial expression, and eye contact. Almost everyone has experienced a conversation where the other person's actions do not fit with his words—a professor, for example, who says there is time for a conference, but who repeatedly looks at the clock. Visually handicapped children are not able to pick up on these signals precisely because of their inability to see them. This not only places them at a disadvantage in terms of interpreting the actions of others, it also places them at a disadvantage when attempting to monitor their own behavior.

Most people, for example, have learned such rules as when it is permissible to scratch or to eat with the fingers. Many children—and adults—stretch this social etiquette to see what would happen. The stares of others, with or without disapproving facial expressions and verbal admonishments, are often enough to discourage future trials. The visually handicapped child does not know when he is behaving improperly unless he is told each time he does it; he cannot read the responses of people around him, nor can he change his behavior, unless someone tells him. And if his behavior is not changed, relationships with peers and other adults will suffer.

Communication

Verbalism in the blind has been noted in the literature for some time. Cutsworth (1951) discusses it, and Warren (1984) has synthesized the available research. A recently published study suggests that verbalism may be an outgrowth of the way adults talk to young blind children. Kekelis and Anderson (1984) recorded the expressive language of four blind youngsters and their parents from early infancy to school age. Their analysis of parents' speech found an unusually high number of single-word utterances—labels, essentially, for the objects around the house. Questions were also frequently used by adults. In spite of the advice given to parents of blind children to explain everything and literally maintain a constant flow of conversation, the authors found instead that very little explanation was provided. The tendency of the four subjects to use labels, to ask questions, to repeat questions of adults without providing an answer, and to speak or question in apparently unrelated situations, or situations totally out of context with the discussion then occurring, did not appear unusual given the conditioning the children had received since early infancy.

Language is certainly one of the developing child's primary means of learning about the environment. It is important that visually handicapped children are exposed to functional language that has meaning and that helps them to make connections and draw relationships. Nonverbal communication is equally as important in language development as it is for the development of social interactions. Sighted children communicate initially by eye contact alone, and later use their eyes to verify what has been said (to look at the apple when daddy says, "apple"). When the baby has shown by his gaze that he understands what daddy wants, daddy can then continue talking about the apple: how good it tastes, where it came from, whether he will make an apple pie, or what father and son will do next time the two of them are out driving and see an apple tree. The father is expanding the conversation and the child's understanding, and such procedures are both effective and necessary with visually handicapped children.

Intersensory Coordination

An area of development about which there is little information in either the handicapped or nonhandicapped literature is that of intersensory coordination and cross-modal transfer. The ability of infants to use all sensory inputs simultaneously, or to take the sensory information obtained in one modality and apply it to another, has serious implications for early education. If infants are not able to use the information presented simultaneously, or if one sensory system is not efficient at processing information, techniques traditionally used to teach infants, such as hand-over-hand manipulation, or the involvement of as many sensory inputs as possible, may not be effective.

One of the reasons the issue is important for visually handicapped children results from the growing use of electronic devices, primarily binaural sensory aids, in early infancy. The theory was first advanced by Bower (1977) that the devices could be used to substitute for the visual system in infants with severe visual impairment. The sound characteristics produced by the aids, which were originally intended to be used as mobility devices for blind adults, provide information to the wearer on distance, location, and surface characteristics (e.g., glass vs. wood) of objects in the environment. Size can often be determined by scanning. Bower felt that blind infants would be able to assimilate this information and, after a period of adjustment and learning, apply it naturally in everyday situations.

Research has not established that binaural sensory aids affect the development of blind infants. One study (Ferrell, 1984; Hart & Ferrell, 1983) suggests that the sensory information provided by binaural sensory aids may even be confusing to the young child and interfere with the child's manner of obtaining information from the environment. In a related study, Ferrell (1983/1984) failed to find evidence of cross-modal transfer in 24 children between the ages of 6

and 24 months on a test of tactual-to-visual transfer. While the subjects were severely visually impaired, each had responded to visual preference techniques for the measurement of visual acuity.

Clearly, much more needs to be studied about the perceptual abilities of visually handicapped infants and the methods by which they obtain and process sensory information. Until such research is available, practitioners should be alert to the inherent problems and sensitive to the individual infant's apparent responses.

STRATEGIES FOR WORKING WITH VISUALLY HANDICAPPED INFANTS AND PRESCHOOLERS

There are several strategies that teachers of the visually handicapped have found useful when working with young visually handicapped children and their parents:

Remember that parents are the most important resource that children have, and that the teacher's influence is transitory. Parents have a history, a present and a future with their child, but teachers come and go. The most successful intervention will be that which provides models for behaviors that are consistent and sustained in the child's environment. The only way to achieve this is to give parents the information and strategies they need in order to structure the best possible home environment that meets the needs of all family members.

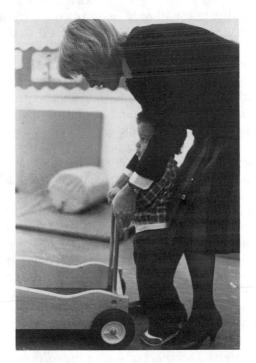

Put the child through the movements, so he knows what you are asking him to do. Babies use vision to observe the movements of others and to monitor their own movements; they can see what they are doing and what they need to change in order to perform a movement or task correctly. A visually handicapped baby may have difficulty doing this. By using a hand-over-hand approach, teachers and parents can demonstrate what the movement feels like and provide valuable sensory and motor information to the child. Soon, the child will know what is expected.

Work from behind. When using this hand-over-hand technique, the child will feel more relaxed and comfortable if the adult is behind him and moving the body parts forward. Using this hand-over-hand technique from the front does not allow the child to feel the natural fluidity of movement, nor does it allow the adult to gauge the child's response. Working from behind also contributes to the visually handicapped child's sense of security, because more of his body is in contact with an adult's.

Use less and less help. Gradually decrease the amount of hand-over-hand assistance being given, so that the child is required to do more and more of the task on his own. This can be done by using less pressure on the child's hands, or by "fading" the technique itself—e.g., begin teaching a child to feed himself with a spoon by first placing your hand completely around his as he grasps the spoon and moving him through the scooping and eating motions. Later, as the child gains control, continue the scooping and eating motions with your hand on his wrist. Gradually move your hand from his wrist, to his arm, to his elbow as you go through the movements with him. Eventually, you will only need to touch his arm to remind him about what he is supposed to do.

Be consistent. Use the same words for the same objects as much as possible. It can be very confusing for a visually handicapped child when one adult refers to "trousers," another to "pants," and another to "slacks."

Use common sense. Teach activities—particularly those of self-care—at a time and in a place that makes sense. A visually handicapped child can be confused if he is toilet-trained on a potty chair in the kitchen, and then has to make the transition to the toilet in the bathroom. The kitchen and bathroom environments are totally different—different smells, different temperatures, different sounds. It makes far more sense to eliminate as many of those transitions as possible by beginning the teaching in the environment where it is most likely to occur. It can be just as confusing to teach activities outside of their logical sequence in time—for example, to teach self-feeding when the child is not hungry, or to work on dressing after the child is dressed.

Parents and teachers of young visually handicapped children need to be spontaneous—to use every possible opportunity to teach new skills and reinforce old ones by using natural interaction times and by taking cues from the child himself.

Ask fewer questions, give more answers, and listen. Use language to describe and expand on the environment, helping the visually handicapped child to make connections and understand relationships. Remember that infants communicate through facial expressions, posture, and respiration—they have much to share with parents and teachers who know to look and listen for their responses. Listen, too, for the every day environmental sounds that are commonplace to you, but lack explanation to the developing child—such as the sound of the closet door opening and closing, the pop of the toaster, or the hum of the refrigerator. Visually handicapped young children do not automatically know what these sounds are, nor do they necessarily connect them to events that follow (putting on a coat, eating a piece of toast, or drinking a glass of milk). Once understood, these sounds can become landmarks in place and time for the visually handicapped child and will help him to organize the environment.

Use touch to guide, reinforce, and reassure the young visually handicapped child. Touch can provide the feedback and security that a visual impairment often denies.

Give feedback. Tell the visually handicapped child, even in infancy, what he is doing right, and what he needs to do better. Visual impairment limits the child's ability to monitor his own actions, and he is dependent on others to do at least some of the monitoring for him.

Keep records of the child's growth and development, either in a baby book or as part of a formal assessment. These records will help parents to see their child's progress and should help teachers to be more accountable for their intervention. Furthermore, without lesson plans and data on the child's response to teaching a particular skill, it is impossible to evaluate both the child's motivation and response mode, and even more difficult to determine if the teaching is both appropriate and effective.

Visually handicapped infant and preschool children can benefit from a systematic early education program that utilizes these strategies to provide the best opportunities for growth and learning. Where an individual child is concerned, the efficacy of early intervention is not at issue; what is important is that the child is given the best chance possible for developing the same skills at the same rate at the same time as all other children. As Strain (1984) states, "We should not be terribly interested, . . . in means, medium, and other actuarial data" (p. 9). We *should* be interested in providing the optimal program based on good practice, and our concern *should* be directed toward closing the gap between those children who are ready for school at age 6 and those who are not.

Study questions

1. What type of early intervention characterized the first educational programs for visually handicapped infants? Why?
2. What are the major outcomes of the Handicapped Children's Early Education Program?
3. Discuss three reasons why the efficacy of early intervention is difficult to prove.
4. What conclusions can be made about visually handicapped children from previous developmental studies?
5. Why is it dangerous to apply data from previous developmental studies to the current population of visually handicapped infants?
6. Discuss the role of vision in infancy and relate it to the developmental difficulties often encountered by visually handicapped infants.
7. What is the "Good Fairy" syndrome and how might it affect motivation in children?
8. How does a visually handicapped infant monitor his actions?
9. Why are consistency and common sense important strategies for adults to use with visually handicapped children? Relate your answer to the child's cognitive development.

Additional readings

Alonso, M.A., Moor, P.M., and Raynor, S. (1978). *Children with visual handicaps. Mainstreaming preschoolers* (Department of Health, Education and Welfare Publication No. 78-31113). Washington, D.C.: U.S. Government Printing Office.

Barraga, N. (1983). *Visual handicaps and learning* (rev. ed.). Austin, Tex.: Exceptional Resources.

Cratty, B.J. (1971). *Movement and spatial awareness in blind children and youth.* Springfield, Ill.: Charles C Thomas.

Finnie, N.R. (1975). *Handling the young cerebral palsied child at home* (2nd ed.). New York, N.Y.: P. Dutton.

Harrison, H. and Kositsky, A. (1984). *The premature baby book: A parents guide to coping and caring in the first years.* New York, N.Y.: St. Martin's Press, Inc.

Hart, V. (1974). *Beginning with the handicapped.* Springfield, Ill.: Charles C Thomas.

Warren, D.H. (1984). *Blindness and early childhood development* (revised 2nd ed.). New York, N.Y.: American Foundation for the Blind, Inc.

Wurster, M. and Mulholland, M. E., eds. (1983). *Help me become everything I can be. Proceedings of the North American Conference on Visually Handicapped Infants and Young Children.* New York, N.Y.: American Foundation for the Blind, Inc.

Additional readings (Parent-Oriented)

Brennan, M. (1982). *Show me how: A manual for parents of preschool visually impaired and blind children.* New York, N.Y.: American Foundation for the Blind, Inc.

Drouillard, R. and Raynor, S. (1977). *Move it!* Lanham, Md.: American Alliance Publications.

Ferrell, K.A. (1984). *Parenting preschoolers: Suggestions for raising young blind and visually impaired children.* New York, N.Y.: American Foundation for the Blind, Inc.

Ferrell, K.A. (1985). *Reach out and teach.* New York, N.Y.: American Foundation for the Blind, Inc.

Kastein, S., Spaulding, I., and Scharf, B. (1980). *Raising the young blind child: A guide for parents and educators.* New York, N.Y.: Human Science Press.

Kekelis, L. and Chernus-Mansfield, N. (1984). *Talk to me: A language guide for parents of blind children.* Los Angeles, Calif.: Blind Children's Center.

Lowenfeld, B. (1971). *Our blind children* (3rd ed.). Springfield, Ill.: Charles C Thomas.

Raynor, S. and Drouillard, R. (1975). *Get a wiggle on.* Lanham, Md.: American Alliance Publications.

Scott, E.P., Jan, J. E., and Freeman, P.D. (1977). *Can't your child see?* Baltimore, Md.: University Park Press.

Ulrich, S. (1972). *Elizabeth.* Ann Arbor, Mich.: University of Michigan Press.

CHAPTER 8

Visual Impairments and Other Exceptionalities

Geraldine T. Scholl

This chapter discusses some of the exceptionalities that may be found in combination with a visual impairment. Definitions, prevalence data when known, and characteristics are noted. Guidelines to help teachers become more sensitive to these variations and their impact on planning to meet educational needs are discussed.

Visually handicapped children and youth may have other, less severe, special educational needs which have an impact on decisions regarding their school placement and on the formulation of individualized education programs to meet all educational needs. The range and combination of these impairments is vast and it is unlikely that any two students will have exactly the same disabilities. (See Chapter 2 for P.L. 94-142 definition.) The following are examples of possible combinations a teacher might find among visually handicapped students:

1. Visual and auditory impairments
2. Visual, auditory, and motor impairments
3. Visual and auditory impairments and mental retardation
4. Visual and motor impairments
5. Visual and motor impairments and mental retardation
6. Visual impairment and mental retardation
7. Visual impairment and emotional disturbance
8. Visual impairment and learning disability

These pupils may be placed in programs for their other disability or may be in a program for visually handicapped pupils. The educational characteristics and needs of severely multiply handicapped students, including deaf-blind children and youth for whom special provisions are essential, are discussed in the following chapter.

The first part of this chapter presents an overview of the limited data on the prevalence of other exceptionalities in visually handicapped children and youth. The second part examines briefly the more common combinations: gifted, mentally retarded, speech impaired, seriously emotionally disturbed, orthopedically and other health impaired, hearing impaired, and learning disabled. Definitions, brief descriptions, and available information related to the visual impairment in combination with each category are included. The third part presents guidelines for helping teachers understand and plans programs to meet the special educational needs of the visually handicapped child with other exceptionalities.

The chapter is designed to supplement information typically included in introductory courses in special education. Selected currently used text books for such courses are included in additional readings at the end of this chapter.

OVERVIEW

Prevalence data for combinations of other exceptionalities with visual impairments are limited. The differences in data reported in Tables 2.2 and 2.3 in Chapter 2, suggest that many visually handicapped pupils are placed in educational settings with other categorical groups but the extent of such placements is not known. Reports from the field seem to indicate that about one-third of the school age population of visually handicapped pupils have at least one additional impairment.

From his extensive survey, Graham (1966) estimated that nation-wide there were about 15,000 multiply handicapped visually handicapped school age pupils; since respondents were asked to report only on the multiply handicapped pupils in their settings, the total population from which the sample was drawn is not known. Table 8.1 reports the additional impairments found in Graham's sample of 8,887 pupils. A total of 21,766 additional impairments was reported. Approximately two-thirds had two and approximately 40 percent had three or more impairments. The most prevalent additional impairment was mental retardation, which is frequently accompanied by other impairments (Graham, 1966; MacMillan, 1982).

Table 8.1   Additional impairments in rank order of frequency   N=8,887

Impairment	Visually Handicapped Sample		Only Additional Impairment	
	N	%	N	%
Mental retardation	7,131	80.2	2,247	25.3
Speech	3,457	38.9	134	1.5
Brain damage	3,116	35.1	91	1.0
Emotional problems	1,479	16.6	222	2.5
Cerebral palsy	1,279	14.4	102	1.1
Epilepsy	1,248	14.0	68	0.8
Crippling or medical	1,248	14.0	68	0.8
Chronic medical	621	7.0		
Crippling	434	4.9		
Hearing impairment	946	10.6	121	1.4
Cosmetic defect	543	6.1	76	0.9
Orthodontic defect	368	4.1	38	0.4
Cleft palate	89	1.0	5	0.1
TOTAL	21,766		3,301	37.2

Adapted from: M.D. Graham, *Multiply impaired blind children: A national problem* (New York, N.Y.: American Foundation for the Blind, Inc., 1966), p. 9.

Reports from the field would indicate that today similar or greater numbers of visually handicapped pupils would be found to have additional impairments.

Descriptions of possible combinations are discussed in the following part.

OTHER CATEGORICAL COMBINATIONS

Gifted

Currently, gifted children are not included among the categories mandated for special education programs and services under P.L. 94-142, The Education for All Handicapped Children Act. Thus, programs and services for gifted children tend to be less well developed in the local schools. The extent of these programs and the numbers of children served are not known since at the present time data are not collected systematically by any national agency. Schools are often reluctant to develop programs for this group, partly because of philosophical issues surrounding elitism and equality. (See Gallagher, 1985; Vail, 1979.)

In the past, giftedness was defined as possessing a high level of intellectual functioning. However, in 1972 the United States Commissioner of Education adopted the following definition which includes a broader range of abilities.

Children capable of high performance include those with demonstrated achievement and/or potential ability in any of the following areas, singly or in combination:

1. General intellectual ability
2. Specific academic aptitude
3. Creative or productive thinking
4. Leadership ability
5. Visual and performing arts (Marland, 1972, p. 10).

The recognition of giftedness among the handicapped population is a recent development (Gallagher, 1985). Issues in providing educational programs for these pupils revolve about identification, curricular adaptations, and the delivery of appropriate professional services to facilitate their education. Frequently, gifted handicapped children and youth do not come to the attention of special education teachers because they are unaccustomed to working with high performance children and tend to scale down their expectations (Gallagher, 1985). In such instances, handicapped gifted pupils frequently remain unchallenged by their educational programs.

Most experienced teachers of visually handicapped learners can recall working with students who meet one or more of the criteria listed above for 'giftedness' and are frustrated in attempting to meet their needs because few programs for gifted children exist in many school districts. Even school districts with well developed identification procedures and educational programs for the gifted may not include handicapped students. Finally, in typical programs for gifted students there are difficulties in adapting the curriculum for the child who has a sensory limitation, such as a visual impairment, since the emphasis is often on enrichment activities that require the use of vision (Gallagher, 1985). Teachers often find the giftedness a greater challenge than the visual impairment when attempting to modify the curriculum. Thus, gifted visually handicapped children and youth are often underserved even when special programs are available for nonhandicapped pupils.

In a position paper adopted by the Council for Exceptional Children: Division for the Visually Handicapped (Corn & Scholl, 1984), four areas were identified as necessary for school programs to respond to the special needs of gifted visually handicapped children: identification procedures, curricular modifications, qualified staff and support services, and psychological needs and counseling.

Identification Procedures Inclusion of children with visual impairments in the identification process available to the regular school population is essential. While standardized measures are often not appropriate for either gifted or visually handicapped pupils, other methods of identification may be used. Parental interviews about activities in the home and community, peer identification, teacher observation, outstanding or unusual performance in a particular area are illustrative of methods that might be used to identify giftedness among visually handicapped children and youth. In the absence of appropriate standardized procedures for assessment, informal methods, particularly observation, should be employed.

Curricular Modifications To meet their special educational needs, curricular and program modifications designed to maximize the achievement of gifted pupils may take place in one or more of the following settings:

1. The regular class with support services from the teacher of visually handicapped pupils and the consultant in education of the gifted;

2. Special classes or programs for the gifted with support services from the teacher of the visually handicapped;

3. Enrichment programs designed for the regular school population both within and outside the school setting and made available to gifted visually handicapped pupils;

4. Acceleration for some or all subject areas;

5. Advanced placement provisions available for all pupils.

The decision about the particular setting and the extent of curricular modifications should be based on the individual needs of the child. The type of setting available, however, will often depend on the available resources within the school district and the community. Children with visual impairments should not be deprived of access to programs or needed services to meet the unique needs of their giftedness.

Staff and Support Services Pre- and inservice training must be available to the school staff who are responsible for the education of the gifted and of visually handicapped children so that both specialists may realize the special needs of gifted visually handicapped children and plan appropriate assessment, placement, and educational programs for them on a cooperative basis. These elements must be included in the planning process: information sharing about the abilities and disabilities of pupils; formulation of adaptive strategies for identification and assessment procedures; creative program planning to meet the special educational needs of both exceptionalities; awareness of the need for social skills and identification of appropriate strategies for their development; and setting realistic expectations.

Psychological Needs and Counseling The special psychological needs and counseling of pupils and their parents must also be considered. Gifted visually handicapped children and youth can lose interest in school and become behavior problems and potential drop-outs just as nonhandicapped gifted children and youth. To prevent such problems cooperative efforts are necessary to meet the needs of gifted visually handicapped children and youth.

Mental Retardation

Mental retardation is defined as "significantly subaverage general intellectual functioning existing concurrently with deficits in adaptive behavior and manifested during the developmental period, which adversely affects a child's educational performance" (DHEW, 1977, p. 42478). There is wide variation in the abilities, characteristics, and educational needs of children labeled "mentally retarded." Various terms are used to describe the levels of severity. Table 8.2 lists the more commonly used descriptive terms.

Visually handicapped children and youth who fall in the severe/profound or custodial groups are discussed in the following chapter on the severely multiply/visually handicapped group. This part discusses those in the mild or educable and moderate or trainable groups who are more likely to be in classes in regular schools.

Grossman (1983) classifies the mentally retarded population into two groups that sometimes overlap: the clinical group who "generally demonstrate some central nervous system pathology, usually have IQs in the moderate or below range, have associated handicaps or stigmata, and can often be diagnosed from birth or early childhood" (p. 12); and those who are "neurologically intact, have no readily detectable physical signs or clinical laboratory evidence related to retardation, function in the mildly retarded range of intelligence, and are heavily concentrated in the lowest socioeconomic segments of society" (p. 13). Since many of the etiological factors in mental retardation,

Table 8.2   Levels of severity in mental retardation

AAMD (Grossman, 1983)		Educational Expectations (Chinn, Drew, & Logan et al., 1979)		Piagetian stages of cognitive development (MacMillan, 1982)
Levels	IQ	Description	IQ	Stages
Mild	50-55 to app. 70	Educable	50-75	Concrete operations
Moderate	35-40 to 50-55	Trainable	20-49	Preoperational
Severe	20-25 to 25-40			Sensorimotor
Profound	Below 20 or 25	Custodial	Below 20	

Adapted from: J. Ardizzone & G.T. Scholl, Mental Retardation. In G.T. Scholl (ed.) *The school psychologist and the exceptional child* (Reston, Va.: Council for Exceptional Children, 1985), p. 854.

e.g., prematurity, low birth weight, infectious diseases, the Rh factor, are also factors that may result in a visual impairment, it is likely that children diagnosed as either mentally retarded or visually impaired due to one or more of these etiological factors may also have the other disability and should be screened and assessed for both (Sadowsky, 1985). Mental retardation seems to occur more frequently in some eye etiologies, such as congenital retinal blindness and bilateral congenital anophthalmos (Warren, 1984). It is not surprising, therefore, that Graham (1966) found the high prevalence of mental retardation in his multiply handicapped study.

Speech Impairments

Communication disorders, including speech and language deficits, are found in about 5 percent of the school population (Kirk & Gallagher, 1983). The definition in the Federal Rules and Regulations includes both speech and language deficits and states that speech impaired "means a communication disorder, such as stuttering, impaired articulation, a language impairment, or a voice impairment, which adversely affects a child's educational performance" (DHEW, 1977, pp. 42478-9). Most specialists in the field divide communication problems into those related to speech and speech production and those related to language.

Language problems include language delay, language deficiency, and childhood aphasia. Language problems are frequently present in pupils with mental retardation, learning disabilities, and hearing impairments (Bloom & Lahey, 1978) and in preschool children (Ulrey, 1982). Some of these are considered developmental delays which tend to improve with maturation and experience.

Communication skills of blind children seem to be similar to those of sighted children when visual cues are not necessary and when there is a limited number of communication encounters (Matsuda, 1984). In his review of research on the language development of visually handicapped children, Warren (1984) also suggests that the lack of visual information and the tendency of parents to provide language forms lacking in linguistic richness place the visually handicapped child at a disadvantage and may account for the verbalism frequently noted in the language of pupils with visual impairments. With regard to remediation for language disorders, Warren, (1984) says "there does not seem to be an effective technology for matching remedial procedures to problem type" (p. 214).

Speech defects include articulation, fluency disorders, and voice disorders. Articulation problems are common in young children and remediation is frequently postponed until it is clear that maturation will not remediate the problem (Emerick & Hatten, 1979; Reynolds & Birch, 1982). There is conflicting information about the prevalence of speech disorders in visually handicapped pupils (Warren, 1984). It would appear, however, that the prevalence of speech problems is no greater than for the nonhandicapped population.

The remediation of both speech and language problems requires the skills of a speech and language specialist. Since therapy is typically conducted on an itinerant basis, visually handicapped pupils in need of such therapy are not removed from their regular school placement.

Seriously Emotionally Disturbed

There is some evidence that autism and autistic-like behavior may be higher in the population with retinopathy of prematurity (retrolental fibroplasia) (Chase, 1972; Warren, 1984). In one study, scores on the Behavior Problem Checklist for a residential school population were higher than the nonhandicapped population but similar to scores of deaf students in a residential setting (Hirshoren & Schnittjer, 1983). Variations in the definition of emotional disturbance, research methodological problems, and confounding variables in studies suggest caution in drawing conclusions. In the absence of data, it is probably safe to assume that emotional problems appear at the same or possibly slightly higher rate among visually handicapped children and youth than among the normal school population.

The Federal Rules and Regulations define seriously emotionally disturbed as follows:
"(i) The term means a condition exhibiting one or more of the following characteristics over a long period of time and to a marked degree, which adversely affects educational performance:

(A) An inability to learn which cannot be explained by intellectual, sensory, or health factors;
(B) An inability to build or maintain satisfactory interpersonal relationships with peers and teachers;
(C) Inappropriate types of behavior or feelings under normal circumstances;
(D) A general pervasive mood of unhappiness or depression; or
(E) A tendency to develop physical symptoms or fears associated with personal or school problems.

(ii) The term includes children who are schizophrenic or autistic. The term does not include children who are socially maladjusted, unless it is determined that they are seriously emotionally disturbed." (DHEW, 1977, p. 42478)

Of the more than 4 million children served during 1982-83 in school programs under P.L. 92-142 and P.L. 89-313, slightly over 8 percent were classified as seriously emotionally disturbed (US-ED, 1983). Applying the same proportion to the visually handicapped population would result in about 2500 visually handicapped children and youth who may be seriously emotionally disturbed. Most are probably being served in classes and programs for visually handicapped pupils with (and many probably without) supportive services from educational personnel qualified to work with emotionally disturbed pupils. Some children with impaired vision are found in residential treatment centers for the emotionally disturbed, typically with limited educational assistance to compensate for their visual impairment. Data to determine accurate figures on this group are lacking.

Orthopedically and Other Health Impaired
A variety of conditions is included under "orthopedically impaired" and "other health impaired." Orthopedically impaired is defined as:
"a severe orthopedic impairment which adversely affects a child's educational performance. The term includes impairments caused by congenital anomaly

(e.g. clubfoot, absence of some member, etc.), impairments caused by disease (e.g. poliomyelitis, bone tuberculosis, etc.), and impairments from other causes (e.g. cerebral palsy, amputations, and fractures or burns which cause contractures)" (DHEW, 1977, p. 42478)

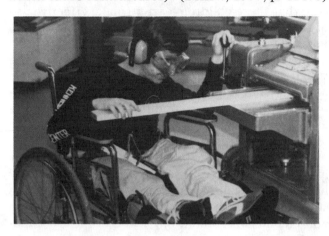

Other health impaired include those "with limited strength, vitality or alertness, due to chronic or acute health problems such as a heart condition, tuberculosis, rheumatic fever, nephritis, asthma, sickle cell anemia, hemophilia, epilepsy, lead poisoning, leukemia, or diabetes, which adversely affects a child's educational performance" (DHEW, 1977, p. 42478).

Some of these conditions, such as cerebral palsy, usually require special education programs and services involving a multidisciplinary team approach. Others, such as amputees, may require some modifications in an educational setting that will enable them to perform school tasks in a regular class. Pupils with conditions such as asthma or rheumatic fever may require physical restrictions but remain in a regular school program. The extent of special educational needs for this very heterogeneous group requires a comprehensive assessment, including vision, by a multidisciplinary team to determine the most appropriate placement and program to meet their needs.

All degrees of visual impairments may be found among orthopedically or physically handicapped and other health impaired, possibly to a greater extent than in the general school population. Vision problems are known to be associated with cerebral palsy (Harley & Altmeyer, 1982; Healy, 1983); and are found in an estimated 30 percent of the multiply handicapped population whose primary diagnosis does not involve vision (Schor, 1983). If such children are not identified as having a visual impairment and appropriate steps are not taken for remediation, then they may not be receiving an appropriate educational program. All children with physical or other health problems should be screened regularly for an assessment of their visual functioning. Such screening must be done by a professional person who has the patience and can communicate with such children since many, especially those with cerebral palsy, do lack verbal communication skills and may require the use of other communication modes. Teachers of visually handicapped learners may serve as consultants to insure that these children learn to make effective use of their vision.

For some children with orthopedic or health impairments and a mild vision problem, remediation of the visual impairment through corrective lenses or use of low vision aids, or simple adaptations and improvements in lighting conditions or monitoring the length of time on visual tasks may assist the child to make better use of vision.

Placement of a child in a wheelchair or on crutches in a special class or residential program for the visually handicapped will often present a challenge to the staff. Usually with the cooperation of the orientation and mobility instructor, physical therapist, occupational therapist, and teacher of the physically handicapped such problems can be resolved. Orientation and mobility instruction is especially important in the educational programs for pupils in wheelchairs or on crutches (Coleman & Weinstock, 1984).

Cooperative efforts on the part of the special education teachers and other support personnel involved will insure that the child receives an appropriate educational program.

Hearing Impaired
Severe hearing impairments in combinaton with severe visual impairments (deaf-blind) are discussed in the following chapter. The appropriate educational setting for others may vary. Pupils with severe hearing impairments but mild to moderate visual impairments would probably be referred to a school or program for the hearing impaired. Pupils with mild hearing impairments in combination with moderate to severe visual impairments might more appropriately be educated in programs for the visually impaired. The Federal Rules and Regulations define hard of hearing

as "a hearing impairment, whether permanent or fluctuating, which adversely affects a child's educational performance." (DHEW, 1977, p. 42478).

The category of hearing impairments shares many of the same problems and issues with the category of visual impairments. Both are low prevalence populations, with high rates of multiple impairments, and a need for specialized teachers and support personnel. In both categories assessment procedures must take into account the age of onset, type of onset, etiology, and degree and type of sensory loss. All these factors must be taken into consideration when working with pupils who have mild to moderate losses in both sensory areas.

Learning Disabled
A specific learning disability is defined as:

a disorder in one or more of the basic psychological processes involved in understanding or in using language, spoken or written, which may manifest itself in an imperfect ability to listen, think, speak, read, write, spell, or to do mathematical calculations. The term includes such conditions as perceptual handicaps, brain injury, minimal brain dysfunction, dyslexia, and developmental aphasia. The term does not include children who have learning problems which are primarily the result of visual, hearing, of motor handicaps, or mental retardation, or of environmental, cultural, or economic disadvantage. (DHEW, 1977, p. 42478)

The definition of learning disability thus excludes children who have learning problems which are primarily the result of a visual impairment. The determination of this latter criterion may be difficult. Little is known about the number of children who are tactile learners and who may also have a learning disability. Daughtery and Moran (1982) in their study of 50 low vision children found that about two-thirds of them could be classified as brain-damaged or learning disabled. In most instances, these children had severe discrepancies between their ability and their achievement.

Learning disabilities may also be found among children and youth who are blind or who have severe visual handicaps and whose major educational disability is their visual impairment. However, the exclusion phrase in the definition cited above may be unfairly eliminating these children, especially those with limited vision, from the services of a specialist in learning disabilities. Teachers of the visually handicapped must know when and to whom a referral should be made for visually handicapped children and youth who may also be learning disabled and should be prepared to work with that specialist in a team approach.

Because of the importance of certain aspects of visual functioning in the process of learning to read, such as focusing, convergence, and using both eyes, children suspected of being learning disabled should have a complete eye examination to rule out the possibility of a visual impairment (Peiser, 1978). Unfortunately, this is not always included in the comprehensive assessment procedure for these children. There are no data concerning the numbers of children diagnosed as learning disabled who also have a visual impairment.

IMPLICATIONS OF THESE DIFFERENCES FOR TEACHERS

The wide range of possible educational variations that may be found in any group of children, as discussed in this chapter, necessitates that teachers of visually handicapped pupils have knowledge of other disabilities, are involved in identification and assessment procedures, and function as vision advocates on behalf of all pupils.

Since exceptionalities in addition to a visual impairment may be found among visually handicapped children and youth probably in the same proportions as in the regular school population, teachers should have sufficient knowledge about other categorical areas so that they may work cooperatively with specialists in those areas in assisting the child to have the best possible educational program. They need to acquire a basic knowledge and understanding of the full range of other disabilities. A single introductory course in special education does not provide sufficient background for teachers to understand the educational needs and characteristics of these specific populations. Additional courses and practicum experiences related to specific categories, particularly mental retardation and emotional disturbance, would enable teachers to work more effectively with other specialists in cooperative planning for the most appropriate educational program for pupils who have multiple exceptionalities.

Teachers of visually handicapped pupils should be aware of signs of other impairments. Children evidencing the characteristics included in the definitions cited in the preceding part should be referred for assessment and possible remedial help. The teacher of the visually handicapped should consult with the school social worker, the school psychologist, teachers of other disability groups, and any other appropriate school personnel to obtain insight and guidance into the seriousness of the noted problem. A referral should be made for assistance through standard school procedures. Because these other school professionals usually have limited experience with children who are visually impaired, it is often necessary for the teacher to function as an advocate and interpreter to professional personnel who work with them. For example, in the case of a possible emotional disturbance, the teacher of the visually handicapped should assist the helping professionals to understand the isolating nature of a visual impairment and difficulties this may cause in initiating social interactions and developing relationships with peers.

Visually handicapped children and youth who also have another impairment require a team approach wherein each specialist interprets the special needs of the specific category to arrive at an appropriate treatment plan for the child.

In the assessment process it is sometimes difficult to determine which is the major educationally handicapping condition. The result may be that the child is placed in the program which is available and does not receive the necessary educational services for the other exceptionality. Such situations point to the necessity for a comprehensive assessment by a multidisciplinary team that will result in the placement appropriate to meet the educational needs for all the exceptionalities the child may evidence. If the most appropriate placement is determined to be a special program for children with another exceptionality, then the child and teacher should have support services from the teacher of visually handicapped pupils; similar support services should be provided by the teacher specialist in the other exceptionality for the child placed in a program for visually handicapped pupils.

An unknown number of children labeled as developmentally disabled, learning disabled, mentally retarded, and cerebral palsied may also have a visual impairment which has not been identified. Knowing this possibility, teachers of visually handicapped pupils should advocate for routine screening programs for visual impairments to be included in the comprehensive assessment for all handicapped pupils. In addition, teachers may also do functional vision assessments that might be useful for these groups. The goal of every teacher should be to identify, assess, and plan the most appropriate program that will meet all the special educational needs of the child.

Study questions

1. Visit a program or school for gifted children or talk to a consultant for the gifted. What problems might a gifted visually handicapped child have in being accepted in that program?

2. Distinguish between visual perceptual problems and visual impairments in the population of learning disabled pupils. Which would be the area where a teacher of the visually handicapped could make the greatest contribution?

3. Interview the director or supervisor of special education in your community about the numbers of children enrolled in other special education categorical programs who also have vision impairments. Ask

whether routine vision assessments are made and if so, what instruments are used for these pupils.

4. Interview the school nurse or community public health nurse about the vision and hearing screening programs or other proceducers used to identify children with visual and hearing impairments for all children. Find out whether handicapped children are included in this process.

5. Visit a program for children with physical impairments that require them to either be in a wheelchair or use crutches. What difficulties might you anticipate in placing a blind child with a severe physical impairment in that program?

6. What difficulties might a visually handicapped child have in adjusting to a residential treatment center placement for severely emotionally disturbed children?

7. What procedures would you suggest for identifying children with visual impairments who are currently enrolled in a program for another categorical group?

8. Visit a program for children with mild to moderate mental retardation. Ask the teacher about any vision problems and what services the children receive for their visual impairment.

9. Describe how you would assess the functional vision of a child who is nonverbal.

10. Visit a residential or day school program for visually handicapped pupils. List other exceptionalities you note in the pupils. Talk with teachers about services these pupils receive.

Additional readings
Selected introductory texts in special education

Berdine, W.J. and Blackhurst, A.E. (1985). *An introduction to special education.* (2nd ed.) Boston, Mass.: Little, Brown & Co.

Blake, K.A. (1981). *Educating exceptional pupils.* Reading, Mass.: Addison-Wesley.

Cartwright, G.P., Cartwright, C.A., and Ward, M.E., (1984). *Educating special learners.* (2nd ed.) Belmont, Calif.: Wadsworth.

Hallahan, D.P. and Kaufman, J.M. (1982). *Exceptional children: Introduction to special education.* Englewood Cliffs, N.J.: Prentice-Hall.

Hardman, M.L., Drew, C.J., and Egan, M.W. (1984). *Human exceptionality: Society, school, and family.* Boston, Mass.: Allyn and Bacon.

Kneedler, R.D. with Hallahan, D.P., and Kauffman, J.M. (1984). *Special education for today.* Englewood Cliffs, N.J.: Prentice-Hall.

Kirk, S.A. and Gallagher, J.J. (1986). *Educating exceptional children.* (5th ed.) Boston, Mass.: Houghton-Mifflin.

Meyen, E.L. (1982). *Exceptional children and youth.* Denver: Love Publishing Co.

Reynolds, M.C. and Birch, J.W. (1982). *Teaching exceptional children in all America's schools.* Reston, Va.: Council for Exceptional Children.

Ysseldyke, J.E. and Algozzine, B. (1984). *Introduction to special education.* Boston, Mass.: Houghton Mifflin.

Selected categorical texts

Barbe, W.B. and Renzulli, J.S. (ed.)(1982). *Psychology and education of the gifted.* (3rd ed.) New York, N.Y.: Todd Publications.

Bigge, J.L. (1976). *Teaching individuals with physical and multiple disabilities.* Columbus, Ohio: C.E. Merrill.

Bleck, E.E. and Nagel, D.A. (eds.) (1983). *Physically handicapped children—A medical atlas for teachers.* (2nd ed.) New York, N.Y.: Grune & Stratton.

Bloom, L. and Lahey, M. (1978). *Language development and language disorders.* New York, N.Y.: John Wiley.

Cegelka, P.T. and Prehm, H.J. (1982). *Mental retardation: From categories to people.* Columbus, Ohio: Charles E. Merrill.

Cruickshank, W.M., Morse, W.C. and Johns, J.K. (1980). *Learning disabilities: The struggle from adolescence toward adulthood.* Syracuse: Syracuse University Press.

Gallagher, J.J. (1985). *Teaching the gifted child.* (3rd ed.) Boston, Mass.: Allyn and Bacon.

Hison, T., Shriberg, L., and Saxman, J. (eds.) (1980). *Introduction to communication disorders.* Englewood Cliffs, N.J.: Prentice-Hall.

Kirk, S.A. and Chalfont, J.C. (1984). *Academic and developmental learning disabilities.* Denver, Colo.: Love Publishing Company.

Kleinberg, S. (1982). *Educating the chronically ill child.* Gaithersburg, Md.: Aspen Systems Corporation.

Long, N., Morse, W.C. and Newman, R. (eds.) (1980). *Conflict in the classroom: The education of emotionally disturbed children.* (4th ed.) Belmont, Calif.: Wadsworth.

MacMillan, D.L. (1982). *Mental retardation in school and society.* Boston, Mass.: Little, Brown & Co.

Maker, C.J. (1984). *Teaching models in education of the gifted.* Rockville, Md.: Aspen Systems Corporation.

McDowell, R.L., Adamson, G.W., and Wood, F.H. (1982). *Teaching emotionally disturbed children.* Boston, Mass.: Little, Brown & Co.

Mullins, J.B. (1979). *A teacher's guide to management of physically handicapped students.* Springfield, Ill.: Charles C Thomas.

Sedlak, R.A. and Sedlak, D.M. (1985). *Teaching the educable mentally retarded.* Albany, N.Y.: State University of New York, N.Y. Press.

CHAPTER 9

Severe Multiple Handicaps

Rosanne K. Silberman

This chapter describes assessment procedures and educational programming, including behavioral objectives, task analysis, behavioral chaining, shaping, prompting, and positioning and handling for severely multiply handicapped students. Specific curriculum areas to be included in the individual education program (IEP) are discussed. The importance of the team approach is emphasized. Several appropriate service delivery models and alternative living arrangements for the population are reviewed. Specific resources are also included.

The range and variety of possible combinations of mild and moderate impairments among visually handicapped children and youth were described in the preceding chapter. This chapter focuses on children and youth who have visual impairments in combination with other disabilities of sufficient severity to classify them as severely multiply handicapped. These pupils usually require modified assessment procedures, placement in special settings designed to facilitate their educational programs, and an individualized education program that will address the broad range of their educational needs. An appropriate education for these multiply handicapped pupils requires a team approach to meet their many and diverse educational needs. This chapter addresses these issues in the education of severely multiply handicapped pupils who also have visual impairments.

ASSESSMENT

Formal and informal assessment of visually handicapped children and youth is discussed in Chapter 11. This chapter highlights the issues, instruments, and procedures that are most appropriate for the severely multiply handicapped population. Because of the great diversity in the possible combinations of impairments only very general guidelines can be presented relative to assessment of the capacities and limitations of each individual pupil.

Assessment of this population presents a challenge to the teacher. Because few instruments have as yet been developed specifically for this group, the teacher must select, adapt, and modify from those available

the items and subtests that will provide information necessary for the IEP. Teachers must then supplement items from available tests with observation and trial teaching as described in Chapter 11. Consultation with other school personnel is essential: the school social worker for assistance in assessing and understanding the family dynamics, the speech and language therapist for assessing language skills in order to plan appropriate stimulation programs, and the physical and occupational therapists for assessing motor development and educational planning to increase skills in this area. The teacher truly becomes the case manager in designing appropriate assessment procedures to form the basis for the individualized education program.

Particular attention must be given to the purpose of the assessment. (See Chart 11.1, Chapter 11.) Through observation, the teacher can determine the priority areas for assessment. Knowledge of normal growth and development will help the teacher to determine the starting point. Since many multiply handicapped students function on the level of Piaget's sensorimotor period of development (birth-two years), infant scales such as the Bayley Scales of Infant Development (1969) or the Learning Accomplishment Profile (Sanford, 1974) might be appropriate for younger pupils. Since these scales rely on observational skills in a variety of settings, the teacher should solicit the assistance of the parents in completing them. Results will provide the teacher with a starting point for educational planning.

For older pupils, however, it is questionable whether a developmental approach is appropriate for multiply handicapped students nearing the end of their education in a school setting. Consideration of the present age of the student and the objective of making him as independent as possible in the shortest time, requires an approach that identifies the critically needed skill areas, and assessment through task analysis of the skill where the teaching must begin. The importance of helping the student become as independent as possible prior to leaving school cannot be overemphasized (Silberman, 1981). Chart 9.1 lists several selected instruments, covering various areas of skill development. Some of these can assess and help the teacher develop instructional programs.

Teachers should select the instrument that would seem to be most appropriate to use for educational planning and then adapt it to the particular pupil's needs. Instruments that are basically observational, for example, the AAMD Scales, are useful for younger children, those who are severely retarded, and those who have limited ability to respond through any mode. Other instruments that require a response from the child may be adapted. Alternate modes of communication must be used by nonverbal students. These may include head or facial movements, body movements, arm-hand movement, visual localizing and scanning, vocalization, gestures, or signing. The teacher should use whatever response mode is appropriate for the child.

Teachers of severely multiply handicapped pupils may find assessment instruments that include curricular applications most useful. *Reach Out and Teach* (Ferrell, 1985) is illustrative of this approach. Although designed for parents, the material is equally useful for teachers in curriculum planning.

Because the development of assessment instruments and procedures for severely multiply handicapped pupils is a growing area, teachers must keep abreast of new developments through reading professional journals and attending conferences.

EDUCATIONAL PROGRAMMING

Results obtained from conducting formal and informal assessment procedures enable the teacher to ascertain the current level of functioning of each severely multiply handicapped student in basic skill areas and with the help of the transdisciplinary team and the student's parents, she can establish instructional priorities and develop individualized education programs. Assessment and program planning are interrelated and must constantly be updated and revised. When working with the child who has severe multiple impairments, development of the IEP must include those goals which are functionally essential in the child's environment whether it be class, home or group home. A behavioral approach with clearly stated objectives is usually most appropriate for teaching such skills. This technique is described in the next part.

Teaching Skills

Snell and Smith (1983, p. 80) identify criteria to select objectives for a specific student:

1. Objectives address practical or functional skills that are most likely to be needed currently or in the near future;
2. Objectives span four instructional domains: domestic, leisure-recreational, community and vocational;
3. Objectives are suitable for the student's chronological age;
4. Objectives must not be so difficult that they cannot be accomplished in a year's time or so simple that they are already in the student's repertoire.

Behavioral Objectives

A behavioral objective is a description of the specific behavior which the student must demonstrate. The criteria for an acceptable behavioral objective are:

1. It must state exactly what the student is to do, must be observable, and must be measurable.
Example: Jennifer will reach for the cup.
2. It must state the conditions under which the behavior is to occur. Level of independence must be incorporated into the objective.
Example: Given verbal or gestural command, Jennifer, a hearing and visually impaired pupil, will reach for the cup; upon seeing the cup, Jennifer will lift it independently.
3. It must specify the criterion level or standard for acceptable performance.
Example: Rob will trail along the hallway for three feet; Jim will stuff five envelopes within a ten-minute period.

Do not use percentages when writing objectives for multiply handicapped students. It is meaningless to say, "Rob will trail along the hallway for three feet 80 percent of the time." It is more appropriate to say, "Rob will trail along the hallway from his class to the lunchroom for three feet, four out of five consecutive

Chart 9.1   Assessment instruments appropriate for multiply handicapped/visually handicapped children and youth

Test	Characteristics	Purpose
Behavioral Characteristic Progression (BCP) (Vort Corp., 1973)	Nonstandardized, criterion-referenced instrument; includes 2400 observable traits grouped into 59 broad categories of skills called "strands"	To identify presence or absence of specific behavioral characteristics To select appropriate learner objectives for each student
Developmental Assessment for the Severely Handicapped (DASH) (Dykes, 1980)	Comprehensive criterion-referenced system; items scored along a continuum of difficulty ranging from completely independent performance to least independent or task resistive performance	To assess the current level of functioning of students on a pinpoint scale in order to translate the assessment data into behavioral objectives To use the cumulative summary sheet and other recording forms for ongoing planning and evaluation
Pennsylvania Training Model Individual Assessment Guide (Somerton-Fair & Turner, 1979)	Skills assessed in five developmental areas on the Pinpoint Scales: Language, Sensorimotor, Social-Emotional, Activities of Daily Living, and Preacademic Comprehensive task-analyzed criterion-referenced tool with four major components: 1. Curriculum Assessment Guide 2. Developmental Taxonomies Section 3. Skill Observation Strategies 4. Individual Prescriptive Planning Sheet Gives detailed sequences of behaviors in the skill areas assessed Transfers information obtained into functional lesson plans Includes antecedents, behavior expected, the consequences given for both the correct and incorrect behavior, and the acceptable criteria for meeting each behavior listed	To assess skill development in 14 areas To help select instructional objectives and implement an educational program To measure short and long term progress
Behavioral Rating Instrument for atypical children (BRIAC). Ruttenberg & Wolf (1977)	Designed to permit observation of integrative functions: ego formation, cognitive attainment, independent functioning Picks up small steps of behavior change	To compare the child with himself over time in acquisition of self-directed behavior
Manual for Assessment of Deaf-Blind Multi-handicapped Children (Rudolph & Collins, 1978)	Based on work at St. Michaelgestel Compares child to self over time Particular attention to language and communication behaviors	To observe the child's interaction with the environment

Chart 9.1   (continued)

Test	Characteristics	Purpose
Callier-Azuza Scale (Stillman et al., 1978)	Comprehensive criterion-referenced assessment tool; Assesses skills in five areas: motor development perceptual abilities daily living skills cognition, communication, and language socialization	To assess adaptive behavior in multiply handicapped pupils To serve as a resource for developing a teaching program
Vineland Adaption Behavior Scale (Sparrow, Balia, & Cicehetti, 1984)	Available in three editions: interview survey form; interview expanded form, and classroom edition Useful as an aid in making decisions about classification, placement, and instructional programming	To assess overall measures of adaptive behavior
AAMD Adaptive Behavior Scale (Lambert, Windmiller, Cole, & Figueros, 1975)	Assesses levels of adaptive behaviors; Standardized on both institutional and public school populations of mentally retarded children and adults; Adapted and used for assessing multiply handicapped pupils	To assess adaptive behavior in 10 domains of personal independence in daily living skills and 14 domains of maladaptive behavior
Los Lunas Curriculum System (Everington, 1982)	Includes curricular suggestions and emphasizes functional activities Focuses on those in the severely impaired range of behavioral performance	To observe functions and construct an intervention program
Developmental Assessment Screening Inventory (DASI) (DuBose & Langley, 1979)	Standardized on a population of severely impaired children with special attention to multiply handicapped, visually handicapped pupils Perceptual and motor items are related to naming by signing, object matching, counting, and following commands	To assess communicative behavioral responses
Functional Skills Screening Inventory (Becker et al., 1984)	Available on the IBM-PC for electronic administration, scoring, and monitoring progress. Designed to be used in natural settings Most appropriate for adolescents and young adults Assesses functioning in 8 areas with 343 items: basic skills and contents personal care community living social awareness communication homemaking work skills concepts	To identify needs of multiply handicapped, visually handicapped pupils To set priorities in basic skills needed for sheltered living and work and for independent living and work

days.'' The objective should include how many (the frequency) or how correct the student must be to achieve criterion level. Criteria for a given objective can be written in terms of:

1. Accuracy level: three out of five times
2. Frequency level: eight times
3. Time limit: within ten minutes

Task Analysis

Once the behavioral objectives are identified for a given student, they must be broken down into small steps or teachable units. There are varying approaches for developing task analyses (Gold, 1976; Popovich, 1981; Williams, 1975). The following describes one meaningful way to develop a task analysis:

1. Identify the terminal goal (behavioral objective) to be accomplished;
2. List all the component skills of the task in sequential order;
3. Identify the entering behaviors or prerequisite skills needed for performing the component skills. Unless these are carefully detailed, a skill to be learned may be too difficult and not be appropriate because the student might not have the prerequisite skill.

One type of format for doing a task analysis is a *vertical listing*. The steps evolve in the order in which they occur when performing a task. This format is easily translated into teaching units and it can be easily understood by profesionals, paraprofessionals, and parents (Van Etten, Arkell, & Van Ellen, 1980). Chart 9.2 is an example of a vertical task analysis of a leisure skill: "Playing Simon," a game which focuses on visual and auditory memory, adapted from Wuerch and Voeltz (1982, p. 106).

The other type of format is the *lattice construction*, a graphic display whereby subgoals are put into a hierarchy (Van Etten et al., 1980). The lowest level skill is placed in a box at the bottom left-hand corner and connected to this box is the component skill of the subgoal that would develop next. The process continues until each of the subgoals is placed in a box connected to another one by a line with a 90-degree angle. The graphic display moves up vertically and to the right in a stepladder format until one reaches the upper right hand corner box which contains the terminal goal of the skills sequence. See Chart 9.2, for an example of a task analysis in lattice format of self-help skill: "Shoes Tied."

In a lattice format, when one skill must be learned before another skill, the boxes are hung directly beneath one another and connected with a straight line. It has an advantage over the vertical listing in that it not only identifies which skills are essential to a task, but it identifies skills that might be helpful to learning the task (Van Etten, 1980).

Teachers find vertical listing more meaningful: it is easier to construct and therefore is likely to be used more frequently; it is easier to add other component skills when needed for individual children; and one can continuously modify the conditions under which a skill should occur.

Chart 9.2   Task analysis: Playing Simon

Behavioral objective: Given Simon, the student will match one visual or auditory signal correctly. Prerequisite skills—press, slide, knowledge of right and left, visual and/or auditory discrimination

Steps: Seated in chair with Simon game on lap or table, student will:

1. Place Simon so that On/Off switch is positioned closest to his body.
2. Slide the On/Off switch to the right to "On."
3. Find Game Selector on the left side of middle surface (at 9 o'clock position).
4. Slide Game Selector to the left (#1).
5. Find Skill Level switch on right side of middle surface (at 3 o'clock position).
6. Slide Skill Level switch to left (#1).
7. Find Start button directly above On/Off switch.
8. Press the Start button.
9. Find the four colored lenses.
10. Press each of the four lenses and look and/or listen to each sound.
11. Press Start button.
12. Look at lighted lens and/or listen to its sound.
13. Press the same lens.
14. If matching error occurs (loud noise will sound), then repeat steps 11, 12, and 13 until response is correct.
15. Locate On/Off switch.
16. Slide On/Off switch to the left to turn off.

Adapted from: B.B. Wuerch, *Longitudinal leisure skills for severely handicapped learners* (Baltimore, Md.: Paul H. Brookes Publishing Co., 1982), p. 106.

Behavioral Chaining

Behavioral chaining is a procedure in which a student learns one step of a task analysis at a time until all the steps are acquired and the student meets the terminal objective.

The two types of behavioral chaining are forward chaining wherein the steps in the task analysis are taught from the first one in the sequence to the last which is the terminal behavior; and backward chaining wherein the steps in the task analysis are taught from the last one occuring in the sequence to the first. (See Chart 9.4 showing forward and backward chaining for the self-help skill of putting on a gym sock).

Shaping

It is highly improbable even with task analysis that a severely multiply handicapped student will learn a new behavior in one lesson. Shaping is a strategy in which the teacher reinforces successive approx-

Chart 9.3   Lattice for "shoe tied" program

Entry Behaviors:
Imitate or model others
Can grasp
Pull against tension

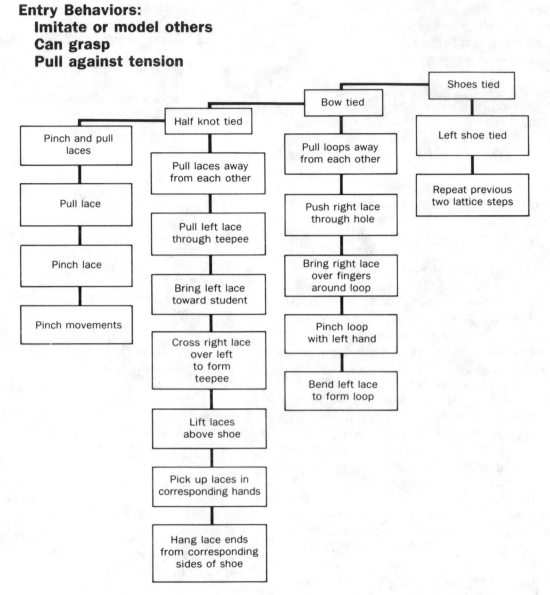

Source: D.D. Smith, J. Smith & E. Edgar, A prototype model for developing instructional materials for the severely handicapped in N.G. Haring and L.J. Brown (Eds.), *Teaching the severely handicapped,* **1** (New York: Grune & Stratton, 1976), p. 167.

imations of a behavior until the terminal behavior is learned. For example, using backward chaining in the task analysis of "Putting on a gym sock," the teacher

Chart 9.4   Chaining

Forward chaining

The student will:
1. Grasp the sock with two hands from the table.
2. Grasp the sock with heel in correct position.
3. Pull the sock over toes when presented with open sock with heel in correct position.
4. Pull the sock over arch of foot (below heel).
5. Pull the sock over heel to ankle.
6. Pull the sock over ankle up to the calf.
7. Pull the sock over the calf up to the knee.

Backward chaining

The student will:
1. With sock on and up to the calf, pull sock over the calf up to the knees.
2. With sock on up to the ankle, pull sock over ankle up to the calf.
3. With sock on to the heel, pull sock over heel to the ankle.
4. With sock on over the toes, pull the sock over arch of foot.
5. When presented with open sock with heel in correct position, pull sock over the toes.
6. When presented with sock, put heel of sock in correct position.
7. Grasp the sock from the table.

would have placed the sock of the student up to the calf aiming to have the student independently pull the sock up to the knee. The teacher would reinforce any close approximation of the student grasping the sock with two hands at the calf. In the next lesson, the teacher might reinforce only if the student pulls up the sock any distance. In the third lesson, the teacher would reinforce the student only if he pulls the sock completely to the knee. The length of time needed to achieve each successive step and number of shaping schedules will vary from student to student depending on the level of responsiveness of each.

Fading

Fading involves the gradual removal of prompts used in teaching a particular skill. At first the student may need physical assistance and a verbal cue on a specific step to achieve success. As the student gains independence, the teacher will fade the physical assistance and give only the verbal cue. A second type of fading is the gradual removal of reinforcing consequences. At first the teacher may give the student a tangible reward and verbal praise. As the student demonstrates success, the teacher will remove the tangible reinforcer and give only a verbal one.

Prompting

Prompts are levels of assistance. It is important for a teacher or assistant not to give more assistance than is needed to work toward independent achievement of a skill. The levels of assistance or prompts range from none at all to total physical guidance.

1. Independent—Sometimes a student is given a single verbal, signed, imitative, or gestural direction and then the student can successfully perform the task in the classroom setting. Later the student may be taken to the lunchroom, gym, or specific work area to demonstrate whether he will do his task successfully in another setting. Success indicates total independence for this specific skill.

2. Verbal, signed, or gestural prompt—This type of prompt provides information to the student in addition to the original direction.

3. Demonstration—If the student does not respond to the above cues, then the teacher demonstrates or models what the expected behavior is. Severely multiply handicapped students who have receptive language difficulties such as those with hearing impairments may be able to imitate a behavior after it is demonstrated.

4. Physical guidance—If the student does not perform after a behavior is modeled, then the teacher gives physical prompts. The teacher coactively performs the activity with the student and physically guides him with hand-over-hand assistance.

Positioning and Handling

Some severely multiply handicapped children including those with cerebral palsy demonstrate little self-initiated motor behavior because of damage to the cerebral cortex and the cerebellum. Their movement is limited by atypical muscle tone and poor coordination among muscle groups (Campbell, 1983). Deviations in postural tone range from an absence or severe limitation in tone (hypotonia or too little tone) to too much postural tone (hypertonia or spasticity).

One intervention approach aimed at facilitating normal tone and inhibiting atypical tone and patterns of movement through proper positioning and handling is the Bobath or neurodevelopmental approach (NDT) (Bobath & Bobath, 1975; Connor, Williamson, & Siepp, 1978). Methods of therapeutic handling are basically designed to:

1. Normalize tactile, proprioceptive, and kinesthetic input
2. Emphasize symmetry of body postures and movements, and encourage midline-oriented activities
3. Inhibit the deteriorating influence of associated reactions
4. Avoid the development of abnormal compensatory movements
5. Prevent contractures and other deformities from developing (Connor, Williamson, & Siepp, 1978).

Since motorically involved multiply handicapped students spend so much of their school day in a sitting position, the teacher must make certain the student is in a comfortable, natural position in order for him to concentrate fully on learning tasks. Considerations to be stressed are the following:

1. Student should be in a right angled sitting position in the chair, sometimes referred to as short sitting. In this position, the child has 90 degrees flexion at the hip, knees, and ankles.

2. The height of the chair should be such that the student's feet rest firmly on the floor or on a footrest. Dangling feet cause postural insecurity.

3. The depth of the chair should extend two inches behind the knee. A chair that is too narrow will rub the back of the student's knees.

4. The tabletop height should be at a level which enables the student's arms to rest naturally on it. If the student has too much flexion, it may be necessary to raise the work surface or provide an inclined tabletop.

There are severely multiply handicapped children with abnormal motor patterns and seizure activity, combined with oculomotor system problems such as strong deviation of the eyes in one direction, with associated abnormal tonic reflex activity of the whole body. They may exhibit primitive compensatory eye movements in the opposite direction of the head movement (Doll's Eyes Phenomenon), resulting in deviation of the eyes every time the unsteady head moves (Fieber, 1977). Therefore, optimum positioning is essential in order for these children to develop the ability to fixate, track, or turn toward objects moving in from the peripheral visual field. Fieber (1977) suggests placing such children in a supine position (on

their back), centering and tilting up the head, and flexing the legs to break up strong extension. Side-lying may also be used to free the eyes from lateral deviation (right side-lying for right deviation of gaze and head turn).

SKILL DEVELOPMENT

The following sections deal with curriculum relevant to planning an instructional program for multiply handicapped visually handicapped students. The specific areas include motor, cognitive, language and communication, self help, prevocational, social, and leisure and recreational skills.

Motor Skills

When assessing and teaching motor skills to a severely multiply handicapped child, the teacher must work with a team including an occupational and physical therapist and an adaptive physical education teacher in order to design a program and develop instructional objectives based upon the student's overall motor development and chronological age. Some skills such as crawling, hopping, and skipping may be appropriate for young children, but unless the achievement of these skills relates to their usefulness in either a recreational, vocational, or community setting, they will be meaningless goals for older multiply handicapped students.

Many multiply handicapped children with central nervous system involvement retain primitive reflexes which interfere with developing higher level motor and cognitive skills. The physical therapist must recommend positioning techniques to inhibit these reflexes and facilitate normal movement patterns.

The following are several important principles applicable to the development of motor skills in visually handicapped children with multiple impairments:

1. Development of postural control against gravity proceeds in a cephalocaudal pattern (from the head down to the feet). Head and upper trunk control is attained prior to control of the pelvis and legs.

2. Development proceeds in a proximal to distal direction. Parts of the body closest to the midline are controlled before the parts toward the extremities. Control of shoulder movements occurs first and then moves to arms, elbows, wrists, and finger movements.

3. Development is sequential. New acquisitions are based on those that have been acquired previously. Skills that a child develops during free play in supine and prone positions prepare him for the skill of sitting.

4. Sequences overlap. While a child is learning locomotor skills such as climbing and running, he still may be developing his walking skills by improving his wide gait or reducing his shuffling steps.

5. Development moves from mass-to-specific.

Dissociation, the breaking up of gross movement patterns involving the total body, into finer, more selective patterns, occurs. Parts of the body can move independently of each other. A child moves from doing a logroll with the entire body moving together to segmented rolling where he turns his head first and then the shoulders, pelvis, and legs sequentially (Connor, Williamson, & Siepps, 1978).

Task analyzed developmental sequences of gross and fine motor development skills based on developmental scales are enumerated in the Callier-Azusa Scale (Stillman, 1978), the Peabody Developmental Motor Scales (Folio & Fewell, 1983), and The Developmental Resource (Chandler, 1979). Teachers of multiply handicapped students should use such sequences of milestones as guidelines in planning intervention strategies. However, they should use caution and not adhere to them too strongly, since many students may not follow the sequence but will successfully achieve higher level motor skills.

Another critical area essential to the development of motor skills is physical fitness. Many deaf-blind students are fearful of exploring their environments sufficiently and need to improve health related abilities such as agility, balance, endurance, flexibility, and strength (particularly upper body in nonambulatory students). The "I Can" Physical Education Program is an intervention program for developing skills in Health/Fitness, Body Management and Control, and Posture (Wessel, 1976; Silberman and Tripodi, 1979).

The development of fine motor skills involving the use of the arms, hands, and fingers, is frequently delayed in severely multiply handicapped students. Reaching, grasping, and release functions are difficult to attain, since vision plays such an important role in encouraging physical contact with the hands or near objects. Its absence or severe reduction necessitates substituting sound stimuli, which is not always appropriate, as in the case of deaf-blind students. Therefore, complete tactual guidance must often be provided. In addition, those with motor impairments may be delayed in fine motor skill development because of the physical restrictions imposed on them as a result of the nature of their disabilities. The occupational therapist must work with the teacher to properly position a student for hand use and provide adaptive aids whenever necessary.

An educational program focusing on fine motor skills must stress age appropriate and useful activities. Requiring older multiply handicapped students to participate in tasks such as stringing beads, stacking blocks, or placing pegs in a pegboard is a waste of time. As indicated earlier, developmental milestones should be used as only guidelines. Chart 9.5 lists the stages of normal fine motor development and presents corresponding functional activities to improve skills which are suitable for older students (Thompson & Rainforth, 1977). A variety of self-help tasks are included, thus providing the student with several opportunities during the day to raise his level of achievement.

Cognitive Skills

The work of Piaget (1954, 1963) and of Uzgiris-Hunt (1975, 1982) with nonhandicapped children has been extremely valuable in serving as the basis for developing curriculum strategies for use with multiply handicapped students in increasing their cognitive skills. (See Chapter 4.)

The teacher of visually handicapped students with multiple impairments must adapt the instructional program to the specific learning styles and cognitive abilities of the students. An analysis of the student's behavior to determine how functional his vision and hearing are in performing the sensorimotor tasks will enable the teacher to adapt the administration of assessment tasks, to structure the environment, and to provide the specific stimuli in intervention activities that permit optimal use of sensory capacities. Alternate responses often need to be taught to the severely handicapped student. For example, a visually handicapped student with a motor impairment may not be able to demonstrate object permanence or to uncover and grasp a covered object, because he lacks the prerequisite skills of visually directed reach, grasp, and visual tracking. Such a student could be given an auditory cue and be taught to turn eyes or body toward the object.

Communication Skills

The development of communication skills in multiply handicapped students is one of the most important areas in an educational program since it overlaps every other curricular domain. Acquisition of a system of communication is essential to the visually handicapped child's participation in a social world (Rogow, 1980). Prior to formal language training in either verbal or nonverbal modes, the student must acquire certain prerequisite skills:

Attending. This begins with getting the child to sit in a chair on the floor and increasing the duration to longer periods of time. This can be combined with visual and auditory training, depending on the characteristics and needs of the student.

Imitation. Since visually handicapped students with multiple impairments have little or no opportunity to copy the behaviors of others due to their disabilities, imitative behaviors need to be specifically taught. Van Dijk's program (1965) provides meaningful strategies.

Functional use of objects. Developmentally, a child first enters the stage of simple object schemes, doing the same thing with all objects, i.e. mouthing, banging,

Chart 9.5   Fine motor development

Age	Normal Development	Functional Activies (S/P Retarded)
Birth	Little purposeful activity Reflex grasp—thumb not included	
4 mos.	Purposeful reach, poor control Objects placed in hand Hands to mouth, objects to mouth Hands to midline "Fingers finger his fingers" Crude grasp—palm and fingers, thumb not utilized	Assist in bringing cup to mouth Finger feeding Assist in face and hand washing
7 mos.	Bilateral hand movements (pick up toy with both hands) Gross grasp—raking grasp (medial side of thumb) No voluntary release Transfer objects hand to hand Neutral forearm position, full palmar grasp	Hold onto glass/cup/tommy-tippy cup Brush and comb hair Set table Assist with dressing, e.g., pull pants up by holding onto waist band
8-9 mos.	Lateral pinch developing Pick up one object, then another Hold up and manipulate two objects simultaneously	Pick up toothbrush and toothpaste Hold toothpaste and remove cap Put toothpaste onto toothbrush Hold onto lotion bottle, remove cover Hold onto zipper; unzip and zip pants
10-12 mos.	Lateral pinch developing Pincer grasp developing Remove objects from container and put them back into a container With one hand, hold object and attempt to pick up another object Poke and probe with index finger Supination	Hang coat on hook Hang clothes on clothesline, using clothespins Open loaf of bread, take out slice, place on plate (crackers, etc.) Open coin purse, take out money Remove and replace silverware from silverware tray With one hand, hold onto toothbrush; pick up toothpaste cap and place it onto toothpaste tube Pick up two pieces of silverware simultaneously Place soap in soap dish
5 mos.	Place round peg in hole Hold crayon with palmar grasp Build tower of two blocks Place pellet into container	Put toothbrush into holder Place utensils into silverware section of dishwasher Stack cups/glasses, bowls, plates Put bread into a toaster
8 mos.	Improve release Stack 3 to 4 blocks Throw ball Turn pages of a book Turn knobs (door, TV, radio) Put pellet into bottle Pour from one container to another	Stack utensils in silverware tray Open and close jar lids Open doors Turn faucets on a sink Turn on washer and dryer Pour milk, pour detergent into measuring cup Pour water into a cake mix

Source: J.W. Thompson, & B. Rainforth, A functional fine motor program for the severely and profoundly retarded. In R. York & E. Edgar (eds.)*Teaching the severely handicapped* **IV**, (New York, N.Y.: Grune & Stratton, 1979), pp. 15-16.

shaking, depending on what is pleasurable. Then he moves to the complex class of schemes, where he examines the properties of objects in more than one way, that is, manually and visually or manually and mouthing. He crumples and tears objects to see what will happen. Finally, he enters the stage of social schemes where he demonstrates functional use of an object and uses it socially and for communication purposes. This marks the beginning of representational behaviors and the student is ready for training in alternative symbol modes (Uzgiris and Hunt, 1975 and Fieber, 1977).

Communication Skills for Deaf-Blind Pupils

Jan Van Dijk's work with language acquisition in deaf-blind children at St. Michielsgestel in Holland has had a widespread positive effect on the education of this population in the United States. The stages of Van Dikj's motor based language program (Van Dikj, 1965a,b) are as follows:

a. Resonance—During this stage the teacher begins to develop a satisfactory relationship with the student. She is building affection and communication between herself and the student. To accomplish this, she selects a motor activity which the student finds pleasurable and is capable of performing. After the child initiates it, the teacher moves together with the student without any physical distance between them. Activities such as rocking, rolling, seat-scooting, knee walking, or walking across a mat are commonly used. An important aim is to develop anticipatory behavior. The teacher should move with the student and then stop for a moment to observe any reactions or cues to begin again. Receptive resonance is evident when the student shows some awareness of their moving together, such as smiling or cooing.

b. Coactive Movement Sequences—The teacher and student still move together at this stage but distance between them emerges. When performing any motor activity, the levels leading to independence by the student are 1) cohesive—where there is no distance between the teacher and student; 2) mirroring—where teacher and student perform the activity opposite from one another; 3) parallel—where the teacher and student perform the activity next to one another; 4) independently—where the child can perform without any motor cue from the teacher. The aim of this stage is to build up imitation through movement sequences on the student's level. The teacher should initiate a familiar movement with the child, introduce new one(s), and always end with the familiar one. The higher the functioning ability of the student, the more complex and lengthy the sequence of activities should be. Movements should first be performed symmetrically, then asymmetrically, then alternatively.

Once a student is successful and comfortable when moving through a variety of sequences using only his body, then objects can be incorporated into the movement, thus creating more distance between the teacher and the student, i.e. movement of body on, next to, or under chair or bench. These activities provide a structure for the student to learn about objects in relation to his body and its movements and help him to use his body as a tool to exploring the world.

c. Nonrepresentational Reference—At this stage the student is first taught to build his body image through the manipulation and reference to specific parts of his body. The teacher points to parts of her own body and then repeats the activity with the student's body until he can model it himself. Once the student can do this consistently, other models such as paper tracing of student's own body, doll figure, clay figure of doll, and finally stick-figure representations should be used. This is a crucial stage because the deaf-blind student needs to be able to imitate a representation of body movements in order to proceed to more refined imitation of signs and thereby develop expressive language (Hammer, 1982).

d. Natural Gestures—In this stage the student learns that refined motor movements can be used to communicate and becomes aware of symbols. The first attempt at teaching natural gestures should involve an object or activity having particular importance or meaning to the student and it should express the movement or action upon the object. Two factors are important to this stage and must occur: decontextualization, when the deaf-blind student uses the gesture in anticipation of something that is going to happen, e.g., getting a drink; and denaturalization, when the student makes a slight movement instead of the complete natural gesture which is taking the form of a symbol.

e. Beginnings of Language—According to Van Dijk (1965), the deaf-blind student is now ready to be taught expressive language via formal signs and/or speech. A student's success in learning sign language will depend on factors such as degree of residual vision, level of fine motor skills including his ability to use two hands, and short term memory. Signs such as the American Sign Language (ASL) or Signed English (Moores, 1974; Wilbur, 1978) can be put directly into the hands of students who are deaf and totally blind. There are several speech and language programs designed for severely and profoundly handicapped students which can be modified, if necessary, to be used with visually handicapped students (Bricker, Ruder, & Vincent, 1975; Guess, Sailor, & Baer, 1976; Kent, 1974).

Other Methods of Communication Used by Deaf-Blind Individuals

Several methods used by high functioning deaf-blind individuals to communicate with sighted individuals are described by Kinney (1977). One method is the alphabet glove, a thin, white cotton glove on which the letters of the alphabet have been printed with indelible ink at definite spots memorized by the deaf-blind wearer. The sighted person spells out his or her words by touching the letters. Kinney (1977) describes the systematic arrangement of the letters and numerals on the glove.

The Braille Alphabet Card, a slow method, enables the deaf-blind person who reads braille to use a pocket-size braille alphabet card which has both the braille and inkprint letters on it to communicate with a sighted person.

The Tellatouch is a device resembling a miniature typewriter that raises corresponding braille letters under the deaf-blind reader's fingertip as the other person types on the keyboard or uses the six braillewriter keys at the bottom of the keyboard.

Communication for Students with Motoric Impairments

Blind or low vision children with cerebral palsy or who have motoric difficulties in their hands may not be able to be taught via aural or manual forms of communication. Communication boards are an alternative system for some. They range in form from simple plywood to sophisticated electronic models, with tactile boards, pictures, pictures and words, the alphabet, numbers, phrases, or some combinations of these possibilities. Alternate modes for responding include: head to mouth pointers, foot pedals, controls which respond to blowing or sucking movements, and other types of microswitches. Examples of battery powered services and switches are described in Burkhart (1980, 1982).

The three basic approaches for providing a means of indication to communicate a message are scanning, encoding, and direct selection. Scanning is a technique in which choices are presented to the student who signals when he sees or touches the correct choice. In the encoding approach, the desired choice is indicated by a pattern or code of input signals which relates to the desired output. In the third approach, direct selection, the child directly indicates the words or pictures to make up his message on the communication board with his hand or headstick.

Self-help Skills

Visually handicapped students with multiple impairments frequently demonstrate delays in self-help skills of feeding/eating, dressing, grooming, and toileting. Reasons for these delays are: 1) the combined sensory impairment(s) and motoric impairment such as cerebral palsy alters the ease and way the self-help skill can be acquired; 2) parents or primary caregivers have not required these individuals to independently perform these skills because of their severe disabilities; 3) many lack prerequisite fine motor skills such as grasping or releasing or cognitive skills such as attending which prevent them from performing the self-help tasks (Van Etten, Schell, & Van Etten, 1980).

Self-help skills should not be taught as single objectives. Since their achievement is interrelated with early motor, cognitive, and language skills, it is essential to

teach all of these skills in combination with each other. For example, an objective could be: When seated in the lunchroom next to the teacher and given a gestural cue of a tap on the hand, the student will reach and grasp the spoon on the table four out of five times.

Since multiply handicapped individuals find it difficult to generalize across settings, it is also important to teach self-help skills in natural environments in a functional manner. For example, eating with a spoon should be taught only at meal or snack time and putting on a jacket should be taught only near the closet or locker room area when the student is going outside.

Selection of targeted skills should be based on what will enable the individual to function as independently as possible within his community. A visually handicapped student with a motor impairment will need a physical or occupational therapist to recommend specific techniques for positioning, transporting, and movement requirements for eating, dressing, and toileting (Finnie, 1975). The aim in every case is always to reduce one's dependence.

Since it is impossible to model a teacher's behavior due to lack of or reduced vision, the teacher should use physical guidance (hand over hand) or coactively perform self-help tasks with her students. Azrin and Armstrong (1973) successfully used a physical assistance fading strategy to teach such skills as spoon and fork usage. The graduated guidance procedure begins with the teacher's hand totally around the student's hand and the utensil during eating. When the student is gaining competence and can grasp by himself, then the teacher lightly guides with her hand and gradually fades the manual assistance up to the forearm, then the elbow, then the upper arm, then the shoulder, and finally the upper back. A light touch is always maintained to prevent any errors until the student can perform the task independently.

Checklists are available to assist in determining the current level of functioning and selecting targeted skills to teach in the self-help domain. These include the Pennsylvania Training Model (Somerton-Fair & Turner, 1979); the Portage Guide (Shearer, 1978); Behavioral Characteristics Progression (Vort, 1973); and the Balthazar Scales of Functional Independence (1971).

Eating Skills

Major skills which need to be developed include sucking, swallowing, chewing, finger feeding, eating with a spoon, drinking with a cup, using a straw, eating with a fork, cutting with a knife, pouring liquids from a container, table manners, and preparing simple foods such as sandwiches.

The earliest developmental abilities of sucking, taking food from a spoon, chewing and swallowing are referred to as prespeech skills. They not only enable the child to eat and drink successfully; they also provide the basis which enables the child to acquire coordination of the muscles and structures around the oral area (Campbell, 1977). Some severely multiply handicapped students have specific oral motor pathologies such as tongue thrust or oral hypersensitivity which prevent them from developing higher level eating and speech skills. It is therefore essential for a speech or occupational therapist to assess a student's oral motor skills and plan intervention strategies with the teacher. Some multiply handicapped students need assistive devices to enable them to eat appropriately and increase their independence. Adaptations of silverware, plates, bowls, and drinking cups are commercially available and they can also be hand made by a creative teacher.

Dressing Skills

Major skills in this area which multiply handicapped students need to acquire include removing and putting on socks, briefs, pants, T-shirt, jacket, shoes, hat, mittens and managing closures such as zippers, buttons, and snaps. Due to severe motoric impairments or severe mental retardation, some may never develop total independence, but it is essential to work on increasing these skills.

Dressing skills must be taught in realistic settings such as arriving and leaving school, before or after gym, and at home or at the group residence upon waking up in the morning or going to sleep at night. Sufficient instructional time and priority must be given to teaching these skills. Undressing is easier than dressing so objectives should be selected to teach removing a garment such as pants prior to putting them on. It is possible and practical to teach to remove or put on several items such as shoes, socks, underwear, and pants during the same instructional period.

A teacher should do a detailed task analysis of her long term goal and teach the student small steps at a time in order to reduce the complexity of the activity and to assure the student's success on each level. (See Chart 9.3, a lattice format task analysis of "Shoes Tied.") Utilization of a backward chaining technique combined with reinforcement is effective since the student is pleased with the end result. For example, when putting on a T-shirt, the student would be taught to pull down the shirt first from his chest or waist over his hips and then to put the shirt over his head.

Some general guidelines include: have the student participate as much as possible; use clothing that is one or two sizes larger at first; and teach only using the student's own body. Dressing dolls and using lacing boards are different skills and have no transfer for visually handicapped students. Velcro fasteners can be used to replace buttons or zippers for students who have severe motor impairments.

Since some multiply handicapped students wear short or long leg braces, teachers must be skilled in removing and putting them on for gross motor or free play activities or when therapeutically indicated. Teachers have to make sure the braces fit because ill fitting ones will cause pressure sores. If red marks last for more than fifteen minutes after the brace is removed, the teacher should report the situation to the therapist.

Toileting Skills

Major skills which multiply handicapped students need to acquire in this area include awareness of being wet or soiled, finding the toilet, sitting on the toilet when supervised and independently, defecating or urinating, using toilet tissue, and flushing the toilet. Also included in this area are dressing skills such as pulling down and pulling up pants, grooming skills such as washing and drying hands, and language skills of indicating by gesture, action, or vocalization when wet or soiled or when one needs to use the toilet.

Teachers should consider toileting skills as a critical component of the multiply handicapped student's educational program. For profoundly retarded or orthopedically handicapped individuals who are incontinent, bladder and bowel management programs should be developed. Dietary considerations should be incorporated, assuring that the student takes in sufficient amounts of roughage and liquid (Bigge, 1982).

Prerequisite skills for toilet training relate to the maturity of the central nervous system and the elimination sphincters. Foxx and Azrin (1973) recommend that a profoundly retarded student be at least five years old before beginning. Since there are adult size diapers and training pants available, maximum age is not a concern.

Grooming Skills

The basic skills that the multiply handicapped student needs to acquire in this area include washing and drying hands and face, toothbrushing, combing and brushing hair, blowing nose, and bathing or showering. Additional ones demanding more complex skills include cleaning nails, shampooing hair, caring for self during menstruation, shaving with an electric razor, and choosing appropriate clothing. Each of these skills

Chart 9.6　Task analysis

Task analysis of toothbrushing	Fine motor analysis
1. Pick up tube of toothpaste	1. Raking grasp, gross grasp
2. With other hand, grasp and hold onto toothpaste cap	2. Pincer grasp, lateral pincer grasp
3. Unscrew cap from toothpaste tube	3. Supination/pronation of forearm, ulnar deviation
4. Put cap on sink	4. Release
5. Hold open tube of toothpaste in one hand and pick up toothbrush in other hand	5. Hold two objects simultaneously Lateral pincer grasp Pincer grasp
6. Bring toothpaste and toothbrush together and squeeze tooth paste out of tube onto toothbrush	6. Bring hands to midline (Bilaterally) Gross grasp
7. Lay toothbrush on sink	7. Release
8. Pick up toothpaste cap from sink	8. Pincer grasp Lateral pincer grasp
9. Put cap on toothpaste tube	9. Bring hands to midline Neutral forearm position
10. Screw cap onto toothpaste tube/screw toothpaste in cap	10. Radial/ulnar deviation, supination/pronation Gross grasp Neutral forearm position Lateral pincer grasp Pincer grasp
11. Lay toothpaste tube on sink	11. Release
12. Pick up toothbrush from sink	12. Pincer grasp, lateral pincer grasp
13. Turn on cold water	13. Ulnar deviation, gross grasp (dependent on type of knob)
14. Brush lower left teeth (back and forth movement)	14. Gross grasp with thumb extended
15. Brush lower right teeth	15. Supination Gross grasp
16. Brush upper left teeth	16. Gross grasp
17. Brush upper right teeth	17. Gross grasp Supination
18. Brush front teeth	18. Gross grasp
19. Rinse off toothbrush under water	19. Gross grasp
20. Turn off cold water	20. Radial deviation Gross grasp
21. Put toothbrush into vertical toothbrush holder	21. Neutral forearm position Release

Source: A.H. Thompson & B. Rainforth, A functional fine motor program for the severely and profoundly retarded. In R. York & E. Edgar (eds.) *Teaching the severely handicapped* IV, (New York, N.Y.: Grune & Stratton, 1979), pp. 18-19.

needs to be sequenced and task analyzed into small steps for instructional purposes and many of them will need to be part of an individual's educational program throughout life. The more independent a student becomes, the more he will be accepted into an adult placement, and the better he will feel about himself.

As with other self-help skill areas, grooming skills need to be taught in functional settings with emphasis on other interrelated skill areas. Chart 9.6 contains a task analysis of toothbrushing combined with an analysis of fine motor skills. This self-help skill provides an older multiply handicapped student with an age-appropriate means of improving his fine motor skills. (See Chapter 20 for additional suggestions on teaching self-help skills to older and higher functioning pupils.)

Social Skills

Multiply handicapped students need to acquire appropriate social interaction skills in order to integrate successfully in their community setting. While many of them develop competencies in activities of daily living and prevocational and vocational skills, their lack of social skills and their excessive maladaptive behaviors prevent them from being accepted into sheltered workshops or group homes.

There are four basic competencies of a social interaction between two or more individuals which multiply handicapped students should learn across curriculum areas (Williams, Hamre-Neitupski, Pumpian, McDaniel-Marx, & Wheeler, 1978). Prerequisite to the four is a recognition of the appropriate time and place for a social interaction.
The components are:
1. Initiating interactions
2. Receiving requests for interactions
3. Sustaining interactions
4. Terminating the interaction

Selection of specific social interaction behaviors should be based upon a student's chronological age and functioning levels, his learning style, and type and severity of the multiple disabilities. Chart 9.7 contains suggested alternatives applicable to verbal and nonverbal students in the four components of social interaction.

Frequently multiply handicapped students exhibit maladaptive behaviors which prevent them from attending to tasks and/or maintaining contact for any considerable amount of time. These behaviors include those that are dangerous to themselves (e.g., self-abuse) or to others (e.g., aggression). Besides resulting in physical damage, they cause disruption in the classroom which makes learning for any of the students almost impossible (Gaylord-Ross, 1980). In addition, aggressive and self-injurious students are avoided by others, which limits the interpersonal contact that might improve their academic and social functioning (Luiselli & Michaud, 1983).

The most effective behavior management strategies are those which are incorporated into the activities of a student on a consistent, daily basis by all who are involved in the educational program. The most desirable strategy for managing severe behavior problems is to have a trained psychologist provide those working with the student with regular consultation on effective techniques for encouraging adaptive skills and discouraging maladaptive acts in the environment (Luiselli & Michaud, 1983).

Behavior modification techniques have been successfully used with visually handicapped students with multiple impairments (Gallagher & Helm, 1974; Hayes & Weinhouse, 1978; Luiselli & Michaud, 1983; Sklar & Rampulla, 1978); Rogow & Rodriguez, (1977) caution that the use of behavior modification programs to eliminate stereotyped behaviors (e.g., rocking, twirling, eyepoking) must be accompanied by alternative activities since the elimination of stereotyped behaviors without substitute activities can result in serious psychological consequences.

An excellent resource for assessing and training basic social skills in a wide variety of settings including residential, educational, activity, and work facilities is *Social Skills for Severely Retarded Adults: An Inventory and Training Program* (McClennen, Hoeckstra, & Bryan, 1980). It includes adaptations for visual, auditory, and motor impairments and the multiplicity of handicaps caused by two or more disabilities. (See also Chapter 20.)

Prevocational Skills

The development of prevocational skills should be incorporated into every multiply handicapped student's individualized education program. Participation in work activities increases the likelihood that this population will be accepted by the nonhandicapped community (Gold, 1973). Research has demonstrated that multiply handicapped individuals have successfully learned complex vocational tasks by the use of task analysis and other systematic training procedures (Bellamy, Horner, & Inman, 1979; Flexer & Martin, 1976; Gold, 1976).

Parents or staff from the student's present or future group home, and community-based rehabilitation personnel are needed to help plan and implement the prevocational program. Rehabilitation teachers and mobility instructors employed by the local Office of Vocational Rehabilitation could serve as excellent resources. Since the curriculum area also incorporates fine motor, language, and social skills, therapeutic personnel are also essential team members.

There are several prevocational assessment tools in task analyzed checklist format which enable the teacher to measure current level of functioning, plan long and short term objectives, and select appropriate

Chart 9.7   Sample social interaction matrices

INITIATE

Nonvocal
1. Looks at object and/or person
2. Reaches for object and/or person
3. Smiles at object and/or person
4. Points to object and/or person
5. Points to picture of object and/or person on a communication board
6. Uses sign language to initiate

Vocal
1. Vocalizes at an object and/or person
2. Says the name of an object and/or person
3. Asks "Do you want to _____?", "Would you _____?", "Please_____." and so on.

RECEIVE

Accepts Initiation	Declines Initiation
Nonvocal 1. Looks at object or person 2. Reaches for object or person 3. Smiles at object or person 4. Shakes head yes 5. Uses communication board to indicate "yes" 6. Uses sign language to indicate "yes"	**Nonvocal** 1. Looks away 2. Pushes object or person away 3. Frowns 4. Shakes head "no" 5. Uses communication board to indicate "no" 6. Uses sign language to indicate "no"
Vocal 1. Makes a sound which indicates "yes" 2. Says "yes"	**Vocal** 1. Makes a sound which indicates "no" 2. Says "no" 3. Says "no, some other time" and/or suggests an alternate activity

SUSTAIN

Chooses an activity appropriate to the skill level of the individual, such as:

    balls
    blocks
    logs
    paddle ball
    bubbles
    table games

TERMINATE

Nonvocal

1. Looks away
2. Pushes object or person away
3. Uses communication board to indicate "done"
4. Uses sign language to indicate "done"

Vocal

1. Says "done," "see you later"

Source: M. Snell (ed.), *Systematic instruction of the moderately and severely handicapped,* 2nd edition (Columbus, Ohio: Charles E. Merrill Publishing Co.), p. 284.

activities. Examples of these instruments include the Prevocational Assessment Curriculum Guide (P.A.C.G.) Inventory (Mithang, Mar, & Stewart, 1978), An Education—Training Guide to Prevocational Skills for Deaf-Blind Persons (Lockett, 1978), and Assessment of Prevocational and Daily Living Skills (Gates, 1978).

Regardless of the functioning level of the students, the prevocational activities selected should be age-appropriate and the amount of time spent should vary according to the student's chronological age and the number of years remaining in an educational program. The setting should be in a workshop area which is separate from other educational activities and it should provide environmental cues that prompt work behavior (Hill, 1982). Whenever possible, attempts should be made to utilize real or simulated materials of jobs that exist in the local community.

It is important to note that while a multiply handicapped student may acquire work skills and be able to complete such tasks as sorting, packaging, assembling, collating, folding and sealing envelopes, making beds, etc., he will only be placed in a workshop situation if he has good work habits. Emphasis must be placed on teaching social skills in combination with prevocational skills. Common problems which exist and need to be reduced include out-of-seat behavior, exhibiting loud noises or mouthing of self or materials, self-stimulatory or abusive behaviors, and refusing to work. (See Hill, 1982 for behavior management strategies for eliminating these inappropriate behaviors.)

Leisure Skills
The importance of including leisure and recreational skills in multiply handicapped students' individualized education programs is increasingly becoming recognized. Teachers should balance instruction in traditional curriculum domains with an equal emphasis on teaching students to use their leisure time efficiently and enjoyably. Programming in this area will enable youth in this population to participate constructively in activities during breaks in routine ("down time"), thereby reducing the need for intense supervision (Wuerch & Voeltz, 1982).

A leisure time activities program should be planned jointly with the family or primary care-givers so that the specific activities selected reflect the values and interests of the home. The teacher should insure that the materials used by the student in school will be made available in the home or group residence (Voeltz & Wuerch, 1981). In addition to the family, a team consisting of a recreation specialist, teacher, adaptive physical education person, and perhaps a staff member from a community-based recreation program should be involved in determining appropriate leisure time activities for each student. All must work cooperatively

to assure that the skills can be learned across settings and will be applicable throughout the individual's lifetime. Provisions must be made for the multiply handicapped student to acquire leisure skills with nonhandicapped students whenever possible (Ford, Brown, Pumpian, Baumgart, Schroeder, & Loomis, 1981).

Since many multiply handicapped students are unable to express their likes and dislikes because of their disabilities and limitations in communication, the team, and particularly the teacher, must introduce several activities to determine the student's

preferences. Teaching a multiply handicapped individual to make choices and to indicate his preferences is extremely important and is too often overlooked in educational programs. The teacher must look for response cues such as whether the student moves toward or away from the materials, whether he smiles or frowns when the material moves, or whether he attends for a brief moment or shows no interest at all. These responses vary from student to student and the teachers must be astute in interpreting their meanings (Wuerch & Voeltz, 1982).

Regardless of functioning level, the multiply handicapped student needs to be provided with a variety of age-appropriate materials. Applying the normalization principle, there is a greater likelihood that he will acquire higher level social skills and be perceived as more competent by others than if he were given to the reactivity of the materials (Granger & Wehman, 1979). Toys or games that have their own reinforcing characteristics such as lighting up, making noises, producing tactile sensations, or moving when manipulated are likely to hold the student's interest and facilitate independent play.

TEAM APPROACH TO SERVING MULTIPLY HANDICAPPED STUDENTS

Numerous disciplines must be involved in the ongoing assessment, management, and programming for multiply handicapped students. Since they have a wide diversity of disabilities, no single profession can meet all their complex needs. A typical team for this population includes an educator, parent or residence manager, paraprofessional aide, physician, occupational, physical, and speech and language therapists, behavioral psychologist, and social worker.

There are three types of team approaches: the multidisciplinary, the interdisciplinary, and the transdisciplinary model. In the multidisciplinary team model approach, each member of the team sees the child individually and then sends a recommendation to the classroom teacher. There is no interaction among the various disciplines. In the interdisciplinary model, each member sees the child individually; however, they discuss their findings in a group and make one set of recommendations which frequently lack consideration of the student's school and home environment or scheduling and program coordination difficulties. In both of these approaches, there is a lack of sufficient follow-up or communication among the disciplines (Hart, 1977).

The transdisciplinary model is truly an integrated team approach which is highly recommended in the field today. The major advantage is its emphasis on sharing among team members. Traditional rigidity of discipline boundaries are broken and members trade skills and learn from one another. Accountability is built into the model through frequent staff meetings and in-service training across skill categories (Haring & Billingsley, 1984; Sirvis, 1978). While the teacher and the family are more directly involved in implementing the team's recommendations, individual members do interact and relate directly with each multiply handicapped child.

The teacher of severely multiply handicapped students has a broader role than that of a typical teacher of visually handicapped students. As the major recipient of the team's cross-disciplinary skill sharing, he has to teach not only his students, but their parents or primary caregivers as well. In addition, he serves as the educational consultant to the other members of the team and must be skilled in working cooperatively with others (Haring & Billingsley, 1984).

SERVICE DELIVERY MODELS FOR MULTIPLY HANDICAPPED STUDENTS

There is great variation in the service delivery models used to provide educational services to visually handicapped students with severe multiple impairments. The Education for All Handicapped Children's Act, P.L. 94-142, has made it possible for many students in this population to move from institutions and private schools to public school programs (Turnbull, 1983). Regardless of the label given to a child, e.g., deaf-blind or mentally retarded-blind, factors such as the available appropriate placement in a community or state, or the type of initial referrral agency or person will largely determine the selection of an educational program. A child with a visual handicap combined with a severe motor impairment and retardation can be placed appropriately in several settings. Administrators of any program should organize service delivery systems to assure that multiply handicapped students acquire functional, age-appropriate skills that enable them to participate to the fullest extent possible in integrated community and school environments (Brown, Branston, Hamre-Nietupski, Pumpian, Certo & Grunewald, 1979).

Hierarchy of service options offered range from the most integrated model to the most segregated model as described in Chapter 13. Those typically used for severely multiply handicapped students include:

A. Special Day Schools—Visually handicapped students with multiple impairments are enrolled in a special day class or school conducted by local education agencies (LEAs) or state education agencies (SEAs). In some communities, agencies such as United Cerebral Palsy or the National Association for Retarded Citizens operate such programs. The success of this alternative is related to the number of interdisciplinary team members available on a regular basis such as physical, speech, and occupational therapists working with the teacher to plan and implement the student programs together (Sirvis, 1978).

B. Hospital or Domiciled Settings—Extremely low functioning visually handicapped individuals with severe and profound multiple impairments who need medical care as well as programming for 24 hours a day are placed in this setting. These facilities, frequently called developmental centers, are often operated by health and welfare agencies.

C. Homebound Instruction—Teachers, social workers or appropriate team members provide instruction to the visually handicapped student with multiple impairments and to the parents in the home to help them work with their child. This type of service delivery should be temporary until an appropriate least restrictive environment is provided. It is particularly valuable for serving preschoolers and it is sometimes used in combination with programs in a special day setting as a support for families.

D. Regional Deaf-Blind Center—This specific service delivery model was established as a result of the sudden increase in the deaf-blind population due to the rubella epidemic in the sixties. Since many children would have been inappropriately referred to institutions for retarded individuals because no programs were available on the local level to meet their special needs, the federal government funded ten centers across the country to provide deaf-blind children with comprehensive diagnostic and evaluative services, a program for adjustment, orientation, and education utilizing a variety of professional and allied services, and consultative services for parents, teachers, and others involved in the lives of these children (U.S. Office of Education, 1975, p. 7415).

Most states, with the assistance of the regional centers, have developed their own resources to meet the educational needs of this population. In 1983, the U.S. Department of Education funded six regional centers to provide technical assistance to the states in developing and supervising deaf-blind programs and provide funds for direct services to deaf-blind children (birth to 21) within each state (American Foundation for the Blind, 1984).

Among the varying types of alternative living arrangements for visually handicapped and multiply impaired children and adults are:

A. Foster Family Care Home—Families take one or more handicapped children into their home to live as a member of the family.

B. Group Homes—A group home is usually a large, single family home where 6-15 handicapped individuals live under the supervision of houseparents. The degree of supervision and training in a group home depends upon the severity of the handicaps of the clients.

C. Residential Schools—Living arrangements may vary. Separate staffs are responsible for supervising residential and educational portions of the program.

D. Institutions—This largest type of residential facility often provides services in a single setting. Residents typically spend their entire day on the grounds of the institution, although they may participate in recreational or educational programs outside the building in which they reside. Living arrangements in institutions typically are organized on a ward basis with sleeping areas and dayrooms for every 20 to 30 individuals. This model is changing as federal guidelines for funding impose standards that require more homelike environments (Meyen, 1982).

E. Community Residential Facilities—The number and variety of small community residential living alternatives has been expanding rapidly since 1970 (Bruinink, Hauber, & Kudla, 1980; Guldager, & Hamill, McGlamery, 1983). These settings provide the needed institutional care required by severely multiply handicapped persons within a smaller setting.

Study questions

1. Visit two service delivery models for students with multiple impairments. Identify pupils with visual impairments. Talk to the teacher about special services they are receiving for the visual impairment.

2. Select a visually handicapped/multiply handicapped student and discuss the effects of the multiple impairments on his development in the following areas: A. Motor (gross and fine); B. Cognitive; C. Communication; D. Self-Help; E. Social Skills.

3. Attend a staff discussion of a team for a visually handicapped student with multiple impairments and prepare a summary report including the recommendations made by each of the team members. Identify the particular type of team approach utilized.

4. Select, administer, score, and interpret a normed or criterion-referenced test typically given to a visually handicapped/multiply handicapped student functioning on Piaget's sensorimotor period of development. What skill areas in object permanence, imitation, causality has he reached? How would you evaluate his skills in attending, imitation and functional use of objects?

5. Develop two age-appropriate behavioral objectives for an adolescent visually handicapped/multiply handicapped student in each of the following skill areas: A. Motor; B. Cognitive; C. Communication; D. Self-help; E. Social Skills; F. Prevocational; and G. Leisure Education.

6. Develop a vertical task analysis for a leisure skill you would teach to a visually handicapped/multiply handicapped student. Develop both forward and backward chaining sequences for teaching a specific self-help skill.

7. Design a sequential instructional program in the area of communication for a visually handicapped/multiply handicapped student, utilizing Van Dijk's principles.

8. Review catalogs from commercial sources and identify five different materials you could use to teach a visually handicapped/multiply handicapped student. Include the particular type of impairments for which the material would be appropriate and the relevant skill area(s).

9. Develop a sequence for teaching a self-help or prevocational skill to a visually handicapped/multiply handicapped student. Include appropriate positioning and handling techniques as well as shaping, fading, and prompting in your program.

Additional readings

Bigge, J. (1982). *Teaching individuals with physical and multiple disabilities.* Columbus, Ohio: Charles E. Merrill Publishing Co.

Finnie, N.R. (1975). *Handling the young cerebral palsied child at home.* New York, N.Y.: E.P. Dutton.

Fredericks, H.B., Baldwin, V.C., Grove, D.N., and Moore, W.G. (1975). *Toilet training the handicapped child.* Monmouth, Oreg.: Instructional Development.

Greer, J.G., Anderson, R.M., and Odle, S.J. (1982). *Strategies for helping severely and multiply handicapped citizens.* Baltimore, Md.: University Park Press.

Gruber, K. and Moor, Pauline. (1963). *No place to go.* New York, N.Y.: American Foundation for the Blind, Inc.

Guldager, V. (1970). *Body image and the severely handicapped rubella child.* Publication No. 27. Watertown, Mass.: Perkins School for the Blind.

Hill, B.K. and Bruininks, R.H. (1981). *Physical and behavioral characteristics and maladaptive behavior of mentally retarded people in residential facilities.* Minneapolis, Minn.: University of Minnesota, Department of Psychoeducational Studies.

Kibler, R.J., Cegala, D.J., Miles, D.T., and Barker, L.L. (1974). *Objectives for instruction and evaluation.* Boston, Mass.: Allyn and Bacon Inc.

Lynch, K.P., Kiernan, W.E., and Stark, J.A. (eds.)(1982). *Prevocational and vocational education for special needs youth.* Baltimore, Md.: Paul H. Brookes.

Mager, R.F. (1962). *Preparing instructional objectives.* Palo Alto, Calif.: Fearon Publishers, Inc.

Mangold, S. (1982). *A teacher's guide to the special educational needs of blind and visually handicapped children.* New York, N.Y.: American Foundation for the Blind, Inc.

McInnes, J.M. and Treffry, J.A. (1982). *Deaf-blind infants and children: A development guide.* Toronto: University of Toronto Press.

Moores, D. (1974). Nonvocal systems of verbal behavior. In R. Schiefelbusch and L. Lloyd (eds.) *Language perspectives—Acquisition, retardation, and intervention.* Baltimore, Md.: University Park Press.

Robinson, C. and Robinson, J.H. (1983). Sensorimotor functions and cognitive development. In M. Snell (ed.) *Systematic instruction of the moderately and severely handicapped,* 2nd edition. Columbus, Ohio: Charles E. Merrill Publishing Company.

Schreerenberger, R.C. (1976). *Managing residential facilities for the developmentally disabled.* Springfield, Ill.: Charles C Thomas.

Utley, B., Holvoet, J., and Barnes, K. (1977). Handling positioning and feeding the physically handicapped. In E. Sontag, J. Smith and N. Certo (eds.) *Educational programming for severely and profoundly handicapped.* Reston, Va.: Council for Exceptional Children.

Van Dijk, J. (1982). *Rubella handicapped children.* Lisse, The Netherlands: Swets & Zeitlinger.

Walsh, S.R. and Holzberg, R. (1981). *Understanding and educating the deaf-blind/severely handicapped.* Springfield, Ill.: Charles C Thomas.

CHAPTER 10

Multicultural Considerations

Geraldine T. Scholl

This chapter summarizes the broad range of cultural differences and socioeconomic and regional variations found among the school population and discusses implications of these multicultural characteristics for the development and implementation of appropriate individualized education programs for visually handicapped children and youth. Suggestions to help teachers become sensitive to these variations are also included.

Attention of educators in recent years has focused on the need for teachers to know and be sensitive to the diverse multicultural needs of children within the school setting. The purpose of this chapter is to present background information that will assist prospective teachers of visually handicapped pupils in adopting a multicultural approach. The chapter is organized around three general principles.

The first part briefly summarizes statistics on cultural variations and socioeconomic and regional characteristics that may be found in the U.S. school population. This part draws primarily on information available about the regular school population since, as noted in Chapter 2, there is limited information about these characteristics among the blind and visually handicapped population.

The second part is designed to give teachers an understanding and appreciation of the variations that children from the various subcultures may evidence and the implications of these multicultural characteristics for education, especially as they are related to planning and implementing individualized education programs.

The third part suggests guidelines to assist teachers in developing a multicultural approach to meet the special educational needs of blind and visually handicapped pupils with diverse backgrounds.

MINORITIES: WHO ARE THEY?

Teachers must have knowledge about the diverse backgrounds of the children they teach (Smitherman, 1981).

Pupils bring to the school setting varying needs derived from their diverse family and cultural backgrounds. Their families are of different racial, ethnic, and religious affiliations; they represent the wide spectrum of socioeconomic differences; and the geographical location of their home communities introduces regional variables, all of which have an impact on the educational needs of the pupils and how these needs may be most effectively met within the school program. Because these characteristics are considered atypical compared with the total population, these groups are sometimes referred to as "minorities." It should be noted, however, that any majority may become a minority under certain circumstances, e.g., Caucasian pupils attending a school with a 75 percent Black population.

Identification of minority groups by race or racial characteristics, or ethnicity, or religious affiliation has limited usefulness when discussing multicultural characteristics in the school-age population because the dividing lines between and among them are blurred. For example, the U.S. census and affirmative action guidelines list Hispanics as a racial minority; in reality they are an ethnic group with several distinct cultural subgroups; Judaism is considered by some an ethnic group, by others a religion and/or culture; classification by race, scientifically speaking, is useful primarily when discussing some distinctive physical characteristic, such as the high prevalence of sickle cell anemia among Blacks. The boundaries of racial, ethnic, and religious groupings are not generally coterminous. The concern in this chapter is not with physical variation, but with the kind of "cultural differences" that distinguish various populations, be they ethnic, religious, regional, or other.

The general information about cultural minority groups in the United States summarized in this part should help sensitize teachers to the broad range of cultural differences that may have an impact on the educational needs of those visually handicapped children and youth who are found among these groups.

Cultural Differences

Immigration into the U.S. was frequently determined, not by the motivation of the immigrants themselves to leave their homelands but rather by external factors in the country of their birth as well as in the U.S. Political factors within the U.S. played a special role in the process and some of these factors will be reviewed first.

Concern about the cultural backgrounds of certain immigrants, changing economic and political conditions in the United States, and the lack of a consistent U.S. immigration policy have had considerable influence on the ebb and flow of immigrants. Until the latter part of the nineteenth century, immigration was largely unrestricted during the time when the country was expanding westward and workers were needed. Large numbers immigrated as a result of famine, poverty, and religious and political oppression in their own countries. In addition, changing economic conditions in the U.S. following the Civil War, and the gradually closing frontier stimulated the passage of the first federal immigration legislation in 1875 which excluded convicts and prostitutes and in 1882 was expanded to include lunatics, idiots, and persons unable to take care of themselves without becoming public charges (Abrams, 1982). The Chinese, and later the Japanese, were specifically excluded partly because of concern about their large numbers in California (Abrams, 1982; Higham, 1956; Martin & Houstoun, 1982). It was not until 1943 that the Chinese Exclusion Act was repealed so that refugees, displaced persons, and war brides/grooms could enter (Abrams, 1982).

The quota system established in 1921 was designed to preserve the Anglo-Saxon nature of this country by giving preference to immigrants from European nations. Concern about the large numbers from less affluent and culturally different nations from the eastern hemisphere, combined with depressed economic conditions, resulted in the passage of the 1952 McCarran-Walter Act which retained a quota system for the eastern hemisphere but allowed unrestricted immigration from the western hemisphere. In 1965 separate limits for eastern and western hemispheres were established and in 1978 these were combined into one worldwide quota (Abrams, 1982). Thus, until 1965, immigration from countries in the Western Hemisphere was unrestricted so that many Mexicans immigrated to the Southwest and Chicago; French Canadians to New England; and Cubans and residents of other Carribean Islands to the southeast (Abrams, 1982). It should be noted that exemptions to the quota were made for those who had

relatives in the U.S., and legislation increasingly gave priority to the reunion of families.

The plight of persons in Europe, particularly Hungary, and Asia, who sustained political and religious oppression and internal upheavals resulted in passage of the Refugee Relief Act in 1953 which admitted those seeking asylum because of political difficulties. The 1980 Refugee Act allowed immigration of refugees who suffered or feared persecution in their own countries to an upper limit of 50,000 annually, although the President can increase those numbers (Abrams, 1982; Stepick, 1982). It is the interpretation of the Haitians' situation which has raised questions about their acceptance, that is, are they truly refugees as defined by the United Nations or are they seeking asylum because of depressed economic conditions in their own country.

The immigration of various groups will be described against this brief summary of the changing conditions in the U.S. There is little question that the U.S. is a nation of immigrants, and it may be useful to know some of the reasons and periods that brought our forefathers here. Various groups came at different times and for different reasons. Even Native Americans may have been immigrants from Asia by way of Alaska 11,000 to 12,000 years ago (Claiborne, 1973). The Spanish settled in the southeast and southwest early in the sixteenth century at about the same time as the English, Dutch, French and Portuguese settled on the east coast. The settlement on the east coast will be traced first because these immigrants played an initial role in the formation of the U.S. as a nation.

Because most of these early settlers on the northeast coast were from England, English became the dominant language (Martin & Houstoun, 1982). During the colonial years, immigrants were welcomed because the colonies were expanding westward. Early Germans, Poles, and Italians arrived during the colonial years but came in greater numbers during the latter part of the nineteenth century, partly because of the unrest, poverty, and other problems in their home countries. The Irish came during the mid-nineteenth century primarily because of a severe famine in Ireland; Scotch-Irish because of religious restrictions; Germans because of political and religious oppression; and Poles because of political upheavals (Cordasco, 1981; Fuchs, 1956; Krolikowski, 1981; Seller, 1982).

The first Jews, primarily of Spanish, Portuguese, and Dutch origins, came in the seventeenth century. They were later joined by Jews of German origin in the latter part of the eighteenth and early part of the nineteenth centuries. Prior to World War I, Jews came from Poland and Russia fleeing persecution (Greeley, 1972; Seller, 1982). Today, Jews may be found in all parts of the United States and represent a variety of national groups.

Blacks came primarily from West Africa as involuntary immigrants (Bronfenbrenner, 1982). They were captured or purchased from their native tribes and transported to Colonial America to be slaves. This slave trade continued until 1808 when it was prohibited by federal law (Higham, 1956). Until the War Between the States, Blacks were found primarily in the south where they worked on the farms and plantations. During the war, some found their way north as far as Canada through the underground railroad system. Following the Emancipation Proclamation on January 1, 1863, when all slaves became free, more migrated to the north where they found employment in factories.

The Spaniards settled in Mexico and the southwest during the colonial period. Many of these early settlers intermarried with Native Americans. Later, other migrations occurred, primarily from Mexico and Central and South America. Residents of Puerto Rico came to escape poverty and unemployment; Cubans began arriving in large numbers in the mid-twentieth century for political reasons. Of the approximately 12 million Hispanics living in the United States in 1978, 60 percent were of Mexican origin, 15 percent were of Puerto Rican background, 5 percent were from Cuba, and the remaining 20 percent were of other Hispanic origin, e.g., Latin America and Spain (Melendez, Melendez, & Molina, 1981). Definitions of "Hispanic" vary: those who speak Spanish, who were born or whose parents were born in Spain or Latin America, whose surnames are Spanish or who identify themselves as Hispanics.

Today there is considerable variation among the Hispanic population relative to place of residence. Mexican-Americans, or Chicanos, are more often found in the southwest in such areas as Albuquerque and Los Angeles; those with Cuban background, in the southeast, particularly around Miami; and those of Puerto Rican background in the the northeast, particularly in New York. However, all three groups may be found in smaller numbers in other parts of the United States. The culture and customs of these three Hispanic groups differ and they tend to refer to themselves as Mexican American (or Chicano or Latino), Puerto Rican, or Cuban, rather than as Hispanic (Advertising Age, 1985).

Asians arrived in the United States in the early 1800s (Yao, 1983). The Chinese came during the gold rush and worked on building the transcontinental railroad. When their numbers increased dramatically in California following completion of the railroad, federal legislation, the Chinese Exclusion Act, was passed in 1882 to exclude them from entrance into this country (Abrams, 1982; Higham, 1956; Martin & Houstoun, 1982). This was expanded to include the Japanese in 1907 (Abrams, 1982). The Japanese came in the latter part of the nineteenth century, imported

for agricultural and construction work. Further declines in the numbers of immigrants from Asia in general beginning after World War I were due primarily to the federal immigration quota legislation passed in 1921 (Abrams, 1982; Jaffe, 1956; Smith, 1982; Spengler, 1956). The collapse of the governments of Laos, Korea, South Vietnam, and Cambodia in the mid-1970s, resulted in a large influx of Asian refugees, particularly to California, Texas, and New York (Dearman & Plisko, 1980).

In the latter part of the nineteenth and early twentieth centuries, immigrants arrived from southern and eastern Europe: Italy, Greece, the Slavic nations, Russia, Roumania, and the Arab world, primarily Lebanon and Syria (Al-Quazzaz, 1975; Higham, 1956).

Later, immigration of these groups too was restricted since the early immigration laws fixed quotas which favored the Northern European and discriminated against the Slavic, Mediterranean, and Jewish people (Jaffe, 1956).

At the present time the United States is receiving more immigrants than at any previous time in the history of the country and more than any other country (Abrams, 1982; Hofstaetter, 1982). Most of these immigrants are from the Third World: Latin America and particularly large numbers from Asia and the Caribbean. Those among the recent immigrants who have a better education fare better than the less well-educated (Waldinger, 1982). A continuing problem is dealing with the undocumented newcomers, of whom there are an estimated three to six million (Corwin, 1982; Smith, 1982).

Attempts were made to assimilate the children of the early immigrants into the American culture through the public school system; many were eager to adopt American ways and to discard the language of their parents and their cultural heritage. The United States became known as the "Melting Pot." Many nineteenth and early twentieth century immigrants were not greeted warmly by the resident population partly because of economic depression and World Wars I and II hysteria directed toward certain groups. As a result, many suffered discrimination. Today, following the consciousness-raising of the 1960s, there is increasing emphasis on bilingual education programs and cultural pluralism wherein diversity is encouraged (Jaffe, 1956; Myers, 1981).

Some groups have resisted assimilation into the mainstream culture. Although three-fourths of Mexican American males are born in this country, almost all have been raised in Spanish-speaking homes and tend to resist Americanization (Bronfenbrenner, 1982). Many newcomers intend to return to their homelands at some later date. Arab immigrants prior to World War II, for example, did not intend to remain in this country and resisted learning English, which isolated them from the mainstream culture (Elkholy, 1974). Following their expulsion from Nova Scotia in the mid-1700s, the Louisiana Cajuns ultimately settled in southwest Louisiana where they have retained aspects of their culture and language. In 1968, after two centuries of struggle to have the French language recognized, the state legislature created the Council for the Development of French in Louisiana to meet the concerns of one-fourth of that state's population who speak some form of this language (Green, 1981).

The preceding summary illustrates the diverse ethnic heritage of people in the United States. In 1979 there were nearly 10 million persons living in the United States who were born in a foreign country (Bronfenbrenner, 1982). Almost all who have come to this country have sustained some discrimination and rejection by the resident population to a greater or lesser degree. Although a few groups continue to resist intermarriage and thus retain a single national background, most persons in the U.S. today can claim ancestors from two or more nations.

The United States is, likewise, a nation of numerous and diverse religions. There is no state religion as there is in some countries. For example, the Church of England is the state religion of England. Many of the early English settlers sought religious freedom which they did not have in their native countries. However, often they brought with them intolerance for religions other than their own (Greeley & Rossi, 1972). Protestantism was the dominant religion during the Colonial period but Catholics were the majority in Maryland and Quakers in Pennsylvania, two colonies settled primarily by these religious groups (Gaustad, 1968).

Irish, German, Polish, and Italian immigrants increased the numbers of Catholics so that by 1850 Catholicism became the largest single religious group (Gaustad, 1968). Many among these immigrants retained their ethnic identification through their religious affiliation and this enabled them to adapt more easily to their new country (Greeley & Rossi, 1972).

Religion in the United States has been characterized as denominational pluralism (Greeley & Rossi, 1972; Wilson, 1968). Different groups of immigrants brought with them varying religions from their native lands. This led to a proliferation of sub-groups among the established religions. For example, there are three major subgroups among Lutherans: American Lutheran Church, Lutheran Church in America, and Lutheran Church-Missouri Synod (Gaustad, 1968). Catholicism holds different meanings for Irish, German, Italian, and Polish members as well as for Hispanic and Asian groups. In addition to the various religions brought from other countries, several have been founded in the United States: Christian Science and the Church of Jesus Christ of Latter Day Saints, or Mormonism (Wilson, 1968).

Table 10.1 lists the stated religious affiliations of the general United States population and those of the world population. Data should be viewed with some skepticism, however. Some religions forbid numbering of members; some persons may declare more than one religion; some religions count only baptized members, primarily adults; some persons do not wish to reveal such information (Goetz, 1984; Lane, 1985). For the U.S., Protestant Church affiliations are broken down by the nine largest; "other" includes 49 smaller denominations. Of the U.S. population, 59.6 percent are reported as members of religious groups (World Almanac, 1985). Based on the estimated world population (U.S. Department of Commerce, 1983), 54.5 have some religious affiliation.

Buddhism, Hinduism, and Islam, while numerous on a world-wide basis, have been present in the United States only in insignificant numbers (Gaustad, 1968). However, there has been a recent increase in the U.S. in the number of followers of Islam, the second largest and most recent of the monotheistic religions on a world-wide basis (Sefein, 1981).

Data regarding numbers of minorities are lacking; as noted above, data reported on religious affiliations have numerous limitations. There are, however, some data regarding numbers of minority pupils in school. Table 10.2 lists the total public school enrollment in the fall of 1982 as reported by the Council of Great City Schools (Casserly, 1983). These 32 schools include 11 percent of the total national public school enrollment; 29.2 percent of the minority school population; and 10.9 percent of the special education students. These data do not include pupils enrolled in private schools nor those from smaller cities and rural areas.

Blacks account for approximately 12 percent of the total population in the United States (Williams, 1983) and approximately 15-16 percent of the public school population under the age of 18 (Children's Defense Fund, 1982; Edelman, 1980; Grant & Eiden, 1982); but approximately 47 percent of the pupils enrolled in the

Great City Schools (Casserly, 1983). Percentages vary from 3.5 percent in Albuquerque to 94.1 percent in Washington, D.C.

The proportion of Hispanics in the Great City Schools ranges from insignificant numbers in Memphis and Nashville to almost half in Los Angeles. (Table 10.2.)

From 1970 to 1982, the proportion of children classified as Asian increased 95.3 percent in the Great City Schools and 256.5 percent on a national level (Casserly, 1983).

Native Americans and the subgroup of Inuits or Eskimos are included under the category of 'Other' in data reporting and represent the smallest minority with .8 percent of the school population on a national level (Casserly, 1983). Of the Great City Schools, the highest proportions are found in Minneapolis (5.0 percent); Seattle (2.9 percent); and Albuquerque (2.8 percent). Eskimos are found primarily in Alaska and Canada. Native Americans tend to be concentrated in those states where there are large Indian Reservations. Since the numbers living in rural areas are higher proportionately than those in urban areas, they are greatly undercounted in the data reported in Table 10.2.

There are limited data about minorities in the school age handicapped population. Except for classes for the educable mentally retarded, where disproportionate numbers of Blacks compared with whites are enrolled (Edelman, 1980), data are limited concerning the number of handicapped children from other categorical groups included in the most widely recognized minorities, namely, Blacks, Hispanics, Asian, and Others. There is some evidence, however, that the total handicapped population includes a disproportionate number of minority group members (Salend, Michael, & Taylor, 1984). Little is known about the extent to which minority groups are represented or whether their numbers are over- or underrepresented in the population labeled as "visually handicapped." Chapter 2 discussed this lack of data on numbers and demographic characteristics of visually handicapped children and youth. In two states where demographic surveys have been conducted, somewhat conflicting data are reported. (See Table 10.3.) Mississippi reported 44.6 percent of visually handicapped pupils as Black (Mann, 1984) compared with 51 percent for the state's total public school population (Plisko, 1983); however, data were missing for 6.5 percent. Nebraska reported 8 percent Black among the visually handicapped pupils (Rawlings, 1983) compared with 5.6 percent for the

Table 10.1   Stated religious affiliations of the United States and world populations.

Religion	United States [1]		World [2]	
	In Thousands	%	In Thousands	%
Total Christian	128,916	95.55	1,056,693	41.28
Roman Catholic	52,089	38.61	621,639	24.29
Eastern Orthodox	4,180	3.10	65,645	2.56
Protestant (total)	72,648	53.84	369,408	14.43
Baptist	25,815	19.13		
Methodist	12,908	9.57		
Episcopal	2,784	2.06		
Lutheran	8,498	6.30		
Pentecostal	3,182	2.36		
Presbyterian	3,458	2.56		
Church of Christ	1,605	1.19		
Mormon	3,725	2.76		
United Church of Christ	1,717	1.27		
Other	8,955	6.64		
Jewish	3,900	2.89	17,320	0.67
Muslim	2,000 (E)	1.48	555,277	21.69
Zoroastrian			246	0.00 +
Shinto			33,050	1.29
Taoist			20,563	0.80
Confucian			163,130	6.37
Buddhist	100 (E)	0.00+	250,952	9.80
Hindu			462,590	18.07
Total	134,916	99.92	2,559,821	99.97

[1] Data from *World Almanac and Book of Facts.* (New York, N.Y.: The New York World Telegraph, 1985), pp. 356-7.
[2] P.W. Goetz (ed.), *Britannica Book of the Year.* (Chicago, Ill.: Encyclopedia Britannica, Inc., 1985), p. 601.

state's total school population (Plisko, 1983). Nevertheless, these data indicate that differences do exist between states in number of minorities as well as their proportion among the school age visually handicapped population.

Socioeconomic/Regional

Families of visually handicapped children and youth share the same social characteristics that are found in the general population. However, these social characteristics may have a different impact on the child depending on the social and cultural context. In 1980, 1 in 5 children was from a one parent family, an increase of 44 percent from 1 in 7 in 1970 (Children's Defense Fund, 1982). More than half of Black children and one in four Hispanic children live in single parent families (Herbers, 1984). Additionally over half of all children have mothers in the labor force, including those from two parent families (Children's Defense Fund, 1982). In the context of an extended family system, a single parent family may not be the disadvantage it would be where the nuclear family is the norm.

There are some data concerning the economic status of minorities. They tend to have a higher rate of unemployment, to live at or below poverty level, and are less likely to be homeowners (Edelman, 1980). In 1983, one-fourth of all children under the age of six lived in families with incomes below the poverty line (Bronfenbrenner, 1984). The rate for minority children is probably higher. Nonwhites have an infant mortality rate twice that of whites; are deficient in dental care; have a higher rate of suicide; and, among children and teenagers, a 25 percent higher death rate than whites from illnesses (Edelman, 1980).

The socioeconomic status of Black pupils tends to be lower than that of white. For example, per capita income of Black families is about half that of white families (Edelman, 1980). Black middle class families constitute 30 percent of all Black families compared with 56 percent of white families, with middle class defined as $20,000 annual family income (Williams, 1983).

Because of their small numbers and thus more limited options for placement in the least restrictive environment, the delivery of services may vary for visually handicapped children and youth depending

Table 10.2   Great Cities Schools: Minority enrollment, Fall 1982

City	White		Minorities		Black		Hispanic		Asian		Other	
	N	%	N	%	N	%	N	%	N	%	N	%
Albuquerque	39,223	53.5	34,035	46.5	2,546	3.5	28,198	38.5	1,264	1.7	2,027	2.8
Atlanta	5,046	7.5	62,520	92.5	61,847	91.5	310	0.5	—	—	363	0.5
Baltimore	24,535	20.5	95,254	79.5	94,206	78.6	228	0.2	604	0.5	216	0.2
Boston	16,631	29.6	39,567	70.4	27,045	48.1	8,496	15.1	3,751	6.7	275	0.5
Buffalo	21,403	45.8	25,354	54.2	22,044	47.2	2,365	5.1	305	0.7	640	1.4
Chicago	71,171	16.3	364,672	83.7	264,530	60.7	88,746	20.4	10,715	2.5	681	0.2
Cleveland	20,498	26.5	56,879	73.5	52,808	68.8	3,190	4.1	658	0.9	223	0.3
Columbus	44,271	63.8	25,146	36.2	24,406	35.2	(220)	0.3	(490)	0.7	(30)	0.0
Dade County	64,044	28.8	158,014	71.2	69,557	31.3	86,165	38.8	2,198	1.0	94	0.0
Dallas	33,543	26.3	94,230	73.8	63,545	49.7	28,050	21.9	2,146	1.7	489	0.4
Denver	24,754	39.4	38,073	60.6	14,388	22.9	20,670	32.9	2,450	3.9	565	0.9
Detroit	22,073	10.9	180,916	89.1	176,251	86.8	3,347	1.7	826	0.4	492	0.2
Long Beach	26,734	47.4	29,679	52.6	11,573	20.5	11,978	21.2	5,787	10.3	341	0.6
Los Angeles	118,120	21.7	426,208	78.3	116,036	21.3	266,958	49.0	41,321	7.6	1,893	0.4
Memphis	24,108	22.9	81,306	77.1	81,306	77.1	—	—	—	—	—	—
Milwaukee	36,140	41.9	50,192	58.1	42,631	49.4	5,700	6.6	1,242	1.4	619	0.7
Minneapolis	26,205	65.2	13,992	34.8	8,985	22.4	578	1.4	2,407	6.0	2,022	5.0
Nashville	43,170	65.1	23,164	34.9	22,209	33.5	—	—	—	—	955	1.4
New Orleans	8,422	10.4	72,896	89.6	68,951	84.8	1,204	1.5	2,716	3.3	25	0.0
New York City	239,496	25.9	684,719	74.1	356,441	38.6	286,173	31.1	40,626	4.4	479	0.1
Norfolk	13,246	37.0	22,630	63.2	21,141	59.0	294	0.8	1,158	3.2	37	0.1
Oakland	5,868	12.2	42,396	87.8	31,120	64.5	5,184	10.7	5,741	11.9	351	0.7
Omaha	29,229	69.2	13,041	30.9	11,122	26.3	1,033	2.4	477	1.1	409	1.0
Philadelphia	55,691	26.8	152,091	73.2	130,803	63.0	16,648	8.0	4,449	2.1	191	0.1
Pittsburgh	20,245	47.9	22,007	52.1	21,662	51.3	(80)	0.2	(260)	0.6	(5)	0.0
Portland	37,311	72.9	13,858	27.1	7,756	15.2	983	1.9	4,238	8.3	881	1.7
Rochester	12,455	36.5	21,410	62.8	17,005	49.9	3,599	10.6	636	1.9	170	0.5
St. Louis	11,249	20.0	45,085	80.0	44,624	79.2	120	0.2	303	0.5	38	0.1
San Francisco	10,143	16.8	50,091	83.2	13,789	22.9	10,328	17.2	25,630	42.6	344	0.6
Seattle	23,377	51.5	22,035	48.5	10,445	23.0	1,986	4.4	8,277	18.2	1,327	2.9
Toledo	26,308	60.3	17,321	39.7	14,968	34.3	1,972	4.5	329	0.8	52	0.1
Washington, DC	3,221	3.5	88,607	96.5	86,368	94.1	1,538	1.7	655	0.7	46	0.1
Council Totals	1,157,513		3,065,570		1,990,479		887,252		171,561		16,278	

Table 10.3   Cultural background of visually handicapped pupils in two states

	White		Black		Hispanic		Other		Not Reported	
	N	%	N	%	N	%	N	%	N	%
Mississippi (Mann, 1984)	215	46.7	205	44.6	1	.2	—	—	39	6.5
Nebraska (Rawlings, 1983)	268	88.0	25	8.0	6	2.0	5	2.0	—	—

on their place of residence. Geographical variations have a great impact on the delivery of services to visually handicapped children and youth because they are a low prevalence categorical group with distinct educational needs that require qualified educational personnel in order to insure their appropriate education. Although P.L. 94-142, the Education of All Handicapped Children Act of 1975, mandates that a continuum of services be made available to every handicapped child, this may not be realistic for children who live in rural or remote areas. Helge (1984b) estimates that 67 percent of all school districts are classified as rural, that is, having a population of less than 150 per square mile or communites of less than 5,000 people. Some of these communities may also be classifed as remote, that is, geographically separated from other communities; or isolated, such as located on islands, mountaintops, or other rugged geographical or climatic regions. Most states west of the Mississippi have some school districts that are classified as rural or remote (Scott, 1984). Rural school districts tend to have higher poverty levels, greater percentages of handicapped children, higher costs for education, lower tax bases, but allocate greater percentages of their resources to education (Helge, 1984b). Many rural communities include diverse subcultural groups and some include populations that tend to be transient.

Illustrative of an identifiable rural minority group are the people who reside in the Appalachian mountains that stretch from upper New York to northern Georgia. Although they share certain characteristics with the majority of American culture—white, Anglo-Saxon, and Protestant—they have been called "the most neglected of minority groups" (Porter, 1981, p. 14). Many have been forced from their home states to seek employment in urban industrial cities in the north where their children are at a disadvantage because they are not of the middle class and they lack many experiences that are essential for school success. English is their native language, but in reality, like some Black children, they speak two languages: that of the mainstream culture and that of the mountains. In addition, many families move back and forth between the industrial city and their former homes which adds further to a disruptive school experience.

The Visually Handicapped Population

As noted in Chapter 2, little is known about the demographic characteristics of the visually handicapped population. Variations in racial, ethnic, and religious background and in social, economic, and regional characteristics, however, are assumed to be present among families of visually handicapped children and youth. There are limited data concerning whether there is a high prevalence rate for visual impairments in racial, ethnic, and socioeconomic groups. Kahn and Moorhead (1973) conclude in their study of data from the Model Reporting Area for 1970 that rates for nonwhites are higher than for whites; that except for glaucoma, diabetic retinopathy, and optic nerve disease, all found in adults, causes of visual impairments are similar for whites and nonwhites. From their review of three data bases that included children and youth: the Health Interview Survey for 1977, Model Reporting Area data for 1970, and the Health and Nutrition Examination Survey (HANES) 1971-72, Kirchner and Peterson (1985) also concluded that the prevalence rate for nonwhites was higher than for whites. Data for specific minority groups were available for adults only in the HANES data base. Based on work with visually handicapped persons in the southwest, Winkley (1971) noted a high prevalence of ptergium among the Hispanic population. (Ptergium is a fleshy nodule encroaching onto the cornea which can be removed surgically). It is found in areas where people spend most of the day outdoors exposed to sun and sand or dust (Vaughan, Cook, & Asbury, 1982). It would appear that, with a few exceptions, the etiology of visual impairments is similar, but that the rates for nonwhites are higher than for whites.

Some of the differences that may be present among these various groups are discussed in the following part.

IMPLICATIONS OF CULTURAL DIVERSITY

The cultural background of all students should be understood, accepted, and respected (Webb, n.d.). Behavior can be misinterpreted if the culture of the child is not known and understood (Peterson, 1983).

All children bring their own language, culture, and customs, which include different attitudes toward education and toward handicapping conditions, any one of which may have an impact on the child's learning, behavior, and progress in school. This part points out some of these differences, many of which cut across more than one minority group described in the preceding part, and how they may have an impact on the child's learning and behavior.

It should be stressed that while there are similarities among those who have a similar background, there are also differences within each group. For example, culture and customs vary among the various tribes of Native Americans. Estimates of the number of different tribes range from 100 (National Advisory Council on the Education of Disadvantaged Children, n.d.) to 500 (Chiago, 1981), each with separate and distinct cultures and languages. Thus, it is not sufficient to identify a child as Native American; teachers must also be aware of tribal and/or regional identifications. In spite of their common language, the three major Hispanic cultures reflect major differences in ethnicity, social class, and cultural identity (Melendez et al, 1981). Teachers cannot assume that a Spanish speaking child is of Mexican, or Puerto Rican, or Cuban heritage.

Similarly, 'Asian' includes a number of distinct groups, each with a different language, varied social and economic backgrounds brought from their native countries, and different experiences in this country. For example, the nineteenth century Japanese immigrants were from middle class agricultural backgrounds where education was highly valued. Although they met with considerable discrimination and prejudice in this country, they gained a reputation for their industrious nature and high achievement in education (Endo & Della-Piana, 1981). In contrast, nineteenth century Chinese immigrants came from a background of hardship in their homeland which included famine, floods, and rebellion; they came as laborers to work on the transcontinental railroad, but when that was completed, they were subjected to considerable discrimination (Kang-Ning, 1981). In recent years, the early immigrants from Vietnam tended to be from the educated professional/ managerial class whereas the

later waves included those who were less well-educated (Kang-Ning, 1981). The Vietnamese children, in particular, bring with them a history of disruptive school experiences from their own country which contribute to difficulties in learning and adjusting to school in this country (Kang-Ning, 1981).

Assumptions based on the socioeconomic status of minority groups cannot be applied to all members of these groups. For example, although in general Blacks may be over-represented in the lower socioeconomic classes, one in three families is considered middle class. In one school district the teacher of a Black middle school boy assumed that he qualifed for the free lunch program; in reality, his mother is a middle level school administrator and his father a university professor. These illustrations emphasize the risk of generalizing and making assumptions based on the particular cultural background of a specific child.

Each community also has its own ethnic characteristics. In some large cities there are pockets of subcultural groups living in close proximity; in other communities, they are dispersed but may be held together by a common religious heritage and affiliation; in still others, they may be integrated within the total community culture. Thus teachers must be aware of not only the multicultural characteristics of the students they teach but also the multicultural characteristics of the community.

This part discusses five major topics: differences in language, in customs, in attitudes, and in place of residence. The final section discusses some social problems that are also important to consider in educational planning.

Language

The language difference found in some minority pupils may be a very critical factor in their school achievement and more particularly in the process of assessment. Academic achievement is hindered by limited knowledge of the language spoken in the school setting. Thus, there is a need for bilingual education for these non-English speaking children. An estimated 20 percent of the population in the United States are nonnative speakers of English (Martinez, 1981). In communities where bilingual programs are available, however, handicapped children are often not included (Cantres, 1981) and thus may have an additional barrier to their right to an equal educational opportunity. Sometimes the language problem presents a greater handicap to school achievement than the child's visual impairment (Gavillan-Torres, 1981).

The provision of effective bilingual educational programs for handicapped children is hindered by several problems. There is a critical need for qualified professionals who are committed to encouraging mainstreaming and integration of the bilingual program into the ongoing educational curriculum of the school district (Ortiz, 1981). Some bilingually trained teachers find difficulty in functioning as advocates on behalf of the pupils involved as they move into the regular classroom (Peterson, 1983). Bilingual education is complicated by the many different languages and dialects, about which knowledge is either lacking

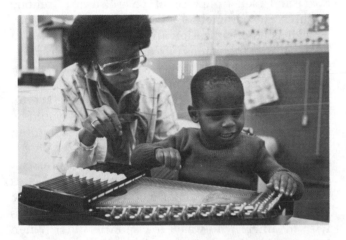

or inadequate, for educators to plan appropriate programs particularly among the Spanish speaking pupils (Gavillan-Torres, 1981). The Spanish spoken by the child with a Puerto Rican background differs from that spoken by the child from a Mexican background. Finally, in some areas, there are so many languages spoken that provision of bilingual education for all creates logistical problems. For example, school officials in the state of Florida estimate that children in their schools speak 50 different languages. In the schools of Chicago there are 75. With increasing populations of new immigrants from Africa and Asia, there is an ever increasing number of languages and dialects being brought to the schools (Nancy Thomas, personal communication, January 1986). It should also be noted that there is no universal agreement that bilingual education is totally beneficial to the children involved.

Minorities in general and bilingual children in particular are disadvantaged especially in assessment. Educators face problems in implementing the requirements of P.L. 94-142 regarding nondiscriminatory testing (DHEW, 1977, 121a. 531). Williams (1978) identifies causal factors in four areas related to multicultural assessment: tests are constructed with little or no consideration given to the diverse cultural backgrounds and sets of experiences among the children in schools today and are standardized on the white majority population; school administrators who purchase the tests seek an easy way to label and sort students into categories for administrative expediency without regard to the weaknesses of the test instruments; school psychologists often have limited knowledge about test construction, including appro-

priate procedures for determining test validity, reliability, and standardization and thus they tend to administer and interpret their results in light of the majority culture with little regard for those within the school district who are not of the majority culture; and finally the students to whom the tests are administered are often misidentified as low achievers and thus misplaced in the educational setting.

Several solutions are proposed for nondiscriminatory assessment including development of special tests for minority groups; modification of existing tests; use of nontest-based procedures; interpretation of tests taking into account cultural factors. The diversity of cultures makes the development of culture-specific tests difficult; tests would need to be developed for innumerable cultures and subcultures in order to be fair to each specific group (Tucker, 1976). Typical procedures for modification of tests and other assessment instruments include the exclusive use of nonverbal tests, translated tests, and development and use of local norms (Weffer, 1981), all of which may be inappropriate procedures for some minority children. Alternative assessment strategies include: observation; rating scales; use of selected subtests of typically used instruments; trial teaching; using the test as a means of teaching the task; and task analysis (Aliotti, 1977). These informal means of assessment are discussed in Chapter 11.

To interpret results of standardized tests accurately for different cultural groups, Weffer (1981) recommends a case study approach that takes into account the difficulties of children learning and using two languages and their "different degrees of bilingualism, biculturalism, acculturation and different socioeconomic levels" (p. 27). Morrow (1979) recommends that teacher education programs include in their curriculum the development of the teacher's skills to participate in an ecological assessment process as one solution to arriving at nondiscriminatory assessment. Such preparation should include familiarity with various assessment instruments, an understanding of the inadequacies of tests, and exposure to practical approaches to assessment (NABSE, 1981b). Finally, teachers should learn to use informal assessment procedures, particularly observation and interviews, as described in Chapter 11.

Customs
Some subcultures may have strong ethnic and religious ties. For example, many among the Hispanic population are Catholic in religious preference and their culture and customs revolve around their religious beliefs and in particular religious feast days. Some religions have strong dietary customs and forbid eating particular foods. For example, some Catholics avoid eating meat on Fridays; many Jews and Muslims

do not eat pork. These customs must be recognized and respected within the school setting and curriculum. School cooking classes should not include the preparation and serving of certain meats, such as pork, or other foods in communities where subcultures exist that prohibit the eating of such foods. Instead, teachers might appropriately incorporate the preparation of ethnic meals in their curriculum. The celebration of holidays that have a religious significance, such as Christmas, might be offensive in communities where non-Christian religions, such as Jewish and Islamic, are present in significant numbers. If Christian holidays are recognized, then holidays of non-Christian groups should also be given appropriate recognition and respect. Teachers should

not schedule special events or examinations on religious holidays or feast days when pupils might be kept at home to celebrate with their families.

Sometimes cultural customs of a minority group may be at variance with the majority. For example, members of Jehovah's Witness religion do not celebrate birthdays. Since observance and recognition of birthdays are typically included in elementary classrooms, teachers must be sensitive to the possible embarrassment for children who may be Jehovah's Witnesses. Such occasions, however, may provide the teacher with an opportunity to discuss cultural differences with the pupils and help them learn respect for such differences.

Appropriate methods of nonverbal communication may also differ from one culture to another. For example, Arabs conduct conversation face to face and consider carrying on a conversation while walking impolite

(Hall, 1969). Touching is important in the Hispanic culture but impolite in the Arabic. For some Native Americans, looking directly in the eyes of another person is unacceptable. Some Asians and native Americans consider assertiveness and speaking up impolite. In India, a man can hold hands in public with another man and a woman with another woman, but a man holding hands with a woman is not acceptable. Space and a sense of personal space also varies among cultures. The parameters of personal and shared space as well as its organization are differently defined in each culture. Intrusions into another person's space, such as close proximity to another's face while speaking, is not acceptable. Notions of privacy also vary. For example, parents in India will never leave an infant or young child alone in a room; this would be considered akin to child abuse. (Eva Friedlander, personal communication, January 1986).

Behavior of children from different cultures can frequently be misunderstood. Peterson (1983) cites the experience of a teacher who was puzzled by the lack of progress of a bright Asian child placed in a class with his uncle who was a few months older. When someone familiar with the culture explained that it was bad manners to excel a senior relative, the children were separated and the nephew began to show gains in academic achievement consistent with his potential. Teachers should seek an explanation for any unexpected behavior that seems to differ from the majority culture, either from the child's family if appropriate, or from school or community personnel who may be familiar with the culture, or from reading. The books by Robert Coles (1967a; 1967b; 1977) in his *Children of Crisis* series are particularly helpful in viewing what it means to live in two cultures from the child's point of view.

Attitudes

Each minority group may have a different attitude toward education. Jews have always had a strong commitment to education as a means of preserving traditions and a way of life, and first generation Jewish parents quickly recognized the role of education as a socializing agent (Lemish, 1981). Generalizations cannot be made about any group, however, so that teachers should be familiar with prevailing attitudes toward education within the community and within the cultural groups represented in the community. With this as a base, teachers can then explore these attitudes within the families of their pupils.

There is little documentation about the different attitudes toward the advent of a child with a handicapping condition into the family constellation. Each culture views deviance differently and these cultural attitudes and expectations can be significant in educational planning for handicapped pupils, particularly in identifying behavioral norms and family expectations (Gil, 1981). In some Black, Hispanic, or Native American families, where there is a strong emphasis on group similarities, an albino child is clearly identifiable and may be rejected by the family and peer groups because of his or her close resemblance to the white majority in appearance. On the other hand, in cultures where the extended family is the norm, the handicapped child may be helped by the presence of many interested and concerned adults.

The minority handicapped child is vulnerable to bias and discrimination on two counts: because of the minority status and because of the handicapping condition (Chinn, 1979; Gliedman & Roth, 1980). Negative stereotypes about minority handicapped pupils can do double disservice to them as low expectations are carried into school planning (Chinn, 1979). Just as special educators attempt to emphasize the abilities rather than the disabilities of their handicapped pupils, so should they also look at abilities rather than skin color, language differences, and other cultural characteristics.

The efforts of the teacher must be directed toward reducing the effects of this double minority status on the child's self-concept and school achievement. To accomplish this, teachers must be aware of the cultural background of the minority pupils enrolled in their classes, the impact the culture may have on behavior, and should integrate the language and culture of the child into the curriculum (Gallegos, Gallegos, & Rodriguez, 1983). Knowledge and appreciation of different cultures and emphasis on respect for diversity should lead to more effective educational programs for all children.

Minority visually handicapped children need understanding and a support system for not only their visual impairment and other exceptionalities, as discussed in Chapters 8 and 9, but also for their minority affiliation. A supportive school environment will enable them to become full participants in society (Gavillan-Torres, 1981). The minority visually handicapped pupil should have equal access to all programs within the school district that are provided for all other pupils including services and programs for those with other exceptionalities. Their school experience should assist them to develop pride in their rich cultural heritage, including their native language, while at the same time helping them to bridge the cultural and language barrier to mutual understanding and respect for the majority culture. The goal must be to foster national unity while rejoicing in diversity (Boyer, 1984).

Place of Residence

Where children live may often determine the quality of the education they receive. Both rural and urban communities have their strengths and weaknesses.

In a survey designed to identify problems in pro-

viding appropriate services for rural handicapped students, Helge (1984a) found that more than 50 percent of respondents listed the following: funding inadequacies; difficulties in recruitment and retention of staff; transportation inadequacies; and provision of services to low prevalence populations.

The quality of instruction in rural, remote, and isolated areas is directly related to the skills of the teacher in individualizing instruction for a variety of pupils and in creatively using local resources. Scott (1984) describes one regular teacher in a remote area who has 48 preparations for 16 students in eight grades; the school is over 100 miles from the central administrative office. The problems faced by regular teachers are compounded for administrators and for teachers of visually handicapped pupils where distances complicate educational planning. The recruitment and retention of teachers to manage such diverse needs is hindered by the fact that teacher certification requirements are inappropriate for preparing teachers for rural areas and few universities are preparing teachers to work in rural and remote areas; thus poorly qualified personnel are often assigned to these programs (Helge, 1984b).

Although P.L. 94-142 has had an impact on the initiation of services to handicapped pupils in rural areas, the low prevalence populations continue to be the most difficult to serve (Helge, 1984b). Different models for service delivery are needed since the traditional continuum of services does not fit into the needs of rural areas. For example, cooperatives and itinerant services are not always appropriate (Helge, 1984a). Helge (1984b) has developed a three dimensional model showing the variables that contribute to the diversity of rural school districts (see Figure 10.1). The two dimensions of population density and topography are critical in planning and implementing an appropriate service delivery system. These two in conjunction with the 19 variables listed for "Other Community and District Variables" increase the variability that may be found in rural communities and make the development and implementation of a single program model impossible.

Helge (1984a) recommends that rural districts develop their own service delivery system based on the variables found in the area which are critical to meeting the educational needs of a particular child. Within each rural area there are certain characteristics which are fixed and cannot be easily manipulated. Designing an appropriate service delivery model requires that creative use be made of those variables that can be manipulated. Figure 10.2 lists the fixed characteristics that form the parameters for developing a program in column one and the variables that can be manipulated to bring student and services together in an appropriate service delivery model in

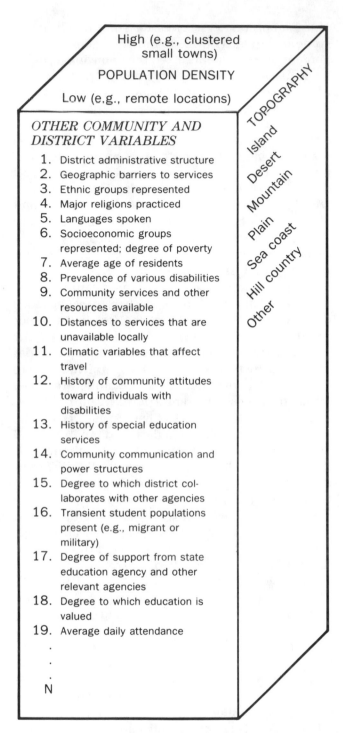

High (e.g., clustered small towns)

POPULATION DENSITY

Low (e.g., remote locations)

TOPOGRAPHY

Island
Desert
Mountain
Plain
Sea coast
Hill country
Other

OTHER COMMUNITY AND DISTRICT VARIABLES

1. District administrative structure
2. Geographic barriers to services
3. Ethnic groups represented
4. Major religions practiced
5. Languages spoken
6. Socioeconomic groups represented; degree of poverty
7. Average age of residents
8. Prevalence of various disabilities
9. Community services and other resources available
10. Distances to services that are unavailable locally
11. Climatic variables that affect travel
12. History of community attitudes toward individuals with disabilities
13. History of special education services
14. Community communication and power structures
15. Degree to which district collaborates with other agencies
16. Transient student populations present (e.g., migrant or military)
17. Degree of support from state education agency and other relevant agencies
18. Degree to which education is valued
19. Average daily attendance
.
.
.
.
N

Figure 10.1   Dimensions of the diversity of rural school systems

Source: D. Helge, The state of the art of rural special education, *Exceptional Children*, **50**, p. 319.

column 2 (Helge, 1984a). Teachers and administrators identify from the first column those which cannot be changed. Within these limitations, the variables in the second column are manipulated in order to develop

an appropriate educational program. Using this model, Helge (1984a) describes a variety of service delivery systems that have been successful. It should be noted, however, that any one of these models might not be appropriate for a school district with a different configuration of variables. (See Figure 10.2.)

Meeting the educational needs of children who reside in urban inner city areas also provides a challenge to special educators and presents a different set of problems. Urban school districts have more school personnel involved in the decision making which tends to increase the bureaucracy and hinder the program's creativity; there tends to be a greater number of problems with discipline, crime, violence, and pollution (Helge, 1984b). Safety is frequently a critical consideration and children must be taught how to cope with the dangers inherent in certain sections of the inner cities (Hechinger & Hechinger, 1984).

In both urban and rural settings, the migrant minority population presents special difficulties for the handicapped child. Appropriate educational services may not be available in certain areas where the migrant worker-parents are employed; the constant mobility results in a fragmented educational program (Salend et al., 1984); the continuing struggle to provide for basic food, clothing, and shelter often leaves parents with little time to devote to their children's welfare (Strazicich, 1983). For migrant children there is a special need for career education, vocational counseling, and vocational education because with the technology explosion, many jobs currently available to unskilled migrant workers will not be available in the future (Strazicich, 1983).

Social Problems

In a complex and heterogenous society it is inevitable that certain social problems arise among the school age population. School administrators face several that are critical: teenage pregnancy, substance abuse, suicide, and child abuse. No one of these is unique to any particular minority group or socioeconomic class, but may be prevalent in some to a greater degree than others. Little is known about the prevalence of the first three within the handicapped population; more is known about child abuse and this will be discussed in greater detail.

Regardless of socioeconomic status, handicapped children are more vulnerable to child abuse than their nonhandicapped peers, partly because they usually require more attention and are less able to strike back at the abusing adults (Kline, 1982; Marion, 1981; Schwarzbeck, 1980). Child abuse is difficult to define because of differing cultural norms (Korbin, 1980). For example, some African tribes scar the faces of their children as a token of attractiveness. For them, this is not child abuse but rather making their child an

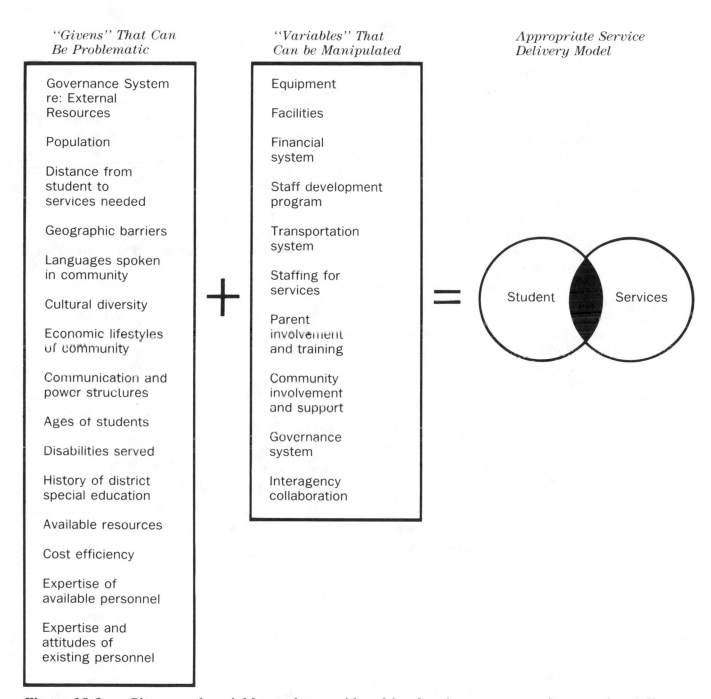

Figure 10.2   Givens and variables to be considered in planning an appropriate service delivery model (1984).

Adapted from: D. Helge. Models for serving rural students with low-incidence handicapped conditions. *Exceptional Children,* **50**, p. 319

acceptable member of the tribe (Korbin, 1980). The National Center on Child Abuse and Neglect proposes this definition: "an abused or neglected child means a child whose physical or mental health or welfare is harmed or threatened with harm by the acts or omissions of his parent or other person responsible for his welfare" (Boardhurst, 1979). States vary, however, in their definitions and teachers should be aware of their own state's definition and laws concerning mandatory reporting of child abuse.

Child abuse is considered a growing problem. The United States Department of Health and Human Services (1981) estimates that over 600,000 children under the age of 18 are abused or neglected annually, only about one-fifth of whom are officially reported to child protective services agencies. Preschool children are most likely to be abused, especially the under three age group. Child abuse is found in all income groups, and rates are approximately the same for whites and nonwhites (USDHHS, 1981). There are some differences: sexual abuse is higher in rural areas, educational neglect is higher in urban areas, and emotional neglect is higher in suburbia (USDHHS, 1981).

Sloan (1983) describes four types of child abuse and neglect: physical abuse; physical neglect; sexual abuse; and emotional maltreatment. Indicators of child abuse in each of these areas are included in Chart 10.1.

Corporal punishment in schools is an officially or unofficially sanctioned form of institutionalized child abuse (Dubanoski, Inaba, & Gerkewicz, 1983; Hyman, 1980). Its use is based on the mistaken beliefs that punishment teaches respect, it is the only thing that some children understand, and problems would increase without it. Some children who are physically abused at home expect to be treated similarly at school and often will bait the teacher to treat them abusively. In working with such children, parents and teachers need to look for positive ways of managing behavior, such as behavior modification, noncorporal means of punishment, and use of rewards.

The causes of child abuse are varied and can be grouped into parental, child, stress-related, and interactional (Schneider, Helfer, & Hoffmeister, 1980). Parental factors include a history of being abused themselves during their own childhood. Abusing mothers tend to be young, single, mentally slow, with frequent pregnancies. Children who are different from siblings in physiology or temperament are typically more vulnerable to abuse. They include those who are handicapped either physically, mentally, neurologically impaired, or who have a congenital defect. Social stress factors form another grouping. Poverty, broken homes, socially isolated families, and unemployment may be contributing factors. Finally, poor parent-child interaction may be a factor. Parents with a tendency toward negative behavior toward children in general are more likely to be abusing parents.

The solution for child abuse lies primarily in the area of prevention (National Committee for Prevention of Child Abuse, 1982). Educational and emotional support programs for young parents to help them cope with the problems encountered in child rearing will frequently help them deal with their problems more effectively. Special attention should be given to parents of handicapped children and to single parents to enable them to cope with the limitations of the child and their own expectations of performance. Communities must have resources for providing emergency aid, temporary shelter, foster care, and crisis services for families.

Teachers should become aware of signs of physical and mental abuse and should know their state and local district laws concerning mandatory reporting of child abuse. Several books on this topic are listed in additional readings at the end of this chapter.

This part has described some of the range of cultural diversity that may be found in the minority populations which were summarized in the first part. It should not be considered exhaustive but rather illustrative of the heterogeneous cultural population that teachers may encounter in their school districts. The range of differences requires that teachers adopt a multicultural perspective for their teaching. Some guidelines for implementing such an approach are presented in the following part.

IMPLEMENTING A MULTICULTURAL EDUCATION

The learning climate of the school must be planned to enhance the social and academic growth of all pupils. The teacher plays a critical role in this process (NABSE, 1981c).

In the past, the attention of the public schools focused on acculturation: the integration or assimilation of pupils with different cultural backgrounds into American society. The price of the assimilation, however, was often the loss of the ethnic identity. Following the consciousness-raising movements during the 1960s, attention shifted to one of respect for diversity through multicultural education (Lemish, 1981). Multicultural education as defined in the standards of the National Council for Accreditation of Teacher Education (1979) "is preparation for the social, political and economic realities that individuals experience in culturally diverse and complex human encounters. . .This preparation provides a process by which an individual develops competencies for perceiving, believing, evaluating, and behaving in differential cultural settings. . ." (NCATE, 1979, p. 4).

Chart 10.1   Physical and behavioral indicators of abuse and neglect

Type of CA/N	Physical Indicators	Behavioral Indicators
Physical abuse	Unexplained bruises and welts - on face, lips, mouth - on torso, back, buttocks, thighs - in various stages of healing - clustered, forming regular patterns - reflecting shape of article used to inflict (electrical cord, belt buckle) - on several different surface areas - regularly appear after absence, weekend or vacation Unexplained burns: - cigar, cigarette burns, especially on soles, palms, back or buttocks - immersion burns (sock-like, glove-like, doughnut shaped on buttocks or genitalia) - patterned like electric burner, iron, etc. - rope burns on arms, legs, neck or torso Unexplained fractures: - to skull, nose, facial structure - in various stages of healing - multiple or spiral fractures Unexplained lacerations or abrasions: - to mouth, lips, gums, eyes - to external genitalia	Wary of adult contacts Apprehensive when other children cry Behavioral extremes: - aggressiveness, or withdrawal Frightened of parents Afraid to go home Reports injury by parents
Physical neglect	Consistent hunger, poor hygiene, inappropriate dress Consistent lack of supervision, especially in dangerous activities or long periods Unattended physical problems or medical needs Abandonment	Begging, stealing food Extended stays at school (early arrival and late departure) Constant fatigue, listlessness or falling asleep in class Alcohol or drug abuse Delinquency (e.g. thefts) States there is no caretaker
Sexual abuse	Difficulty in walking or sitting Torn, stained or bloody underclothing Pain or itching in genital area Bruises or bleeding in external genitalia, vaginal or anal areas Pregnancy	Unwilling to change for gym or participate in P.E. class Withdrawal, fantasy or infantile behavior Bizarre, sophisticated, or unusual sexual behavior or knowledge Poor peer relationships Delinquent or runaway Reports sexual assault by caretaker
Emotional Maltreatment	Speech disorders Lags in physical development Failure-to-thrive	Habit disorders (sucking, biting, rocking, etc.) Conduct disorders (anti-social, destructive, etc.) Neurotic traits (sleep disorders, inhibition of play) Psychoneurotic reactions (hysteria, obsession, compulsion, phobias, hypochondria)

Source: D.D. Broadhurst, *The educator's role in the prevention and treatment of child abuse and neglect.* (Washington, D.C.: National Center for Child Abuse and Neglect, Children's Bureau, Administration of Children, Youth, and Families, U.S. Dept. of Health, Education & Welfare, 1979), p. 9.

The goal must be to assist teachers to prepare pupils to live in a pluralistic society where diverse groups retain their traditional culture "within the confines of a common society" (Myers, 1981, p. 2).

This part discusses attitudes, respect for differences, and work with families as they relate to children from different backgrounds.

Attitudes

Attitudes are viewed as a critical element in the success of P.L. 94-142, The Education of All Handicapped Children Act of 1975 (Jones & Guskin, 1984). Successful mainstreaming depends in large measure on the attitudes of regular educators (Jamison, 1984). Attitudes of professionals toward visually handicapped persons tend to be more negative than positive (Siller, 1984; Strohmer, Grand, & Purcell, 1984) and may by related to historical and psychosocial factors (Monbeck, 1973). The teacher of visually handicapped pupils needs to be aware of any negative attitudes on the part of regular educators who may have visually handicapped pupils in their classrooms. In a culturally diverse society, attitudes are an important consideration, particularly for the minority handicapped student.

Modifying attitudes, however, is a complex process (Watts, 1984) and may not always occur with increased information and direct contact (Jamison, 1984; Towner, 1984). Teachers of visually handicapped minority pupils should, however, use a variety of techniques that may assist them in changing attitudes of regular teachers toward minority visually handicapped pupils. Direct contact with minority visually handicapped pupils; group discussions with teachers, parents or primary caregivers, and other school personnel; role playing; and contact through the media appear to be techniques useful for attitude change (Towner, 1984; Strohmer, Grand, & Purcell, 1984). In the classroom, the teacher's attitudes and expectations of the handicapped minority child provide the model for the other students (NABSE, 1981). Students look to their teacher for cues on behavior toward their peers. Regular teachers may need the assistance of the teacher of the visually handicapped in structuring how the minority visually handicapped child should be treated in the regular classroom.

Respect for Cultural Differences

Incorporating a multicultural focus in the preparation of teachers represents an attempt to help teachers recognize students as individuals in order to develop educational equity (Baptiste, Baptiste, & Gollnick, 1980). It should lead to a better understanding of the educational needs of children with diverse cultural backgrounds and to more effective programming for them, as well as to the elimination of stereotypic thinking about such

groups. Multicultural education is essential in a society of cultural pluralism (Baptiste & Baptiste, n.d.).

Teachers should learn about the cultural differences among all children in their school districts and should respect the right of the children and their families to those differences even when they are inconsistent with the teachers' own cultural background. Teachers

of visually handicapped pupils must be prepared to interpret the multicultural needs of their pupils to regular teachers. The preceding two parts in this chapter provided basic information about the differences that may be found in the regular school population and implications those differences may have on the parents' and child's behavior. Teachers should study which of these differences are found in their communities and among the children with whom they work. The greater the knowledge in these areas, the more likely the teacher, in collaboration with parents or primary caregivers, can plan appropriate educational programs to meet the needs of minority visually handicapped pupils.

The teacher should identify the particular components within a child's culture, other than the obvious ones such as dress and diet, that might facilitate or impede their school achievement. For example, assertiveness and questioning are valued in school and society. The passive nonquestioning behavior of some Asian children must be viewed within the context of that culture, namely, respect and obedience to elders (Kang-Ning, 1981). The child's self-concept will be enhanced when the teacher works within the majority culture, by respecting cultural differences.

Even if it were desirable, schools would have difficulty in teaching the American way of life to children from some cultural backgrounds (Carter & Segura, 1979). As noted earlier, some minority groups, e.g., Mexican-Americans, retain much of their native culture and language. Cultural patterns, even for some who have been resident in this country for long periods of time, may persist for several generations. Because a child was born in the community does not necessarily mean that the family has been acculturated. Work with the parents or primary caregivers may help determine the degree to which the educational program must be modified to meet the needs of a particular minority visually handicapped pupil.

Work With Families

Teachers must be sensitive to the needs of the child's family. Depending upon experiences in the home country, some may be suspicious of persons representing the authority of the school, view them as intruders, and may resent advice that may appear to them to be at variance with their beliefs. Some, fearful that their children will abandon their cultural heritage, may even undermine the work of the school. Some parents, such as those from Arabic nations, view females as having lower status; fathers in particular, may resent advice and counseling from a female teacher. These problems require patience and understanding so that mutual confidence is developed, and so that the teacher's interest in the child and the sincerity of the school personnel in the child's welfare are conveyed.

Teachers and students should seek information and knowledge about the cultural backgrounds of each other. All students should be encouraged to take pride in their rich cultural heritage. With knowledge, acceptance, and respect for the cultural backgrounds of their classmates, students will learn to appreciate the diversity of the American cultural heritage (NABSE, 1981d; Webb, n.d.).

Multicultural education is good teaching (Payne, 1981). The various subject matter disciplines taught in schools are essential for all cultural groups but the process by which knowledge and skill in these disciplines is acquired may vary according to the culture. Thus, teachers must adapt methodology to meet the particular needs of their pupils. For some, this may be an emphasis on enhancement of psycho-motor skills within each discipline; for others it may mean a focus on a cooperative rather than a competitive learning environment. The school curriculum and how it is taught should be individualized to meet the unique needs of all pupils.

Study questions

1. From the U.S. Census compare data on the minority composition of your state with the national figures. Compare data on the minority composition of your city and your school district with the state and nation. Can you explain any differences?

2. Obtain data from census reports about your community and school district concerning the racial, ethnic, and religious characteristics of your community. Tell what implications these characteristics might have for visually handicapped pupils in your community.

3. Select any cultural difference discussed in this chapter. Describe how you would help other visually handicapped pupils and regular pupils learn about and acquire respect for that difference.

4. Obtain the data on the ethnic composition of your community and your school district. How do they compare? How do you account for any differences?

5. Interview the school nurse or community public health nurse about the health status of pupils in your community. How does the health status of the major minority groups compare with that of the school district as a whole. How do you account for any differences?

6. Interview the leader of some minority group in your community such as a minister, head of an advocate group, leading spokesperson for the group, etc. Find out about the problems of being a member of that minority group in your community.

7. Interview the state education consultant for the visually handicapped in your state about how visually handicapped children residing in rural and remote areas of your state are being served. How does the model of service delivery differ from that in urban areas in your state?

8. Review individual items on any published test. Select those which would be biased for any three minority groups discussed in this chapter and explain why.

9. To what extent has your teacher education preparation program prepared you to work with children from diverse backgrounds?

10. Plan a unit on multicultural education for your classmates or for pupils at the grade level you plan to teach. Include your goals and objectives, content, instructional procedures, and evaluation procedures.

11. Find out about the prevalence of substance abuse, teenage pregnancy, and teenage suicide in your community. To what extent are these problems also present in the handicapped population?

12. Find out about mandatory reporting of child abuse in your state. How does the state definition of child abuse differ from that included in this chapter? Talk to a social worker about preventive measures being taken in your community to reduce the prevalence of child abuse. Are there any cultural assumptions involved in those measures? What are they?

Additional readings

Baptiste, H.P., Baptiste, M.L. and Gollnick, D.M., (eds.) (1980). *Multicultural teacher education: Preparing educators to provide educational equity.* Washington, D.C.: Commission on Multicultural Education, American Association of Colleges for Teacher Education.

Banks, J.A. and Joyce, W.W. (1971). *Teaching social studies to culturally different children.* Reading, Mass.: Addison Wesley.

Broadhurst, D.D. (1979). *The educator's role in the prevention and treatment of child abuse and neglect.* Washington, D.C.: National Center for Child Abuse and Neglect, Children's Bureau, Administration for Children, Youth and Families, U.S. Department of Health, Education and Welfare.

Coles, R. (1977). Eskimos, Chicanos, Indians. Vol IV of *Children of Crisis.* Boston, Mass.: Little, Brown & Co.

Coles, R. (1967a). Migrants, Sharecropper, Mountaineers. Vol. II of *Children of Crisis.* Boston, Mass.: Little, Brown & Co.

Coles, R. (1967b). The South Goes North. Vol. III of *Children of Crisis.* Boston, Mass.: Little, Brown & Co.

Cross, D.E., Baker, G.C., and Stiles, L.J. (1977). *Teaching in a multicultural society: Perspectives and professional strategies.* New York, N.Y.: The Free Press.

Gliedman, J. and Roth, W. (1980). *The unexpected minority: Handicapped children in America.* New York, N.Y.: Harcourt Brace Jovanovich.

Harrison, R. and Edwards, J. (1984). *Child abuse.* Portland, Ore.: Ednick Publications.

Jones, R.L. (ed.)(1984). *Attitudes and attitude change in special education: Theory and practice.* Reston, Va.: Council for Exceptional Children.

Kempe, C.H. and Helfer, R.E. (ed.)(1980). *The battered child*(3rd Ed.). Chicago, Ill.: University of Chicago Press.

Kline, D.F. (1977). *Child abuse and neglect: A primer for school personnel.* Reston, Va.: Council for Exceptional Children.

Kline, D.F. (1982). *The disabled child and child abuse.* Chicago, Ill.: National Committee on Child Abuse.

Kunjufu, J. (1985). *Developing positive self-images and discipline in Black children.* Chicago, Ill.: African American Images.

Moody, C.D., and Vergon, C.B. (eds). *Approaches for achieving a multicultural curriculum.* Ann Arbor, Mich.: The University of Michigan, School of Education, Program for Equal Educational Opportunity.

National Alliance of Black School Educators. (1981). *Structuring the learning climate for minority handicapped students.* Washington, D.C.: NABSE.

Omark D.R. and Erickson, J.G. (1984). *The bilingual exceptional child.* San Diego, Calif.: College-Hill Press.

Plata, M. (1982). *Assessment, placement, and programming of bilingual exceptional pupils: A practical approach.* Reston, Va.: Council for Exceptional Children.

Sloan, I.J. (1983). *Child abuse: Governing law and legislation.* New York, N.Y.: Oceana Publications, Inc.

PART 2

COMPONENTS
OF A
QUALITY
EDUCATIONAL PROGRAM

INTRODUCTION

Chapters in the preceding section described the population of visually handicapped children and youth: who and how many there are and their demographic characteristics; their growth and development and variations that may be expected because of their visual impairment; the visual impairment itself: its etiology, how it is assessed and how vision may be used more efficiently; and the challenges presented by those with special needs: infants and young children, the severely multiply handicapped, those with other exceptionalities, and those from multicultural backgrounds. The influence of these considerations as they relate to the individual visually handicapped child is applied to the process of planning an appropriate educational program in the seven chapters included in this part.

Formal assessment measures have certain limitations when applied to any population of handicapped children. To supplement and complement formal assessment, teachers must know nontest-based or informal measures and procedures that are helpful not only in assessment but also for program planning and for classroom instruction. These procedures and how teachers can use them for both assessment and planning educational strategies are described and discussed together with procedures for assessment based on the use of standardized or formal instruments. Teachers must know and understand the limitations and strengths of a broad range of available assessment tools so that they can interpret and make use of the results in planning the individualized education program. In addition, suggestions for teachers to work in a team relationship with other school personnel who may be involved in the formal assessment process, particularly the school psychologist, are described in Chapter 11.

Chapter 12 examines how teachers use the results from both formal and informal assessment in the development of the Individualized Education Program (IEP), as required in P.L. 94-142. The chapter includes an examination of the formulation of goals and objectives based on the results of the assessment; the decision making process; and the factors that are related to the selection of appropriate instructional strategies to implement the IEP for each individual child.

Chapter 13 describes the various settings in the continuum of services that should be available to each child so that the IEP may be implemented most effectively. Five service delivery models are described and compared. Each child should be placed in the least restrictive environment most appropriate for that child. Teachers should know and understand the characteristics of the various settings so that the best decision regarding placement may be made for the child.

Chapter 14 examines the roles and functions of the teacher of the visually handicapped in the various settings discussed in the preceding chapter. The chapter also includes a summary of stress as it relates specifically to teachers of the visually handicapped.

Chapter 15 discusses the role of parents in the educational process. Under P.L. 94-142 parents have increased involvement in educational decisions that affect their child. Teachers must know this role and how best to work with parents in an effective relationship.

Successful educational programs for visually handicapped children and youth require a good working relationship among parents, the student when appropriate, and members of the educational professional team. The team approach to this advocacy relationship is described in Chapter 16.

The implementation of a good program for visually handicapped children and youth depends in large measure on the teacher's knowledge and ability to tap various available resources that will enhance the educational process. Chapter 17 reviews the various materials, aids, and equipment that can be employed in the educational program and how to obtain them.

CHAPTER 11

Psychoeducational Assessment

Amanda Hall
Geraldine T. Scholl
Rose-Marie Swallow

This chapter reviews the major issues related to psychoeducational assessment of visually handicapped children and youth. The first part discusses definition, purposes, types of instruments, the process, and current issues in assessment; the second addresses the availability of published instruments that may be useful in a comprehensive educational assessment; the third identifies informal or nontest based instruments and procedures that teachers use in the instructional program. The importance of adopting an ecological approach in the assessment process is emphasized.

Assessment is an essential component in educational programming for all children and youth. Results of a comprehensive assessment involving members of the multidisciplinary team form the basis for making decisions regarding educational placement and for the development of the Individualized Education Program (IEP) as mandated by P.L. 94-142, the Education for All Handicapped Children Act of 1975. (See Chapter 12). A comprehensive educational assessment employs a combination of tools and techniques selected to be consistent with the purposes of the assessment. These tools and techniques include a summary of the developmental history; observation in the various settings of the child's environment or ecology; and administration of appropriate published tests and teacher-made tests and checklists in the areas of educational need. A key factor in comprehensive assessment is the interpretation and integration of information gathered from these various sources in order to make educational decisions (Bennett, 1981). To participate fully in this process, the teacher must have an understanding of the growth and development of visually handicapped children and youth and their educational needs (see Chapter 4); knowledge of the potential impact of the visual impairment on behavior and functioning (see Chapters 3, 5, & 6); and a thorough understanding of the assessment instruments and procedures, including their purpose,

available standardization data, and their strengths and weaknesses in assessing the educational needs of visually handicapped pupils. This chapter is not intended to take the place of a course in assessment of handicapped pupils.

The first section of this chapter provides a general overview of assessment: definition, purposes, types of instruments, the process, and current issues and trends in assessment. The second section describes published instruments and discusses the role of the teacher in working with other members of the multidisciplinary team who may administer some of these instruments. The third section presents information concerning informal and nontest based instruments and procedures that typically are employed by the teacher of visually handicapped children and youth. Appendix B includes a glossary that should help in understanding the measurement terms used in this chapter.

GENERAL CONSIDERATIONS

Definition

Assessment is a multifaceted process of gathering information by using appropriate tools and techniques in order to make educational decisions about placement and the educational program for a particular pupil (Ysseldyke, 1979). It is more than administering tests designed to yield a score. In the past, results from a single test were typically used as a basis for educational decision-making. This approach did not yield educationally meaningful information for the teacher about the pupil. Current practice stresses a more comprehensive approach to pupil assessment which takes into account the following:

1. Current life circumstances, such as health, nutritional status, family attitudes and values, family constellation and level of acculturation which can influence performance;
2. Developmental history, including significant events in early physical, mental, and emotional development; physical and sensory limitations; and evaluation of parental attitudes, behavior, and performance;
3. Outside factors, such as the philosophical orientation of the caregivers and professional personnel, including the teacher, and the consistency of that orientation with that of the parents; conditions under which the child is observed which can influence interpretation of pupil behavior and performance;
4. Interpretation of behavior and performance based on the clinical experience and best judgement of the evaluator; and
5. Prognosis or prediction of future performance based on two alternatives: the child continuing to live in the current environment (home, school, community) and the child placed in a remedial environment, such as a special class (Salvia & Ysseldyke, 1981).

A comprehensive assessment then is the process of collecting and interpreting a variety of information on which to make informed decisions about the individualized education program for visually handicapped children and youth.

Purposes of Assessment

Salvia and Ysseldyke (1981) list five purposes of assessment. This part summarizes these purposes as they relate to educational programming for visually handicapped children and youth.

Identification and Screening

Routine vision screening should be an accepted part of the regular school district screening and identification program. Because of the prevalence of visual impairments in other categories of handicapped pupils (see Chapters 8 & 9), school districts should screen for possible visual impairments all pupils enrolled in special education programs at more frequent intervals. Measures useful for vision screening are described in the second section of this chapter.

Classification

Although screening and identification measures may indicate the likelihood of a visual impairment, additional assessment is often necessary to determine

eligibility for a specific special education placement and/or services. As noted in Chapter 2, states vary in their eligibility requirements for special education programs and services for visually handicapped children and youth. An eye examination by an appropriate specialist, usually an ophthalmologist or optometrist, is typically required to determine whether a pupil is sufficiently different to be eligible for special education programs and services according to the regulations of the particular state. Determination of eligibility on the basis of vision for pupils with severe multiple impairments may be difficult, and often a functional vision assessment by teachers of visually handicapped pupils may be of greater value for screening and identification than the medical examination. If the pupil's major disability is vision, then the measure of visual functioning may suffice for the placement decision. Assessment of selected environmental variables may be necessary to determine whether the best placement is in a residential or a day school program. If the pupil has or appears to have other disabilities, then additional assessment may be required to determine the impact of these on educational functioning and whether the visual impairment or the other disability is the major educationally handicapping condition. For example, a child who has a visual impairment and a hearing impairment might be placed in a program for visually handicapped, or hearing impaired, or deaf-blind children. To arrive at a decision of the most appropriate placement, an assessment of hearing and vision would be necessary to determine the extent of the two sensory impairments. Assessment instruments and procedures in all areas of educational need must be used to determine placement in the least restrictive environment.

Instructional Planning

A comprehensive assessment in all areas of educational need is necessary to determine what and how to teach. Measures of functional vision, aptitude or intelligence, and achievement are commonly used for this purpose. The strengths and weaknesses of these instruments and the controversy over their use is discussed later in this section. Such assessment data are used to determine the student's present level of performance, to develop the long and short term objectives for the individualized education program, and sometimes to predict future performance. This latter purpose is especially important when students are about to move to another level or type of program, such as graduation from high school.

Pupil Evaluation

Assessment is a means to examine change over time, to monitor student progress, and to determine the effects and usefulness of specific intervention strategies. Such assessment must be ongoing and an integral part of instruction. Instruments and procedures used for instructional planning are often appropriate for this purpose.

Program Evaluation

Finally, assessment is necessary to determine the effectiveness of a particular education program or instructional strategy or program of intervention within a school or school district. Individual pupil achievement, progress in the program, and success on completion of the program are often used as part of program evaluation data collected by administrators.

This chapter focuses primarily on assessment for instructional planning and pupil evaluation.

Types of Instruments

There are several ways of classifying instruments used in assessment: formal or informal or nontest based; standardized or nonstandardized; norm-referenced or criterion-referenced; group or individual; verbal or performance. There is some overlap among the groupings and also between the groupings. For additional information, selected texts in assessment are included in the additional readings at the end of this chapter.

Formal/Informal

Formal instruments are typically those which require strict adherence to instructions for administration and scoring, frequently have time limits, and yield a quantitative score, usually expressed in comparison with a group. Informal instruments have less rigid instructions for administration, have no time limits, and frequently yield no quantitative score. The results are expressed in qualitative terms and the validity of the results often depends on the clinical skills of the individual administering and interpreting the results.

Standardized/Nonstandardized

Standardized instruments are formal instruments that have been standardized, that is, they have been administered to large groups of pupils with similar backgrounds, ages, and other demographic characteristics and the results are reported as norms derived from this process of standardization. The value of results from a standardized test depends in large measure on the characteristics of the normative group (Salvia & Ysseldyke, 1981). Teachers, in interpreting results from standardized tests, should determine whether the individual pupil is similar to or different from the population on which the test was standardized since results obtained from the pupil are compared with this norm group. If the pupil is

significantly different, then the validity of the comparisons can be questioned. This issue will be discussed more fully in the following section.

Norm-Referenced/Criterion-Referenced

Assessment results typically have two dimensions: the descriptive data and the evaluative component. Descriptive data are the numerical results from the assessment instruments; the evaluative component is the interpretation of what the results mean. Raw scores, the number of correct items obtained on the test, have little meaning. For example, a raw score of 20 (descriptive) on a test would not be useful for educational planning. However, if the raw score of 20 means a score at the 80th percentile level (evaluative), then the teacher has useful information in order to make an educational decision. When raw scores are reported in comparison with the scores attained by members of the group on whom the test was standardized, tests are called norm-referenced. When raw scores are reported in relationship to the extent that a student has acquired mastery of a skill, the tests are called criterion referenced. Both types of tests are useful for educational planning; both have specific purposes; and both have limitations (Salvia & Ysseldyke, 1981).

Norm-referenced tests report a student's status relative to other students of similar age or grade and allow controlled comparisons with other students tested. Because a norm-referenced test is standardized around the mean score of the norm group, the assumption is made that half will attain scores above and half will attain scores below the mean or in other words, there are some high achievers and some low achievers. The raw score of an individual pupil is compared with the average or mean for a similar grade or age group. Grade or age equivalents are frequently used for this purpose, especially for tests of achievement. Scores may also be expressed in a quotient in comparison with a standard. For example, an IQ is computed by dividing the child's mental age as obtained from a standardized test of intelligence by the chronological age, and multiplying by 100.

Teachers of visually handicapped pupils must be cautious in interpreting the results of norm-referenced tests because there are few tests standardized on the visually handicapped population and thus the comparisons may not be valid. Scores alone should not be used to make educational decisions or for educational planning; the teacher can only infer the true meaning of the score in relationship to the learning task and circumstances. The score does not define the skills in terms of behaviors learned or to be learned.

Criterion-referenced tests are a more recent development in assessment (Salvia & Ysseldyke, 1981). These tests report results of a student's development of a specific skill in terms of total mastery. They provide descriptive data, that is, the number of correct responses but the evaluative dimension is different. Students must meet a predetermined criterion level to be successful. Scoring at or above the set criterion means mastery of the task and thus success; scoring below indicates nonmastery. Teachers frequently adopt a numerical point of reference which indicates if a student has successfully learned a skill, usually the 80 percent criterion level. This signifies the instructional level but not mastery. There may be certain subjects or skills where reaching 100 percent mastery is required before introducing the next level of learning. However, because learning is cumulative, it is assumed that the student will have other opportunities to be exposed to the skill.

Criterion-referenced testing is popular in special education. Criterion-referenced tests do not make comparisons between and among students; they usually are simpler to administer and score; the items more nearly reflect daily classroom tasks; the results are more applicable to establishing learning goals and educational objectives; they are considered more effective than norm-referenced tests for assessing the effects of instruction (Morgan, 1981). In addition, curriculum materials, especially in the basic skill subjects of reading, arithmetic, and language arts, are readily available, and many incorporate criterion-referenced tests to determine level of mastery. Teachers should be cautioned, however, to select programs based on a careful examination of the curriculum to determine whether it is appropriate for a particular student. There are increasing numbers of computer-based instructional systems which utilize criterion-referenced items for the evaluative base. Caution is urged in selecting and evaluating these developments as well.

Group/Individual
Group tests are those typically administered to two or more children at the same time; individual tests are administered on a one-on-one basis. Group tests usually have lower reliability ratings. They may be administered as individual tests but in doing so, interpretation should take into consideration the possible differences that may be obtained in reliability since they are designed to be used with groups rather than individuals (Salvia & Ysseldyke, 1981). In general, individual tests are preferred for use with visually handicapped children and youth.

Verbal/Performance
Verbal tests are those which rely on verbal instructions and responses, such as a vocabulary test. Performance tests provide opportunities for abilities to be demonstrated by doing something, such as putting cards in a sequence to tell a story or making a design with blocks from a picture. Most tests for visually handicapped pupils are verbal tests and thus a visually handicapped child who is not verbal or oriented to words may be at a disadvantage.

The Process of Assessment
As noted above an assessment should be directed toward achieving some objective. The objective to be achieved for most blind and visually handicapped pupils is to plan an appropriate educational program. To achieve this objective, a comprehensive educational evaluation must be completed. This process includes six steps as listed in Chart 11.1. The objectives, procedure, persons involved, expected outcomes, and evaluation are explained for each step.

Determine the referral concerns.
Visually handicapped pupils present a wide range of problems and abilities so that sometimes it is difficult to know where to begin with an assessment. One way is to have parents or teachers formulate specific questions or describe specifically the problem area or concern. For a specific problem, such as a lack of motivation to learn braille, a summary of what has been done and what alternatives have been tried should also be included. The more clearly the question, problem, or concern is described, the more likely the assessment will answer the question and the less likelihood there will be for overassessment to occur.

Gather background data.
Rarely is it necessary to start without any information about the pupil. Therefore, the next step is to gather all relevant data related to the question, problem area, or concern from an examination of school records and from interviews with parents and the child if appropriate, with teachers, and with others who are familiar with the child. Items should be selected from the interview instruments included in Appendix C that are appropriate to the question, problem area, or concern. Observations by the teacher or other professional who will conduct the assessment should be made particularly in the setting where the problem is most likely to occur; these observations should be compared with those in other settings where the problem is not evident. Chart 11.2 lists components in a comprehensive assessment. Only those areas should be assessed where there is missing information. There is little need to test for testing's sake. A comprehensive assessment in all the areas listed should be done when there is a reason to do so, such as initial admission to the program or movement from one level to another.

Chart 11.1   The process of assessment

Steps	Objective	Procedure	Persons Typically Involved	Outcome
Determine reason(s) for assessment	To describe the parameters of the problem clearly and concisely	Interview relevant persons for description of the problem Observe in problem and non-problem settings Describe behavior or performance specifically Describe alternatives or attempted interventions	Teacher Parents	Clearly defined problem/concern
Gather background data related to the defined problem/ concern	To obtain background information related to the problem/concern To determine areas where assessments have been completed To determine areas where assessment is necessary	Review school records Obtain developmental history Describe characteristics of various settings (ecology) in which the child functions	Teacher Psychologist Social Worker Nurse Parent	Determination of possible causes that may influence subsequent steps Determine areas for assessment
Conduct assessment	To obtain missing qualitative and quantitative data To identify areas of strength/weakness	Select and administer formal/standardized informal/nontest based assessments Modify/adapt procedures and scoring with caution but as necessary	Teacher Psychologist Ophthalmologist/ Optometrist Social Worker Functional vision specialist	Qualitative and quantitative supporting data
Integrate and interpret results	To describe the whole child within his/her present ecological setting	Review all data Discuss alternative strategies Determine most appropriate strategy	Multidisciplinary team members, including parents	Plan of action with priorities and specific strategies
Implementation	To remediate or alleviate the problem	Assign case manager Develop objectives for remediation Assign responsibilities to carry out plan Provide concerned persons with information and resources to carry out plan	Teachers Parents and family Outside support systems	Problem elimination or reduction
Evaluation of progress	To monitor progress of intervention	Follow-up procedures, e.g., phone call, reports, visits, etc.	Case manager	Revision of plan or termination of intervention

Chart 11.2 Components in a comprehensive assessment

Vision
  Eye examination by an ophthalmologist or
    optometrist
  Functional vision assessment
  Assessment of visual efficiency
  Low vision aids evaluation

Intelligence/Aptitude
  Cognitive development
  Intellectual functioning

Sensory/Motor Skills
  Gross and fine motor development
  Perceptual learning

Academic Skills/Concept Development
  Achievement in reading, writing, spelling,
    mathematics
  Language development
  Listening and auding skills
  Concepts: temporal, quantitative, positional,
    directional, and sequential
  Study skills

Social/Emotional/Affective
  Behavioral control
  Social and affective learning
  Adaptive living skills
  Recreation and leisure skills

Functional Living Skills
  Daily living skills
  Orientation and mobility skills
  Community travel and use
  Career and pre-vocational skills

background concerning assessment instruments and procedures to serve as consultants to the school psychologist or other professional who will be assessing the child.

Since it is increasingly apparent that the value of the individualized education program is dependent on the proper selection and utilization of both formal and informal assessment techniques, appropriate instruments and procedures should be selected that will address the question, problems, or concern. The teacher may begin this process by using selected formal and informal instruments. If more sophisticated assessment instruments and procedures are required, the teacher may refer the child to the school psychologist or other community specialist or agency for a more comprehensive assessment in specific areas of need. Since only a small number of formal assessment instruments specifically designed to assess the educational needs of visually handicapped pupils are available, the teacher and school psychologist must often adapt available tools by modifying instructions, lengthening time limits, and liberalizing scoring. In so doing, however, there are limitations in interpreting results particularly in the application of norms to a population not included in the standardization samples. In this instance, the teacher should work with the specialist to interpret the special characteristics of the visual impairment that may have an impact on the student's performance during the assessment since many school psychologists are reluctant to assess visually handicapped pupils (Ward, 1982).

Chart 11.3 presents suggested guidelines for assessing visually handicapped children and youth (Bauman, 1974, Langley, 1978; Scholl and Schnur, 1976). The second and third sections of this chapter discuss suggested formal and informal instruments and procedures that are useful for assessing particular areas of educational need.

Conduct the assessment.
The reasons underlying the referral for the assessment should influence the direction of the assessment, including the selection of appropriate instruments and procedures. Since the needs of visually handicapped students are so varied, it is difficult to design a fixed battery of assessment instruments and procedures that would consistently address the needs of all students. Indeed, a survey of school psychologists indicated that there is little agreement on what should be included in an assessment battery for visually handicapped pupils (Bauman & Kropf, 1979). Teachers of visually handicapped pupils are usually the most knowledgeable about the learning style, instructional needs, and development of children and youth with visual impairments. They should have sufficient

Integrate and interpret results.
The data gathered from the preceding steps must then be integrated into an educational report that will summarize the findings, interpret the results, and recommend appropriate placement and contents for the individualized education program (IEP). Interpretation must take into consideration factors related to the visual impairment. A student's degree of vision, and age at onset of the visual impairment may result in a different range of experiences and different processing methods that may be reflected in responses to certain test items, such as vocabulary. Poor performance on a reading inventory administered in dim illumination might be an indication of decreased visual ability in low light rather than a problem with reading skills. Familiarity with test materials, the testing process, and test content may also have an influence. For

Chart 11.3   Guidelines for assessment of blind and visually handicapped children and youth

Greet the pupil and initiate physical contact appropriate to the age of the pupil, e.g., a pat on the head; a hand on the shoulder; a handshake

Describe the room, if it is unfamiliar to the pupil, and allow him to explore if he expresses an interest in doing so

Guide the pupil to the chair and table where the assessment is to take place and allow him time to get acquainted with the setting

Position the pupil to promote comfort, alertness, maximum range of motion and optimal use of vision; establish optimal physical positioning to obtain control for severely multiply handicapped pupils

Allow time for initial contact, including physical manipulation for nonresponsive and severely multiply handicapped pupils to achieve maximum attention and alertness

Explain what you will be doing and for older pupils what you will do with the information you gain from the assessment

Allow the pupil an opportunity to explore any materials that will be used in the assessment prior to initiating each test; tap the object, or cue verbally, or touch the child slightly to assist in locating materials

Assist the pupil through the task demands to make certain directions are understood

Provide verbal and tactual guidance to imitate body actions when assessing motor or self-care skills

Add sound elements to tasks when possible to stimulate interest

At the conclusion of the assessment, thank the pupil and engage in some closing comments that demonstrate interest in him and what he has done

example, raised line drawings may be familiar to some visually handicapped students but not to others. Timed tests may pose a problem for students with low vision because of the reduced rate of reading. All of these factors may influence performance on the assessment and thus the interpretation. (See Chapters 4, 5, and 6.)

Multidisciplinary team members then review the results of all the assessments and discuss alternative strategies related to the question, problem, or concern. The teacher of visually handicapped pupils contributes to the interpretation of the findings by pointing out behaviors and responses common to visually handicapped students. Input from other team members contributes to the teacher's understanding of other factors, such as an interpretation of the influence of the home and parental attitudes from the school social worker. This interchange of ideas and expertise leads to insightful and useful recommendations.

Determine strategies for intervention.
The teacher translates the IEP which results from the assessment and the conclusions of the multidisciplinary team into the short and long term instructional objectives which will form the base for the daily educational program of the pupil. (See Chapter 12.)

Evaluate progress.
Monitoring progress is typically accomplished through some of the informal assessment strategies which are discussed in the third section of this chapter. Modifications in the IEP are made as indicated from this process.

Current Issues in Assessment
The passage of P.L. 94-142 with its provisions regarding evaluation procedures for handicapped pupils has stimulated considerable controversy about tests as they apply to certain handicapped pupils (Scholl, 1984). P.L. 94-142 requires that pupils be assessed with instruments validated for the particular purpose for which they are used, that no one procedure be used exclusively, and that tests are tailored to assess specific areas of educational need (DHEW, 1977). There are several trends in special education that are resulting from these nondiscriminatory provisions: the move away from standardized instruments that emphasize a comparison with norms toward a more functional assessment through nontest-based approaches, and increasing interest in the ecological approach, that is, assessing pupils in relationship to their environment.

The application of the nondiscriminatory provision to pupils with sensory impairments is difficult to implement since there is a limited number of tests specifically designed and standardized for these groups. Thus, when tests designed and standardized on nonhandicapped or on pupils with other categories of handicapping conditions are used with the visually handicapped population, results must be interpreted in light of the limitations the visual impairment may impose on the behavior and functioning of the pupil. Test items on all formal and informal instruments should be scrutinized carefully to determine whether they may be discriminatory when used with visually handicapped pupils.

One response to the discriminatory aspect of many published tests is to use them in nonstandardized ways, such as modifying the administration procedures by providing additional cues, eliminating time limits, or scoring on the basis of limited experiential background. This is an appropriate procedure if the information sought is related to the learning potential. However, if there is a need for drawing comparisons with the nonhandicapped population, this is not considered appropriate. Thus, the reason for administering the assessment should determine whether this approach is useful (Scarr, 1981; Glaser, 1981).

The adoption of an informal assessment approach which focuses more directly on the child's environment (school, home and community) is also being used with many handicapped groups (Oakland, 1981; Oka & Scholl, 1984; Ross & Holvert, 1984; Smith, 1980). These strategies are often more productive particularly in identifying appropriate ways to assist pupils in mainstreamed programs to become integrated. They are also very useful for assessing the multiply handicapped and preschool age populations. Some of these techniques are described in the third section of this chapter.

There is increasing interest in applying an ecological approach to assessment. Conventional assessment procedures are child-centered, that is they focus on isolated aspects of the child's functioning and attempt to identify deficits in the child (Carlson, Scott, & Eklund, 1980). The ecological approach recognizes the importance of taking the environment into account. It assumes that the individual does not function in a vacuum but rather is influenced by the setting in which the individual is functioning and which provides both positive and negative influences. Therefore, the environment should also be assessed as well as the child. Chart 11.4 lists some instruments that have been found useful in environmental assessment for the nonhandicapped population and which should also be useful in assessing the setting in which visually handicapped children and youth live (Oka & Scholl, 1984). Looking at the environment of the visually handicapped child is especially important because of the limited range of experiences many have in their home and community living.

The next two sections describe some useful instruments and procedures for assessment.

PUBLISHED INSTRUMENTS

This section summarizes available published instruments that may be useful in the comprehensive assessment of visually handicapped children and youth. In the selection of appropriate instruments several characteristics of the tests are important and should be considered.

All standardized instruments must demonstrate adequate validity and reliability, if their results are to be considered useful for educational planning. Validity refers to the degree to which a test measures what it purports to measure and is considered the most important criterion of a test instrument (Wisland, 1974). Validity is determined by several methods, three of which will be described here. In *face validity* items are examined by professionals to ascertain whether they appear to measure what the test is designed to measure (Wisland, 1974). For example, a panel of experts would review the items and decide whether they are appropriate for the purposes of the test. *Content validity* is determined by an examina-

tion of the content of the test using such criteria as the appropriateness of the items, the completeness of the item sample, and the method by which each item assesses the content (Salvia & Ysseldyke, 1981). For example, are the items included in the test appropriate for the subject matter the test is designed to assess? *Criterion related validity* uses a criterion measure that has accepted validity and correlates the new test with the accepted one (Salvia & Ysseldyke, 1981). For example, a new achievement test is corrected with a well-known achievement test. Validity may be affected in a number of ways: by the reliability of the test; by possible systematic bias in method of measurement; by item selection; or by errors made during administration or scoring. Test manuals should include a description of the validity of the test and how it was determined. This information helps teachers to know whether the test is appropriate for their purpose.

Reliability is the degree to which approximately the same results would be obtained if the test were administered again. It is the consistency with which the test measures what it is supposed to measure. Unless a test is valid, it cannot be reliable (Salvia & Ysseldyke, 1981). Reliability is determined by the *test-retest* method (the same test is administered to the same group after a time interval); by the *split-half* method (alternate items of the same test are administered and the results compared); and by administering *alternate forms* of the test to the same population. Several factors influence reliability. A longer test has greater reliability; a shorter interval between tests in the test-retest method increases the reliability index; any variation in the two testing situations lowers the reliability. A reliability coefficient of .90 is considered minimum for making decisions about a particular student (Salvia & Ysseldyke, 1981). Test manuals should include information about the reliability and how this was determined.

All norm-referenced instruments must be standardized, that is, administered to a population that is as similar as possible to the population for whom the test is designed. The sample from whom the norms are derived should be sufficiently large to provide a full range of scores; should describe age, sex, socioeconomic status, geographical distribution, demographic characteristics, and any other relevant variables that will allow for comparisons to be made with the population to whom the test will be administered (Salvia & Ysseldyke, 1981).

Implications for Assessment of Visually Handicapped Pupils

Unless a standardized test has normative data for blind and visually handicapped pupils, results should not be interpreted using the norms published with the

Chart 11.4   Observation instruments for ecological assessment

Instrument	Description	Comments
Social Climate Scales (Moos, 1974, 1975, 1979)	Measures the environment from the participant's perspective. Scales include Family, Classroom, Work, Ward Atmosphere, Community-Oriented, and Group Environmental Programs, Scales.	Compares answers from different respondents (pupils, parents, teachers) to develop a profile of environmental characteristics.
Stern Personality and Environment Indexes (J.L. Richman & Co.,Syracuse, N.Y.)	Measures personality needs and environmental characteristics. Scales available are Classroom Environmental Index, Elementary and Secondary School Index, and High School Characteristics Index.	Compares "needs" inferred from daily activities and behaviors to "press," the social and physical characteristics of the environment.
Classroom Interaction Analysis (Bradfield & Criner, 1975)	Measures interactive behavior in the classroom. Scales include Teacher Style, Teacher Attention, and Pupil Behavior.	Provides an objective method for measuring interaction within the classroom.
Henderson Environmental Learning Process Scale (Henderson, Bergen, & Hurt, 1972)	Measures characteristics of the home setting.	Provides a measure of characteristics of the home that are related to intellectual and scholastic performance of young children.
Home Observation for Measurement of the Environment (Bradley & Caldwell, 1976, 1977)	Measures aspects of social, affective, and cognitive support to the child in the home. Looks at emotional and verbal responsiveness of mother; avoidance of punishment; provision of adequate play materials; language stimulation and pride, affection, and warmth.	Includes infant and preschool versions with interview and observation of parent and child in their home.

test. Further, if test items are omitted because they cannot be completed by visually handicapped pupils, or if the administration and scoring protocols are modified, or if items are adapted, or time limits lengthened, results cannot legitimately be compared with the norms. However, the results may provide valuable diagnostic information concerning a pupil's behavior and performance, may be helpful in identifying strengths and weaknesses that can be addressed in an instructional program, and can be used for identifying additional areas for assessment.

There is some disagreement among professionals regarding the development of separate norms for visually handicapped pupils for commonly used instruments (Bauman, 1973; 1974; Scholl & Schnur, 1976; Vander Kolk, 1981; Warren, 1978, 1984). The argument in favor of using regular norms is related to the fact that visually handicapped pupils live in a sighted world and therefore should be measured on that standard. However, Warren (1984) summarizes the issue when he says that with regard to intelligence tests "the need for separate norming for blind samples has to do with the validity of the test, not with the type of environment that has to be met" (p. 180). Furthermore, there is little information as to whether tactual and auditory experiences are analogous to visual experiences and lead to similar developmental sequences. In addition, the influences of different sensory systems on learning patterns and styles are not well understood. (See Chapter 5). In conclusion, the use of published norms is a question which must be determined by the purpose of the assessment.

Areas typically included in a comprehensive assessment include: functional vision, intellectual and cognitive development, concept development, psychomotor skills, social and daily living skills, academic achievement, and pre-career and career skills. The lists of assessment tools in this part stress measures developed or adapted specifically for the visually handicapped population. Instruments that require some modification for use with visually handicapped students but which have been found very helpful are also included. It should be noted that the areas included here do overlap and some instruments may be useful for several purposes. Publishers of tests are included in Appendix D. For additional lists of assessment tools in common use, see Bauman & Kropf (1979); Chabot (1977); Dronek (1977); Genshaft, Dare and O'Malley (1980); Langley (1978); Ray, O'Neill and Morris, (1983); Scholl and Schnur (1976); Swallow (1981); Yarnall and Carlton, (1981).

Functional Vision

Assessment of functional vision is a necessary complement to the medical eye examination because it focuses on how the child uses his vision. Functional vision is typically assessed by the teacher and uncovers ways in which students use vision to perform various educational, daily living skills, and orientation and mobility tasks. Areas in which training to improve functional vision might be useful can then be identified and procedures designed to increase use of vision. Examples of functional vision assessment tools are included in Chart 11.5. The first seven are useful for screening and identification of a visual impairment. The Holmgren Yarn Test is helpful in identifying children who are color-blind, a frequent concern of early elementary teachers. Additional information on the remaining instruments and procedures for increasing visual efficiency is included in Chapter 6.

Intelligence

Intelligence tests are norm-referenced measures that include items thought to sample the domain of behaviors that reflect intelligence. Since definitions of intelligence vary, behaviors sampled in different intelligence tests also vary. Salvia and Ysseldyke (1981) stress that the same test items may create different psychological demands for children with different background experiences and learning opportunities. Since a visual impairment can lead to experiential and learning differences and deficits, it is important to examine items on intelligence tests critically to determine applicability to visually handicapped pupils.

Tests of intelligence should be administered by a qualified psychologist or psychometrist preferably with experience in assessing visually handicapped pupils. Teachers of visually handicapped pupils must often work with the school psychologist particularly in interpreting the special characteristics and needs of these pupils that have an impact on educational functioning (Spungin & Swallow, 1975). Uses and limitations of tests not standardized on visually handicapped pupils were discussed earlier. Teachers and school psychologists should exercise caution in interpreting results from any of these instruments. Chart 11.6 lists intelligence tests commonly used with visually handicapped pupils.

Concept Development

Concept development is closely related to intellectual and cognitive development. This area includes the assessment of concepts that are basic to the visually handicapped child's performance in school tasks, daily living skills, and orientation and mobility. Assessment instruments are typically administered by teachers and orientation and mobility instructors to identify needed areas of instruction and to monitor progress in the acquisition of skills. Chapter 19 includes information on the interpretation and use of these instruments with visually handicapped pupils in teaching concepts basic for orientation. Chart 11.7 lists tests in this area.

Chart 11.5   Functional vision assessments

Assessment Tool	Publisher	Developed For Visually Impaired	Adapted For Visually Impaired	Purpose
Flash Card Vision Test for Children	New York Association for the Blind	yes	—	distance visual acuity
Eye Chart for Children	New York Association for the Blind	yes	—	distance visual acuity
Near Vision Test for Children	New York Association for the Blind	yes	—	near visual acuity
Near Vision Test—Numbers	New York Association for the Blind	yes	—	near visual acuity
Sloan Test Reading Cards for Low Vision Patients	New York Association for the Blind	yes	—	near visual acuity
STYCAR Vision Tests	Institute of Psychological Research	no	no	distance visual acuity screening
Testing the Untestable (A Vision Screening Program for Exceptional Children)	ERIC Document Reproduction Service	no	no	distance visual acuity screening
Holmgren Yarn Test (Wool Color Test)	Bernell Corporation	no	no	color discrimination
Functional Vision Screening for Severely Handicapped Children	New Outlook for the Blind	yes	—	functional vision
Peabody Model Vision Project: Functional Vision Inventory	Stoelting Company	yes	—	functional vision
Visual Functioning Assessment Tool	Stoelting Company	yes	—	functional vision
Diagnostic Assessment: Program to Develop Efficiency in Visual Functioning	American Printing House for the Blind	yes	—	functional vision

Chart 11.6   Intelligence and aptitude assessments

Assessment Tool	Publisher	Developed For Visually Impaired	Adapted For Visually Impaired	Purpose
Wechsler Preschool and Primary Scale of Intelligence	Psychological Corporation	no	no	intelligence
McCarthy Scales of Children's Abilities	Psychological Corporation	no	no	intelligence
Wechsler Intelligence Scale for Children	Psychological Corporation	no	no	intelligence
Williams Intelligence Test for Children with Defective Vision	Institute for Psychological Research	yes	—	intelligence
Blind Learning Aptitude Test	University of Illinois Press	yes	—	aptitude
Stanford-Owaki-Kohs Block Design Intelligence Test for the Blind	Western Psychological Services	yes	—	intelligence
Haptic Intelligence Scale	Stoelting Company	yes	—	intelligence

Chart 11.7   Assessments of conceptual understanding

Assessment Tool	Publisher	Developed For Visually Impaired	Adapted For Visually Impaired	Purpose
Developmental Activities Screening Inventory	Teaching Resources Corporation	yes	—	early childhood screening
Learning Accomplishment Profile—Diagnostic Edition	Kaplan Corporation	no	no	developmental assessment includes concept items
Reynell—Zinkin Scale for Visually Impaired and Blind Preschool Children	Stoelting Company	yes	—	cognition and language
Brigance Inventory of Early Development	Curriculum Associates	no	no	developmental assessment includes concept items
Body Image of Blind Children	American Foundation for the Blind	yes	—	body image, spatial, and positional concepts
Hill Performance Test of Selected Positional Concepts	Stoelting Company	yes	—	positional concepts
Preparatory Reading Program for Visually Handicapped Children	American Printing House for the Blind	yes	—	pre-reading and reading concepts
Tactile Test of Basic Concepts	American Printing House for the Blind	yes	—	concepts needed to understand instructions in early grades
Piagetian Assessment Battery and Training Manual for Teachers of the Visually Handicapped	Stoelting Company	yes	—	Piagetian indices of cognitive development
Peabody Individual Achievement Test	American Guidance Service	no	no	general information subtest
Peabody Mobility Kits—Concept Development Scales	Stoelting Company	yes	—	pre-mobility concepts
Assessing Basic Competencies: Visually Impaired	American Printing House for the Blind	yes	—	skills and concepts needed for success in society

Psychomotor Skills

Assessment of psychomotor skills is an essential component particularly in the comprehensive assessment of preschool and multiply handicapped children with visual impairments. Chart 11.8 includes a selection of these instruments.

Gross and fine motor skills are essential for later school learning and particularly to the acquisition of orientation and mobility skills. Chapter 7 discusses use of these assessment tools with preschool children; Chapter 9 describes modifications necessary in administering several of these instruments to children with severe multiple impairments. Chapter 19 describes the use of these instruments in orientation and mobility skill development.

Social and Daily Living Skills

Tests assessing social skills include measures of overall social development and acquisition of specific skills such as following directions, working independently, and appropriate interaction with others. Daily living skills include such areas as cooking, house cleaning, leisure skills, money management, personal hygiene, and eating. Tests for these areas are listed in Chart 11.9. These tests typically rely on interviewing either the student or the caregiver. There is conflicting evidence concerning the accuracy of the informant's response, with some evidence of overestimating abilities (Fewell, Langley, & Roll, 1982) and no significant differences between informant's and actual performance measures (Sexton, Kelley, & Scott, 1982). The difference may be attributed to the nature of the test items, a student's handicapping condition, and the relationship of the informant to the student, all of which may have an impact on the informant's response accuracy. Conflicting information from different sources can provide valuable data for the examiner, however, and can lead to confirmation or questioning of a student's actual performance on specific tasks. Discrepant information can also disclose varying expectations for a student on the part of the persons interviewed.

Application of these instruments to the preschool population is included in Chapter 7, to those with severe multiple impairments in Chapter 9, and to culturally different children in Chapter 10. Additional procedures for assessment and instruction in daily living skills are described in Chapter 20.

Academic Achievement

Achievement tests measure mastery in specific content areas. Students are compared with other students on norm-referenced tests. One weakness with such tests is that they may include content not taught in schools and may then become a measure of intelligence (Popham, 1975).

Criterion-referenced achievement tests are concerned with a student's attainment of specific skills and measure the degree to which students have mastered skills in the content area. Both types of tests are typically administered to monitor the child's progress in school. Tests of reading and arithmetic achievement are the areas most commonly used in achievement assessment. It should be noted that the American Printing House for the Blind will print in large type short runs of any special achievement tests used in a school district.

Reading can be broken down into several prerequisite skills to consider for educational assessment: pre-reading and reading concepts, tracking (visual or tactual), phonics, letter recognition, word recognition, comprehension, understanding the purposes of reading, and comparing the effectiveness of two or more reading modes for a particular student (e.g., auditory, braille, regular print, large print). Examples of assessment tools can be found in Chart 11.10.

Assessment skill in mathematics incorporates pre-math concepts including Piagetian concepts such as seriation and one-to-one correspondence. Also included are simple to advanced computation skills, word problems, graphs, geometry, algebra and more advanced skills. Chart 11.11 presents some useful mathematics assessment tools.

Achievement tests can be used as diagnostic tests. This requires an analysis of student responses. For example, on an achievement test item,

$$\begin{array}{r} 9 \\ +\ 2 \\ \hline \end{array} \quad \text{a student answers:} \quad \begin{array}{r} 9 \\ +\ 2 \\ \hline 1 \end{array}$$

The answer is wrong for the achievement test but the teacher should look further into why. Did he add and forget to write down the "10?" Did his vision blur and he saw the + as a −? Does he know what + means? Does he simply not know the answer? The teacher can thus examine incorrect responses as a diagnostic procedure.

Career and Prevocational

As students approach transition from school into the adult world, assessment is useful to determine their understanding of the world of work; qualities necessary to hold a job, such as organizational skills, motivation, timeliness; and performance in vocation-related tasks. Few formal assessment tools provide sufficient information for a full picture of career skills for the visually handicapped adolescent. It is usually necessary to administer items from a variety of assessment measures which may include academic, social, orientation and mobility, and daily living skills to obtain a complete picture. Some assessment tools for this area are listed in Chart 11.12. Most of these measures

Chart 11.8   Psychomotor skills assessments

Assessment Tool	Publisher	Developed For Visually Impaired	Adapted For Visually Impaired	Purpose
Callier-Azusa Scale	Callier Center for Communication Disorders	yes	—	developmental assessment includes motor and perceptual skills
Developmental Activities Screening Inventory	Teaching Resources Corporation	yes	—	early childhood screening includes fine motor
Koontz Child Development Program	Western Psychological Services	no	suggestions for visually impaired	developmental assessment includes gross and fine motor
Brigance Diagnostic Inventory of Early Development	Curriculum Associates	no	no	developmental assessment includes gross and fine motor
Oregon Project for Visually Impaired and Blind Preschool Children	Jackson County Education Service District	yes	—	developmental assessment includes gross and fine motor
GUIDE Developmental Skills	Educational Products and Training Foundation	yes	—	developmental assessment
Frostig Developmental Test of Visual Perception	Consulting Psychologists	no	no	visual perception
Developmental Test of Visual Motor Integration	Follett Educational Corporation	no	no	geometric form reproduction
Motor Free Visual Perception Test	Academic Therapy Publications	no	no	visual perception
Peabody Mobility Programs	Stoelting Company	yes	—	orientation and mobility
Stanford Multi-Modality Imagery Test	American Foundation for the Blind	yes	—	functional imagery related to orientation and mobility

Chart 11.9   Social and daily living skills assessments

Assessment Tool	Publisher	Developed For Visually Impaired	Adapted For Visually Impaired	Purpose
Callier-Azusa Scale	Callier Center for Communication Disorders	yes	—	developmental assessment includes daily living and social development
Koontz Child Development Program	Western Psychological Services	no	suggestions for visually impaired	developmental assessment includes social skills
Brigance Diagnostic Inventory of Early Development	Curriculum Associates	no	no	developmental assessment includes self help skills
Learning Accomplishment Profile—Diagnostic Edition	Kaplan Corporation	no	no	developmental assessment
Oregon Project for Visually Impaired and Blind Preschool Children	Jackson County Education Service District	yes	—	developmental assessment includes self-help and socialization
GUIDE Developmental Skills	Educational Products and Training Foundation	yes	—	developmental assessment
Maxfield-Buchholz Scale of Social Maturity for Use with Preschool Blind Children	American Foundation for the Blind	yes	—	social maturity
Vineland Social Maturity Scale	Western Psychological Services	no	no	social maturity
Developmental Profile by Alpern and Boll	Psychological Development Publications	no	no	developmental screening includes self-help and social skills
Assessing Basic Competencies: Visually Impaired	American Printing House for the Blind	yes	—	basic skills for success in society includes coping skills
Overbrook Social Competency Scale	Nevil Interagency Referral Service	yes	—	social skills

are classified as value scales which determine an individual's weighted preference for things, ideas, people, or behavior (Kerlinger, 1971). Reliable answers and an understanding of the content are necessary for these types of measures. The limited knowledge about the world of work of many visually handicapped pupils may be to their disadvantage in responding to this type of instrument. For example, a teenage girl may state that she wants to work with young children without first-hand knowledge of the responsibilities and commitments required for this type of work. Teachers who use these instruments should make certain that the student does understand the items.

In using any of the instruments included in this part, teachers should recognize that administration protocols must often be adapted to accommodate the special visual, tactual, or auditory needs of visually handicapped pupils; additional cueing, physical guidance, or additional verbal explanations to supplement test directions may be necessary; timing requirements may need modification; and response format and modification of pictures may be required. The teacher must keep in mind the impact of any of the modifications on the results and should be cautious in interpreting the results in comparison with the published norms, particularly for tests that are standardized.

INFORMAL NONTEST-BASED ASSESSMENT

Informal assessment should be considered an essential adjunct to the use of the formal measures and published instruments discussed in the previous section. It is a means by which the teacher gains insight into students' behavior and growth, analyzes the instructional setting, and determines educational needs. A dynamic learning process takes place through interactions among the teacher, other students, the educational setting, and the material to be learned. Learning is not static, but rather ongoing; neither is it sporadic, but rather continuous; it is not isolated, but rather cumulative. For the teacher, collecting meaningful assessment information about the student should also be ongoing, continuous, and cumulative. The products, interactions, and behaviors of the student within the ecological setting generate the information needed for educational decisions based upon reasoned assessment practices.

This section focuses on some useful informal nontest-based assessment approaches and procedures which aid teachers of visually handicapped pupils to identify educational needs and plan instructional programs to meet those needs. The application of selected procedures are intended to illustrate how to monitor student behavior and learning. Through the use of systematic data collection, the teacher not only evaluates learning, but also determines appropriate modifications or strategies to ensure continued development. Informal assessment does not need to be time consuming and when performed properly, it can be most efficient. A skilled teacher informally assesses the student, the task, and the learning environment during instruction or while monitoring student progress.

This section discusses the role of the teacher in the informal assessment process; information that can be gathered from informal assessment; and types of informal assessment.

Role of the Teacher

The teacher of visually handicapped students is the most appropriate person to informally assess functional learning. As the specialist in visual impairments, she can observe the entire range of student behaviors, skills, and attitudes; select and utilize appropriate assessment strategies and/or materials; and when in direct contact with the student and the classroom, can assess the educational as well as the visual needs of pupils. Informal assessment is often an integral part of the teaching activity and utilizes ordinary skills that should be possessed by all teachers. These skills are continuously refined through pre- and in-service training and experience. Effective educational programs require that teachers be specialists in psychoeducational assessment.

Information Gathered from Informal Assessment

Information generated by most informal assessment practices is natural to the educational setting and to the student's daily learning environment. This is a major advantage of informal assessment in that it considers the pupil in relationship to his ecological setting. Prior to beginning any informal assessment, teachers should first review readily available information from the school records: eye examination reports, psychological reports of formal standardized tests, and other data recorded in the school records. (See Chart 11.1.) The teacher then selects tools and strategies for informal assessment to determine variables which affect the child's learning; to identify the most appropriate learning strategies that can be used by the child; to study the interrelationship of the child within the learning environment; to determine learning and behavioral needs; and finally to evaluate what the child has learned. Chart 11.13 lists questions related to these headings that might be explored through informal assessment procedures.

Types of Informal Assessment

There are three major types of informal assessment practices that are, in varying degrees, components of the instructional process. These include interviews, observation, and curriculum-based procedures.

Chart 11.10   Reading assessments

Assessment Tool	Publisher	Developed For Visually Impaired	Adapted For Visually Impaired	Purpose
Roughness Discrimination Test	American Printing House for the Blind	yes	—	tactile discrimination
Mangold Developmental Program of Tactile Perception and Braille Letter Recognition— Criterion Tests	Exceptional Teaching Aids	yes	—	tactile discrimination and letter recognition
Visual Pattern Recognition Test and Diagnostic Schedule	Institute of Psychological Research	no	no	visual pattern recognition
Preparatory Reading Program for Visually Handicapped Children	American Printing House for the Blind	yes	—	pre-reading and reading concepts
Dolch Word Cards	American Printing House for the Blind	no	braille, large print	whole word recognition
Braille Code Recognition Test	American Printing House for the Blind	yes	—	braille code recognition
Brigance Inventory of Basic Skills	Curriculum Associates	no	no	range of reading readiness and reading skills
Brigance Inventory of Essential Skills	Curriculum Associates	no	no	reading skills necessary for independence
Sucher-Allred Reading Placement Inventory	Economy Company	no	no	reading level
Durrell Listening-Reading Series	American Printing House for the Blind (adapted version)	no	braille	reading and listening levels

Wide Range Achievement Test	American Printing House for the Blind (adapted version)	no	braille, large print	reading and spelling levels
Cooperative Sequential Tests of Educational Progress	American Printing House for the Blind (adapted version braille) / National Association for Visually Handicapped (adapted version—large print)	no	braille, large print, normative data for visually impaired grades 4 to 6	reading and listening levels

Chart 11.11   Mathematics assessments

Assessment Tool	Publisher	Developed For Visually Impaired	Adapted For Visually Impaired	Purpose
Piagetian Assessment Battery in Training Manual for Teachers of the Visually Impaired	Stoetling Company	yes	—	Piagetian indices of cognitive development
Key Math Diagnostic Arithmetic Test	American Printing House for the Blind (adapted version)	no	braille	range of math skills
Brigance Inventory of Basic Skills	Curriculum Associates	no	no	range of math skills
Brigance Inventory of Essential Skills	Curriculum Associates	no	no	math skills needed for independence
Wide Range Achievement Test	American Printing House for the Blind (adapted version)	no	braille	math level
Cooperative Sequential Tests of Educational Progress	American Printing House for the Blind (adapted version - braille) / National Association for Visually Handicapped (adapted version - large print)	no	braille, large print, normative data for visually impaired grades 4 to 6	math level

Chart 11.12   Pre-career/career skills assessments

Assessment Tool Tool	Publisher	Developed For Visually Impaired	Adapted For Visually Impaired	Purpose
Brigance Inventory of Essential Skills	Curriculum Associates	no	no	functional skills needed for independence
Assessing Basic Competencies: Visually Impaired	American Printing House for the Blind	yes	—	basic skills needed for success
Kuder Preference Record	Science Research Associates	no	braille form available from Perkins School for the Blind	vocational preference
Hall Occupational Orientation Inventory	Scholastic Testing Service	no	no	career orientation
Crawford Small Parts Dexterity Test	Psychological Corporation	no	no	manipulation
Manipulative Aptitude Test	Western Psychological Services	no	no	manipulation

Chart 11.13   Questions that can be explored in informal assessment

What is the student's functional level?
What can the student do? What specific skills are performed adequately? What skills are not performed adequately? What areas of assessment are needed?

What are the variables which affect this student's learning? How does the student respond to reward? Does the student need more concrete learning experiences? Is the curriculum paced too fast or too slow? Will the student benefit from extended school year experiences? Are additional services required? What about the student's vision, visual functioning, and optimal visual environment?

What learning strategies help the student?
Which educational aids or devices assist learning? Does the student require instruction in slate and stylus skills? Does the student need a functional, critical skills curriculum? What about aural reading? What is the reading rate and/or level of comprehension in the preferred reading mode? Which reading method is most effective? When should certain aids and devices be introduced? Will the student benefit from utilizing a microcomputer or paperless braille system?

How does the student effectively utilize the environment? Does the student require any low vision aids? How well is the student integrated into the community? How well does he function independently? Does the student utilize community resources? How, when, and where does the student apply his orientation and mobility skills? Is the time allocated for school activities sufficient to enable the student to acquire needed skills within the regular school day or does he require an extended school experience?

What are the learning and behavioral needs of students? Which are the high priority skills needed at this point in the student's schooling? What sub-tasks are required for these high priority skills to ensure successful progression in the educational program?

Has the student learned?
How much progress has been made? How can progress be facilitated? What measures have been most appropriate for assessing progress for this student?

Interviews

Interviews can be used for a variety of assessment related purposes (Tucker, n.d.). Parents can be interviewed to identify any problem areas prior to admission of their child into a program; students can be interviewed to determine their attitudes toward admission to the program, toward school, and any other aspect of the student's life; teachers can be interviewed to determine any anticipated problem areas.

Successful interviewing requires skills in interper-

sonal relationships. The interviewer must be able to establish rapport with the person being interviewed; have skill in communicating, including both listening and nonverbal communication; have a focus or purpose for the interview so that rambling is reduced to a minimum; and be able to question judiciously especially when there is any indication that the topic touches on a sensitive issue. Finally, the interviewer must be able to interpret the content of the interview in order to make it useful for the intended purpose. Although unstructured interviews may be useful in some instances, for example in attempting to narrow down the concern expressed by the interviewee, structured interviews directed toward some purpose are more effective. Appendix C includes two illustrative interview instruments, one for interviewing parents to obtain a developmental history; and one for interviewing students that the teacher of visually handicapped pupils may find useful for identifying school problems. Teachers should select only those items which are relevant to the problem being identified.

Although interviewing is useful, there are problem areas. Aside from the issues of validity and reliability, questioning around sensitive areas during an interview may inhibit expressiveness and honesty (Dillon, 1981). Teachers should avoid continuous questions and make judicious use of silence and declarative phrasings during the interview.

Observation

Good teachers use casual, indirect, and continuous observation to monitor what is happening during a lesson. This procedure is usually sufficient when learning is progressing normally. However, when learning is not progressing normally, a more systematic approach is needed in order to define, analyze, or pinpoint a problem. More intensive observation requires that the behavior be viewed and recorded systematically using a predetermined data collection plan. The first step is to target the behavior, that is, determine which behavior is to be observed more closely. Next, the most appropriate type of recording must be selected for the observation in order to identify a behavioral strategy for remediation. Chart 11.14 summarizes three recording procedures.

Chronolog. In the chronolog method, the student is observed during a specified period of time and all activities are recorded. This method is particularly useful to identify behaviors which are antecedent, that is, those that precede the problem behavior, and those which are consequent, that is, those that come after the behavior. Figure 11.1 illustrates a typical chronolog form. The reason for the observation is stated, the classroom activity is specified, and the time period of observation is recorded on the data sheet. Behavioral statements are written in short

Student _____ Date _____

Observer _____ Time _____

Reason for observation _____

_____

_____

Activity period _____

Time	Event

Figure 11.1   Continuous observation

Chart 11.14   Recording behavior during an observation

	Process	Advantages	Disadvantages
Chronolog	Observer writes a detailed account of what student does during a specified time period. (See Figure 11.1.)	Provides information concerning variables which help to identify pattern of behavior; takes into account antecedent and consequent behaviors.	Requires recorder's attention totally centered on one student.
Frequency Recording	Observer tracks occurrence of behavior by event recording used for a discreet behavior (See Figure 11.2.) or duration recording used to determine length of time of the behavior. (See Figure 11.3.)	Useful to establish prevalence of a behavior or to monitor success of a behavioral strategy.	Does not take into account antecedent and consequent behaviors.
Frequency Tally	Observer takes a tally for a specified period of time for one or more specific behaviors. (See Figures 11.4 and 11.5.)	Useful to establish a baseline and monitor success of a behavioral strategy.	Does not take into account antecedent and consequent behaviors.

Figure 11.2   Event recording

Behavior: Patrick pokes his eyes in math class.

Dimension: Number of times Patrick pokes his eyes during 7th grade math, Period III.

When measured: Period III, November _____ to November _____, 1985.

Day 1	Day 2	Day 3	Day 4	Day 5
IIII	IIII I	(absent)	III	(absent)
(Total 4)	(Total 5)	(Total 0)	(Total 3)	(Total 0)

Grand total for 3 days in school = 12 times. Daily average = 4.

Figure 11.3   Duration recording

Behavior: Mary sits alone during nutrition.

Dimension: Number of minutes Mary sits alone during nutrition.

When measured: Nutrition, 10:00 a.m.-10:20 a.m., November _____ to November _____, 1985.

Day 1	Day 2	Day 3	Day 4	Day 5
10:05-10:20	10:12-10:20	10:03-10:07 10:15-10:20	10:08-10:15	10:05-10:20
(Total 15 min.)	(Total 8 min.)	(Total 9 min.)	(Total 7 min.)	(Total 15 min.)

Grand total for 5 days = 54 minutes/100 minutes.

simple language. Judgmental statements that show intent, imply purpose, or draw conclusions are to be avoided. Conversations are recorded as accurately as possible. The completed chronolog provides a comprehensive and accurate recording of all events that should then be summarized to discover the pattern to the behavior and what are the significant variables which directly affect the student's behavior.

Frequency Recording. This method requires that a specific behavior be identified for the observation. The behavior should have a clearly delineated beginning and end. For example, Patrick pokes his eyes in class (Figure 11.2) or Mary sits alone during nutrition class (Figure 11.3).

Frequency Tallies. In this method a set of disruptive behaviors may be tracked concurrently. (See Figure 11.4). The observer tallies the number of times each of the four behaviors occurs during a specified period. A weekly average is then computed for each behavior. After initiating a management control system, graphing may be useful to monitor the success of the intervention strategy. Figure 11.5 used the event recording in Figure 11.4 to chart the daily average for the week.

To implement a total management system, conferencing may be appropriate. Parents, students, school staff, other students if appropriate, meet weekly to review progress on the problem behavior. Often the student can suggest means of helping him control the problem behavior.

	Pokes Eyes	Gets Out of Seat	Talks Out	Incomplete Assignments
11/11 Period III	1111	1111	11	1
11/12	1111 1	111	1	1
11/13	111	111	111	0
11/14	1111	1111	1	0
11/15	1111	11	11	1
Total	23	16	9	3
Average	4.4	3.2	1.8	.6

Figure 11.4   Frequency tally

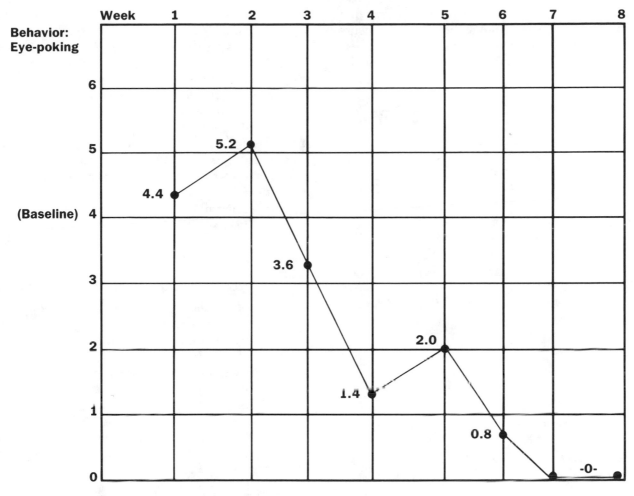

Student: Patrick
Behavior: Eye-poking
Date: November-December, 1985

Figure 11.5 Graphing

Classroom observation may also be helpful in determining the climate of the classroom. The classroom is the ecological environment in which the child lives and to determine a fit between the ecology and the student, interactions should be noted: between visually handicapped student and teacher, visually handicapped student and other students, visually handicapped student and the learning tasks, and visually handicapped student and classroom materials. Chart 11.4 included structured observation instruments that may be useful for this purpose. Sociograms are a useful device to determine the relationship between the visually handicapped pupil and his classmates (Hargrove & Poteet, 1984).

To understand the child as a learner is to recognize the supportive influences and potentially destructive demands upon the student: teaching style of the teacher, peer influences, learning tasks, environmental demands. A shift in any one of these factors may have an effect on the child's learning and behavior.

The teacher of visually handicapped pupils may wish to seek permission of the regular teachers to observe the total classroom ecology in order to facilitate better integration of the visually handicapped pupil in the regular classroom.

Curriculum-Based Procedures

Curriculum based assessment compares favorably with other more formal assessment procedures in problem identification and remediation (Marston, Mirkin, & Deno, 1984). Error analysis and task analysis are two curriculum based methods useful in assessment. *Error Analysis.* Error analysis is directed towards determining the types and patterns of learning difficulties students may be experiencing. Computation error in mathematics is the most frequent error made by students (Reisman, 1972). However, the regular classroom teacher without knowledge of Nemeth Code cannot analyze mathematical errors easily for the blind pupil. Using interview techniques may be a useful substitute. For example, the teacher presents Shawn with some problems and says, "Please do these problems aloud and tell me how you figured out the answer."

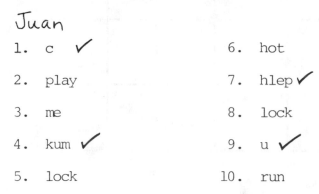

In the first problem, Shawn explains "5×7=35. I put my 5 here and carry the 3. 3+2=5 and 5×5=25." Each problem was explained the same way. The teacher is now able to diagnose Shawn's error pattern, can teach the correct algorithm, and can assist Shawn to develop an understanding of the multiplication process (Mercer & Mercer, 1981).

Juan

1. c ✓   6. hot

2. play   7. hlep ✓

3. me   8. lock

4. kum ✓   9. u ✓

5. lock   10. run

Figure 11.6   Juan's typewritten spelling lesson.

Error analysis of Juan's typewritten spelling paper (Figure 11.6) yielded the following errors:
1. The letter used in place of a word, e.g., "c" for "see;" "u" for "you."
2. Substituted "k" for "c" and deleted silent "e".
3. Reversed two middle letters: "le" for "el."
Error analysis of Juan's braille writing (Figure 11.7) yielded the same types of errors:
1. The letter used in place of the word, e.g., "c" for "see;" "u" for you.

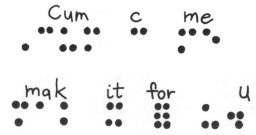

Figure 11.7   Error analysis of Juan's braille writing

2. Omitted silent "e;" "k" for "c;" "Kum" for "come;" "mak" for "make."

Problems with the silent "e" after a consonant-vowel-consonant combination (CVC-e) were also diagnosed in Juan's reading. Pattern errors can be assessed not only within a subject but also across subject areas. Additional instruction in CVC-e is needed by Juan before he can master this concept and apply it to his reading, spelling, and writing.

Error analysis is a powerful informal assessment tool. It enables the teacher to determine which skills are critically needed and what content is necessary to maximize learning. The process itself involves eight steps included in Chart 11.15.

Task Analysis. Task analysis is the process of breaking down a learning task into sequential subskills. It is an essential skill for teachers when developing learning programs, particularly those for multiply handicapped pupils. Chapter 9 explains the procedure in detail for teaching multiply handicapped pupils and Chapter 20 shows its application to the teaching of social skills.

Most curriculum guides and instructional programs have as their basis a task analysis approach to learning units. Scope and sequence charts help teachers develop their own learning tasks. Each subtask has an objective with a stated criterion level. A scope and sequence chart easily lends itself to the development of instructional objectives. See Chart 11.16.

Chart 11.15   Steps in error analysis

Correct the work sample

Note the error(s)

Identify any patterns of error

Analyze interrelationships across skill areas

Formulate behavioral objectives for missing skill(s)

Teach to short term objectives within each skill

Show students the relationships across skill areas

Reassess skills along with the generalized application of the skills

Guidelines for the selection of informal assessment instruments and procedures include:
1. The informal approach or procedure selected depends upon the purpose for the assessment and the efficiency of the technique, including its quality. If the instrument does not address the purpose, then the results are not a valid measure of that behavior.
2. If a selected informal technique requires some ratings or observations, there should be as little difference as possible from one rater to another; otherwise the results are not reliable.

3. Assessment outcome should have direct application to the learning process or to the environment in which the student learns so that intervention strategies can be developed.

Chart 11.16   Reading comprehension scope and sequence list

1. Summarizes main ideas and selects facts to support main ideas.
2. Selects an appropriate title after reading.
3. Answers specific detailed questions.
4. Finds factual and inferential information.
5. Interprets descriptive words and phrases.
6. Recognizes shifts of meaning caused by using words in different context.
7. Selects the meaning of a specific word when the meaning is implied.
8. Interprets literal and figurative meaning.
9. Draws logical conclusions.
10. Predicts possible endings based on previous events.
11. Identifies relationships among characters in a story.
12. Recognizes that characters change as a story develops.
13. Makes inferences about materials read
14. Recognizes structure of plot.
15. Compares similar elements in different stories.

Comprehensive educational assessment utilizes a variety of complementary techniques that allow information to be placed into proper perspective. The determination of which techniques to use and how to interpret results requires a broad understanding of curricular demands, developmental needs, unique needs related to the visual impairment, and a broad knowledge of assessment instruments and procedures.

Study questions
1. Select a visually handicapped child from your practicum setting. What question, problem area, or concern would require a comprehensive assessment. Formulate your question, list areas you would want included in the assessment, and tell what assessment instruments and procedures, both formal and informal, you think would be appropriate.
2. The school psychologist in your school district has never assessed a visually handicapped child before and has come to you for advice on instruments and procedures that are appropriate for visually handicapped children and youth. Summarize what you would include in your discussions with her.
3. Select some assessment instrument described in this

chapter. Look up three reviews of that instrument from the texts and test references listed in additional readings and interpret to your classmates the validity, reliability, and standardization data of that instrument.
4. Select some criterion-referenced test used with nonhandicapped pupils. Review the test and evaluate its appropriateness for visually handicapped pupils. Tell how it would need to be modified for such pupils.
5. Review items on some individual test of intelligence, such as the Wechsler Intelligence Scale for Children Revised. Select items that you think would be discriminatory for a visually handicapped child.
6. In a role playing situation, interview a set of parents about the early development of their child using the interview guide in Appendix C.
7. Ask your supervisor's permission to observe a particular child. Decide what behavior you will observe and select the most appropriate system for recording that behavior. Discuss the results of your observation with your supervisor.
8. Describe the uses and limitations of criterion-referenced tests for visually handicapped pupils.
9. Describe the uses and limitations of norm-referenced tests for visually handicapped pupils.
10. Tell how you would decide on the areas for an assessment of a multiply handicapped pupil with low vision and developmental delay who is enrolled in a special class for the mildly mentally retarded at the junior high school level.
11. Tell how you would decide on the areas for an assessment of a 4 year old child who is totally blind, appears to be developing at a rate appropriate for his chronological age, and who will be entering kindergarten in the fall.
12. Select some assessment instrument and administer it to a visually handicapped child, if possible. If that is not possible, role play such an assessment with one of your classmates.

Additional readings
The following general texts in assessment are listed for supplementary reading.

Goldman, J., L'Engle Stein, C., and Guerry, S. (1983). *Psychological methods of child assessment.* New York, N.Y.: Brunner/Mazel.

Guerin, G.R. and Maier, A.S. (1983). *Informal assessment in education.* Palo Alto, Calif.: Mayfield Publishing Co.

Hargrove, L.J. and Poteet, J.A. (1984). *Assessment in special education.* Englewood Cliffs, N.J.: Prentice-Hall.

McLoughlin, J.A. and Lewis, R.B. (1981). *Assessing special students: Strategies and procedures.* Columbus, Ohio: Charles E. Merrill.

Salvia, J. and Ysseldyke, J.E. (1981). *Assessment in special and remedial education.* 2nd ed. Boston: Houghton Mifflin.

Scholl, G.T. (ed.). (1985). *The school psychologist and the exceptional child.* Reston, Va.: Council for Exceptional Children.

Swanson, H.L. and Watson, B.L. (1982). *Educational and psychological assessment.* St. Louis, Mo.: C.V. Mosby Co.

Taylor, R.L. (1984). *Assessment of exceptional students.* Englewood Cliffs, N.J.: Prentice-Hall.

Wallace, G. and Larsen, S. C. (1978). *Educational assessment of learning problems: Testing for teaching.* Boston, Mass.: Allyn and Bacon.

Wisland, M.V. *Psychoeducational diagnosis of exceptional children.* Springfield, Ill.: Charles C Thomas.

Zigmond, N., Vallecorsa, A., and Silverman, R. (1983). *Assessment for instructional planning in special education.* Englewood Cliffs, N.J.: Prentice-Hall, Inc.

The following are good resources for review of tests.
Buros, O.K. (ed.). (1978). *The eighth mental measurements yearbook.* Highland Park, N.J.: Gryphon Press.

Johnson, O.G. (ed.). (1976). *Tests and measurements in child development.* Vol. I & II. Washington, D.C.: Jossey-Bass.

Kayser, D.J. and Sweetland, R.C. (eds.). (1985). *Test critiques: Volumes I, II, and III.* Kansas City, Mo.: Test Corporation.

Mitchell, J.V., (ed.). (1983). *Tests in print III.* Lincoln, Nebr.: The University of Nebraska Press.

Scholl, G.T. and Schnur, R. (1976). *Measures of psychological, vocational and educational functioning in the blind and visually handicapped.* New York, N.Y.: American Foundation for the Blind, Inc.

Sweetland, R.C. and Kayser, D.J. (eds.). (1984). *Tests: Supplement: A comprehensive reference for assessments in psychology, education and business.* Kansas City, Mo.: Test Corporation.

Sweetland, R.C., O'Connor, W.A., and Pirnazar, (ed.). (1983). *Tests.* Kansas City, Mo.: Test Corporation.

Yarnall, G.D. and Carlton (1981). *Guidelines and manual of tests for educators interested in the assessment of handicapped children.* Dallas, Tex.: South Central Regional Center for Service to Deaf-blind Children.

The following are additional recommended resources.
Jastrzembska, Z. (1982). *Model for a workshop on assessment of blind and visually impaired students.* New York, N.Y.: American Foundation for the Blind, Inc.

Langley, M.B. (1978). *Assessment of multihandicapped visually impaired children.* Nashville, Tenn.: George Peabody College for Teachers.

Ray, S., O'Neill, M.J., and Morris, N.T. (eds.). (1983). *Low incidence children: A guide to psychoeducational assessment.* Natchitoches, La.: Steven Ray Publishing.

Reynolds, C.R. and Clark, J.H. (eds.). (1983). *Assessment and programming for young children with low-incidence handicaps.* New York, N.Y.: Plenum Press.

Scholl, G. and Schnur, R. (1976). *Measures of psychological, recreational, and educational functioning in the blind and visually handicapped.* New York, N.Y.: American Foundation for the Blind, Inc.

Swallow, R.M. (ed.). (1977). *Assessment for visually handicapped children and youth.* New York, N.Y.: American Foundation for the Blind, Inc.

Swallow, R.M., Mangold, S., and Mangold, P. (eds.). (1978). *Informal assessment of developmental skills for visually handicapped students.* New York, N.Y.: American Foundation for the Blind, Inc.

Vander Kolk, C.J. (1981). *Assessment and planning with the visually impaired.* Baltimore, Md.: University Park Press.

CHAPTER 12

Planning the Individualized Education Program

Marjorie E. Ward

This chapter describes the process of formulating an Individualized Education Program (IEP) for a visually handicapped child and illustrates how the IEP goals and objectives are based firmly on the data gathered during the assessment procedures. A second purpose is to point out some assumptions that underlie the decisions that are a part of the IEP process, and to highlight some factors that can influence the design of instructional strategies from which teachers can select those appropriate for their particular students.

In the previous chapter the authors explained the importance of specifying the purpose for the assessment of a visually handicapped child and then for carefully planning assessment procedures, selecting appropriate formal and informal assessment instruments, and interpreting the results in light of that purpose. The purpose for the assessment may be to determine eligibility for service, to predict performance, to monitor academic progress or social and/or motor development over time, or to suggest appropriate placement in the least restrictive setting. Another important purpose for assessment is to specify a child's present levels of performance as accurately as possible. It is this last purpose on which this chapter will focus.

The careful specification of present levels of performance is essential before a teacher can prepare a program of instruction with any degree of assurance that there will be a link between what the child already knows and what the teacher plans for the child to have the opportunities to learn next. Using the information collected during the assessment the teacher can formulate a clear and systematic plan of action or instructional strategy to guide what she will do and what the student will do during the instructional session to show that learning is taking place.

The plan of instruction for handicapped children has been described in P.L. 94-142, The Education of All Handicapped Children Act of 1975, and is known as the Individualized Education Program (IEP). Although the format for an IEP may vary from school district to school district, the process for preparing

the IEP and its contents should be the same from district to district as both process and basic content have been laid out in the Act.

The purpose of this chapter is to describe the process of formulating an IEP for a visually handicapped child and to illustrate that the IEP is based firmly on the data gathered during the assessment procedures described in the previous chapter. A major portion of the chapter will focus on the selection of instructional strategies. It should be obvious that the quality of the instructional plan is closely related to the quality of the assessment data on which the plan is based.

THE INDIVIDUALIZED EDUCATION PROGRAM

At the heart of the instructional program for each handicapped child must be, according to federal law, the individualized education program or IEP. The IEP has been called a "management tool" to be developed to assure that, when a child does require special education, it is appropriate to his special learning needs, is actually delivered, and is carefully monitored (Torres, 1977).

IEP Team

P.L. 94-142 specifies that the IEP be a written statement designed by those persons who are most knowledgeable about the child's educational needs (DHEW, 1977, p. 42490). It is to be developed at a meeting attended by the members of the IEP team as specified in Chart 12.1.

Certain features of this description of who prepares an IEP are of special importance when visually handi-

Chart 12.1 Members of the IEP Team as specified in P.L. 94-142

- Representative of local education agency or intermediate unit, other than the child's teacher, qualified in area of child's need
- Child's teacher
- Child's parent(s) or guardian or surrogate parent
- Child, as appropriate
- Others at parents' or school's request

capped children are involved. First, the representative of the local district or intermediate unit other than the child's teacher is to be present, and that person should know about appropriate services for visually handicapped children. In some districts, especially those in sparsely populated areas, there may be no such person. In these cases, a county teacher of visually handicapped children or program supervisor who is knowledgeable should be involved in the IEP deliberations. Sometimes it is necessary to go well beyond the county of residence to locate a qualified person. Some districts find it necessary to purchase service from another county or district where a qualified person is employed.

The child's teacher is also a member of the IEP team. If the child is presently in the regular classroom, the teacher may have only minimal understanding of the educational and instructional needs of visually handicapped children. If the child is already receiving special education services because of a visual impairment, then at least one of the child's teachers who knows how the child functions visually as well as academically should be a member of the IEP team.

Most parents are rich sources of information regarding the patterns of development, present skills, behavior styles, and needs of their children and certainly parents of visually handicapped youngsters are no exception. P.L. 94-142 recognizes the valuable contribution parents can make to the pool of information on which the IEP for their child is based and, in fact, requires that parents be encouraged to participate in the deliberations. If parents elect not to participate, then districts need to document their attempts to have parents involved. When a parent or both parents do participate, it is encumbent on the school personnel to create an atmosphere in which parents feel comfortable and free to ask questions, offer information, and serve as a functional member of the IEP team for their child.

A handicapped student at the secondary level is more likely to attend the IEP meeting than a younger child, although the Act permits the latter where appropriate. Certainly it makes sense for the individual

most affected by the IEP to be a part of its formation. Other team members need to hear from the student's perspective what instructional needs are perceived as critical. Use of low vision aids, orientation and mobility training, or career and vocational counseling may be uppermost on the high school student's list of needs, and those needs should be identified along with needs others have noted.

Other persons may also attend the formal IEP meeting at the discretion of the parents or school district. Frequently the parents will bring along an advocate, friend, or in some cases even a legal advisor. The district may request the presence of the school psychologist or educational diagnostician.

P.L. 94-142 specifies that there be agreement among those preparing a student's IEP. To facilitate arrival at this agreement, the IEP should be written down for all to examine. There are procedures to be followed if parties cannot come to an agreement, and these are spelled out in P.L. 94-142 as procedural safeguards and due process procedures. Explanations of these procedures are beyond the purview of this discussion; for further information the reader is encouraged to consult *A Primer on Due Process* (Abeson, Bolick, and Hass, 1975) and the due process procedures drawn up by each state to assure compliance with the Federal regulations for implementation of P.L. 94-142.

IEP Content

The Education of All Handicapped Children Act also spells out what each IEP is to contain (DHEW, 1977, p. 42491). These components, as mentioned earlier, are to be written down for all to examine, discuss, and finally approve formally (see Chart 12.2). The specific components are:

1. *A statement of the child's present levels of educational performance.* Here is where information from both formal and informal assessment feeds into the IEP process. While test results and scores taken individually may yield information about one aspect of academic performance and social behavior, they become more valuable to the process of designing instruction when they are added to other assessment information such as observation data, attitude scales, analysis of errors on work samples, and descriptions of functional vision in specific school situations. IEP team members can look for inconsistencies in academic performance or social behavior and may be more likely as a team rather than acting alone to identify information that is perhaps an indication of poor vision more than it is an indication of typical or maximum performance. Such an open forum with all information subject to the scrutiny of all team members, including parents, requires that team members be competent in their specialties and that

each have respect for the contributions and ideas of other team members. When team members vie for power and influence, the vulnerable one is the child.

2. *A statement of annual goals, including short term instructional objectives.* Both annual goals and short term objectives should follow logically from assessment of present levels of performance. If a low vision child is having difficulty with reading, then one annual goal might be identified as improvement in oral reading and one short term objective might be the mastery of a list of sight words not presently recognized accurately on the first attempt. Of course, an objective such as this example assumes that the teacher has assured himself the child can see the printed words well enough to distinguish them; that is, the teacher must be certain the problem is interpreting the written symbols and not registering the visual stimuli.

3. *A statement of the specific special education and related services to be provided to the child, and the extent to which the child will be able to participate in the regular education program of the school.* The first part of this component calls for a description of what the particular child needs that is different from or in addition to the education program provided for nonhandicapped students. For visually handicapped students these services might include orientation and mobility instruction both on and off the school property, a program to stimulate the use of low vision, instruction in the use of special equipment such as the abacus or Optacon, special vocational assessment, typing during the elementary grades, provision of optical enlargement devices and instruction in their proper use, other special reading or writing aids and materials, and any special teaching strategies called for when vision is limited or absent. It is here that the value judgments of team members enter into decisions on what should be taught next. It is one question to ask *how* best to teach a particular bit of information or skill or to stimulate thought along a particular line; it is another to ask *what* among the many things a handicapped child needs to learn to function as independently as possible should be taught at this particular point in time.

The second part of this element of the IEP is aimed at the issue of appropriate placement in the least restrictive environment for the child, given his present levels of performance and current goals and objectives. Placement should not be viewed as a one-time decision; rather, appropriate placements may change as the child learns and grows during the school years. The IEP team is required to describe the extent to which the visually handicapped child will be able to join other children in the regular school activities and participate in the social and extracurricular life

of the school as well as the academic life. Children are to be removed from the regular school program only when they cannot profit from, participate in, and contribute to the activities and atmosphere of the program. Their capacity to do so, not surprisingly, may change over time, and thus changes in placement may be justified as the child progresses through the school years. One student by age 21 may have attended a residential school for visually handicapped children, a special class in the public day school program, and regular classes with the assistance of a resource and/or itinerant teacher.

4. *The projected date for initiation and anticipated duration of such service.* The people who helped write P.L. 94-142 wanted to avoid the unnecessary delays in providing needed services for children that in the past had sometimes plagued parents and slowed down student progress. With the IEP, team members are to specify dates on which services will begin and the approximate period of time they will be required. Some services, such as transportation to and from school, may be required as long as placement continues in that setting. Other services such as initial instruction in the use of an optical enlarger may be for a limited time with periodic follow-up to assure maintenance of skills.

5. *Appropriate objective criteria and evaluation procedures and schedules for determining on at least an annual basis whether the short term instructional objectives are being achieved.* Accountability has become a prime concern among many educators, in part perhaps because of pressures from the community to demonstrate that schools make the kind of difference in the lives of children that the community wishes. P.L. 94-142 calls for at least an annual review of the IEP to determine whether or not the goals are being met and the services specified are being provided and are still necessary. IEP team members must specify what criteria will be used to make such determinations and what procedures will be followed to

collect the necessary data. At this point the IEP process comes full circle; as new data are gathered and evaluated, revisions that are needed in the annual goals and short term objectives should become evident. The IEP team can initiate the process of preparing a new IEP for the next school year or reasonable time period for the particular child.

Chart 12.2   Components of the IEP for a handicapped child

- A statement of the child's present levels of educational performance.

- A statement of annual goals, including short term instructional objectives.

- A statement of the specific special education and related services to be provided to the child, and the extent to which the child will be able to participate in the regular educational program of the school.

- The projected date for initiation and anticipated duration of such service.

- Appropriate objective criteria and evaluation procedures and schedules for determining on at least an annual basis whether the short-term instructional objectives are being achieved.

While the format of an IEP may vary from district to district, as was mentioned before, the content is to be the same as is the process for determining that content. In Figure 12.1 is a sample of an IEP cover sheet on which identifying information for the child is reported, IEP team members listed, special and related services spelled out, and annual and short-term goals summarized. Space is also provided for parents to sign to indicate their having examined and approved the IEP, if that is their decision. In Figure 12.2 another IEP format is illustrated. Figure 12.3 shows an IEP process and content evaluation form which one state, Ohio, drew up to determine compliance with the requirements laid out in P.L. 94-142. Note that the focus is compliance rather than program quality. Program quality demands a different type of evaluation, one that ideally would include observations of the program in operation.

IEPs FOR VISUALLY HANDICAPPED CHILDREN

Now that the major components of the IEP have been explained, some specific considerations regarding IEPs for visually handicapped children should be mentioned. Among these considerations are some basic assumptions about the context or framework within which planning instruction occurs in order to increase the probability that the children will master the objectives that lead to annual goals outlined in their IEPs.

Assumptions Underlying IEP Preparation

The first assumption that underlies instructional planning for visually handicapped children is that careful consideration will be given to the question: given all this child has to learn to achieve his maximum potential, why should he work to master this objective at this time? The greater the severity of the visual impairment, the more critical this question becomes since opportunities for incidental learning are fewer and possibilities for distorted or incomplete sensory input are greater when sensory input is limited than when vision is within the normal range. When reviewing assessment data the IEP team must consider the areas on which to concentrate at that point in the child's life, given the knowledge base and repertoire of skills the child has already acquired and the relevant information and array of skills that lie ahead. For example, a six-year old blind child who functions at a retarded level may have, as a priority in her IEP, the development of toileting, hand-washing, and finger-feeding skills; tactile differentiation and discrimination skills; and standing alone, turning toward, and walking to a person calling her name, objectives that are quite different from those selected for a typical youngster about ready to enter first grade.

Inherent in this first assumption is the question of just what kinds of objectives to include or what kinds of related developmental, corrective, and supportive services to incorporate into the IEP. Since the IEP is supposed to specify an appropriate program for the handicapped child, whatever is listed in the IEP must be provided at no cost to the parents and cannot be omitted because of that cost. P.L. 94-142 makes it clear that such services ". . .as are required to assist a handicapped child benefit from special education" are to be provided; special education is defined as "specially designed instruction, at no cost to the parent, to meet the unique needs of a handicapped child. . ." (DHEW, 1977, p. 42480). For visually handicapped children such services as mobility training, Optacon instruction, instruction with special equipment and materials to stimulate use of low vision, low vision evaluations, provision of optical enlargers or electronic reading aids and the necessary instruction and supervision in their use, and reader service may be required. If such services or special materials are not available locally, they are not to be left out of the IEP if they are what are called for so a particular child can benefit from his education program. At issue is who pays, and especially in sparsely populated areas, where providers can be found. Of course, what is not often recognized unfortunately is who pays and at what cost, if necessary services are *not* provided so a child can profit from the time he spends in school.

What has happened in some instances when services are not currently available because of cost or

INDIVIDUALIZED EDUCATION PROGRAM PLAN

Student's Name: _____

Birth Date: _____

Present Date: _____

Grade/Program: _____

Teacher(s): _____

School: _____

Primary Assignment(s):	Date Started	Expected Duration of Services	Special Media or Materials
_____	_____	_____	_____
_____	_____	_____	_____

Extent to which the
child will Participate
in Regular Education

_____

_____

_____

Services:

_____

_____

_____

IEP Planning Meeting Participants: Name
*Local Education Agency Representative: _____
*Parent, Guardian or Surrogate Parent: _____
 Student: _____
*Teacher(s): _____
**Evaluator(s): _____
 Other(s): _____
        _____

Dates for review and/or revision of the Individualized Education Program Plan: _____

Person responsible for the maintenance and implementation of the IEP plan: _____

*Must attend. If the parent, guardian or surrogate parent does not attend, documentation of attempts to gain their participation should be attached.
**Must attend if the student is newly identified as exceptional.

Figure 12.1   Sample IEP Program Plan

PRESENT EDUCATION LEVELS

Directions: Using as many pages as necessary, describe the student's present educational levels in appropriate curricular areas. These may include but are not limited to:

Academic Achievement	Pre-Vocational Skills
Emotional Maturity	Vocational Skills
Self-Help Skills	Psychomotor Skills
Social Adaptation	Other:

SHORT-TERM OBJECTIVE	INSTRUCTIONAL METHODS MEDIA/MATERIAL TITLES(S) (OPTIONAL)	EVALUATION OF INSTRUCTIONAL OBJECTIVES	
		TESTS, MATERIALS EVALUATION PROCEDURES TO BE USED	CRITERIA OF SUCCESSFUL PERFORMANCE

School District
Responsible _____

Student _____
          (name or number)

Current
placement _____

Eligibility
certified _____
               (date)

Period of individualized education program

_____ to _____

Date(s) of meeting: _____

_____

_____

Persons present	Relationship to child

Curriculum areas* requiring special education and related services	Present level(s) of performance	Annual goals	Short term objectives	Time required	Objectives attained (dates)		
Area 1							
Area 2							

*If more space is required, use an additional sheet.

Figure 12.2   Sample Individualized Education Program form

A. List any special instructional material or media necessary to implement this individualized education program.

Special education and related services recommended	Personnel responsible (name and title)	Date services begin	Duration
Curriculum area 1			
Curriculum area 2			

Student name or number _____

B. Describe the extent to which the child will participate in regular education programs

_____

_____

_____

_____

C. Recommended type of placement: _____
(include physical education)
_____

D. Provide justification for the type of educational placement

_____

_____

_____

_____

E. Actual placement: _____

_____

F. List the criteria, evaluating procedures, and schedule for determining whether the short term objectives are met.

Short term objectives	Objective criteria	Education procedures	Schedule

Date of parental acceptance/rejection _____

Signature _____

Signature _____

IEP EVALUATION — (Classroom)

DOES THE IEP
    Key: ✔ =Yes   X=No

DOCUMENT	COMMENT

☐ It was developed in a conference?
    ☐ District representative(s)
    ☐ Teacher(s)
    ☐ Parent(s)
    ☐ Child (when appropriate)
    ☐ Evaluation Team Member (initial placement)	

☐ That the parent(s) were provided a copy of the IEP?
    ☐ Yes
    ☐ No
    ☐ Unknown
☐ The IEP is readily accessible to the teacher?
☐ The IEP was completed and in place prior to the child's placement?
☐ There is only one IEP?	

CONTAIN
☐ A statement of child's level of educational performance (LEP)?
    ☐ Based upon the MFE for initial IEPs?
    ☐ Based upon objective data collected by the child's teacher(s)?	

☐ Annual Goals for all specially designed instruction
    and related services?
    ☐ Are they based upon the LEP?
    ☐ Do they describe student behaviors to be achieved?
    ☐ Is there a statement of when the goals will be achieved if less
        than one year?	

☐ Short-term instructional objectives?
    ☐ Do they relate to the annual goals?
    ☐ Are they stated as intermediate steps
        which will lead to the respective annual goal?
    ☐ Is there a criterion for success?
    ☐ Are they reflected in the lesson plan?	

☐ Specific educational services to be provided?
    ☐ Is the date of initiation and projected duration shown for
        each service required?
    ☐ Are goals and objectives developed for each service required?	

☐ Extent to which child will participate in regular educational program?	

☐ Criteria, procedures and schedules for
    evaluating achievement of instructional objectives?
    ☐ Is there standardized and/or criterion/referenced evaluation
        for each objective?	

Figure 12.3   Sample IEP evaluation form

staff, has been the decision not to write into a child's IEP what is really needed for the child to profit from special education. When this happens, it is grounds for the parents to refuse to sign the IEP, thus registering their disapproval of the IEP contents. But certainly cost cannot be ignored as eventually the bill arrives.

By exerting their rights to due process and requesting a due process hearing before an impartial hearing officer, parents may succeed in adding to the IEP the appropriate and necessary services their child's condition warrants. Still, the issue of payment for services and trained staff to offer them remains. In his discussion of a situation involving the provision of interpreter service for a deaf child (Board of Education vs. Rowley, 1982), one educational diagnostician, in pointing out the dilemma faced by all parties when federal intent of legislation, in this case P.L. 94-142, is to mandate services but the monies to pay for them are scarce, has observed that:

> . . . Services should not be judicially provided or denied based on their price tag. If funds are not available to provide all of that which the Act entitled to handicapped children, then it is a problem for Congress to resolve by appropriating different monies or by amending the Act accordingly. It is not for the Supreme Court to adjust spending priorities by interpreting the scope of the Act so narrowly. (Heaney, 1984, p. 461)

Closely related to the first assumption regarding selection of objectives is a second that presumes the selection of instructional objectives and strategies to achieve them has occurred within the context of a systematic process of designing instruction. One model for systematic instruction appears in Figure 12.4. In this model, the first step is the identification of relevant attributes of the learner. Based on that assessment of attributes, appropriate instructional goals and objectives can be specified. Then comes the focus of concern in the next part of this chapter, the selection of an appropriate instructional strategy. The subsequent steps in the model are addressed in later chapters in this text and include the selection of

instructional media and materials, the actual implementation of the instructional strategy, and the evaluation of the results of instruction. A summative evaluation at the end of instruction can yield information not only about the competence of the student in reaching the particular objective but also about the efficacy of the instructional program; we may in retrospect, for example, find that learning did not occur as had been anticipated because there was a breakdown in the match between student and objective, between student and strategy, between student and materials, or between student and evaluation process.

A third assumption is that those persons preparing the IEP have examined their philosophical positions regarding how children learn, various theories of child development including cognitive theories as represented by Piaget, maturational theories as espoused by Freud and Gesell, and behavioral theories with which Skinner, Bandura, and Engelmann are associated. While a teacher who views a child's behavior to be the product of his biology, predetermined by genetic patterns, and strongly directed by inner thought and feelings might actually select teaching strategies similar to those of a teacher who views behavior as a product of an individual's own design and heavily influenced by the child's own choices and active participation in the instructional activities, the rationales the two teachers might give for their choices may be quite different. In the ideal situation, theories about how children learn will issue from the philosophical view a teacher holds about children and their relation to their environment and those people around them (Seaver and Cartwright, 1977). Unless time is spent in thinking through a philosophical position and then analyzing what theories of learning logically follow and what repertoire of instructional practice could result, planning instruction may be reduced to trial and error.

For purposes of this discussion, learning will be defined as the acquisition of new skills or information and the acquisition of skills to manipulate that information in new ways. Gagne has described learning as a "change in disposition or capabilities which persist over a period of time and which is not simply ascribed to processes of growth" (1977, p. 3). The goal for teachers, then, is to design instruction and choose strategies that lead to changes in skills, size of knowledge base, and level of abilities to manipulate information that last over time and that cannot be attributed only to physical changes in the learner.

One final assumption regarding the process of designing instruction has to do with the recognition that no one instructional procedure or strategy so far has been found adequate and effective for all children or learning environments. Some teachers may espouse one particular method or technique or set of materials

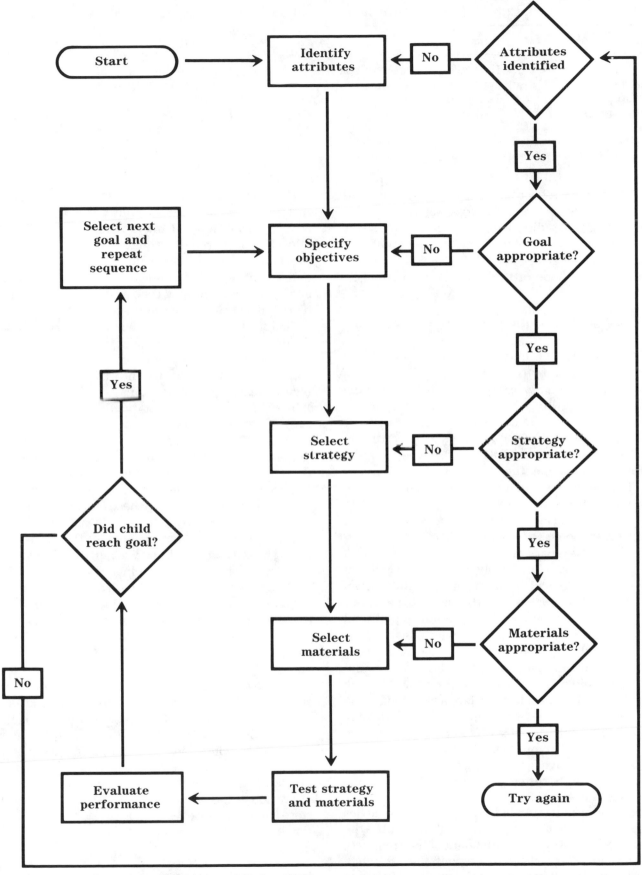

Figure 12.4   Diagnostic Teaching model   Source: M.E. Ward, *Educating special learners* (Belmont, Calif.: Wadsworth, 1981), p. 388.

Chart 12.3   Factors influencing selection of instructional strategies

Setting	Task	Learner
Residential program	Time allotted, needed, spent	Input channels available
Private placement	Type of learning outcome	Output channels available
Institution	Degree of involvement with others	Degree of useful vision
Regular class		Repertoire of experience and knowledge
Resource room		Level of function in areas relevant to task
Special class		

to use with students, but research to date has not revealed conclusive evidence that there is one way without rival to arrange the conditions for youngsters to master bodies of information, develop cognitive and problem-solving skills or performance skills, control their own behavior, or develop attitudes and value systems.

Factors Relevant to the Selection of Instructional Strategies

There are many methods teachers can employ to promote learning by their students. Although the selection of one method or strategy depends upon the particular situation, there are several important factors that can influence what strategy is finally chosen. (See Chart 12.3) These are the setting in which instruction will take place in the event no space options are available, the specific task, the type of learning outcome expected, and the desired degree of involvement with other learners.

First, the setting in which instruction is to take place may preclude some activities but add to the effectiveness of others. What can be done, for example, in a self-contained class for visually handicapped children may be more difficult in a resource room program where children come and go throughout the day or in a regular class where a visually handicapped child is one of fifteen to thirty children whose teacher has access periodically to the services of a consulting or itinerant teacher. The physical facilities and equipment available will also permit or limit the selection of activities. Here a teacher may face a serious dilemma if the setting, facilities, or equipment is not available that would enable the most effective strategies to be used. If too much compromise is necessary, over time, the results can have far-reaching effects on the overall education of the visually handicapped child, or any child, for that matter.

Next, the task itself will suggest some approaches to instruction. For example, time plays a role—the amount of time available, the amount of time required, and the amount of time actually spent (Carroll, 1963). A child may be allotted a certain amount of time to master a task. But the amount of time that child may need to master that task may exceed the amount

allotted. Or, the child may not need that much time. In addition, the amount of time and effort the child is willing or able to spend may be less than that allotted.

Reading rate may be slow due to the extra time needed to follow a line of print, the limited number of letters or words in the field of view at each fixation, the amount of additional processing time required to interpret a blurry or distorted image, or the length of time needed to find the beginning of the next line of print. So the child with low vision in a regular class setting may fall behind or not complete work on time because of time constraints, unless the teacher considers the time factor in planning instruction.

In addition to time, the type of learning outcome can influence the selection of teaching strategies. Gagne (1977) has identified five major kinds of learning (see Chart 12.4) and the external conditions that can enhance their development: intellectual skills, cognitive skills, verbal information, motor skills, and attitudes. While several of these learning outcomes may be a part of a particular task, one may be the primary concern as, for example, in the mastery of typing where motor skills may dominate but cognitive skills and attitudes are also involved.

The degree of involvement with other learners that would be desirable also can influence instructional decisions. In some instances a child needs to work independently or needs to learn to work independently. At other times, a child may profit from cooperative enterprises or perhaps competitive situations. Certainly the strategies for independent work will be different from those for cooperative and competitive efforts.

Finally, characteristics of the learner discussed in earlier chapters, play a role in the final selection of instructional strategies to facilitate learning. They include the degree of useful vision, other input channels available and their efficiency, the output modes available, the repertoire of previous experiences and knowledge the child has stored and can retrieve, and the present level of function in areas relevant to the task at hand.

Instructional Strategies

Most teachers upon reflection would agree that the instructional strategies they design for any given

Chart 12.4   Five major categories of learned capabilities, including subordinate types, and examples of each

Capability (Learning Outcome)	Examples of Performance Made Possible
Intellectual Skill	Demonstrating symbol use, as in the following:
Discrimination	Distinguishing printed m's and n's
Concrete Concept	Identifying the spatial relation "underneath"; identifying a "side" of an object
Defined Concept Rule	Classifying a "family," using a definition
	Demonstrating the agreement in number of subject and verb in sentences
Higher-Order Rule	Generating a rule for predicting the size of an image, given the distance of a light source and the curvature of a lens
Cognitive Strategy	Using an efficient method for recalling names; originating a solution for the problem of conserving gasoline
Verbal Information	Stating the provisions of the first Amendment to the U.S. Constitution
Motor Skill	Printing the letter R
	Skating a figure eight
Attitude	Choosing to listen to classical music

Source: R.M. Gagne, *Conditions of learning* 3rd edition (New York, N.Y.: Holt, Rinehart, & Winston, 1977), p. 47.

instructional session incorporate elements of telling, leading, showing, probing, and verifying. It is important for the teacher to be aware of what is happening during instruction and to make conscious decisions based on sound reasoning about what strategy or mix of strategies to employ. Since we cannot depend upon students learning all they need to know by osmosis, by coincidence, or by other ways not fully identified, we need to arrange conditions that will increase the probability for learning to occur; we need to plan for systematic instruction. Our interest must focus on the arrangement of activities and conditions external to the learner that promote learning (Gagne, 1977; Gagne & Briggs, 1974) and the instructional strategies that lead to the outcomes we desire.

The strategies to be discussed in this section can be placed along the "telling-discovery methods continuum" (Glennon, 1981, p. 38) depicted in Figure 12.5.

Lecture. The "telling" method where the teacher presents information and the student takes in what is said is possibly the most used (and abused) strategy found in classrooms. For visually handicapped students whose repertoire of experiences may be limited, a discrepancy may develop between what message the teacher presents and what message is received by the students. For example, if the topic for the lesson is the changing of the seasons and their relationship to the earth's rotations and revolution around the sun and students have no understanding of "rotation" and "revolution" or at least the meaning of "revolution" in this context, little learning and much confusion may occur.

Demonstration. Often teachers plan to illustrate their ideas with demonstrations to show what happens, how

it works, or the sequence of events. Frequently these demonstrations are used in conjunction with lectures and they can be effective in increasing the level of understanding of otherwise abstract concepts as, for example, illustrating the earth's rotation and revolution. For the low vision child, a demonstration may be very helpful but only if the child can clearly see it. For the functionally blind child, a demonstration must be accompanied by an accurate verbal description of what is happening and ample opportunity to handle the materials being used and to ask questions to clarify and verify what is happening. Even then demonstrations may not have the same power for the blind learner as for those who have some vision.

Question and probe. Frequently a teacher will use questions to check students' understanding during the process of instruction. Responses to probes serve as feedback to the astute teacher and provide data on which the teacher can base immediate or later revisions in instruction. For example, a teacher lecturing on the earth's rotation may quickly realize a change in strategy is necessarily based on responses, or lack of responses, to questions about the earth's tilt, the position of the hemisphere in relation to the sun during rotation and revolution, etc.

Guided discussion and discovery. With this strategy the teacher has the end point in mind and leads the comments, questions, and observations of the students so they eventually arrive at that predetermined point. Some teachers rely heavily on this strategy in the study of literature, history, and social studies as well as in the physical, earth, and life sciences. The method can be quite effective as long as the students have the necessary background knowledge of the topic and can follow the logic of the discussion.

	Guided discovery	?
"Pure" telling		"Pure" discovery

Figure 12.5   **The telling-discovery methods continuum** (Source: V.J. Glennon, (ed.), *The mathematical education of exceptional children and youth: An interdisciplinary approach.* (Reston, Va.: National Council of Teachers of Mathematics 1981), p. 38.

While these four strategies usually are illustrated with a picture of a live teacher before a group of students whose attention is riveted on that teacher, permutations also exist. Programmed instruction is a form of guided discussion where student responses are used to determine progress through material to a predetermined point. It can be a linear format with one path followed by all students or a branching format with various paths selected for students dependent upon student response to set questions. Another variation of guided instruction is computer-assisted instruction or CAI. With CAI, the traditional interface of teacher and pupil takes on a different character as the pupil interacts with the subject matter via a computer terminal of some type rather than via another person. While the teacher's physical presence may not be required during the instructional period, the amount of instructional planning and the sequencing of ideas as well as the management of correct and incorrect responses reveal the quality and extent to which the instructor has analyzed and anticipated what could happen during the interaction between student and material.

Other strategies can also enhance the acquisition of knowledge and skills. Modeling behavior that is appropriate may enable a youngster to learn by imitation. The model may be the teacher, another child, or an individual in a film, video tape, story, or simulation. Of course, careful selection of the model is imperative; the model should be "good" and acceptable for the child (Walker & Shea, 1976). For visually handicapped children the effectiveness of models again depends on how accurately the children can see, touch, and/or hear what is going on.

Some learning for all children calls for the mastery of motor skills. For blind children as well as low vision children, and actually others who may see in fact quite well, it is effective to lead the student physically through the moves and positions the task requires. In some cases actual physical manipulation of the body may be necessary as, for example, in printing or cursive writing, lifting heavy objects without straining

muscles, cutting with scissors, plucking guitar strings, holding a long cane, or setting a book on the viewing table of an electronic visual aid. Physical manipulation may be an appropriate substitute for modeling in many cases.

Peer tutors may also be chosen as a means of delivering instruction. The behavior of peer tutors can also vary from side to side on the telling-discovery methods continuum shown in Figure 12.5. The strategies peer tutors use are typically those of the teachers who train them. While the "delivery system" may be new, the instructional strategies usually are not.

Having a sighted child work together with a visually handicapped child may be a very effective way to having both children come to recognize, respect, and complement each other's strengths and weaknesses. In some instances the visually handicapped child may take the role of the tutor, while in others the sighted child may. There is often as much benefit for the tutor as for the tutee since one of the best way to learn something is to teach it to another person.

In reality, the instructional strategies and variations mentioned here are rarely pure. Elements of telling emerge during demonstrations, examples creep into lectures to demonstrate specific points, and guided discussions may be halted while particular ideas are clarified. That probably does not matter unless the teacher is not aware of what is happening and does not realize if certain strategies are not as effective as others.

> . . . In general, it can be said that the method of teaching through telling is most appropriate for arbitrary associations and the simpler types of conceptual learning. As the kind of learning increases in complexity through the higher concepts, generalizations, and problem-solving, the method should shift increasingly to the right of center on the (telling-discovery methods) continuum . . . (Glennon, 1981, p. 39)

Direct Instruction

Prior to the design of an instructional session, the decision should be made regarding what role the teacher will play during instruction. At times the teacher will want to control very openly what goes on and what students do, in which case, in large measure, students "receive" instruction; they listen, they read, they respond, and they watch as directed. At other times the teacher assumes what to observers might be a more passive role and the learners appear to be in charge. The teacher facilitates learning by presenting opportunities, offering suggestions at critical junctions, and providing materials that stimulate thought in the desired direction. The teacher's role may fluctuate during the course of a day as well as within one instructional period.

When the teacher wishes to manage and monitor the instructional session closely, the direct instruction approach is very effective. Direct instruction calls for "precise, measurable objectives for each child and setting up instructional environments and procedures in such a way that both the child and the teacher know exactly what is to be learned and what criteria will be used to judge the learning" (Cartwright, Cartwright, & Ward, 1981, p. 392). Essential elements of direct instruction are systematic assessment of behavior, careful planning of instruction with regard for the identification of prerequisite skills, and the use of objective evaluation procedures so it is clear when instructional goals have been achieved. Careful sequencing of instructional activities and pacing are also ingredients of successful direct instruction. The diagnostic teaching model (see Figure 12.4) is one way to approach direct instruction.

Another popular technique, contingent on detailed analysis of behavior, is applied behavior analysis. Applied behavior analysis techniques rely on careful and precise observation and accurate measurement of behavior and then make use of consequences to maintain or modify particular behavior (Hall, 1971). The focus is on what might be done to increase, decrease, maintain, or develop a specific or target behavior. Of critical importance are the ABCs of behavior analysis: the antecedent stimuli or events that precede the target behavior and set the occasion for the behavior to occur, the target behavior itself, and the consequences of that behavior that immediately follow. Behaviorists try to control the consequences by selecting reinforcers and the schedule for their presentation that will affect the strength of the target behavior in the desired direction. A reinforcer is "any event or stimulus consequence that increases the strength or future probability of the behavior it follows" (Hall, 1975, p. 2).

Behavior Modification Steps

The basic steps for planning systematic changes in behavior using techniques of behavior modification and management have been summarized as follows:
1. Select the target behavior to be changed. This behavior must be precisely described so when it occurs there is no problem in recognizing it. The selection process should include a consideration of the frequency, intensity, duration, and type of behavior as well as, naturally, the determination of the direction for the change in that behavior.
2. Collect and record baseline data, that is, data about frequency and/or duration of the target behavior before any intervention is used.
3. Identify appropriate reinforcers for the individual or group by observing what is reinforcing or by asking what would be reinforcing. Reinforcers serve as the consequences of the target behavior. If the consequences of a behavior are positive from the viewpoint of the student, the probability of that behavior

occurring again under similar circumstances is greater than it would be without those consequences. Positive reinforcers may be external and tangible symbols of success such as a star, a point, a check, a pat, smile, wink, or word of praise or encouragement. Reinforcers may also be internal satisfaction, a feeling of accomplishment, the solution to a puzzling question. The goal is to have the child "perform the desired behavior, not for a tangible reward, but for the satisfaction he receives as a result of personal achievement" (Walker & Shea, 1976, pp. 14-15).
4. Collect and record data to demonstrate the effects of the intervention upon the target behavior. One way to determine if change in the desired direction has occurred is to compare data after intervention with the baseline data. Data may be collected and recorded in a variety of ways to show frequency of response, rate of response, or percentage of responses that are correct. (See Chapter 11.) A variety of designs are used in applying techniques of behavior analysis to demonstrate a causal link between teaching behavior tactics and student improvement (Cooper, 1981). Cooper has prepared a detailed discussion of the array of procedures to measure and report school-related behavior for the reader who wishes more specific information (Cooper, 1981).

To increase the frequency or strength of desirable behavior with techniques of behavior modification, there are four strategies that are common and effective.
1. Shaping—the systematic and immediate reinforcement of successive approximations of the target behavior until the target behavior is achieved.
2. Modeling—the provision of an example of behavior to be imitated.
3. Contingency contracting—the formation of an agreement, written or oral, between student and teacher that specifies the responsibilities of each in relation to an agreed upon activity: in simple terms, "If you do X, then you can do or get Y."
4. Token economy—a system of exchange of earned symbolic things like check marks or cards for specific rewards (Walker & Shea, 1976, pp. 43-63).

To decrease the likelihood that undesirable behavior will continue, there are six main strategies used in behavior modification.
1. Extinction—removal or withdrawal of reinforcers that have previously maintained or increased a behavior.
2. Time-out reinforcement—removal of an individual from an opportunity to receive reinforcement to one where no reinforcing event is available for a specific period of time.
3. Satiation—in common parlance, "getting too much of a good thing;" continued and increasing reinforce-

ment of a behavior to the point where the behavior is decreased or eliminated.

4. Punishment—presentation of an unpleasant or aversive stimulus to decrease an undesirable behavior; leads to a decrease in frequency of response in presence of the same antecedents.

5. Reinforcement of incompatible behavior(s)—rewarding a behavior that is in opposition to or incompatible with the undesired behavior.

6. Desensitization—systematic procedure to lessen a specific fear that an individual has learned (Walker & Shea, 1976, pp. 64-84).

Management of behavior that is deemed inappropriate or incompatible with the desired behavior can present a challenge to experienced as well as to new teachers. Results of research have clearly demonstrated that programs of behavior modification using contingency management based on reinforcement theories have been implemented successfully with visually handicapped children to reduce the frequency of self-injuring behaviors (Barton & LaGrow, 1983; Luiselli & Michaud, 1983; Longo, Rotatori, Kapperman, & Heinze, 1981) and manneristic behaviors such as rocking and head-wagging (Simpson, Sasso, & Bump, 1982; Sklar & Rampulla, 1973; Caetano & Kaufman, 1975; Miller & Miller, 1976) as well as to increase the frequency of time spent working on academic tasks (Swanson, 1977; Roades, Pisch, & Axelrod, 1974) and waiting on command (Yarnell & Dodgion-Ensir, 1980; Kornsweit & Yarnell, 1981). With severely multiply handicapped visually handicapped children who have limited repertoires of behavior to begin with, behavior modification programs may be necessary just to elicit any type of response. Belcastro (1977-78) has reviewed research done with visually handicapped children and youth using single-subject research designs and has pointed out the characteristics of good studies that readers should copy in their own efforts to decrease inappropriate behaviors and increase desirable behaviors of visually handicapped youngsters.

All students, including those with impaired vision, need to learn that their behavior leads to consequences. Teachers need to be able to determine when to apply the systematic techniques of behavior management and when to try other strategies. A critical component that can often sway an opinion for or against a behavior modification program is the degree to which the subject, the person whose behavior is to be modified, has control over what happens to him and to the amount of say he has in determining what behavior will be changed and how. The less control and input the subject has, the more uncomfortable some teachers become with the instigation of tightly controlled behavior management programs and the more ethical questions they pose. A major concern is what appears to some to be the treatment of people, especially whose capabilities are very limited, as objects rather than as people (Allen, 1979; Augenstein, 1979). While this is not the intent of behavior management techniques, the risk, nevertheless, is there.

Another concern expressed by teachers is the degree of stress given to the evaluation of learning based solely on behavior immediately after instruction. Bruner (1977) has observed that performance is really a "surface expression" of competence; we assume that performance on the tasks we select and in the situation we devise accurately indicates student competence. For low vision children and children with no usable vision, that assumption may be violated unless strategies are appropriate so students have ample opportunity to learn what we have decided that they should learn and to demonstrate in a variety of ways that they have mastered the task or know the information. For example, correct responses to a test of multiple choice questions may reveal one level of mastery, while questions that probe for specific applications, analyses, or use of the information to solve problems may uncover, to a greater extent, the degree to which that information has been assimilated and can be drawn upon in various situations.

Instructional strategies relying primarily on a sequence of stimulus presentation, student response, and immediate reinforcement of the desired response are considered especially good for encouraging and shaping behavior (Briggs, Campeau, Gagne, & May, 1967). For development of concepts, rules, and problem-solving skills, other strategies may be just as or more effective and efficient.

EXAMPLES OF IEPs AND INSTRUCTIONAL STRATEGIES FOR VISUALLY HANDICAPPED CHILDREN

To illustrate the major points in this chapter about systematic planning of instruction in accord with the information about a child and the goals and objectives selected for that child as outlined on his IEP, three descriptions of instructional sessions follow. The teacher has planned instruction according to the curriculum of the regular class in Ben's case or in accord with the contents of the IEPs in the cases of Bruce and Lucretia. Instructional strategies vary to meet the needs of the child and the purpose of the lesson. Given that no one way is necessarily the best way to carry out instruction, consider what alternative plans and strategies might be used with these students.

Ben

Mrs. Petrie has arranged a science learning center in her regular fifth grade class where each afternoon four children gather while their classmates read or work on their social studies class project assignments. Ben, who has low vision due to congenital cataracts and glaucoma, takes his place with the other three children around the table where two balances and two boxes of various gram pieces have been set out. The children start to explore the gram pieces and immediately comment on the different colors and sizes. Ben and Carlos begin sorting the plastic gram

weights by size. Ben is very much a part of the activities. He leaves the regular class just four times per week for the resource room where he is learning to type and to use an optical enlarger for his reading assignments (see Figure 12.6).

Mrs. Petrie wants the students to see how the balances can be used to verify the youngsters' estimates of the weights of the gram pieces. Since the students seem interested in color and size, Mrs. Petrie elects to guide their activity by asking "What else can you observe about the gram pieces besides their color and size?" Several children mention that the pieces of the same color and size fit together. Several others match the one-gram pieces with the two-gram pieces, and Paula announces that the sets are now equivalent but not equal in size and heaviness. These terms the children had used in a previous science lesson and also in their arithmetic.

Micky, who has been taking apart the balances during the discussion, suggests that they might check out weights with the balances if the holding cups with magnets used in an earlier activity were exchanged for cups with no magnets. Mrs. Petrie supplies the necessary cups and helps the children set up the balances and check their calibration. The children together make up a chart to indicate how many one-gram pieces balance with the two-gram pieces and how many ten-gram pieces balance with the twenty-gram pieces. Ben is put in charge of sorting and selecting the pieces to balance. Paula records the data, Carlos verifies the position of each balance indicator and announces what balances with what, and Micky manages the assembly of all the equipment. At the end of the activity, Mrs. Petrie has the children explain

how many ways they can judge equivalency using the gram pieces and the meaning of the terms balance, variable, and calibration.

Bruce

Miss Cassidy, the resource room teacher, has observed herself and in conjunction with Mr. Jacoly that Bruce, age eight and very nearsighted, has had difficulty reading cursive writing and has not yet mastered writing the letters in his name. Mastery of cursive writing is one of the language arts goals on Bruce's IEP for the year (see Figure 12.7). She decides to have Bruce spend fifteen minutes after lunch recess practicing first his name and then the other letters on which his classmates in the regular second grade are working. Bruce has said that Mr. Jacoly wants him to write his name "the right way" on his spelling paper from now on.

Miss Cassidy has Bruce print his name first. Then she has him select the vowels in his name from a set of cards on which the vowels have been written in cursive style. Next she has him select the consonants, starting with the capital 'B.' Bruce confuses the 'B' with the 'R' and 'P', so Miss Cassidy has Bruce talk about similarities between the three letters and describe where they are different. Bruce then arranges all the letters in the correct order to spell his name, traces the letters with his finger as he describes them, and finally starts writing on wide-lined paper with a medium-width marking pen. He uses his assembled letters as a guide when necessary. Miss Cassidy also has available for Bruce several practice sheets on which she has written his name on the top line as a model. She physically guides Bruce's hand to practice the 'B' several times, each time doing less of the actual manipulation of his hand. She uses a similar strategy for the letters of Bruce's last name and then proceeds to the remaining letters of the alphabet. Bruce checks off on a chart each letter he has mastered in cursive at the end of each week. He decides that he wants to be finished in a month with all the letters.

Lucretia

Lucretia, age eleven and in the special class for visually handicapped children, is reading on the fourth grade level. She uses braille for most of her reading but has also started Optacon lessons. Mr. Orpheus has observed that Lucretia does not read along for more than one minute without asking for help which she really does not need, getting out of her seat, or speaking to the youngsters next to her. Lucretia's IEP (see Figure 12.8) calls for her to improve her study skills, one of which is ability to work independently. Mr. Orpheus has decided to initiate a behavior management program to increase Lucretia's independent reading time and decrease her off-task behavior.

INDIVIDUALIZED EDUCATION PROGRAM PLAN

Student's Name: Ben Martin

Grade/Program: 5th grade and resource room for VH chn

Birth Date: 2/17/73

Teacher(s): Mrs. M. Petrie & Mr. J. Gibson

Present Date: 9/25/83

School: Livermore Elem.

Primary Assignment(s):	Date Started	Expected Duration of Services	Special Media or Materials
Reg. 5th grade and resource room (4 times per wk, 45 min. per time	9/83	6/84	Talking Books, tapes, typewriter, Visualte..
Regular class – for all academic work, gym, and art			

Extent to which the child will Participate in Regular Education

Resource room – for study time with special media, for typing lessons and practice, and for development of listening skills

Services:

Bus transportation	9/83	ongoing
Mobility evaluation	3/84	to be determined
Low vision evaluation	4/84	

IEP Planning Meeting Participants: Name

*Local Education Agency Representative: Mrs. Shana Lowry

*Parent, Guardian or Surrogate Parent: Mr. & Mrs. Benjamin Martin

Student:

*Teacher(s): Mrs. Margo Petrie & Mr. Jesse Gibson

**Evaluator(s): Mrs. Carrie Davis, School Psychologist

Other(s): intern (with permission of parents)

Dates for review and/or revision of the Individualized Education Program Plan: 9/84

Person responsible for the maintenance and implementation of the IEP plan:

*Must attend. If the parent, guardian or surrogate parent does not attend, documentation of attempts to gain their participation should be attached.
**Must attend if the student is newly identified as exceptional.

Figure 12.6   IEP cover sheet for Ben Martin

Short term objectives	Objective criteria	Education procedures	Schedule
1. Write UC and LC letter in cursive writing	1. correct formation of letters upon request	3 lessons of 15 minutes in length each week after lunch period; chart for student to make; materials- marking pen, letter models, wide lens and regular desk line paper.	To be completed by 1. 10/31
2. Use cursive writing for spelling tests.	2. Correct formation of letters on weekly spelling tests.		2. 1/15
3. Use cursive writing for all language arts written work.	3. Correct formation of letters of random sample of written work during mid March		3. 3/31

Date of parental acceptance/rejection 8/24/83

Signature _Bruce J. Genog, Jr._

Signature _Rosemary L. Genog_

Figure 12.7   Excerpt from IEP for Bruce Genog.

Mr. Orpheus charts on a simple histogram Lucretia's frequency of on-task behavior for five days during the fifteen-minute periods of independent reading time each morning. When Mr. Orpheus shows Lucretia the histogram and the felt markers that indicate how many minutes she worked on her reading without any interruptions, she agrees that she is not getting much reading done. Together they plan a program to help Lucretia spend more time reading and less time fussing. Mr. Orpheus shows Lucretia his timer and explains that he will set it for one minute at the beginning of the next reading period. If Lucretia is reading appropriately when the timer stops, she will get a small card put on her desk and the timer will be set again. Lucretia suggests that once she has earned five cards she be allowed to stop reading. Mr. Orpheus continues their negotiations with the counteroffer that as soon as she has earned five cards without a 'fault' she can take a two-minute break. Then they will increase to seven cards after which she can have a break of two minutes. Lucretia, who in the past has enjoyed keeping track of her progress by using charts and string graphs, asks Mr. Orpheus if she can make her own chart and promptly spends her thirty minutes of free time at lunch that day designing and making her chart without a single pause. Mr. Orpheus notes, not without some amusement, her intense concentration. At the end of three weeks, Lucretia's chart shows the progress she has made toward her goal of fifteen minutes (see Figure 12.9).

The process of planning instruction for visually handicapped children corresponds essentially to the process of planning instruction for all children. The process, to be effective, demands that conscientious professionals devote considerable intellectual effort and physical energy to focus with each child's parents on the special education needs of the child and on how those needs can be appropriately met in school. That "how" then must be detailed in the individualized education program for the child. For the low vision or blind child, the quality of the IEP goals and objectives rests heavily on the quality of the assessment data. As has been emphasized in earlier chapters, the IEP team members need to verify that the assessment data give evidence of the abilities and achievement levels of the child accurately and not merely reflect the fact that a child has impaired vision.

In this chapter, the intent has been to describe the process of preparing an IEP for a visually handicapped child and to highlight some important assumptions underlying the decisions that are a part of that process. In addition, factors that can influence decisions regarding instructional strategies used with visually handicapped children have been described in terms of the telling-discovery methods continuum. Finally, to breathe some life into the discussion, Ben, Bruce, and Lucretia and their teachers were introduced to illustrate how the contents of IEPs can be translated into interactions between students and teachers during the actual process of instruction.

Instructional Area: Study skills

Annual Goal: Lucretia will increase her ability to work independently once a task has been presented to her

SHORT-TERM OBJECTIVE	INSTRUCTIONAL METHODS MEDIA/MATERIAL TITLE(S) (OPTIONAL)	EVALUATION OF INSTRUCTIONAL OBJECTIVES	
		TESTS, MATERIALS EVALUATION PROCEDURES TO BE USED	CRITERIA OF SUCCESSFUL PERFORMANCE
Lucretia will - read silently with no off-task* behaviors for periods of 15 minutes *Off task behaviors: leaving seat talking aloud nudging child to left or right asking for help when none required	Ginn 720 reader, 4th level "Patterns" supplementary stories	changing criterion design to increase on-task behavior Progress to be charted on chart made by Lucretia Mastery — to be determined by comparing behavior to criterion	15 minutes of reading with no off-task behavior during independent reading time

Figure 12.8   Sample instructional objective from Lucretia's IEP

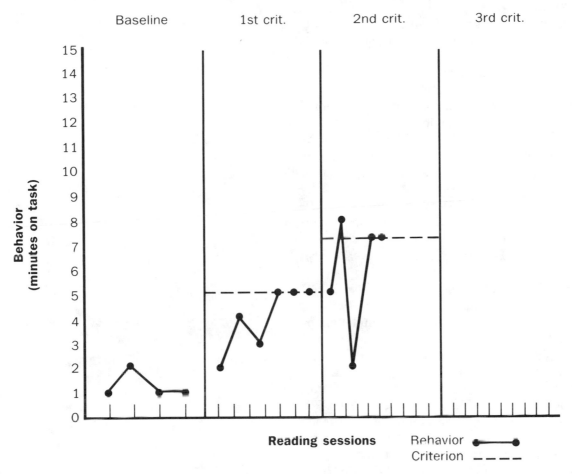

Figure 12.9   **Effects of reinforcement on Lucretia's time spent reading independently.**

Study questions

1. Explain the intent of the Individualized Education Program for handicapped children.

2. Who is to participate in the preparation of an IEP for a handicapped child? What types of information do you think each should contribute to an IEP for a visually handicapped child?

3. What related services might be necessary for a low vision or blind child? What issues surround whether or not these services are actually written into the child's IEP?

4. What is your position relative to this statement: "Cost and availability of services should dictate where visually handicapped children are placed for their education."

5. What assumptions underlie the planning of instruction for visually handicapped children? What are some implications if any of these assumptions are violated?

6. What influences can the instructional setting, the specific task, and the amount of time allotted for mastery of a specific task have on the selection of instructional strategies for visually handicapped children?

7. Describe the major instructional strategies along the telling-discovery continuum and explain the role of the teacher and the student as each strategy is implemented.

8. What is direct instruction? What are three critical elements in direct instruction?

9. Describe the ABCs of applied behavior analysis. What are some techniques of applied behavior analysis that can be used to increase the frequency of a target behavior? decrease it?

10. What do you see as the major responsibilities of the teacher of visually handicapped pupils in the design of instruction for visually handicapped children?

Additional readings

Bruner, J. (1981). *Toward a theory of instruction.* Cambridge, Mass.: Belknap Press of Harvard University Press.

Cooper, J.O. (1981). *Measuring behavior.* Columbus, Ohio: Charles E. Merrill Publishing Company.

Gagne, R.M. (1977). *Conditions of learning.* New York, N.Y.: Holt, Rinehart, and Winston.

Glennon, V.J. (ed.). (1981). *The mathematical education of exceptional children and youth: An interdisciplinary approach.* Reston, Va.: National Council of Teachers of Mathematics.

Hall, R.V. (1975). *Managing behavior: Behavior modification—Basic principles.* Lawrence, Kans.: Hand H. Enterprises, Inc.

Keller, F.S. (1969). *Learning: Reinforcement theory.* New York, N.Y.: Random House, Inc.

Mangold, S. (ed.). (1982). *A teacher's guide to the special education needs of blind and visually handicapped children.* New York, N.Y.: American Foundation for the Blind, Inc.

Mills, A. E. (ed.). (1983). *Language acquisition in the blind child: Normal and deficient.* London: College Hill Press.

Swallow, R.M., Mangold, S., and Mangold, P. (1978). *Informal asssessment of developmental skills for visually handicapped students.* New York, N.Y.: American Foundation for the Blind, Inc.

Torres, S., (ed.). (1977). *A primer on individualized education programs for handicapped children.* Reston, Va.: Foundation for Exceptional Children.

Walker, J.E. and Shea, T.M. (1976). *Behavior modification: A practical approach for educators.* St. Louis, Mo.: The C.V. Mosby Company.

CHAPTER 13

Educational Programming

Dean W. Tuttle

This chapter discusses educational programming to meet the general and unique needs of visually handicapped students, regardless of the multiplicity of handicaps. The chapter summarizes philosophy and purpose; program provisions for visually handicapped students; the process of program implementation; traditional service delivery models; and administrative issues and concerns.

The topic of educational programming for visually handicapped students must be viewed in the context of special education, and even more broadly, general education. Special education complements the services and programs provided by general education and together they serve common goals established for the education of all children and youth. Therefore, a brief consideration of the general goals of education is appropriate.

Bower (1966) has suggested that the purpose of education is to assist children and youth to acquire life competencies enabling them to love, to work, and to play. Learning to love involves the process of developing enough of self to be able to share it with another as well as cultivating the desire and willingness to share another's self; work refers to the ability to contribute to the welfare of another; and play, the ability to participate in recreational activities for the purpose of enjoyment and renewal. Children and youth must learn to exercise these life competencies within a cohesive system of acceptable cultural and personal values.

The purpose of education just described applies equally to all children and youth whether disabled or non-disabled. However, handicapped children and youth have some unique needs which prevent the attainment of these life competencies through the ordinary provisions of general education. Special education provides the modifications required to meet the unique needs, thus enabling them to acquire the skills essential to becoming fully functioning, fully participating members of society. Modifications will generally be required in one or more of the following categories.

1. Curriculum (partial or total)
2. Learning strategies (compensatory or adaptive skills)
3. Materials and devices (media)
4. Classroom management (teaching techniques)
5. Environment (architectural and other physical barriers)

A child whose handicap is interfering with or disrupting adequate educational progress will require at least one and frequently more than one of these modifications. The more severe the handicap or the more severe the multiplicity of handicaps, the greater is the number of modifications that are required to meet the educational needs of that child. The discussion of educational programming to meet the general and unique needs of visually handicapped children, regardless of the multiplicity of handicaps is divided into the following sections: philosophy and purpose; program provisions for visually handicapped students; the process of program implementation; traditional service delivery models; and administrative issues and concerns.

PHILOSOPHY AND PURPOSE

As stated above, the purpose of education is to equip children and youth with life competencies that enable them to love, to work, and to play within the context of an acceptable system of values. This purpose is equally applicable to the education of visually handicapped children and youth. All too often, unfortunately, visually handicapped students do not acquire these requisite independent living skills. For example, Morrison (1974) described some visually handicapped young adults who did not know that eggs come twelve to a carton, did not know how to make a bed, did not know that exact change was not needed when making a purchase. "What good does it do to know about the Boer War, if you can't make your bed?" (Morrison, 1974, p. 459). Education of the visually handicapped is more than academics, more than passing one grade level after the other (Tuttle, 1981). Only with the well-established competencies of life can visually handicapped individuals be expected to become fully functioning, fully participating members of society.

To accomplish this task most effectively, visually handicapped children should be educated in as normal and natural an environment as possible. For many, this means being educated with sighted peers and living at home. If either of these settings appears to jeopardize optimum growth and development in

the cognitive (academics), behavioral (independent living skills including compensatory or adaptive skills) or affective (self-concept including self-esteem) domains (Tuttle, 1984), then other program alternatives may be more appropriate (Stager, 1978). For some, the residential school may provide the essential components for optimal growth and development (Miller, 1984; Silverstein, 1985).

One of the basic philosophical positions underlying educational programming for visually handicapped students is that the visually handicapped child "is first of all a child, more clearly resembling all other children than differing from them, and that the similarity of his 'childness' must never be allowed to be obscured by the difference of his blindness. . . . The emphasis of his educational program must be not on the differences due to his blindness, but on the commonalities that he shares with all children, with provisions made for variations due to his own individuality and the limitations of his blindness" (Stratton, 1977, xi, xii, xiv).

Although most educators would agree that assimilation of visually handicapped students into the sighted community is desirable and necessary, time to interact and learn from other visually handicapped children and youth is essential to the development of a healthy and realistic self-concept. The fundamental principle that visually handicapped children should be educated with sighted children to the maximum extent possible must be balanced with another principle that they also need to learn some adaptive coping behaviors as well as certain things about themselves from others who are visually handicapped.

Educational programming for visually handicapped students does not begin when the child formally enters school at age six. Optimally, programming starts at birth or as soon as possible after the visual loss has been diagnosed since the most critical period of the visually handicapped child's educational program is the early preschool years when his basic attitudes, feelings, and approaches to problem-solving are established. (See Chapter 7.) O'Brien (1975) felt that "it is extremely important that visually impaired children be given ample time to grow in a richly stimulating and supportive setting until they are developmentally ready for a meaningful and successful school experience" (p. 201). In some states there are preschool counselors available to families with visually handicapped preschoolers. In other states, depending on state and district guidelines, the teacher of visually handicapped may begin working with visually handicapped infants at birth or at age three.

During the school years, general education plays a primary role in the education of most visually handicapped children. "Children with visual limitations, like all school-age children, are first and foremost the responsibility of general education. Only when it is clear that the regular educational provisions provided for all children are inadequate to meet the needs of children who are blind or partially seeing should special programming be sought" (Ashcroft & Zambone-Ashley, 1980, p. 29). Even those children who are placed temporarily in self-contained special education classes or in residential schools will return, it is anticipated, to the general education setting. As a general rule, the curriculum needs of visually handicapped children are the same as those of their sighted peers. Therefore, "the overall curriculum and standards should not be different for the child with visual impairments" (Ashcroft and Zambone-Ashley, 1980, p. 33).

PROGRAM PROVISIONS FOR VISUALLY HANDICAPPED STUDENTS

Although the overall curricular needs of visually handicapped children and youth are the same, access to that curriculum is achieved through the implementation of the types of special education modifications described earlier in this chapter. There are four key participants involved in the process of providing the required modifications to the visually handicapped student: the federal government; the state department of education; the local education agency; and the national, state and local agencies, and organizations.

The Federal Government

In addition to P.L. 89-313, "The Aid to Education of Handicapped Children in State-Operated Institutions Act" and P.L. 94-142, "The Education for All Handicapped Children Act" discussed previously in this book, the legislative branch has enacted, the executive branch has implemented, and the judicial branch has interpreted many other laws designed to support and equalize educational opportunities available to visually handicapped children and youth in the United States. For example, in 1887 Congress passed a bill which established the American Printing House for the Blind for the purpose of producing and distributing textbooks and other educational material in the media appropriate for visually handicapped children. The most significant piece of legislation to be passed in recent years is Section 504 of P.L. 93-112, the Vocational Rehabilitation Act of 1973 and the federal rules and regulations which were released in 1977 by the former U.S. Department of Health, Education and Welfare. This law protects the civil rights of all handicapped individuals, children and adults, and prohibits discrimination in education, housing, transportation, and employment on the basis of the handicap. In addition to the passage and implementation of these laws, the Federal government has a responsibility to monitor and enforce state and local compliance.

State Department of Education

Every state has enacted its equivalent of the Education for All Handicapped Children Act to be implemented through the State Department of Education. As a general rule, someone in the State Department of Education is charged with the responsibilities of the state consultant for education of visually handicapped children.

The state's consultant for the visually handicapped is the state's primary advocate for and facilitator of appropriate, quality education for all its visually handicapped children and youth and the state's primary monitor of local compliance with state and federal regulations. Some of the responsibilities include: providing leadership and on-going professional development for teachers of visually handicapped students; designing child search plans; serving as consultants to local districts in the development of appropriate program models with adequate funding for the requisite teaching staff, educational materials and equipment, and related services; and maintaining communication and facilitating cooperative efforts with the public, other agencies, the medical community, U.S. Office of Education, teacher training institutions, national professional organizations and consumer groups (SECVH, 1984).

The Local Education Agency (LEA) or Residential School

At the local level, the teacher of visually handicapped students is the primary advocate for and facilitator of appropriate, quality education for all visually

handicapped children and youth within the district or residential school. It is the program administrator's responsibility to secure the services of a qualified and certified teacher of visually handicapped students; to obtain and manage the necessary fiscal resources to make available related services, as required; to provide the structure and guidelines for the efficient implementation of the program; and to evaluate periodically its effectiveness (Florida AEVH, 1977; Moore and Peabody, 1976; Spungin, 1981).

The residential school serves a unique role, distinct from the local education agency. The law holds the LEA responsible for all handicapped children within their jurisdiction, even children attending residential schools. The residential school serves as an educational resource to all school districts within the state (Miller, 1984; Silverstein, 1985).

National, State, and Local Agencies and Organizations

There are many public and private agencies and organizations that offer support services or provide specialized materials and/or equipment for visually handicapped students. The effective utilization of these other resources enhance the quality of the educational experience for visually handicapped students. Many states have established an instructional materials center for visually handicapped students which assists local education agencies to find sources and secure appropriate educational materials for visually handicapped students. (See Chapter 17.) In many local communities, volunteers and service clubs are actively involved in the special education programs for visually handicapped students.

When the four participants (the federal government, the state education agency, the local education agency, and the national, state, and local resources) work together toward the common goal of quality educational programs for visually handicapped children and youth, the free and appropriate public education promised by the law indeed becomes a reality. If any one or more of the participants is ineffective or work at cross-purposes, the quality of the educational experience suffers and is in danger of being less than adequate.

THE PROCESS OF PROGRAM IMPLEMENTATION

The recent federal and concomitant state laws which address the educational needs of handicapped children are designed to provide a free and appropriate education for all handicapped children, to assure parent participation in the decision-making process, and to protect the rights of handicapped children and their parents. The educational program deemed appropriate must be provided without charge to the parent and must include any related support services such as transportation, therapies, mental health services, etc. essential to the child's educational growth.

The intent is to serve all handicapped children and youth 3 through 21 years of age. However, the mandate of P.L. 94-142 "does not apply to children aged 3 to 5 years or 18 to 21 years if such requirement is inconsistent with state law or practice or any applicable court decree" (Gearheart, 1980, p. 40). To assure that every handicapped child is provided with a free and appropriate educational program, every school unit needs to establish procedures for each phase of the process.

Child-find
In order to reach every potentially eligible handicapped child and parent, extensive and aggressive childfind procedures must be implemented in the school and the community. Mass media informational campaigns, school and community vision screening programs, behavioral checklists for teachers and parents, and informative programs at service clubs and other organizations are a few of the activities to serve this purpose. Although referrals are handled differently in each school district, procedures to refer a child for further consideration must be clearly communicated to agencies and organizations which may make referrals.

Assessment
Parental permission is required before any assessment can be conducted. The law provides for regular, complete, and nondiscriminatory assessment to minimize erroneous diagnoses which, in turn, result in incorrect placements and inappropriate programming. The diverse range of needs among visually handicapped children and the unique set of needs of each child require careful and thorough assessment. (See Chapter 11.)

Low vision children and children who are primarily tactile and auditory learners must not be placed at a disadvantage during the evaluation process because of their lack of vision. Appropriate adaptations and modifications must be made available to assure valid and reliable findings.

Since children's needs change from month to month and from year to year, regular periodic assessment must be conducted. For children already receiving special education, a complete reassessment must be undertaken at least every three years to permit appropriate alterations, when necessary, in the programs. Of course, less comprehensive assessment of children's progress takes place all year long.

Eligibility
The first question to be answered from the assessment findings is whether the child is eligible for special education services. At a meeting frequently referred to as a staffing or multidisciplinary team meeting, educational, psychological, medical, and other professionals along with the parents make this determination. If it can be demonstrated that the child has a visual impairment, then there must be sufficient evidence to indicate that the visual impairment is indeed an educational handicap and that it is interfering with the child's adequate functioning in the regular classroom. A measured reduction in visual acuity or visual fields is insufficient in and of itself to determine eligibility; only when both conditions are met is the child eligible for special education services.

The Individualized Educational Program
After the child's needs have been assessed and a determination of eligibility for special education services has been made, the staffing team is responsible for the development in writing, and the maintenance of an Individualized Educational Program (IEP). Chapter 12 examined the process of formulating the IEP and of selecting appropriate instructional strategies for implementation.

Placement
With the identification of needs, services, and service providers, there remains the question of which is the most appropriate educational setting or service delivery model. The law stipulates that the visually handicapped child should be placed in the "least restrictive environment," the environment that least restricts the child's educational growth. It might be referred to as the child's "most productive environment." The specialized needs represented among visually handicapped children vary considerably in both type and intensity. Therefore, a variety of service delivery models is required to accommodate this diversity. "The law does require that there be a continuum of alternative placements available, which ensure that the child has available to him an educational program commensurate with his needs" (Champion, 1979, p. 247).

In fact, when the team is making a placement decision, all possible alternatives must be considered to assure the parents and professionals that the least restrictive or most productive environment is being selected.

Bryant (1984) grouped program alternatives for visually handicapped students as: 1. self-contained classrooms in either residential or public schools; 2. cooperative programs between residential schools or special classes in the public schools and regular education classrooms; 3. resource programs including resource room, itinerant and residential school short-term special purpose provisions; and 4. consultative programs providing support to regular classroom teachers. She stated that "a continuum of services must allow for movement between program units of various design depending upon student need at any point throughout his or her school years. It may be more administratively efficient to adopt a single plan...but such a rigid plan is limiting and defeats the existence of a true, working continuum" (p. 15).

The placement decision is influenced by a number of factors. Each child's unique set of needs and circumstances must be considered individually. The fundamental issues are the extent of the child's needs and the services required to meet those needs adequately. The variables listed below impact upon the team's decision.

1. *Extent of the child's need for specialized instruction:* Visually handicapped children who are involved in learning many compensatory or adaptive skills will require intensive instructional time from the teacher of the visually handicapped. For example, a child in need of intensive instruction in beginning braille, typewriting, or visual functioning may require a service pattern that enables daily contact.

2. *Developmental level or grade placement:* As a general rule, the younger the child, the greater his needs. A child in the primary grades who is still developing basic skills has greater need for specialized instruction than a youth at the secondary level.

3. *Degree of independence and maturity:* Visually handicapped children who have failed to develop compensatory skills, personal study habits, or personal management skills require more supervision and instructional time.

4. *Nature and extent of visual handicap:* The type and degree of the visual impairment determines in part the nature and extent of the specialized services required. For example, a low vision youth with diminishing vision may have more intense needs than a low vision youth with stable vision. (See Chapters 3-6.)

5. *Nature and extent of additional handicaps:* Each additional handicap further compounds and exacerbates the basic needs of the visually handicapped child. As a general rule, severely multiply handicapped blind children require a special education program for most if not all of the day. (See Chapter 9.)

6. *Recency of onset of visual handicaps:* The more recent the visual loss, the more critical is the need for learning new adaptive behaviors and coping skills. A recently blinded teenager would need to focus more time and energy on the acquisition of new compensatory skills than a congenitally blind teenager.

7. *Quality of home and community support:* A positive and accepting home and community environment is essential for maximum growth and development. A home environment that is not conducive to the child's welfare may suggest a need for an alternative placement.

8. *Quality of specialized services and resources:* Sometimes placement decisions are based on the availability of specialized services such as orientation and mobility instruction or physical therapy. When administrative convenience is the sole criterion for placement, it is a violation of the intent of P.L. 94-142.

9. *Nature of the available adapted educational materials and equipment:* Well equipped special class or resource rooms have a greater concentration of specialized materials and devices. A child who needs continuous access to braille reference books, electronic devices, and adapted curriculum materials will need to be placed where these are accessible.

10. *Geographic circumstances and the extent of travel required:* Parents who live in rural, sparsely populated regions have fewer program alternatives. A child who could profit from placement in a resource room but lives 50 or 100 miles away, will require multi-disciplinary creative program planning. (See Chapter 10.)

11. *The preferences of the parent and child:* The preferences of parent and child must play a significant role in placement decisions.

12. *Results from previous placements:* If the previous year's placement successfully met the child's needs, there is probably little reason to change unless the child's needs have changed.

The key to successful placement is the flexibility to utilize the best of several traditional service delivery models in combinations for varied lengths of time in order to meet the unique needs of a specific child. "Essential to the effectiveness of such plans is the flexibility of individual placements and opportunity to modify the plans for an individual child when the situation calls for such modification. Placement in one type of program or the other should not imply a total or permanent commitment to that placement" (Ashcroft & Zambone-Ashley, 1980, p. 29).

Due Process
Due process procedures are designed to protect the rights of each handicapped child. Parents may protest any decision felt to be detrimental to their handicapped child's welfare. Under the same provisions, school officials have equal rights to protest actions of

parents that seem to endanger their handicapped child's best interest. There are three possible courses of action to resolve any disagreements: 1. a hearing by an impartial hearing officer; 2. appeal to the state department of education; and 3. litigation in the courts.

The rights of handicapped children and their parents are protected in several other ways. Consent of parents is required for the initial assessment and for placement decisions. If the parents disagree with the assessment findings of a district, they can request an independent evaluation to be paid for by the district. If a handicapped child's parents are either unavailable or unwilling to participate in the staffing process, provisions have been made for surrogate or substitute parents. Parents are entitled to a written notification before any changes in program goals or program placements are implemented. It is clear that the checks and balances available through the due process procedures serve to protect the handicapped child's welfare.

TRADITIONAL SERVICE DELIVERY MODELS

The oldest educational program for visually handicapped children in the United States is the residential school for the blind, a model that was first established in the early 1830s and continues to be available in most states today. At the turn of the century, other program models began to emerge—first, the self-contained class in the public schools, then the resource room, and finally the itinerant teacher and teacher-consultant organizational patterns. (See Chapter 1 for a description of the historical development of educational programs for the visually handicapped.) Each new model that emerged allowed for greater and fuller assimilation into the regular educational program. Rather than replacing former models, each new model became another alternative from which to choose.

For years, the visually handicapped child and his parents have had a choice: the child could either enroll in a residential school for the blind or attend the local public school which, if large enough, would probably have the services of a trained teacher of visually handicapped students. However, there were and still are children, particularly low vision children, who chose to attend the local public school even without special education support. If the visual limitation was not interfering with educational progress and the child was indeed functioning efficiently and independently, then this choice may have been appropriate. Unfortunately, far too many visually handicapped students still attend public schools without the services of a trained teacher of visually handicapped persons even though they could profit from some or all of the special education modifications described earlier in this chapter.

Five of the traditional service delivery models will be analyzed: 1. the teacher-consultant model; 2. the itinerant teacher model; 3. the resource room model; 4. the self-contained class model; and 5. the residential school model. The essential features of each model will be described and then this section will conclude with a comparison of all five models.

The Teacher-Consultant Model

The teacher-consultant is a special educator specifically prepared to work with visually handicapped students, a role that is more consultative than instructional. In its purest form, the teacher-consultant emphasizes supportive and administrative functions to equip the regular classroom teachers and aides, their administrators, and other school personnel to meet most if not all of the visually handicapped child's needs. Obviously, the student who is served in this manner must be relatively independent and, therefore, would have little need of intensive training in the compensatory skills or other coping behaviors associated with the visual handicap.

Typically, the teacher-consultant serves multiple school districts through a regional administrative unit. Since restricted vision is a low prevalence handicap and since many parts of the United States are rural and sparsely populated, some of these regions span several counties. Usually, the special education office and storage space for the materials not currently in use are centrally located. Nonetheless, the special teacher may, on occasion, find it necessary to spend the night when visiting visually handicapped children in distant communities.

The major advantages of this program model are that the visually handicapped child remains in his home community, attends the local school with sighted peers, and is taught almost exclusively by the regular school personnel thus minimizing the stigma associated with special education. There are two primary disadvantages: 1. minimal time for direct instruction of the visually handicapped child by the specialist; and 2. the time and fatigue involved in traveling great distances.

The Itinerant Teacher Model

The itinerant teacher model is the most common and, from an administrative point of view, perhaps the most convenient way to serve visually handicapped children in the U.S. public schools. Under this plan, the visually handicapped child lives at home and attends classes in the local public school with other neighborhood sighted peers and, for most of the school curriculum, is taught by the regular classroom teachers. As the name implies, the itinerant teacher for visually handicapped students travels from school to school to provide the special education modifications required by each visually handicapped child. Frequently there is only one teacher of visually handicapped students per district, supervised by the director of special education.

Moore and Peabody (1976) studied the specific functions of itinerant teachers for the visually handicapped in Pennsylvania. "Itinerant teachers reported an average of approximately 59% of their time in direct instruction of children, 11% in consultation relating to the children, and 16.5% driving. The remaining 13.5% of their time was utilized in administrative duties such as procuring materials, record keeping, meetings, reviewing referral materials, and screening referrals" (p. 48). Naturally, the amount of time available for direct instruction of visually handicapped children depends on the number of different schools and the geographic distances involved.

The work space provided for this instruction varies from one school to the next and, at times, from one week to the next. It would not be surprising to find the itinerant teacher and child working in the corner of the regular classroom, the library, the hall, the nurse's office, or even a janitorial closet. Unfortunately, the work space is not always assigned with reference to the physical environmental needs of the child, a reality that puts pressure on itinerant teachers to be creative and assertive in their role as advocates.

The itinerant teacher's office and storage for housing the adapted educational materials and devices is usually located either in a district administrative office building or in one of the schools being served. Because the adapted educational materials and devices must be transported, it requires careful planning and coordination with the classroom teachers.

Although the itinerant teacher's visits are more frequent (every second or third day) than the teacher-consultant's, this model still requires that the visually handicapped student function in the regular classroom with a fair degree of freedom and independence. "If a child has had the advantage of a stimulating family and preschool experience, has high levels of ability and motivation in school, and has demonstrated emotional stability and adaptability, it may be possible for him to succeed adequately in an itinerant program from kindergarten through grade 12" (O'Brien, 1973, p. 364). Unfortunately, there are visually handicapped students being served on an itinerant basis for the sake of administrative convenience but whose more intense needs could be better served by another program model.

The success of the itinerant teacher model and, for that matter, the teacher-consultant model, depends on the attitudes of the regular classroom teachers and their willingness to adapt to some special needs and to assimilate the visually handicapped child into the classroom activities. Kielbaugh (1977) studied the attitudes of elementary school classroom teachers toward mainstreamed visually impaired children and found them to be, in general, positive.

The Resource Room Model

Jones and Collins (1966) described the resource room as a "specially staffed and equipped room to which blind and/or partially seeing children who are enrolled or registered in regular classrooms come at scheduled intervals or as the need arises" (p. 6). Once again, there is the cooperative effort between general education and special education to meet the needs of the visually handicapped child. As in the previous models described, the regular classroom teacher has the responsibility of providing for the general curricular areas for all children in her care including the visually handicapped child while the resource room teacher has the responsibility of providing for specialized compensatory skill instruction, information counseling about blindness, and academic remediation necessitated by the visual loss.

Unlike previous models, the fully equipped resource room and specialists in education of visually handicapped students are always available to the visually handicapped children and their regular classroom teachers. If problems arise during the day, they can be addressed immediately without waiting for the

next scheduled visit from the specialist. There is a danger, however, that too much assistance is offered thus restricting the vital and essential growth toward independence. Because there are usually several visually handicapped children attending the school where the resource room is located, specialized instruction can take place in small groups as well as individually. The resource room provides an opportunity for visually handicapped children to interact and learn from each other as well as from their sighted peers.

"The resource room teacher and aide are full members of the faculty in the elementary school in which they are based. Hall duty, bus duty, lunch room duty, playground duty, faculty meetings, and in-school committees are shared equally with regular staff" (O'Brien, 1973, p. 367). As a result, the special educator can gain a real sense of belonging to a single professional team that remains fairly constant.

Most resource rooms for the visually handicapped are located in the more densely populated urban and suburban sections of the country. Children usually travel away from their home neighborhood to attend the school that houses the resource room and thus do not attend school with the other neighborhood children.

The Self-Contained Classroom Model

The self-contained classroom for visually handicapped students in the public schools is a specially staffed and specially equipped room that serves visually handicapped children for most if not all of their instructional needs for both the general curriculum and special education. The teacher of the visually handicapped and aide, if any, are able to design and implement a program that focuses exclusively on the unique needs of each child for the entire school day. The staff are considered members of the professional team at the school and are expected to share equally in the many school duties and activities.

For the 1962-63 school year, Jones and Collins (1966) reported that 21 percent of the programs for visually handicapped students provided self-contained classes. Over the past two decades the use of this model has greatly diminished with the exception of some larger metropolitan areas where very young or severely multihandicapped blind children are served. Generally, the visually handicapped children are not educated with their home neighborhood children but are usually bussed across town or between towns to one school in order to have sufficient enrollment for a class. Interaction with sighted peers occurs in the halls, the cafeteria, and on the playground.

The Residential School Model

The oldest, the most comprehensive, and the most expensive service delivery model is the residential school. Most states have at least one residential school and these schools vary in enrollment from less than 10 to over 250 students. Some are located on the same campus as the school for the deaf and are frequently referred to as dual schools. Parents of children who are enrolled in state operated residential schools are not charged for tuition, board, room, or transportation as the schools are fully funded by their respective legislatures. Private schools do charge but these fees are frequently paid by the sending district.

Whether the school is large or small, it provides the same basic array of services:

1. Instructional services including classrooms, educa-

tional materials and equipment, offices and storage, teachers, aides, and other specialists;
2. Food services including fully equipped kitchen, dining room, cooks, and other personnel;
3. Residential services including furnished rooms, linens, laundry, houseparents, and other personnel;
4. Extracurricular and recreational services both on campus and in the community;
5. Health care services including clinic and medical staff;
6. Transportation services for students' travel home, field trips, etc;
7. Maintenance services for upkeep and repairs for the buildings, grounds, vehicles, and other equipment;
8. Administrative services including superintendent, supervisors, accountants, secretaries, and other personnel.

The entire campus of the residential school is designed, equipped, and staffed specificially to meet the needs of visually handicapped children. In addition to the classroom teachers, there may be other specialists in physical education, music, industrial arts, home economics, orientation and mobility, speech, physical and occupational therapy, vocational education, social work, and psychology. The educational materials, adaptive devices, and specialized equipment are accessible to the visually handicapped children not only in the classroom but throughout the campus (Welsh, 1982).

With trained staff on duty 24 hours a day, it is possible to design and implement a highly structured, consistent learning environment for the children who need it. In addition to providing for compensatory skill and personal management instruction, informational counseling about blindness, and academic remediation, the teachers are responsible for the design and implementation of the basic educational program. The houseparent is an essential and integral part of the educational team to encourage and reinforce the child's skills of independence (Brasher, 1980). Simon (1979) conducted a survey to determine the competencies required of houseparents and found that they care for the students' health, discipline, counsel, train in daily living skills, monitor safety conditions, and supervise residential routines.

Because of its unique position within the state, multiple demands are placed on the residential school. Almost by default, if the service or program is not available elsewhere in the state, the residential school is expected to provide for the need (Spungin, 1982). As a result, every residential school throughout the country has addressed most if not all of the following areas:
1. A comprehensive kindergarten through 12th grade educational program;
2. A comprehensive ungraded program for multiply handicapped children through the age of 21;

3. Short-term special needs programs either during the year or the summer for the recently blind, braille remediation, orientation and mobility, home management, career education, or other specific short-term objectives;

4. Comprehensive educational assessments for any visually handicapped child whether on campus or from the LEA;

5. Instructional materials service for both campus and LEA children in order to acquire and distribute appropriately adapted educational materials;

6. Parent education particularly for parents of preschool visually handicapped children;

7. Consultations and inservice training.

The chief administrator of a residential school is usually referred to as a superintendent. Typically the school activities are coordinated by a principal and the nonschool activities are supervised and coordinated by a dean of students or supervisor of home life. Teaching staff and dormitory staff need to work closely together to assure continuity and consistency for each child's program.

Summary Comparison of Program Models

Chart 13.1 compares all five models with respect to ten critical characteristics.

a. *Extent of specialized student's needs:* Each individual visually handicapped child has a unique constellation of needs. The more intense the needs are, the more severe special education modifications are required to meet those needs. Each service delivery model can accommodate a different range of needs.

b. *Adapted educational materials and devices:* Textbooks and other supplementary materials need to be made available in a medium appropriate to the needs of the specific child. Frequently, specialized equipment or devices are required to accomplish certain educational tasks. Sometimes, the visually handicapped child has access to these specialized materials and devices within his assigned classroom. At other times, the child may need to travel to another room or facility. There are still other times when the materials and devices will need to be brought to the child for temporary use on a day by day basis.

c. *Physical facilities:* Some visually handicapped children require modifications in the physical learning environment with respect to work space, lighting, electrical outlets, storage, etc., to facilitate efficiency in the accomplishment of certain educational tasks. The location for the specialized instructional time with the teacher of visually handicapped students may be carefully chosen and suited to the unique needs of a visually handicapped child or it may be on a space available basis from one day to the next with little regard to the specific needs of the child.

d. *Special education instructional time:* The amount of specialized instructional time available to each child from a teacher trained in education of visually handicapped students will vary from one service delivery model to another. The extent of the child's needs should dictate the amount of time scheduled for specialized instruction.

e. *Peer interaction:* A visually handicapped child's social and emotional development is enhanced through opportunities to relate to sighted classmates. The amount of time available for interaction with nonhandicapped peers varies from one program pattern to another. At the same time, a visually handicapped child also needs to relate to other visually handicapped children as a means of refining and reinforcing a healthy self-concept and as a means of learning appropriate problem-solving techniques and approaches.

f. *Home and community support:* To be most effective, the education of visually handicapped children requires cooperative efforts among general education, special education, the home, and community organizations. Caring, accepting yet realistically demanding parents can and should facilitate the reinforcement of skills learned at school. Community organizations (scouting, church youth groups, parks and recreation programs) also provide essential opportunities for visually handicapped children to learn and practice cognitive, behavioral, and affective skills.

g. *Student's travel time:* The travel demands placed on visually handicapped students will vary from one service delivery model to another. Some students walk to the neighborhood school, some travel across town or between towns on buses or vans, while still others travel across an entire state by plane.

h. *Teacher's travel time:* Travel demands placed on the teacher of visually handicapped children will also vary from one service delivery model to another. In some programs, no travel is required of the teacher while in others travel among several counties is necessary. Teachers who are required to travel are usually reimbursed on a per-mile basis for travel between the first school of the day and the last. When serving a low prevalence population, a fundamental issue is whether the child travels to the teacher or the teacher to the child.

i. *Average student case load:* The average student-teacher ratio varies from one model to another. From the author's own surveys it appears that the student load ranges from a high of 50 children all of whom require minimal support service from the teacher consultant to a low of two severely multiply handicapped deaf-blind children. It should be noted that when student-teacher ratios are given, they reflect the range of averages among several states rather than minimums or maximums.

j. *Professional identity and supervision:* The program models vary from highly structured and closely super-

Chart 13.1   Comparison of program models

Characteristics	Teacher Consultant	Itinerant	Resource	Self-contained	Residential
a. Extent of specialized student needs	Relatively few needs; must be independent and resourceful	Mild to moderate needs; fairly independent	More severe needs	Severe needs and/or chronic unsupportive home environment	All levels of needs
b. Adapted educational materials/devices	Limited; designed primarily for children with vision	On loan to school; needs met by frequent visits to the school	Available at all times during the school day	Multi-level standard or adapted materials available at all times during the school day	Multi-level standard and adapted materials available day and night
c. Physical facilities	Limited often temporary space; learning environment designed for children with vision	Some modifications possible; classroom designed for children with vision	Resource room specially designed; regular class designed for children with vision	Classroom specially designed or modified	Entire campus specially designed
d. Special education instructional time	1% or less of student's school time	5-10% student's school time	25-50% of student's time	All or nearly all of student's school time	Potentially 24 hours a day
e. Peer interaction	Almost exclusively with sighted peers	Usually exclusively with sighted peers	Predominantly with sighted peers; some with other visually handicapped peers	Predominantly with visually handicapped peers; some with sighted children on the play ground and in the cafeteria	Almost exclusively with visually handicapped peers
f. Home and community support	Heavy reliance on local public school personnel for home contacts	Frequent contacts possible; responsibility for home contacts shared between general and special educator	Home contacts cultivated more by special educator than the regular educator	Home contacts primarily through special educator	More infrequent home contacts; administrators, teachers, and houseparents all play a role
g. Student travel time	Same as for nonhandicapped children living in the same neighborhood	Same as for nonhandicapped chidren living in the same neighborhood	Possibly across town or between towns	Usually across town or between towns	Weekends or monthly; potentially across the entire state
h. Teacher travel time	Extensive; up to 50% of teacher work time	Average of 5 hours per week	None	None	None
i. Average student case load	15-20 students	10-14 students	6-9 students	3-5 students	3-5 students
j. Professional identity and supervision	Relates to multiple administrators, multiple staffs at multiple sites; minimal supervision	Multiple professional teams at multiple sites; moderate structure and supervision	Single professional team; single site; immediate supervision	Single professional team; single site; immediate supervision	Single campus-wide team; immediate and usually more knowledgeable supervision

vised to unstructured and minimally supervised. Some provide the teacher with a team of professionals with which to identify at a single site, while others require the teacher to relate to multiple administrators, multiple teams at multiple sites. The teacher's need for structure, for the consistency of a professional team with which to identify, and for strong administrative supervision and support must be carefully matched to the characteristics of the service delivery model.

In actual fact, very few programs reflect exclusively one model. To do so would be to force children's needs to be met by some predetermined, pre-existing service delivery model. More realistically, children's needs should be assessed periodically to determine the extent and type of need before prescribing an appropriate combination of service deliveries.

The focus of the preceding discussion regarding traditional program models has tended to emphasize the visually handicapped child participating, to whatever extent possible, in the regular educational program. Multiply handicapped blind children are not usually placed in the regular classroom. Instead many are enrolled in special eduction self-contained classrooms serving related disability groups considered to be the primary handicap, while receiving services from an itinerant teacher of the visually handicapped and other specialists. This multidisciplinary approach provides the greatest amount of flexibility for meeting the widest range of needs at the local education agency level. (See Chapter 9.)

As a result, in some states many programs may provide a combination or mix of models. An itinerant teacher may actually be serving many of the students on a consultative basis. A resource room teacher may spend part of every day serving some children on an itinerant basis. Children in residential schools may attend the local public school for part or all of the school day. Creative resourcefulness and flexibility are the keys to effective programming for visually handicapped children.

ADMINISTRATIVE ISSUES AND CONCERNS

Despite the provisions of recent legislation and the efforts of advocacy groups, there are still issues that have not yet been resolved. The intensity of each of these concerns varies with prevailing public attitudes, national and state policy regarding special education, the strength of advocacy efforts, additional legislative activities, and general economic conditions. The concerns have been grouped under program management issues, program effectiveness issues, and program evaluation issues.

Program Management Issues

One of the recent controversies has centered around the legislative mandate and its interpretation regarding placement. Champion (1979) explained that "P.L. 94-142 requires that a child be placed according to an Individualized Educational Program (IEP) in the least restrictive environment (LRE)" (p. 247). Unfortunately many educators began equating the phrase "least restrictive environment" with the popular term "mainstreaming" and felt or feared that the law precluded placement in segregated self-contained classrooms or in residential schools. Others argued that to mainstream a blind child in an unprepared, uncooperative, and unresponsive local public school setting would be more restrictive than a segregated placement (Bishoff, 1977; Hapeman, 1977). Champion (1979) attempted to clarify the issue by indicating that LRE "refers to the milieu where a child will be least restricted in attaining his or her potential for educational growth" (p. 247).

It is true that the intent of the law was to facilitate the integration of handicapped children into the regular classroom since so many of them had been previously excluded simply on the basis of the handicap. The handicapped child is to be provided with as much interaction with nonhandicapped peers as possible with just enough special education support to enable and promote independent functioning in the classroom. This experience provides the visually handicapped child with the opportunity for the reality testing of adaptive behaviors and coping skills so necessary for life (Maron, 1977).

However, the law also recognizes that handicapped children represent a wide range of intensity of needs which requires a full continuum of service delivery models. Not all visually handicapped children can or should be served by the same delivery pattern. Theoretically, a special program should be developed to meet the unique needs of each child rather than attempting to serve all children in the same way. In practice, the options are more limited because of the small number of children being served. Frequently, a child in a rural, sparsely populated district may be offered the option of either services of an itinerant teacher or attending a residential school for the blind (see Chapter 10).

Just as the needs of one child are distinct and unique from those of all other children and therefore require a specially designed program, so too, any child's needs will vary over time, requiring a modification in the program offered. Taylor's observations in 1973 are still relevant: "After a long arduous period of program prejudice, which included not only the controversy over residential versus local school programs, but also attacks on and defenses of the various patterns of local school programs, present practices show a definite trend toward recognition that each may be beneficial to some children at some period of their school careers" (p. 164). Placement decisions must be made in response to a particular set of needs demonstrated by a given child at a specific time in his school career and subject to review and modification after limited duration.

P.L. 94-142 provides for a free and appropriate public education for all handicapped children. Another issue surrounds the word "appropriate." An appropriate education is the development of a program which adequately meets all of the child's identified needs. Although the professionals in education of visually handicapped strive for excellence in education, the term "appropriate" does not mandate the ideal or the maximum.

On the other hand, the word "appropriate" carries with it the mandate that all of the child's general and special educational needs must be met. Some visually handicapped children are currently being served by a generalist in special education, someone purportedly prepared to work with all handicaps. Especially in rural areas of the country, special education services tend to be generic, concentrating on the common elements across all disabilities. They seldom address the unique needs of visually handicapped children and their parents. "Generic approaches. . .are of value up to the point where they need to be specific. After that point is reached, they can actually be damaging" (Long, 1984, p. 28). Teachers who are untrained to teach the specialized compensatory skills, e.g. braille, electronic reading aids, abacus, and mobility, are unable to promote the visually handicapped child's independence, so essential for becoming a fully functioning assimilated member of society.

There are two other practices that fail the test of "appropriateness." Some administrators misconstrue the role of the teacher of the visually handicapped to be exclusively academic tutoring, to provide the support necessary to enable the child to pass all subjects. As important as this goal may be, the academic tutor tends to ignore the child's social, affective, recreational, and vocational needs. The other practice that fails to contribute to an "appropriate" program is simply not to recognize the child's needs in some areas, especially those areas classified under related services such as occupational therapy, physical therapy, mental health, etc. If the need is not identified, it is reasoned, the district cannot be held accountable and thereby avoid additional expenses.

The last program management issue to be discussed is related to funding. Most residential schools have budgets established with respect to services provided and enrollment, budgets that are independent of the local education agency. The per capita costs in some residential schools exceed $30,000. The local education agency is reimbursed through one of a number of enrollment- or class-based formulae from state and federal sources to cover a portion of the extra costs involved in educating a handicapped child. Many of these funding formulae fail to credit the teacher of the visually handicapped for children placed in other special eduction classes but who still require consultative and direct services from the teacher of visually handicapped. This inequality diminishes the funding base for the program costs for visually handicapped children. Since the funding base for both the residential school and the local education agency are based on enrollment, a climate of competition rather than cooperation tends to dominate in some states.

As the special education area with the fewest numbers, education of the visually handicapped tends to receive less than a proportional share of the state and federal money designated for special education (Corder & Walker, 1969; Rand Study, 1954). In an effort to achieve some equality, the following guidelines were proposed by Long (1984): 1. funds supporting general education activities should extend to visually handicapped children when appropriate; 2. funds supporting special education activities should address unique needs of visually handicapped children; 3. generic special education funds should be proportionally available for programs for the visually handicapped and multiply handicapped blind children; and 4. preferential funding must occasionally be provided due to low prevalence and unique needs. Because of the limited resources, agencies and service providers must plan and work cooperatively to provide the best possible free appropriate public education for visually handicapped children (Champion, 1979; Risley, 1971).

Program Effectiveness Issues

For most of the twentieth century, controversies have surfaced from time to time regarding the relative merits of one service delivery model over another. The debate was rekindled soon after the passage of P.L. 94-142. To raise this issue again would be both foolish and irrelevant since, as has already been stated, each program pattern has special characteristics uniquely applicable to meeting the needs of specific children at certain times during their school careers.

The intent of this section is to highlight a few observations from recent literature which contribute to a better understanding of the characteristics of each program pattern. Generalized conclusions regarding the relative effectiveness of programs cannot be made from the specific observations cited. It must be remembered that what appears as a deterrent to meeting one child's needs may be the very characteristic that serves to meet the needs of another child.

Interaction with sighted peers is one of the basic reasons given for mainstreaming. However, mere physical presence in the regular classroom does not guarantee that this goal has been accomplished. Hoben and Lindstrom (1980) found that mainstreamed visually handicapped children were more socially isolated than their nonhandicapped peers. Furthermore, non-disabled children feel some discomfort in face-to-face relationships with blind children with the possible consequence that interactions with blind children are avoided or aborted, thus minimizing the blind children's full social development (Jones, Lavinc, & Shell, 1972). The goals of mainstreaming are not fully achieved until the visually handicapped children have equal opportunity to participate mentally, socially, physically, and emotionally in classroom, cafeteria, playground, and extra-curricular activities.

Standards of behavior must not be different for the child who is visually handicapped (Ashcroft & Zambone-Ashley, 1980). There is evidence which suggests that great variability exists in the mainstream settings with respect to the standard applied to visually handicapped children. After researching this problem, Keilbaugh (1977) observed that "the most interesting outcome of this study was the extent to which regular classroom teachers disagreed about standards the exceptional child should meet in the regular classroom" (p. 434). Special treatment and inconsistent standards tend to produce false expectations, unrealistic perceptions, and resentments.

Some researchers studied certain characteristics or variables with reference to service delivery models. The type of program pattern appears to have little influence on the relative level of visually handicapped children's self-esteem (Coker, 1979; Head, 1979). Blind children, 10 to 12 years of age, in local public school programs were perceived by their teachers to be more mobile than visually handicapped children in residential schools (Blackhurst & Marks, 1977). On the other hand, graduates of local public school programs appear to have greater difficulty with personal and home management tasks than graduates of residential schools (Hapeman, 1977; Ohlsen, 1971). The morale of teachers of visually handicapped students does not seem to be a function of program pattern (Bina, 1982).

With respect to programs for severely and profoundly handicapped blind children, there are still many unmet needs (Gates, 1983). A majority of the visually handicapped children in both residential and local public school programs have more than one handicap. Bourgeault, Harley and DuBose (1977) found drastic inconsistencies in services for multiply handicapped blind children, overlapping and redundant services to some children and inappropriate services to many others. They also reported that professionals primarily responsible for serving visually handicapped children felt inadequate to serve children with additional handicaps, while professionals serving other handicaps felt inadequate to deal with blindness. Improvements in both services and personnel are essential to meet the needs of multiply handicapped children. (See Chapter 9.)

Program Evaluation Issues

The evaluation of program effectiveness is a complex process with many components. Federal and state government personnel, LEA administrators and teachers, residential school staff, visually handicapped children and their parents all participate in one or more facets of evaluation. Some of the components are unrelated to each other thus contributing to fragmentation of the process. Some components address qualitative issues better than others.

The federal government is responsible for protecting the rights of handicapped children and assuring equal opportunity for a free appropriate education for each handicapped child. The evaluation of compliance with established regulations is accomplished through reviewing required reports and making periodic on-site visits. Each state government, in turn, has similar responsibilities and monitors the LEA's compliance with state and federal regulations. Unfortunately, most of the federal and state evaluation procedures tend to focus more on adherence to regulations rather than qualitative issues. A few state departments of education are beginning to follow the example set by Massachusetts and California (Stager, 1978; California State Department of Education, 1985) to establish guidelines that evaluate program quality in the local public schools.

Accreditation, on the other hand, provides opportunity to address qualitative standards. The National Accreditation Council for Agencies and Schools Serving the Blind and Visually Handicapped is recognized by the U.S. Department of Education as the only accrediting body that has specialized standards for residential schools for the visually handicapped. Professionals who represent the education of visually handicapped serve on committees to establish and periodically revise the standards and the review procedures. The most valuable part of the accrediting process is the self-study and evaluation which involves the entire residential school staff and community and provides an opportunity to identify the school's strengths and weaknesses (Scholl, Long, & Tuttle, 1980).

Accreditation, according to Scholl (1971) "is a means by which the general public. . .can recognize quality schools that are worthy of their support; it gives assurances to public and private funding agencies that programs meet accepted standards; it signifies to parents who are concerned with obtaining a quality education for their children that the school meets the minimum standards for similar programs" (p. 220). Scholl concluded that accreditation "assures school personnel that their experience is acquired in a quality setting, thereby making the school a desirable and sought-after place of employment" (p. 220). None-theless, accreditation in the United States is typically voluntary, with the inevitable result that not all residential schools choose to apply for accreditation.

At the local public school level, administrators responsible for program evaluation are frequently not as knowledgeable about education of the visually handicapped as they are about the larger special education programs. Consequently, the teacher of the visually handicapped must, of necessity, assume a greater responsibility for program evaluation. Spungin's (1981) *Guidelines for Public School Programs Serving Visually Handicapped Children* provides the administrator and teacher with the essentials of quality programming, particularly with respect to assessment procedures, personnel and program requirements, teacher responsibilities, teacher-student ratios, unique curriculum needs, and program support (facilities, materials and equipment, ancillary services). By using Spungin's (1977) list of competencies and the revised list included in Appendix E considered essential to be an effective teacher of visually handicapped children, an administrator or teacher is able to identify skills in need of further development (Stager, 1981).

In response to the need for a program evaluation tool specifically for local public schools serving the visually handicapped, Scholl (1981) developed a *Self-Study and Evaluation Guide for Day School Programs for Visually Handicapped Pupils: A Guide for Program Improvement*. This document is designed to assist district personnel to specify the program philosophy, goals, and objectives, and to identify programmatic strengths and weaknesses. Scholl suggested that the self-study and evaluation guide can be used in conjunction with an existing state or national accreditation process or it can be used simply as a tool for self-evaluation and program improvement, independent of any other evaluation procedure.

Study questions

1. What goals do general education and special education have in common? What is special about special education for visually handicapped children and youth?

2. Discuss the philosophy underlying educational programming for visually handicapped children, including a comparison between visually handicapped and sighted children, the importance of preschool programming, and special curriculum needs.

3. List the four key participants who share the responsibility for educational programming for visually handi-capped students. What are some major areas of responsibility for each?

4. What is the importance of each of the following in implementing an appropriate program for a visually handicapped child: child-find, assessment, eligibility, the individualized educational program, placement, due process.

5. List the five traditional service delivery models. Describe three advantages and three disadvantages of each.

6. Visit two different service delivery models in your state. Compare your evaluation of their programs, advantages and disadvantages, etc. to the content of this chapter.

7. Interview a residential school and a day school teacher about their respective views on the settings. Compare their views with those expressed in this chapter.

8. Describe how you would provide contact with nonhandicapped pupils if you were a teacher in a self-contained classroom.

9. Describe how you would provide contact with other visually handicapped pupils if you were an itinerant or teacher consultant.

10. Obtain your state's regulations for educational programs for visually handicapped pupils. What similarities and differences are there compared to the "ideal" as described in this chapter.

Additional readings

American Printing House for the Blind. (1981). *Handbook for teachers of the visually handicapped*. Louisville, Ky.: Author.

Ashcroft, S.C., and Zambone-Ashley, A.M. (1980). Mainstreaming children with visual impairments. *Journal of Research and Development in Education*, **13**(40), pp. 22-36.

Hatlen, P.H. (1980). *Important concerns in the education of visually impaired children*, MAVIS Sourcebook 5. Boulder, Colo.: Social Science Education Consortium, Inc.

Leslie, M. *Teaching the visually impaired child in the regular classroom*, MAVIS Sourcebook 3. Boulder, Colo.: Social Science Education Consortium, Inc.

Lowenfeld, B. (1981) *Berthold Lowenfeld on blindness and blind people*. New York, N.Y.: American Foundation for the Blind, Inc.

Orlansky, M.D. (1980). *Encouraging successful mainstreaming of the visually impaired child*, MAVIS Sourcebook 2. Boulder, Colo.: Social Science Education Consortium, Inc.

National Accreditation Council. (1979). *Self-study and*

evaluation guides. New York, N.Y.: NAC.

Scholl, G.T. (1981). *Self-study and evaluation guide for day school programs for visually handicapped pupils. A guide for program improvement.* Reston, Va.: Council for Exceptional Children.

Scholl, G.T. (Ed.) (1984). *Quality services for the blind and visually handicapped learners: Statements of position.* Reston, Va.: Council for Exceptional Children.

Spungin, S.J. (1981). *Guidelines for public school programs serving visually handicapped children,* New York, N.Y.: American Foundation for the Blind, Inc.

Spungin, S.J. (1982). The future role of residential schools for visually handicapped children. *Journal of Visual Impairment & Blindness,* **76**(6), pp. 229-233.

Tuttle, D.W. (1984). *Self-esteem and adjusting with blindness.* Springfield, Ill.: Charles C Thomas.

CHAPTER **14**

The Teacher

Susan Jay Spungin
Josephine L. Taylor

This chapter reviews the roles and functions of teachers for visually handicapped children and youth in residential and day school programs. The development of various patterns in serving this population is related to the characteristics of the population served, geographic distribution of students, and teachers' perception of their role. An historical summary of teacher preparation programs in past years and a discussion of burnout and stress management are included.

Until the early twentieth century, residential schools were the only settings where blind and visually handicapped children and youth of school age in the United States could receive a formal education which recognized their special education needs. The need to become integrated into society, as well as recognition of the importance of family life for healthy growth and development led to the establishment of day school programs. The first day school program began in 1902 but they began to proliferate in the 1920s and 30s. (See Chapter 1.)

By 1948, day school classes for blind and visually handicapped children served less than 10 percent of the total identified school age population. From 1949 to 1956, as a result of retinopathy of prematurity (ROP), formerly retrolental fibroplasia (RLF), the blind and visually handicapped school age population increased by 39 percent. In 1956 about 25 percent of all visually handicapped children attended public school classes. By the mid-1980s, more than 80 percent of all blind and visually handicapped children were attending local day school programs.

The increase of public school programs for visually handicapped children as well as the shift in student population to a more multiply handicapped group of pupils has greatly influenced both the service delivery system as well as the roles of those teachers working with them. In the 1980s, teachers of the visually handicapped in public schools report that more than 50 percent of their pupils are multiply handicapped. Teachers in over 50 percent of residential schools for the blind are teaching almost exclusively multiply

handicapped/visually handicapped children. Teacher preparation programs have had to become flexible, training teachers for a wide variety of educational settings, and a student population with diverse and complex educational needs. Over the past thirty years, for example, teacher training programs have merged the two traditionally separate and distinct preparation programs: one for teachers of blind students and one for partially seeing students. The most common pattern now is to train and employ teachers who are certified to instruct the broad range of visually handicapped pupils, including blind children, children with limited vision, and low vision children.

TEACHER ROLES

In looking at specific roles and functions of teachers of visually handicapped children and critical factors in the preparation of these teachers, it has long been recognized that professional roles differ according to the kind of educational setting in which the teacher functions and the amount of supervision provided (Mackie & Dunn, 1955). In residential schools, teachers have lengthy periods of time for one-on-one student contact; indeed the teacher is often the primary intervening professional in the student's life, responsible for all aspects of his growth and development. In contrast, various public school programs serving this population are moving away from direct teaching in a self-contained classroom to case management in an itinerant or teacher consultant program. This wide variation in teaching roles requires not only a knowledge of regular education and special education as it relates to the blind and visually handicapped child, but administrative and organizational skills as well.

It is the very diversity of the roles and demands made on the teacher of visually handicapped pupils that makes this teaching profession unique. Teachers of visually handicapped children and youth can choose to have comparative autonomy, as in an itinerant program, or a close tutorial educational experience, as in a residential school setting or a special self-contained class. These varied settings provide teachers with an opportunity to develop a variety of skills in team teaching, management, community organization, and public education. The different organizational patterns and settings allow teachers to choose one best suited to their personality, talents, and preferred working environment. Because of this wide range of options, professional teacher preparation programs have attempted to become more relevant to the necessary teacher competencies and to the demands of the various actual teaching situations (Connor, Rusalem, Baker & Joan, 1971). The curriculum is designed to prepare students to function competently in a variety of educational settings with a heterogeneous population ranging in age from birth to adulthood, and in all roles related to and essential for the performance of professional functions (Bowers, 1965).

TEACHER PREPARATION FOR THE VISUALLY HANDICAPPED

In the past the preparation of teachers for children who are visually handicapped has been influenced by many factors: Leadership of outstanding people, changes in general education, the numbers and types of handicapping conditions of visually handicapped children entering schools, state and federal legislation requiring equal educational opportunity for all children, and federal student financial support in the form of fellowships and grants for preparation in higher education. Historically it has been assumed that teacher roles are more or less defined by the system and often conflicts emerged between well established teaching patterns and new teacher functions. Predictions of teacher roles cannot rely on theoretical role expectations but must be complemented by observation of the teacher's actual behavior. Various projects related to needed competencies and role definition are summarized in the following section.

COMPETENCIES OF TEACHERS OF VISUALLY HANDICAPPED STUDENTS

Background

In 1918, the American Association of Instructors of the Blind (AAIB) identified a list of goals which would help to make the education of visually handicapped pupils more effective. The list included:

1. The adoption of a Uniform Type for the blind of the English speaking world.
2. The gradual elimination of pupils of very low mentality from our schools.
3. The introduction of sight-saving classes for the partially blind in institutions for the blind and in public schools.
4. The regular and scientific training of our girls in homemaking.
5. The systematic physical training given our pupils in the gymnasium, the swimming pool and on the athletic field, the holding of competitive athletic meets which has done much to promote self-confidence and school pride.
6. The education of the blind with the seeing in high schools and universities, as well as in special classes for the blind in public schools.
7. The introduction of new courses of study which are more elastic and which give equal opportunity for the development of the bright as well as the dull child.
8. The establishment of separate kindergartens for the young blind.
9. Greater attention to vocational work, especially for those of lower mentality (Abel, 1967, p. 107).

A review of this list in light of current needs shows that some have been accomplished or are good practice today (1, 4, 6, 7, 9); others have been emphasized in the past but are not so relevant today because of changing philosophy and population (2, 3); and two are still in need of emphasis (5, 9). (See Chapter 1.) It should be noted that there were no teacher preparation programs at the time this list was adopted. Soon thereafter, the first formal program was established at Perkins in cooperation with the Harvard Graduate School of Education. (See Chapter 1.)

Some years later, Merry (1933) in a doctoral dissertation which surveyed the field of educating blind children at that time, listed these basic qualifications which experienced educators of the blind should possess: four year high school course, three or four years of normal training, special training for non-academic courses, a course in the history of education for the blind, and in psychological and educational problems in blindness.

Between 1950-1955, the United States Office of Education established a national committee to identify the competencies needed by teachers of handicapped children, including teachers of blind and of partially seeing children. The committee suggested that specialized teachers of the blind need:

1. the same competencies required of qualified teachers of sighted children plus a sequence of specialized preparation;

2. medical knowledge involving the anatomy of the eye and the implications for education and development of visually handicapped pupils;

3. guidance and counseling skills;

4. knowledge of instructional strategies;

5. skills in teaching orientation and mobility;

6. ability to teach communication skills, braille, typing, and listening;

7. curriculum adaptation and development;

8. assessment and evaluation;

9. knowledge of role and ability to work with other specialists, agencies and appropriate organizations (Mackie & Dunn, 1955, pp. 76-77).

Between 1957-1959, the American Foundation for the Blind held two conferences with the assistance of its Teacher Education Advisory Committee, a group of special educators, to discuss the objectives of a

Office of Education Committe for Teachers of the Blind, 1955

functional, competency-based teacher education program (AFB, 1961). Historically, the teacher roles had often been merely a reflection of the degree of impairment of the visually handicapped student: totally blind and a braille reader, or partially sighted and a print reader. These two neat categories, however, were not always easy to define due to visual, psychological, and sociological factors which affect each individual (AFB, 1961).

The special educators convened by AFB (1961) stated that the growing number of professional educators and types of educational settings for whom teacher education centers must provide professional preparation should have as a structure for their basic courses "...various types of educational programs for blind children," courses for "...administrative and consultative personnel at all levels," "...intensive and well planned short term orientation and field work type of observation," teacher education courses for working with blind children and courses for those "...who will act in various leadership roles at national as well as at other levels..." (AFB, 1961, p. 18).

Thus by the early 1960s the role of the teacher of

visually handicapped children and youth, regardless of educational settings, was already viewed in a much broader sense than that of instructor. In addition to developing proficiency skill areas, the teacher must be able to work with a wide range of age and educational levels, varying degrees of vision loss, as well as highly individual and educational needs. In addition, such a teacher might be expected to work in a variety of educational settings and must be knowledgeable about administrative problems, be able to work cooperatively with personnel from other professions, and be skilled in parent counseling. Not least, she or he is called upon to work closely with appropriate community agencies and often to locate or even create community resources relevant to the program (AFB, 1961).

In 1961, concerned that the generic approach for both programming for pupils and for teacher education then being espoused by many special educators would undermine quality, AFB, in a second conference of special educators, began to look at basic and often unique competencies for teachers of visually handicapped students which include:

1. An understanding of exceptionality as a personal, psychological and social problem, particularly as it affects the blind person.

2. A knowledge of problems for educating and meeting the needs of all exceptional children with specific emphasis upon those directly concerned with the visually handicapped plus the understanding of the importance of the relationship of these specialized services to general educational services for all children.

3. Knowledge and skill in the use of tools and procedures relating to diagnosis, guidance and counseling.

4. Skill in the interpretation of federal, state, and local legislation affecting administrative organization of services.

5. Familiarity with resources, aids and materials, and skill in adapting, modifying, and creating needed teaching aids.

6. An understanding of general curriculum and a working capacity to make the special adaptations needed for developing and implementing a program for blind pupils.

7. A basic understanding of learning: how it occurs and what problems are inherent in learning for visually handicapped.

8. A clear perception of interpersonal relations and the role demanded of the teacher as he establishes positive communication with blind or visually handicapped persons and provides interpretation to other professional personnel who function in the total program.

9. Insight in understanding the communication process as it functions with the family, the community,

and society at large when they are confronted with problems related to the visually handicapped.

10. Ability to identify valid existing research affecting the needs and programs of the visually handicapped as well as an understanding of problems yet unsolved and awaiting further study (AFB, 1961, pp. 22-23).

In 1969, the Council for Exceptional Children (CEC) initiated its own study of competencies for special education teachers. The committee developing preparation programs for teachers of visually handicapped students listed the following:

1. Knowledge of the influence that various types or degrees of visual impairment have on children;

2. Knowledge of the educational implications of eye conditions;

3. Ability to identify and correctly place visually handicapped children;

4. Knowledge of educational procedures for children who are visually handicapped;

5. Ability to teach communication skills;

6. Knowledge and skill in teaching educational appraisal and remedial techniques in the basic skill subjects;

7. Evidence of appropriate practicum experiences with visually handicapped children;

8. Information on local, state, and national resources for the education and assistance of children who are visually handicapped (CEC, 1974).

Concurrently with those developments during the 1960s, federal legislation began to provide funds to institutions of higher education for the preparation of special education personnel. This stimulated the growth of teacher education programs in the various colleges and universities. P.L. 85-926, an act to encourage expansion of teaching in the education of mentally retarded children through grants to institutions of higher learning and state educational agencies, provided funds for personnel in the area of mental retardation. This was expanded in 1961 to include personnel in the area of the deaf (P.L. 87-276, an act to make available to children who are handicapped by deafness the specially trained teachers of the deaf needed to develop their abilities and to make available to individuals suffering speech and hearing impairments the specially trained speech pathologists and audiologists needed to help them overcome their handicaps) and in 1963, to all areas of special education (P.L. 88-164, Mental Retardation Facilities and Community Mental Health Centers Construction Act of 1963). This funding led to an increased number of full time students in teacher preparation programs for the visually handicapped, stimulated the unification of the curriculum in education of the blind and partially seeing, and increased the number of preparation programs for leadership personnel (Holman & Scholl, 1982). With encouragement from the Bureau

of Education for the Handicapped in the Department of Health, Education and Welfare (now the Office of Special Education and Rehabilitation Services) colleges and universities began to move in the direction of competency based programs in their teacher preparation, a movement already underway in the field of the visually handicapped.

Establishing a Competency-Based Teacher Education Program

In order to examine the preparation of teachers relative to actual tasks performed and to functionally redefine roles, in 1973 AFB initiated and sponsored the first in a series of six meetings with representatives from 22 colleges and/or universities offering preparation programs for teachers of visually handicapped students. The product of these work sessions was a draft edition of the competencies which these teacher educators agreed were essential. The competencies were assigned to 12 goal areas reflecting seven

teaching activities: assessment and evaluation; educational and instructional strategies; guidance and counseling; administration and supervision; media and technology; schools, agencies, community relations; and research.

The twelve goals that emerged were:

1.0 Teacher will demonstrate knowledge of normal and atypical developmental patterns in visually handicapped learners.

2.0 Teacher will demonstrate the ability to assess visually handicapped learners using a variety of informal and formal procedures.

3.0 Teacher will demonstrate the ability to select, design and/or modify specialized curricula for visually handicapped learners.

4.0 Teacher will demonstrate proficiency in the operation of media and devices necessary for the education of the visually handicapped learner.

5.0 Teacher will utilize instructional strategies to facilitate learning in visually handicapped children.

6.0 Teacher can effectively utilize instructional materials, media, devices, aids, etc. appropriate to the individual needs of visually handicapped children.

7.0 Teacher will demonstrate ability to identify and provide appropriate counseling and guidance services to visually handicapped learners, and significant others.

8.0 Teacher will demonstrate ability to utilize local, state and national resources to assist in the delivery of services to the visually handicapped learner.

9.0 Teacher will demonstrate knowledge of and opportunity for research with visually handicapped learners.

10.0 Teacher will accept responsibilities of being a member of the teaching profession and will make a commitment to improve services for visually handicapped learners.

11.0 Teacher will demonstrate ability to administer and/or supervise programs for visually handicapped learners, including ancillary personnel, para-professionals, and volunteers.

12.0 Teacher can demonstrate the ability to evaluate both instructional sequences and overall program effectiveness of various school programs and agencies serving visually handicapped learners (Spungin, 1977, p. 12).

The competencies were then field tested with teachers actually working with visually handicapped pupils in a variety of settings. Variables that were studied included: the role and function of the teachers in the field compared to the training competencies; the relationship between time spent on various activities and competencies. The questionnaire designed to seek this information was sent to 1,993 teachers in residential and day schools throughout the country—807 teachers returned the questionnaire, a response rate of 41 percent (Spungin, 1977).

The recommendations of the AFB project led to the initiation of a three-year project at the University of Michigan. The major objective of the Michigan project was to expand the mastery task/achievement indicator portion of the Spungin competency document and to create an end-product which could be utilized by college and/or university professionals in designing and modifying their training programs; by state education consultants for the visually handicapped in planning and implementing programs for the professional development of teachers of the visually handicapped; and by state departments of education in reviewing and revising the then very heterogeneous teacher certification requirements (Holman & Scholl, 1982).

In October 1979, and again in March 1980, 12 university faculty members who volunteered to work on this project met to revise the competencies, and

to develop a draft of mastery tasks. The original 12 goals were collapsed into 10 and some knowledge and skill statements were combined. The mastery task/achievement indicator section for all competencies was revised and greatly expanded—to 191 statements—to include more specific indications of how achievement of the competency would be measured. The competency statements, on the other hand, were reduced from 82 to 70, and ten goal areas were defined as a framework for the competencies:

1. Teacher will demonstrate knowledge of developmental patterns in visually handicapped learners.

2. Teacher will demonstrate the ability to assess visually handicapped learners using a variety of informal and formal procedures.

3. Teacher will demonstrate the ability to select, design and/or modify specialized curricula for visually handicapped learners with varying degrees of visual impairments and at all developmental levels.

4. Teacher will demonstrate proficiency in the operation of media and devices necessary for the education of the visually handicapped learner.

5. Teacher will utilize instructional strategies to facilitate learning in visually handicapped children.

6. Teacher can effectively utilize instructional materials, media, devices, etc. appropriate to the individual needs of visually handicapped children.

7. Teacher will demonstrate ability to identify and provide appropriate counseling and guidance services to visually handicapped learners and significant others.

8. Teacher will demonstrate ability to utilize local, state, and national legislation, policy, and resources to assist in the delivery of services to the visually handicapped learner.

9. Teacher will demonstrate knowledge of and need for research with visually handicapped learners.

10. Teacher will accept responsibilities of being a member of the teaching profession and will make a commitment to improve services for visually handicapped learners with varying degrees of visual loss and at all developmental levels (Holman & Scholl, 1982).

Some interesting perspectives in the work of the Michigan study emerged in Holman's (1983) survey of four groups of administrators, (superintendents of residential schools, state education consultants for the visually handicapped, supervisors of large programs, and heads of the instructional resource centers). Asked to determine the degree to which they viewed the 10 goal areas and 70 competency statements as being essential for teachers, 99 of the 159 administrators responded. There was considerable agreement that 7 of the 10 goal statements were essential. Only half of the respondents viewed Goal 9 as essen tial and responses for Goal statements 7 and 8 varied according to the type of administrator, with a significant difference in responses of residential school administrators to Goal 8. In general, the consensus of administrators was that the competencies are needed and appropriate for teachers in various settings.

One of the weaknesses in the competencies was the limited attention to the affective component. As a result of a review by professionals (Scholl, 1982), 44 competencies in this domain were added. Subsequently, following a review of the competencies by selected teachers in the field (Scholl, 1982), the mastery task segment was also expanded. The revised document thus includes 10 goal areas, 70 competencies, and 225 mastery tasks. (See Appendix E.)

TEACHER ROLES IN VARIOUS EDUCATIONAL SETTINGS

Review of the literature regarding the various teaching roles as they relate to different organizational patterns found in residential and public day school programs for the visually handicapped indicated that clear, precise, functional descriptions are lacking.

The literature describes the role of teachers in residential schools for the blind as attempting to meet the needs of the visually handicapped multiply handicapped child, as well as those of children from geographic areas with such sparse populations that adequate educational programs are limited in numbers. The staff is also expected to be competent in skills concerned with the development of the whole child and his total life adjustment (Best, 1963). This range can be far-reaching indeed and for a period of time led to an examination of the changing role of the residential school:

> In states where day school programs are well developed, relations between residential and day schools vary. . .[residential school] services include diagnostic appraisal of visually impaired children with other handicaps; remedial educational programs for children with severe and/or unique educational programs; consultant services to teachers in local programs; a center for distribution of instructional materials including books; summer and/or short term academic year programs for children who need intensive instruction in such areas as typewriting, braille reading and writing, physical education, home economics, daily living skills, orientation, and mobility; and materials and programs for parents of preschool visually handicapped children. (Scholl, 1968, p. 20)

Residential schools are continuing to examine the needs in the field and are responding by modifying current programs and initiating new ones in order to meet the educational needs of blind and visually handicapped pupils in the geographical areas they serve (Dietz, 1977; McIntire, 1985; Miller, 1984, 1985; Silverstein, 1985; Spungin, 1982).

There is more discussion in the literature about teachers' roles and competencies in day school programs. Teachers of the visually handicapped child, working in a special class situation, need to be competent at least to some extent in communication devices, instructional strategies, curriculum development, and public education (Adams, 1908; Curtis, 1908; Clark, 1935).

The most widely discussed educational pattern for visually handicapped children attending public schools is the resource room. The following competencies gathered from different resources have been considered necessary for resource teachers of visually handicapped students (Barber, 1960; Bourgeault, 1960; Enright, 1953; Fortner, 1945; Gilmore, 1956; Grant, 1966; Heimbuch, 1962; Irwin, 1961; Johnson, 1961; Meyer, 1925; Paterson, 1913; Root, 1961).

1. Knowledge of communication skills and utilization of devices.
2. Understanding the educational implications of eye conditions.
3. Skills in curriculum development and adaptation.
4. Skill in public education.
5. Skill in guidance and counseling.
6. Skill in orientation and mobility.
7. Knowledge of how to utilize and develop local, state and national resources.
8. Ability to do teacher consultation.
9. Understanding of the sociological and the psychological needs of children.
10. Skill in paper and record keeping.
11. Knowledge and procurement of educational equipment.
12. Knowledge of child growth and development.
13. Background in general education.
14. Ability to develop and provide supplementary devices, e.g., readers, tutors, class activities, etc.
15. Skill in classroom observation.

The competencies specified for the itinerant teacher are similar to those of a resource teacher, with the following additions (AFB, 1956; Avery, 1968; Bryan & Barthman, 1958; Johnson, 1961; Lowenfeld, 1956; Root, 1960).

1. Ability to visit several schools on a regular basis.
2. Serve as a catalyst to improve vision screening standards for all schools.
3. Ability to travel expeditiously, allowing for flexible scheduling.
4. Accompany all class field trips.
5. Attend and organize all teacher conferences.

The role of the teacher-consultant for visually handicapped students in public schools—as distinct from the itinerant or special education teacher—first developed in Oregon in the 1940s (Fortner, 1945;

Jones, 1953)—was essentially supervisory in nature. Due to the shortage of qualified teachers, this type of specialist frequently assumes the role of an itinerant teacher. The literature cites an ideal mix of direct and indirect responsibilities for the true teacher-consultant (Fortner, 1945; Jones, 1953).

1. Determine the type of education placement for visually handicapped students.
2. Arrange for special services.
3. Be knowledgeable about public education, systems, personnel, and resources.
4. Sponsor and conduct workshops.
5. Supply materials and aids.
6. Resolve individual and general problems in eye care, visual hygiene, lighting, seating, and posture.
7. Work with students in orientation and mobility.
8. Work with regular classroom teachers.
9. Guidance and counseling.

As more and more responsibility is placed on community schools under mandatory legislation to educate all handicapped children, the position of teacher-consultant has become increasingly more complex. As individual regular classroom teachers accept their responsiblity to serve all children, the teacher consultant may assume more of an indirect relationship with selected visually handicapped students and a closer relationship with the regular classroom teacher.

PRESENT AND FUTURE ROLES

Over thirty years have passed since the ROP population of children helped shape public day school and residential educational patterns. The rubella children of the sixties and the new retinopathy of prematurity newborns of the 1980s along with P.L. 94-142 (The Education for All Handicapped Children Act of 1975) have been major influences on the changing role of the teacher preparation programs.

The 1980s bring special challenges to define the role and function of teachers of the visually handicapped, especially in the light of growing acceptance of general special educators and generic program models developed to serve all handicapped children including, in some cases, the low prevalence population of visually handicapped children. To justify the need for specially trained teachers, teachers and teacher educators alike feel a need to articulate clearly what skills are truly necessary for a teacher of the visually handicapped. Consequently, the Division for the Visually Handicapped of the Council for Exceptional Children (CEC) adopted a national position statement on the role and function of the teacher of the visually handicapped (Spungin, 1984). (See Appendix F.)

The position statement makes no attempt to specify differences of teacher role and function as it relates to one of the five organizational service delivery models described in Chapter 13. Although the areas of assessment and evaluation, educational and instructional strategies, guidance and counseling, administration and supervision, and school community relations are viewed as basic for all teachers of the visually handicapped, there are unique and changing roles for teachers of the visually handicapped in each of the five educational settings.

Any discussion of the role and function of teachers of the visually handicapped must always be viewed against historical factors that have had an impact on teacher training programs and their graduates. Not only have the increased numbers of multiply handicapped/visually handicapped children helped shape new roles for the teacher; the methodological philosophy has changed from sight-saving in the early part of the century to an emphasis on increasing visual efficiency from the 1960s onward. (See Chapters 5 and 6.) Teachers of the visually handicapped students have had to learn effective methods for functional visual assessment and development of orientation and mobility (see Chapter 19), of visual efficiency programs (see Chapters 5 and 6) as well as behavior management skills for the more severely multiply handicapped student (see Chapter 9). Added to these new areas is also training in technology and computer accessibility for their students, not to mention evaluation and development of appropriate software. (See Chapter 17.)

It is necessary, therefore, to realize the continual evolution of the roles of teachers of visually handicapped pupils in the context of the ever-changing population of children to be served, the organizational patterns available to serve them, as well as the availability of teachers.

Residential School Teachers

Since the 1950s, teachers in residential schools for the blind, more than in any other setting, have had to change their role dramatically, from academic teachers in traditional self-contained classrooms, to behavior management and self-care instructors for severely multiply handicapped youngsters, some of whom may not even have a vision loss or having one, the vision loss may not be seen as the primary educationally handicapping condition. (Chapter 9.)

There continues to remain, however few, a group of more academically able children, many of whom reside at the residential school but attend the neighborhood community day school programs with sighted peers. When this occurs, the residential school teacher must serve as a liaison between two educational settings, a role similar to that of an itinerant teacher or teacher consultant.

In states where day school programs are well developed, the residential school and its staff often provide statewide services which include diagnostic and assessment services for pupils in local school programs, consultant services to teachers in local school programs, instructional materials center, orientation and mobility, respite care, preschool outreach service and summer courses in communication skills (Spungin, 1982). Many of these services and roles of teachers working in residential schools should sound familiar since they were identified as needed and in some states already happening as early as the 1960s (Scholl, 1967).

Special Class Teacher

The special teacher continues to work in a self-contained classroom frequently with severely multiply handicapped visually handicapped children somewhere in the range of four to six children per class with a teacher aide. Heavy emphasis is placed on parent counseling and materials development with few attempts to mainstream children into regular class settings. The special teacher comes best

prepared to this type of program with heavy emphasis on training in mental retardation, emotional disturbance, and behavior management techniques. The program is often nonacademic in nature with intense training in self-care and daily living skills. (See Chapter 9.)

The Resource Room Teacher

The average size of a class in the resource room is seven to ten students, who, in the past, spent a relatively small part of the day with resource teachers learning special skills. Although her role is sometimes remedial in nature, it is generally believed the teacher of visually handicapped pupils cannot and should not serve as an academic tutor but rather deal with those unique educational needs required as a direct result of the visual impairment. Visually handicapped children are often bused across school district lines in order to receive this service making traveling to

families in a variety of different community settings imperative for a resource teacher. As a consequence, the combination of a resource/itinerant teaching model is growing throughout the country. However, in this case, the student contact remains more direct and on a more frequent basis.

Itinerant and Teacher Consultants

Presently, the largest numbers of teachers trained to teach visually handicapped students in public schools are itinerant teachers (Report to Congress, 1984). This group often serves in a teacher consultant capacity due to large caseloads and geographic area to be covered. Unlike the teacher consultant who may serve thirty-five students on the average and travel some 1300 miles per month, the itinerant teacher sees an average of fifteen children and travels 900 miles monthly. Although they both function as case managers, the itinerant teacher has more direct contact with the student as well as the family. Both types of teachers require high levels of training in administration, time management, and interpersonal skills in that they must work with and coordinate the services of many types of professionals from occupational therapists to physical therapists to low vision and orientation and mobility specialists (Spungin, 1977).

VARIATIONS ON A THEME

With the growing emphasis on generic program models often viewed as economically efficient, some visually handicapped children in public schools may be receiving no services whatsoever, or services by special educators not trained in the field of education for the visually handicapped. Anecdotal reports from teachers and administrators of programs for visually handicapped pupils report that increasing numbers of visually handicapped youngsters are being placed in other regular or special education programs, and are receiving no, or very limited, specialized services for their visual impairment. In cases of multiply handicapped visually handicapped children, placement in classes for mentally retarded or developmentally delayed may be appropriate, but the educational needs created by the visual impairment still demand some contact on either an itinerant or teacher consultant basis, to insure that all their educational needs resulting from a visual impairment are being met. Consequently, many teachers of visually handicapped pupils are required to wear many hats in different combinations (Huebner & Ferrell, in press).

As a consequence, teachers are becoming dual or multi-competency trained professionals, required to have competencies not only in education but in orientation and mobility, in work with other disability groups, in preschool education, and in deaf/blind as well. These multi-competency trained professionals are in great demand—answering, in many cases, the need to hire one instead of three teachers to serve a highly complex low prevalence population of visually handicapped children. Because of this variety of

professional experiences, the teacher of the visually handicapped child is routinely exposed to career options and variations within the job requirements which can make this occupation an extremely attractive one. Career paths from teacher to supervisor to coordinator of an instructional materials center for the visually handicapped are only a few of the job possibilities. Professionally, the teacher not only works directly with students, but also serves as a case manager and member of an interdisciplinary team. He or she must not only relate well to the child, his family, and community but to the special education director, regular or residential school principal, regular classroom teacher, school psychologist, social worker, and volunteers, to mention only a few. With the many challenges and opportunities for professional growth and development which this position offers come complex problems so that management of stress and potential burnout becomes yet another competency to be mastered.

MANAGEMENT OF STRESS

Maslach (1978) defines burnout as "an emotional exhaustion resulting from stress of interpersonal contact" (pp. 56-58). A person's ability to cope with stress determines the effect on the individual's job performance and health. Many of the environmental sources of stress are unavoidable for teachers of the visually handicapped. Work overload and time pressures abound: planning and implementing an individualized educational program for each student, conferring with each child's parents, attending meetings, counseling parents, working through school and agency bureaucracies, to mention a few. Job tension increases as job satisfaction decreases. Teachers of the

visually handicapped can become disillusioned and burned out while working with students, perceiving only one visually handicapped child's problems and failing to see any progress or success.

Much of the stress is due to the low prevalence of a heterogeneous population to be served over a large geographic area. For example, because there are few visually handicapped children in the general population, the teacher of the visually handicapped child may be the only such specialist in the district. The teacher may feel isolated and unable to share problems, solutions, and personal feelings with other specialists. The type of service delivery in which teachers are employed also contributes to their stress. Itinerant teachers spend significant amounts of time driving from school to school. Residential school teachers, especially those who are young and energetic, may become rapidly depressed about the limited potential they see for making significant impact on the established program. The nature and severity of the student's handicap may be another source of stress. The student's progress, especially in the case of multiply handicapped blind children may be slow in spite of the significant amounts of time, effort, and patience spent by the teacher (Bina, 1982). Whatever the setting, there are four basic areas of stress for these teachers:

1. Economic factors—the teachers' feelings of being underpaid and thus, undervalued;
2. Repetition— serving the same children year after year using the same materials;
3. Overload— geographic areas and caseloads become too large, paperwork too prolific, and personal time too scarce;
4. Isolation—although itinerant teachers are isolated, they do encounter a greater number of other professionals than do resource or residential school teachers. Special efforts must be made for all teachers of visually handicapped students to come together at workshops and conferences (Olson, 1982).

Effective ways to deal with stress fall within two categories: actions to improve the environment so that it is less stressful and ways to improve personal resistance to stress (Muldoon, 1980). Improvement of the environment can involve political action such as joining negotiation committees where salary decisons are made. Even when one doesn't achieve a specific financial request, the personal satisfaction can come from having been heard. Teachers can also choose to become involved in program or administrative committees, deciding how and when they will serve the children, instead of simply feeling intimidated by administrators who tell them how it will be. Low administrator support and salary have been typically listed by teachers of the visually handicapped as major attrition factors (Bina, 1982). Stress on the job itself may be diminished in other ways—when stress accumulates, the teacher can be aware of it and try to list antecedent factors, pinpointing causes, and then experimenting with solutions.

Effective stress management is the sense of control of one's environment. Awareness and resistance to one's own loss of control and avoidance of behavior that produces feelings of helplessness and uselessness help in alleviating stress.

CONCLUDING REMARKS

Over the years, the role of the teacher of visually handicapped students has changed from that of an academic teacher to one of case manager, often multiply certified in two or more of the following: regular elementary or secondary education, preschool education, orientation and mobility, rehabilitation, mental retardation, and multiply handicapped. P.L. 94-142, the Education for All Handicapped Children Act of 1975, established a right to a free appropriate public education in the least restrictive setting for all handicapped children regardless of the type of disability. In low density population areas, it is not always possible to offer a full continuum of placement options to low prevalence handicapped children. It is also difficult to provide adequate services for visually handicapped infants and their parents and to blind and visually handicapped adults. If all visually handicapped pupils and adults are to be given appropriate services, it may be necessary in the future to prepare personnel as teachers of children, O&M specialists, and teachers of multiply handicapped pupils as well as to expand the training to include infants and their parents. These specialists with extended and more intensive training would have a specialist degree, qualify for higher salaries, and would have a greater number of available employment options. As the ROP and rubella populations of the not so distant past dictated these multiple competency training needs, the national trends of the 1980s toward cost effectiveness and use of computer technology will undoubtedly have an impact upon teacher roles and competencies in the future.

Study questions

1. Describe the setting you would most prefer for your first job considering your own personality and background.
2. Describe the age group with whom you would prefer to work, considering your personality and background.
3. Review the competencies for teachers of visually handicapped pupils included in Appendix E. Select the five that you feel you meet to the greatest degree. Tell how you would demonstrate to an administrator your achievement of these competencies.
4. Select the five competencies you feel you meet to the least degree. List those that are necessary for you to perform the job you would prefer and tell how you will acquire these competencies.
5. Select five competencies you would like to acquire during your student teaching or internship. Tell how you will go about acquiring these competencies.
6. Select five competencies you would like to acquire during your first year of teaching visually handicapped pupils. Tell how you would go about acquiring these competencies.
7. What career goals would you like to accomplish in five years? Ten years?

Additional readings

Burns, D.D. (1980). *Feeling good: The new mood therapy.* New York, N.Y.: New American Library.
Corn, A.L. and Martinez I. (1977). *When you have a visually handicapped child in your classroom.* New York, N.Y.: American Foundation for the Blind, Inc..
Harris, A.B. and Harris, T.A. (1985). *Staying OK.* New York, N.Y.: Harper & Row.
Lazarus, R.S. and Folkman, S. (1984). *Stress, appraisal and coping.* New York, N.Y.: Springer Publishing Co.
Lowenfeld, B. (1981). *Berthold Lowenfeld on blindness and blind people.* New York, N.Y.: American Foundation for the Blind, Inc.
Spungin, S.J. (1977). *Competency-based curriculum for teachers of the visually handicapped: A national study.* New York, N.Y.: American Foundation for the Blind, Inc.
Spungin, S.J. (1977). *Guidelines for public school programs serving visually handicapped children,* 2nd edition. New York, N.Y.: American Foundation for the Blind, Inc.

CHAPTER 15

Working with Parents

Kay Alicyn Ferrell

Parents of visually handicapped children play a major role in their education. Working with parents is no longer an ideal—it is a mandate. This chapter examines factors affecting attitudes of parents of visually handicapped children, levels of parent involvement in education, and common myths about parents. Strategies for increasing parent involvement and ensuring cooperation are explored.

Working with parents is no longer an ideal—it is a mandate. Teachers of blind and visually handicapped children will find their professional lives inexorably tied to those of the parents of their students as they work toward the best education possible for all visually handicapped children and youth. It is parents who can make or break a program; who can make the difference between a one-time exposure to a skill and its generalization to other areas of a student's life; who can pressure the school administration for more materials and smaller caseloads; and who can either add to or subtract from a teacher's successful career. Parents should be viewed as neither friends nor enemies; they are colleagues, and as such they deserve the same respect, training, patience, understanding, vacation, and sick leave given to any co-worker. The only difference is that their hours are longer, and their remuneration, if it comes at all, is usually intangible.

Too often, however, educators view parents from a distance and "surrender to an impulse to blame all family problems on parents" (Featherstone, 1980). It is not uncommon for teachers to report that over-correction procedures aimed at eliminating a child's rocking or eyepoking do not work because "the parents don't follow through at home;" that self-care skills are difficult to teach because "his parents do everything for him;" that parents fail to enforce good study habits or are negligent about the care of low vision aids. "His parents baby him." "His parents refuse to send him to the store on his own." Parents seem to be caught in a Catch-22, where they either do too much or too little for their children. Their actions seem to be under constant scrutiny by the very professionals that they depend on to help them help their children.

Such attitudes toward and judgments of parents are unacceptable, given today's requirments in both federal and state law for parent involvement, training, participation, and counseling. Until the mid-1970s, parent involvement in education was marked by a laissez-faire attitude on the part of both parents and school personnel. In contrast to the roots of public education—where parents were both the administrators and supervisors of the local one-room schoolhouse—school officials had come to expect parents to give up their responsibilities for their children's education at the point they entered the school system. Special education had become notorious for its failure to involve parents in the educational process:

> Special education used to be a game played over the heads of parents. They were not allowed to see most records. They received few notices about their child's program. These notices were usually incomprehensible and often came after the program had already begun or been changed. Their consent was engineered by telling them that if they wanted any service at all for their child they had to consent to the school's recommendations. Parents were seldom invited to staff conferences about the child and evaluations of student progress were not shared with them. (Martin, 1979, p. 8)

To some extent, this attitude still prevails. The parent of a blind child recently wrote,

> I was told by a pompous psychologist...and an over-worked classroom teacher that it was unlikely that [my daughter] would ever achieve even the rudiments of academic skills, and, moreover, that she was an incorrigibly ill-behaved child. However, my own experience with [her] told me that the so-called experts were mistaken, that [my daughter's] potential had not been tapped, and that her rambunctiousness stemmed from boredom. Unfortunately, any time I "rocked the boat," I was patronized, or hit with veiled and not-so-veiled

threats that [my daughter] would be removed from the program, or that the program would be completely shut down to the detriment of other students. (Parent communication [name withheld], March 24, 1985)

A teacher who complains about the lack of follow-through in the home has an obligation to see that parents know *how* to follow through—whether it means training the parents themselves or finding someone who can. This places tremendous strain on

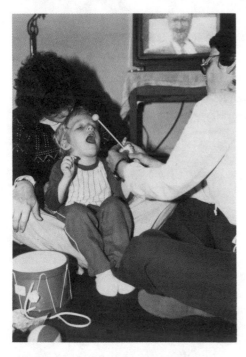

the teacher-parent relationship, however, where expectations and demands can run high on both sides. It is incumbent on both parents and teachers to understand and respect the other's perspective.

FACTORS INFLUENCING PARENT ATTITUDES

All individuals bring their own values and experiences to a situation, and parenting is no exception. In addition, because the meaning of parenthood is so deeply involved with all aspects of personality (Ware, 1981), the birth of a handicapped infant can challenge an individual's basic system of values, beliefs, and trust, as well as his sense of control over his own life. How that individual responds to the situation will depend on his or her strengths and weaknesses, the help given by other family members (Wills, 1979) and by professionals, and the influence of many different factors.

The Changing Status of the Family

The American family is in a state of transition. Twenty years ago, the most predominant family unit in this country was composed of a working father, full-time

mother, and two or more children. Recent statistics, however, reflect a quite different family composition (U.S. Department of Labor, 1985):

Six out of 10 women with children under 18 years old are in the labor force.
Almost 48% of women with children under age 3 work outside the home.
Almost half the children in two-parent families in 1984 had both an employed mother and father.
The number of families maintained by women grew more than 84% between 1970 and 1984. One-fifth of all current families with children are maintained by mothers. Over 16% of all families in the United States—10.3 million—had as their principal support women who were divorced, separated, widowed, or never married. Sixty percent of these woman-maintained families had children under the age of 18.
10.9 million children in 1984 lived in single-parent families. In 1981, 1 out of every 5 babies was born to a single mother.

Today's family is thus likely to consist of one or more working parents. This does not reflect a major change in family relationships: When women are employed, the majority of them are working because of economic need, not because of a desire to abandon their children or their household responsibilities. Nearly two-thirds of all women in the civilian labor force in 1984 were either single (26%), divorced (11%), widowed (5%), separated (4%), or had husbands whose incomes in 1983 were less than $15,000 (19%). When families are the sole responsibility of women, they are also more likely to live below the poverty line than other families.

Today's families are more mobile than they were in the 1960s and 1970s, both because it is easier to move and because seeking viable employment often necessitates a move. It is not uncommon for children to attend two or three different schools during their elementary years. But increased family mobility can lead to erosion of the family support network; no longer do children, parents, and grandparents live in close proximity to one another, and it has become increasingly difficult to rely on family members for guidance and support in times of trouble (Umansky, 1983). Extended families also served as the training ground for developing parenting and child-care skills. Children learned to care for their younger siblings in large families, and their parents and grandparents were models for nurturing, loving, and other support roles.

But statistics and changing mores do not mean that the American family is in trouble—it is simply in transition. At the same time that all these change were taking place, crime rates were decreasing, more children were completing high school and achieving better grades, and integration of both racial and other minorities into society was succeeding (Vincent, 1985). Today's families are different, but they are just that—different. There is no typical family in the 1980s.

This does mean, however, that typical approaches

to parental involvement—those that were developed in the 1960s and early 1970s—are no longer valid. Many of the expectations professionals have for parent participation may be based on memories of their own family interactions, or on images of the ideal family popularized by television series. Understanding that parents may not be available during school hours, that they may not want to spend their limited time at home working with their children on therapy or homework, that they cannot adjust work and social schedules to accommodate IEP meetings, or that they may not be able to drive their children to numerous medical and educational appointments, may be difficult for a generation of professionals who grew up in a different economic, political, and social environment. "The greater disparity between a teacher's background and a child's lifestyle, the greater is the likelihood that the teacher may misinterpret the needs and behaviors of the child and family members" (Umansky, 1985).

Stages of Grief

Parents are frequently said to go through certain stages as they come to terms with a child's handicap. The model most frequently referred to was originally developed to rationalize the actions of terminally ill patients (Kubler-Ross, 1969). While this theory is frequently used to describe parents' emotional and coping status along an imaginary continuum of acceptance, there is little empirical evidence that parents of handicapped children actually go through these stages.

Certainly, all parents at one time or another experience these feelings, but whether they experience them in this sequence or to this degree is open to conjecture. Further, while the stages may very well apply to individuals who are dying, the underlying premise—that parents will or should one day achieve acceptance—may be suspect. In most cases, professionals try to force parents to accept their child's blindness when they do not even know what acceptance is (Ferrell, 1984), or they offer platitudes and injunctions to accept the handicap that are embedded in Norman Rockwell family images (Featherstone, 1980).

As applied to parents of handicapped children, the model frequently includes the following stages:

1. *Denial and isolation*—This can be manifested as a denial that the handicap exists, or an effort to minimize the implications of the handicap. This stage can provide momentary escape for the parent, who is attempting to cope with feelings of guilt and shock while trying to carry out daily routines—including parenting the very child that is provoking the feelings to begin with. Many professionals attempt to move families out of this stage quickly, but as Ware (1981) warns, this can be "a serious mistake," since this stage generally coincides with the newborn period

and efforts should be directed toward enhancing attachment and encouraging confidence in parenting skills. Occasionally, this stage can occur throughout the child's lifetime, such as when a parent dismisses a child's reading difficulties with the comment, "I was the same way at that age. He'll grow out of it."

2. *Anger*—During this stage anger can be directed toward the professionals who did either too much or not enough; toward the family genes; toward fate; or simply toward anyone and anything. "Early on, it seems that the anger is so intense that it touches almost everyone, because it is triggered by feelings of *grief* and inexplicable *loss* that one does not know how to explain, nor how to deal with" (Smith, 1984, p. 1). Anger in itself is not bad; it can be helpful. If anger is not allowed to be expressed, however, it can eventually be directed toward the child (Ware, 1981).

3. *Bargaining*—This stage may be characterized by a search for a cure, another doctor, or a different educational program. While it is difficult to distinguish this stage from the recommended practice of seeking a second or third opinion, it reflects the anguish parents can experience in finding answers to questions about their child's health, handicapping condition, or educational potential.

4. *Depression*—The handicapping condition has begun to have its full impact on the family during this stage, and depression seems to permeate all aspects of the family's relationships. It is during this period that parents may measure their expectations for their child before learning of the handicap against what appears to be a limited potential for growth and development. Depression can also be expressed as feelings of inferiority—'I'm not a good parent. I can't help. It's hopeless.'—or as pessimism about the future: "Maybe it's worse than they're letting on. What if it keeps getting worse? What can I expect from the future?"

5. *Acceptance*—Parents are at peace with themselves as people and as parents, and see their child as an individual with his own strengths and weaknesses. Lairy & Harrison-Covello (1973) suggest that parents who have reached this stage are more likely to have further pregnancies, which may imply that the parents no longer see blindness as an overwhelming handicap or fear that other children will be born with the same condition. Reaching a point of acceptance, however, does not necessarily imply competent parenting. Parents can be at peace with a child's handicap, yet not change the manner in which they relate to their child or enforce behavior. By the same token, parents who never accept their child's handicapping condition can be highly successful and intuitive parents who

seem to know how to obtain optimal performance from their child. Ortiz (1973) found that mothers of children with rubella syndrome tended to be neither overly accepting nor rejecting, nor were they martyrs, but they still were able to carry out their child's educational program.

As Ware (1981) stated:

> Acceptance does not mean liking the handicap. It does not mean that the anguish and lost dreams will be forgotten. They will always be remembered but relived with less frequency and with lessening intensity. Acceptance does not mean enjoying the necessity for special programs and agencies. Instead, you learn to appreciate the existence of good programs and agencies and develop confidence in your ability to make the judgments which are best for your child. It does not mean never wishing your child can see. Of course, you would like for him to have sight! You simply abandon this as an *ever-present* wish, because you know it is a fact that he cannot see and you know you love him dearly even though he cannot see. It does not mean never crying or feeling angry and depressed. These feelings will periodically return. Their recurrence does not mean that you have not adjusted or that you are losing your ability to cope. It means you are human. (Ware, 1981, p. 46)

Severity of the Handicap

Schell (1981) and Marion (1981) have stated that the severity of the child's handicap often influences the attitudes and feelings of parents. The more obvious the handicap, the less socially acceptable it is. Parents of blind and visually handicapped children may be particularly vulnerable to such social pressures, since many eye disorders are accompanied by obvious physical manifestations, such as cataracts, deviated eyes, and nystagmus.

Different children affect parent-child interactions in different ways and require different parenting techniques. The more severe the handicap, the greater influence certain factors will have on parents' self-concept and sense of control over the situation. Some of the factors that influence parents' responses to handicapped children include: (a) the reward that parents derive from parenting; (b) how difficult and time-consuming routine caregiving tasks (dressing, feeding, etc.) are or become; (c) how frequently the child needs to be hospitalized, and how life-threatening and stressful those hospitalizations are; (d) the additional financial resources that are required to support the child's medical needs; (e) parents' expectations for the child's future, which may be pessimistic, even if unfounded; (f) the isolation of parents from family and friends because of the time and financial commitments, as well as the social stigma associated with the handicap; and (h) less time for sleeping, recreational activities, and performing routine household chores (Moroney, 1981; Ramey, Beckman-Bell, & Gowan, 1980). The impact of these factors increases geometrically with the severity of the handicap. Parents of blind and visually handicapped children may feel the impact even more, because blindness is often perceived to be one of the most limiting of handicaps.

Age At Onset

According to Mori (1983), the older a child is when the handicap is diagnosed, the more difficult it is for the parents. Parents of children with congenital blindness have never known their child any other way. When the visual handicap occurs later, either due to an accident or because a diagnosis was not possible earlier, parents must adjust to a new concept of their child. The process parents of older children go through may be no different from that of parents of newborns, but the family has already developed dreams and goals for the child which may need to be fundamentally altered because of the diagnosis of impairment. Even if the child has been diagnosed as handicapped previously, a subsequent but new diagnosis of blindness on top of the other handicapping conditions may be particularly difficult for parents because of the myth and stigma usually attached to visually handicapping conditions (see Chapter 2).

Socioeconomic Status

Schell (1981) and Marion (1981) state that the higher the socioeconomic status of the family, the more adverse the reaction to the birth of a handicapped child. Certainly, parents of all socioeconomic levels share similar feelings about the birth of a handicapped child, but some feelings may relate directly to the value placed by adults on childhood and on the development of children into responsible adults (Umansky, 1983). In pre-industrial society, children were important to the family to help generate family income or as extra hands to maintain the family farm. The more children a family had, the more prosperity it enjoyed.

In today's society, however, parents have children primarily for emotional satisfaction, not for financial security. Higher socioeconomic families may also see children as a means of continuing the family name and fortune, while lower socioeconomic parents may wish for a better life for their children. In either case, the birth of a handicapped child can raise difficult questions about the child's ability to reproduce and to hold gainful employment. Higher educational levels in parents do not necessarily guarantee enlightened attitudes toward persons with handicaps, either; college graduates are just as likely to have been exposed to and to sustain common myths about blindness.

How Information Was Received

The manner in which parents are first told about their child's handicap can also influence parent attitudes

(Mori, 1983). Parents enter the situation with the anxiety of knowing that they had to consult a specialist about their child, a fact that automatically makes them different and focuses on the child's abnormality. This in itself creates an atmosphere of hope, fear, and uncertainty, and what parents take away from that meeting can hinge on how they were told as much as on what they were told.

"Ask any five parents of visually impaired children how they first learned their child had vision problems and you will get five different horror stories" (Stotland, 1984). Physicians have notorious reputations for being cold and distant at such times. Usually, their training has not prepared them for delivering the type of news that shatters parental dreams of the perfect child. The hurried, aloof manner frequently exhibited by medical professionals may result from a need to avoid their own pain and feelings of inadequacy in dealing with the situation (Mori, 1981). Featherstone (1980) supported this view when she pointed out that professionals often feel far less powerful than they appear to parents.

Financial Hardships

Financial matters are of concern to all families and range from providing food, shelter, and warmth, to planning for college education for the children. As life expectancy rises, parents are also concerned about their own retirement. The stress is particularly hard on one-parent families, many of whom are women, and the majority of whom are in low paying or less skilled jobs (U.S. Department of Labor, 1985). Families maintained by women are also more likely to live in poverty. The United States Department of Labor reports that, in 1983, more than 1 out of 3 families maintained by a woman was poor, compared with 1 out of 13 other families.

The financial stress on already overburdened families rises concomitantly with the birth of a handicapped child (Moroney, 1981). The average monthly medical bill for a severely handicapped child, for example, has been estimated at $650.90, while the average monthly medical bill for a nonhandicapped child is estimated at approximately $25.00 (Shankaran, 1985). The additional costs of special day care programs, transportation to and from therapy services, and special equipment have not been estimated. It is understandable that parents may not want or be able to purchase toys, consult another physician, or even to attend a parent group, given their limited financial resources and the necessities that must be provided for all their children. Educators must be sensitive to the financial implications of the recommendations and requests they make to parents and should make those recommendations and requests only when they can also refer the family to financial aid.

Time

The lack of time frequently contributes to stress, which can be manifested as anger, impatience, or tension among family members. Families with handicapped children report that time is a rare commodity in their daily lives. Parents frequently state that they have less sleeping time, particularly during the infant and preschool years, and that basic caregiving chores (dressing, bathing, eating) take longer to accomplish. They also feel that a great deal of time is spent in transit to various therapies, educational programs, and recreational opportunities (Moroney, 1981; Ramey, Beckman-Bell, & Gowan, 1980). Parents rely on professional guidance as to which programs their children could benefit from, but sometimes those recommendations are made without an awareness of where the programs are located or when they are offered. Efforts should be made to refer parents to comprehensive center-based services as much as possible, and to locate alternate transportation sources, such as other parents or community vans, to relieve some of the time pressure parents often experience.

The emphasis that educators often place on parents as teachers can place an added burden on parents to perform at home, when they are asked to set aside a special instructional period during which the parent and child work together. Many parents—of both nonhandicapped and handicapped children—do devote daily time to working with their children on homework. The difference is that a special instructional period is an assignment, while working on homework is only a suggestion; the first is mandatory, while the second is voluntary. The first case also carries with it an implication that the parent will be judged by his child's progress. In such cases, the time that is given by the parent is likely to be resented and loaded with anxiety. Teachers do not teach all day long; parents should not be expected to do so either.

Critical Events

At different periods in the life of a family, parent-child and parent-professional relationships may be particularly difficult to maintain because of the stress of certain events. Hammer (1972) has identified six critical events in the life of the famiy with a handicapped child:

- The child is born or the handicap is suspected.
- The diagnosis is being made and the handicap is being treated.
- The child is ready to enter a school program.
- The child reaches puberty.
- The child reaches the age of vocational planning.
- The parents grow old and worry that the child will outlive them.

At least three of these critical events are key periods

in the lives of all families, whether the children are handicapped or not. They take on more significance, however, when the child is impaired, because the standard resolutions are not available. When the nonhandicapped child is ready to enter school, reaches puberty, or begins vocational planning, parents generally know what to expect because they have had similar experiences themselves. When these same events occur with a handicapped child, it is a new experience entirely for the parents, and the same concerns and fears are raised all over again. Educators need to be aware of these critical periods in the life of a family and be able to respond appropriately; information and assistance in locating resources will help parents combat their fear of the unknown.

Lack of Control

Feeling in control of one's life is a natural desire. Parents of children with handicaps, however, frequently feel powerless to change what is happening around them. Mori (1983) suggested that one of the most critical and debilitating aspects of having a handicapped child is the uncertainty. Parents do not know what to expect from the future—will the child be able to attend school, will she ever learn, go to college, or raise a family? What effect will the child with a handicap have on the other children? What will happen after the parents die? Parents may believe that the child's condition is the worst it could possibly be. Or they may fear that society will reject the child. Few of these questions or fears are ever answered immediately. The uncertainty and questioning lasts for many years and continuously contributes to feelings that one is not in control of one's own life.

Most people approach parenthood with the certainty that they are responsible for their children, that they will make the best possible choices for them, and that their rights as parents are grounded in common law and cannot be removed unless they do something horrible to their children. Yet parents of handicapped children suddenly find themselves forced to rely on the judgments, opinions, and recommendations of experts. "Compounding the problem is that these others are often strangers with whom no bond of trust has yet been established" (Smith, 1984, p. 2), and that attention is focused on the abnormality of the child and the situation simply because specialists have to be consulted in the first place (Ware, 1981).

A sense of control is not fostered if parents feel that they are under constant scrutiny. One mother wrote,

> I am always aware that any remarks that I make, even replies to routine questions, are being automatically weighed to see if they are really concealing hidden meanings, and I used to feel considerable resentment that my views were not accepted at their face value. (Lairy & Harrison-Covello, 1973, p. 36)

A sense of the feeling of lack of control has been expressed by parents as they discuss the difference between professionals who choose to work with handicapped children, and parents who have no choice:

> People who are in this profession of working with the handicapped have chosen it, and it is a profession that gives you a lot of self-esteem and a lot of good feelings. Everybody likes people and admires people who work with handicapped children. ...It's such an enobling profession. ...[T]his is something that if they get into and they pursue, they have chosen and it makes them feel good. *The parents have not chosen this.* No parent would choose to have a child that is anything less than normal and whole. And so while we both want the best for our child, the best program, we also have to realize that we're coming from different places. You're coming from a place that gives you a lot of self-esteem. A parent of a handicapped child does not have that self-esteem. (Kupfer, 1985, pp. 24-25)

A parent's sense of being out of control can affect the parent-child relationship. It can also place unrealistic expectations that professionals have all the answers. Professionals working with parents of handicapped children need to examine how their actions, language, and judgments contribute to this insecurity while at the same time develop strategies to help parents gain control over their lives.

Parents as an In-group

To a certain extent, parent attitudes toward professionals are formed from bonding with other parents, by sharing experiences and feelings about their children and about the professionals they have encountered. Parents cannot share these feelings with most professionals, simply because most professionals simply do not know what it is like to have a handicapped child (Kupfer, 1985). As long as professionals withhold information or attempt to make decisions for parents, there will be cause for parents to discuss insensitive, uncaring professionals and to dismiss their recommendations.

The dichotomy between "those who know" and "those who cannot even imagine" will grow. Extreme examples of this dichotomy can be debilitating to parent-professional relationships, because it may lead to an unwillingness to listen—"No one is going to tell me about my child!"—and an inability to take advantage of the professional's training and expertise.

The Myth of Cure

Another factor that influences the parent-professional relationship is the belief that the child can be made better through medical or educational intervention. In most other phases of life, this does occur. Individuals visit a doctor to cure an illness and attend school to obtain an education and a chance at a better life.

When dealing with issues of disability, this does not happen. Nevertheless, the expectation for cure, for making things better, is still there. Kupfer (1985) stated it best:

> There is a certain animosity that is just *there* between parents and professionals that will *always* be there because you have these intervention programs, you can do this diagnosis, but you can't make our kids better. ...The bottom line is, he can't be fixed. And that always makes a parent sad. And as a professional that's something you have to understand. (p. 22-23)

THE CONTINUUM OF FAMILY INVOLVEMENT

Federal laws mandating parent involvement are based on three major assumptions: (a) parents should make decisions about their child's education; (b) parent participation ensures the rights of the child under Public Laws 94-142 and 98-199; and (c) parents are capable of teaching and already function as their children's teachers (Turnbull, Turnbull, & Wheat, 1982). Mori (1983) views family involvement in the education of children with handicaps as developmental in nature. Families are composed of individuals with differing backgrounds who will respond to an educator's efforts to involve them in the educational process along a continuum of options. Different members of the same

family may function at different places along this continuum at any one time, and the needs of both the family member and the educational system may change periodically and cause shifts along the continuum. Mori suggests the following levels of family involvement:

1. *Passive receptivity to the child's participation in the program.* Parents allow the child to participate in the educational program and may or may not attend conferences.

2. *Minimal involvement in the child's program.* The parents have more personal contact with the professionals involved in the program, including discussions about the program itself. Parents may participate in parent groups and training sessions.

3. *Involvement as a trainee in intervention strategies.* The parents receive instruction in working with their child.

4. *Involvement as a fully participating member of an interdisciplinary team.* Parents participate in the educational process by exchanging meaningful information with professionals, selecting goals for the child, teaching, measuring, and evaluating the child's progress.

5. *Involvement as a counselor of other families with handicapped children.* Parents are willing not only to share their own feelings, but to provide emotional support and encouragement to other parents.

6. *Involvement as both advocate and policy maker.* Parents have become thoroughly integrated into the agency or educational program, and a high level of mutual trust and respect exists. Parents help to formulate policy and can interpret that policy to the larger community.

7. *Involvement as program initiator and developer.* Parents take on the responsibility of starting new programs, either for their own children or for others.

It is critical for professionals to understand that an individual parent's involvement at any given point in time is dependent on a great many factors. But parents can and do involve themselves in the educational programs of children, and a sensitive professional will not only recognize and accept the level of participation desired at that point, but will also strive to help parents along to the next level.

Stile, Cole, and Garner (1979) have identified several factors associated with parent attrition:

Meetings are held at inconvenient times and/or locations.
Financial pressures may necessitate parents' working double or split shifts, and distant locations may be difficult—or too expensive—to reach. Try to schedule parent group meetings at different times of the day, or on weekends. When possible, plan the parent meeting around a meal, and include all children; all families have to eat, and including siblings reduces the need for babysitters.

Parents are not asked for their input.
Everyone likes to be asked for input. It increases self-concept and helps parents to feel more in control of the situation. Research has shown, moreover, that parents really do know their children best. Parent and teacher assessments of the same child do not differ significantly regarding the child's level of performance (Vincent, 1985).

Professionals make unwarranted assumptions regarding parents' prerequisite skills.
Teachers may assume either too much or too little

about what a parent brings into the educational environment. Frequently this is expressed as "parents do not follow through at home," when in fact the parents may not be aware of what they are supposed to be doing at home, or the strategies they can utilize to provide follow-up. When too little is assumed, professionals may adopt a condescending attitude toward parents. Both approaches discourage parent involvement.

Parents are not given consistent and ongoing feedback on their efforts or the child's progress.
Reinforcement is a critical feature of all educational programs and working with parents is no exception. Adults respond to positive reinforcement as well as children, and both parents and teachers need feedback on how well they are doing.

Parents feel threatened.
It is easy, too, for parents to feel intimidated when they are forced to turn to highly-trained individuals who use educational jargon and seem totally competent, particularly at a time when parents feel incompetent and insecure. One parent has stated that during her child's earliest years, all the successes belonged to professionals; "only the failures were mine" (Oster, 1985).

Parents have unrealistic expectations for results within the program.
Parents turn to an educational program for help with their child. Education has become a cure-all in our society, and parents hope that the situation will improve with educational intervention. When that does not occur, disappointment prevails. Both program and child goals need to be continually reviewed with parents so that realistic expectations can evolve.

Parents are burned out from previous efforts.
For various reasons, past involvement in educational programs may have been unsuccessful and discouraging for parents, or it may have required so much of their energy that they need a vacation. Parents do have a right not to be involved; in many cases, they may seek involvement at a later time after they have had a chance to rest, to spend some time alone, and to evaluate the current program.

The program neglects the social needs of parents.
Parent involvement is more than meeting the child's needs; it also means meeting the parent's needs for time off, activities with other adults, and respite care.

Reluctance of parents of mildly involved children to associate with parents of severely impaired children.
Parents of mildly handicapped children may understandably feel that they have little in common

with parents of children who are severely impaired. This is sometimes observed in groups of parents of visually handicapped children, some of whom may have children who are "just blind," while others have multiply impaired visually handicapped children who

require different degrees of care and who have varying educational potentials. The emphasis in parent groups may be better placed on the parents' needs for sharing and support on common issues and concerns, rather than on those with which only limited numbers of parents can identify.

GUIDELINES FOR PROFESSIONALS IN DEALING WITH PARENTS

Professionals hold the power in the parent-professional relationship; they affect parents' self-concept, confidence, and level of involvement in the educational program by what information they choose to share and how they share it. But educators have just as much responsibility under special education law to educate and be responsive to the parent as they do to the child, and they will find that employing strategies to share their power will enhance parent participation in and support of the educational program, while strengthening the parent-professional relationship.

Beckett (1985), Featherstone (1980), Gorham (1975), Mori (1983), and Oster (1985) have suggested the following guidelines for professionals to employ when dealing with parents:

1. Involve parents in every step.
2. Talk face-to-face, and eliminate any physical barriers (such as a desk or telephone) when communicating with parents. Maintain eye contact.
3. Ask parents what their needs are.
4. Be attentive and use active listening skills as necessary. Show respect and concern for both the parent and the child. Learning to listen better conveys respect and demonstrates to parents that you think they can contribute valuable information. Good

listeners discover strengths as well as weaknesses.

5. Share any and all information. Make no assumptions about what families want or need, and do not try to judge when parents are ready for new information and when they are not. They are adults.

6. Be specific and objective about presenting information. Give how-to advice, including helping to devise a realistic management plan with suggestions for living on a daily basis.

7. Help parents understand the child's abilities and assets. What the child can do is much more important to both the child and the parent than what he cannot do. Help parents to think positively by reiterating that there is no such thing as a final diagnosis.

8. Use everyday language, and minimize use of jargon or acronyms. Give parents a glossary of educational and medical terms to help them interpret the language of other professionals.

9. Answer all questions honestly, but sensitively. Admit that you don't have answers to all questions.

10. Plan future goals—and meetings—cooperatively.

11. Clarify and summarize the results of any meeting or conference before concluding, and follow up with a written summary.

12. Give copies of all reports to parents (they must stay informed to stay involved). Remember that any written materials should be in the parents' native language and in an accessible mode of communication if the parent is sensorily handicapped.

13. Create opportunities for parents to talk with other parents. "The most realistic way to decrease families' isolation is by providing them with access to their peers" (Oster, 1985, p. 31). Parents offer parents respect with empathy and without the burden of clinical assessment.

14. Warn the family of any gaps in service or inadequacies in the community.

Umansky (1983), in a position paper developed for the Association for Childhood Education International, has given a three-pronged charge to educators:

(a) Children must be given a sense of heritage—pride in the uniqueness of each population group, with continual support for the similarities among people who live and work together.

(b) The curriculum must reflect children's current and future needs in family and society.

(c) Educators and parents must become more familiar with each other. Children do things at home they don't do at school and vice versa.

The charge is really no different for teachers of blind and visually handicapped children. They, too, must convey a sense of pride of self to blind and visually handicapped children, and they must employ a curriculum based on a lifelong perspective. Just as im-portantly, they must become familiar with and learn to experience the educational process from the parent's point of view—and work to assure that that process is just as rewarding for parents as it is for teachers and children.

Study questions

1. What differences can you identify between your present family unit and your parents' family units?

2. Discuss acceptance of a child's handicap from both a professional's and a parent's point of view.

3. How does the child's age affect a parent's response to a diagnosis of visual impairment?

4. How could physicians be better prepared for dealing with parents?

5. Are parents their child's best teacher? Discuss why or why not.

6. How would a teacher of visually handicapped children counter a parent's question that, "My child will always be blind. What can you do to make a difference?"

7. Plan the time, place, and agenda for a series of meetings for parents of visually handicapped children.

Additional readings

Bailey, D.B., Jr. and Simeonsson, R.J. (1984). Critical issues underlying research and intervention with families of young handicapped children. *Journal of the Division for Early Childhood,* **9**, pp. 38-48.

Barton, D.D. (1984). Uncharted course: Mothering the blind child. *Journal of Visual Impairment & Blindness,* **78**(2), pp. 66-69.

Brennan, M. (1982). *Show me how: A manual for parents of preschool visually impaired children.* New York, N.Y.: American Foundation for the Blind, Inc.

Bromwich, R.M. (1981). *Working with parents and infants: An interactional approach.* Baltimore, Md.: University Park Press.

Buscaglia, L. (1975). *The disabled and their parents: A counseling challenge.* Thorofare, N.J.: Charles B. Slack, Inc.

Dickman, I.R. and Gordon, S. (1983). *Getting help for a disabled child—advice from parents* (Public Affairs Pamphlet No. 615). New York, N.Y.: Public Affairs Committee, Inc.

Ferrell, K. (1985). *Reach out and teach.* New York, N.Y.: American Foundation for the Blind, Inc.

Hart, V. and Ferrell, K.A. (1985). Parent/educator cooperative efforts in education of the visually handicapped. In G.T. Scholl (ed.), *Quality Services for blind and visually handicapped learners: Statements of position.* Reston, Va.: Council for Exceptional Children.

Kershman, S.M. (1982). The training needs of parents of deaf-blind multihandicapped children, part two: Factors associated with parental responses. *Education of the visually handicapped,* **14**, pp. 4-14.

Kershman, S.M. (1982). The training needs of parents of deaf-blind multihandicapped children, part one: The parent competencies. *Education of the Visually Handicapped,* **13**, pp. 98-108.

Nousanen, D. and Robinson, L.W. (1980). *Take charge! A guide to resources for Parents of the visually impaired.* Austin, Tex.: National Association for parents of the Visually Impaired, Inc.

Robinson, L.W. (1982). *Parents to the rescue.* Austin, Tex.: National Association for Parents of the Visually Impaired, Inc.

Turnbull, H.R. and Turnbull, A.P. (1984). *Parents speak out: Then and now* (2nd ed.). Columbus, Ohio: Charles E. Merrrill Publishing Co.

CHAPTER **16**

The Team Approach to Advocacy

Jack Hazekamp

This chapter addresses the roles and responsibilities of the various professionals in advocating for an appropriate quality education for visually handicapped students. It includes suggestions for encouraging students to become effective self-advocates through the use of a team approach in implementing P.L. 94-142. Techniques for promoting and improving parent-professional partnerships in advocacy are described.

The education of visually handicapped children and youth involves many key individuals—school staff, parents, administrators, and the students themselves. It is essential that these individuals work together as a team, using their collective knowledge and experience, to identify and meet the unique needs of this special population. A team approach to advocacy is an effective way to advocate for visually handicapped students.

The synonym for the verb *advocate* is *support*. The goal of advocacy, therefore, is to support students by providing them with the knowledge, skills, abilities, and attitudes necessary for them to become self-advocates who are willing and able to support themselves as responsible contributing members of the society.

The team approach to advocacy is a major factor in providing a quality education to visually handicapped students as well as complying with the mandates of P.L. 94-142, the Education for All Handicapped Children Act of 1975 and other federal and state legislation. The team should become aware of federal and state laws and regulations by contacting local and state education agencies. It is important that all team members be informed regarding specific state requirements and local procedures including local terminology and acronyms.

This chapter addresses the roles and responsibilities of parents and professionals in advocating for an appropriate quality education for visually handicapped students through a team approach in implementing P.L. 94-142 as it pertains to visually handicapped students; of professionals in promoting and improving parent-professional partnership; and of the teacher of the visually handicapped student as the primary education advocate for visually handicapped students.

ROLES AND RESPONSIBILITIES IN USING THE TEAM APPROACH TO IMPLEMENT P.L. 94-142 FOR VISUALLY HANDICAPPED STUDENTS

The following procedures for using a team approach as mandated by P.L. 94-142 can provide an effective process for advocating an appropriate quality education for visually handicapped students when professionals, parents, and students understand their roles and responsibilities in identification; assessment; development; implementation of the IEP; annual review; and due process hearings.

Identification

The team approach begins with identification of visually handicapped students, including referrals for special education from vision screening programs, eye specialists, and other medical professions or public and private agencies, as well as from teachers and parents.

The teachers of visually handicapped students and medical specialists, particularly the eye specialist, and the school nurse, will often play key roles in identifying visually handicapped students. Professionals have the responsiblity of providing information to all parents and teachers through written communication, in-service training and parent education regarding the signs which may indicate a visual impairment and the procedures for making a referral.

Assessment

Once a student has been referred for special education, a comprehensive assessment must be conducted by a multidisciplinary team. This assessment must address all areas related to the suspected disability.

For visually handicapped students, assessment should include, as appropriate, the following areas:
- Vision/low vision
- Concept development and academic skills
- Social/emotional skills
- Daily living skills
- Orientation and mobility
- Communication skills
- Sensory/motor skills
- Career and vocational skills

Chart 16.1 provides a model for determining the areas to be included in the assessment and the professionals who should be involved, depending upon the needs of each student who is referred. Specific information about assessing these three areas may be found in Chapters 3, 6, 11, 19, 20, and 22.

The team approach is crucial in assessing visually handicapped students. Parents should be involved with professionals in identifying the areas of need to be assessed. Throughout the assessment process,

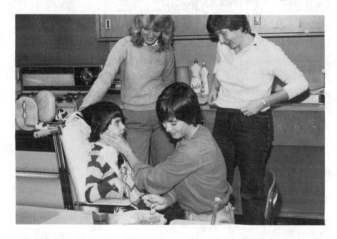

parents should be encouraged to provide information about the current skill levels and needs of their child. To assist them in becoming involved, parents should be provided with basic information regarding assessment of the specialized needs of visually handicapped students, including assessment strategies and formal and informal assessment instruments which can be used to identify those specialized needs.

Parents should be fully informed of the assessment to be conducted and should be made aware of the instruments to be used. Parents must give written consent before the assessment is conducted.

Professionals conducting the assessment must be knowledgeable about the special needs of visually handicapped students and ensure that assessment does not discriminate against the student because of a visual handicap. The multidisciplinary team conducting the assessments must work together, sharing their knowledge and expertise. For example, when a psychologist is a part of the team and has not had

training or experience assessing visually handicapped students, it is important that he or she work closely with the teacher of the visually handicapped student who can share knowledge and expertise regarding the visual impairment, including the implications for selecting, administering, and interpreting the results of the assessment instruments.

The results of the assessments should be provided to the parents prior to the Individualized Education Program (IEP) team meeting so that the parents can participate fully as members of that team. Any information which may have an emotional impact on parents should be shared prior to the IEP meeting, giving sufficient time for them to deal with this information privately before it is discussed publicly.

The visually handicapped student, when sufficiently mature to understand, should also be provided with the results of the assessment in language the student understands, particularly if he will be participating in all or part of the IEP meeting. (See Chapter 12.)

Individualized Education Program Development Including Placement in the Least Restrictive Environment

The team approach is particularly crucial in developing the student's IEP. Chart 16.1 provides a model for planning a program based on the assessed needs of each student.

It is important that all members of the team, including the parents and, when appropriate, the students, participate fully in determining present levels of performance, developing appropriate goals and objectives, and selecting the appropriate placement which is least restrictive to the student in implementing IEP goals and objectives.

As they reach each level in the maturation process, students become increasingly involved in decisions which affect them. For example, a student's ideas and feelings regarding the content of the IEP should be heard and considered. Students should also be allowed and encouraged to take increasing responsibility for their personal as well as their educational needs in order to prepare them to become independent and responsible adults. Parents and professionals should recognize the importance of preparing the students for the transition from school to the world of work, which includes the transition from childhood to adulthood. The team should also use the IEP as a focus in providing the students with knowledge, skills, abilities and attitudes necessary for these transitions.

Implementation of the IEP

The team approach is crucial for the successful implementation of the IEP. First, cooperation and coordination among and between professsionals who

Chart 16.1   Role of professionals in meeting unique needs of visually handicapped pupils

Areas of Unique Needs Which May Result From a a Visual Impairment	Assessment Should Address, when Appropriate:	Key Professionals Who May Be Involved in Assessment, Planning, and/or Provision of Needed Instruction and Services Include
Vision (for all visually handicapped students)	Eye Examination and Report • Near and distant acuity • Field of vision, including peripheral field • Etiology and prognosis • Recommendations for educators and parents	Eye Specialist* (Ophthalmologist or Optometrist) School Nurse Teacher of the Visually Handicapped
Low Vision (for students with residual vision)	Functional Vision Assessment • Observations of how student functions in educational situations • Modifications necessary for visual efficiency including -Task modifications, time requirements -Specialized materials and equipment -Desired seating, lighting, and physical arrangements -Recommendations for further low vision assessment by an eye specialist Low Vision Assessment	Teacher of the Visually Handicapped* Orientation and Mobility Specialist Eye Specialist Classroom Teacher(s) (regular and special education) Eye Specialist* who has training and expertise in low vision, including appropriate low vision aids Teacher of the Visually Handicapped Orientation and Mobility Specialist
Concept Development/ Academic Skills	Student's Mode of Functioning in Academic Tasks Basic Concepts Listening Skills	Teacher of the Visually Handicapped* Classroom Teacher(s)
Communication Skills	Typing Signature Basic Communication Equipment Use of Computers Use of Visual Aids Slate and Stylus Abacus Use of Specialized Equipment	Teacher of the Visually Handicapped* Classroom Teacher(s) Language, Speech and Hearing Specialist
Social/Emotional Skills	Socialization Skills Affective Education Recreation Sex Education Psychological Implications	Teacher of the Visually Handicapped* Counselor Psychologist Social Worker Recreation Specialist Classroom Teacher(s)

(Continued on next page)

Chart 16.1   Role of professionals in meeting unique needs of visually handicapped pupils

Areas of Unique Needs Which May Result From a a Visual Impairment	Assessment Should Address, when Appropriate:	Key Professionals Who May Be Involved in Assessment, Planning, and/or Provision of Needed Instruction and Services Include
Daily Living Skills	Personal Hygiene Dressing Skills Clothing Care Food Preparation Eating Skills Money Management Social Communications Telephone Skills Written Communications Time Skills Organization Skills	Teacher of the Visually Handicapped* Orientation and Mobility Specialist Classroom Teacher(s)
Sensory/Motor Skills	Gross and fine motor skills Alternate sensory discriminations and integration Posture, balance, strength, movement and coordination	Teacher of the Visually Handicapped* Orientation and Mobiity Specialist* Physical Education Specialist School Nurse Occupational/Physical Therapist
Orientation and Mobility	Concepts Body Image, control and movement Orientation/Mobility Skills in the home, school and community Use of residual vision Interaction with the public Acquiring and remembering necessary information Related Daily Living Skills	Orientation and Mobility Specialist* Teacher of the Visually Handicapped Physical Education Specialist Eye Specialist Occupational/Physical Therapist
Career/Vocational Education	Career Education Pre-vocational Skills including work habits, attitudes and motivation Interests/Aptitudes Vocational Skills	Teacher of the Visually Handicapped* Orientation and Mobility Specialist Career/Vocational Education Teacher(s) and Specialists Classroom Teacher(s) School Counselor Rehabilitation Counselor*

*Professional(s) with primary responsibility

work with the visually handicapped student are essential to ensure that all instruction and services focus on the needs of the student. Chart 16.1 provides a model for professionals who may be involved in implementing the IEP, based on each student's assessed needs.

Second, a parent-teacher partnership is essential in implementing the IEP; particularly follow-through in the home. This partnership can be enhanced through

communication between home and school. Ongoing progress reports to parents from teachers and feedback from parents will enhance this home-school partnership. Examples of how this can be accomplished include formal conferences, informal notes, telephone calls, and home visits. (See Chapter 15.)

Annual Reviews

At least annually, the IEP must be reviewed and revised as appropriate by the IEP team, using a team approach similar to that used to develop the IEP. IEP reviews will be facilitated by ongoing communication between parents and teachers.

Whenever additional assessment is needed, or for mandated reassessment every three years, the same procedure is followed as outlined in the initial comprehensive assessment.

Due process hearings

When using a team approach, differences of opinion will occur. These should be respected, openly shared, and resolved through a team approach to reach a consensus agreement. It is important to remember that "Irritants Make Pearls." When there is mutual respect and cooperation, most differences of opinion and misunderstandings can be resolved within the team process.

However, when there is a serious difference of opinion or disagreement which cannot be resolved through a team approach, a due process hearing should be requested to resolve the disagreement.

Throughout the team process, and particularly during a due process hearing, it is very important that disagreements not develop into adversarial relationships, which could seriously impair the functioning of the team and thereby seriously affect the education of the visually handicapped student.

The key to avoiding adversarial relationships between and among team members is to focus consistently on the needs of the students.

ROLES AND RESPONSIBILITIES OF PROFESSIONALS IN PROMOTING AND IMPROVING THE PARENT-PROFESSIONAL PARTNERSHIP

Communication is the key to establishing and maintaining an effective parent-professional partnership. This communication must be two-way and open; professionals must openly communicate with parents and parents must openly communicate with professionals.

This communication involves the exchange of information regarding the student. Professionals have the responsibility of providing information to parents to enable them to effectively participate as team members as well as parents in meeting the needs of their handicapped child. Information to parents should be presented in a way which is understandable, and the use of educational jargon and acronyms should be avoided or clearly explained.

Parents should receive information which relates to the specific needs of their child. Unnecessary or irrelevant information should be omitted on any report. When parents request copies of student records or other information, assistance should be provided, as needed, in interpreting and understanding this information.

Parents also have a responsibility to share pertinent information with professionals which will assist in assuring appropriate assessment and instruction and services, including medical information, feedback regarding the instruction and services being provided, information about how the child is functioning at home, and approaches they have found effective in teaching their child. This information is invaluable to all professionals serving the child and should be documented as a part of the assessment and in the IEP, particularly the present levels of performance section.

Parents and professionals, through a team approach, should be assisted to understand that the education of the visually handicapped child is a joint responsibility. The most effective approach in meeting this responsibility is for parents and professionals to work together in identifying and meeting the changing needs of each visually handicapped child.

Parents and professionals should also establish and maintain positive and realistic expectations of one another so together they may cooperatively establish positive realistic expectations for the visually handicapped student.

Parental expectations of professionals are often based on previous experiences with professionals especially those in the medical community. Sometimes these experiences may tend to be negative especially since the professional may be associated with the initial and painful discovery of their child's handicap. It is therefore important that the partnership between education professionals and parents begin as early as possible to establish a positive relationship, and ideally when the infant is first identified as having a visual impairment.

Professional expectations of parents should be realistic. Although it is necessary for parents to understand the importance of their involvement and such involvement should be encouraged, it is essential for the professional to be sensitive to the factors which will influence the degree to which parents are willing or able to be involved.

These factors not only include those relating to adjustment to parenting a visually handicapped child as outlined in Chapter 15, but also a variety of other factors, including time constraints because of work, family or other responsibilities, and stress related to coping with marriage, financial, job, health or other problems.

Through the parent-professional partnership, professionals should become sensitive to the needs of parents and the entire family so they can assist parents to become as involved as possible in the education of their child within the constraints imposed by these special needs.

Finally, parents and professionals should jointly establish realistic and consistent expectations for the visually handicapped student. These expectations should be discussed with the student so that he or she is aware of what is expected at home and school. Ongoing communication will be important to assure that expectations are consistently applied, are high enough so the student is motivated, but are realistic enough so they may be achieved.

It is essential that students develop high, but reasonable expectations of themselves in order to be effective self advocates.

ROLES AND RESPONSIBILITIES OF PROFESSIONALS IN COORDINATING INSTRUCTION AND SERVICES

Because the needs of visually handicapped students are complex, particularly those students with multiple impairments, many staff may be involved in providing instruction and services depending on the needs of students, including:
- the teacher of the visually handicapped
- the classroom teacher (regular and special education)
- the orientation and mobility specialist
- the eye specialist
- the regular or adaptive physical education instructor
- the school nurse
- the career/vocational education specialist
- the speech, language and hearing specialist
- the counselor, psychologist or social worker
- the transcriber
- the reader
- the aide
- ancillary staff in residential programs
  dormitory/ward personnel
  food services staff
  health services staff

Communication among all of the individuals and agencies working with the visually handicapped student is essential to assure the coordination of all instruction and services to focus on the individual needs of the student.

In working as a team throughout the identification, assessment, IEP planning, review, and implementation process, it is important that individuals share their particular knowledge and skills with other members of the team. Chart 16.1 may be helpful in identifying professionals with expertise related to the unique needs of visually handicapped students.

It is important that those staff who have not had training or experience in the special needs of visually handicapped students work with individuals who have this knowledge so that instruction and services meet all of the needs including the specialized needs of visually handicapped students.

When a student is multiply handicapped or has other special needs, expertise will also be needed in other areas. Through the use of the team approach the complex needs of these students can effectively be identified and met. For example, when a visually handicapped student is also orthopedically impaired, gifted, and has limited proficiency in English, the team should include individuals with expertise in these areas to assure that the student's needs are identified and instruction and services coordinated to focus on these needs. (See Chapters 8 & 9.)

The IEP should be the focus for coordinating instruction and services. However, ongoing communication will also be necessary to assure that instruction and services are coordinated. Formal and informal meetings and written communication will assist this coordination.

The most effective way to facilitate communication is to designate one individual to be responsible for coordinating instruction and services and facilitating communication with parents. For visually handicapped students, the teacher of the visually handicapped is usually the most effective person to act as a "case coordinator" in facilitating this communication and coordination.

THE ROLE AND RESPONSIBILITIES OF THE TEACHER OF THE VISUALLY HANDICAPPED

Because of their special training and expertise, teachers of visually handicapped children and youth will play key roles as the primary educational advocates for visually handicapped students when working with the team. This section lists how the teacher should take primary responsibility for supporting the team approach in educating visually handicapped students.

Identification

• Assist in the identification of visually handicapped students by working with the school nurse, eye specialists, and community agencies in the child find activities and the referral process.
• Provide information to parents and teachers through the use of written information, in-service, and parent education regarding signs which may indicate a visual impairment.

Assessment

• Provide information to parents about assessing visually handicapped students and coordinate input from parents in the assessment of visually handicapped students.
• Conduct assessments and provide assistance to other members of the assessment team.
• Assist parents in understanding the results of the assessment prior to the IEP meeting and, particularly for the first IEP meeting, prepare parents for the meeting by explaining the purpose of the IEP meeting, who will be present, and how they can effectively participate in the development of the IEP, emphasizing the importance of their participation.

IEP Development and Review

• Assist parents to participate in IEP meetings by providing information about the needs of visually handicapped students, including local, state or national guidelines and other literature.

• Attend IEP meetings to provide assistance and information to parents and other IEP team members.
• Encourage parental involvement including, when appropriate, writing parent responsibilities into the IEP.

IEP Implementation

• Provide specialized instruction and services to meet the unique educational needs of visually handicapped students as appropriate.
• Communicate with other staff who are serving the student to ensure the coordination of instruction and services.
• Communicate with parents about the instruction and services being provided and follow-through at home including progress reports, parent-teacher conferences, and home visits.
• Select and obtain the appropriate braille or large type textbooks, educational aids, materials, and equipment needed by the visually handicapped student including working with the transcriber, other individuals, and the student, to obtain necessary materials, media, and equipment in a timely manner.
• When the student is placed into a regular classroom, work with the regular teacher, the site administrator, and sighted peers to facilitate maximum appropriate integration.
• Work with the classroom teacher in environmental adaptations and provide assistance in adapting classroom activities and assignments.

Due Process Hearings

• Provide information which will facilitate the due process hearing including referring parents to sources for assistance, particularly parent organizations.

Responsibilities of the teacher of the visually handicapped related to encouraging the parent-professional partnership include:
• Maintaining ongoing two way communication with parents and other family members regarding realistic and consistent expectations of each visually handicapped student consistent with abilities, progress and future goals;
• Facilitating communication between parents and other staff and administrators;
• Providing ongoing information to parents and, when appropriate, students, including referrals to other sources of information and services to assist them in their primary advocacy roles;
• Assisting in organizing local meetings for parents to provide information to parents and to facilitate parents assisting one another. Providing an opportunity to parents, as well as students, to meet with visually handicapped adults is particularly useful in developing realistic long range expectations;

• Providing information about state or national organizations which can also provide information and support to parents of visually handicapped children; and
• Referring parents to other parents of visually handicapped children or individuals who can act as sources of information and support, particularly when attending IEP meetings.

Responsibilities of the teacher of the visually handicapped in coordinating instruction and services include:
• Facilitating the coordination among all staff serving each visually handicapped student throughout the identification, assessment, IEP development, review and implementation by serving as the ''case coordinator'' for these students; and
• Providing ongoing information and in-service to staff regarding the education of visually handicapped students.

As the primary information source for parents, staff, and administrators regarding the specialized needs of visually handicapped students, the teacher of the visually handicapped has the professional responsibilities to maintain current knowledge and skills in the following areas:
• Skills in working with parents of visually handicapped children, including the unique needs of families which include a visually handicapped child;
• Assessment strategies and instruments to identify unique needs of visually handicapped students;
• Appropriate instructional strategies and educational materials, media, and equipment including the current technology, which can be effective in meeting the needs of visually handicapped students;
• Appropriate placement options for visually handicapped students in the least restrictive environment;
• Local resources available to visually handicapped students within the regular and special education programs, community resources, and state and national resources.

The teacher of the visually handicapped should work with administrative staff and parents in continuous evaluation of the effectiveness of the program in meeting the needs of visually handicapped students.

The teacher of the visually handicapped in coordination with the orientation and mobility specialist should provide ongoing information to parents, administrators, regular and special education staff and the community regarding the needs of visually handicapped students and instruction and services available to meet these needs.

The teacher of the visually handicapped should maintain a library of current professional materials and be aware of pamphlets, films, and other materials which could be useful in providing inservice and parent education.

The teacher of the visually handicapped should be aware of current research, new development, and technology through professional journals, workshops, and conferences and through membership in professional organizations.

Finally, the teacher of the visually handicapped should advocate for maintaining and improving the quality of services to visually handicapped students by becoming involved in boards and committees at the local level and, through professional and parent groups and organizations, become involved politically at state and national levels to advocate for an appropriate education for all visually handicapped students.

Each individual involved in the education of visually handicapped children and youth—the parent, the administrator, the staff member, and the student—has responsibilities as an advocate. By working together as a team, these individuals can increase their effectiveness in reaching the common goal of providing an appropriate quality education for each visually handicapped student, and thus providing each student with the skills, abilities, and attitudes to become an effective self advocate. The following story illustrates how a team approach can assist Johnnie in becoming an advocate for himself:
See Johnnie. (Identification)
See through Johnnie. (Assessment)
See Johnnie through. (IEP Planning and Implementation)
See Johnnie able to see himself through. (The Goal—Self Advocacy)

PROFESSIONAL RESPONSIBILITIES IN ASSESSING, PLANNING, AND PROVIDING INSTRUCTION AND SERVICES

Chart 16.1 is by no means intended to be complete or all inclusive, but rather is presented, as a general guide or model for using a team approach to assess, plan, and provide instruction and services to meet the unique needs of each visually handicapped student. It should be understood that parents, and when appropriate, students will also be involved, as well as other staff members, including transcribers, aides, readers, bus drivers, etc. It should also be understood that it is the responsibility of administrators and program specialists to provide support necessary for the team to carry out their responsiblities.

The chart does not include the needs of all students including basic curriculum, courses of study, standards of behavior and discipline, etc. Visually handicapped students should, as much as possible, meet the standards and expectations established for all students.

The chart also does not include needs resulting from

an additional disability or disabilities or other special needs of students served in programs for bilingual, gifted, disadvantaged, etc., since the needs of these students and the professionals involved are so numerous, varied, and complex, that it precludes including them in this chart.

Study questions

1. How can you as a professional use the team approach to increase your effectiveness in identifying, assessing, planning, and/or providing instruction and services to visually handicapped students?
2. Which other members of the team should you be working with in your responsibilities to serve visually handicapped students?
3. What are some ways you can foster a more effective relationship with the parents of students you serve?
4. How successful has your program been in providing visually handicapped students with the skills, abilities, and attitudes to become independent and productive after leaving school?
5. How can you become more effective in assisting the students you serve to make a successful transition from school to the world of work and become more effective self advocates?

Additional readings

Ban, J.R., and Masoodi, B.A. (1980). School administrators and the visually handicapped, *NASSP Bulletin,* **74**, pp. 64-69.

Genshaft, J.L., Dare, N.L., and O'Malley, P.L. (1980) Assessing the visually impaired child: A school psychology view. *Journal of Visual Impairment & Blindness,* **74**(8), p. 344.

Rioux, W.J. (1978). Parents and educators—A forced or natural partnership? *The Directive Teacher,* **1**(2).

Risley, B.L. (1971). Toward more effective services: cooperation and coordination as the imperative for relevance. *Education of the Visually Handicapped,* **3**(3), pp. 73-79.

Sawyer, H.W., and Sawyer, S.H. (1981) A teacher/parent communication training approach. *Exceptional Children,* **47**, p. 305.

Seligman, M. and Seligman, P.A. (1980). The professional dilemma: Learning to work with parents. *Exceptional Parent,* **10**(5), p. 11

Spungin, S.J. (1978). *Competency based curriculum for teachers of the visually handicapped: A national study.* New York, N.Y.: American Foundation for the Blind, Inc.

Wardell, K.T. (1976). Parental assistance in orientation and mobility instruction. *The New Outlook for the Blind,* **70**(7), p. 321.

Wolfe, J. and Troup, J. (1980). Strategy for parent involvement: Improving the IEP process, *Exceptional Parent,* **10**(1), p. 31.

CHAPTER **17**

Resources, Media, and Technology

Julia Holton Todd

Parents and teachers face an exciting challenge in selecting the appropriate media, equipment, and resources to assist in implementing the IEP goals for a visually handicapped student. Appropriate identification and utilization of resources will make a significant difference in the education of visually handicapped students and their preparation for independent, successful living as adults in a sighted world.

Providing an appropriate education for a visually handicapped child requires cooperative effort among school personnel, parents, and other agency persons in order to ensure that the needs of the students are properly identified and that all possible resources are secured and utilized. The visually handicapped student may need specialized materials and equipment to access information readily available to students who are not visually handicapped. Appropriate identification and utilization of resources will make a significant difference in the education of visually handicapped students and their preparation for independent, successful living as adults in a sighted world.

Due to the rapid development of new media and technology, it is difficult for parents and teachers to keep up-to-date with the latest information. In the past, there were many fewer special materials available for use of visually handicapped students— braille, tape recording, large print, the braillewriter, slate and stylus, and the abacus. Now, a host of new technology for blind and low vision students is emerging. Advances in computer technology and electronics have the potential for giving a visually handicapped person almost total access to the printed and electronic word. Concurrently, the American Foundation for the Blind has established a National Technology Center at its New York City headquarters, where detailed information on all types of devices, basic as well as sophisticated, is available on request.

The National Technology Center also maintains a register of local sites for training in the use of technical aids, lists of users of such kinds of products, and makes evaluations of new and existing devices.

This chapter discusses various materials which will assist the teacher in identifying specialized materials and equipment needed by a visually handicapped student for a complete appropriate education. New developments will be addressed and briefly summarized; however, a comprehensive overview of electronic and computer technology will be impossible since this area is changing so rapidly. Information presently available will be outdated by the time this book is published. Orientation and mobility materials will be discussed in Chapter 19. Parents and educators must accept the challenge of remaining knowledgeable about current developments through attending meetings and exhibits, as well as reading professional and parent journals.

After determining the necessary resources for an appropriate education, school personnel and parents must investigate the service delivery system which identifies and provides resources to visually handicapped students. The service delivery system varies from state to state and is dependent upon local, regional, and state policies and resources. In this chapter, service delivery systems will be discussed along with information to aid in determining the systems used in a given area.

The parents and the school must work cooperatively to identify and obtain all necessary resources. The possibilities are so vast and the service delivery system so complex that no one school or person can adequately serve a visually handicapped child in an isolated context.

IDENTIFICATION AND SELECTION OF SPECIALIZED MEDIA AND EQUIPMENT

After the educational needs of the student have been identified as a result of a multifaceted evaluation, school personnel and the parents develop an individualized educational program (IEP) for the child. Parents and school personnel should discuss the necessity of utilizing specialized equipment and media for the implementation of the IEP. Before selecting specialized materials or equipment for a visually handicapped child, the teachers must investigate all aspects for the use and applications of the particular material in order to ensure that it is the most legally appropriate for the student and that it can assist in meeting the goals outlined in the student's IEP. In the following section are listed some of the factors to be considered in determining the usefulness of materials such as closed circuit televisions (CCTV), electronic travel aids, or braille books.

Student Considerations
• Which IEP goal does the use of this material facilitate?
• Will the material aid the child in becoming more independent?
• Will the student be able to use the device anywhere in the school, at home, and/or during the summer?
• Will the item assist the student with vocational preparation?
• Is it a consumable item?
• If yes, and it is borrowed from an agency, what are the agency's policies about the consumption of loaned items?
• Can the item be used by the student independently?
• How will the item affect the student's reading speed?
• Will the device contribute to or alleviate user fatigue?
• Will the material be available to the student after graduation?
  —In the case of aids and devices, will the student be able to keep them upon graduation?
  —In the case of large print, braille, and tape, will the student have access to materials in these formats after graduation?

Alternatives
• Are there alternative brands?
• If the student does not receive this material what can be used in its place?
• What might be the result if the student is not supplied with this material or any alternative?

Training
• Does the teacher and/or student need training in order to utilize the material properly and effectively?
• If yes, who will provide the training and, if costs are involved, who will pay for it?

Classroom Considerations
• What type of storage will be needed?
• Will the student have free access to the storage area, or will the student be dependent upon the teacher to get the material from the storage area?
• What type of space and other facilities (electrical outlets, desks, etc.) are needed in order for the child to use the material?
• Will the material create confusion and/or distraction in the classroom?
• Will it be necessary for the teacher and/or parent to closely monitor the use of the material?

Manufacturer Information
• Who manufactures the product?
• What is the initial cost to the school district and/or parents?
• Will there be any other costs after purchase (service agreement, consumable/expendable components)?
• What is the delivery time?
• How much lead time is necessary for the order?

Maintenance and Service
• What kind of care/maintenance is required?
• Where is service available?
• What are the procedures for having an item serviced?
• If the item needs service, will a back-up/replacement be available?
• Who pays for service agreements, maintenance and/or expendable/consumable items?

VISUAL, TACTUAL, AND AUDITORY MEDIA EQUIPMENT

Parents and teachers face a challenge in the selection of appropriate media and equipment. Not all visually handicapped students can or should use all the materials listed in the next pages. There are hundreds of materials available from publishers and companies such as the American Printing House for the Blind, the American Foundation for the Blind, and Science Products. Rapid developments in technology have led to many applications for the visually handicapped person and advances in computer technology have greatly accelerated the introduction of new devices. Parents and teachers should consider these carefully and choose which are the most appropriate for the handicapped child. Some of these materials are listed in the following sections with their descriptions. They are categorized into Visual Aids, Tactual Aids, and Auditory Aids. The addresses of some of the companies which provide these materials are listed in Appendix G.

Visual Aids
Visual aids make it easier for visually handicapped students to see print and other images. Nonoptical aids which do not require special prescriptions or training to use are presented here. Optical visual aids, those prescribed by an eye specialist, are described in Chapter 6. Use of these optical aids usually requires special training.

Acetate: Yellow acetate can be placed over print to increase print darkness and contrast. (Source: office supply stores)

Bold Line Paper: Bold line paper may be used in writing, mathematics (graphs), or music to enable a student to see the lines better. This paper is available in many different forms. The lines can vary in width, color, and contrast with the paper. (Source: American Printing House for the Blind, Modern Education, or teachers can make their own by going over lines on primary paper or other heavy paper with a marking pen).

Bookstands: Bookstands make it possible to elevate, angle, and/or bring print closer to student's eyes. The use of bookstands may reduce the amount of neck and back fatigue caused by bending over to get close to a book on a desk. (Source: American Foundation for the Blind, homemade).

Closed Circuit Television: The closed circuit television (CCTV) projects an enlarged image onto a television screen. Most systems have a zoom lens which allows for variable magnification. Polarity switches on many CCTVs enable the user to select a white image on a

Portable model of a closed circuit television system

black background or a black image on a white background. Contrast and illumination can also be varied. Some systems have adaptations which enable them to be used with typewriters, microfiche readers, and computer terminals. (See Chapter 6.)
Considerations: The user is able to see/read almost any printed material or images and has instant access to the material. The user does not have to wait for the material to be reproduced in large print. However, closed circuit televisions are expensive and not all models are portable. Students must receive training in order to utilize the equipment correctly. The user must be able to move the material under the camera while reading the print on the television screen. The teacher should investigate service agreements and the

length of time required for maintenance or repair. (Source: Apollo, Pelco, Visualtek)

Felt Tip Pens: The use of felt tip pens, usually black, by the teacher and the student is often beneficial due to the dark, bold line produced by the pens. (Source: office supply stores)

High Intensity Lamps: These often provide the amount and angle of light needed by the student for maximum reading efficiency. Light sources with variable rheostats allow the student to make necessary adjustments depending upon the light conditions in the classroom. (Source: American Foundation for the Blind, American Printing House for the Blind, Bernell, office supply stores)

Large Print Textbooks: Many visually handicapped students can read standard print; others will require books with larger print. The need for large print may not be apparent until the third grade when the print size becomes smaller in textbooks and other classroom materials. Large print (or large type) generally refers to letters which are 14 to 30 points high. Large print can be produced by photo enlarging standard type, resetting standard type in large sizes, or typing on a large-type typewriter.
Considerations: Not all visually handicapped students need large print. A student may use large print for some subject areas (e.g., mathematics and science) and regular print for others. Holding materials closer to the eye may also be done instead of using large print. Many students use large print in combination with other aids, such as tapes, magnifiers, and/or closed circuit television systems. The quality of the print is important in large print as well as regular print. Making the print larger does not guarantee that a student will be able to read it. Spacing, boldness of letters, and paper color and quality are also vital to reading efficiency.

Lack of color, and often, the poor quality of pictures make them less informative or motivating than regular books. Large print may be more time-consuming and tiring for the reader due to the total head sweep, place confusion, and the tendency to see small parts of words or phrases at one time. The weight and size of some large print books make them difficult for children to carry and store. Relatively little is available in the way of supplementary, reference, or recreational reading material for children; not all text series are available through the American Printing House for the Blind; and volunteer groups produce books with a wide range of quality. Once the child leaves school, considerably less is available.

Markers and Reading "Windows": These types of masks and markers will assist the student in following the text without losing the place. The teacher or parent can use a heavy piece of paper and cut out a "window" that will expose the amount of material/text that can be easily handled by the student (e.g., one word at a time or one line at a time).

Microfiche: This sheet of microfilm containing rows of micro-images of pages of printed matter may be used with the standard lens or lens with higher magnification. (Source: office and library equipment companies)

Viewscan: This portable electronic magnifying system consists of a small hand-held camera that the user moves across the printed material. A bright, magnified image is displayed on a screen. The Viewscan can be connected to a computer with a computer interface. (Source: Wormald International Sensory Aids)

Viewscan

Tactual Aids

Tactual aids enable the blind individual to obtain information through the sense of touch.

Braille Books: Braille texts are produced by publishers, volunteers and paid transcribers and the American Printing House for the Blind under the Federal Quota Program (p. 292). Transcription by computer is also possible and is becoming more feasible and cost efficient as the technology develops and is readily available.

Considerations: Braille textbooks are very expensive and not all titles are available in braille. Students should be taught to read braille by a certified teacher just as a sighted child should be taught reading in print by a certified teacher. The student must learn special codes in order to be able to read mathematics and science books in braille. The quality and completeness of a braille textbook should be examined before it is given to a student. Teachers should know whether or not the book was proofread after transcription and if all tables, charts, and explanations for pictures in

the print text were included. Braille materials are not readily available to adults; therefore, visually handicapped students must learn to use other aids and equipment. Learning to use auditory aids is extremely important for the braille user. Although braille is only one of the many options for the student, it is an important one which releases a person from dependence on equipment or people.

Braille Readiness Materials: Readiness materials are designed to aid the teacher in preparing a student for braille instruction. (Source: American Printing House for the Blind, Exceptional Teaching Aids)

Braille Ruler, Compass, Protractor, and Tapes: The embossed markings on these and other similar measuring devices enable the visually handicapped student to read measurements. (Source: American Foundation for the Blind, American Printing House for the Blind, Science Products)

Braillewriter: This six-key machine is operated manually by the student and produces raised dots on paper inserted into the machine by the student. (Source: American Printing House for the Blind, Howe Press)

Cranmer Abacus: An adaptation of the oriental abacus, the Cranmer abacus has a special backing which prevents accidental movement of the beads. (Source: American Printing House for the Blind, American Foundation for the Blind)

Cubarithm Slate: The slate enables the blind student to perform arithmetic computations using standard braille characters. This, however, is rarely used now. (Source: American Printing House for the Blind, American Foundation for the Blind)

Optacon: (Optical-to-Tactual-Converter) This electronic reading device transforms print into vibrating letter configurations that are read tactually. It consists of three parts: a camera, an electronics section, and the tactile array. The blind person moves a miniature camera across a line of print with the right hand, while feeling a tactile representation of the individual letters or numbers with the index finger of the left hand resting on the tactile array which consists of 144 vibrating pins.

Considerations: The greatest advantage of the Optacon is the accessibility to printed material which would otherwise be unavailable without an intermediary reader or a reading machine. Disadvantages of the Optacon center around its slow speed and lack of flexibility. Secondly, the Optacon cannot handle a wide variety of printed information such as script, poor quality print, pictures, and elaborate unorganized formats. It can handle a range of print sizes and styles, and a number of adaptations allow the reader to work with typewriters, computer terminals, electronic calculators, and especially small print. Teachers and students must both receive extensive training in the effective use of the Optacon. The cost of purchase, repairs, adjustment, and maintenance must be considered. (Source: Telesensory Systems, Inc.)

Optacon

Paperless Braille: The phrase paperless braille describes the product of several pieces of equipment which store information on audio cassette tapes and are presented in a display ranging from 12-32 braille cells in length. The reader runs his fingers over the display cells and simply pushes a button to bring up the next segment of recorded braille. The reader can also produce and record his own braille, edit, and interface with an increasing variety of computers, typewriters, and calculators. For example, a student linking a VersaBraille to a microcomputer would be able to read that computer's information output in paperless braille, instead of using a cathode ray tube (CRT) screen. In addition to cassette braille, technology is increasing the means of braille production. Several print to braille translation systems exist (e.g. Maryland Computer Services Triformations, Inc., and Cranmer's Modified Perkins Brailler), and their flexibility increases continuously. These systems can be accessed through a variety of input modes and can interface with a number of other technological devices. These two developments alone—cassette braille and computerized braille production—greatly increase the availability and flexibility of materials for braille readers.

Considerations: The advantages of a cassette brailler are: (a) reduced storage space since one cassette can typically store 300-500 pages of braille; (b) usability of the machine for a variety of reading and writing tasks; and (c) portability. In a study of the San Diego City Schools' use of cassette braille, the following additional advantages were cited: (a) the editing or correctability feature; (b) less noise; (c) electronic keyboard which cuts down on fatigue; (d) higher reading rates when compared to braille reading; (e) word search capabilities (Doorlag & Doorlag, 1983). Problems discovered in this pilot study include: (a) the limited interfacing abilities which presently exist; (b) weight for continuous carrying; (c) sensitivity to being knocked around. Experienced users would also like to see the display enlarged so they can have immediate access to more information at one time, thereby increasing their reading speed. (Source: Telesensory Systems, Inc., Triformation Systems, Inc.)

Raised Line Drawing Kit (Sewall): A board covered with rubber on which acetate is placed enables the blind child and the teacher to produce raised lines. (Source: American Foundation for the Blind, American Printing House for the Blind)

Raised Line Paper: This specially embossed paper helps students to write on lines. (Source: American Printing House for the Blind, Modern Education Corporation)

Sensory Quill: The Sensory Quill enables the user to produce lines by moving a stylus across a page. (Source: Traylor Enterprises, Inc.)

Slate and Stylus

Slate and Stylus: The slate is a metal frame with openings through which braille dots are punched with a pointed stylus. Slates are available in many sizes from a pocket sized single line to eight lines and 18 cell to 40 cell. Note: Writing with the slate and stylus must be done from right to left. To read the raised dots, the paper is usually turned over. (Source: American Printing House for the Blind, American Foundation for the Blind)

Tactile Graphics Kit: The tools in this kit can be used to produce various textures for use in tactual drawings such as maps. (Source: American Printing House for the Blind)

Tactual Maps and Globes: Maps and globes with raised surfaces and different textures aid the blind child in learning map concepts. (Source: American Printing House for the Blind, Map publishers, homemade with rope caulk, tracing wheel, yarn and glue, or other materials)

Templates and Writing Guides: These guides assist the blind individual in writing on lines and in specified spaces. (Source: American Printing House for the Blind, American Foundation for the Blind, homemade)

Thermoform machine: The thermoform duplicator is utilized to produce copies of braille. In addition, it can be used to produce raised reproductions of some materials. (Source: American Thermoform Corporation)

Auditory Aids

Auditory aids are those which enable an individual to learn how to utilize hearing and good listening skills. Auditory devices are often used in conjunction with visual and/or tactual aids.

Kurzweil Reading Machine: The Kurzweil Reading Machine utilizes computer technology to translate print into synthetic speech output. The device is extremely expensive and requires extensive training. Most state schools and colleges have a Kurzweil Reading Machine in their libraries. (Source: Kurzweil Computer Products)

Speech Compressor: The speech compressor is a device which makes it possible for the user to control the speed of the audio output of a tape to produce compressed speech. Minute bits of recorded speech are discarded by deleting minute segments every x amount of time through time-sampling, or by deleting pauses between words and sentences, or by shortening all vowel sounds; the material is then re-recorded in its shortened form. Intelligibility is preserved, tonal quality is not adversely affected, and listening time for the same material is reduced. There are several devices for randomly selecting and discarding speech segments including the Tempo-Regulator and several computerized techniques. Accelerated speech refers to material which is recorded at one speed and reproduced and played back at an increased speed. While this approach is somewhat functional for small rate increments, larger increases in speed produce a "Donald Duck" distortion in tonal quality, and seriously limit the usability of the recorded material. There are now successful devices which can control this pitch-altering effect of accelerated speech. While it is often easier and less expensive to accelerate the speech, compressed speech offers better quality and flexibility to the listener.

Considerations: Visually handicapped individuals have been using accelerated or compressed speech for many years because of its increased efficiency. In fact, speech compressed from 175 wpm (normal speaking rate) upward to 275 wpm has consistently resulted in no appreciable loss (often an increase) in comprehension or recall (Bancroft & Bendenelli, 1982; Foulke, 1968). In some cases comprehension did suffer at rates greater than 275 wpm, and Foulke has postulated that adequate perception time was not available at those speeds. Rates of about 250-274 wpm are nevertheless, several times faster than average rates for braille or large print readers in grade school—children could listen to selections a second time to pick up missed points and still use less than that required by braille or large print. (Source: American Printing House for the Blind, Varispeech II—sold by audio-visual companies)

Synthetic Speech: This is the computerized production of phonemes into words based on a variety of programming formats. Presently, synthetic speech is used in a variety of ways, most notably as a) reading machines for printed books, articles or other typed pages (e.g., Kurzweil Reading Machine, Cognodictor); b) an output mode for computer terminals (Triformations, Total Talk, Echo II); and c) feedback for typing (Talking Typewriter, Spellex II).

Considerations: There are some real advantages to the increasing availability of synthetic speech. It is relatively easy to understand, offers the reader some control over translation of material (rate, spelling, etc.) and requires limited special training (Goodrich, Bennett, Paul, & Wiley, 1980; Ryhne, 1982; Selvin, 1981). At this writing, there are still several limitations which restrict the flexibility of synthetic speech. For example, reading machines usually require printed materials with high quality print and a relatively full and simply organized format. Highly technical materials present difficulties because of the occasional inaccuracy and symbolic vocabulary of the translation. When used as an output mode for the computer terminals, graphics cannot be translated because of the present inability to translate such information into auditory display. (Source: Computer Aids Corporation, Telesensory Systems, Street Electronics, Digital Equipment Corporation)

Talking Books: Books recorded on tape and/or records are called Talking Books. These are produced and recorded under the talking book program which provides public funds through the Library of Congress for the production of talking books to be made available free to thousands of visually handicapped adults and children. Aside from talking books, there are numerous "books-on-tape" produced by commercial publishers and available for all modes of car and home cassette players. (Source: Talking Books—National Library Service for the Blind and Physically Handicapped, Library of Congress, Regional Libraries; "Books-on-tape"—bookstores)

Talking Calculators, Clocks, etc.: Technology is advancing so quickly that many "silent" machines are now available with audio output. (Source: American Foundation for the Blind, American Printing House for the Blind, Science Products, office supply stores, department stores)

Tapes: Tapes and the tape recorder are useful for taking class notes, recording homework, recording test answers, listening to assignments, and "reading" assigned books. (Source: American Printing House for the Blind, Recording for the Blind, National Library Service, office supply stores, audio-visual stores)

Large Print Computer

Computer Applications

As stated earlier, the rapid developments in computer technology are making a significant change in the accessibility of computers for visually handicapped individuals. Just as sighted persons are utilizing computers at home, on the job, and for education, the visually handicapped person can also use computers in these areas. Microcomputers, with the appropriate peripherals (add-ons) and software (programs), enable the visually handicapped individual to function alongside the sighted person in the acquisition and manipulation of information.

Computers can be accessed through hardware and/or software that is designed specifically for the

visually handicapped or with commercially available components. Unfortunately, there is no one system that will fit all the needs of a visually handicapped user. The type of system used and the adaptations needed will depend upon the application and the hardware and software that will be interfaced (connected) to enable the visually handicapped user to do the necessary tasks.

In the area of large print, a large print computer system can be purchased or software that produces large print on the screen of a conventional computer system can be used. Closed circuit television systems and large print readout devices, such as the Viewscan, can be connected to a computer to allow for a large printed readout. Many large print programs/systems do not allow for the display of graphics or animation. Some programs that produce large print allow for not only a variation in the height of characters, but also in the width of characters. Also, modifications to standard computer systems can be made to accommodate the needs of the visually handicapped user.

Graphics and color can be used for vision stimulation and tracking exercises. For this type of use, monitors/screens and graphics programs with high resolution are preferable to those with low resolution. High resolution results in clearer, more precise definition of shapes and characters.

Perhaps the most exciting and rapidly expanding area is the utilization of microcomputers by braille users. Speech synthesis and braille input and output devices enable the blind person to manipulate data—printed, spoken, and tactual. Through the use of appropriate hardware, software, and peripherals, the blind person can use word processing programs to enter data through the regular keyboard by using a braille keyboard

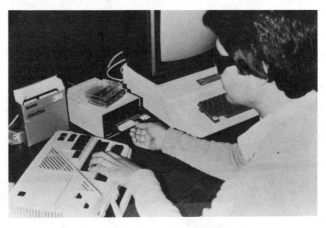
VersaBraille interface with Apple II computer system

simulated on the standard keyboard, or with an alternate device such as the Versabraille II. Information can be retrieved (output) in braille, print, or speech.

This has very exciting applications for students and teachers. Teachers can type a lesson or test and then, using the appropriate hardware or software, convert the material to large print, braille, regular print, or speech, depending upon the needs of the student. The student, on the other hand, could do homework or tests in braille and convert it to print for the teacher.

When selecting software or hardware for use by visually handicapped individuals, the parent or teacher must follow all the general guidelines for selection and use of computer items. Many books and articles have been written on the subject. Lawrence Scadden's *Blindness in the Information Age: Equality or Irony* (1984) discusses how a visually handicapped person can make the most out of living in the computer age.

Hardware/Software Considerations
• How flexible is the hardware/software? (e.g., can it be used for more than one purpose and more than one person at a time?)
• Can it be used by sighted and visually handicapped individuals interchangeably?
• How does the program/hardware handle graphics?
• Does the system lose its flexibility as peripherals/extra pieces are added?
• Can the computer be easily adapted so that a variety of methods can be used for input and output (e.g., braille, voice, tape, disc)?
• Does the speech synthesizer work with all hardware and software being used?
• What is the voice quality?
• Can the voice output be modified to refine the pronunciation of words?

Speech Synthesizer
• Word processing programs: is the editing flexible?
  —one line at a time
  —one character at a time
  —full screen

SERVICE DELIVERY SYSTEMS
Parents and teachers should take time to carefully determine the service delivery system that has been designed to provide specialized materials and equipment to visually handicapped students in the school system and state. Some states have very formally organized delivery systems that entail minimum cost to the school district and require little effort on the teachers' or parents' part beyond requesting the items needed. Other states, however, have no formal system and it is the responsiblity of the teachers and/or parents to work out all the details of delivering materials and other resources to visually handicapped students. Often the system that has been developed is dependent upon the administration of the Federal Quota Allocation within the state.

The Federal Quota Allocation
Since the passage of the Act to Promote the Education of the Blind in 1879, Congress has allocated monies annually for the production of specialized books, equipment, and instructional aids for the legally blind. This national program is known as the Federal Quota Program and is administered by the American Printing House for the Blind (APH) in Louisville, Kentucky. Agencies providing educational programs for legally blind students who function below college level are eligible to receive a portion of the Federal Quota Allocation, funds allocated by Congress, on the number of legally blind students registered in an annual survey (The Annual Registration of Legally Blind Pupils). This annual registration requires that all agencies serving legally blind individuals below college level register those individuals served as of the first Monday of each January. Eligible agencies include state departments of education, residential schools for the blind, state commissions for the blind, and rehabilitation agencies.

Of the more than 44,000 individuals registered annually, approximately 66 percent are served by state departments of education, 21 percent by residential schools for the blind, and 13 percent by other agencies. 7,100 individuals read braille, 14,000 use large type, 16,000 use both (American Printing House for the Blind, January, 1984 registration).

After verification of the students' names is submitted, the agency is allocated monies for the purchase of items produced by the American Printing House for the Blind. The Federal Quota Allocation can be used only at the American Printing House for the Blind. Between fiscal years 1977 and 1983, the annual allocation averaged $116 a year for each legally blind student registered (APH, 1984). For additional information, contact the State Department of Education, Division of Special Education.

Which Delivery System Model Is in Use?
As stated earlier, the resources delivery system in many states is dependent upon the method of administering the Federal Quota Allocation. The Association of Instructional Resource Centers for the Visually Handicapped (AIRC/VH, 1984) has identified three models for the delivery of materials available with Federal Quota Funds: 1) the Acquisition/Delivery Model—the agency administering the Federal Quota Allocation receives requests for materials, processes them, and arranges for the shipment of the materials to the requestor; 2) the Clearinghouse Model—the agency with this structure receives and processes requests, arranges for shipment to the requestor, and maintains an inventory of the materials so that they may be recirculated if necessary; and 3) the Depository Model—the Depository Model offers all the

services listed previously and, in addition, houses unused books and equipment. Borrowers are required to return the materials after use to the Depository so that they may be reshipped immediately upon the receipt of another request. In addition to the administration of the Federal Quota Allocation, many of the agencies with one of the above models offer other services such as information dissemination, inservice training, materials production and/or duplication, and loan of materials not available from the American Printing House for the Blind.

One of the challenges facing parents and teachers is that the materials delivery system may consist of services and resources from several agencies such as the state department of education, the state commission for the blind, residential school for the blind, local school districts, intermediate school districts, instructional materials center, private agencies, volunteer agencies, service organizations, and federal agencies. Instructional materials centers (IMC) for the visually handicapped, found in several states, for example, are designed as instructional materials coordinating units and resource centers for the coordination, cataloging, standardizing, production, procurement, storage, and distribution of educational materials needed by visually handicapped students. It is the responsibility of teachers and parents to know of the services and resources offered by each of these agencies so that the visually handicapped child receives all the needed materials and equipment in an expedient manner.

Questions to Ask When Determining the Materials and Resources Delivery System

The following information should be requested of the supervisor or director of special education. If necessary, the State Department of Education, Division of Special Education, should be contacted for additional information. (Refer to section on additional information for teachers in this chapter for an explanation of terms used below.)

Federal Quota Program

• How do I acquire materials and equipment produced by the American Printing House for the Blind (APH) and available with Federal Quota Funds?
• What procedures must be followed in requesting items?
• What may I order and when?
• What policies exist concerning maintenance agreement, repair (particularly when materials must be returned to manufacturers), maintenance of records of location of materials, retrieval, and return of materials?
• What are the procedures and timeline for the APH Annual Registration of Legally Blind Pupils? How are these procedures different from the annual count required by provision in P.L. 94-142?
• What are my responsibilities as a teacher/parent?

Additional Materials, Resources, and Services

• What services are offered in addition to the administration of the Federal Quota Allocation?
—inservice training
—information dissemination
—newsletter
—books for parents and/or professionals on loan
—audio-visual programs on loan
—equipment repair
—SpecialNet
—other
• Does the agency provide any items (equipment and/or books) that are not available with Federal Quota Funds? If yes, what are the details concerning items available, eligibility requirements, repair and maintenance policies, cost, restrictions on the use of the item and/or parent and school responsibilities for maintenance and provision of consumable or expendable items?
• Are materials, equipment, and services provided for visually handicapped students who are not legally blind and, therefore, not registered on the Annual Registration of Legally Blind Pupils? If yes, what services, materials, and equipment are available and what are the procedures for receiving them? (See above question.)

Questions About Transcription of Large Print, Braille, and Tape

• If I need textbooks transcribed into any of these media, what are the procedures for the following:
—filing the "Intent to Braille, Large Type, or Record" with APH;
—locating the transcriber, typist, or recorder (are these persons paid or is a volunteer network established);
—securing supplies needed by the persons listed above;
—monitoring the progress of the work;
—insuring the quality and accuracy of the work;
—duplicating the finished product, and
—storing and inventorying of the master.

Other Miscellaneous Questions

• Are there existing networks, volunteers, and/or service organizations in the state and/or in the area?
• Are there other agencies that offer services for school-age visually handicapped children?
—residential school for the blind
—clinics for evaluation
    low vision/equipment and materials evaluation
—state commission for the blind
—state rehabilitation agency
—service organization
—volunteer groups

When securing materials and/or resources, it is extremely important to consider the time that may lapse between the initial request for services and/or materials and delivery to the student. This is especially critical when ordering textbooks in large print, braille, and/or on tape. Depending upon the source and the delivery system, it may take two weeks to six months to secure a textbook. Figure 17.1 illustrates the number of alternatives and the steps between request and delivery.

ADDITIONAL INFORMATION FOR TEACHERS

Parents and teachers will encounter many terms that may be unfamiliar, which will be briefly discussed here. *Brailon Exchange:* Many agencies will provide an individual with a copy of a braille book in exchange for Brailon (thermoform paper) equal to the number of pages in the book. Brailon is a trade name for the plastic "paper" used when thermoforming (making copies of braille masters).

Central Catalog: The Central Catalog is a listing of sources of books which are available in large print, braille, and/or tape from commercial, volunteer, and nonprofit groups including APH. This national directory is published by the American Printing House for the Blind.

Certified Braillist/Proofreader: A person becomes a certified braillist or proofreader after completing course work and having a manuscript approved by the National Library Service for the Blind and Physically Handicapped, a Division of the Library of Congress.

Copyright Permission: Copyright permission must be granted by a publisher for the transcription of a title into large print, braille, or tape. Although many copyright owners allow for free transcription of their materials into braille, large print, or tape for use of the handicapped population, the Copyright law protects the authors' rights to their works and the use of these materials without the necessary permission is a violation of this law.

Ex-Officio Trustee (American Printing House for the Blind): Each eligible agency appoints an Ex-Officio Trustee for the Federal Quota Account at the American Printing House for the Blind. Sometimes this trustee is the superintendent of a residential school or someone he appoints, appointees from the State Department of Education, and the various agencies. This person is responsible for the expenditure of the Federal Quota Allocation and the Annual Registration of Legally Blind Pupils.

Filing an Intent: A person who intends to transcribe a book into large print, tape, or braille should *file an*

intent with the Central Catalog at the American Printing House for the Blind (APH). Information such as title, copyright date, author, and publisher is indicated. This prevents duplication of effort. As mentioned earlier APH serves as a national clearinghouse for information on the availability of books in large print, braille, and tape. Upon receipt of an *intent* for a title already available in the specified format, APH will notify the person that the book is already available and provide the name and address of the source.

Free Matter for the Blind: Educational or other materials or devices specifically designed or adapted for use by a blind person can be mailed through the U.S. Mail at no cost if it is labeled "Free Matter for the Blind." (Refer to the U.S. Domestic Mail Manual—Regulation 135 for additional information.) This free matter mailing should be used appropriately. It was intended to relieve the burden of extra cost of mailing bulky and heavy braille and large print books and other items designed or adapted for use by a blind person. There are size and weight restrictions that must be considered when packaging materials. This method of shipment can be extremely slow because it is the lowest priority for movement by the U.S. Postal Service.

Intent Forms: Intent forms are used to notify the American Printing House for the Blind (APH) of a person's "intent" to transcribe a title into large print, braille, or tape. Forms are available from APH. (See also "Filing an Intent.")

Master: The original large print, braille, or tape book is called a master. Copies are made from the master which usually is not circulated. APH will store master copies of items for groups that do not maintain their own master libraries.

SpecialNet: SpecialNet is a computer-based communication network. It provides current information and instant communication for persons concerned with educational services and programs. Educators of visually handicapped children use *SpecialNet* to locate braille and large print books throughout the country.

Transcribing: This is the process of changing a standard print title into large print, braille, or tape.

Parents and teachers are largely responsible for the selection of appropriate media, equipment, and resources for the education of visually handicapped students. It is their responsibility to identify and select specialized media and equipment namely visual, tactual, and auditory aids, computer applications and service delivery systems available and determine this

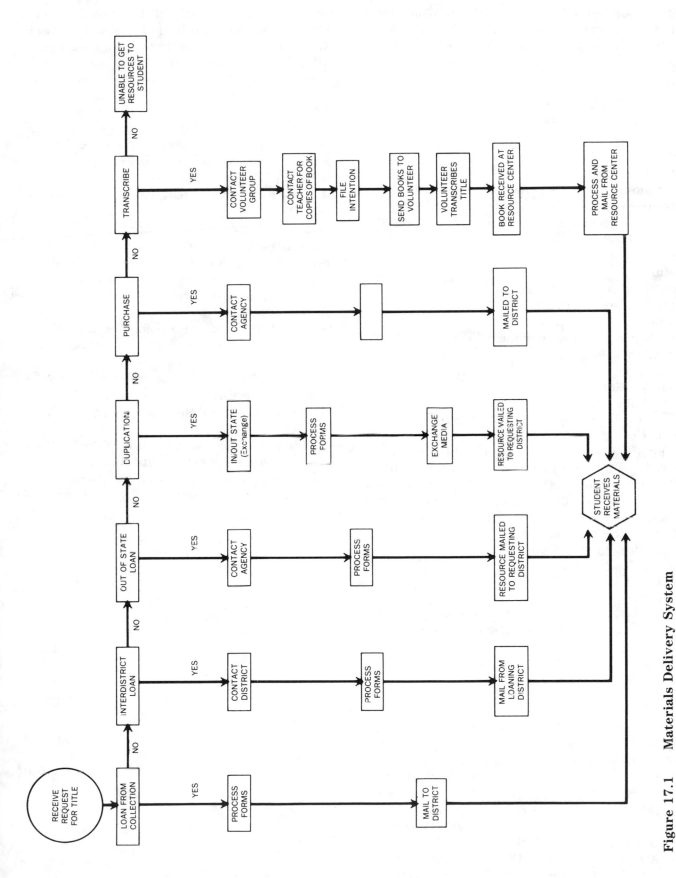

Figure 17.1   Materials Delivery System

Source: J.H. Todd, *Assessing resources for school-age visually handicapped students: A resource book* (Columbus, Ohio: Association of Instructional Resource Centers for the Visually Handicapped, 1981), p. 3.

which is most appropriate and readily available for the individual preferences of a visually handicapped student and his preparation for independent, successful living as an adult in a sighted world.

Study questions

1. List questions that need to be answered when determining the appropriateness of an item for a student. Indicate two questions in each of the following areas:
—Student considerations
—Alternatives
—Training
—Classroom considerations
—Manufacturer information
—Maintenance and service

2. Name four aids in each of the following areas and describe their uses.
—Visual aids
—Auditory aids
—Tactual aids

3. Describe ways in which visually handicapped individuals could use computers.

4. Why is it important to identify and utilize the service delivery system in a school district and state?

5. List ten questions that should be asked when identifying the service delivery system in a school district and state.

6. Define the following terms:
—Federal Quota Allocation
—Central Catalog
—Master
—Transcribing

7. What are some of the recent developments of resources, media, and technology in the field.

Dennison, A.L., Kappan, D.L., Napier, G.D., Schrotberger, W.L., and Tuttle, D. (1974). *Handbook for teachers of the visually handicapped*. Louisville, Ky.: American Printing House for the Blind.

Goldenberg, E.P. (1970). *Special technology for special children: Computers to serve communication and autonomy in the education of handicapped children*. Baltimore, Md.: University Park Press.

Journal of Visual Impairment & Blindness. (1984). Special Issue on Microcomputers, **78**(9), pp. 393-470.

Scott, E.P. (1982). *Your visually impaired students: A guide for teachers*. Baltimore, Md.: University Park Press.

State of Florida Department of Education. (1982). *A resource manual for the development and evaluation of special programs for exceptional students (Volume 111-F: Electronic communication devices for visually impaired students)*. Tallahassee, Fla.: Author.

Taber, F.M. (1981). The microcomputer: Its applicability to special education. *Focus on Exceptional Children*, **14**.

Todd, J.H. (1981). *Visually impaired students in a regular classroom: A resource book*. Columbus, Ohio: Ohio Resource Center for Low Incidence and Severely Handicapped.

Todd, J.H. (1981). *Accessing resources for school-age visually handicapped students: A resource book*. Columbus, Ohio: Association of Instructional Resource Centers for the Visually Handicapped.

Additional readings

Braille and computers. (1984). In *Aids and Appliances Review*. Boston, Mass.: Carroll Center for the Blind.

Brown, J.W. and Redden, M.R. (1979). *A research agenda on science and technology for the handicapped*. Washington, D.C.: American Association for the Advancement of Science.

Corn, A.L. and Martinez, I. (1977). *When you have a visually handicapped student in your classroom: Suggestions for teachers*. New York, N.Y.: American Foundation for the Blind, Inc.

PART 3

SPECIAL
CURRICULUM
CONSIDERATIONS

INTRODUCTION

In general, educational programs for visually handicapped children and youth follow the same curriculum as that offered in regular schools and classes. Each child studies those subject areas necessary to achieve the educational goals and objectives detailed in the individualized education program. This section discusses the typical curricular areas in the school program.

The first three chapters present areas that require the expertise of a qualified teacher of visually handicapped pupils, regardless of the educational setting. Chapter 18 examines communication skills, particularly specialized techniques, aids, and materials for reading and writing by both blind children who must rely on the sense of touch for reading and for children with limited vision who can make use of visual materials. For these pupils, the modifications and techniques described in Chapter 6 are especially applicable to instruction in communication skills.

Chapter 19 examines the knowledge, skills, and techniques that are employed to help visually handicapped children and youth become oriented to their environment and to move safely, efficiently, independently, and gracefully within that environment.

Chapter 20 describes social skills and the techniques that may be used to teach these skills. The acquisition of these skills by visually handicapped children and youth is essential for their ultimate adult adjustment.

Visually handicapped children and youth attending regular schools study some curricular subjects in the classroom with their sighted peers. Chapter 21 examines modifications and adaptations for these subject areas included in the regular curriculum: social studies, mathematics, science, foreign languages, creative arts, and physical education.

The chapters in this section focus on the essential elements in the school curriculum that should be included in the individualized education program. Inclusion of these elements will assist blind and visually handicapped children and youth to enter adulthood with an academic background appropriate to their abilities and future needs.

CHAPTER 18

Communication Skills

Toni Heinze

This chapter describes receptive avenues, including print reading possibly with magnification or electronic reading devices, listening and auding, and braille; and expressive avenues including typing, handwriting, and braille, as well as the use of nonverbal cues. While there are similarities in the ways visually handicapped children and youth develop some skills, others may require different teaching/learning approaches and specialized equipment.

Communication is a two way process involving the sharing of feelings, ideas, or other information. The various ways in which a "speaker" and a "receiver" interact and communicate are through talking and listening, gesturing, or possibly through signing. However, a great amount of information-sharing takes place across time and space, when ideas are preserved in a written, recorded, or electronically stored manner, and communication occurs through such media as books, newspapers and magazines, mail, radio and television, and computer output. In all cases, for communication to take place, both the speaker and the receiver must have a common experience base and attribute similar meaning to whatever language system or symbol is being used.

Our educational system is designed to establish this common experience and promote the crucial communication skills of reading, writing, speaking, and listening. The child with a visual impairment is no less dependent on such skills as any other child; indeed, with his restricted opportunities for incidental learning, he must rely even more so on avenues of information-sharing which are open to him.

This chapter focuses on the major communication modes which are critical to visually handicapped children and youth. It begins with an overview of the general reading process and elements common in all types of reading followed by a discussion of different receptive/reading modes used by visually handicapped children and youth, including listening and aural reading, print and braille reading, and the use of electronic reading machines. Special aspects of each reading mode, its advantages and disadvantages, and educational implications are emphasized. Expressive communication skills of braille writing, typing, and

handwriting are also discussed with emphasis on those elements specific to their use with visually handicapped children and youth.

THE READING PROCESS

Reading has been defined as "the process of constructing meaning through the dynamic interaction among the reader's existing knowledge, the information suggested by the written language, and the context of the reading situation" (Wixon & Peters, 1983). The process of reading is, therefore, interactive: it depends on the knowledge and skill of the author and of the reader; constructive: the meaning must be actively created in the mind of the reader based on previous knowledge; and dynamic: the process is variable and must adapt to the demands of the reading experience (Finn, 1985; Wixon & Peters, 1983). Meaning is acquired by the integration of the percept, which is derived from sensory input (visual, tactual, or auditory depending on the medium used for reading), with the prior knowledge base of the reader. The goal of reading instruction is to develop readers who can process written language for meaning. (Finn, 1985; Duffy, Roehler, & Mason, 1984; Wixon & Peters, 1983).

The term "reading" is traditionally used to refer to a nonhandicapped person's visual understanding of the printed word but a broader interpretation includes reading pictures, diagrams, or a variety of other graphic material. The blind child may also tactually read raised symbols and diagrams or read print words after they have been converted to tactual sensations through an electronic reading machine or to auditory sensations through recorded or computerized speech. In all these instances, the process of perception of a symbol to comprehension of an idea takes place, though the stimuli and input channels may differ. Each type of stimulus presents a different perceptual unit (the amount of information that can be perceived at a given time). The size of this perceptual unit and the time required for its recognition have much to do with the efficiency of the various reading modes. For example, for the normally-sighted child, the perceptual unit in reading may be several letters or perhaps a phrase (Foulke, 1969), but for the low vision child who requires extremely close proximity or magnification and additional effort to discriminate symbols, the perceptual unit may be two or three letters or even a single letter (Marmolin, Nilsson, & Smedshammer, 1979). Therefore, while both children "read" print, they may do so with varying levels of efficiency. While speed is not the only critical variable, it can enhance or restrict the reader's ability to make use of helpful language cues such as syntax and context. This same process operates for the braille reader. The perceptual unit is the individual braille character which symbolizes a letter, number, or group of letters. The reader must synthesize these smaller units into larger units as quickly as possible so that language cues can assist in decoding the message. For the aural reader, the perceptual unit depends on the rate of the speaker; however, a similar synthesis must take place for the "reader" to receive the message.

Teaching Considerations

Readiness. While different reading modes (visual, tactual, aural) necessitate specific readiness skills, the reading process itself requires several prerequisites. First, the child must have a variety of concrete experiences involving many objects, actions, people, places, and cause and effect relationships. Next, the child needs a growing language base to correspond with his experiences; this language base should include both receptive and expressive vocabulary. The child also needs to develop auditory skills of discrimination, localization, identification, closure, sequence, and memory for stories. The print reader will need visual skills such as tracking, discrimination, identification, matching, categorizing and comparing, and closure. Children using other reading modes need corresponding perceptual/cognitive skills. The beginning reader also needs enough maturity to be able to concentrate, exert some self-control, listen to and follow simple directions. He will also benefit from opportunities to see reading symbols used in his environment in the form of signs, stories, messages, and letters. Still another important readiness factor is motivation—a sense of excitement and curiosity about the intriguing relationship between experiences and ideas and the symbols which represent them.

Reading Methodology. Once the child has a sufficient experiential and language background, he can par-

ticipate in a more structured reading program. Such a program should involve a reinforcement and expansion of readiness experiences, an introduction to the reading process which employs general principles of good reading and fosters comprehension and efficient reading behaviors, a wide gamut of special skills to handle a variety of reading tasks and materials, an ongoing interaction with other language arts areas, and diagnostic and remedial techniques for specific reading problems.

There are many effective teaching methods for facilitating good reading habits. The competent teacher must be knowledgeable about a vast array of good reading methods in order to choose, combine, and adapt them as students demonstrate individual needs. Several approaches/techniques and their advantages are listed here (Harris & Sipay, 1985):

Reading Approach	Advantages
1. language experience Ashton-Warner (1963) approach	helps to build experiential background
2. unit approach	can assist incidental learning
3. individualized approach	personal and individual, increasing meaningfulness, ties reading to wide range of academic and life areas
4. directed reading approach	focuses attention on specific comprehension and recall skills, provides structure via anticipation and review, emphasizes knowing the purpose of the reading task
5. cloze procedures	promotes comprehension through use of context and syntax clues
6. phonics	strengthens auditory skills effective synthetic approach
7. structural analysis	provides added expectancy clues, decreases field of choices, effective synthetic approach
8. multisensory approaches (e.g., Fernald (1943), Ashton-Warner (1963) adapted for low vision students	capitalizes on and derives support from several senses, personal and individual increasing meaningfulness
9. "linguistic" approach	capitalizes on structural and organizational language cues, supports use of orthographic context, and syntax clues, synthetic approach

READING MODES

In the following sections are discussed various reading modes used by visually handicapped students: braille reading; listening including the use of recorded materials and readers; and print reading using various aids such as magnifiers and the Viewscan.

Braille Reading

Braille reading is still the most widely used means of reading and writing for severely visually handicapped and functionally blind individuals. Since braille takes more time to read and space to store, a contracted form of braille, called Grade 2, is most often used by braille readers. The advantages of braille as a reading/writing system are:

1. it can be used by blind readers as a tool for daily living skills, or as a major communication tool;
2. it provides both a reading and a writing system;
3. it provides many deaf-blind individuals with a workable communication tool;
4. it provides the user with easier control over material via scanning, using format clues, and reviewing, than does a reader or recorded material;
5. developing technology will assist the braille reader by making material more readily available, more easily stored and retrieved and by providing added input and output modes for computer terminals.

The disadvantages include:

1. reading speed is significantly slower than that for print reading or recorded materials;
2. daily current and readily available printed information (as well as texts, reference materials, etc.) is not readily available;
3. braille materials are expensive to produce;
4. it takes up considerable space and presents portability and storage problems (though the technology of cassette braille alleviates this problem to some degree);
5. the multiple usage of only 63 available characters causes some confusion and ambiguity, since the same symbol may stand for letters, words, punctuation, numbers, musical symbols, etc.
6. spelling skills require special attention because of the contractions;
7. braille requires a great amount of remembering and synthesizing since a gestalt of phrases, sentences, page format, and pictures is not available to the reader;
8. specific elements of braille present serious problems to a number of multiply handicapped individuals (e.g., contractions and multiple cell usage for mentally retarded persons, and tactual discrimination for stroke and advanced diabetic readers).

Teaching Considerations

Teaching approaches for braille reading should be based on the following premises:

1. for most braille readers, the perceptual unit is considered to be the individual braille character or cell, in contrast to the word or phrase for most print readers (Foulke, 1971; Nolan & Kederis, 1969).
2. the noticeable shape or arrangement of dots—rather than the number of dots—in the braille character is one of the most critical variables in the reader's ability to recognize it (Bürklen, 1932; Henderson, 1967; Nolan & Kederis, 1969).
3. braille readers necessarily use a serial or synthetic approach; they must recognize individual characters in a series, remember them in sequence, and then integrate them to form the "whole" word (Foulke, 1982).
4. context and syntax clues are more helpful for somewhat familiar material while phonetic and structural analysis clues are more helpful for difficult material (Harley, Henderson, & Truan, 1979; Nolan & Kederis, 1969).
5. lower functioning readers have greater difficulty with individual character recognition and subsequent integration into actual words, use of contractions, and use of peripheral cues such as spatial position of characters, syntax, and context; Nolan and Kederis (1969) suggest that the level of intellectual ability needed for efficient braille reading is greater than that for print reading.
6. reading rates of braille readers (90-120 wpm during high school years) are considerably slower than reading rates of normally sighted print readers (250-300 wpm in upper grades) or than compressed aural reading rates (275 wpm) (Lowenfeld, 1945; Nolan, 1966); greater time is also required to tactually explore special formats and to scan for specific pieces of information that can be almost instantly perceived by the print reader.

If the teacher considers these factors, she will include certain key elements in her approach to working with braille readers. For example, she will emphasize training in quick and accurate character recognition in order to increase (a) the reading rate without lowering comprehension; and (b) the reader's opportunities for using spelling, context, and syntax clues. In an early study of elementary and middle grade braille readers, such character recognition training resulted in a reduction of reading time by almost half and a reduction of mean number of errors by over 80 percent (Henderson, 1967). Similar training with high schoolers resulted in a 30 percent increase of reading speed with a 60 percent reduction of errors (Umsted, 1970). One of the most promising results of the latter study was that the poor readers made the greatest gains from the training. Some teachers have found that braille readers can recognize specific letters or braille signs much more quickly when searching for them within words; therefore, they promote the use of whole words and the clues offered by them during character recognition training (Krueger & Ward, 1983).

Other efforts at increasing at least the reading rate have included controlled exposure devices and experiential use of hands and fingers to pick up information (McBride, 1974; Olson, 1975; Wallace, 1973). Such techniques have led to the following observations regarding very fast readers: (1) they read "intermittently" or only parts of the presented material; and (2) time rather than the braille cell is the perceptual unit.

Mangold (1977) has developed a program of sequentially presented exercises involving tracking skills, coordinated and independent use of the hands, orienting skills, same/different discrimination, and introduction of the braille alphabet characters. This training program (available through Exceptional Teaching Aids) is intended to be part of the overall braille reading program, and can be used with beginning readers as well as braille readers who are experiencing related difficulties. Olson (1976, 1979, 1981) has also provided numerous suggestions for instilling efficient behaviors early in a braille reading program. Including such activities from the beginning should result in the prevention of many troublesome reading behaviors.

The braille reading program necessarily shares several common elements with any reading program. For example, a strong readiness component is critical and would include an experiential and language base, auditory and attention skills, and motivational experiences. Braille reading, however, differs from other reading programs in many ways, especially with regard to perceptual and mechanical skills, and the need for a synthetic approach to the reading process. Chart 18.1 presents a sample of such skills, or emphases which are especially pertinent to the braille reader's success.

For many years, beginning braille readers used basal readers transcribed into braille and/or specially prepared materials designed by their teachers. However, a number of educators of visually handicapped children questioned this approach because basal readers were designed to introduce print letters, words, sounds according to a systematic sequence of difficulty level, frequency of occurrence, and so on. Transcribing these readers into braille failed to take into account the differences in the braille code. Consequently, first graders were confronted with up to 90 percent of the more than 200 contractions and short forms, as well as many other difficult and confusing characters (Rex, 1971). In addition, the infrequency of occurrence of some of these difficult characters and contractions did not allow for regular practice once the characters were introduced. The emphasis on pictures and visual imagery also presented problems when basal readers were transcribed into braille (Bleiberg, 1970). Teachers often developed their own supplementary materials to compensate for these difficulties. In 1980, Caton, Pestor, and Bradley presented *Patterns*, a reading program specially designed with the beginning braille reader in mind. *Patterns* is based on a systematic presentation of contractions and other special characters from easier to harder, a built-in frequency of occurrence to allow for needed repetition, and stories which relate to the young child's developing experience base, as well as vocabulary and language development activities (Caton, 1979). The program (available from the American Printing House for the Blind) is intended as the primary reading program during early skill building. It has been used successfully with mainstreamed children who also participate in the regular classroom's reading program. Even if the teacher uses a specially designed braille series such as *Patterns*, she must be cognizant of the wide variety of good reading approaches that exist so that she can draw from them to meet individual student differences in learning style and possible reading problems.

New Technology

New developments in technology have provided the visually handicapped student with various reading modes aside from braille. The paperless or cassette braille takes up less storage space and is more portable (see Chapter 17 for further discussion). In addition to this, technology is increasing the means of braille production. Several print to braille translation systems

Chart 18.1. Emphases in a braille reading program

Readiness Level:
- opportunities to see braille symbols in the child's everyday environment
- manipulative and search skills to explore and operate items within the environment
- positional concepts to organize the environment and later the reading page
- tactual discrimination, identification, matching, categorizing, closure skills
- finger and hand coordination, strength, and dexterity

Beginning Reading Level:
- associate sounds and meaning with the braille symbols, choosing characters which allow for ease of configuration discrimination, motivation, and use of language clues
- introduction to Grade 2 braille in a logical and sequential manner
- develop efficient mechanical skills—coordinated use of both hands, use of index fingers and next several fingers to contact dots, tracking skills, light and even pressure applied to braille dots, continuous left to right movement across braille cells, efficient techniques for handling pages

Building Skills Level:
- character recognition training
- efficiency in handling reading materials
- spelling skills to accompany learning of braille contractions
- emphasis on word attack skills (phonics, syllabication, structural analysis) and comprehension skills (cloze procedures, directed reading approaches, use of language clues)
- using above approaches to improve synthesizing of letters into words, words into complete messages

Flexibility Skills:
- using a variety of formats
- note taking
- scanning and skimming
- coordination of braille with alternative communication tools such as recordings, Optacon, typing, possibly closed circuit TV
- reference skills
- use of Grade 3 braille (with additional contractions) when appropriate

*Diagnosis and Remediation of
Braille Reading Problems*

exist and their flexibility increases continuously. Another reading device, the Optacon, translates written materials to tactual representations which the visually handicapped student can read. A miniature camera is moved across a line of print with one hand while a tactile representation of the individual letters or numbers is felt with the other. For example, as the camera is moved over an upper case E, the reader first feels the vertical line and then three emanating horizontal lines with the index finger of his opposite hand (Orlansky & Rhyne, 1981).

The increased accessibility to printed information coupled with the Optacon's portability provide blind individuals with a real aid to communication and overall independence. Reading rates with the Optacon vary considerably, ranging from only a couple of words per minute after basic training (Link, 1980) to as much as 90 words per minute for experienced readers with certain types of materials. Even if the Optacon reader is only able to read several words per minute, the additional avenue of communication can make a significant difference in one's ability to perform certain tasks independently (Goldish & Taylor, 1974).

An appropriate training program is necessary for the efficient use of these new devices. For example, in training the visually handicapped student in the use of the Optacon, some factors to be considered are the general readiness factors, the individual's potential for reading with the Optacon, management of the reading aid itself, specific reading skills including mastery of print symbols and use of language cues, exposure to a variety of print style and formats, and special considerations for multiply handicapped readers (Moore & Bliss, 1975; Link, 1980). An important part of early Optacon training involves learning the "critical features" of print letters and numbers (TSI, 1977). This process involves analyzing the components on the tactual array and identifying the symbol by the process of elimination. Early use of language cues (orthography, syntax, and context) are also emphasized. Application to relevant tasks is encouraged as soon as possible. A sequential approach is used to aid students in the management and coordinated use of the Optacon and its special attachments, with students concentrating first on perceptual/cognitive skills and gradually adding mechanical and motor skills.

The Optacon has been found to be a useful tool for some multiply handicapped individuals. It may well be appropriate for those deaf-blind individuals with the necessary tactual and cognitive abilities, considering the restricted avenues of auditory and print information available to them (Moore & Hunt, 1981; Telesensory Systems, 1977; Thurman & Weiss-Kapp, 1977). Poss (1980) demonstrates how an individual with the loss of most fingers on both hands is able to read a variety of materials with the Optacon.

All or some of these can be very useful tools for the multiply handicapped student. As with any student, the approach to training them in the use of these tools must emphasize flexibility and an open-minded approach to problem solving.

Listening

Listening involves several steps—an awareness of and attention to relevant sound discrimination, identification of that sound, and finally, assignment of meaning to the sound—in order for the listener to receive his "message." Through listening, we develop environmental concepts, spatial relationships, receptive vocabulary (and subsequently, expressive vocabulary), and speech patterns. We gather subtle emotional-social information from intonation and intensity, and security and enjoyment from familiarity. Throughout our school experiences, an increasing amount of information is communicated from teacher to student, and from student to student, through speaking and listening. Other sources such as radio, television, and specific recorded material also provide valuable information.

Listening is usually the preferred means of learning for elementary level students since listening comprehension is typically above reading comprehension. Since listening is a more natural process than developing reading skills, it allows better comprehension and retention (Taylor, 1973). This preference for listening often continues until after the seventh grade. If the student's reading development is slow, preference for listening continues even longer. Listening and aural reading (auding) play an important role for the sighted child, but this method of information-gathering is critical to the visually handicapped student whose visual channel provides limited, sometimes incomplete information, and requires more time and work. Listening and auding then become a major source for learning. Henderson (1973) states that, for some severely visually handicapped students, listening may actually take the place of reading due to the limited graphic material available and the additional time required in reading braille. Willis (1979), in a survey of reading media used by visually handicapped students, found that the proportion who used listening as their primary mode of reading had doubled since 1972. With the increasing availability and quality of tape recordings, indexing systems, compressed speech, and computerized print to speech options, listening promises to take on an even greater and more critical role in the learning process (Orlansky & Rhyne, 1981).

Advantages of Listening

Listening has a number of advantages as a communication skill. Listening vocabulary is typically broader than speaking, reading, or writing vocabulary (Hender-son, 1973). Listening therefore supports the development of the speaking, reading, and writing vocabulary. For the multiply handicapped learner or one who has difficulties with print or braille reading, the listening vocabulary is the critical communication tool.

Speed is another advantage of listening. Nolan (1966) found that, while high school braille readers may attain reading speeds of about 90 words or more per minute with good comprehension, they can easily handle recorded material of 150-175 words per minute, and in some cases, compressed speeds of 275 words per minute without loss of comprehension. Day and Beach (1971) found that delayed recall (long-term memory) for audio-read information was better than for print material. While listening may not always be a better means of handling verbal information, when time saved is considered, it is a very efficient means of gathering and processing such information. Visually handicapped print readers, while having access to a wider range of informational displays, can achieve increased efficiency in use of time when gathering information from prose materials through listening.

Difficulties for the Listener

Listening does present some significant problems as a communication skill. For example, reading by listening, or auding, limits the display, or the manner in which information is presented to the receiver at any given time. This is especially noticeable when working with graphs, charts, etc. Referability is also restricted. One cannot listen ahead, skim, review or carefully analyze, or get a gestalt of the information as easily. Even available recorded indexing systems require more time and money than that required by the sighted reader who can scan ahead, quickly review or get a quick overview through headings, paragraphing, and other special format cues.

The rate, intensity, pitch, and temporal spacing are controlled by the speaker, not the listener. Electronic technology does provide the listener with increasing flexibility through the use of compressed speech, variable speed and tonal controls, and other adjustments, but some control over the material is still lost to him. This reduced control over rate can affect the listener's attention level since thinking is typically faster than speaking. To maintain concentration, the time lag must be dealt with efficiently by using active listening techniques or compressed speech.

Still another disadvantage of listening is the limited availability of auditory material. A majority of the average student's school day involves listening activities and much of the auditory information available to the sighted student is equally available to the visually handicapped child, although supportive information in the form of blackboard presentations, graphics, facial expressions, and gestures may be missed.

The limited availability of readers and of recorded text and supplementary material as an alternative to print material can place the visually handicapped student at a further disadvantage.

Despite its limitations, listening is destined to remain, and even expand, as a critical avenue of learning for the visually handicapped student with the rapidly expanding technology for recording, indexing, compressing speech and producing synthetic speech (see Chapter 17). The fact that the visually handicapped student is not always an efficient listener (Bischoff, 1979; Hanninen, 1975; Hatlen, 1976), suggests a need for systematic training in this area.

Curriculum Considerations

The need for a strong listening curriculum in the visually handicapped child's educational program seems obvious. Yet, listening skills often receive more token attention than implementation (Bischoff, 1979; Hatlen, 1976; Swallow & Connor, 1982). Listening efficiency requires that specific strategies be systematically taught. Chart 18.2 presents several elements of such a training program. Since abilities listed as "readiness" have a range of levels, it is difficult to designate at what point skills are at a readiness level and at what point they should be considered part of a structured program to develop listening and aural reading as communication tools. Therefore, there is some overlap in Table 18.2. This is appropriate since children must continue to refine even their most basic listening abilities.

The suggested training components of a listening program are not exhaustive, but are representative of several programs which have been developed for the visually handicapped learner (Alber, 1974; APH, 1973; Bischoff, 1967; Bishop, 1971; Henderson, 1973; Stocker, 1973; Swallow, 1982). These training components are not presented in a sequential order; a student may be working at different levels of several skills simultaneously. The importance of organizing a systematic, sequential program with continuity and application to a variety of everyday learning situations cannot be overemphasized. The teacher can use a variety of curricula already available. Some include listening skills for both communication and orientation and mobility (Rathgaber, 1969). Others are based on a psycholinguistic approach to auditory skills (Alber, 1974). Some are geared toward children while others are most appropriate for older students and adults because of their vocabulary and practice activities (Stocker, 1973).

In addition to teaching critical listening and aural reading skills, a good listening program should involve techniques which are most likely to lead to efficient use of these skills. For example, research has shown that "active" listening is more efficient than "passive" listening (Henderson, 1973; Nolan & Morris, 1969). Since listening by itself does not require active partici-

Chart 18.2.   Readiness and training components of a listening program

Readiness Components
- Awareness of environmental sounds
- Discrimination of sound patterns
- Identification of sounds
- Vocalization of environmental sounds
- Functional interpretation of environmental sounds
- Basic receptive vocabulary
- Basic level of attention and concentration
- Association of meaning to sounds
- Auditory memory (recognition)
- Awareness of emotional information from voice variations
- Ability to follow simple verbal directions

Continue with Training Components
- Fine discrimination of letter sounds
- Vocabulary development
- Auditory closure and use of context
- Listening for specific purposes including: (a) the main idea, (b) critical analysis, (c) logical conclusions and outcomes, (d) opinion versus fact, (e) word meaning, and (f) directions
- Auditory memory skills—especially important when using recorded materials—including: (a) recall of important facts/details, and (b) sequential recall
- Organizational skills, perception of format cues
- Selective listening
- Efficiency and flexibility with a variety of auditory materials, equipment, and aids, including: (a) recorded tapes, (b) compressed speech, (c) synthetic speech, and (d) human readers
- Perception of subtle cues which affect meaning including: (a) intonation, (b) intensity, (c) pitch, and (d) pauses

pation, the implication is that the listener must actively intervene on his own behalf. This can be done by taking notes, by breaking material into smaller segments and mentally reviewing it, or by solving problems which require information gained through the listening act. It would also seem appropriate to use a directed listening approach (Keller, 1969; Cobb, 1977) in which students learn to listen for specific purposes, to skim and locate specific information, to focus attention on the listening material by using study questions before the selection or review questions after the selection. Providing relevant motivation for listening tasks is also effective (Nolan & Morris, 1969; Swallow & Connor, 1982).

Appropriate spacing of auditory material over time also helps. While long periods of aural reading of literature and social studies material do not seem to impede comprehension or recall (Brothers, 1971), more technical material may require shorter periods. Furthermore, familiar and well-organized material is more suited to the listening mode (Day & Beach, 1971).

Use of Recorded Materials

Recording material on cassette tapes, open-reel tapes, and discs (records) has long been an important source of educational material for the visually handicapped child. Recorded textbook material, literature, recreational and vocational information, and teacher-made supplementary lessons allow the visually handicapped student to use an alternative and sometimes more efficient, learning channel. However, to use recorded materials efficiently, the student should have carefully planned instruction in aural reading or auding skills (Swallow, 1982). Many of the skills mentioned previously as components of a good listening program (see Chart 18.2) are appropriate here, as they specifically relate to working with recorded materials. Techniques for maximizing control over the listening mode, and for flexibility with a variety of equipment and indexing techniques must also be emphasized. Specific training objectives and suggestions for implementation are available in the literature (APH, 1973; Swallow & Connor, 1982).

New technology such as compressed or accelerated speech, and synthetic speech (see Chapter 17) have been developed to increase efficiency in the use of recorded materials.

The need of special training for the most efficient use of compressed speech must be considered. Specific guidelines, however, still need development (Bischoff, 1979; Foulke, 1974; Grumpelt & Rubin, 1972; Hanninen, 1975; Orr & Freedman, 1967). At this point, instructional strategies have primarily consisted of a gradual increase of speed with accompanying questions to measure comprehension and recall. Promoting good aural reading skills in general, including directed listening tasks and use of content clues, would be appropriate. However, as compressed speech becomes more commonly used and readily available, research must address itself to techniques for most effective usage.

Computer technology is providing visually handicapped readers with another promising communication tool—synthetic speech (see Chapter 17). As a communication tool, synthetic speech is available with a variety of adjustable controls for adjusting speed and pitch of the electronic voice, spelling out words that may have been misunderstood, scanning the page for format or specific topics (Orlansky & Ryhne, 1981), and utilizing a variety of foreign languages.

Reading machines are presently most appropriate for reading informational materials which are nontechnical, and do not require total accuracy of each character or symbol (Goodrich et al., 1979). They are also excellent for skimming for particular passages, and for some editing tasks (Selvin, 1981). They provide increased accessibility to printed materials for the severely visually handicapped reader; the increased reading rates also provide an advantage over braille or Optacon. In some cases, the technology itself has been used to teach reading to students who were previously slow or nonreaders (Wilhelm, 1980). Broadened research into critical variables, effect of student-machine interaction, and use of recorded translations from reading machines, will further advance the efficiency of such devices (Ryhne, 1982).

Use of Readers

Often the visually handicapped student will need information from a printed source which has not been recorded. If such alternatives as magnification or Optacon or electronic reading machines are not possible or efficient in such a situation, the student must rely on a reader. In this case, the inherent limitations of listening as a communication tool are evident (speed, referability), but the student as listener can increase his control to some extent. For example, he can tell the reader ahead of time what kind of information he is looking for and what his goals are. He can ask the reader to describe the organizational format, special graphic displays, and any cues for emphasis that might be helpful. He can occasionally stop and review or summarize important points. Such steps will give the visually handicapped listener added control over the material. It is important that a comprehensive listening program include opportunities to develop such directive structuring skills to enhance the student's efficiency in working with readers.

Print Reading

By far the greatest amount of information used in schools is in the form of printed materials: regular printed text, pictures, diagrams, charts, maps, microfiche, signs, labels, etc. Therefore, the individual who is able to use printed materials, even if only for short periods of time or for very specific purposes, has significantly greater accessibility to a wider variety of information. Fortunately, the majority of visually handicapped individuals, an estimated 70-80 percent of the legally blind readers in this country, are able to read print, with or without the use of low vision aids, at least in small amounts. These low-vision readers share both similarities and differences with print readers. Similarities include a need for adequate experiential, language, and visual discrimination readiness skills, and generally good reading habits including tracking, word attack, and comprehension skills. Of special importance to the low-vision print reader is the influence of such variables as the eye condition, environmental conditions, and types of reading materials as noted in Chapter 6, the need for emphasis on an effective synthetic approach to reading and word attack skills (Henderson, 1973), and difficulties with pictures and other supportive information.

The individual's eye condition can have varying effects on his method and efficiency of reading. For example, some conditions may influence the amount and type of preferred lighting on the reading task and in the surrounding environment. Some conditions affecting the reader's field may influence his angle of eccentric viewing, positioning of materials, amount of information viewed at one time, and use of magnification aids. Other conditions may specifically influence the reader's need for orientation aids and consideration of fatigue. Chapters 3 and 6 provide specific implications and suggestions in this area.

As mentioned in the discussion on the general reading process, the perceptual unit for low-vision print readers is smaller than that for readers with normal vision—perhaps only a single letter or small group of letters. A similar difficulty arises when the low-vision reader attempts to get information from pictures, charts, and diagrams. Ocular condition, required proximity, and/or magnification can prevent the reader from perceiving the whole or even major parts at once. The low-vision reader is placed at a disadvantage in three ways: (1) he loses the orientation aids of the gestalt, prominent features, and defined areas making it more difficult to understand where the part he is seeing fits into the whole; (2) locating the specific area which will provide him with desired detailed information can be more difficult; and (3) time required to locate and process these partial bits of information is lengthened. Because of these difficulties, the low-vision print reader must take a more synthetic approach to working with graphic materials, whether in reading prose or in examining pictures or diagrams. It becomes critical to emphasize the types of reading skills which will provide support to such a synthetic approach. These include all the important skills that belong in any good readiness and reading program with special emphasis on the following:

1. broadened experiential base to compensate for difficulties with incidental learning; accompanying vocabulary.

2. visual efficiency skills including tracking skills, attention to critical features of symbols and pictures; closure; figure-ground; systematic search patterns for pictures, charts, maps, diagrams, headings (see Chapter 6 for specific suggestions).

3. specific reading skills such as cues to sight vocabulary; orthographic, syntax, and context clues; structural analysis and phonics clues; reference skills (Bateman, 1963; Henderson, 1973; Rhyne, 1981).

4. appropriate use of optical and nonoptical aids (see Chapter 6 for specific suggestions).

5. flexibility with a variety of printed materials.

The low-vision reader will also benefit from special attention to working conditions for reading tasks. Some children may require increased lighting while others may operate better with reduced levels of illumination. Many children will benefit from using a reading stand to hold materials up and off the desk top, thereby allowing a closer viewing range without the fatigue often caused by bending over work for long periods of time. Eccentric viewing techniques which allow the child to use his best acuity may help. Another factor is the size of print type. Visually handicapped youngsters may be able to handle a variety of print sizes depending on such variables as type style, spacing, contrast, use of optical aids, lighting and glare, and length and difficulty of task. (See Chapter 6.)

The low-vision reader's ability to use pictures, charts, or diagrams efficiently also depends on the quality of the reproduction, spatial layout, boldness and contrast of color, and amount of clutter and detail. Difficulty can arise when print is placed immediately next to or over a distracting background. Structuring such reading situations through the use of typoscopes, outlining, or calling attention to important points will help to some extent.

The low-vision student must exert considerable energy during the reading process. Therefore, effort, time, and fatigue must also be considered. Extra time must be allotted for some visual tasks. A carefully chosen sample of visual tasks might substitute for a greater number of redundant examples and long visual tasks can be broken up by short periods of auditory/oral or motor tasks to allow for rest.

Magnification and Print Reading

A number of low vision students are able to read the regular print without magnification; they may need especially appropriate lighting and perhaps occasionally a marker or typoscope when additional structure is needed. Other students may use a variety of magnification aids, especially when special symbols, reference works with smaller print or supplementary materials are being used in the classroom, or special directions or labels need to be read. Such aids are described in detail in Chapter 6.

Large Print

A number of students use large print materials for some or most of their school work. Again, individual needs vary; while one child may use large print for much of his classwork, another may use it mostly as reference material for specific times when regular print is difficult to use efficiently. At one time, large print was frequently recommended for low-vision students. However, such widespread use has come under close scrutiny since there are several disadvantages for the reader (Stokes, 1979).

Large print is not always the most appropriate choice. Children can learn to use their remaining vision more efficiently, and use a variety of aids for specific tasks making them more flexible as to the types of materials they can handle. It can, however, be appropriate for children who cannot use optical aids efficiently, or it may be used along with such aids for children with greatly reduced acuity. Large type might also be helpful when using materials at a distance from the eye as when typing or reading music (Stokes, 1976). When attempting to decide which type of print to use, the teacher must consider: reading accuracy and rates, comprehension, reading comfort, and the fatigue factor for varying lengths and types of materials.

Optical and Electronic Magnification Aids

A large number of low-vision students are able to read regular print with a variety of magnification aids. (See Chapters 6 & 17.) These include stand and hand-held aids, spectacle mounted aids, telescopes, closed circuit television systems (CCTVs), and the Viewscan. Each of these aids has specific advantages and their use should be determined by the user's acuity and functioning level, specific tasks to be accomplished, and motivation to use the aids efficiently.

Stand and hand-held aids and telescopes are best for mildly to moderately visually handicapped individuals for short reading tasks, reference tasks, or checking detail. The close circuit television system allows the user to place reading and writing material under an adjustable camera zoom lens and read the magnified image as it is projected on a TV monitor. The closed circuit TV is best for moderately to severely visually handicapped individuals because of its wide range of magnification levels, vertical presentation for less fatigue, relatively large field of view (useful with charts, pictures, etc.) brightness and contrast control and reverse polarity, and zoom possibilities. The user's ability to use the CCTV to monitor his own writing makes it a doubly useful communication tool.

The Viewscan is an electronic device that magnifies typed print about 4-9 times the size of the original material (see Chapter 17). While its display is smaller that the CCTV, its portability and mobile camera are advantages. Both CCTVs and the Viewscan have computer access capability.

EXPRESSIVE MODES

Just as reading (whether tactually, auditorally, or visually) provides an individual with a means for receiving messages, a system for sending messages is also needed. The following discussion emphasizes several expressive modes which have special relevance to visually handicapped students.

Braille Writing

One of the earlier cited advantages of braille for the functionally blind individual is that it offers a means of writing as well as a means of reading. In fact, braille and typing will probably be the most efficient methods for writing. Braille writing instruction is usually begun at approximately the same time as braille reading, in the first grade or as soon as the

Perkins Braillewriter

student is ready (Harley, Henderson, & Truan, 1979). The beginning student typically uses the Perkins braillewriter (Lowenfeld, Abel, & Hatlen, 1969) because it offers the child several advantages: (a) greater efficiency, especially in speed and spatial flexibility; (b) less demand for very fine motor skills required by the slate and stylus; and (c) an immediate opportunity to read his own work as he produces it—an important motivator to the beginning reader. Learning to write as he learns to read also reinforces braille character formation and word recognition, since the child knows what he wrote.

The actual production of braille characters on the brailler is accomplished by simultaneously depressing keys to correspond with the dots in the braille character. Teachers have used a variety of ways to help their students learn to produce the braille characters correctly. Some have emphasized learning the dot numbers of the characters, while others have emphasized a more kinesthetic approach to character shapes. Still others use a swing cell which allows the child to relate the shape of the character to the corresponding keys on the braillewriter. Since the student is likely to be starting to read with Grade 2 braille, he will also begin to write Grade 2 braille or a modified version in the beginning (Harley, Henderson, & Truan, 1979). The student must also learn how to handle and adjust the various parts of the machine, how to make corrections, how to keep place, and how to organize for special spatial formats. From the beginning, good habits should be developed. Motoric and conceptual readiness is critical. The beginning braille writer needs fine motor strength and dexterity, as well as a working relationship with the positional concepts related to the brailler, the page, and to the braille characters themselves. Writing should be experienced as a relevant and meaningful part of the child's communication system. Harley, Henderson, and Truan (1979) and Olson and Mangold (1981) offer excellent suggestions for emphasizing the overall language process during the development of braille writing skills.

When the student has mastered the braille code, the slate and stylus (see Chapter 17) can be introduced. When using this tool, dots are depressed individually and from right to left so that when the paper is turned over and read from left to right, the characters will be raised and in the proper sequence. Additional ways to prevent confusion are: a) start with letters that are not likely to cause reversals; and b) emphasize the dots or shapes of the characters as the stylus approaches each new cue. In that way the character can retain its identity even though the writer is progressing from right to left (Henderson, 1973). The student should be familiar with the braille code in general to prevent confusion when forming the letters on the slate and stylus.

While the slate and stylus is much smaller, lighter, quieter, and more portable, it has severe limitations in setting up spatial displays. While such tasks are not easy on the brailler either, they are possible. The efficient student will be able to use both techniques as appropriate. Students must be given sufficient time and opportunities to develop accuracy and efficiency with both the braillewriter and the slate and stylus so he can use either as the situation demands.

Typing Skills

Typing skills are essential for all visually handicapped youth and adults who are capable of learning them and can be considered a "survival" communication skill for many severely multiply handicapped individuals. Efficient typing skills allow the visually handicapped student to communicate with classroom teachers in mainstreamed settings, to communicate with friends, family, classroom peers, to take and leave notes/messages for others, to communicate by mail with others, and to broaden their vocational options. Additional benefits of typing skills can be felt in the reinforcement of spelling skills (Henderson, 1973), especially for braille readers and those who have relied heavily on aural reading, and in the motivational impact on reading. Students enjoy reading material they have "produced" themselves, and typing tied with individualized reading approaches can provide added impetus to strengthening students' reading skills. Since typing is typically taught by the

touch method, it is a skill which should be included in the visually handicapped student's curriculum beginning in the elementary grades as soon as the necessary readiness level is reached.

Teaching Considerations

Some major considerations in the teaching of typing skills are readiness level, skills emphases, and general teaching approaches or methods. The student's readiness for learning to type depends on a variety of skills such as finger dexterity and coordination and a basic level of concentration. Language ability is also important, particularly consistent letter recognition and a fairly developed reading vocabulary. Usually youngsters have attained the necessary readiness skills by about third or fourth grade and typing instruction can begin. Because of the increased independence and communicative control that typing can afford, teaching of this skill should not be delayed for either low-vision or blind students.

Skills which would be appropriate for any typing student would also be appropriate for the visually handicapped typing student. Additional skills involving special adaptive equipment should also be included. Therefore, an effective typing program for visually handicapped youngsters should enable the student to:

1. achieve accurate and consistent keyboard mastery;
2. be familiar with the machinery and able to "fix" and reset inappropriate settings;
3. copy material from a variety of modes (print, braille, recorded, etc.);
4. use appropriate modifications (reading stands, light probes, carbon paper, position cues, etc.);
5. compose at the typewriter because of the difficulty of continuously transferring from braille or print to the typewriter;
6. use recording machinery (taped formats, notes, dictaphone, foot pedals, etc.) in conjunction with typing;
7. set a variety of formats including centering, tabulating, spacing, outlining letters, etc.;
8. proofread and correct errors, including the use of Optacon and CCTV adaptive equipment, and other appropriate aids (Hanninen, 1979; Rhyne, 1981).

The actual teaching approach will have much to do with the visually handicapped student's success in developing efficient typing skills. Motivation is very important and is not usually a problem. Students often enjoy the motoric skill, the manipulation of the machine, and the production of a product. It is also important that the teacher emphasize the difference that typing can make in their independence and social interactions.

Standard touch typing programs are often appropriate and are available in a variety of reading modes. Supplementary exercises may be useful for motivational purposes and to provide the necessary opportunities for application. Accuracy should be stressed from the beginning. This is especially important since students will be using their skill to communicate in a variety of subject matter areas, preparing assignments, responding to tests, etc.

Handwriting

The ability to write or at least to make a signature, is a valued sign of literacy. Writing is tied closely to the self-concept, and a signature is an important means of self-expression. This is as true for a visually handicapped individual as for the nonhandicapped individual. Determining the most appropriate level and type of handwriting skills for a visually handicapped child or young adult depends on the answers to several questions:

1. How much handwriting should be taught?
Considerations: Signature for checks, legal documents, the alphabet for taking messages.

2. Should cursive or manuscript be stressed?
Considerations: Cursive or a modified version might be more appropriate for legal signatures, but manuscript may do for individual letters or note-taking.
Cursive may be easier to write because of the connected flow of letters to make a single word or unit, but may be more difficult to read (by a visually handicapped student or others).
Manuscript may be more difficult to write because of the many interruptions in pencil/paper interaction, but may be easier to read (by the visually handicapped writer and others).

3. What is the potential for efficiency of the handwriting skill?
Considerations: Legibility to oneself and others, consistency and accuracy and time involved in the development of a usable product.

4. What is the potential for use of the handwriting skill?
Considerations: Opportunities and inclination to develop, practice, and maintain the skill at an efficient level.

5. What is the learner's level of motivation to develop the handwriting skill?
Considerations: Previous success or failure with this skill, attitudes of significant others, self-concept.

Before the teacher can design an appropriate program for teaching handwriting skills, the student's visual status, age of onset of visual impairment, and previous knowledge of writing must also be considered. Chart 18.3 presents some of these considerations. Once these factors have been considered, the teacher can choose from a variety of teaching techniques which have proven effective for students with various backgrounds and needs. For low vision children standard

handwriting programs such as those produced by Zaner-Bloser can be very effective. The teacher may have to spend additional time calling the student's visual attention to critical features of similar letters and spacing patterns; choice of appropriate writing utensils will also be important.

Chart 18.3.   Teaching implications of specific student characteristics (Becker, 1963; Stark, 1970; Stocker, 1963)

Student	Areas Needing Emphasis
Student with considerable usable vision	calling attention to visual critical features of letters monitoring one's writing using appropriate aids
Adventitiously blinded student with some visual memory and previous knowledge of writing	staying on a line when providing proper spacing between words and other symbols crossing t's and dotting i's maintaining kinesthetic memory of how letters/ symbols are shaped and joined using appropriate aids
Congenitally blind student	developing a kinesthetic knowledge and formation of letters and other symbols developing spatial orientation within letters, within words, on lines, and on pages retracing when necessary connecting letters crossing t's and dotting i's

Stark (1970) provides an extensive description of techniques and writing aids which can assist the adventitiously blind to maintain their kinesthetic memory for letter formation and for orienting their writing to the available space. Stocker (1963, 1970) and McCoy and Leader (1980) have found success with kinesthetic tracing as long as they provided sequential steps to insure transfer to increasingly smaller and more appropriate writing sizes. Freund's *Longhand Writing for the Blind* (1970) and the *Mark's Method* (1956) emphasize specific guidelines for forming each letter while Huckins (1965) provides a very specific sequence and letter formation guideline, as well as readiness requirements. Still another approach is the *square hand* which uses a block formation of letters for those having extreme difficulty making curving and diagonal lines and connectors. Some teachers have added a forward chaining approach to teaching signature writing, that is, the student writes *D* until that letter is mastered, then *Da*, then *Dav*, until *David* is mastered.

Whichever teaching technique is used or modified, important elements in the teaching approach are motivation, feedback, and opportunities to practice and maintain the skill one is developing. Using writing skills in daily personal activities and classroom tasks can assist in this process. In addition to choosing appropriate teaching techniques, the teacher will

need to select from a variety of aids that can assist the student in both learning and independently using his writing skill. These include materials to help form letters, the Sewell Raised Line Kit for providing tactual feedback, bold line and raised line writing papers, templates and clipboards for maintaining orientation, and a variety of magnification aids (see Chapter 17 on Resources, and Chapter 6 on Visual Efficiency for specific suggestions and resources). Usually, an individual will benefit from not just one aid, but a variety of aids which are appropriate for different tasks under different conditions. It is up to the teacher to acquaint the student with several aids so that he can choose the appropriate ones.

NONVERBAL COMMUNICATION

Communication between or among individuals involves more than the use of verbal symbols in braille, speech, or print. For example, a great deal of communication takes place via sign language systems, whether they emphasize whole ideas or individual language components such as vocabulary and syntax. Another important means of communication is not verbal at all; rather, it involves the use of the face and body to express ideas and feelings. This can be done with eye contact, facial expressions, head nodding, shoulder shrugs, posture, and a wide variety of hand, arm, even foot gestures. These expressive techniques are difficult for the visually handicapped individual to perceive, to use, and to learn (Apple, 1972). Often when they are used, they are used inappropriately (Parke, Shallcross, & Anderson, 1980). In fact, even after blind children have received training, they have used gestures ineffectively—behind their backs or with their hands lowered at their sides, not aware that sighted individuals do not see all sides of an object as they do when exploring tactually (Bonfanti, 1979). Because of the value sighted persons place on nonverbal expressions, attempts have been made to encourage visually handicapped individuals to use these behaviors. Simple approaches such as eccentric viewing techniques which assist the individual in facing his partner, increasing familiarity and ease of body movements through expressive music and imagery, and training of specific gestures for specific purposes (Bonfanti, 1979; Apple, 1972) have met with varying degrees of success. It is, however, important that visually handicapped students realize that people do use their bodies to communicate with each other. Calling attention to such behaviors can increase the likelihood that they will be able to communicate more effectively with sighted persons.

Areas of nonverbal communication and strategies for assisting blind and visually handicapped children and youth to acquire and appropriately utilize nonverbal communication skills are described in greater detail in Chapter 20.

Study questions

1. Provide several examples of how a visually handicapped student might have limited access to various sources of information.

2. Discuss why it is so important that a visually handicapped student develop a *range* of both receptive and expressive communications skills. Provide several examples of appropriate combinations of such skills and devices.

3. Compare and contrast the reading process for braille, auding, and print on the following bases:

	braille	*auding*	*print*
similarities			
differences			
equipment			
advantages for efficiency			
disadvantages for efficiency			

4. List readiness elements which are necessary for any "reading" mode (visual, tactual, auditory).

5. List five types of aids that can assist the low vision youngster to read print more efficiently.

6. Provide examples of how the visually handicapped student can increase control over his use of listening as a communication tool.

7. Why is so much emphasis placed on teaching the braille reader/writer to be as efficient as possible?

8. Why is typing referred to as a "survival" skill for the visually handicapped student?

9. What are some variables that would help determine a teaching approach to use for handwriting skills with a visually handicapped individual?

10. List some nonverbal techniques that we use in our everyday communication. Why might these be difficult for the visually handicapped individual to develop?

11. How can the developing electronic technology assist the visually handicapped individual in his communication opportunities? How might it restrict his communication opportunities?

Additional readings

Bateman, B. (1973). *Reading and psycholinguistic processes of partially seeing children*. Reston, Va.: Council for Exceptional Children, Monograph Series A, No. 5.

Baumann, J.F. and Johnson, D.D. (ed.). (1984). *Reading instruction and the beginning teacher*. Minneapolis, Minn.: Burgess Publishing Co.

Caton, H., Pester, E., and Bradley, E.J. (1980). *Patterns: The primary braille reading program*. Louisville, Ky.: American Printing House for the Blind.

Finn, P.J. (1985). *Helping children learn to read*, New York, N.Y.: Random House.

Harley, R.K., Henderson, F.M. and Truan, M.B. (1979). *The teaching of braille reading*. Springfield, Ill.: Charles C Thomas.

Mangold, S. (1977). *The Mangold developmental program of tactile perception and braille letter recognition*. Castro Valley, Calif.: Exceptional Teaching Aids.

Mangold, S.S. (ed.). (1982). *A teachers' guide to the special educational needs of blind and visually handicapped children*. New York, N.Y.: American Foundation for the Blind, Inc.

Nolan, C.Y. and Kederis, C.J. (1969). *Perceptual factors in braille word recognition* (Research Series No. 20). New York, N.Y.: American Foundation for the Blind, Inc.

Olson, M.R. (1981). *Guildelines and games for teaching efficient braille reading*. New York, N.Y.: American Foundation for the Blind, Inc.

Searfoss, L.W. and Readence, J.E. (1985). *Helping Children Learn to read*. Englewood Cliffs, N.J.: Prentice-Hall.

CHAPTER 19

Orientation and Mobility

Everett W. Hill

Instruction in orientation and mobility is an essential component in the educational service delivery system for blind and visually handicapped children and youth. This chapter presents basic information for teachers on the concepts underlying orientation and mobility, assessment strategies, instructional procedures, and techniques for teaching these skills. Special considerations for preschool and multiply handicapped children are included.

In 1948 Lowenfeld stated that blindness imposes three basic limitations on the individual:

1. In the range and variety of concepts
2. In the ability to get about
3. In the control of the environment and the self in relation to it.

It is interesting to note that all three of Lowenfeld's basic limitations are related to orientation and mobility (O&M); specifically limitations two and three.

Traditionally, orientation has been defined as the process of using the senses to establish one's position and relationship to all other significant objects in one's environment. Mobility has been traditionally defined as the capacity, readiness, and facility to move about in one's environment as opposed to reading or sitting or turning in place. Orientation skills and mobility skills are so closely related that in order to be an efficient traveler, one must be proficient in both areas (Hill & Ponder, 1976).

Lowenfeld (1981, p. 72) states,

Mobility which is the capacity or facility of movement has two components. One is mental orientation and the other is physical locomotion. Mental orientation has been defined as the ability of an individual to recognize his surroundings and their temporal or spatial relations to himself, and locomotion as the movement of an organism from place to place by means of its organic mechanism.

Lowenfeld goes on to state that both mental orientation and movement are essential for mobility but are not separate functions.

It is evident from the above definitions that orientation and mobility are interdependent. If one is mobile but not oriented, there is no purpose or meaning to the movement. Conversely, if one is oriented but not mobile, one cannot get to where one desires.

The ultimate goal of orientation and mobility instruction is to enable the student to move purposefully in any environment, familiar or unfamiliar, and to function safely, efficiently, gracefully, and independently (Hill & Ponder, 1976). Promoting independence through O&M instruction has many inherent values and can positively impact on the individual in a number of ways.

VALUES OF INSTRUCTION IN O&M

Psychological
Orientation and mobility can contribute positively to one's self-concept. The idea of being able to move efficiently and independently in various environments enhances not only self-esteem but also self-confidence.

Physical
Since O&M involves movement in space, the body is "exercised" in the process. Both gross motor skills, e.g., walking and fine motor skills, e.g., using a cane, are continually taught and reinforced throughout the O&M process.

Social
Possessing good O&M skills creates more social opportunities for the individual. One who does not possess good O&M skills is restricted (socially) in the amount, diversity, and spontaneity of social encounters.

Economic
Having good O&M skills may help one economically from two perspectives. First, being mobile should create more employment opportunities for the indi-

vidual. Secondly, the options to walk or use public transportation systems versus using a taxi to get somewhere certainly should save the individual money.

Daily Living Skills
Many activities of daily living are enhanced and facilitated by O&M. For example, shopping requires O&M skills in order to locate the stores as well as to travel within the store. Retrieving a lost object and sweeping the floor are examples of daily living activities that rely heavily on systematic search patterns which are part of O&M instruction.

EXPANDING THE DEFINITION OF ORIENTATION AND MOBILITY

Orientation and mobility is a relatively young profession. The first formalized O&M program attempted with blind people in the United States was at Seeing Eye Inc., in 1929 (Whitstock, 1980). In the 1940s, Richard Hoover developed a program of "foot travel" (utilizing the long cane) for blinded veterans at Valley Forge Army Hospital (Bledsoe, 1980). Hoover's training methods and cane techniques were later refined and improved at Hines Veteran's Hospital in Chicago, Illinois during the 1950s.

In the early 1960s, two university training programs, Boston College and Western Michigan University, were started to prepare O&M instructors to primarily work with adventitiously blinded adults. Orientation and mobility with this population consisted of sensory training activities and formal O&M skills. As more university training programs were developed in the mid to late 1960s, systematic O&M instruction was extended to children and concept development became an integral part of the O&M curriculum (Weiner & Welsh, 1980).

In the 1970s, a great deal of emphasis was placed on providing O&M services to low vision individuals. Assessment and training of functional distance vision as well as the use of low vision aids became part of the repertoire of the practicing O&M specialist. Prior to this, many low vision persons went through the O&M training sequence blindfolded (Apple, Apple, & Blasch, 1980).

In the late 1970s and in the 1980s, a great deal of programmatic emphasis was placed on the delivery of O&M services to preschool and multiply handicapped populations. Presently, there also exists a need to provide O&M services to the geriatric blind population.

SYSTEMS OF MOBILITY

The four generally accepted systems of O&M are the human guide, long cane, dog guide, and electronic travel aids (ETAs). These systems are not mutually exclusive, as many blind travelers use more than one system or a combination of them. In some instances,

low vision aids may also be considered a system of mobility. For a complete treatment of low vision aids, see Chapter 6.

Human Guide

Skills that enable a visually handicapped person to travel with a sighted person are called sighted guide skills. Sighted guide skills can also be used in combination with other mobility systems such as the cane and dog guide. As shown in Figure 19.1, the visually handicapped person grasps the guide's arm just above the elbow. The visually handicapped person's upper and lower arm form an angle of approximately 90 degrees which positions the traveler one-half step behind the guide. There are also several special sighted guide techniques for different environmental situations such as going through doors, up and down steps, etc., (see Formal Mobility Skills section in this chapter). For a more complete treatment of the subject, see Hill and Ponder (1976).

Figure 19.1   Human Guide Technique

Advantages:
1. When the sighted guide techniques are used correctly with a proficient sighted guide, travel is very safe and efficient.
2. The guide can be a constant source of information about the environment.
3. The sighted guide skills can be used to develop and reinforce such skills as kinesthetic awareness, orientation concepts, etc.

Disadvantages:
1. Many sighted persons are not knowledgeable in how to guide visually handicapped persons.
2. Sighted guide travel used as the only mobility system may foster dependence rather than independence.

3. Some handicapped travelers may not pay attention to environmental information and orientation when traveling with a sighted guide.

The Long Cane

There are several types of canes available for visually handicapped travelers. There are various orthopedic canes, folding canes, and long canes. Canes have been made out of materials such as wood, various metals, fiberglass, boron, and plastic.

Prior to the development of formal cane skills, many visually handicapped persons used short wooden canes.

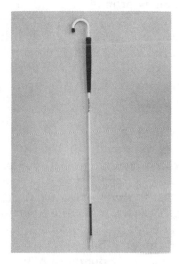

Figure 19.2   Long Cane

Most often, these short canes were used for identification purposes. The information and protection provided by these canes were limited because of their length.

A version of the present day long cane was used by Richard Hoover at Valley Forge Army Hospital in the 1940s (Bledsoe, 1980). In 1964, the Veteran's Administration published specifications for the long cane which helped establish standards for a model long cane (see Farmer, 1980; Hill & Ponder, 1976). Most long canes used today are made from aluminum, have a rubber grip, a nylon tip, and a crook (see Figure 19.2). They should be rigid, durable, conductive, lightweight (average 8-10 ounces), and relatively attractive and inexpensive (Hill & Ponder, 1976). The length of the cane will vary according to the user's height, stride, and speed of reaction time.

Advantages
1. It provides advance information about objects and the walking surface.
2. It is highly maneuverable.
3. It is inexpensive and requires very little maintenance.
4. It identifies the user as visually handicapped (this may also be a disadvantage).

Disadvantages
1. The upper part of the body is unprotected, particularly from suspended objects, e.g. tree branches.
2. It is not collapsible and can be difficult to store.
3. It is difficult to use in strong winds.
4. It identifies the user as visually handicapped.

Dog Guides

According to Whitstock (1980), systematic training of dog guides for the visually handicapped began sometime in the 18th century. During World War I, the first dog guide school was established in Germany to train blinded veterans of the German Army. The first dog guide school in the United States, the Seeing Eye, Inc. was established in 1929 in Nashville, Tennessee (Putnam, 1963). Later in the same year, the Seeing Eye, Inc. was moved to Morristown, New Jersey where it is presently located.

Although the dog guide as a method of mobility has been well publicized, less than 2 percent of visually handicapped persons use it for the following reasons: first, the majority of visually handicapped persons have good travel vision; second, most dog guides walk between three to four miles per hour, a speed which eliminates many elderly and physically handicapped, visually handicapped persons as dog guide candidates; third, most dog guide training schools require that applicants be at least 16 years of age because of the responsibility of caring for a dog; finally, some visually handicapped persons do not like dogs or simply prefer another system of mobility.

Advantages
1. A well-trained dog guide will circumnavigate objects in the travel path, including overhanging objects at head level, so physical contact is avoided.
2. A dog guide will intelligently disobey its master or mistress if she makes a wrong safety decision when traveling, e.g., crossing against traffic.
3. The dog walks between 3-4 miles per hour, and many visually handicapped persons who use dogs enjoy walking confidently at a good, quick pace.
4. Many dog guide users report greater ease in negotiating unfamiliar terrains because they are able to concentrate on orientation rather than being concerned about their safety.
5. The presence of the dog guide may facilitate social contacts and interactions.

Disadvantages
1. It is inconvenient and it takes time to care for, groom, and feed the dog guide.
2. The dog guide is not very "collapsible." In certain social situations, small spaces, etc., it might be difficult or not feasible to use a dog.

3. Sometimes, the dog guide gets most of the attention rather than the master or mistress in a social situation.
4. Certain landmarks and environmental clues, e.g., intersecting sidewalks, are not readily available for use by dog guide users.

Electronic Travel Aids (ETAs)

Electronic travel aids (ETAs) are relatively new devices in comparison to the cane or dog guide systems of mobility. Farmer (1980) stated:

> An ETA may be described as a device that sends out signals to sense the environment within a certain range or distance, processes the information received, and furnishes the user with certain relevant bits of this information about the immediate environment. (p. 372)

In the 1970s, ETAs received a great deal of attention as a supplemental orientation and mobility system for blind adult travelers. Cane travelers, for example, can use an ETA to circumnavigate an obstacle in the travel path without making physical contact with the obstacle. Besides the obstacle detection capabilities of ETAs, some ETAs, such as the Sonicguide™, are classified as environmental sensing devices because they provide information about the surface properties of objects in the environment. Therefore, in recent years, attention has been focused on using ETAs to teach environmental and spatial concepts to congenitally blind children.

Although examples of ETAs can be found as early as 1897, very few of the 30 prototypical devices have survived the rigors of field testing (Farmer, 1980). The devices discussed in this section (Pathsounder, Mowat Sensor, Sonicguide™, and Laser Cane) are the most widely used and represent the state of the art in ETA technology for blind persons.

The Lindsay Russell Model E Pathsounder

The Pathsounder is a box-like sonar obstacle detecting device which was developed by Russell as a secondary aid for the long cane traveler. The Pathsounder emits and receives sonar waves to provide the user with information about obstacles in the line of travel. The device is chest mounted, weighs about 16 ounces, and is supported by a neck strap.

The Pathsounder has automatic near-far range settings and manual sensory mode (auditory, tactual, or both) controls. The maximum area of coverage is slightly below the waist to above the head and just outside the shoulder width.

Although the Pathsounder is not widely used by independent long cane travelers (the original target population), it appears to be potentially useful to multiply handicapped blind populations. It would appear that deaf-blind persons might find the Pathsounder useful since environmental information can be received through the device's tactual sensory

mode. Conversely, blind diabetics with poor tactual sensation might find the auditory sensory mode useful. Furthermore, because the device is a simple obstacle detector with very few controls to manipulate, it might be useful with mentally retarded blind persons. Farmer (1980) and Russell (1975) reported case studies which support the notion of using the Pathsounder with multiply handicapped blind individuals.

Baird (1977) used the device in a different context and described the Pathsounder as a concept development and mobility skill building tool for young blind children. Although there are no studies which examine the Pathsounder as a concept development teaching device, the idea is promising. Logically, concepts of distance, such as near, far, specific units of measurement (inches, feet, yards), width and height could easily be related to the signals of the Pathsounder. However, the expense, weight, and appearance of the device may be constrictive factors in using the device with very young blind children.

The Mowat Sensor

The Mowat Sensor was developed by G.C. Mowat in New Zealand as a supplement to the long cane and dog guide systems of mobility. It can be used to locate signs, poles, pedestrians, and other landmarks away from the travel paths. It is hand held and measures 6 inches × 2 inches × 1 inch (see Figure 19.3), and weighs a little over 6 ounces (Farmer, 1980). The Sensor has a manually operated range setting (near range—1 meter; far range—4 meters).

Figure 19.3   Mowat Sensor

Like the Pathsounder, the Mowat Sensor utilizes sonar waves to provide obstacle detection information. When an object is detected in its field, the entire device vibrates; the Sensor provides information about the distance of the user from an object through the ramp effect (the device vibrates faster as the user approaches closer to an object).

The Mowat Sensor has potentially the same applications for use as the Pathsounder with multiply handicapped blind populations. However, in comparison to the Pathsounder, the Mowat Sensor is relatively inexpensive, lightweight, unobtrusive, and can be easily stored in a pocket or purse when not in use.

The Sonicguide™

The Binaural Sensory Aid (later known as the Sonicguide™) was developed in 1966 by Leslie Kay (Farmer, 1980). This device, like the Pathsounder and Mowat Sensor, is operated using sonar waves which are transmitted and received and then translated into auditory signals. The electronics are mounted in spectacle frames (see Figure 19.4) with an accompanying power pack.

The Sonicguide™ differs from the Pathsounder and Mowat Sensor in that it is capable of being used both as an obstacle detector and environmental sensor. According to Farmer (1980), one can use the

Figure 19.4   Sonicguide™

Sonicguide™ to: (a) estimate distance from objects by relating it to the pitch (pitch gets lower as the user approaches an object); (b) determine the direction/location of objects by amplitude differences (an object on the user's right side produces a louder sound in the right ear); and (c) identify object's surfaces through tonal characteristics (a round metal pole will reflect echoes that have pure tone quality).

In the late 1970s, a growing interest in the use of the Sonicguide™ as a tool for expanding contact with the external world for infants and toddlers widened the number of studies (Bower, 1977; Ferrell, 1980; Strelow, Kay, & Kay, 1978) which have been reported. The Sonicguide™ in its original form was

not satisfactory for use with very young children. The physical structure of the device was unsuitable and the range was too long for practical use with infants. Two devices, the Infant Sonicguide™ (Smith & Dailey, 1978) and the Canterbury Children's Aid (Strelow et al., 1978) were developed to make the ETA accessible to the young blind population.

Researchers (Bower, 1977; Ferrell, 1980; Strelow et al., 1978) have examined the Infant Sonicguide™ as it related to behaviors such as object/person location, reaching to sound, motor tasks, and stereotypic mannerisms. Ferrell (1980) reported the use of the device with four young children and found that all subjects could use the aid. The benefits of the Sonicguide™ were qualified but some improvement in use of language, social interaction, gross and fine motor, and cognitive abilities were noted for some of the children. An increase in stereotypic mannerisms was noted when the subjects were not wearing the device. Bower (1977) used the Infant Sonicguide™ with babies to facilitate social interaction, object location, and reach-grasp. Strelow et al. (1978) used the device as a mobility aid for two young children and found that travel skills increased for both subjects. Carter, Carter, and Ferrell (1980) prepared a manual for program implementation of the Infant Sonicguide™ which includes localization, reaching, and object avoidance.

The Sonicguide™ has been used for concept development activities with children (Baird, 1977; Kay, Strelow & Kay, 1977; Newcomer, 1977; Scione, 1978). The aid not only offers the potential for teaching several spatial concepts such as front, up, down, left, right, center, perpendicular, parallel, etc., but also the unique tonal sound qualities created by various object surfaces that should stimulate young children to explore their environment. Furthermore, it is conceivable that blind children using the aid would be able to classify and categorize environmental objects by their sonic tonal qualities.

Finally, several other applications and uses of the Sonicguide™ have been explored—with multiply handicapped children (Kitzhoffer, 1983); as a way of stimulating vision in partially seeing children (Carter, 1975); in adverse weather (Farmer, 1975); and as a complementary travel aid to the dog guide (Jacobson, 1979).

The C-5 Laser Cane

The C-5 Laser (Light by Stimulated Emission of Radiation) Cane was invented by J. Malvarn Benjamin of Bionic Instruments, Inc., and works on the principle of infrared light. The C-5 Laser Cane (see Figure 19.5) is an adapted long cane and is used in the same manner. "The cane was designed to enhance the environmental probing ability of the long cane, to reduce tension while traveling, enabling the user to make more graceful progress" (Farmer, 1980, p. 382).

The electronic components are mounted near the top of the cane with auditory and vibratory modes providing information from three beams.

The up channel detects objects at head level, the forward channel functions at waist level (adjustable range 5 to 12 feet), and the down channel operates at ground level, three feet in front of the cane tip. High (2600Hz), Middle (1600Hz), and Low (200Hz) sounding

Figure 19.5   C–5 Laser Cane

tones are emitted from the respective channels when an object is in range and interrupts the "pencil-thin" beams transmitted from the cane (Farmer, 1980). The forward channel is the only channel with a tactual display (a tiny pin vibrates against the index finger when placed on the side of the cane).

The Laser Cane weighs approximately 16 ounces. It has a rechargeable battery, charging unit, and telemetry unit which is used to monitor the cane's signals during training.

Because of its size and weight, the current model Laser Cane does not appear to have a great deal of relevance for young blind children. Goldie (1977) trained four junior and senior high school students in the use of the cane. She concluded that in order to benefit from utilizing the device, one must have good long cane techniques and understanding of the spatial layout structures of the environment.

Other Devices
In addition to the aids discussed, two other devices are also currently available or in prototypical form. The Nottingham Obstacle Detector (Dodds, Armstrong, & Shingledecker, 1981), with a range of 7 feet, is similar to the Mowat Sensor except that it has audio output only. The output is in the form of eight musical notes that indicate different distances. The Computerized Travel Aid (Maure, Mellor, & Uslan, 1981) utilizes the transducer from the Polaroid One-Step camera and micro-processors to provide distance information about obstacles in the travel path.

The Use of ETAs
The majority of ETAs described in this section were originally designed to be used as supplementary mobility systems with the cane or dog guide for the purposes of advanced obstacle detection. It appears, however, that relatively few visually handicapped travelers use ETAs as supplemental mobility systems (Hill & Bradfield, 1983; Jacobson, 1979). Probably the quality and type of information provided, size, weight, appearance, cost, and maintenance of the devices are contributing factors in their nonuse.

More recently the notion of using ETAs with visually handicapped children to teach spatial and environmental concepts is becoming more widespread (Hill & Bradfield, 1983). Additionally, ETAs have been used in the teaching of specific O&M skills such as establishing and maintaining straight lines of travel. There probably will be a limited market for present ETAs with visually handicapped adults and school age children to be used as supplemental systems. However, it appears that the future of ETAs lies in their application and relevance to enhancing concept, sensory, and motor development as well as specific O&M skills with visually handicapped children (Hill & Bradfield, 1984).

CONCEPT DEVELOPMENT
Concept development is the process of utilizing sensory information to form ideas of space and the environment. Piaget and Inhelder (1948) stated that cognitive abilities develop as children interact with their environment and develop concepts of space in which visual activity plays an important role. Congenitally blind children, however, are often restricted in the range and variety of experiences needed to develop these concepts (Lowenfeld, 1948, 1981). Hapeman (1967) stated that congenitally blind children lack the necessary concrete knowledge of their environment and the necessary basic concepts of distance, direction, and environmental changes.

Piaget (1960) postulated a hierarchical sequence of stages and concepts within stages through which children progress in the process of cognitive development. These stages are sensorimotor, preoperational, concrete operations, and formal operations. It appears that visually impaired children go through the same stages of cognitive development, but at a much slower rate. Studies by Simpkins and Stephens (1974) have shown that blind children demonstrate a lag of as much as four to eight years in the developmental stages postulated by Piaget. This is consistent with earlier studies based upon the developmental levels of Piaget (Friedman & Pasnak, 1973; Gottesman, 1973; Higgins, 1973; Tobin, 1972). (For more information on concept development see Chapter 4.)

Vision and Conceptual Development (Hill & Hill, 1980)

Vision is an important perceptual system in developing awareness of objects and one's own body, including its parts, relationships, movements, and functions. (See Chapter 5.) It is also an efficient system for developing the concept of how other people look as well as forming object-to-object relationships. The visually handicapped child must develop these concepts primarily through the haptic sense. Through vision, one can view the totality of objects and develop relationships quickly; whereas, the haptic sense is not as efficient, particularly when examining parts of relatively large objects. Garry and Ascarelli (1960) found that visually handicapped children seemed to be unaware of, or at least unconcerned about, the upright position and the top, bottom, left, right, and back of objects—that is, with position, both relative and absolute.

Temporal and spatial relationships are particularly difficult for visually handicapped children to master, especially when distance is involved. In their investigation of teaching topographical and spatial orientation to congenitally blind children, Garry and Ascarelli (1960) found that to these children, "here" was synonymous with "now," not place. In other words, congenitally blind children often form temporal rather than spatial relationships—a relationship that is only as extensive as their span of auditory and kinesthetic attention rather than a reciprocal, face-to-face relationship with an environment that always faces one.

Sighted people use vision to experience, stabilize, control, and monitor an ever-changing environment. Because visually handicapped children must rely on their remaining senses, the task of developing and assessing spatial concepts is more difficult and time consuming.

In addition to being very diverse and complex, certain spatial concepts are also extremely ambiguous (Hill, 1970). Common concepts such as near and far appear to be quite simple, but if one analyzes the spatial implications of these terms, they become extremely difficult to define. In fact, many visually handicapped children have difficulty developing meaningful concepts of near and far because they are unable to conceive of body mass. As Garry and Ascarelli (1960) pointed out, one must first be aware of the body as an object existing in space that is occupied by other objects. This awareness of body mass is essential to developing a sense of objective rather than subjective space because it:

> provides a basis for comparison of size and space, and enters into an ability to orient other objects to the body. Lacking this ability, near and far are reduced to what is touchable or out-of-reach, and perception is restricted to a temporal sequence of sensation and movement as they must be until a given consistency of positional orientation is established in reference to the body as an object in space. (Garry & Ascarelli, 1960, p. 12)

Cutsforth (1951) and Harley (1963) wrote extensively about the ability of many congenitally blind children to verbalize certain concepts without directly experiencing them sensorially. Hill (1970) reported that many of these children develop concepts at the verbal level only because they have not directly experienced the concepts in a variety of ways. Not surprisingly, Rubin (1964) found that congenitally blind children performed less well on tests of abstraction than did adventitiously blind or sighted subjects.

Language development plays an important role in assigning labels to concepts. According to Cutsforth (1951), congenitally blind children frequently have language problems because of limited concrete experiences, which in turn limits their base of reference from which to derive and associate the meaning of words. Congenitally blind children develop much of their language through rote learning. Spatial words, in particular, present problems since they are often derived from and associated with visual space. Because these children have no ready reference in their experience (Garry & Ascarelli, 1960), they take longer to develop language that is experientially based than do sighted children. In addition, because blind children live in a "visual world," they are expected to use visual terms despite their lack of visual experience (Cutsforth, 1951).

Classification of Concepts

There are many important concepts for visually handicapped children to acquire which are related to O&M. The reader is directed to Hill and Blasch (1980), Lydon and McGraw (1973), Wardell (1976), and Hall (1982) for extensive listings of important concepts.

Hill and Blasch (1980) classified concepts into three broad areas—body concepts, spatial concepts, and environmental concepts. Information the child acquires in developing a body concept includes the ability to identify parts of the body and knowing the locations, movement, relationships, and functions of the various body parts. Body awareness, perceptual body schema (Frostig & Horne, 1964; Garry & Ascarelli, 1960), and body image (Cratty & Sams, 1968; Hapeman, 1967; Lydon & McGraw, 1973) are terms similar in meaning to the term body concept. Adequate knowledge of body concepts may be viewed as central to the development of spatial concepts and to the process of orienting oneself to the environment and being mobile (Hill & Blasch, 1980).

Hill and Blasch (1980) discussed and classified three types of spatial concept categories—positional/relational, shapes, and measurement. Examples of positional/relational spatial concepts include: front, back, top, bottom, left, right, between, parallel, etc. The category of shape includes such concepts as round, circle, rectangle, square, etc. Finally, measure-

Table 19.1   Age ranges of published spatial concepts/O&M instruments for VI populations

Instrument	Authors	Age Range	Source
The Body Image of Blind Children	Cratty & Sims, 1968	5-12	AFB
The Orientation and Mobility Scale for Young Blind Children	Lord, 1969	3-12	CEC
Stanford Multi-Modality Imagery Test	Dauterman, 1972	16+	AFB
The Kephart Scale	Kephart, Kephart, & Schwartz, 1974	5-7	CEC
The Tactile Analog to the Boehm Test of Basic Concepts Form A	Caton, 1977	K-2nd grade	APH
Concepts Involved in Body Position in Space	Hill, 1970	6-14	EVH
Hill Performance Test of Selected Positional Concepts	Hill, 1981	6-10	Stoelting
Peabody Mobility Kit	Harley, Wood, & Merbler, 1981	Preschool-Adult	Stoelting

ment concepts include distance, amount, weight, volume, width, length, and size. Measurement concepts can be incremental, e.g., inch, foot, pound, etc., or relative in nature, e.g., large, small, narrow, far, near, etc. Time certainly is another measurement category but is usually not considered spatial.

Anything one perceives through one's senses could be considered an environmental concept. Hill and Blasch (1980) generated an extensive list of O&M related environmental concepts, e.g., street, traffic light, safety island, etc. They also discussed environmental concepts relating to topography, e.g., hilly, ramp, tilt, etc.; textures, e.g., cement, stone, smooth, hard, etc.; and temperature, e.g., hot, cold, humid, dry, etc. Hapeman (1967), in discussing environmental concepts, added the notion that understanding the nature of and differences among fixed, movable, and moving objects is very important for congenitally blind children. Finally, it is also important for blind children to understand that certain environmental concepts have multiple labels but have the same meaning. For example, the area between the sidewalk and the street can be called a gutter, shoreline, parkway, boulevard, tree lawn area, and city property.

Assessment of Conceptual Development

To develop accurate and diverse concepts, a linkage must occur between sensory interaction with the environment and terminology before meaningful concepts can evolve (Hill, 1970); a good vocabulary is not sufficient. Furthermore, to identify the visually handicapped child's actual level of conceptual attainments, concepts should be assessed on the basis of performance. In the next section, published concept development instruments designed for visually handicapped and sighted children are briefly described and discussed. Procedures for designing informal concept development instruments are also presented. This information supplements those presented in Chapter 11.

Instruments Designed to Assess Conceptual Abilities of Visually Handicapped Populations

Currently, there are eight published concept development/O&M type instruments available for visually handicapped populations (see Table 19.1). Six instruments are reviewed in depth here.

The Body Image of Blind Children (BIBC) (Cratty & Sams, 1968). This instrument for the evaluation of blind children's body image can be used to assess: the child's ability to identify body parts; the left-right dimensions of his body and body parts; body planes (sides, back, front, etc.); ability to respond to requests for specific bodily movements; and ascertain the movements of a person who is touching him. In addition to assessing an individual's ability to make left-right discriminations about her body, questions are used to assess the ability to differentiate between another person's left and right body parts. Finally, the ability with which the child can accurately judge the location of objects relative to his body and the manner in which he can accurately place his body relative to objects may also be assessed.

This instrument is based upon a 16-step body-image training sequence for sighted children (Cratty, 1967). It is an attempt at assessing the body-image of blind children in a systematic fashion and goes beyond just asking the child to name body parts. Its major weaknesses are: (a) the limited amount of data presented on reliability and validity; (b) the pass-fail system which, while being easy to administer, does not give any value to approximations of a correct response; and, (c) the sequence of body planes and their body parts because the use of some body parts is in the body plane section.

The Stanford Multi-Modality Imagery Test (SMIT) (Dauterman, 1972). This test was designed to assess the functional imagery of blind persons. The multi-modality aspect of this test involves the use of haptic (tactile and kinesthetic) and verbal stimuli for imagery stimulation. The test method chosen is a measure of imagery involving geometric patterns. The test has three phases, the first two of which are the learning phases and involve the subject in the construction of simple three-sided and four-sided figures by placing rubber bands around a rectangular-shaped board.

The SMIT is the only spatial concept instrument specifically designed for visually handicapped adults. The tasks, however, become increasingly complex and its utility is questionable with lower functioning adults and its use with children would definitely be questioned.

The Kephart Scale (Kephart & Kephart, 1973; Kephart, Kephart, & Schwartz, 1974).
This instrument was designed to measure body and environmental concepts of visually handicapped children. The child is asked to verbally construct an "imaginary" boy or girl by naming body parts and an "imaginary" environment by describing a house, its rooms, yard, and neighborhood. The child is encouraged to be spontaneous, but assistance in the form of prompting may be provided by the examiner.

The informal approach to obtaining verbal information about the child and the environment is the major strength of the scale. However, the lack of sound research techniques in the development of the Kephart Scale makes its use questionable. The lack of validity and reliability evidence as well as scoring criteria are definite weaknesses of this instrument.

The Tactile Analog to the Boehm Test of Basic Concepts, Form A (Caton, 1977).
The Boehm Test of Basic Concepts (BTBC) developed by Boehm (1971) is designed to measure children's mastery of concepts considered necessary in the primary school years. The test is intended for use with nonhandicapped children in kindergarten, first, and second grades. Its purpose is to identify children whose overall level of concept mastery is low and who may need special attention. An additional purpose is to identify individual spatial and quantitative concepts with which large numbers of children in a class may be unfamiliar. Form A of the BTBC was translated into a haptic format called the Tactile Test of Basic Concepts (TTBC) developed by Caton (1977) for use with visually impaired children.

The BTBC consists of a series of 50 picture items and could easily be used with many low vision children. The TTBC is composed of 50 plastic sheets on which 50 items of the BTBC are presented in raised outline drawings. The TTBC is individually administered and may be used as a criterion-referenced test. Its major weakness (as in the BTBC) lies in the lack of validity data.

Concepts Involved in Body Position in Space (Hill, 1970).
This instrument was developed to assess a variety of selected spatial concepts (positional terms) of visually handicapped children ages 6 to 14 years. This performance test consists of 75 items divided into three parts. Selected positional concepts such as front, back, left, right, etc., are tested in different ways in each part. In the first part, the child identifies the relationship of various body parts as she follows spoken directions to move and position those parts. In the second part, the child is asked to demonstrate the same concepts by moving herself in relationship to objects. The third part consists of the child demonstrating the same concepts by moving objects in relationship to each other. Hill (1970) postulated that if certain spatial concepts could be assessed in a variety of ways, a formalized instructional program could be developed to remediate concept deficiencies. There are no validity, reliability, or normative data reported on Hill's (1970) original instrument (Concepts Involved in Body Position in Space).

The Hill Performance Test of Selected Positional Concepts (Hill & Hill, 1980; Hill, 1981).
This instrument is a revised edition of *Concepts Involved in Body Position in Space* (Hill, 1971). The original instrument and manual were revised utilizing item analysis techniques (Kerlinger, 1972) on data obtained from previous studies done by the author. Preliminary revision involved a reduction in the number of spatial concepts assessed and the division of the test into four parts: Part I-Ability to identify positional relationships of body parts; Part II-Ability to move various body parts in relationship to one another to demonstrate positional concepts; Part III-Ability to move the body in relationship to objects to demonstrate positional concepts; and Part IV-Ability to form object-to-object relationships. Test items were reduced from 75 to 72 and the more complex concepts, such as parallel, perpendicular, etc., were deleted to make the instrument more age appropriate (to ages 6-10 years). Validity, reliability, and normative data are available in Hill and Hill (1980) and Hill (1981).

The Peabody Mobility Scales (PMS) (Harley, Wood, & Merbler, 1981). The PMS was designed for multiply handicapped visually handicapped persons. The concept development subtest includes the following: body image, spatial relations (front/back, up/down, on/under, left/right discriminations, shape discrimination, size discrimination, and organization). A review of the PMS is contained in the mobility assessment section of this chapter.

The O&M Scale for Young Blind Children—The Short Form (Lord, 1969).
Lord's scale is a comprehensive assessment of O&M including some self-help items. It is reviewed in detail

in the mobility assesment section of this chapter. The Lord Scale does assess such spatial concepts as left and right (turns) and compass directions.

Summary of Published Instruments for Assessment of Conceptual Development

Six of the published instruments reviewed primarily assess various spatial conceptual abilities. Lord's scale (1969) and the Peabody Mobility Kit (1981) assess some orientation and mobility skills, but also assess some areas of concept development. Lord (1969), Dauterman (1973), Caton (1977), Hill (1981), and Hill and Hill (1980) have reported reliability, validity and normative data.

Instruments Designed to Assess Spatial Concepts and/or O&M Abilities

There are several instruments designed for handicapped children which assess spatial concepts and/or O&M directly or in part. Many of these instruments can be adapted for use with visually handicapped children and require little or no modification. The following is a brief review of some of these instruments.

The Ayres Space Test (Ayres, 1972)

This test identifies individuals with learning disabilities due to sensory integrative dysfunction. The major purpose of the test is to evaluate the dimensions of perceptual speed and space visualization. It is intended for use with individuals 3 years of age to adult. Standardization data on the Ayres Space Test have been severely criticized in reviews in Buros (1972). Extensive modification would be necessary, however, if the Ayres Test were used with totally blind children.

The Basic Inventory (BCI) (Engelmann, 1967).

This criterion-referenced inventory by Engelman (1967) taps a series of concepts subjectively selected as being basic for success in first grade. The inventory purports to evaluate the instructions in certain beginning academically-related concepts as well as the instructions given an individual child. The BCI is designed for nonhandicapped children who are preparing for beginning academic tasks. It is primarily intended for culturally disadvantaged preschool and kindergarten children. The instructions for administering and scoring the BCI are explicit, detailed, and item specific. Much of the manual is devoted to classroom applications of the inventory. This inventory is designed for nonhandicapped children so adaptations for visually handicapped children are necessary. There are no data on validity, reliability, and age norms.

Marianne Frostig Developmental Test of Visual Perception (Frostig, Lefever, & Whittlesey, 1966).

This test is intended for children between the ages of 3 to 8 years and can be administered to small groups or individuals. It measures five operationally defined perceptual skills: eye-motor coordination, figure ground, constancy of shape, position in space, and spatial relationships. Validity data are suspect as the test does not appear to measure each of the five operationally defined perceptual skills (Buros, 1972).

Boehm Test of Basic Concepts (BTBC) (Boehm, 1971).

The BTBC is designed to measure children's mastery of concepts considered necessary for achievement in kindergarten through second grade. The BTBC assesses such directional concepts as below, different, middle, top, last, etc. The BTBC has two forms. Each form consists of 50 pictorial items arranged in approximate order to increasing difficulty. Each item consists of a set of three pictures, about which statements are read aloud to the children by the examiner. The statements briefly describe the pictures and instruct children to mark one that illustrates the concept being listed. The BTBC is a group administered test. It is possible that some low vision children may be able to use the BTBC without modifications.

Informal Conceptual Assessment

There are many excellent informal checklists that have been developed by O&M instructors and teachers of visually handicapped pupils such as the one published by the Illinois Office of Education (1974), Curriculum Guide for the Development of Body and Sensory Awareness for the Visually Handicapped. Since there are so few published formal instruments for visually handicapped populations which are valid, reliable, and norm-referenced, teachers and O&M instructors may need to develop their own performance measures to assess concept development. The following guidelines are offered when developing such assessments in the concept development area:

1. Be specific when identifying and defining the domains to be assessed. For example, the domain of "body concepts" may be too general to assess.

2. Review existing (formal and informal) assessments for identifying specific domains and items. Frequently, several items can be used from existing assessments or could easily be modified for use. Other sources of assessments can be found in books listed in additional readings at the end of this chapter.

3. Define the format of the assessment items at the appropriate level of the population being assessed. For example, will the assessment be administered individually, orally, etc.

4. Write the specific assessment items and instructions. Care should be taken that individual assessment items do not test too many concepts. Also, items and instructions should be analyzed to determine if any necessary prerequisite skills are needed by the respondents, e.g., receptive language skills.

5. Define the criteria for acceptable responses.
6. Consider time factors, attention span, and notification of respondents.

The Role of the Teacher in the Development of Concepts

Spatial and environmental deficiencies of visually handicapped children may not only impede their progress in O&M, but may also cause problems for them in performing academic tasks. Classroom activities, such as understanding the directions of the teacher, moving within the classroom and throughout the school, and completing assignments, all require some understanding of spatial concepts. Concept development is not the exclusive responsibility of the O&M specialist; teachers should share in the responsibility of teaching concepts. In fact, teachers may be in a better position to take the lead in teaching concepts because they may have more contact time with greater numbers of children.

Orientation and mobility specialists generally teach concepts in two ways. One way is to teach concepts on an individual basis in the context of O&M lessons. These lessons generally range from one-half hour to one hour each, 2 to 5 days per week. In the past, this approach has been a reactive one because the child may not be able to progress normally through the O&M sequence. More recently, O&M instruction has started at an earlier age with a strong emphasis on concept development. Another way that O&M specialists have taught concepts, particularly in residential school settings, has been with small groups of children. Mills and Adamschick (1969), Hill (1970, 1971), and Webster (1976) describe formalized concept development programs at various residential schools where the O&M specialist taught "concept classes." Basically these programs consisted of teaching body, spatial, and environmental concepts to small homogeneous groups of students using a multisensory approach.

An Interactive Approach

Certainly the teacher may utilize the individual or small group approach to teaching concepts. In fact, these strategies may be preferred with some children and in some service delivery models. However, another approach is to teach concepts through the child's subject matter, e.g., science, math, social studies, physical education, etc.; specialized skills areas, e.g., braille, typing, activities of daily living, etc.; and typical school activities, e.g., transition activities in the classroom, lining up, running errands, putting things away, etc. This integrative strategy could be utilized with any service delivery model. If the child is in a regular public school classroom, it would involve the regular classroom teacher(s) and other teachers the child has, specialized teachers, and parents, with the teacher of the visually handicapped and the O&M instructor taking the lead and coordinating the instruction.

Many regular classroom teachers teach concepts. However, they may not be aware of the important body, spatial, and environmental concepts for visually handicapped children. Because the regular class teacher must teach many things and also be concerned about the nonhandicapped students in the class, it is important that the teacher of the visually handicapped develop and coordinate the integrative strategy in a time efficient and nondisruptive manner. The following procedure is an example of how the teacher of the visually handicapped can develop, coordinate, and implement an integrative concept development strategy:
1. Utilize formal and informal instruments, developmental norms, observation, school records, and feedback from school personnel and parents, to assess the child in the area of concept development.
2. Develop a list of important concepts which need to be acquired.
3. Communicate assessment findings to the classroom teacher, key school personnel, and parents.
4. Assist the classroom teacher in task analyzing subject matter for the inclusion of important concepts to be learned, reinforced, and/or emphasized. Subjects such as math contain many spatial concepts, e.g., basic geometric shapes, parallel and perpendicular, etc. The idea is to help the classroom teacher to be cognizant of the concepts contained within various subject matter so they can be emphasized for the child.
5. Provide the classroom teacher with specific suggestions and activities which can introduce and reinforce important concepts within the context of various subject matter. For example, Randolph (1971) suggested activities such as rearranging the classroom seating arrangement to form circles, squares, etc. with the chairs when teaching a unit on basic shapes in math class.
6. Assist the classroom teacher in identifying opportunities for teaching and reinforcing concepts in the classroom that are not directly related to subject matter. For example, Hill (1971) suggested such activities as:
(a) During question and answer session, inform children that if they want to be called on they should, "Raise your *right* hand," "Put your hands on *top* of your head," "Touch your *left shoulder*," etc.
(b) Vary where the child signs her name on assignments. For example, have children sign their names in the *lower right-hand corner, top middle* of the paper, etc.
(c) Emphasize the use of spatial concepts when giving directions to put things away, e.g., the *left*-hand side of the *big* shelf; running errands, e.g., the principal's office is *next* to the small lobby; and travel within the classroom, e.g., stand *up*, turn *left*, and walk a *few feet straight ahead*, etc.

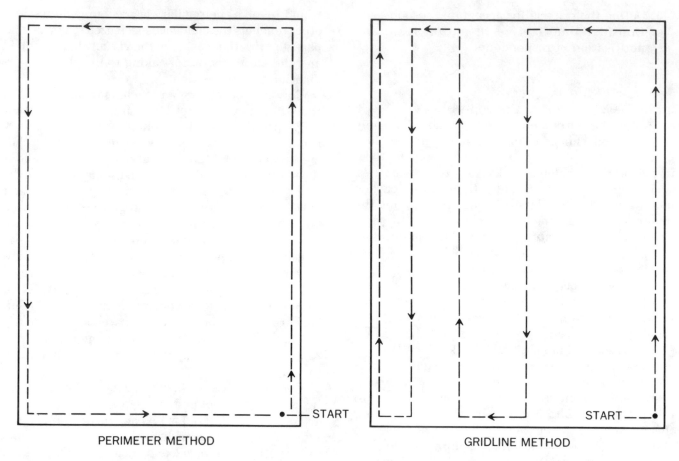

PERIMETER METHOD   GRIDLINE METHOD

Figure 19.6   Examples of systematic search patterns

7. Keep other school personnel, specialists, and parents informed of the child's progress and provide appropriate suggestions for reinforcement activities. For example, if the classroom teacher is emphasizing the concepts of left and right, the speech therapist might use the words "left" and "right" in articulation exercises, the O&M instructor might work on left and right turns with the child, and the parent might reinforce left and right when foods are being passed at the dinner table. The basic notion is to have a coordinated team effort which systematically exposes the child to different dimensions of the concept.

ORIENTATION

Theory

Orientation involves both perceptual and cognitive processes. Rieser, Guth, and Hill (1982) identified and discussed three component processes of spatial orientation—knowledge of spatial layout, spatial updating, and knowledge of spatial concepts and systems of concepts. Similarly, Hill and Ponder (1976) discussed three principles of orientation in a question format—(a) Where am I? This requires that the individual know his present position in space (updating); (b) Where is my objective? (layout knowledge); and (c) How do I get there? (spatial concepts and systems).

Knowledge of Spatial Layout

Another name for spatial layout knowledge is object-to-object relationship knowledge, e.g., knowing the relative positions of different objects or places. The utilization of perimeter and gridline search patterns (Hill & Ponder, 1976) is a practical method for the visually handicapped traveler to systematically acquire spatial layout knowledge (see Figure 19.6). The perimeter search pattern is used to explore the boundaries of an area in order to identify the size, shape, and important features around the perimeter of the area and to explore the internal features of the area to establish object-to-object relationships.

Another method of acquiring spatial layout knowledge is by soliciting aid (Hill & Ponder, 1976). Systematic questioning strategies can be very useful in obtaining much spatial relationship information about an area in a short period of time.

Repeated travel within an area may also facilitate

spatial layout knowledge. Rieser, Guth, and Hill (1982) state:

> a traveler may memorize the routes traveled, mentally listing the distances walked and directions of turns taken from object-to-object. With knowledge organized like this, the traveler would be limited to those routes, unable to figure detours or shortcuts. (p. 214)

This path or route knowledge is undoubtedly the most frequent method of orientation employed by blind people (Siegel & White, 1975). A critical factor in the use of path knowledge for orientation is the accurate detection of the extent of distances walked and the degree of turns made. If you are unable to detect how far you walk and how much you turn, then you have no basis for determining how such movements affect your orientation.

A great deal of effort is currently focused on understanding the "perceptual" (automatic) versus "cognitive" (strategic) nature and use of path knowledge and toward plotting the accuracy of path knowledge-based orientation across systematic variations of route configuration. Recent findings make it clear that the accuracy of path knowledge-based orientation is inversely related to the number of turns in a route (Lindberg & Garling, 1981) and the overall length of a route (Thomson, 1983). The ability of blind persons to use this method of orientation has been repeatedly demonstrated. For example, Worchel (1951) found no differences in the performances of sighted and blind subjects who were guided along two sides of a right triangle and then asked to walk back along the hypotenuse to their starting point.

Knowledge of the spatial patterns or shapes of different paths traveled is a somewhat more versatile method of spatial organization. Rieser, Guth, and Hill (1982) state:

> . . .a person who knows that two places are arranged at the ends of an "L" shaped route can figure the direction to take if a shortcut is desired, whereas, a person knowing only a mental listing (e.g., go 10 steps straight, ahead, turn left, and go 20 more steps) would not be able to identify the direction of a shortcut. However, a person who learned the spatial pattern of each route separately would not be able to figure novel paths from places previously learned along one route to other places previously learned along another route. (p. 214)

The most versatile system of establishing spatial knowledge is the use of a reference system. Here the traveler is able to determine the direction of a straight-line path from the endpoint of a route back to its start when the route traveled between the two points is not itself direct (see Figure 19.7). Siegel and White (1975) described the ability to integrate numerous spatially patterned routes within a common frame of reference as resembling a survey map.

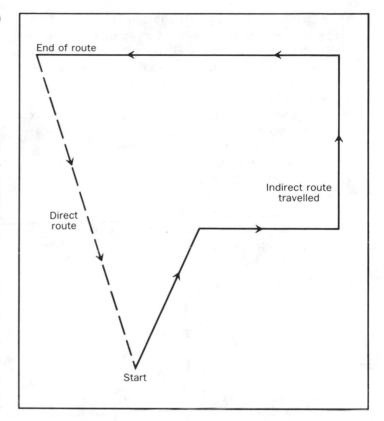

Figure 19.7   **An indirect route and the most direct route between two points.**

Spatial Updating

Spatial updating refers to the processes of establishing self-to-object relationships and being able to keep track of those relationships while moving. The cognitive process described by Hill and Ponder (1976) reflects one method of updating (see Figure 19.8). In other words, updating involves the confirmation of various travel hypotheses based upon the availability and usefulness of environmental information.

There is also some evidence that spatial updating does not involve cognitive processes. Under some conditions, it appears that travelers are able to perceptually (automatically) relate their own locomotion to knowledge of their surroundings (Rieser, Guth, & Hill, 1982).

Cognitive Process

The cognitive process is actually a cycle of five processes which the student uses while performing orientation skills. The steps interact, and any or all may be repeated each time the cognitive process is performed. The amount of time the cognitive process requires can vary. It is imperative that the student be capable of performing all steps in the cognitive process and integrating them while performing orientation skills. The five steps of the cognitive process are as follows:

1. Perception: The process of assimilating data from the environment through the remaining senses: odors, sounds, tactual, kinesthetic perceptions, or change in brightness level.

2. Analysis: The process of organizing perceived data into categories according to consistency, dependability, familiarity, source, sensory type, and intensity.

3. Selection: The process of choosing the analyzed data that best fulfills the orientation needs of the present environmental situation.

4. Plan: The process of designing a course of action based on the sensory data selected as most relevant to the present environmental situation.

5. Execution: The process of performing the planned course of action.

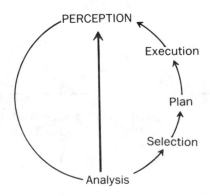

Figure 19.8   Cognitive Process

Source: E. Hill & P. Ponder, *Orientation and mobility techniques* (New York: American Foundation for the Blind, Inc., 1976), p. 4.

Knowledge of Spatial Concepts and Systems of Concepts

Several of the important prerequisite concepts necessary for independent travel have been discussed in the concept development section. However, knowledge of rules, principles, and systems of spatial concepts is important in establishing and maintaining orientation during travel. Teachers of visually handicapped children can integrate the instruction of orientation concepts and systems within the curriculum. For example, landmarks and clues could be taught with a unit in science, measurement concepts and skills in math and science, compass directions in geography, and numbering systems in math, geography, and social studies. A brief description of some of these systems (see Chart 19.1) summarized from Hill & Ponder (1976)

follows. Numbering systems have been described in detail to illustrate the interrelatedness of several of these systems.

Numbering Systems

Numbering systems provide an order and structure to our environment. For example, knowing the interstate numbering system which is constructed in a logical progression would help determine the directions of a particular interstate as well as its approximate location.

Buildings usually have their own numbering system. There is an originating point where the number begins and numbers should get progressively larger as one moves away from it. Most buildings also follow an odd-even sequence wherein even numbers are consistently on one side and odd numbers on another. Generally there is a pattern to the system and bathrooms, closets, storage rooms are excluded.

Patterns in outdoor numbering systems also help blind and visually handicapped persons as well as nonhandicapped persons find their bearings. City dividing lines are usually located in the "downtown" area and are often main streets or bodies of water. Numbers should get bigger as one moves away from them. It is extremely important to develop questioning strategies by visually handicapped persons to inquire about the numbering system of a city.

The odd-even sequence is followed outdoors as well as indoors. It is important for visually handicapped persons to establish patterns in numbering systems and to be aware of long or short blocks, parks, angular streets, etc. which may cause deviations in the numbering system.

Knowing the principles of city numbering systems allows one to pinpoint and find an address correctly. For example one can determine a great deal of information about the address, 1215 W. Green Street, by having previous knowledge of the city numbering system. Analysis of 1215 W. Green Street:

a. Green is an East-West Street.
b. It is approximately 13 blocks west of the North-South dividing lines of the city.
c. 15 in the address would indicate the directional side of the street and the relative position in the block, e.g., closer to the beginning of the block.

Visually handicapped persons should be aware of appropriate sources from which to obtain information about a city's numbering system, e.g. the Fire Department, City Planning, taxi companies, Chamber of Commerce, etc.

Although numbering systems are not constant or universal across environments, they can lend order, provide a structure, and facilitate the establishment of object-to-object relationships in a particular building, city, or locale within a given city.

Chart 19.1   Systems of spatial concepts

Landmarks

—A landmark is any familiar object, sound, odor, temperature or tactual clue that is easily recognized, is constant, and that has a known, permanent location in the environment.
—Landmarks are constant and permanent.
—A landmark's use is dependent upon knowledge of at least one direction or one object in the environment in relation to it.
—A landmark has at least one unique characteristic to differentiate it from other objects in the environment.
—Landmarks may be recognizable by their visual, tactual, olfactory, kinesthetic, or auditory characteristics or a combination thereof.

Clues

—A clue is any auditory (including object perception), olfactory, tactile (including temperature), kinesthetic, or visual (including color, brightness, and contrast) stimulus affecting the senses which can be readily converted to give the student information necessary to determine his/her position or a line of direction.
—A clue may be dynamic or stationary.
—The functional use of a clue depends upon the user's familiarity and knowledge of its source.
—Certain clues may be transferable from one environment to another.
—All stimuli do not have equal value as clues; some will most adequately fulfill the informational needs of the moment (dominant clues), some will be useful but to a lesser degree, and some will have negative value (masking sounds).
—Measuring is a skill which involves ascertaining the exact or approximate dimensions of an object or space, using a given unit.
—Everything in the environment is measurable.
—Linear measurements are constant.
—There are standard increments or units of measurement; those commonly used indoors are: inch, foot, yard, rod, and any fraction or approximation thereof.
—Standard units of measurement have fixed, definite, interchangeable relationships to each other (e.g., 12 inches = one foot), and appropriate increments should be chosen according to the distance to be measured (e.g., use feet to measure length of table, use inches to measure length of pencil).
—Measurements may be divided into three broad classes: (a) measurements using standard units, (b) comparative measurements, and (c) nonstandardized (paces, knee high).
—Comparative measurements compare the length or distance of two things; for example, longer than, wider than, less than.
—Linear measurement is applied to the three basic dimensions: length, height, width.
—Standard or nonstandard units may be used for approximate measurements (e.g., approximately 7 yards, waist-high, 3 paces).

Compass Directions

—A direction is a line on which something is moving, along which something is pointed, in which something is aimed, or toward which something is facing. Compass directions are specialized directions which are dictated by the magnetic fields of the earth. The four main compass directions are cardinal points, and are spaced with 90° intervals around the circle of the compass; they are north, east, south, and west.
—Compass directions are constant.
—Compass directions are transferable from one environment to another. Compass directions allow the student to relate to the distant environment. Compass directions allow the student to relate environment-to-environment concepts in a more positive and definitive manner.
—An east-west line of direction is perpendicular and at right angles to a north-south line.
—All east-west lines are parallel; all north-south lines are parallel.
—Travel may be either east or west on an east-west line, and north or south on a north-south line.

Adapted from: E.W. Hill & P. Ponder, *Orientation and mobility techniqes* (New York, N.Y.: American Foundation for the Blind, Inc., 1979), pp. 4-9.

Formal Orientation and Sensory Skills

The development of orientation and sensory skills greatly facilitates independent travel. A list of the important orientation and sensory skills is shown in Chart 19.2. Some of the orientation skills are described in other sections of this chapter. For a complete and detailed description, consult Welsh and Blasch (1980), Hill and Ponder (1976), Weisgerber and Hall (1975) and Lydon and McGraw (1973).

Chart 19.2   Orientation and sensory skills

---

1. Auditory Skills
   1.1. Sound Localization
   1.2. Sound Identification
   1.3. Sound Discrimination
   1.4. Echo Location
   1.5. Use of Sound Shadows

2. Tactual
   2.1. Tactual Discrimination (hands and feet)
   2.2. Tactual Identification

3. Olfactory
   3.1. Discrimination
   3.2. Identification

4. Kinesthetic and Proprioceptive Awareness

5. Turns
   5.1. 90 degrees
   5.2. 180 degrees
   5.3 Various angles

6. Establishing and Maintaining a Straight Line of Travel
   6.1. Perpendicular Alignment (squaring off)
   6.2. Parallel Alignment

7. Search Patterns
   7.1. Perimeter Method
   7.2. Gridline Method

8. Recovery Skills

9. Use of Reference Points and Systems

10. Soliciting Aid

11. Time/Distance Estimation

Familiarization Process

Many visually handicapped persons do not have great difficulty traveling in familiar areas. However, learning and traveling in novel environments can be difficult and stressful (Barth & Foulke, 1979). A skilled O&M specialist or teacher of the visually handicapped can systematically and efficiently familiarize the child to a novel environment. Typically, this process involves the teacher systematically guiding the child through the novel area and pointing out its salient features. Combinations of other methods such as verbally describing the environment and the use of various orientation aids (Bentzen, 1980), e.g., tactual maps and models are also used frequently.

The act of familiarizing a person to a new environment is an important skill for teachers. Usually the important landmarks, clues, and spatial relationships of the area are pointed out. Familiarization by the teacher is particularly appropriate when the environment is complex, dangerous, or there is little time for the visually handicapped person to learn it on his own. Also, some persons, e.g., multiply handicapped persons, may not be able to acquaint themselves (independently) with novel environments. Whenever possible, however, great care should be taken to instruct visually handicapped persons in how to systematically explore and learn novel environments independently. This process is known as self-familiarization (Hill & Ponder, 1976) and should start at an early age. Otherwise, visually handicapped persons may always have to rely on a sighted person to familiarize them to new environments.

The self-familiarization process should start with preschool children by teaching them the idea of a reference point and how to employ systematic search patterns on flat surfaces, such as trays, table tops, floors, and walls. Sequentially, the notion of reference points and search patterns is extended to larger and more complex areas, i.e., small rooms, large rooms, hallways, floors of buildings, buildings, an area around school or home, a shopping mall, etc. Obviously, as the environment is expanded and becomes more complex, the visually handicapped person will also be using formal O&M skills to implement the self-familiarization process.

The self-familiarization process is time consuming and involves many skills. When familiarizing oneself to a new environment, one should keep three basic questions in mind: (a) What information do I need in order to travel or function in a particular area? (b) How do I obtain this information? and (c) How will I utilize this information? (Hill & Ponder, 1976). It is very important that teachers encourage exploration of novel environments in a systematic way. The self-familiarization process not only involves many O&M skills, but also facilitates decision making and problem solving.

Assessment and Teaching of Orientation

Drop-off and standard lesson plan procedures are two methods of assessing "clusters" of O&M skills and are discussed in the Formal Mobility Skills section of this chapter. Certain instruments already discussed in the Concept Development section also assess orientation skills, e.g., Lord's Scale and the Peabody Mobility Scales. There are other informal procedures that teachers may use to assess and teach orientation, particularly, spatial layout knowledge. A list and brief description of these procedures follows:

1. Have the student describe the area and highlight its important features and spatial relationships.
2. Question the student about the area.

3. Ask the student to point to different objects or locations in the environment to demonstrate spatial relationships.

4. Ask the student to imagine that she is in a particular environment and to point to different objects or locations.

5. Ask the student to do (3) and (4) above and to use clockface dividings, e.g., the gym is at 1:00 from me, or cardinal directions.

6. Ask the student to describe routes and travel to different locations within the area.

7. Ask the student to describe alternative routes and to travel to different locations within the area.

8. Ask the student to construct a tactual model or map of an area.

9. Ask the student to describe the area and/or give directions to someone unfamiliar with the area.

10. Ask the student to travel a particular route and then point back to the start.

11. Ask the student to make straight line distance judgments about triads of objects within the area. For example, "Think of the main door to the gym, principal's office, and cafeteria. Which two locations are closest together? Which two locations are farthest apart?"

12. Ask the student to do step 11 but to make judgments on the walking distances between triads rather than straight-line distance judgments.

13. Rearrange objects in an area, e.g., a room, and ask the student to put the objects back in their original locations.

14. Administer a quiz to the student about the area.

Many of the above assessment procedures may also be used for teaching orientation. Teachers can incorporate the teaching of orientation concepts, systems, and skills through various curricula and subject matter, for example, the use of the sun and wind in science class; measurement skills in math and science; compass directions, distance, spatial layout of environment in geography; the nature of cities, towns, and numbering systems in social studies, etc.

FORMAL MOBILITY SKILLS

One of the major goals of O&M is to provide visually handicapped persons with skills and techniques which will enable them to move safely about their environment. The first comprehensive and systematic text delineating mobility techniques was written by Hill and Ponder in 1976. This text was followed in 1977 by another techniques book written in the form of behavioral objectives (Allen, Griffith, & Shaw, 1977). A book by Tooze (1980) followed with an emphasis on mobility techniques and training for children.

Most teacher training and/or certification programs in the education of the visually handicapped offer at least one course in orientation and mobility or a similar subject. Typically, teachers are trained in the understanding and use of "pre-cane skills." The teacher is expected to be familiar with the various sighted guide skills, hand and forearm techniques (protective skills), and training techniques. For a detailed description of these techniques, see Hill and Ponder (1976), Allen, Griffith, and Shaw (1977), and Tooze (1980). A brief overview of formal mobility techniques follows.

Sighted Guide Techniques

It is important for blind travelers to utilize different sighted guides safely and efficiently within varying environments and under different conditions. Using a sighted guide is an excellent way for visually handicapped children to develop basic skills such as kinesthetic awareness or sensory awareness in preparation for independent travel. During sighted guide skill instruction, the use of nonverbal cues and interpreting the information received through the guide and environment are stressed. It is also important that visually handicapped persons are able to instruct individuals whom they choose to use as a guide in the proper skills of guiding.

A description of Basic Sighted Guide, Narrow Passageway, and Stairway Techniques follow. There are also several other sighted guide techniques which are used to negotiate different environmental situations, e.g., doors, seating, etc. For a complete description of these techniques, consult Hill and Ponder (1976) and Allen, Griffith, and Shaw (1977).

Figure 19.9   Basic Sighted Guide Technique

Basic Sighted Guide (see Figure 19.9). The student grasps the guide's arm just above the elbow with the thumb to the outside and the four fingers to the inside of the guide's arm. The grip should be secure, yet comfortable for the guide. The student's upper arm is positioned parallel and close to the side of the body, forming approximately a 90° angle with the lower arm. The shoulder of the student's grip arm is directly behind the shoulder of the guide's arm, positioning the student approximately one-half step behind the guide. For comfort and ease, it may be advisable for small children to grasp the guide's wrist rather than just above the elbow.

Narrow Passageways (see Figure 19.10). The purpose of the narrow passageway technique is to allow safe and efficient passage through a restricted space that

Figure 19.10   Narrow Passageway

cannot be negotiated in the basic sighted guide procedure. Prior to negotiating the restricted space, the guide moves his guiding arm behind and toward the small of his back. In response to this guide-initiated nonverbal cue, the student straightens her arm and moves directly behind the guide. After traversing the restricted space, the guide returns his arm to a normal position and the student resumes the normal guiding position.

Stairways (see Figure 19.11). The purpose of this skill is to enable the student and guide to safely and efficiently negotiate stairs by avoiding verbalizations on the part of the guide such as informing the student of the vertical direction of the stairs, how many steps there are, etc. The guide approaches the edge of the steps squarely and pauses at the edge of the first step. The student evenly aligns herself beside the guide. The guide takes the first step and the student follows at the guide's pace remaining one step behind. The guide pauses after completing the stairs, indicating to the student she has one more step left to negotiate.

Protective Techniques

For the most part, protective techniques (hand and forearm skills and trailing) are primarily utilized in familiar indoor environments. Protective techniques

should be utilized selectively and are generally not used for traveling great distances. Descriptions of the major protective techniques follows.

Figure 19.11   Negotiating Stairways

Upper Hand and Forearm (see Figure 19.12). The purpose of this skill is to detect objects which may be encountered by the upper region of the body. It is accomplished by positioning the arm parallel to the floor at shoulder level. The forearm is flexed at the elbow forming an obtuse angle of approximately 120°. The fingers are relaxed, held together and extended approximately one inch outside of the opposite shoulder with the palm outwardly rotated.

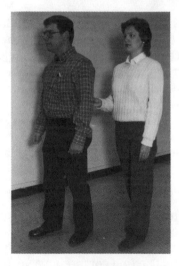

Figure 19.12   Upper Hand and Forearm Technique

Lower Hand and Forearm (see Figure 19.13). The purpose of this skill is to locate and provide protection from waist level objects. To accomplish this technique, the upper arm, forearm, and fingers are extended. The hand is positioned downward at body midline, approximately 6 to 8 inches away from the body. The palm is rotated inward with the fingers relaxed and positioned close together.

Figure 19.13   Lower Hand and Forearm

Trailing (see Figure 19.14). The purposes of trailing are to establish and maintain a straight line of travel and to locate a specific objective on or along the trailing surface. Facing the desired line of travel, the student is positioned parallel and close to the object being trailed. The arm nearest the object is extended downward and forward at an approximate angle of 45°. Light contact with the little and ring fingers are maintained on the trailing surface as the hand is cupped slightly toward the trailing surface with the fingers relaxed and held close together.

Figure 19.14   Trailing

Assessment of Formal Mobility Skills

There are few published instruments available which assess formal mobility skills. A common practice is for O&M specialists to teach formal mobility skills and then systematically observe visually handicapped students using them under different conditions and varying environments. Since orientation skills are frequently taught with mobility skills, they are generally assessed together. One such assessment procedure is the "drop-off" lesson. The "drop-off" lesson is usually conducted in a larger outdoor space than the student has previously spent time traveling within. The student is taken by the instructor (usually by car) to an unknown location within the space and then asked to locate a specific objective, e.g., an address. The student is not allowed to solicit aid during the "drop-off." The instructor observes the student from a distance and only intervenes for safety reasons. For a complete description of "drop-off" procedures, see Hill and Ponder (1976).

Another assessment procedure of formal O&M skills is the notion of standard evaluation lesson plans (Kappan, 1971). The idea here is for the O&M specialist to develop a series of sequenced O&M evaluation lessons which would assess clusters of O&M skills. For example, after students had learned sighted guide skills, they would be evaluated on their performance of the sighted guide skills over a predetermined route or course. Although some assessment would naturally take place during each O&M lesson and after the introduction of individual skills, the standard lesson plan approach allows the O&M instructor the opportunity to systematically evaluate several skills at one time. Clusters of O&M skills are first assessed in simple indoor environments then assessed in progressively more complex environments outside.

Published Formal Mobility Assessments

Lord's Scale (1969) and the Peabody Mobility Kit (Harley, Wood, & Merbler, 1981) were briefly mentioned in the Concept Development Assessment section of this chapter. They are reviewed in more depth here.

The Orientation and Mobility Scale for Young Children—Short Form (Lord, 1969).
This scale was developed to assess the relevant behavior skills of orientation and mobility with visually handicapped individuals. The scale contains 24 items relating to directions and turns, movement in space, and self-help (see Chart 19.3). These items were selected from an original 124 items administered to 173 blind children ranging in age from 3 to 12 years. This instrument offers some guidance to the mobility specialist and teacher when assessing behaviors directly related to mobility; however, it is not helpful in identifying prerequisite spatial concepts if the child fails certain tasks. In addition, no validity data are available.

The Peabody Mobility Scales (PMS) (Harley, Wood, & Merbler, 1981). The development of the PMS (which includes the scales, as well as training activities) was the outgrowth of a Bureau of Education for the Handi-

Chart 19.3   Summary of the orientation and mobility scale for young blind children: Short form

Turns and Directions

Correctly turns left
Describes R-L turns
Points out cardinal directions
North is in front of you
—a. Point to the South
—b. Point to the East
—c. Point to the West
Travels route using cardinal directions
—Take three steps to the North, two steps East, and two more steps North.

Movement in Space

Points toes in direction of travel
Walks with relaxed gait
Up steps—alternating feet
Down steps—alternating feet
Hops—one foot
Hops—alternating feet
Skips
Runs freely by himself
Simple jumping—both feet
Jumps off chair

Self-Help

Demonstrates working part of door
Uses door key
Puts on sweater—unassisted
Buttons sweater
Puts on sweater—one sleeve inside out
Puts on belt—fastens
Dials telephone numbers
Identifies simple tools
Uses helping hand efficiently—getting on chair

Source: F.E. Lord, Development of scales for the measurement of orientation and mobility for young children in *Exceptional Children*, 1969, **36**, pp. 77-81.

Chart 19.4   Peabody Mobility Scale categories and major skills

I. Motor Development
    1.1 Basic Movement
    1.2 Creeping
    1.3 Standing
    1.4 Walking
    1.5 Ascending Stairs
    1.6 Descending Stairs
    1.7 Running
    1.8 Jumping
    1.9 Climbing

II. Sensory Skills
    2.1 Sound Localization
    2.2 Tactual Discrimination (Hands)
    2.3 Tactual Discrimination (Feet)
    2.4 Olfactory Discrimination

III. Concept Development
    3.1 Body Image
    3.2 Spatial Relations (Front/Back, Up/Down, On/Under)
    3.3 Left-Right Discrimination
    3.4 Shape Discrimination
    3.5 Size Discrimination
    3.6 Organization

IV. Mobility Skills
    4.1 Sighted Guide
    4.2 Seating
    4.3 Turning and Maintaining Orientation
    4.4 Trailing
    4.5 Utilization of Discriminable Landmarks
    4.6 Environmental Travel

Source: R.K. Harley, T.A. Word & J. B. Merbler, *Peabody Mobility Scale*, (Chicago, Ill.: Stoelting Company, 1981), p. 68.

capped (BEH) grant entitled, "The Development of a Program in Orientation and Mobility for Multiply Impaired Blind Children."

The PMS is criterion-referenced and covers the following skills areas: (a) motor development; (b) sensory skills; (c) concept development; and (d) mobility skills. The categories and major skills of the PMS are summarized in Chart 19.4.

The Peabody Mobility Kit is applicable to students with severe sensory, physical, and developmental impairments. There is also a kit for sighted and low vision persons which covers four areas: motor skills, vision skills, concept skills, and mobility skills. The Kit emphasizes utilization of vision, eye-foot coordination, color, and direct discrimination.

No validity, reliability, or normative data are available on the Peabody Mobility Scales; however, it is currently the only instrument that assesses multiply handicapped/visually handicapped persons (preschool through adult). The Scales and instructional programs (for both kits) may be utilized by both O&M instructors and teachers.

Several published instruments were described and reviewed. Many of these instruments assess a limited range of spatial O&M related concepts. Many of the instruments are designed to assess concepts of school age visually handicapped children. Teachers and O&M instructors may need to design their own informal methods of assessing spatial concepts because of the limited scope and age range of available published instruments. Identifying the range and variety of concepts important for visually handicapped children and constructing valid and reliable instruments to assess such concepts is a difficult task. By their nature, spatial concepts are often ambiguous, diversified in meaning, and complex. The assessment of concepts may involve the use of existing published instruments, adapting concept instruments that are designed for other populations, and constructing informal procedures. Care should be taken to assess concepts systematically in a variety of ways so appropriate teaching activities can be developed.

Role of the Teacher in the Development of Formal Mobility Skills

Historically, the teacher of the visually handicapped has been responsible for teaching basic formal mobility skills, such as sighted guide techniques, protective techniques, and teaching these skills in the absence of or in coordination with a qualified O&M specialist. It is also good practice for teachers to work cooperatively with the O&M specialist to reinforce appropriate mobility techniques in the school and home environment (Hill, 1984).

The issue of whether teachers should teach advanced mobility skills, e.g., cane techniques, is long standing. The arguments against the practice have centered around lack of time, expertise, and liability. These concerns have contributed to the trend of preparing dual competency (O&M and teaching) personnel in preparation programs. There are several arguments in favor of dual competency preparation for teachers of visually handicapped pupils. Many school districts with small enrollments of visually handicapped pupils cannot afford to employ two professionals. This is especially true in rural areas where there are few pupils scattered over a wide geographical area. A teacher with dual competency can meet the comprehensive educational needs of these visually handicapped pupils. Finally, some professionals maintain that orientation and mobility instructors are prepared to work primarily with adults. Studies show that increasing numbers of O&M specialists are working with school age children (Uslan, Hill, & Peck, in preparation).

It is important that all teachers of visually handicapped pupils have a basic understanding of advanced mobility skills such as diagonal and the touch technique (Hill & Ponder, 1976) in order to reinforce appropriate cane skills. The diagonal and the touch technique are probably the cane techniques most frequently used within the school and on the school grounds.

When using the diagonal technique, the cane is held diagonally across the body so it acts like a "bumper" (see Figure 19.15). The cane is angled away from the body so the tip is approximately one inch above the ground and one to two inches outside the widest part of the body.

The diagonal technique provides advance warning of low objects and can be thought of as an extension of the hand and forearm techniques. The diagonal is used primarily in a familiar, indoor environment.

The touch technique allows the traveler to detect drop offs (curbs, steps, etc.) and objects in the travel path. It is used in both familiar and unfamiliar environments. When using the cane in touch technique

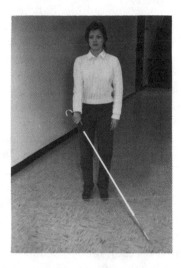

Figure 19.15   Diagonal Technique

fashion, the cane is held in the midline of the body and swung from side to side in a low, flat arc. The cane tip contacts the walking surface at a point one inch outside the widest part of the body. The cane is swung in a rhythmic manner with cane tip striking the walking surface on the side opposite the forward foot (see Figure 19.16). The basic notion behind the touch technique is for the traveler to clear the area (with the cane) for his next step.

Figure 19.16   Touch Technique

It is also important that teachers understand such techniques as cane placement, e.g., how the cane is positioned under chairs, tables, in a car, etc.; how the cane is held while using a sighted guide, e.g., going through doors; and the proper cane techniques used when going up and down stairs. (See Allen, Griffith, & Shaw, 1977; Hill & Ponder, 1976 for a comprehensive treatment of cane techniques.)

DEVELOPMENTAL PERSPECTIVES OF ORIENTATION AND MOBILITY

It appears that teachers and O&M specialists are serving more preschool age and multiply handicapped children than ever before. Perhaps child find programs through P.L. 94-142 and progressive state laws such as in Michigan (mandatory services for handicapped children from birth to 26 years of age) have provided the impetus for comprehensive services to all age groups.

O&M should be broadly defined within the developmental perspective for both preschool and multiply handicapped populations. It is particularly important that the teacher, O&M instructor, and other professionals (occupational therapists, physical therapists, adapted physical education teachers, etc.) and parents work as a coordinated team when designing and implementing O&M services for preschool and multiply handicapped, visually handicapped populations (Hill, Rosen, Correa, & Langley, 1984; Langley, 1980). The following brief overview of motor development and other developmental skills specifically related to O&M supplements information presented in Chapters 4, 7, and 9.

Motor Development

The motor development of congenitally blind children is not markedly different from that of sighted children in the first few months of life (Warren, 1984). However, there is a reported lag of crawling and walking with these children (Fraiberg, Smith, & Adelson, 1969; Norris, Spaulding and Brodie, 1957). Langley's (1977) summary of some important development motor milestones in relationship to sighted children appear in Table 19.2.

Table 19.2   Developmental milestones in motor patterns among young blind children

Motor Behavior	Expected Age	Blind
Head up from prone	1 month	4 months
Elevates self on elbows	4 months	8.75 months
Reaches	3-5 months	8 months
Sits	6-8 months	8 months
Raises to sitting	8 months	11 months
Creeps	7 months	13 months
Stepping movements when supported	8.8 months	10.75 months
Stands by using furniture	8.6 months	13 months
Stands alone	11 months	13 months
Walks three steps	11.7 months	15 months
Walks alone	12-15 months	19 months

Adapted from: M.B. Langley, Developmental guidelines for teachers and evaluators of multihandicapped children in *An introduction to assessment of severely profoundly handicapped children: Module III* Austin, Tex.: Education Service Center, Region XIII.

The development of good gross and fine motor abilities are important prerequisites for formal O&M skill training. Efficient gross motor skills facilitate environmental exploration and movement through the environment. Efficient fine motor skills facilitate the exploration and manipulation of objects and are necessary as well for learning how to use a cane. Good posture and gait are particularly important prerequisites for utilizing any system of mobility such as the cane or dog guide.

A Guide to Developmental Skills Related to O&M

Correa (1982) and Correa and Hill (in progress) have developed (from the literature and practical experience) guidelines to developmental skills related to O&M (see Chart 19.5). The purpose of the guidelines is to provide teachers and O&M specialists with an understanding of developmental sequences in areas which closely pertain to O&M, such as gross motor, fine motor, sensory-motor, and concept development. In addition, the more traditional O&M skills applicable to preschool visually handicapped children are included. The guidelines should serve as a quick reference list for pinpointing general assessment and intervention areas when working with preschool and/or multiply handicapped visually handicapped populations.

Orientation and Mobility is an important support service in the comprehensive delivery of services to visually handicapped children. With the implementation of P.L. 94-142, the O&M instructor serves as an integral part of the multidisciplinary team in developing and implementing individualized educational programs (IEPs) for visually handicapped children.

Orientation is the process of utilizing sensory information to establish and maintain one's position in the environment. Mobility is the process of moving safely, efficiently, and gracefully within one's environment. The ultimate goal of O&M instruction is for visually handicapped persons to be able to travel in any environment as independently as possible. Because of the heterogeneous nature of the visually handicapped population being served, e.g., multiply handicapped, low vision, preschool, etc., the definition of O&M must be broad. The process of O&M instruction encompasses much more than the teaching of traditional, formal O&M skills and techniques. Concept development, sensory training, and motor development are all an integral part of O&M instruction. Orientation and Mobility is an important life span process which cannot be taught in isolation. A team approach involving the O&M instructor, teacher of the visually handicapped, other school personnel, and parents is necessary in order for visually handicapped children to realize their full potential in the area of O&M.

Many visually handicapped children need formal instruction in concept development before they are able to master advanced travel skills and techniques. Body image concept (knowledge of body parts, relationships of body parts, function and movement of body parts); spatial concepts (concept of position, shape, size, and measurement); and environmental concepts, (corner street, block, etc.), are all important prerequisite concepts which enhance safe, efficient, and independent O&M. Although it is the role of the O&M instructor to design and implement instruction in this area, concept development is not, and neither should it be, the exclusive domain of O&M. In order for concept development instruction to be effective with visually handicapped children, a coordinated effort of concept development instruction must be implemented. The teacher of the visually handicapped, regular class teacher(s), other key professionals, and the parents must work cooperatively with the O&M instructor in order for such instruction to be effective.

The senses play an important role in identifying, interpreting, and utilizing environmental information for purposeful movement. The teacher can assist the O&M instructor in developing, implementing, and coordinating instructional activities in the area of sensory skills training. Some of the important areas are: (a) auditory—sound localization, identification, discrimination, and echolocation; (b) tactile (textures and temperatures)—identification and discrimination; (c) kinesthetic and proprioceptive; (d) olfactory; and (e) vision—teaching low vision children what, how, and when to look for things in their environment as well as reinforce the proper use of low vision aids when applicable. (See Chapters 5 & 6.)

Formal orientation instruction entails such skills areas as the following: (a) identifying and utilizing landmarks and clues; (b) knowledge and use of compass directions; (c) knowledge and use of indoor and city numbering systems; (d) the ability to align the body to objects and with sounds for the purpose of establishing and/or maintaining a straight line of travel; (e) the use of systematic search patterns to explore novel objects or environments; (f) recovery skills; and (g) the knowledge and use of where, when, and how to solicit aid. The teacher can reinforce many of these formal orientation skills by integrating them in such subject matter as science, math, and social studies. The teacher can play an important role in introducing and reinforcing such formal mobility skills as sighted guide skills and protective techniques. It is also important for the teacher to reinforce the proper use of cane skills when applicable.

The development of gross and fine motor abilities is of particular importance when working with preschool and multiply handicapped/visually handicapped children. The teacher and O&M instructor should work cooperatively with the occupational therapist, physical therapist, and adapted physical education instructor, in implementing an instructional program in the area of motor development.

The development of good gross and fine motor abilities are important prerequisites for formal O&M skill training. Good posture and gait are particularly important prerequisites for utilizing any system of O&M such as the cane or dog guide.

Finally, the teacher should be aware of the important developmental milestones which affect O&M. The teacher can play a critical role in developing many of the prerequisite skills necessary for independent travel.

Study questions

1. What are some of the inherent values in O&M instruction?

2. Why has the definition of O&M become broader in recent years? Besides formal O&M skills, what other curricular areas should be included in the broader definition of O&M?

3. Discuss the advantages and disadvantages of the various mobility systems. Is it possible for visually handicapped persons to use more than one system? Why or why not?

4. Which Electronic Travel Aid(s) has/have both obstacle detection and environmental sensing capabilities? Discuss the implications of sensory training and concept development for visually handicapped children with the various electronic travel aids.

5. Why is the development of spatial and environmental concepts difficult for visually handicapped children? What is the relationship of concept development to formal O&M skills? How can teachers assist in the development of concepts in the context of their role?

6. Discuss some of the strengths and weaknesses of the formal instruments which assess spatial concepts. What are some informal assessment procedures a teacher could use to assess concept development?

7. Describe the three component processes of orientation. Discuss the role of the teacher in facilitating the development of orientation processes. Describe and discuss some informal procedures that a teacher might use in assessing orientation.

8. Discuss the role of the teacher in the instruction and reinforcement of formal mobility skills.

9. Identify and describe the important developmental prerequisites which are necessary prior to formal instruction of the long cane.

10. Identify a developmental skill or cluster of skills related to O&M. Design a team approach strategy to facilitate the development of the skill(s) you have identified.

Chart 19.5   A guide to the development of skills related to orientation and mobility.

	Gross Motor Activities	Fine Motor/Activities	Concept Activities	Formal Orientation Skills Activities	Formal Mobility Skills Activities
Birth-6 months	Reflex integration Head control Protective responses Balance Rolling Sitting Pushing up in prone Backward crawling Pivot movement	Grasping (ulnar palmer) Reaching Inspects hands/fingers Beginning midline skills Hitting/banging/raking Holds objects in both hands Responds to touch of different texture Head turning to sound	Body awareness (exploration of own body) Curiosity of events in environment		
6-12 months	Beginning of locomotion Up on hands-knees Creeping Sits unsupported Trunk rotation Cruises furniture Stands unsupported	Reach-grasps (radial & pincer) Releases toys Imitates actions with objects Picks up small objects Strikes one object with other Transfers objects Puts objects in container	Awareness of self and others: social Beginning of spatial relations with objects Object Permanence		
12-24 months	Walks-wide gait Runs Pushes/pulls toys Climbs Maneuvers steps Jumps	Trial and error exploration Wrist rotation (door knob) Plays with pop-beads, stacking rings, formboards	Object identification (object concept) Points to own body parts		
2-3 years	Good balance (stands on one foot) Walks upstairs: one foot on each step	Unbuttons Puzzles Copies shapes/prewriting Stacks rings/correct sequence	Big and little Object function Matches textures In, on, under Wet, dry	Establishes idea of a reference point Systematic search patterns with hands Uses landmarks and clues	Simple sighted guide skills Trailing

Age					
3-4 years	Pedals tricycle Walks on tiptoes Walks backwards and sideways Uses jungle gym	Strings small beads Removes/inserts small pegs Opens & closes doors, cabinets, drawers, and windows	Names shapes Sorts different textures Identifies smells Names top, bottom, front, back and sides of object Matches sounds Matches long and short toys Knows heavy/light Association of objects Same-different Number concepts Names body parts on doll/others Names body planes (top of head, etc.) Transfers image to body movement	Develops echolocation skills Travels Simple Routes Perpendicular and Parallel Alignment	Intermediate to advanced sighted guide skills Upper hand and forearm Lower hand and forearm
4-5 years	Uses teeter-totter Pedals tricycle, turning corner Hops on one foot Runs changing direction	Wraps object in foil Cuts 2"curve on paper Makes clay shapes Laces sewing cards Uses pinch clothes pins Locates with sound cue: near or far Locates dropped objects with sound cue	Tells function of body parts Describes objects as soft, rough, or smooth Names textures/fabrics First, middle, and last Loud/soft sounds	Reserves routes Problem solving skills	Advanced sighted guide skills Diagonal cane technique

Additional readings

Hill, E. (1976). *Orientation and mobility techniques: A guide for the practitioner.* New York, N.Y.: American Foundation for the Blind, Inc.

Hill, E.W. and Blasch, B.B. (1980). Concept development. In R.L. Welsh & B.B. Blasch (eds.). *Foundations of orientation and mobility.* New York, N.Y.: American Foundation for the Blind, Inc.

Illinois Office of Education (1974). *A curriculum guide for the development of body and sensory awareness for the visually impaired.* Springfield, Ill.: Author.

Langley, M.B. (1980). *Assessment of multihandicapped, visually impaired children.* Chicago, Ill.: Stoelting Company.

Leary, B. and von Schneden, M. (1982). *"Simon says" is not the only game.* New York, N.Y.: American Foundation for the Blind, Inc.

Lowenfeld, B. (1981). *Berthold Lowenfeld on blindness and blind people.* New York, N.Y.: American Foundation for the Blind, Inc.

Swallow, R., Mangold, S., and Mangold, P. (1978). *Informal assessment of the visually impaired.* New York, N.Y.: American Foundation for the Blind, Inc.

Tooze, D. (1980). *Independence training for visually handicapped children.* Baltimore, Md.: University Park Press.

Warren, D.H. (1984). *Blindness and early childhood development.* New York, N.Y.: American Foundation for the Blind, Inc.

Welsh, R.L. and Blasch, B.B. (eds.). (1980). *Foundations of orientation and mobility.* New York, N.Y.: American Foundation for the Blind, Inc.

Welsh, R.L. and Weiner, W. (1976). *Travel in adverse weather conditions.* New York, N.Y.: American Foundation for the Blind, Inc.

CHAPTER 20

Social Skills

Kathleen Mary Huebner

This chapter provides guidelines for learning experiences in social skill areas. It addresses components, content areas, methods, and strategies which can be applied by teachers, parents, and other significant adults in the following social skill areas: daily living skills, interpersonal skill development, nonverbal communication, sex education, dating, recreation and leisure.

GENERAL GUIDELINES

The following general guidelines apply to all areas of social skills dealt with in this chapter. The guidelines presented are assessment, age appropriateness of skills taught, orientation to surroundings and materials, transference of learned skills to new situations and settings, and task analysis.

Assessment

Before instruction begins for any given skill, students should be assessed to determine their levels of ability in the skill or task in question. They should be observed in natural environments to determine which skills have already been acquired. Since there are many ways of accomplishing tasks, flexiblity of methods must be allowed. Students will often develop their own techniques and strategies through discovery learning. Whether students need to receive initial or continued instruction, or reinforcement or practice of any task can be determined by observing whether they complete the task with: (1) safety; (2) poise; (3) independence; (4) confidence; and (5) in a traditional manner.

Safety

Students must perform tasks safely, that is, without harm to themselves or others.

Poise

Poise is synonymous with self-possessed assurance, composure, and dignity. Poise while performing tasks helps those who interact with children to view them as competent, and thereby reinforces their self-confidence. Children who appear nervous or hesitant while performing a task such as pouring a glass of milk will often be offered assistance. Even if they know they can do it, they may view such offers as signs of incompetence. When children are poised, it is less likely that someone will offer to do things for them, and this trust reinforces their self confidence.

Independence

Students should perform tasks independently, that is, without the assistance of others and without relying on someone else for guidance.

Confidence

Confidence is a conscious feeling of certainty, surety, and self-reliance. The students' confidence in their ability to perform tasks assists in the development of their self-concept and self-worth (McMakin, 1976).

Traditional Manner

"Traditional manner" means that the task is performed in a way which is socially acceptable in the student's culture. It is possible to eat warm oatmeal, safely, independently, with confidence and poise, by scooping the cereal up to the mouth using only the fingers. However, in cultures similar to those of the United States, this is not the traditional manner.

It is critical that teachers be sensitive, that is, aware and responsive to students' and parents' cultures, customs, traditions, religious beliefs, abilities, needs, concerns, and feelings. (See Chapter 10.)

Age Appropriateness

Most skills are developmental; therefore students' ages, experiences, and maturation should be considered when deciding when to initiate instruction of specific skills. Age appropriate tasks are those that match children's developmental age, abilities, and interests rather than just their chronological age. Early instruction must begin at home. The parents and ideally a teacher qualified in early education of the visually handicapped provide the first training. Later instruction should be integrated into students' programs throughout the school years (Schultz, 1968). Learning experiences and instruction should be given in a clear, concise, and timely manner so visually handicapped students have the opportunity for parallel development with their peers.

Orientation

Orient students to the immediate surroundings in which the instruction will be given. The setting should be as realistic as possible. For example, when teaching how to spread various food products, e.g., butter on bread, the setting should be a kitchen table, counter, or dining-room table. The objective should be explained. Students should be oriented to and knowledgeable about equipment and materials, and be able to recognize them.

Transference

To transfer a learned skill to a new setting, students must understand all the concepts involved in mastering a skill and apply and demonstrate their understanding and ability in various situations. Once the skill is learned, students should have the opportunity to apply the skills in different ways. Give students the opportunity to practice a skill in other settings, such as in the cafeteria or the kitchen.

As students acquire competencies, they should be incorporated into realistic experiences. For example, students who learned to travel independently in small business areas, to identify money and keep it organized in their wallets, to cut meat, and to interact with waitresses, could be assigned to a neighborhood restaurant, order a meal that includes food which requires cutting, and pay their bill. This requires students to use old and new learning, and apply planning, organizational, and decision-making skills.

Task Analysis

A process that can be used with virtually every activity from relatively simple ones like buttoning a shirt to complex ones like ironing a shirt, is task analysis. This process breaks a task into subtasks and identifies each component behavior to be performed in the natural sequence of activity. It gives students the opportunity to experience a sequence of successes while learning to complete an entire task. Task analysis can be used to guide decisions and help identify:
(1) the steps necessary to complete a task;

(2) the sequence of steps to complete a task;
(3) the next step to be taught in a task sequence;
(4) the part(s) of a task a student is having difficulty with and thereby requires further instruction;
(5) the part(s) of a task learned but requiring continued practice;
(6) the part(s) of a task learned and performed independently;
(7) the adaptations necessary for a particular child to successfully complete a task; and
(8) the options possible when independent completion of a task is not feasible (Bigge, 1982).

Before analyzing a specific task to determine the instructional sequence, the teacher should determine the terminal behavior or objective to be met by the students, and the prerequisite skills students must have to proceed smoothly through the process. Prerequisite skills vary depending on the task. Some general categories are self-help, fine motor, gross motor, safety awareness, body-image concepts, spatial relationships, sensory awareness concepts, and familiarity with materials to be used. Once terminal behaviors, objectives, and prerequisite skills are determined, analyzing the task to determine the instructional sequence begins.

Assemble all equipment and materials needed to perform the task to be analyzed and place them on a work space in an organized fashion. Several strategies can be used to develop a task analysis. With the first two strategies a blindfold or low vision stimulator is worn. Each step is recorded in the sequence used to complete the task. The first strategy employs the use of a tape recorder which leaves the hands free to perform the task. Every step is spoken and recorded. The second strategy uses a blindfolded partner who performs the task while the nonblindfolded person verbally records and writes down every observed step. With the third strategy the task is performed without wearing the blindfold and each step is recorded as it is completed. This last strategy is generally the least effective and should only be used when a tape recorder or partner is unavailable.

Once the steps are recorded, try to complete the activity exactly as outlined, doing no more and no less. Repeat the process until the task can be completed by following the identified steps. (Examples of task analyses are also provided in Chapter 9.)

As the task analysis is used with students, changes may be needed. In writing it, include only one action in each step. Some students naturally combine steps, others require a single action breakdown. The terms dominant and nondominant or preferred and nonpreferred hands should be used in writing task analyses, not the instructions, so that they will apply to right- and left-handed students.

Once a task is analyzed into its sequential component parts, the identified subskills can be used to collect baseline data and develop checklists, goals and objectives (Bigge, 1982). Avoid unnecessary repetitions and delays in progress by developing goals and objectives, teaching tasks in sequential and definitive steps, providing appropriate reinforcement, and maintaining records.

DAILY LIVING SKILLS

The ability to perform routine activities of daily living is critical for one's well being and self-concept. Every-day countless activities are performed which are essential to self-care and personal management. Visual observation and incidental learning are not accessible avenues of learning for children who have neither sight or limited sight. These children cannot observe movements, actions, or manipulation of objects performed by others. Thus, it is critical for visually handicapped students to actively participate in age appropriate routine activities in the home, school, and other environments. If adults restrict and overprotect, then the result will be dependent children who lack the ability to perform routine tasks.

Several synonymous terms are used for formal curricula which address skills of daily living: daily living skills (DLS), activities of daily living (ADL), techniques of daily living (TDL), self-care, self-help, and personal management. The curricula provide students with skills needed to perform routine activities including table etiquette; eating; hygiene; personal grooming, organization, and clothing care; food preparation, house care; money management; shopping; sewing; telephone use; time-telling; child care; and minor household maintenance. (American Foundation for the Blind, 1974; Inkster, 1977; Wehrum, 1977; Yeadon, 1974).

Learning activities of daily living is, however, an ongoing process, and their teaching goes beyond a formal curricula which is presented in school. Teaching daily living skills is the responsibility of all significant adults in students' lives. The content of this section applies to both a formal daily living skill curricula and the day-to-day experiences students should have in the home, educational setting, and community.

Table Etiquette

Mealtimes should be relaxing and pleasurable. Regardless of the setting or occasion, social etiquette behaviors such as the use of napkins, appropriate voice level, and orientation to table settings remain constant. Other table etiquette behaviors such as posture and placement positions of glass and silver-ware vary depending on the formality of the occasion.

Visually handicapped students' training in table behaviors and skills should include graceful sitting at the table; posture; purpose, placement and handling of napkins, utensils, dishes, glassware, and serving containers; conversation; self-orientation to table settings and common areas of the table; voice level; table manners; and ordering food in restaurants. (American Foundation for the Blind, 1974; Davidow, 1974; Wehrum, 1977; Yeadon, 1974).

Sufficient instruction and practice in a variety of settings must be provided in all aspects of table etiquette until appropriate skills become routine habits and students feel confident, relaxed, and enjoy the social aspects of mealtime.

Eating Skills

For visually handicapped students, eating can be a difficult, embarrassing, and stressful experience if thoughtful and consistent instruction is not provided. If students do not learn eating skills appropriate to their age, and as a result must receive instruction in skills generally reserved for younger children, eating will not be pleasurable, and may become associated with feelings of inadequacy, apprehension, shame, and guilt (Mangold, 1980).

Many young visually handicapped children need to be taught how to finger feed themselves; sometimes even basic chewing motions must be taught. Eating skills should be introduced at mealtime, at the table with the family present, so that the social aspects of mealtime can also be learned.

Several curriculum guides are available which describe specific, and slightly different techniques for teaching eating skills to the blind student. (See additional readings).

Some techniques are the same or similar to those used by sighted persons; others are modified or have been developed for visually handicapped individuals. An example of a modified technique is one used for scooping foods with a fork. A sighted person uses a fork to scoop foods such as peas, corn kernels, or jellied vegetable salad by putting the tips of the tines of the fork directly into the food to be scooped. Visually handicapped students may have difficulty in doing the same without inadvertently pushing the food being scooped into another food on the plate, or pushing it off the dish. Therefore, a technique often taught is the use of a piece of bread, knife, or sometimes a spoon depending on the food, as a back-up, support, or wall in conjunction with the fork. (See curricular guides for detailed techniques.)

An example of a technique which has been developed specifically for visually handicapped individuals is one which is used to locate and differentiate among various foods on a dinner plate. A sighted individual looks at a plate of food to determine what or where the various portions are. In the home setting the menu should be made known to the student. In a restaurant, the student chooses his food so it is not necessary to determine what is on the plate, but where it is. Visually handicapped students are taught to use a systematic investigative procedure, by holding the fork horizontally with the prongs facing up and gently tapping and moving the bottom of the length of the tines of the fork across the food portions in a clockwise fashion around the inner circumference of the plate. They must learn to interpret the sensory information received through the fork, as to the size, shape, texture, and consistency of the foods. Therefore, they are able to distinguish the location and proportions of various products on the plate.

Whenever possible, use real food and let students consume it as they learn. This provides direct feedback.

With instruction and reinforcement they will learn to hold the utensil level and judge the weight of an appropriately filled utensil. Learning to cut meats and other foods into bite size pieces can be a lengthy process and takes more practice than mealtimes allow. This skill is often taught and practiced with only clay or sliced raw potatoes. Frequently the continental method of cutting and lifting meat products to the mouth is simpler for visually handicapped persons. Uncooked rice or sand can be used to teach scooping, serving oneself from bowls, and pouring. Sliced raw potatoes may be used to teach serving oneself from a platter. Teachers should check for allergies before using real foods.

Once students have learned various eating skills, feedback and reinforcement should be provided during meals.

Hygiene, Personal Grooming/ Organization, and Clothing Care

Hygiene, personal grooming/organization, and clothing care skills often overlap. Explanations of the need for, and the effects of hygiene and personal grooming/ organization, and clothing care on health and interpersonal relationships should be provided. Generally techniques are taught which will assist students in performing the following activities:

The use and care of bathroom fixtures—sink, toilet, urinal, bathtub, and shower

Use of soaps, powders, and towels—washing, bathing, and drying of body parts and body

The care of teeth—brushing, rinsing, flossing, and use of mouthwash

The use of deodorants—creams, roll-ons, and sprays

The removal of unwanted body hair—dipilatories, electric and safety razors, shaving creams, gels, foams, after-shave lotions, tweezers, and styptic pencils

The care of prosthetic eyes—removal, cleaning, and insertion

Nail care—manicure, pedicure, and application/ removal of polish

The use of cosmetics—lotions, creams, skin freshener, astringents and moisturizers, foundations, rouge and blushers, face powders, lipstick, gloss, eye shadow, eyebrow make-up, and eye liner

Hair care—brushing, combing, styling, cutting, washing, blow drying, and setting

The use and self-administration of medication—pills, capsules, liquids, and injection (with the cooperative efforts of medical personnel)

The organization of toiletries, cosmetics, clothing, and personal belongings

Clothing care—washing, drying, brushing, dry cleaning, and repair

Shoe care—polishing, repair, and purchasing

Clothing storage—methods for identification and organization, folding, hanging, and packing

Appropriateness of clothing—seasonal, informal, semi-formal and formal, styles and fads

Apparel shopping—where, when, how, why.

Reinforcement of visually handicapped students' efforts must be both intrinsic and extrinsic. Sighted persons get feedback for efforts to "look good" by glancing in a mirror. Visually handicapped students need to learn to appreciate their efforts through the use of other senses, as well as from the reactions of others toward them. In our society cleanliness and good grooming are the norm. Poorly groomed sighted persons are often considered "lazy, rude, ignorant or lacking in self-respect." Poorly groomed blind persons are "usually pitied as being incompetent in maintaining basic standards" (Wehrum, 1977, p. 40).

Instruction in hygiene, grooming, and clothing care provides many opportunities to teach or reinforce basic concepts. Identification of body parts, their functions, range of motion, and relationship to each other and others can easily be incorporated into lessons such as washing hands, make-up application, and folding shirts. Spatial concepts such as under, over, above, below, front, side, left, and right should also be incorporated into lessons.

Learning experiences in hygiene and grooming should be presented in their entirety as often as possible, particularly to congenitally blind children. For example, if the objective of a particular day's lesson is to apply toothpaste to a toothbrush, the entire sequence of brushing the teeth should be completed.

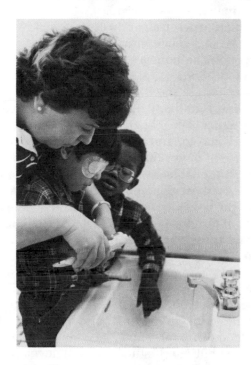

Appropriate reinforcement should be given to students as they proceed to the step in which they are to be instructed. Instruction is then provided, repeated as necessary, in the technique to be used for applying an appropriate amount of toothpaste on the brush. The teacher should assist the students as necessary, in completing the task. When the students are able to perform the complete task with safety, confidence, independence, poise, and in a traditional manner, begin to teach a new task. Check from time to time to determine whether students have retained learned tasks and incorporated newly acquired skills into their daily routine.

Food Preparation

Learning about foods and their preparation begins at home as part of the daily routine. Most toddlers enjoy playing with pots, pans, plastic dishes, cups, tumblers, and wooden spoons on the kitchen floor while dinner is prepared. Visually handicapped toddlers should be given the same opportunities to learn about kitchen items and begin to associate the smells, sounds, and activities of food preparation with mealtime and eating.

Although it can be stressful, parents should be encouraged to take their visually handicapped children on shopping trips. The children should be permitted to examine food on display. Parts should be identified, uses explained, and methods for determining quality taught. When the children are older, the cost and weight of items and methods of preparation should also be explained. Special trips to farm or produce markets where food is displayed without protective coverings are recommended. Products such as meat should be examined with protective coverings in the market and then at home without them. Fat, bones, and meaty portions should be tactually examined and shapes of various cuts of meat explained. Participation in helping to put groceries away gives children further sensory exposure and helps them learn which products require refrigeration, freezing, or dry storage. Methods for labeling canned, frozen, and dry food products should be introduced when students have learned to read and write.

Age appropriate responsibilities should be given to students. If children do not have these experiences while growing up, it is difficult to compensate for the knowledge which would have been acquired routinely. If their only exposure to food is when it is cooked and served in portions, it is not unusual for them to be unable to identify products in their natural state.

There are curricular guides which can be used to familiarize the visually handicapped student with their food. Guides developed for other populations, such as standard household arts and home economics courses, and those for use with developmentally delayed students can be used with modifications to allow for use of the other senses. Many residential schools for the visually handicapped have also developed curricular guides. (See additional readings.)

Parents are often fearful of the dangers of food preparation tasks. These fears must be dispelled by demonstrating safety techniques. The students should be instructed until they have the ability to perform tasks safely.

The teacher of visually handicapped students is responsible for assisting the parents and the home economics teachers with the unique needs and safety techniques involved. The teacher of visually handicapped children should intermittently accompany students to home economics classes to observe, demonstrate, and assist as necessary, and to develop and maintain an ongoing and effective line of communication with the teacher and parents.

House Care

Basic house care routines should be learned through instruction from parents and teachers. The children should be taught care for toys, books, and clothing, and learn to put things where they belong so they can be located when wanted. This is more important for visually handicapped children than for sighted children. Visually handicapped children cannot walk into a room and visually scan its contents to locate the desired toy, book, or garment. Having good organizational skills will minimize the children's frustration as well as that of other members of the household. Therefore, organization should be an integral part of all daily living skill learning experiences.

As children mature, age appropriate responsibilities for which they are accountable should be added. Children should be encouraged to do small jobs both in the home and in the community. Adults responsible for educating students need to keep in mind that they will someday be responsible for their belongings, dormitory room, apartment, and home; therefore, they need to learn all the skills required to maintain their households.

Teachers should encourage parents to involve their visually handicapped children in all routine household care procedures, to carefully explain why they are performing maintenance activities, and demonstrate how each activity is accomplished. The teacher should communicate frequently with the students and parents to determine: (1) in which household maintenance activities children are participating; (2) the quality of the work being done by the students; and (3) if the parents need any assistance in determining an effective and efficient technique for the children to use.

Money Management/Shopping

Tactual identification of United States coins is not difficult. The size, thickness, and smooth versus serrated edges makes accurate identification simple. When students learn to count money and make change in the classroom, they often use worksheets with pictorial representations of coins. Visually handicapped students need real coins and currency for counting and making change exercises.

Since tactual determination of United States paper currency is not possible, visually handicapped students must rely on the honesty of sighted persons for its initial identification. A paper money identifier is available through the American Foundation for the Blind, but it is unlikely that students will have such a device available to them on a daily basis. Students will need some general guidelines: (1) cash checks or money orders, or get change for bills of large denominations, in a reliable establishment; (2) pay for items with the smallest denomination of bills possible to increase the possibility of getting correct change. For example, if purchasing an $8.00 item, give the clerk a five and three one dollar bills or a ten dollar bill, not a twenty if it is avoidable.

There are various methods of folding identified paper currency and organizing it in the wallet. Generally because the one dollar bill is used most frequently it is left unfolded. The remaining denominations are each folded differently and placed in different positions in the billfold. If students have developed and use a particular system consistently, effectively, and efficiently, do not change it.

Visually handicapped students should have many shopping and bill paying experiences and learn general costs of products ranging from candy bars, hamburgers, and soft drinks, to furniture, appliances, utilities, and housing costs. They need to learn where to shop for food, clothing, and household products as well.

Students also need to learn to appreciate the cost of things and become intelligent consumers. Parents should give them tasks and responsibilities around the home and an allowance. They should learn that they will need to work, be responsible, and save what they earn to purchase items for themselves or as gifts for family and friends.

Students should become familiar with the layouts of neighborhood markets and stores and, as they become independent travelers, sent on shopping errands. They should be given opportunities to develop communication skills with clerks in order to locate items, select clothing, and match colors and accessories. Students should be familiar with local radio-reading services which announce sales or read newspaper advertisements. They should learn comparative shopping skills and how to maintain financial records and budgets.

Sewing

Both male and female visually handicapped students should be able to do minor mending and clothing repairs, such as sewing on buttons, mending seams, and repairing hems. Various techniques for threading a needle, such as using a wire loop needle threader, automatic needle threaders or self-threading needles need to be taught. Students will need to learn how to estimate thread lengths, cut, and knot; tactually and accurately locate button placements and holes of buttons, and use straight or cross sewing techniques to replace two and four hole and shank type buttons; sew on snaps, hooks and eyes; identify right and wrong sides of fabrics, accurately mark and turn up hems with pins, sew various stitches and hems; evenly adjust seam edges, pin pieces of fabric together, and sew seams together (Markle, 1977; Yeadon & Newman, 1980).

If students are interested in advanced sewing skills, including use of sewing machines and constructing garments, they should be encouraged. Modifications will be necessary and the tactual sense will be used as a substitute for vision. For students with low vision, high contrast helps. Patterns can be prepared so that visually handicapped students can lay out, pin, cut, and recut fabrics independently.

Telephone Use

Communicating with someone who is not physically present is a difficult concept for most children to understand. This difficulty is often intensified by a lack of or limited vision. Direct instruction is needed to involve children with the telephone. They should be encouraged to play with a toy telephone and included in real telephone conversations with parents, family members, and others they know.

Later, students should learn reliable techniques for using push button, rotary dial, and pay telephones. They must learn to accurately dial telephone numbers, including area codes, within the time

allotted so they will not be disconnected before completing the connection. Encourage them to call friends and relatives. They should also learn to use the telephone to gather information and to accurately record important facts. For example, students should make calls to determine the time at which a movie or sporting event starts. They can record this information in braille, large print, or on audio tape. They should gradually gather more complex information, such as bus stop location, time of departure, travel time, and return bus stop and time schedules. This information is most easily recorded by repeating the information to the person giving the information while making an audio tape recording. The student confirms the information and records it for future reference simultaneously.

The student should also be taught to compile and maintain a personal telephone directory and use phone directories with a magnification or optical scanning device. He should be familiar with the cost of purchasing and/or renting telephones, and monthly and long distance call charges.

Although large print dials and large push button phones are available, students with low vision should become proficient in a tactile method so they will be confident in using public telephones—which are not equipped with large print.

Time Telling

Direct intervention is required to teach the visually handicapped student time concepts. Students should learn to use and accurately read the time on tactual or large print clocks and watches, estimate passages of time during active and inactive periods, and the length of time needed to accomplish various tasks so that planning and organization of time can be achieved (Kimbrough, Huebner, & Lowry, 1976). Encourage the use of speech output clocks and watches early in children's time experiences. They can be fun, motivating, and helpful in instruction.

Child Care

Parents and teachers should encourage visually handicapped children to play with infant-like dolls and be shown how to pick up, hold, feed, burp, change, bathe and powder, dress, and demonstrate affection. As children grow older they should be guided how to do the same with real babies (Rahn, 1972). Visually handicapped children should also help with siblings and children of relatives, family, friends, and neighbors. Parents need to encourage their visually handicapped children to participate in scouting and community sponsored school child care courses. Skills needed by responsible and trusted baby sitters must be taught throughout students' early years. After visually handicapped children have completed child care training, parents should encourage them to baby sit for younger siblings, relatives, and neighbors.

Minor Household Maintenance

Minor household repairs such as labeling and switching circuit breakers, replacing fuses, hammering a nail, hanging pictures and other wall ornamentation, putting up curtain rods, screwing "C" hooks into cabinets, tightening screwed items such as chair legs, and replacing light bulbs are procedures which most individuals complete routinely. Most households have basic screwdrivers, hammers, pliers, nails, and screws handy so that minor repairs can be completed as the need arises. Visually handicapped students should receive basic instruction which will enable them to safely, independently, and confidently complete such basic household maintenance activities.

The teacher of visually handicapped students should communicate regularly with the parents, the industrial arts teacher, metal and wood shop teachers and others who teach household maintenance skills. Some residential schools for the blind have developed curricula and techniques which may be helpful. Parents and teachers should also get visually handicapped students involved in work experience programs.

Teachers of visually handicapped students must observe their students in all types of situations in order to observe their strengths and weaknesses in daily living skills. In addition, it is critical that they incorporate daily living skill objectives in the student's individualized education program (see Chapter 12). Students' development of daily living skills should not be left to chance. Communication among all the significant adults in

children's lives is critical. Time must be found in the teachers', children's, and parents' schedules to provide meaningful learning experiences in daily living activities.

INTERPERSONAL SKILL DEVELOPMENT

This section discusses problems unique to visually handicapped students in interpersonal skill development and suggests strategies to minimize or circumvent the difficulties. Specific topics covered are stereotypic behaviors, nonverbal communication, sex education, and dating.

There is little significant research on the development of social interaction of visually handicapped children and youth, but it has been studied in other areas of exceptionality. La Greca and Mesibov (1979) noted that a significant factor contributing to the

psychosocial adjustment of children is the quality of their peer relationships. Others have found that peer acceptance is positively related to good mental health (Glidwell, Kantor, Smith, and Steinger, 1966). Early intervention strategies which positively affect visually handicapped students' peer relationships are important for social and emotional growth and development. As students grow older, the demands and skills required for successful social interactions become increasingly complex" (La Greca & Mesibov, 1979, p. 234).

Stereotypic Behaviors

Repetitive motor behaviors, such as body rocking, head swaying, and eye rubbing, which are socially inappropriate because of their *quality, frequency*, and *intensity* are commonly referred to as blind mannerisms or blindisms (Jan, Freeman, & Scott, 1977). These terms are misnomers, because these behaviors are observed in many children (Burlingham, 1965; Gruber & Moore, 1963; Warren, 1984). Various types of stereotypic behaviors and factors which relate to the probable causation of such behaviors on social interactions, factors to consider prior to intervention, and strategies of prevention and extinction are presented here.

Effects of Stereotypic Behaviors

Regardless of the factors which cause visually handicapped children and youth to engage in stereotypic behaviors, one must consider their effects on the children and others. Such behaviors can lead parents and others to fear children, fear for them, or falsely believe that they are developmentally delayed, autistic, or emotionally disturbed. They can lead to teasing by other children and social segregation. If stereotypic behaviors are frequent, they may interfere with the children's ability to be receptive to learning or other stimulation in the environment. The children may also become increasingly withdrawn from reality. Such behaviors are unsightly, abusive, and can lead to physical injury (Warren, 1984). Constant eye rubbing and eye gouging can discolor the skin around the eye and cause it to become callous-like. Intervention to reduce and dispel such behaviors is nearly always indicated.

Considerations Prior to Intervention

Before intervention, several factors should be considered. How serious is the behavior? Assess the frequency of the behavior, determine when and why it occurs, and the results of the particular behavior.

Who is affected by the behavior? Are the children affected because they withdraw from reality when involved in stereotypic behaviors? Do teachers find it difficult to instruct children when they are actively performing stereotypic behaviors? Do parents and other care givers react negatively and does this affect their interactions with the children? Do siblings and peers become fearful when observing such behaviors? Do peers hesitate to engage in conversation and interactions with the children?

Are such behaviors interfering with the children's learning (Caetano & Kauffman, 1975; Hoshmand, 1975)? Will you do more harm than good by interfering and extinguishing them? What will happen if you do not intervene? What are the children's levels of understanding? Can you rationalize with them? Can they control, or learn to control their behaviors? Can they understand the effects of their behaviors on others?

Consider Piaget's theory of normal development in respect to self-manipulation to object manipulation. If you extend the self-manipulation period, you delay normal development. If children engage in stereotypic behaviors in novel situations, they will tend not to sustain contact with the novel stimulus or situation and will therefore be delayed in the quality and quantity of such experiences (Warren, 1984).

Keep in mind the long and short term effects on social interactions should the stereotypic behavior continue through childhood, adolescence, and adulthood. All of these factors should be considered before planning and implementing a program designed to extinguish the undesirable behavior.

Intervention Strategies

Cutsforth (1951) stated in reference to "blindisms" that "correction, prohibition, punishment are utterly futile unless a child can find a substitute activity" (p. 6); therefore, physical activity needs to be redirected. Since the 1950s many parents, teachers, researchers, and other professionals have implemented programs to either prevent stereotypic behaviors from starting or extinguish those which have developed and persist. Causal factors of stereotypic behaviors include sensory deprivation, restricted locomotion, social deprivation, inadequate primary child caregiver-child relationships, photophobia, limited motor/physical activity, lack of ability to imitate, and lack of variety of activities.

Prevention Although research is limited, it is a rational conclusion that appropriate early intervention will reduce stereotypic behaviors. Objectives designed for visually handicapped infants and young children should equip primary child caregivers with the skills and abilities to provide the youngsters with adequate sensory stimulation, ambulatory and social skills, physical activities, and exposure to a variety of environments and their components. (See Chapter 7).

Visually handicapped children should receive instruction from a qualified orientation and mobility instructor, knowledgeable in early childhood education, when they start to walk, if not before. An early education program should be planned by a qualified teacher of visually handicapped children to develop efficient, accurate, and effective use of the senses (Ferrell, 1984; O'Brien, 1976).

Eichel (1979) observed that when visually handicapped children swing on swings they do not rock and recommended that children who rock repetitively be given rocking furniture and swings to use. Sandler (1963) recommended that visually handicapped children observed engaging in repetitive stereotypic behaviors be diverted to a meaningful activity. The same parts of the body used in the inappropriate behavior should be used in the substitute activity. For example, eye rubbing or hand flapping can be substituted with meaningful object manipulation activities such as playing with a xylophone, pots and pans, or plush toys.

By providing children with appropriate early education programs, engaging them in meaningful activities, and encouraging them to play with objects in their environment which provide sensory feedback, the potential for self-stimulation behavior should be reduced. When children show signs of habit forming repetitive stereotypic behaviors, correct them, remind them of what they are doing, explain to them what they are doing and how it affects them and others, and provide them with instruction and opportunities to seek out and participate in meaningful activities (Ferrell, 1984). It is essential that intervention be consistent, and that reinforcement be given to the children not only when correcting inappropriate behaviors but also for appropriate behaviors.

Students who become visually handicapped later in life may not develop repetitive stereotypic behaviors the same degree as those who are born with severe visual limitations do. They may, however, tend to lose previously acquired body and facial gestures, or other body language "vocabulary". These students should be made aware of such changes and encouraged to make a conscious effort to maintain their body and facial language repetoire (see section on nonverbal communication in this chapter).

Extinction Research conducted to determine effective strategies to reduce and extinguish inappropriate stereotypic behaviors is reported in the literature more frequently than research to support specific preventive strategies. The most commonly reported approach involves the application of behavior modification techniques (Blasch, 1975; Caetano & Kauffman, 1975; Miller & Miller, 1976; Sklar & Rampulla, 1973). Behavior modification programs use token reinforcers, peer pressure, praise and encouragement, reprimands, point systems, food reinforcers, and the like. Some programs combine positive reinforcement with additional strategies such as aversive stimulation, praise and encouragement, the introduction of alternative behaviors, and reprimands and punishment.

Eichel (1979) analyzed and classified stereotypic behaviors by body parts and recommended an instructional program which introduces meaningful activities utilizing the involved body parts. Chrisholm (1966) recommended relaxation techniques and purposeful exaggeration and repetition of undesirable behaviors to give the children conscious awareness of their actions. Morse (1965) supported Cutsforth's (1951) theory of substitute activity. Igarashi (1971) recommended encouraging children to become interested in their environment, and to expose them to a variety of experiences. Knight (1972) recommended increased instruction in basic movement skills and orientation and mobility training to encourage and enable children to increase their independent travel skills, and thereby widen accessibility to their world.

Five suggested approaches are made by Holland (1971);

1. If the behaviors appear to be overt expressions of internal conflict and insecurity, then a psychiatric consultation may be the most appropriate action (Carroll, 1961);

2. Provide instruction to develop alternative socially acceptable behaviors (Morse, 1965);

3. Provide instruction to increase the child's awareness of his body stucture and movements (Knight, 1972);

4. Provide instruction to enable him to utilize his body as an appropriate expressive instrument; and

5. Provide consistent verbal reinforcement as necessary.

It is important that efforts to extinguish inappropriate behaviors be consistent. Every adult involved with the student should be aware of the instructional programs and methods used. Everyone must be sensitive to the children's needs, ego, self-concept, and self-esteem. It is important to provide the children with overt recognition of their appropriate behaviors, not just correction of inappropriate behaviors. Communication about progress, or the lack of it, needs to be ongoing among the children, parents, family members, and instructional staff to determine if methodologies are effective and to plan program changes. Extinguishing inappropriate stereotypic behaviors can be a tedious process. It is essential to continually remind oneself of the long term goal of providing the children with opportunities to develop social skills.

Nonverbal Communication

Human communication is complex. As noted in Chapter 18, communication includes speaking, listening, reading, and writing. Nonverbal communication is an inseparable part of dynamic communications and interactions. We communicate through appearances, dress, facial expressions, body postures and positions, gestures, eye behaviors, vocal cues, and the distance we maintain between ourselves and others. By observing nonverbal signals we can often tell whether our audience is interested or bored, agrees or disagrees, is pleased or angry; understands a parent's stare that means "No" as well as a smile which means "I am so proud". We learn to send nonverbal cues which convey specific meanings in our culture through observing, testing, and mimicking. Thus, the inability of visually handicapped children to observe subtle nonverbal communication cues can make personal and social interaction difficult.

Nonverbal communication has been delineated into seven areas by Knapp (1978): (1) body motion or kinesics; (2) physical characteristics; (3) touching behaviors; (4) vocal qualities and vocalizations; (5) proxemics; (6) artifacts; and (7) environment. These areas serve well as categories for a curriculum for teaching visually handicapped students nonverbal communication skills. A brief description of these areas with suggested activities follows.

Body Motion or Kinesics

Body motion or kinesic behaviors, includes gestures, body, limb, hand, feet, and leg movements, eye behaviors, facial expressions, and posture. Visually handicapped students should learn how to express themselves nonverbally as well as realize that individuals may be sending them nonverbal cues without realizing that they are not being received, interpreted, and acted upon. Such misunderstandings can lead to confusion, awkwardness, and difficulties in communication. Although visually handicapped students may not be able to receive nonverbal signals, they should know how to send them. For example, they should know how to wave to an idling car whose driver is waiting for them to cross the street.

Because sighted individuals are accustomed to communicating by using their bodies as a means of expression, they sometimes become uncomfortable relating to visually handicapped individuals whose bodies remain static. Visually handicapped students should learn to use body motions to illustrate and emphasize points and be taught such gestures within a social skills curriculum and as opportunities in daily activities present themselves.

Although facial expressions are perhaps the most common way of expressing affect nonverbally, the body is also used. A drooping head means sadness, a quick walk with head held high is a signal of confidence. If visually handicapped students are not using their bodies to correctly express the appropriate affect for the situation, they may be sending contradictory messages. Dolls, puppets, or dramatization may help in teaching visually handicapped children affective body motions. Participation in speech, drama, dance classes, and school plays should also be encouraged.

Nonverbal body motions also serve as conversation regulators. Persistent lack of eye contact, glancing away, shifting body weight from one leg to the other signal the speaker that the listener is disinterested or bored. Such behaviors regulate conversations because they communicate whether the subject or interchange should be continued or terminated. Visually handicapped students often send these signals effectively. However, they do not tend to be aware that they are being sent. Therefore, conversation skills need to include such strategies as interjecting open ended questions and listening for body movement in order to determine the listener's interest.

Other body motions include manipulation of one's own body parts or objects which may be satisfying but can irritate others.

Physical Characteristics

The second category of nonverbal communication is physical characteristics. The cues included in this category are physique or body shape, body or breath odors, attractiveness, height, weight, hair, and skin color. Our society is very conscious of physical appearance, condition, and hygiene. Sighted individuals tend to evaluate others by their appearance. Visually handicapped children may not because of the lack of vision; however, they must learn to realize that others may judge them on their appearance. When visually handicapped children experience successful and unsuccessful conversations and relationships the contributing factors should be discussed. This should include the possible aversion of peers because of the visual impairment. (See the section on Daily Living Skills in this chapter).

Touching Behaviors

The third category, touching, includes physical contact. Our society has many touching taboos. Visually handicapped students should be taught how to firmly shake hands, and how, and when, and where, it is appropriate to hug, kiss, cuddle, and stroke others. (See the section in this chapter on Sex Education). Role playing activities and situational simulations can be useful strategies.

Vocal Qualities

The fourth area of vocal qualities and vocalizations relates to how something is said not what is said. The pitch range and control, tempo, articulation, and resonance give definite cues about meaning. Vocalizations include laughing, sighing, crying, yawning, coughing, groaning, clearing of the throat, vocal qualifiers such as intense pitch, and segregates such as "um", "ah", and "uh-huh". Because visually handicapped students are unable to see facial expressions they may have difficulty understanding the meaning of the voice quality or vocalizations, sarcasm, expressions which have double meanings, sexual connotations, or that sometimes what is meant is the exact opposite of what is said. Role-playing can help in teaching visually handicapped students that an identical phrase can have different meanings depending on how it is said and the situation in which it is expressed. Use identical phrases with different intonations and have the student describe the meaning of the statements; then have the students vocalize the same statements using various vocal qualities to convey different meanings.

Proxemics

The fifth category is proxemics, the study of the use and perception of personal and social space and territoriality. Humans tend to delineate personal territory and maintain certain spatial distances from others depending on the situation and the culture. Americans tend to maintain less distance with friends than with strangers. If a stranger comes too close, we feel uneasy and distracted from the content of the communication. Visually handicapped students need to become sensitive to our culture's proxemics. They tend not to be upset by others coming too close to them, but may themselves distract others by impinging on another's personal space. Demonstrations and situational experiences, including attention to appropriate loudness of voice used in different situations and types of conversation should be provided. The term "broadcast voice" has been applied to visually handicapped students who have not learned to adjust the volume of their voice for varying situations.

Artifacts

The sixth category is artifacts, the manipulation of objects which may act as nonverbal stimuli. Perfume, makeup, clothes, wigs, the whole repertoire of beauty aids, and falsies are artifacts. Visually handicapped students should learn to apply the artifacts they choose to use and be made aware of possible reactions to under- or over-use of artifacts. For example, too much perfume or aftershave may result in negative reactions.

Environment

The seventh category is environmental factors such as furniture, interior decorating, lighting, smells, colors, noise or music, and temperature. The environment can be an influential factor during personal communications. Visually handicapped students can learn about these factors through discussions. An ideal time is when parents are explaining the need to keep rooms neat, or put the light on when someone enters the room. It is also appropriate to discuss the environmental factors which influence communication in home economics classes.

Strategies which can be used in teaching nonverbal communication skills include but are not limited to:

Direct physical manipulation of facial and body parts with accompanying explanations
Use of dolls and puppets
Dramatization
Demonstration
Role playing
Situational simulations
Assertiveness training
Speech, debate, elocution, drama, and dance classes
Participation in school plays, musicals, and other performing arts
Direct instruction in spoken communication skills
Direct instruction in hygiene and grooming skills
Teaching visually handicapped students nonverbal communication skills is the responsibility of both parents and teachers. It is an ongoing process that fits into various components of an education plan and is most effective when done daily as specific situations arise. Noticing the application of appropriate nonverbal skills and acknowledging the students' efforts are as important as noting deficits and teaching appropriate remedial skills.

SEX EDUCATION

Sexuality is integral to humanity. It is a holistic concept that has intellectual, mental, emotional, social, and physical aspects (Selvin, 1979; Gendel, 1973). As a holistic concept, sexuality is more than a physical expression; it is a function of the entire personality. It is a communication process which includes conversation, shared interests, the expression of feelings, as well as engagement in sexual behaviors and activities (De Loach & Greer, 1982). It is affected by and affects the individual's capacity to be sensitive, caring, concerned, and affectionate (Hicks, 1980).

Romano (1982) views sexuality as a combination of attitudes and behaviors which express the "manliness or womanliness" of each individual. The attitudinal aspect includes self-image, internalized values and expectations resulting from religious, cultural, and ethnic backgrounds, and the degree to which the individual has internalized societal values and expectations. The behavioral aspect includes social interaction skills, the action and verbal manifestations of attitudes, and the physical or erogenous and genital components of sexuality.

It is a "human right to be a feeling and informed sexual being" (Neff, 1982, p. 63). Sex education is a life-long process. Sex education curricula represent just one effort, a formal one, to provide structure in an academic setting by which students may come to a better understanding of sexuality. If sexuality is conceptualized holistically, parents, general educators, sex education and special education teachers, family members, clergy, peers, acquaintances, friends, and sexual partners will all affect students' sexual development to some degree. Some influence the students' moral development and values, some provide information about sexual anatomy or alleviate fears which accompany menses or wet-dreams. Others give instruction in self-care and social skills, help in understanding the difference between platonic and sexual relationships, and serve as role models. In addition to affecting development of sexuality through incidental learning, parents and teachers have a responsibility to provide direct instruction which will enable visually handicapped students to become feeling and informed sexual beings.

Appropriate sex education includes factual and philosophical aspects of sexuality. An appropriate sex education can assist visually handicapped students to:
realize that sex is something we are, not something we do;
eliminate sexual anxieties and misconceptions;
acquire an adequate knowledge of physical, mental, emotional, and social processes as they relate to sex;
develop attitudes, knowledge, and understanding necessary for interpersonal relationships;
develop a healthy self-image;

acquire adequate knowledge of sexual preferences and deviations for decision making and self-protection (Dickman, 1975; Neff, 1975).

Planning a Sex Education Program

Factors to consider when planning a sex education program for visually handicapped students fall into four general areas: (1) intrinsic; (2) extrinsic; (3) age of onset of visual handicap; and (4) the disabling process (Glass, 1984; Scholl, 1975). Intrinsic factors include personality, temperament, attitudes, education, intellectual abilities, and the presence of additional handicapping conditions. Extrinsic factors stem from the student's family, marital status of parents, environment, social, community, religious, cultural, and ethnic influences. The age of onset of the visual impairment is important. Did it take place at birth, before learning social and sexual behaviors, or after social and sexual patterns and behaviors were established? Aspects of the disabling process matter as well. Is the visual impairment progressive or stable? Was onset gradual, acute, or sudden? Are there any accompanying debilitating diseases? What is the degree of visual loss?

Glass (1984) states that there is "strong evidence that healthy sexuality is dependent on a healthy self-image" (p. 1). Visually handicapped children whose impairment occurs at birth or before puberty may grow up with a poor self-image and a lack of sexual identity if appropriate steps are not taken. Visually handicapped students who are perpetually treated as children without expectations for dating, romance, marriage, and parenting will have difficulty developing healthy self-images and sexuality.

By the age of three, sighted children have compared the anatomical features of their parents' bodies, their own, and those of siblings and peers. These experiences and others such as seeing peers in locker rooms and baths, adults on beaches, in magazines, movies, and even pornographic publications are not accessible to blind students and may be inadequately visible to low vision students. Warren (1984) confirms this in stating that "probably the most severe aspect of the sex learning problem with blind children involves access to information" (p. 238).

Visually handicapped students know their own bodies if they are allowed to explore them freely. They may have experience with the bodies of peers, usually of their own sex, through play but they often know little about the bodies of the opposite sex, or of adults of either sex (Selvin, 1979). Touching or exploring other bodies, except in the most private and intimate situations, is not considered socially acceptable in our culture. Visually handicapped students often create "bizarre theories concerning the anatomy and functions of sex" through ignorance due to a lack of accurate information, experience, and curiosity (Foulke & Uhde, 1975, p. 9). Significant adults must assume the responsibility for providing accurate sexual information to visually handicapped students.

Availability of Programs

In the early 1970s approximately 10 percent of public school systems provided sex education. In the late 1970s this increased to approximately 37 percent (Kirby, Alter, & Scales, 1979). A 1982 study of large city school districts (cities with populations over 100,000) found that sex education in some form was provided in 80 percent of such districts and 85 percent of the 9.3 million students enrolled in large city schools received it. Most districts reported that sex education curriculum material is integrated into other courses. Therefore both at the elementary and secondary levels "some form of sex education is generally available in most large city schools" (Sonenstein and Pittman, 1984, p. 20).

Sex education courses or integrated programs have a variety of titles such as family life education, human growth and development, health education, and in some instances, sex education. School personnel with the primary responsibility for presenting the sex education curricula include health, home economics, science, physical education, and sex education (one who teaches no other courses) teachers. The most predominant goals of the curricula include objectives to: (1) promote informed and rational decision-making with regard to sexuality; (2) increase knowledge about reproduction; (3) facilitate a positive and satisfying sexuality; (4) reduce unwanted teenage pregnancy; (5) reduce sexual activity among teenagers; and, (6) reduce childbearing among teenagers (Sonenstein & Pittman, 1984).

Sonenstein and Pittman (1984) found the following trends through their study of large city school district sex education programs.

Grades	Topics Covered
5th & 6th	Physical Differences; Changes at Puberty
7th & 8th	Intercourse; Pregnancy Cycle; Pregnancy and Childbirth; Consequences of Teen Pregnancy; Sexually Transmitted Diseases; Sexual Feelings and Attraction; Communication with Opposite Sex; Communication with Parents; Sexual Decision Making; Personal Values; Media Messages about Sex; Resistance to Peer Pressure; Masturbation;
9th & 10th	Responsibilities of Parenthood; Teen Marriage; Love Relationships/ Commitments; Family Planning Sources; Contraception; Gynecological Examination; Abortion; Homosexuality; Rape; Sexual Abuse

The progression, therefore, generally moves from physiological facts to reproductive facts and issues, to complicated and value laden issues. It is also based more on age appropriateness than the controversial nature of the subject. The time allotted to sex education also was found to increase with school level. There is great variety in sex education programs across the country. Some schools have none, some offer basic physiological information, while others provide intensive discussions on a broad range of topics.

Sex Education for Visually Handicapped Students

Torbett (1975) recommends that the first step to developing appropriate sex education programs is to expose visually handicapped students to the sexual culture in which they live. Experiences should include tactual exploration of their own and other children's bodies; playing with anatomically correct dolls representing both sexes; and reading literature and experiencing other forms of mass media material available to any student. Activities which should take place at home with parental guidance include tactual exploration of adult bodies of both sexes; observation and instruction in appropriate ways people demonstrate affection toward each other; when, where, and with whom different types of affection are appropriate and inappropriate; and explanations of colloquial or slang sexual terms. Teachers in infant and early intervention programs can help parents become aware of the children's need to develop a healthy self-image, including sexuality. Teachers of elementary and secondary school aged children should consult with parents and other teachers about their students' sexuality development.

The family provides the most significant role models. Research suggests that sex education is often the most neglected area in the family. Parental hesitancy "is even more striking for blind children" (Torbett, 1975, p. 33). Parents may have to read sexual material aloud to visually handicapped children, bathe with them, and provide living or graphic models for tactual exploration. Learning at home by touching bodies of family members seems to be most appropriate, but embarrassment and fear of incest may make this difficult (Glass, 1984). Modesty is a topic which requires direct discussion with visually handicapped students, particularly those who are blind.

Anatomy and Function of Sexual Organs

Learning about the structure and function of sexual organs should take place at an early age and in consultation with parents (van'T Hooft and Heslinga, 1975). Without such experiences, the child will lack physical anatomy concepts. Graphic dolls or live models are recommended as teaching aids (van'T Hooft

and Heslinga, 1975). Graphic dolls or constructed models are not as realistic as humans. However, social resistance to live models may be strong. Models should be life size, made of material approximating texture of the human form, and include all sexual features which are clearly tactually discernable. Torsos used in medical schools and mannequins can be used though they lack reality. Anatomic models of sexual organs provide life-size examples of parts of external sexual organs such as the clitoris and scrotum, and permit tactual examination of internal sexual organs such as the uterus and vas deferens. Constructed penis models are available in flacid, circumsized, uncircumsized, and erect form. Constructed models can be used to practice placement of both male and female contraceptive devices. (See Appendix H for resources.)

The function of sexual organs and different physical feelings of arousal of both genders should be explained to visually handicapped children as they reach puberty. Topics for discussion include physical manifestations of arousal, menstruation, ovulation, wet dreams, erection, ejaculation, masturbation, intercourse, climax, contraception, pregnancy, and childbearing. Young girls generally begin menstruation between 11 and 14 years of age. They should be prepared for its beginning, including hygiene, keeping track of their cycle, and use of sanitary pads and tampons.

Sexuality Awareness

Establishing a solid gender identity, essential to a healthy self-image, is one of the initial goals of sex education leading to awareness of sexuality. Visually handicapped children may need direct instruction to establish gender identification because of the lack or limited response to visual stimuli accessible to other children. Visually handicapped students need direct instruction about differences in men and women's clothing, body stature, stances, and movements. Neff (1975) suggests activities which may increase visually handicapped students' awareness of their own sexuality such as examining differences in clothing, constructing forms of male and female bodies, dressing male and female dolls, and examining sculptures which graphically represent differences in the genders.

Vocabulary

Another objective is the establishment of a developmentally appropriate sexual vocabulary. This includes correct terminology. It is no more difficult to learn the correct names than it is to learn meaningless and "cute" terms. The meaning of slang terms, derogatory implications, and inappropriateness or appropriateness of their use in various situations and settings should be explained. (Foukle & Uhde, 1975; Neff, 1982.)

Social Aspects

We are constantly exposed to manifestations of sexual behaviors. Whether or not we observe physical manifestations of affection at home, we see kissing, petting, sexually arousing behaviors and language, and if we choose to, intercourse through television, films, or sexually graphic publications. Visually handicapped youngsters do not have these opportunities. It is essential to advise visually handicapped youngsters that certain activities are acceptable, normal, and pleasurable in private, at certain times, and with certain individuals.

Visually handicapped children must learn how to protect themselves from inappropriate sexual advances. They must be taught what an inappropriate sexual advance is, how to recognize, and how to deal with it. Parents and teachers may also consider enrolling visually handicapped students in self-defense classes which may be offered in the school or through community center organizations. Students must also be given the opportunities to discuss their feelings, disappointments, and joys related to their sexuality and expression of it. If the visual impairment, or concomitant impairments, are hereditary, they should be informed about genetic counseling. Regardless of parental or religious beliefs it is essential that visually handicapped students have the knowledge to become accurately informed sexual beings so that they can make intelligent decisions. Yet, teachers must respect the students' cultural and religious heritage. (See Chapter 10.)

DATING

"Adolescence is a time of turmoil as well as first love, of self-doubt as well as discovery" (Kent, 1983, p. 247). Attraction and desire to spend time and share experiences with members of the opposite sex, awareness of social pressures, and the need to be accepted by peers is heightened during adolescence. Being asked or asking someone for a date is especially important to adolescents, including visually handicapped ones. Dating is a significant part of social, psychological, and emotional development. It can be pleasurable, exciting, fun, and stressful. Visually handicapped students need social contacts with members of the opposite sex just as much as their sighted peers. They need parents and teachers to provide guidance, direction, and instruction in all the social skill areas to be well prepared for dating as adolescents and/or adults.

Preparing visually handicapped students for dating should begin during childhood and continue indefinitely. For example, if stereotypic behaviors are not prevented or extinguished, their demonstration will detract from attractiveness and will therefore interfere with acceptance by peers or a potential date.

If visually handicapped adolescents have limited recreation interests and abilities, they may be considered uninteresting or incompetent, and receive few invitations from peers. If they dress inappropriately

or are not well groomed, they may be considered unaware and uncaring, and peers may choose not to associate with them or shun them. If their eating skills are below par, peers may view them as undesirable companions. Families' cultural and religious values must be known and considered before broaching subjects such as dating behaviors and customs with students. (See Chapter 10.)

Choosing Potential Dates

A large nonverbal communication repertoire is associated with predating and dating behaviors. Flirting is accomplished primarily through nonverbal eye and facial gestures. Nonverbal behaviors can indicate whether someone is interested in being a potential date. Visually handicapped students can learn how to send nonverbal communication behaviors but do not have the ability to receive those expressed by others. They depend on interpreting verbal communication, direct physical contact, and information from friends. (See section on Nonverbal Communication Skills.) Therefore, they have "much less freedom in choosing and approaching" potential dates (Lowenfeld, 1959, p. 391).

At a school sports event or the local burger shop sighted adolescents can scan the environment, determine who is there, locate someone they want to be with, attract their attention, determine through nonverbal communication if they respond positively, and then join them. Visually handicapped students are at a distinct disadvantage in this scenario. They must ask a sighted friend to identify who is beyond their hearing or visual capability or ask if specific individuals are present and then be directed toward them; or accompany a sighted friend and "settle" for the sighted friend's selection; or sit, hope, and wait for peers to approach them.

Visually handicapped students are in a position of being selected as a friend or date far more frequently than in a position of selecting friends and dates unless they make an effort to be appropriately extroverted and assertive. Before they can seek out companionship, they need good interpersonal skills, confidence in social skills, and a healthy self-concept.

Mobility

Independent mobility skills are essential for visually handicapped adolescents. These skills must be learned, practiced, and used throughout childhood. (See Chapter 19.) Driving a car is often a symbol of independence and prestige for adolescents. The car provides freedom of movement and privacy. Visually handicapped adolescents will need to find alternatives to driving. Tandem bicycle riding is appropriate for casual dates such as picnics and the movies. Parents, older siblings, or friends may need to provide rides to and from parties, concerts, beaches, and dances. Double dating and public transportation (where it is available) are other alternatives. Most communities have cab companies which can be used for special occasions.

The car provides a private place where teenagers can talk and freely express their feelings for each other. Visually handicapped adolescents must have alternative environments such as the family room or den. They may become acutely aware of their "difference" through such experiences and will need to discuss anxieties, fears, angers, frustrations, and joys.

Attitudes of Sighted Peers and Their Parents

Attitudes are discussed in Chapter 2 but there are some considerations unique to dating. For example, parents of sighted youngsters may discourage dating visually handicapped youths. Visually handicapped students need to be able to deal with the resistance of parents of sighted dating partners. It helps to stage scenarios and use role playing to provide visually handicapped students with concrete examples of how to handle questions and concerns parents may have. Discussions with older visually handicapped individuals who have dated may also be helpful.

In an informal survey of seven blind women Kent (1983) found that they recalled as teenagers they felt "they were not considered appropriate partners of the dating game" by their peers (p. 249). Because a date is often a status symbol, sighted adolescents may be unwilling to date a visually handicapped youngster. Even students who are popular may "fall too far below the norms of physical perfection to be a proper showcase" (Kent, 1983, p. 249). Popularity held in elementary school often wanes as adolescence is reached and criteria change.

Because of a lack of research, this author conducted an informal survey of young visually handicapped adults.

Male and female interviewees expressed similar feelings. They felt peer pressure deterred sighted youngsters from dating students who were visually handicapped. Generally, the adults interviewed found that while in high school, it was easier to date graduates than school mates. Several found that participation in activities at local organizations for the visually handicapped provided supportive supplementary social and dating experiences. Others did not. A number of the interviewees felt isolated and defensively withdrew from social activities. The majority found that dates which they initiated were more successful than those initiated by school aged peers and that post high school dating was easier and more satisfying than high school dating.

The feminist movement has had an impact on dating practices. At one time the male played a more aggressive role than the female in dating. Today it is acceptable for either males or females to initiate a date. Young women no longer need to wait and hope someone will ask them on a date. Today, young women can initiate contact and extend an invitation. Visually handicapped students should be encouraged to pursue desired friendships and appropriately assert themselves with potential dating partners. Those in residential schools tend to be more comfortable dating schoolmates. It is essential that residential school students participate in home community recreation activities so they learn to socialize and develop friendships with sighted youngsters. (See section on Recreation and Leisure Time.)

Strategies

Parents and teachers must be sensitive to visually handicapped students' need for privacy, to discuss feelings openly, to understand dating behaviors and customs, and sexuality. (See section on Sex Education.) The teacher should observe students in all types of situations, not just the classroom. Informal observations in school hallways, cafeteria, at dances, and other activities provide information about the quality of students' social life. The teacher should also communicate with students and parents to determine the quality of leisure time and involvement in social and recreation activities with family, friends, and members of the community.

Students may be uncomfortable seeking information about dating from family members or teachers who need to be sensitive and inititate discussion, guidance, and instruction. Role playing may be a particularly effective teaching strategy to utilize. Books about teenagers and dating experiences can be read and discussed. Assertiveness training may also help. Parents and teachers must address the social and emotional needs of visually handicapped youths and provide them with the skills they need to socialize and date on an equal level with their sighted peers.

**Chart 20.1   Representative list of recreation activities
in which visually handicapped individuals are able to participate**

acting	gardening	sewing
archery	golf	singing
auto repair	gymnastics	sculpture
badminton	ham radio	shopping
baking	handball	skating
ball games	hiking	skiing
biliards/pool	horseback riding	spectator sports
bingo	horseshoe pitching	squash
boating	hunting	stamp collecting
bicycle riding	instrumental music	swimming
bowling	jogging	table games
camping	judo	theatre going
ceramics	karate	table tennis
cooking	kite flying	track and field
crafts	knitting	traveling
cricket	leatherwork	touring
crocheting	model building	walking
dancing	mountain climbing	watching television
dinner parties	museum going	water sports
dining out	needlework	weaving
dramatics	painting	weight lifting
fencing	picture taking	woodworking
fishing	puzzle solving	wrestling
flower arranging	reading	writing
gambling	sailing	yoga

RECREATION AND LEISURE

The contribution of play and recreation to the growth and development of visually handicapped students cannot be minimized. Meaningful play and recreation experiences during the formative years can have a positive effect on health, fitness, intellectual growth and development, creativity and self-expression, social and emotional adjustment, and personal satisfaction and fulfillment (Luxton & Kelley, 1981). Play is characterized as behavior in which visually handicapped children are "freed as far as possible from any imposed constraints or expectations to elicit specific response" (Tibaudo, 1976, p. 1). Play permits optimum exploration of the unknown. It is unpredictable, and thus helps to develop the capacity to generate new and unexpected thoughts and responses to situations and stimuli. To take the fullest advantage of play, visually handicapped children must be given freedom and opportunities to make self-regulatory decisions. The "recreation experience" should ultimately be one in which visually handicapped students voluntarily participate because they find it pleasurable. The "recreation experience" should be one of "self-fulfillment, freedom, and mastery that requires no other justification" (Kelley & Ludwig, 1984, p. 1).

The primary goals of leisure are first, that students develop the skills and attitudes needed to fully participate in recreation activities; and second, that they become knowledgeable of recreational choices so they can intelligently select how they spend their leisure time. Visually handicapped children often live a highly structured life. Too often, too many decisions are made and activities are selected for them. Inherent in any effort to help students develop a repertoire of recreational activities must be the encouragement of freedom of choice, exploration, and decision making skills. It is essential to their development that they have time to engage in recreational pursuits.

Recreational Activities

Visually handicapped students can participate in many recreation activities. The list of representative activities provided in Chart 20.1 is not inclusive of all possible activities. In many instances visually handicapped individuals can participate in most recreation activities with few or no modifications (Buell, 1975; Martinez & Grayson, 1981). Modifications and adaptations need not detract from the pleasure derived from participating in the activity.

Recreation Delivery Systems

The Family

Parents should include visually handicapped children in all recreation activities in which the family participates (Lowenfeld, 1964). Visually handicapped children should be exposed to a wide variety of recreation activities beginning with those in which the family has a particular interest.

The family which enjoys Monopoly, backgammon, chess, or Scrabble, should get adapted games. Visually handicapped children can take along a portable radio and listen to the play-by-play calls while enjoying the enthusiasm of the crowd, hot dogs, and peanuts at spectator sports. Significant adults should show them the equipment and body positions of players, as well as explain the objectives and rules of the game. On a weekend camping and hiking trip visually handicapped children should be given age-appropriate responsibilities such as fetching and carrying water from the stream, collecting and chopping kindling, baiting and catching fish, assisting in food preparation and cleanup, and telling their share of ghost stories around the camp fire.

The teacher of visually handicapped children should discuss the family's recreation activities with the parents and students. Parents may need guidance about techniques the students should use and be familiarized with adapted games and equipment which will enable full participation in specific activities. Gradually, the children will begin to select those activities from which they derive the most pleasure and satisfaction.

The Community

All communities have recreational resources. An informal survey of available recreational resources can help to identify available programs (Carter & Kelley, 1981). Directories published by the local Chamber of Commerce, Better Business Bureau, local newspapers, community welfare council, tourist bureau, local and/or state government offices, telephone companies, realtors, and community service organizations list recreation resources, special events, and activities. Parents and teachers should be familiar with the community recreation resources so they can involve the children in meaningful programs and activities.

From an early age, visually handicapped children should be in play groups and taken to neighborhood playgrounds where they can interact, play, and establish friendships with other children. At an appropriate age they should participate in supervised playground activities provided by the local department of parks and recreation. Older students should be encouraged to explore recreation choices in the community and to participate in those which will best satisfy their developmental and social needs. Many local community resources, for example, YMCA and YWCAs, Red Cross, scouting associations, church and synagogue groups, and service organizations, offer structured recreation experiences and programs for children, youth, and adults. Programs include club activities, drop-in centers, classes, parties, dances, picnics, special events, contests, field trips and tours, day camps, and overnight camps.

Agencies for the Visually Handicapped

Local agencies for the visually handicapped as well as other disability groups may have recreation programs. They may be similar to those offered through other community organizations. Before enrolling students in special recreation programs for the visually handicapped, Lowenfeld (1964) recommends that parents "weigh carefully all the circumstances" (p. 127). For example, if a child attends a public or private school in the mainstream, perhaps he should be involved in both community recreation activities and special programs. If the child is the only, or one of a few visually handicapped children in his school, it may be advantageous for her to have the opportunities to socialize and interact with other students and adults who are also visually handicapped and who may serve as role models.

Students who attend a residential school for the visually handicapped may be provided recreation activities with its community organizations through the school. When students go home on weekends and during vacations, it would be to their advantage to participate in recreation activities with the family and within the community among sighted peers.

National Organizations

Several national organizations offer sport and recreation programs specifically for visually handicapped individuals. These organizations are for the most part restricted to visually handicapped individuals. However, in some instances sighted individuals are included in competitive events. Visually handicapped students should know about these organizations and be encouraged to send for program descriptions. (See Appendix H.)

Guidelines and Adaptations

It is beyond the purview of this text to present specific modifications and adaptations to make recreation activities accessible to visually handicapped students. However, some general guidelines follow (for specific information see Appendix H). Adaptations and modifications should only be made when absolutely necessary.

Either provide the student with a thorough orientation, or encourage the student to orient himself, to the environment in which the recreation activity is to take place.

Familiarize the student with the activity through demonstration, tactual exploration, and verbal descriptions.

Present a new activity by presenting it in its entirety, then breaking it down into small parts, and then again in its entirety. (See section on Task Analysis in this chapter.)

Develop and utilize an effective communication system to provide cues and signals to start, stop, give warning, direction, or change actions.

Use a multisensory approach.

Use concrete realistic examples.

Utilize the buddy system when appropriate, rotating the visually handicapped student's buddies.

Provide a variety of recreation experiences for the visually handicapped student but allow him to select the ones he prefers and give him the opportunity to develop skills that will enable him to enjoy selected recreation activities as an adult.

Carefully analyze activities to determine if they need to be modified to enable the visually handicapped student and nonimpaired students to participate on an equal basis.

Modify procedures and intellectual behaviors used in activities if they will help the visually handicapped student achieve the objectives of the recreation activity. As the student learns, gradually eliminate the modifications.

Modify rules for recreation activities as they apply to contests, structured group games, table games, informal play, and mass activities. As the student becomes competent, gradually reinstate the true rules of the activity.

Modify equipment or procure commercially available modified equipment which may be helpful or necessary for the visually handicapped student's participation in table games, ball games, and other recreation activities (Buell, 1982; Carter & Kelley, 1981).

Pursuits of recreation activities should not be taken lightly because they do not fall into the traditional category of educational academics. Recreation activities can be a pleasurable vehicle by which visually handicapped students further develop muscle tone, balance, flexibility, fine and gross motor coordination, posture, gait, team spirit, orientation and mobility skills, and interpersonal skills. Countless learning experiences can be provided through recreation activities which will enhance visually handicapped students' cognitive, social, academic, emotional, and physical development. In order to provide a well conceived and meaningful recreation program for visually handicapped students, the following basic steps should be applied: assess cognitive, motor, psychosocial needs and interests; formulate purposes, goals, and objectives; develop program content, procedures, and implementation strategies; execute and monitor programs; and evaluate the student's progress and program effectiveness (Carter & Kelley, 1981; Kelley & Ludwig, 1984). (See Chapter 12.)

The teacher of visually handicapped children, in working with students, parents, and recreational specialists, must know and communicate students' "culture, needs, wishes, social patterns, lifestyle, and level of ability (or disability)" (Carter & Kelley, 1981, p. 73). The teacher must also be aware of these same attributes of the groups with whom the student most often interacts.

Spending leisure time in self-fulfilling recreation activities is essential to visually handicapped individuals' well-being. Visually handicapped individuals have a right to learn what options are available. Whether they decide to use their leisure time reading a novel on the best seller list, going fishing, gambling, or mountain climbing is unimportant. What is important is that they be provided with the learning experiences which will help them develop the needed skills to actively participate in the recreation activities of their choice.

Parents and teachers must share the responsibility for helping visually handicapped students reach their maximum social skill potential. With teaching time constraints and the pressures of teaching unique skill areas such as braille, use of low vision aids and technological devices, orientation and mobility, etc., it is often difficult to "find the time" to teach social skills, but the time must be found. If teachers do not make an overt effort to observe their students outside the classroom and communicate with the students and their parents, they will be unable to plan and implement relevant social skill programs. Teachers clearly must take the time to reflect on students' long range needs and consistently provide learning experiences in all social skills areas.

Daily living skill content areas for inclusion in individualized education programs are presented in this chapter. Criteria to be used to determine if instruction is warranted include students' demonstrated ability to perform the given task safely, independently, with confidence, poise, and in a traditional manner. The analysis should be completed by the teacher prior to providing instruction in daily living skills. Interpersonal skills presented in this chapter include discussion of the effects of and intervention strategies for the prevention and extinction of stereotypic behaviors, nonverbal communication skills, sex education, and dating. Recreation and leisure time activities, delivery systems, and guidelines for modifications and adaptations are presented. Instruction in social skills is clearly an ongoing process which crosses the boundaries of the classroom and school. The development of an adequate social skill repertoire is essential to each visually handicapped student's ability to reach his self-selected level of independence and interdependence.

Study questions

1. Write an Individualized Education Program for a third grade visually handicapped student in the area of daily living skills. Use your local school district's format.

2. Do three detailed task analyses for daily living skills of your choice.

3. What factors should you consider before applying an intervention program to visually handicapped adolescent students who demonstrate repetitive stereotypic behaviors? Explain why the factors you have identified should be considered.

4. Describe your personal philosophy regarding the application of intervention programs to extinguish stereotypic behaviors which are demonstrated by visually handicapped students. Explain the reasons for your philosophy.

5. You are a teacher of visually handicapped students enrolled in a residential school for the blind. You have the first grade students, several of whom have consistently demonstrated stereotypic behaviors involving hands and arms. Write a detailed behavior modification plan which you will implement. Also include a description of additional adults you will involve and a rationale for their inclusion in the program.

6. You are a teacher of infant and preschool visually handicapped students. You have just been assigned to work with a three year old, totally blind child, Joshua. Joshua and his parents have never before been provided with instructional services from a teacher certified in education of the visually handicapped. You visit Joshua and his parents three afternoons a week. Joshua demonstrates excessive stereotypic behaviors such as rocking, head rolling, and finger flapping. You note that occasionally he demonstrates stereotypic behaviors such as eye gouging, eye rubbing, and eyelid pulling. Describe the strategies and intervention program you would establish. Include how you would involve the parents.

7. As a teacher of visually handicapped students you are assigned to work with a congenitally blind seventh grade boy and girl who have poor nonverbal communication skills. Write a section for the IEP which will address their needs. Use the IEP format used by your local school district.

8. List twenty activities which you would incorporate into visually handicapped student's social skills program which deal specifically with nonverbal communication skills. For each activity, list the nonverbal communication skill, the setting(s) in which it will be taught, the strategy which will be used, who will be responsible for teaching it, and how you will evaluate the student's ability to transfer and apply the skill.

9. As an itinerant teacher of the visually handicapped, you have two students in high school who are enrolled in the school's sex education program. One student,

Jeremy, is a young man who has had low vision since birth and is able to use his sight to read enlarged print materials. Sarah has been blind since birth. The science teacher who will be teaching sex education has requested that you meet with him to discuss the two students and modifications you might suggest. In preparation for the meeting you plan to review the sex education curriculum. Obtain such a curriculum which is presently being used in your local school district. Prepare a list of suggested adaptations and modifications which you will present and discuss with the science teacher.

10. You have just taken a job as a teacher of visually handicapped children in a new school district and you have a junior high school student who is going through puberty. The student has started to ask you questions regarding sexuality. You know very little about the student's family background, and in reviewing school records find that no specific coursework has been offered in the area of sex education. Describe your course of action.

11. The parents of one of your visually handicapped high school students has shared with you their concern for their son's lack of a social life and the fact that he has never dated. Describe what you would do to determine his social lifestyle and what you would do to help him improve it.

12. Identify your favorite "recreation experience" which involves physical activity. Describe how you would introduce this activity to a totally and congenitally blind high school freshman. Include all strategies, adaptations, and modifications.

13. As a teacher of visually handicapped students you plan to take an adventitiously blinded student to his first live football game since his blindness occurred. Describe how you would prepare him for the outing.

14. Develop an outline for a social skills curricula for use with elementary or secondary school aged visually handicapped students. The outline should be inclusive of all appropriate social skill areas for the school level selected.

15. You are an itinerant teacher of visually handicapped children. You have recently accepted a new position in a school district in which you are the only vision teacher and you have a supervisor who does not have any experience in the field of blindness. You find that there is insufficient time to spend with your students and they are all in need of varying degrees of instruction in social skills. In preparation for a meeting with your supervisor, develop a thorough rationale as to why your students need more instructional time from you and why you need more time to consult with your students' other teachers and parents to effect a meaningful social skills training program.

16. You are a teacher of visually handicapped students who has accepted a teaching position at a residential

school for the blind. After four months on the job you have noted general deficiencies in the students' social skills. The only formal instruction is provided to junior and senior high school students and this is a once a week, forty minute class. You have determined that daily living skills are taught primarily by houseparents who, though well intended, have never received any training from the staff. You also note that formal recreation skill training is provided by volunteers, on weekends and some weekday evenings, who are knowledgeable in specific recreation activities but not in effects of visual impairment on learning. You decide that there is a need to develop and present a plan to incorporate a formal social skills curricula into the school's routine. Develop the plan as you would present it to the principal and superintendent.

Additional readings & resources

Daily Living Skills

Bender, D. (1985). *Everyone, everywhere, everyday needs the tools of the trade called living: Home Economics/Daily Living Skills Assessment.* Nebraska City, Nebr.: Nebraska School for the Visually Handicapped.

Pennsylvania Materials Center for the Visually Handicapped (1977). *Focus on individualized programming for the visually handicapped: Part II.* Harrisburg, Pa.: Pennsylvania Materials Center for the Visually Handicapped.

Tremble, J. and Wilson, F. (1970). *Manual for a work-experience program.* Hartford, Conn.: Oak Hill School.

Willoughby, D.M. (1979). *A resource guide for parents and educators of blind children.* Baltimore, Md.: National Federation of the Blind.

Yeadon, A. and Grayson, D. (1979). *Living with impaired vision: An introduction.* New York, N.Y.: American Foundation for the Blind, Inc.

Stereotypic Behaviors

Berkson, G. (1973). Visual defect does not produce stereotyped movement. *American Journal of Mental Deficiency,* **78**, pp. 89-94.

Chase, J.B. (1972). *Retrolental fibroplasia and autistic symptomatology.* Research Series #24. New York, N.Y.: American Foundation for the Blind, Inc.

Eichel, V.J. (1978). Mannerisms of the blind: A review of the literature. *Journal of Visual Impairment & Blindness,* **72** (4), pp. 125-130.

Guess, D. (1966). The influence of visual and ambulation restrictions on stereotyped behavior. *American Journal of Mental Deficiency,* **70**, pp. 542-547.

Guess, D. and Rutherford, G. (1967). Experimental attempts to reduce stereotyping among blind students. *American Journal of Mental Deficiency,* **71**, pp. 984-986.

Thurell, R. and Rice, D. (1970) Eye rubbing in blind children: Application of a sensory deprivation model. *Exceptional Children,* **36**, pp. 325-330.

Nonverbal Communication

Argyle, M. (1975). *Bodily communication.* New York, N.Y.: International Universities Press.

Eibl-Eibesfeldt, I. (1973). The expressive behavior of the deaf-and-blind-born. In von Cranach, M. and Vine, I. (eds.). *Social communication and movement.* New York, N.Y.: Academic Press.

Fast, J. (1970). *Body language.* New York, N.Y.: M. Evans.

Goldberg, G.N., Kiesler, C.A., & Collins, B.E. (1969). Visual behavior and face-to-face distance during interaction. *Sociometry,* **32**, pp. 43-53.

Harrison, R.P. (1974). *Beyond words.* Englewood Cliffs, N.J.: Prentice-Hall.

Lerner, R.M., Karabenick, S.A., and Meisel, M. (1975). Effect of age and sex on the development of personal space schemata towards body build. *Journal of Genetic Psychology,* **127**, pp. 91-101.

Mehrabian, A., and Diamond, S.G. (1971). The effects of furniture arrangement, props, and personality on social interaction. *Journal of Personality and Social Psychology,* **20**, pp. 18-30.

Meisels, M. and Guardo, C. (1969). Development of personal space schemata. *Child Development,* **40**, pp. 1167-1178.

Rosenfeld, L.B. and Plax, T.G. (1977). Clothing as communication. *Journal of Communication,* **27**, pp. 24-31.

Scheflen, A.E. (1964). The significance of posture in communicative systems. *Psychiatry,* **27**, pp. 316-331.

Smith, A.I. (1970). Non-verbal communication through touch. Unpublished doctoral dissertation, Georgia State University.

Walker, D.N. (1971). Openness to touching: A study of strangers in nonverbal interaction. Unpublished doctoral dissertation, University of Connecticut.

Williams, F. and Tolch, J. (1965). Communication by facial expression. *Journal of Communication,* **15**, pp. 17-21.

Sex Education

Blum, G. and Blum, G. (1981). *Feeling good about yourself: A guide for people working with people who have disabilities.* Second Edition. Calif.: Feeling Good Associates.

Chipouras, S., Cornelius, D., Daniels, S., and Makas,

E. (1982). *Who cares? A handbook on sex education and counseling services for disabled people.* Second Edition. Baltimore, Md.: University Park Press.

Crutcher, R., Chaton, M., and Koser, L. (1982). *The emerging male: A man's handbook.* Calif.: Everyman's Center.

Greengross, W. (n.d.). *Sex and the handicapped child.* Rugby, England: National Marriage Guidance Council, Little Church Street.

Hallingby, L. (1982). *Bibliographies of holdings of the SIECUS information service & library: Sexuality and illness, disability, or aging.* New York, N.Y.: SIECUS.

Knight, S.E. and Thornton, C.E. (1983). *Teacher workbook for family life education.* ERIC Documents Reproduction Service. Document No. ED 229-685.

Sexuality and the family life span. Proceedings from changing family conference XI (1982). Iowa: Division of Continuing Education, University of Iowa.

Smith E., Silver, P., and Hughes, K. (1981). *Sex and disability: A resource guide to books, pamphlets, articles, and audio, visual, and tactile materials.* Alameda/San Francisco, Calif.: Planned Parenthood.

Throckmorton, T. (1980). *Becoming me: A personal adjustment guide for secondary students.* Grand Rapids, Mich.: Grand Rapids Public Schools.

Woods, N.F. (1984). *Human sexuality in health and illness,* Third Edition. St. Louis, Mo.: C.V. Mosby.

Braille and Large-Print Pamphlets

Birth control: All the methods that work and the ones that don't, (n.d.). New York, N.Y.: Planned Parenthood.

Braille edition: Iowa Commission for the Blind (1977) 4th and Keosauqua Way, Des Moines, Iowa 50309.

Large Type Edition: Foundation for Blind Children (1977) 1201 North 85th Place, Scottsdale, Arizona 85257.

For boys: A book about girls, (1980). Milltown, N.J.: Personal Products Co.

Growing up and liking it, (1980). Milltown, N.J.: Personal Products Co.

Large print birth control information sheets, (n.d.) Alameda/San Francisco, Calif.: Planned Parenthood.

Constructed Models

Gender Dolls/Models of Human Genital Anatomy
Jim Jackson and Company
16 Laurel Street
Arlington, Mass. 02174

Dating

Kent, Deborah (1978). *Belonging.* New York, N.Y.: The Dial Press.

Recreation and Leisure Time

Amphlett, E.M. (1969). Blind horsemanship. *New Beacon,* **53** (621), pp. 4-6.

Bellinger, J. (1971). Skating for the sightless. *Rehabilitation Teacher,* **3** (3), pp. 23-25.

Cordellos, H.C. (1976). *Aquatic recreation for the blind.* Washington, D.C.: Physical education and recreation for the handicapped, Information and Research Utilization Center.

Deschamps, G. (1969). Teaching blind beginners how to ski. *Rehabilitation Bulletin,* **16**, pp. 8-10.

Di Mattia, R. (1970). Sailing: A new experience. *The New Outlook for the Blind,* **64** (5), pp. 138-141.

Fisher, D. (1972). Blind students learn karate. *Journal of Rehabilitation.* **38** (4), pp. 26-27.

Hartman, R.E. (1974). Ball Games for visually handicapped children. *The New Outlook for the Blind.* **68** (8), pp. 348-355.

Heyes, A.D. (1974). Blindness and yoga. *The New Outlook for the Blind.* **68** (9), pp. 385-393.

Hyman, D. (1969). Teaching the blind student archery skills. *Journal of Health, Physical Education, Recreation,* **40**, pp. 85-86.

McNaughton, J.D. (1972). Bicycle riding practices of blind and partially sighted children. *The Chronicle.* **11** (7), pp. 6-7.

Sonka, J.J. and Bina, M.J. (1978). Cross country running for visually impaired adults. *Journal of Visual Impairment & Blindness.* **72** (6), pp. 212-214.

Waffa, J. (1963). Fencing as an aid to the habilitation or rehabilitation of blind persons. *The New Outlook for the Blind.* **57** (2), pp. 39-43.

Zok, J.E. (1970). *Instructional manual for blind bowlers,* Washington, D.C.: American University and American Blind Bowling Association.

CHAPTER 21

Curricular Adaptations

Kathleen Mary Huebner, Coordinator

June E. Morris
Pete Rossi
Linda De Lucchi
Larry Malone
Myrna R. Olson
Rona Shaw
Diane H. Craft

This chapter describes background information and presents suggestions for modifications in social studies, mathematics, science, foreign languages, creative arts, and physical education for use by blind and visually handicapped children and youth in regular classes

Regular teachers are usually not experts in the education of visually handicapped pupils and teachers of visually handicapped pupils are not special content area experts. The basic information and modifications suggested in this chapter should, however, provide information that will enable the special and the regular teachers to work together toward assisting visually handicapped children and youth to derive maximum benefit from their school experiences in these curricular areas. The areas included are social studies, mathematics, science, foreign languages, creative arts, and physical education. Guidelines included in several parts of the chapter are also applicable for subject areas such as computer science, industrial arts, and home economics.

SOCIAL STUDIES
June E. Morris

What are the social studies? Where are their roots? What are their goals? How are they taught? What problems are encountered by visually handicapped students studying them?

Social studies is defined in the *Webster's New World Dictionary* (1982) as "a course of study, esp. in elementary and secondary schools, including history, civics, geography, etc." (p. 1352). It is defined similarly in *The American Heritage Dictionary* (1982) as "a course of study including geography, history, government, and sociology, taught in secondary and elementary schools" (p. 1160). Webster codes the term as an Americanism, meaning it originated or first came into use in this country. According to Barr, Barth, and Shermis (1977), "the most enduring definition was developed by Edgar Wesley some forty years ago. 'The Social Studies' said Wesley, 'are the social sciences simplified for pedagogical purposes' " (pp. 1-2). Later in the text, the authors propose their own definition which states, "The social studies is an integration of experience and knowledge concerning human relations for the purpose of citizenship education" (p. 69).

Barr, Barth, and Shermis (1977), in a National Council for the Social Studies publication, trace the history and development of social studies. They report social studies to be a relatively new and evolving discipline having its early roots in history. It was not until after 1900 that social scientists formally broke away from historians to form their own separate disciplines.

Coursework prescribed by the different states for social studies varies. Nevertheless, a common theme found includes geography (state, United States, world), history (state, United States, world), and government/civics (state, United States, world). Other courses sometimes required or offered as electives at the secondary level include anthropology, archaeology, career education, citizenship, conservation, consumer education/economics, culture, economics, humanities, international relations, law, minority studies, psychology, religion, and sociology. The sequence of study generally moves from focusing on home/family, to school, to neighborhood, to community/city, to state/region, to United States/nations, to hemisphere, and to the world (National Survey, 1976).

How They Are Taught

It is immediately apparent that a course of study including as wide an array of subjects as social studies must, by its very nature, lend itself to virtually all teaching techniques. However, according to Barr, Barth, and Shermis (1977), three distinct social studies teaching traditions have evolved and are currently in use. These include transmission, discovery, and reflective inquiry. Each addresses citizenship as its goal. The three traditions, respectively, and their purposes are:

1. *Social Studies Taught as Citizenship Transmission* Citizenship is best promoted by inculcating right values as a framework for making decisions.

2. *Social Studies Taught as Social Science* Citizenship is best promoted by decision making based on mastery of social science concepts, processes, and problems.

3. *Social Studies Taught as Reflective Inquiry* Citizenship is best promoted through a process of inquiry in which knowledge is derived from what citizens need to know to make decisions and solve problems (p. 67).

Special Concerns for Visually Handicapped Students and Their Teachers

Students who are visually handicapped should have no inordinate problems handling the verbal content of social studies curricula regardless of the media they use (braille, recordings, large type, regular type with or without magnification) for text materials. Generally, the verbal content of social studies courses can be "taken in stride." However, commonly used nonverbal formats often present major problems—particularly for those who require tactile materials. A review of two 1982 social studies textbook series available in both braille and large type (Scott Foresman [for grades 2 through 6] and Tiegs-Adams Series [for grades 3 through 6]) showed extensive use of pictures, maps, globes, graphs, and diagrams. Such graphic presentations are common to social studies textbooks at all levels and are effective ways of presenting information to

sighted students but are often obstacles to communication for visually handicapped persons. Social studies is highly dependent on graphics; therefore, it is this pervasive concern to which teachers of visually handicapped students studying social studies must be most vigilant.

The Blind (Tactual) Student

Nolan and Morris (1971) conducted a series of studies relating to tactile maps and their use. One objective of the project was to develop a pilot training program to teach blind students to use tactile maps. The authors found an existing vicious circle of problems in teaching the geographic component of social studies curricula. Due to lack of design information, tactile maps often have poor legibility; therefore, teachers do not use them widely nor teach their students how to read them; therefore, blind students do not learn basic geographic concepts and map reading skills; therefore, attempts to improve the design of tactile maps are frustrated because the students with whom they must be tried lack the concepts and skills needed to use the new designs. Franks and Nolan (1970) documented the severe deficit existing for this group in knowledge of geographic terms and concepts. Although researchers have addressed questions of tactual perception, map design, symbol legibility, means of producing better quality maps, and training techniques during the ensuing years, those problems previously identified are still prevalent.

Nevertheless, the need for tactile maps should not be ignored nor their value diminished. Brambring (1977) evaluated three ways of conveying information from maps to blind persons. These were (a) use of a tactile map; (b) use of a verbal description of a map; and; (c) a combination of the two. Results indicated both methods employing use of tactile maps were more effective than just a verbal description. Similar findings were reported by Nolan (1966) and Morris and Nolan (1970). Using structured interview techniques to elicit information from legally blind students who customarily used recorded text materials, 38 percent of those in the Brambring study stated they found descriptions of graphics of little or no use and usually skipped them while 35 percent said they found it necessary to use supplemental materials, usually the braille or print edition of the text. In the latter study, legally blind college students were unanimous in finding recorded graphics inadequate. Of this group 61 percent stated a preference for having graphics in written form.

Information related to design and use of tactile graphics is provided by Berla (1982). In an excellent review of pertinent research he assimilates and discusses the research of physical features contributing to symbol legibility; and identifies design considerations that contribute to tactile clarity. These include size, figure-ground features, orientation of shapes, use of symmetrical vs. asymmetrical figures, and redundancy of tactile stimuli. He notes that other research on use of tactile maps points out the critical need for users to have basic map reading concepts (e.g., that maps represent real things and spatial and time-distance relationships) and the perceptual-motor skills needed to read tactile displays.

Franks (1983) reviewed research relating to tactile maps and graphics to determine guidelines for tactile map design and related training materials. These data-based guidelines address complexity of design, use of symbols, spacing between symbols and patterns, the need for tactile edges, the value of stimulus redundancy, and scanning.

Closely related to the problems blind students have with tactile maps are their problems with tactile graphs. Barth (1983b), in reporting research on tactile graphics, noted the paucity of attention given to graphic interpretation training, particularly for graphs.

Several factors are basic to the problems blind students have with social studies curricula. One of these is the geographic content of the curricula with its intrinsic reliance on maps and globes. Another is the pervasive use of graphs and diagrams in textbooks to relate data and other information. A third is the common use of tables, the braille to print ratio of which may be as much as 6 to 1, meaning a table may extend over several pages. The implications for teachers are not to be taken lightly. First, and at an early age, blind students need to be taught the basic concepts necessary for map use. This is also critical for orientation and mobility training. Second, students need specific training to help them attain geographic concepts necessary for understanding what maps portray. Sighted people look at a river and gain the concept. For blind people it is not so easy. Third, students will need to be taught how to read maps and other graphic materials. For instance, they will need to be taught to explore graphics systematically and thoroughly and how to follow an unwieldly table from page to page. But, probably the most demanding of the implications for teachers are the needs their students will have for them to provide tactile graphics where not otherwise available. This means teachers will need to learn how to design and create such. Fortunately, materials and tools are available to help.

The Low Vision Student

Graphics found in regular print editions of social studies textbooks are often large enough to enable the student with low vision to use them with or without low vision aids. Additionally, they frequently are printed in bright colors which may contribute to their

visibility. Nevertheless, it is not possible to generalize that all low vision students will be able to use them nor that any one student will be able to use all graphics. Whether using the regular print edition of a textbook or the large type edition, this is a concern. Visual ability will vary over the entire range possible between students and may vary within the same student from time to time. Some students will be able to see only small parts of a graphic at a time and may have trouble gaining the gestalt. Consequently, teachers must be alert to the needs for assistance low vision students may have and be aware that most will require more time to use graphics and tables than will their normally sighted peers.

A technique a teacher can use to monitor students is to periodically review selected graphics with them. By asking pertinent questions and directing use, a teacher can determine the student's level of skill and learn whether the student is able to see the graphic well enough to use it. Another advantage to directed use is that it can help a student who is having trouble putting the pieces together to form the gestalt.

Even though students will undoubtedly be using whatever optical aids or low vision devices they normally use, on occasion it may be necessary for a teacher to enlarge either part or all of a graphic or to redraw it for greater clarity. When redrawing, general rules would be to enlarge it, to eliminate all nonessential elements (background clutter), and to reproduce it with bold lines offering high visual contrast to the background. Where feasible, enlargers may meet the need. Students who have a marked field restriction may benefit from the reduction of certain graphic representations. In this case, the best possible copy of the original should be used for reduced size reproduction.

Curricular Adaptations

Research Addressing Format

Two major federally funded research projects have been undertaken specifically addressing special formats for social studies curricular materials. The first was the development of an Aural Study System by the American Printing House for the Blind (Morris, Nolan, & Brothers, 1973; Morris, Nolan, & Phelps, 1973). The second was Materials Adaptations for Visually Impaired in the Social Studies (MAVIS) by the Social Science Education Consortium (Social Studies Materials, 1981).

Because many legally blind students depend upon recorded text materials (whether recorded by personal readers, volunteers, or professionals) and because learning achieved through listening is known to compare favorably with that achieved through reading braille or large type, an aural study system was designed and evaluated. It contained three coordinated components and met specified study needs of visually handicapped students previously identified (Morris & Nolan, 1970; Nolan, 1966)—a major one being the need to locate specific places (e.g., pages) within a recorded text. The content for the experimental material was a unit on Latin America taken from a world history textbook. The components of the system were (a) an indexed record; (b) a specially designed record player (the forerunner of the Indexing Cassette Player used with *The World Book Encyclopedia,* Recorded Edition) enabling rapid search and precise identification of pages; and (c) a braille supplement containing the kinds of information visually handicapped students had stated they preferred in written form. The supplement contained a title page, a table of contents, an outline of headings from the text, spelling lists, study questions, all graphics, the unit activities, references, and an index. Evaluation included two phases and results showed all blind students used as subjects were able to learn to operate the Aural Study System and were able to use it to accomplish typical study tasks.

The MAVIS project had as a purpose the adaptation of "social studies curriculum materials for use by visually handicapped students in grades K-6 in both integrated and self-contained classrooms" (Social Studies Materials, 1981, p. 1). The materials included adaptations of two 1-6 textbook series, two nontext kits (one for primary students, one for elementary), and a fifth grade component of a career awareness program. Teacher and student materials were prepared with the latter being readied in braille, large print, and recorded forms. The most important conclusion regarding application of results was that "the resulting materials are well-liked and usable by teachers and students, but such a literal adaptation is too expensive and too quickly dated to be feasible on any broad-scale basis" (Social Studies Materials, 1981, p. 53).

The results of these studies offer both useful information and a frustrating encounter with reality for teachers of visually handicapped students. On the positive side, the results indicate students can learn social studies from a variety of media, particularly if information to which they may need to refer is readily available in written form. This is extremely important when the breadth and scope of potential required readings are considered. On the negative side, results indicate that needed materials are not likely to be readily available when readings go beyond the few social studies series available in braille and large type.

The Blind (Tactual) Student

The primary concern for teachers of students requiring tactile materials in teaching social studies is the provision of graphics in tactile form. As indicated by the research, a mere description is of limited usefulness. Consequently, it is essential that important graphic materials be presented in a form blind students can use, a tactile form. Additionally, many students feel it is helpful to have descriptions of the graphics to use with them. Teachers of social studies should arrange to have such graphics prepared to accompany any material used that does not come with them. One source is Recording for the Blind, Inc. If feasible, and when requested, this organization will provide a supplement of raised line drawings to accompany their recorded texts. In addition to needing tactile graphics, students using recorded materials may find it helpful to have their teachers provide, in written form, such things as spelling lists, study questions, and important references for them.

Two pervasive concerns relating to tactile graphics are their design and use. Information and tools are available for the creation of legible, well designed graphics by teachers and volunteers. The people responsible for making tactile graphics should invest the little additional time required to learn how to do so to assure that the considerable time needed in actually making them results in useful products. The other concern is that students be instructed how to use tactile graphics. At a minimum, they should be taught to be analytical, systematic, and thorough in their approach and instructed how to track lines and analyze shapes by looking for distinctive features (Nolan, 1979).

The Low Vision Student

Many low vision students will use a large type edition or recorded text for social studies. Just as blind students using recorded materials may find it helpful to have their teachers provide, in written form, spelling lists, study questions, important references, and other information to which they may need to refer, so may the low vision student. Those using recorded materials will also need access to print graphics. Often those in the regular print edition of the text will be usable. If not, they may need to be enlarged, reduced, or redrawn for greater clarity. As with tactual readers, low vision students should be instructed to be analytical, systematic, and thorough in using graphics.

Special Social Studies Materials

Fortunately, materials have been developed and are available to help meet the special needs of visually handicapped students in social studies and their teachers. Those developed by the American Printing House for the Blind represent a sequential program for teaching what maps are, the concepts necessary for their use, and the needed skills. Although specific training in map use may not be necesary for some normally sighted students, it is for blind students. In addition to classroom applications, such skills are essential for orientation and mobility.

For use with students
• Maps Represent Real Places: Map Study I—(APH)—teaches that maps stand for real things
• Basic Map Reading Concepts: Map Study II—(APH)—teaches 30 fundamental map reading concepts related to location and direction
• Recognizing Landforms: An Audio-Tutorial Program in Map Study—(APH)—teaches 40 basic geographical concepts (Miller, 1982a)
• Simplified Continental Relief Map Cassette Programs—(APH)—self-instructional audio programs including geographic, special features, and socio-historic information about each of the six continents (Miller, 1982b)
• Tangible Graphs—(APH)—teaches skills and concepts needed to use tactile graphs (Barth, 1983a)

For the teacher
• *Social Studies for the Visually Impaired Child: MAVIS Sourcebook 4* (Singleton, 1979)—(SSEC)—includes suggestions for teachers
• *Resources for Teaching Social Studies in the Mainstreamed Classroom: MAVIS Sourcebook 6* (Singleton & Leslie, 1979)—(SSEC) includes suggestions for sources of materials
• Tactile Graphics Kit—(APH)—a kit of specialized tools for making foil masters for thermoforming (Barth, 1982)
• *Tactile Graphics Kit Guidebook* (Barth, Berla, & Davis, 1981)—(APH)—provides information on how to design and make tactile graphics and how to teach tactual readers to use them (available with Tactile Graphics Kit and separately)

Sources
APH   American Printing House for the Blind, P.O. Box 6085, Louisville, Ky. 40206
RFB   Recording for the Blind, 20 Roszel Rd., Princeton, N.J. 08540
SSEC Social Science Education Consortium, 855 Broadway, Boulder, Colo. 80302

Study questions
1. What is the primary goal of social studies curricula?
2. What is the single most pervasive concern of teachers of visually handicapped students studying social studies?
3. In what form do visually handicapped students need their graphic materials?
4. What are the three critical needs for instruction specific to blind (tactual) students studying social studies that teachers must address?
5. What types of information do visually handicapped students studying from recorded social studies materials find helpful in written form?

Additional readings
Barth, J.L., Berla, E.P., and Davis, G.L. (1981). *Tactile graphics guidebook*. Louisville, Ky.: American Printing House for the Blind.
Berla, E.P. (1982). Haptic perception of tangible graphic displays. In W. Schiff and E. Foulke (eds.), *Tactual perception: A sourcebook*. pp. 364-386. Cambridge, Mass.: Cambridge University Press.

MATHEMATICS
Pete Rossi

Indications of forms of elementary mathematics have been associated with early civilizations in history. The apparent need to count is indicated by marks drawn on cave walls. Higher forms of mathematics such as plane and solid geometry were practiced by the Greeks over 2000 years ago. At the turn of the century mathematics was taught for such various reasons as training the mind to develop reasoning ability and powers of abstraction.

The fifties are associated with a great awareness of mathematics and its technological advances as well as the "new math." Most people associate the new math with the orbiting of Sputnik I by the USSR. In fact the new math was already on its way. However, it was the associated publicity of Sputnik that helped publicize the new math. It was also this same publicity that motivated the federal government and large private foundations to give financial support to various mathematical study groups for the development of different aspects of teacher training programs in mathematics and curriculum changes on the elementary, secondary, and college levels.

These groups, as a whole, were responsible for new and changed coursework for probability and statistics, logic, trigonometry, as well as plane and solid geometry. They also advocated an emphasis on structure in numerical systems, greater precision in language used in definitions, and increasing the use of such concepts as variable, solution set, ordered pairs, scientific notation, and proof. They recommended the use of the "discovery" method of teaching, a general compressing of subject matter content from the college level to the elementary level, and the elimination of drill for other than repeated computations (Kinsella, 1965). The influence of these groups is noted in present day practices despite a lesser emphasis on certain course content and a return to drill.

Mathematics has evolved to more than just the arithmetic of numbers and the four basic algorithms of addition, subtraction, multiplication, and division. It is now a study of symbols with respect to quantity, form, algorithms, sequencing, measuring, graphing, and the methods for processing these concepts.

Special Concerns for Visually Handicapped Students

Adapted Textbooks

Why some children learn mathematics readily and others do not is a valid question. There are probably many interrelated factors. Some children are more intelligent than others as manifested by scores on intelligence tests and school achievement scores. Some students are believed to have an ability for mathematics. Whether this is true or not, one must accept that there are different skills involved for mathematics and verbal skills as noted by varying scores on such tests as the college boards.

It is generally accepted that students who are visually handicapped lag behind their sighted peers in computational skills (Brothers, 1972; Nolan, 1959). There are undoubtedly many factors such as natural aptitude and the need for adapted equipment, textbooks, and techniques to teach even such basic concepts as size, distance, and measurement.

Braille textbooks are not as easily procured as print textbooks. This is especially true for mathematics and science textbooks since there are fewer certified mathematics transcribers than literary transcribers. There is a separate code for mathematics and a separate computer code. Imagine needing to learn three separate languages while in school—English for literature, Italian for mathematics, and Spanish for computer class!

Mathematics textbooks tend to have items that are spatially arranged and color coded. For the low vision reader who needs photographically enlarged textbooks, spatial arrangement may not be a severe problem but absence of color (due to the enlargement process) may or may not hinder the learning situation and should be pointed out to the classroom teacher.

The implication of spatial arrangement and color coding present problems for the braille reader. For an elementary grade student, the incorrect answer to the question "How many red balloons are on the page?" may be caused by his missing one of the raised line drawings of the balloon rather than not counting

correctly; or it may be due to the fact that the student does not recognize the representation of the balloon; if the word balloon is used, the lower grade student may not know it; the word may be above his vocabulary level. The above discussion presumes that the transcriber is able to reproduce the raised line drawing at all which is not the general rule.

Children read from left to right in a straight line. Materials should be transcribed as such as opposed to vertical and spatially indented presentations of pictures or problems. Also, transcribers should not be forced to guess that the required word or letter is for a picture of an item to be counted (or any pictures in all books for that matter). The teacher of the visually handicapped along with the classroom teacher should make notes in the book as to what to use to represent the picture. Another suggestion is that the transcriber be given the teacher's edition with the words already printed or at least be given a photocopy of the necessary pages with the printed words.

Adapted Educational Aids

In addition to the need for special textbooks, appropriately adapted educational aids are a necessary component of any mathematics class. Aids are needed for two purposes. They are needed to supplement portions of textbooks that have been omitted due to an impracticality of tactually representing them. Besides pictures, an example of this might be any kind of graph. They are also needed to fulfill the same purpose that sighted counterparts need aids: to help in interpreting mathematical concepts.

Most adapted mathematical aids are used for graphing, representing geometric shapes, measuring, and computing. For graphing, besides braille graph paper, two popular aids are the Graphic Aid For Mathematics and the Sewell Kit (Raised Line Drawing Kit). The former of the two is a rubberized raised grid graph board. It can be used in representing: the plotting of points, bar graphs, straight lines, curved figures, plus it has applications in arithmetic, geometry, and trigonometry. The Graphic Aid for Mathematics is available from the American Printing House for the Blind, Inc. (APH).

The Sewell Kit consists of a rubberized pad and polyester paper. The paper, when placed on the pad and written on, creates raised lines. The Sewell Kit differs from the Graphic Aid for Mathematics in that it does not have a raised line grid but it does yield a permanent copy of the problem whereas the latter does not. The Sewell Kit is available from the American Foundation for the Blind, Inc. (AFB).

It should be noted that some children and teachers prefer the use of brailon paper with the Sewell Kit rather than the less expensive polyester paper that comes with the kit. It seems as if the copy is clearer and is less likely to wrinkle on brailon paper. These two aids have an advantage over braille graph paper in that graphing is done in what is referred to as the positive mode as contrasted to the negative mode. What this means is that the user does not have to think about graphing "backwards" as he does when using braille graph paper because the user does not need to press down on the back of the paper and then turn it over to feel the raised line.

There is an abundance of adapted and nonadapted aids available to teach the recognition of standard shapes. It is safe to assume that almost every teacher of mathematics who will be teaching the basic shapes has access to the appropriate blocks, planes, and wire figures. In addition for the visually handicapped, the Mitchell Wire Forms with Matched Planes and Volumes (APH) is a collection of the basic shapes presented in wire, plane, and three dimensional forms.

To show the relationship between two and three dimensions, the Geometric Forms (APH) aid is suggested. This aid consists of a plastic sheet with a raised line drawing of a square, a triangle, and a circle and solid pieces consisting of a square, triangle, circle, cube, pyramid, hemisphere, and a sphere. The solids have proportional dimensions such that they can be placed exactly on the appropriate raised line drawings.

As indicated previously, the Sewell Kit can also be used to construct raised line drawings of geometric shapes. The existing body of research pertaining to map reading and the recognition of shapes indicated that raised line drawings should be simple (Franks, 1979). In other words, there should not be a one to one correspondence between the crowded and colorful print picture and the raised line drawing. Rather, many raised line drawings should be considered in representing a complicated picture, chart, diagram, or graph if the print is trying to show several concepts at the same time.

Counting is the first formal concept in mathematics to be learned. Besides verbal repetition as characterized by children's television shows, it is suggested that actual objects be counted. Since psychologists indicate that learning progresses from concrete to abstract, familiar to unfamiliar, and self to nonself, counting should be taught as such. Count physical objects by starting with body parts (fingers, toes, eyes), then body parts in motion (steps, hops, skips, and waves), progressing to toys (blocks, beads, and pegs), household objects (chairs, windows, and utensils), and to symbolic representation using available educational aids. Nonadapted aids used for this type of symbolic representation are called manipulatives and they are part of standard curricula to varying degrees. Adapted aids are such items as the combination large print and braille APH Number Line. This device is designed for simultaneous use by the braille reader and the

classroom teacher who does not know braille. It consists of ten different number lines with both braille and print numbers.

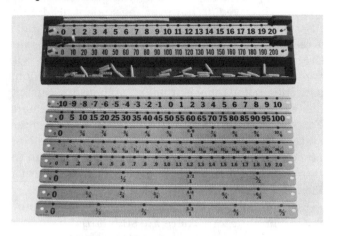

APH Number Line

After counting is understood, the child will be able to quantify the concept of measuring. Up to this point, the child will probably have developed a concept of some type of measurement. For example, the child may realize that one television show is longer than another or that the school building is further away than the child living next door. As indicated above, with the concept of counting mastered, the child is ready to quantify the measurement. The child should be able to indicate that the thirty minute comedy show is shorter than the one hour special, the two block walk to the candy store is not as long as the one mile mobility lesson to school, the forty pound dog weighs more than the twelve pound cat, and eighty degrees Farenheit (or 26.6 degrees Celsius) is warm enough to swim and thirty-two degrees Farenheit (or zero degrees Celsius) is cold enough to have snow.

In order to perform the act of measuring, adapted devices are necessary if the student is a large print or braille reader. In choosing and using an aid the teacher of the visually handicapped must maintain communication with the classroom teacher. Specifically, what is the objective of the lesson. For example, a braille protractor can be used to teach the concept of measuring the degrees in a given angle but the accuracy may not be as exact as the visual counterpart. The same accuracy requires significantly more expensive and sophisticated equipment which may be unnecessary for the immediate objective. For other forms of measuring (metric and nonmetric), rulers, thermometers, balance scales, and timers are available in various adapted forms including larger print, braille dots, and spoken output.

The use of these aids can be easily integrated into a standard mathematics curriculum. It should be noted that most of these adapted aids for measuring are designed so that the classroom teacher does not need to know braille because print is also part of the device, or braille dots are used to establish a pattern only as opposed to symbolizing a braille character, or speech is involved. If, however, the student needs more instruction in learning the concept of measuring, it is recommended that the Introduction to Measurement in Mathematics (APH item) be used. This is a kit with three sets of tactile aids and three sets of instructional activities in linear measurement, volume and capacity measurement, and mass and weight measurement. For specifically learning the metric measurement system, the Metric Measurment Program is recommended as it encompasses all of the materials in the Introduction Program but uses metric units (American Printing House for the Blind, 1984).

Another concept that follows the mastery of counting is computation. There are standard devices that can be used in teaching computation. One aid is the abacus which, although not used nearly as much in standard curricula is still used in teaching visually handicapped students. One reason for this is that the modified Cranmer Abacus (APH) is designed with a backing so that the numbers do not "erase" if the device is tilted.

The brailler is still the most popularly used device for working out computations. The arithmetical computations are performed in a manner similar to how one would type a computation problem on a typewriter. Attention would have to be paid to the horizontal and vertical alignments as well as the need to back space due to the rightward motion of the typewriter and the leftward motion of solving the problem. It is for this reason that it is recommended that the vision teacher give the student practice problems filling in the blanks on spatially formatted problems. Once the child knows how to format and braille the number exactly where it is to be placed, incorrect answers can be isolated to misunderstandings of the concept and not due to brailling errors.

After the student understands what it means arithmetically to perform the four basic operations, calculators are considered in standard curricula. For the low vision student, there are several workable options. Besides holding the calculator closer, it is suggested that magnifiers which rest on the visual display be used. Unlike hand-held magnifiers, this will allow the free use of the hands. Some students also use standard calculators with enlarged visual displays. Another inexpensive alternative is the calculator with synthesized speech output. Not only do they say the key name when the key is struck but they also read the answer number by number or with appropriate place value. For example, 1,245 can be read as 1-2-4-5 or one thousand two hundred forty five. Obviously, this latter suggestion, along with somewhat more

expensive braille output devices, is appropriate for the totally blind student as well.

Chisenbop (a system of using fingers for calculating) has been suggested as a method that is applicable to visually handicapped students (Struve, Cheney, & Rudd 1979-80). Although it is a workable supplementary method, it is not as such a standard part of most school curricula. Thus, the factor of time in an already crowded school day must be considered, unless an alternative such as summer camp is used for instruction.

Oral arithmetic is practiced by and encouraged for sighted and visually handicapped students. The range of application goes from using flash cards and reciting the multiplication tables to using certain algebraic procedures. It is not a practical substitute for problems needing a calculator but it is very helpful for quick calculations involving daily arithmetic computations. For example, the addition of two digit numbers is made easier if the second is thought of as a multiple of ten plus the ones digit. Thus, adding 35 plus 47 is simplified if the 47 is thought of as 40 and 7. First add the 35 and 40 and obtain 75. Then add the seven. The answer is 82. For multiplying certain numbers such as 31 times 29, the recognition of this as a problem that can be written algebraically as the difference of two squares makes mental computation easy. That is, 31 times 29 is the same as $(30+1)(30-1)$ which is the product of the difference of two squares. The answer is always the first number squared minus the second number squared, that is, 30 squared minus 1 squared which is 900 minus 1 or 899.

Since fractions and decimals are part of any standard curriculum, mathematical concepts of fractions or decimals should be taught. The written representations of fractions and decimals are also an established part of the mathematical code. What the vision teacher has to do is to teach braille written representation and suggest to the mathematics teacher methods by which the student can tactually work with fractions and decimals. Payne and Scholl (1981) suggest that one method of showing students fractions is to begin with concrete objects such as strips of paper folded into different numbers of equal parts. Using the written names for the parts (half, third, fourth, etc.) helps in properly naming the fractions. If this method is used, it is suggested that the student help in folding the papers for some of the fractions so they understand what the whole was and can contrast the resultant part to it.

The use of nested containers is helpful in teaching equal fractional parts. For example, use the top of a shoebox and cut a cardboard (for rigidity and the smooth meeting of edges) that is to be nested as equal fractional parts. The Fractional Parts of Wholes (APH) aid uses a similar concept using three nested circles that are divided into differing fractional sectors. Use body parts and count one half (one out of two) of the student's fingers. Have the student count every third hop while an adult counts every hop until the student is told to stop at an appropriate number (multiple of three). Count every fourth block of a pile consisting of a multiple of four. Create new piles and ask which pile is larger. Using two thirds of the number of forks in the kitchen cabinet drawer, are there enough forks to set the table?

Have the student braille thirty "for" signs across the top of a page. On a separate line have the student braille one "for" sign for every two he counts on the top line. Which line is longer? Repeat this for every one out of three, two out of three, one out of six, two out of six, three out of six, etc. Have the child label each line by naming it its fractional equivalent. Which lines are equal in length and which are longer?

To show that five-sixths is more than one-half, the teacher of the visually handicapped should select a passage consisting of exactly sixty words (just stop when this number is reached). Then, have the child braille one out of two words (every other one as read by the teacher) and then have the child braille five out of six words (as read by the teacher). Which one makes more sense since it has more words?

The use of time is also suggested in teaching fractions to visually handicapped students. It is a concept they can relate to and can easily estimate. There are sixty minutes in an hour and thirty minutes in one half hour, thus 30 over 60 equals one half. Since 2, 3, 4, 5, 6, and 10 are factors of sixty, there are many fractions that can be related to an hour.

Since there exists an arithmetical relationship between fractions and decimals, an understanding of fractions helps in understanding decimals. The use of money and the fractional equivalent of coins to a dollar helps to equate decimals and fractions. For example, a dime is one tenth of a dollar and is written .10 whereas the quarter is written as .25 and is one fourth of a dollar. It should be noted that this is a monetary relationship only and has no physical relationship with comparing metallic coins to paper dollars.

Computer Software

Although they are a relatively recent addition to the school and society, computers now permeate all aspects of society. It is impossible to live a day without some type of computer contact. Computer chips are now found in watches, clocks, radios, microwave ovens, washing machines, typewriters, cash registers, check-out counters, photocopy equipment, and the list goes on and will continue to grow. It has been stated that more "computers" are now manufactured each year than people are born.

Computers are a subject with which many people are unfamiliar. Even those who are "experts" with computers find it difficult to keep up because new products are rapidly being introduced. This unfamiliarity carries over to teachers of the visually handicapped. There are valid reasons. The present curriculum for training teachers of the visually handicapped is already a full course of study. While performing the tasks for which they were trained, experienced teachers have found technology changing rapidly.

Despite these reasons, it is necessary that teachers of the visually handicapped learn about computers in order to work with their students. Computers are more involved than the average household appliance. Unlike a television set, the user cannot just turn it on and find what they want with one turn of the knob. However, it is not required that the computer user learn about how the central processing unit works or how to program. The teacher needs to know what the computer can do, what controls are needed to tell it to perform the task, and how it interfaces with the other equipment the student may be using.

In mathematics, computers are used for problem solving because of their ability to quickly store and process vast amounts of information. There are three approaches classroom teachers can employ. They can either use any of the thousands of existing software programs, teach their students to write their own programs, or a combination of these. The existing software programs take on many different formats ranging from tutorial lessons, computerized assisted instruction (CAI), educational games, to arcade games.

The existing mathematical software programs are written on such diverse topics as counting and number recognition, addition, subtraction, multiplication, division, word problems, fractions, decimals, mixed numbers, percentages, geometry, graphing, algebra, trigonometry, probability and statistics, and other concepts too numerous to list.

The students can also be taught how to write their own programs to solve simple problems (as opposed to writing an accounts payable software program). In order to do this, the student must learn how to program using any one of several languages. The student may program in one of the many popular programming languages such as FORTRAN, PILOT, BASIC, or PASCAL, with the possible exception of LOGO because it is so visual. Also, the programming use of the computer in the graphic mode may cause similar problems due to its visual nature.

Computer Hardware

Most classroom teachers will be using one of the popular brands of microcomputers as opposed to a business mainframe. The reason for this is that a microcomputer is a portable desktop computer (also referred to as a personal computer). The business mainframe is a huge system that many people in different buildings and states may be accessing simultaneously. As a teacher of the visually handicapped, the primary role will be related to having the student access the microcomputer.

Most microcomputers (and mainframes) are accessible by the visually handicapped. Student access can be broken into two categories: input and output. Input is the act of getting information into the computer memory. Output is the logical opposite. The most popular methods of input pertinent to this discussion are typing at the keyboard, with and without synthesized speech, and brailling on an electronic braille display. The most popular types of output are inkprinters, braille embossing devices, visual displays (monitors), electronic displays, and synthesized speech.

For a low vision student, input can be accomplished using low vision aids and closed circuit television devices with and without synthesized speech. There is also a full monitor magnifier that, although not designed for the low vision student, is very helpful. It is called a Beamscope (available from Independent Living Aids, Inc.) and its main purpose is for enlarging the screen image for group viewing.

For reading output, the low vision student can use the same devices used for input, plus using magnifying aids to read output from a regular inkprinter. Some students have had success sitting closer to the monitor and using an oversized monitor as opposed to the smaller sizes. This will yield a practical and highly efficient method of obtaining increased magnification.

For the braille reader, input can be accomplished using an electronic braille display or using the regular computer keyboard with a synthetic speech adaptor. For reading output, the braille reading student can use the same devices used for input plus employ a braille embossing device which will yield a paper copy.

Role of the Teacher of the Visually Handicapped

There is an ongoing need to communicate with the classroom teacher with respect to the role of the teacher of the visually handicapped. Effective communication will result in better understanding of the mathematical concepts to be taught and appropriate recommendations for special techniques and educational aids. With respect to this latter point, the earlier the teacher knows what will be taught during the year, the sooner textbooks and aids can be ordered. The need to order materials as early as possible (preferably before the school year begins) is crucial since these books and aids are not always readily available. The more communication and working together, the better the understanding (and correction) of problems. Is the child getting an incorrect answer because of a problem related to braille, or a misunderstood mathematical concept?

Vocabulary itself can be the problem. For example, one student and mathematics teacher became frustrated with each other while working together trying to perform "cross" multiplication. Since this is only a valid concept in print and not in braille because of the formatting, their frustration was understandable. It was the role of the teacher of the visually handicapped to discover this cause of frustration and explain to the teacher how the fractions are spatially formatted in braille. A mutually agreed upon solution was to use the term product of the means times the extremes which is really the correct terminology rather than cross multiplication.

The classroom teacher will probably not have the time to work individually with the visually handicapped student above the usual time given to other students. Thus, when necessary, it is suggested that the teacher of the visually handicapped consider recommending supplemental instruction or individualized tutoring (or whatever term is used in a particular state). There are various eligibility criteria with respect to different legislative mandates. This instruction may be supplemental to the class or in lieu of the class as circumstances require.

Following are some suggestions which the teacher of the visually handicapped can make to the classroom teacher. Since homework may present a problem because of the significantly longer length of time it may take a blind or visually handicapped student to do computational problems, it is suggested that the student be given only a representative sample of all the homework problems. This balance will help save time while allowing reinforcement of the problems. For taking notes from the board, teachers may verbalize what is written as it is written (most teachers do this automatically). Teachers may also involve sighted students by asking them to make carbon copies of their notes and having a reader read them to the visually handicapped student as necessary. Or the classroom teacher may photocopy the lesson plans for the supplemental mathematics teacher to use.

For classroom test taking, the student may utilize braille, and/or various aids, be given the test orally, or a combination of these. Since rate of work and time is a factor, it is also generally accepted that more time be allotted to the actual test taking. In many states there are mandates which allow blind students twice the time and low vision time and a half. These suggestions should carry over to standardized tests as well as the classroom tests. However, on occasion teachers of the visually handicapped have experienced problems in this area. Many times problems are solved by the written suggestion that certain test items be eliminated from the scoring because they are testing solely visual concepts. Other times, it may involve the written suggestion that the blind student be allowed to take certain aids into the testing situation. Like the sighted child who is at least allowed paper and pencil, the blind and visually handicapped student needs some equipment such as a brailler, braille paper, and at times, depending upon the test, an abacus or a calculator.

It may be appropriate for the blind or visually handicapped child to be given the test separate from the group due to needed extra time, use of aids, or the ordering of the test in a specialized media such as braille or large print.

The Future

Acknowledging that no one can accurately predict the future, there are some probable and possible events that may occur. Computers will become more accessible and special problems will be overcome. For example, totally blind students will be able to read columns on a monitor and tactually interpret graphic displays on the monitor. Besides the existing literary braille translation programs, there will be mathematical code and computer code translation programs. Thus, textbooks will become more quickly and readily available. There will be an increase in available software specifically designed for the handicapped with respect to educational learning and tutorial lessons. Vocationally, employment opportunities at home and on the job will increase. Unlike a barrier associated with blindness, the computer will make society more accessible to the visually handicapped.

Mathematical Code and Computer Codes

The Nemeth Code is the mathematical braille code used by students in performing arithmetical computations and mathematical problem solving. It differs from the Computer Code (which is not to be confused with computer braille translation programs). All codes use the standard cell design but assign different meanings to the same symbol. There are hundreds of symbols in the codes. The main reason for this is that for print programs that have to be transcribed into braille, exact programming spacing must be maintained and of course no numeric indicators and capital signs are used in regular print. The most common symbols are included in Chart 21.1. It should be noted that due to the need to standardize all computer operational commands for different pieces of equipment, the Braille Authority of North America is reviewing the Computer Code.

The numbers used in the mathematical codes use the same pattern as the literary code but the pattern is dropped one line.

The teaching of mathematical concepts to blind and visually handicapped students is a group effort with each member giving individual help. The classroom or mathematics teacher brings the mathematical expertise. The teacher of the visually handicapped must bridge the gap between his specialty and that of the classroom or mathematics teacher. In addition to knowledge and concept development, the knowledge and use of specialized adapted equipment and educational aids is necessary.

Study questions

1. Why is the learning of mathematics generally more difficult for a visually handicapped person than a sighted person?
2. Explain how the teacher of visually handicapped students would assist the teacher of mathematics with respect to the teaching of graphing.
3. Select one teaching aid and explain its strengths and weaknesses.
4. List alternative strategies for teaching fractions to a totally blind student.
5. List the adapted methods by which a low vision student can access a microcomputer.

Additional readings

National Council of Teachers of Mathematics. (1986). *Arithmetic teacher.* Reston, Va.: Author.

Bureau of Education for Exceptional Students. (1983). *A resource manual for the development and evaluation of special programs for exceptional students* (Volume 111-F: Electronic Communication Devices for Visually Impaired Students, Part 1; Computer Accessibility for the Visually Impaired). Tallahassee, Fla.: Author.

McGillivray, R. (ed.). (1983). Voice output for computer access by the blind and visually impaired. *Aids and Appliances Review,* Nos. 9 & 10. Boston, Mass.: The Carroll Center for the Blind.

Chart 21.1   Selected braille mathematical symbols

In the literary braille code, numbers are preceded by the numeral sign: ⠼ followed by the first ten letters of the alphabet in their normal position.
In the braille code for mathematics and science notations, numbers are placed in the lower cells:

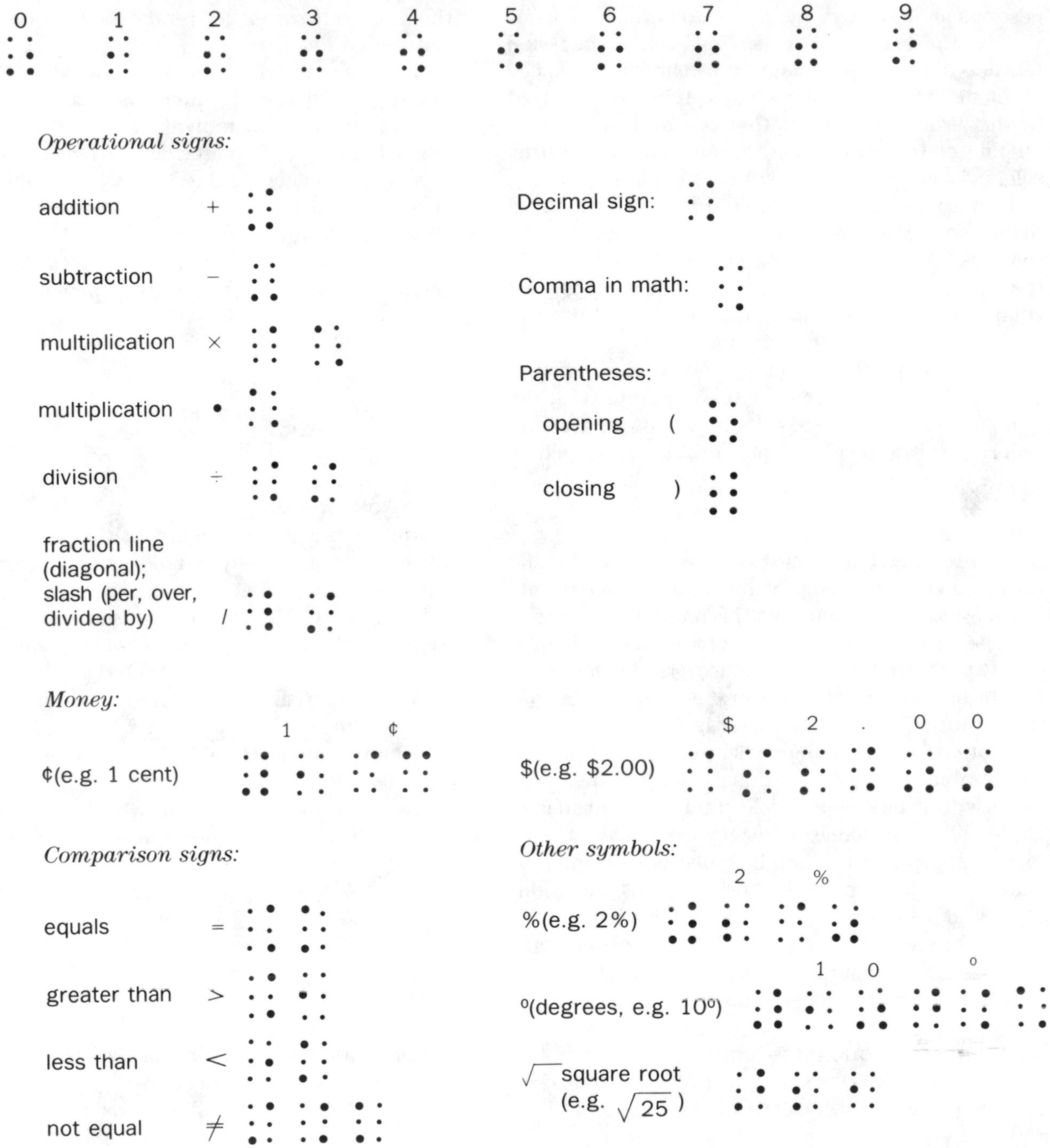

0   1   2   3   4   5   6   7   8   9

Operational signs:

addition   +

subtraction   –

multiplication ×

multiplication •

division   ÷

fraction line
(diagonal);
slash (per, over,
divided by)   /

Decimal sign:

Comma in math:

Parentheses:

opening   (

closing   )

Money:

1   ¢

¢(e.g. 1 cent)

$ 2   .   0   0

$(e.g. $2.00)

Comparison signs:

equals   =

greater than   >

less than   <

not equal   ≠

Other symbols:

2   %

%(e.g. 2%)

1   0   °

°(degrees, e.g. 10°)

√ square root
(e.g. √25)

Source: American Printing House for the Blind, *The Nemeth braille code for mathematics and science notation.* Louisville, Ky.: Author, 1980.

SCIENCE
Kathleen Mary Huebner with Linda De Lucchi, Larry Malone and Myrna R. Olson

This section describes the purpose of science teaching in K-12 education; what adaptations in equipment and teaching procedures are necessary to teach science to blind and visually handicapped students; guidelines for teachers, both in special settings and in mainstreamed classrooms, and resources for supplies and equipment for teaching science. Developments in technological adaptations and instruction and the important role of computers in enabling visually handicapped students to work in science are outlined.

Science, the search for evidence and knowledge; technology, the application of scientific principles; and societal issues, the influences of science and technology on people, are important themes in the education of all citizens.

A position paper endorsed by the National Science Teachers Association (1982) emphasizes the need for scientific and technological literacy for all citizens and recommends that science teaching emphasize the; development of knowledge and of process and inquiry skills; application of the knowledge and skills to personal and social decision making; enhancement of attitudes, values, and appreciations of science and technology; and interactions of science and technology in the context of science-related societal issues.

To this end the contemporary science curriculum for all students should provide not only activities for the development of physical and life science concepts, and of science processes, but also an appreciation of the world. Students should participate in learning activities that develop science knowledge and process skills and that provide opportunities to apply these skills in the solution of problems and the exploration of science-technology-societal issues. The outcome of good science teaching should develop scientific and technological literacy, and enable students to prepare for either further study in science-related areas or for informed participation in modern society. Knowledge in science is continually advancing and expanding the understanding of the universe; citizens must be able to incorporate these discoveries into appropriate aspects of their lives.

Science should be recognized as a fundamental component in the education of all children. Youngsters by nature question and test their environment to understand themselves better and their relationship to their surroundings. They are curious to find out how systems work and where things come from. This systematic accumulation of such information and inquiry into the nature of things is one of the objectives of science education.

This part discusses the considerations related to teaching science to visually handicapped pupils, adaptations necessary for effective science education, and resources that will assist teachers to ensure that their visually handicapped students acquire competencies necessary for scientific and technological literacy.

General Considerations Related to Teaching Science to Visually Handicapped Pupils

If visually handicapped students are to derive maximum benefit from the science curriculum, their instruction must be soundly based in a multisensory approach directed toward the acquisition of information from other sources of sensory input to compensate at least partially for the reduced visual sensory input. The development of concepts can thus flow more readily from the varied sources of sensory input.

A Multisensory Approach

Students with normal vision learn a great deal through incidental and planned observation of the activities of other people. They can see that a seed has sprouted, how wires are connected to get a complete circuit, and that bubbles form in a cup when certain liquid materials are mixed. Visually handicapped students cannot learn from remote visual observation. They must have direct access to objects, materials, organisms, procedures, and operations through a multisensory approach in order to gain knowledge and integrate information into concepts.

Understanding the processes of science depends on the ability of the students to make observations and to quantify those observations. Observation is a multisensory process, the integration of input from auditory, tactile, and olfactory as well as visual sources (Thier, 1979). Low vision students should be encouraged to incorporate the use of their vision whenever possible. The teacher of visually handicapped children should explain to the science teacher, as well as other instructional staff, the types of objects and actions students are able to see and under what conditions, that is, their functional vision. (See Chapter 3.) Specific examples relative to the individual should be given, rather than mere interpretation of quantitative clinical information about the degree of vision. Other sensory losses should also be noted, such as the reduced tactile sense in diabetic children.

A multisensory approach to learning science is diverse and active. It can open new avenues for expression and creativity, and serve to motivate students by helping to stimulate interest and realize potential.

Concept Development

Concept development in science for visually handicapped students follows the same cognitive sequence as for any other student: observation, data collection and recording, and analysis. Visually handicapped students need to touch objects, materials, and organisms in order to observe size, shape, texture, pattern, and change. They must smell sprouting seeds,

products, reactions, and fruits in order to observe variety and evidence of change. They must listen to scurrying isopods, fizzing reactions, and tuning forks, in order to observe movement, variety and change.

Data are information; science is built on creating, recording, and manipulating data. In order to understand data the fundamental process must be grounded in direct sensory experiences. For example, students learn the concept of weight from a simple two-pan balance with a tactile balance indicator that lets them compare objects to numbers of gram pieces. After a variety of weighing experiences students will understand how the weight of objects is determined and will internalize the concept of weight. The process is similar for developing other concepts such as temperature, distance, and volume. Internalization of concepts provides a basis for further study. Advanced visually handicapped students can make measurements with remote sensing instruments and record the results of such measurements with computers. The key to developing the concept is direct sensory experiences with a variety of application activities.

Analysis is an intellectual process that is dependent on skill and cognitive development. The process of analysis is facilitated if information has been effec-

tively gathered and recorded for efficient retrieval and study.

Thoughtful sequencing of experiences can facilitate concept formation. Each activity should be carefully sequenced as to its component parts. (See Chapters 9, 12, & 20 on Task Analysis.) Further, science activities should be presented in hierarchical sequence. There are two ways to think about an activity sequence, horizontal sequencing and vertical sequencing. Both have a definite place in the science program and both contribute to concept formation.

Horizontal sequencing is the process of putting together a series of activities that converge on a concept. Each activity reinforces the same concept. For example, if students successfully complete a variety of experiences such as swinging pendulums, sinking rafts, flying wind-up airplanes, and monitoring heart rates, their concepts of variables and controlled experiments are reinforced. In other words, the concepts presented do not depend or build upon each other, but they do have common facets. Visually handicapped students can often benefit from the kind of reinforcement of concepts provided by horizontal sequencing of activities, especially when the concepts are fundamental to all science and set the stage for effective experimentation.

Vertical sequencing is the process of putting together a series of activities that build toward a higher concept. Each activity is prerequisite to the ones that follow. An example of this kind of sequencing is found in the study of magnetism and electricity. Students are first introduced to the concept of magnetism. Next the students experience the basic concepts of electricity: open and closed circuit, conductors, insulators. The third activity builds on these concepts, introducing students to the concept of electromagnetism. The final activity puts it all together to make a telegraph unit which they use to communicate with a code of their own design. Each activity develops a concept that is critical for understanding subsequent concepts.

To facilitate concept formation, certain components in the educational process must be considered. These are described in the next part.

The Teacher

The teacher of the visually handicapped is a facilitator for the teaching of science. Teachers of visually handicapped pupils vary greatly in their interest in and ability to teach science. Many feel intimidated by science because they do not know the content. For example, they cannot explain why a candle burns, or why it gets hot in the process. Or they are fearful of working with an electrical experiment because they do not know what electricity is or how it works.

In contrast, other teachers incorporate science into

the curriculum regularly. They understand that the challenge of science is the *process*, rather than the knowledge of facts, or *content*. These teachers do not limit themselves to readings from the science text, or lectures on science facts; instead they encourage students to find things out for themselves. They provide materials to explore and manipulate, and build the skills of observation, experimentation, and inquiry that follow from student investigation. They integrate the core curricular basic skills of reading, communication, writing, computation, and artistic expression into the science experience, and use the science activity as a springboard to practice these skills.

Visually handicapped pupils need teachers who:

are skilled in using the processes of science to enrich the total curriculum for the students;

are sensitive to each student's cognitive learning style and provide science experiences that match that style;

use hands-on materials to help students with concept formation;

know where and how to obtain appropriate materials to use in science teaching;

provide verbal descriptions of diagrams and photographs, demonstrations, and visual observations of experimental outcomes; utilize whenever possible, materials and procedures that provide access to the concepts under investigation.

The involvement of teachers of visually handicapped pupils in the teaching of science depends in large measure on the setting in which they are employed. In some residential settings and in self-contained day school classes, teachers, especially at the elementary level, may teach science as part of the regular curriculum. Such teachers will require greater depth in the content of science. In other residential settings, classes may be taught by specialists; if these teachers are not knowledgeable about the education of visually handicapped pupils, other teachers in the school are available to assist them in selecting materials and methods appropriate to the needs of the pupils.

In day school resource room and itinerant programs, teachers of visually handicapped pupils will rarely teach science since this curricular area is typically taught by regular classroom teachers or special science teachers. In these settings, the teacher of the visually handicapped usually serves as a consultant to the regular teacher on selection of appropriate methods and materials and any other instructional problems related to the teaching of science concepts to visually handicapped pupils. In-depth knowledge of science is desirable but not essential for teachers in these settings.

Planned professional development experiences for teachers of visually handicapped pupils, however, are highly recommended. These include:

special workshops on the teaching of science conducted by colleges and universities for regular teachers;

attendance and participation in conventions and workshops sponsored by professional organizations;

inservice sessions conducted by personnel in instructional materials centers, usually under the aegis of state departments of education;

readings in professional journals both in special education and science education;

participation in special SAVI/SELPH workshops.

Teachers who have an opportunity to participate in the latter activity are introduced to a planned sequence of inservice education. The program Science Activities for the Visually Impaired (SAVI) began as a federally funded three-year project to develop science activities for upper-elementary and junior-high school aged blind and visually handicapped students. It was expanded and revised to be a suitable resource for physically handicapped and learning disabled students in a project called Science Enrichment for Learners with Physical Handicaps (SELPH). The resulting product, SAVI/SELPH, is a generalizable special education science resource (De Lucchi & Malone, 1982). It includes:

1. Detailed teacher guides for 40 science activities, including background, materials list, lesson plan, evaluation, language development, and science extension.

2. Student materials, available in complete kits, or as individual line items, including measuring tools, specialized equipment, and student record sheets.

3. Other print resources including a list of student reading and listening materials to complement each activity.

In the special workshops, teachers learn about the background, information, instructional methods, and the use of materials. The program includes the following components:

1. *Teachers enroll for training in pairs*—ideally, each pair includes a special educator and a regular educator from the same school, so they can support each other.

2. *Training spans several months.* A thirty-two contact-hour course, meeting for four hours once a month for eight months provides the participants with time to try out the activities and methods with their students and report back about their experiences.

3. *Hands-on experiences with materials.* Teachers do the experiments and set up the materials themselves in a structured learning situation so that their experiences may serve as a model when they instruct their students.

4. *Instructors available to the teachers.* Inservice programs address the specific needs of individuals through individualized consultation. The more personalized and responsive the training is, the more effective the performance of the trainee.

Teachers not able to make use of this special program can nevertheless apply many of the same common sense principles to organizing their own science curriculum and class procedures for the blind and visually handicapped students. Appendix H presents a sample SAVI scientific reasoning module.

The Curriculum

The most effective science activities are those including numerous tactile and auditory interactions, and extensive manipulation of equipment, materials, and organisms.

For an example of a multisensory science experience, consider the popular activity of sprouting seeds. Typically, milk cartons are cut in half, or yogurt cups gathered, soil is metered in, seeds are planted and watered, and time and nature take their course. In due time plants appear and students observe (visually) the wonder of plant growth. Such activities need enrichment for blind and visually handicapped students. First of all, not just any seed will do. Seeds should be large and tactually distinct. Beans, peas, sunflowers, corn, and squash are excellent seeds for a multisensory program.

For visually handicapped students to observe the process of seed germination, soil is not appropriate. Seeds should be sprouted in water in pans or commercially available sprouters. Students should feel and smell changes daily to understand the germination process. Finally, when the germinated seedlings are about a week old, several can be grown further using a hydroponic setup (see Figure 21.1). The hydroponic approach is desirable because students can continue to monitor root growth as well as shoot growth without sacrificing the plant in the process. The whole plant is available for multisensory observation as it continues to grow through its entire life cycle.

Similarly, curriculum planning for science education at more advanced levels should be within a multisensory framework. The visually handicapped student should be allowed to explore concepts via tactile methods whenever possible, and encouraged to relate her acquired skills and knowledge to her own sensory environment. Consultation with other teachers and specialists will be vital in choosing and adapting appropriate science curriculum at all levels.

Figure 21.1   Hydroponic seed sprouting

Tools, Materials, and Setting

Access to both the process and content of science depends on the ability of the students to make observations and to quantify those observations. Specialized tools and carefully selected material are called for. Because a great deal of information will be received through tactile channels, materials must be chosen that meet a number of criteria. Objects such as beads, seeds, washers, wires, and threads should not be very small. Small objects that need to be counted or organized are tedious or impossible to keep track of. When dropped or misplaced, small objects are difficult to find. Small organisms that move quickly or fly are not appropriate. Instead, use larger objects: seeds such as beans, peas, and sunflowers, and heavy twine. Large, sturdy organisms such as crayfish (with pincher guards), isopods, and snails can introduce blind youngsters to many behaviors and interactions of animals without the danger of injury to the organisms, or the frustration of escape.

A critically important process in science, such as measuring, requires special tools in order to provide access for blind students. A semi-rigid meter tape, possessing properties of both a meter *stick* and a meter *tape* is ideal for visually handicapped students. Centimeters are indicated by raised lines, and numbers

Chart 21.2   Basic subject areas and science activities

	Concept/Subject areas	Specific tools/Activities
Primary ages 3-8	World around us: nature, animals, liquid, movement, reaction sequence	Seed sprouting, animal visits, pendulum work, magnets, tuning forks
Intermediate ages 8-14	Biology Chemistry Scientific method	Lab work: tools, procedures for measuring, weighing, comparing, recording data and results; introduction to computers
Advanced ages 14-18	Physics Chemistry Biology	Computers Electricity Dissection

are presented in both braille and large print. Students can easily measure distance along flat horizontal surfaces, vertical distance, or curved surfaces (circumference of a basketball).

Most of the above suggestions hold for low vision students as well, except that in most cases the low vision students will use visual rather than tactile input for dealing with written language. Labels and instructions will need to be prepared in a print size that is appropriate for the visual acuity and perception of each individual student. Contrast between objects and backgrounds should be strong, and color should have strong values rather than being weak pastel shades. As with any subject, the science lessons should be taught under uniform, diffuse lighting, with no glare, no shadows, and no strong backlighting.

The most effective organization of the setting for science work depends on whether the student is in a mainstreamed or a special class situation.

Visually handicapped students learn science in the regular classroom where the visually handicapped student has his own experimental set-up or shares with just one other student, and the regular students share equipment in groups of up to five students per set-up. An alternative to whole-class instruction is to subdivide the class and teach science to half of the class while the other half does seat work or participates in some alternative active learning. Instruction can be provided by the regular classroom teacher, or in some cases by an aide, paraprofessional, or interested parent. Subdivided classes allow the instructor to focus more attention on the special needs of the visually handicapped student and for this reason is a recommended practice when resources permit.

Organizational schemes for students in residential or self-contained setting can be even more individualized. In small self-contained groups of one to four students, each student should have a complete experimental set-up. This amount of material is manageable and this number of work stations can be continuously monitored with relative ease. The most

effective way for the instructor to operate in this situation is on the opposite side of a roomy table, or from inside a "horseshoe" shaped arrangement of tables. Such an arrangement allows for continuous monitoring of student behaviors and efficient introduction and removal of materials, resulting in rapid progress by the students. Every student is involved in every step of the lesson simultaneously.

With larger groups of visually handicapped students it is possible to operate in a similar manner with the same amount of equipment but the students will have to form partnerships. Progress will necessarily be slower because partners will have to share equipment. This does not mean that one student will complete step A, the second step B while the first watches, and so forth, as sighted students do. Each student will need a chance to do step A, then both will follow with step B, and so on to guarantee an uninterrupted sequence of actions. An exception to this general rule would be when an experimental sequence is repeated a number of times, such as when students investigate magnets to see how the number of spacers between two magnets affects the force of attraction. One student can do the experiment with one spacer, the second student can try two spacers, the first can do the experiment with three spacers, etc. The process is known by both through direct experience and they can share results. In this case it is not necessary for both students to repeat the experiment with each and every spacer to fully apprehend the concept under investigation.

Chart 21.2 outlines some of the basic subject areas and science activities by very rough age and ability ranges. These will vary greatly according to the type of school, student, and whether there are both academic and vocational track students enrolled.

Summary Guidelines: Method, Strategy, Materials

On the following page are guidelines that should provide guidance for teachers of visually handicapped pupils as they work with pupils in science education.

Method

Orient students to work area, materials, equipment, etc., and provide them with a controlled work space.

Set up instructional settings to assure the most advantageous position between the teacher and students for effective monitoring.

Develop science activities to meet the needs of visually handicapped students as well as modify standard experiments for meaningful, multisensory experiences.

Strategy

Encourage every student to be involved in every step of the lesson simultaneously. Do not encourage visually handicapped students to play a passive role, or to act only as the recorder in experiments with sighted partners.

Select sighted team members carefully to work along with visually handicapped students. Rotating partners for the entire class may be an appropriate strategy.

Observe visually handicapped students participating in the science class periodically. After class offer suggestions to both the visually handicapped students and the teacher.

Maintain a close working relationship with the science teacher to encourage frequent feedback and mutual consultation.

Materials

Provide real objects, organisms, and materials for classroom use and experiments as often as possible.

Use sturdy objects and organisms of appropriate size for tactual examination, such as beans, peas, sunflower seeds, crayfish, isopods, snails, etc.

Describe or provide alternatives to chalkboard work, printed diagrams, photographs, etc. Provide clear, high contrast printed materials for low vision students.

Germinate seeds in water rather than soil so students can observe the growth process through many senses.

Adapt or modify tools and materials for effective use by visually handicapped students. For example, fix a physical stop to a large syringe so the plunger can be pulled out at pre-set measures such as 10, 25, or 50 ml., or tactile notches can be cut in edges of the plunger of a syringe to determine a variety of volumes.

Acquire specialized tools, data recording materials and other materials when necessary, e.g, braille rulers, thermometers, speech output calculators, scales, cell models, etc.

Implement the use of organizational containers such as muffin tins or egg cartons.

Use stable and nonbreakable materials.

Label containers and materials in braille and large print.

Use high contrast between materials and work surfaces whenever possible.

Be certain that written materials are accessible to the students. These include textbooks, science journal articles, teacher handouts, etc.

Make use of braille, audio tapes, large print, and sighted readers for the students.

With the ideas and methods covered in this section in mind, teachers of visually handicapped students will find they can become excellent *science* teachers as well. We need more trainers, but we also need more skilled master teachers to spread the word and to teach the courses. There is no greater nurturer of a student's curiosity about the world, no greater incentive toward interaction with one's environment, than an early introduction to science. The concepts, contents, and methodology of science education can be an important contribution to student self-expression and confident judgment.

Study questions

1. Select a specific science concept from any grade level and describe how a multisensory approach would be incorporated into the learning experience.
2. List the benefits visually handicapped students should derive from science education.
3. Prepare a list of regular science teachers who are teaching visually handicapped students in mainstream classes. You may select either elementary or secondary level. Interview one or more of those teachers about the experiences.
4. Select one item from a general science materials catalog and tell how you would adapt it for visually handicapped pupils.
5. Select one science experiment from any elementary or secondary science textbook and tell how you would adapt it for visually handicapped pupils.

Additional readings

De Lucchi, L. and Malone, L. (1982). Science Activities for the visually impaired. In G. Mangold, (ed.), *A teacher's guide to the special educational needs of blind and visually handicapped children*. New York, N.Y.: American Foundation for the Blind, Inc.

Malone, L. and De Lucchi, L. (1981). Multisensory science education—Meeting special challenges. In Corrick, B. (ed.), *Teaching handicapped students Science* Washington, D.C.: NEA.

National Science Teachers Association (1982). *Science-Technology-Society, Science education for the 1980s*. Washington, D.C.: National Science Teachers Association.

Thier, H.D. (1979). Fostering Observations in a Science Program for the Young Blind Student. In Hofman and Richer (eds.), *Sourcebook: Science education and the physically handicapped*. Washington, D.C.: Natinal Science Teachers Association.

Vernon, D. (1981). The use of activity-centered science activities to facilitate the mainstreaming of elementary school children with special needs. *Science Education*, **65** (5), pp. 467-475.

FOREIGN LANGUAGES
Kathleen Mary Huebner

Visually handicapped students study foreign languages during their elementary, secondary, and post secondary education. Languages frequently, but certainly not exclusively, studied include Spanish, French, German, Italian, Russian, and Hebrew. Both educators in the fields of visual handicaps and foreign languages have observed that visually handicapped students are at no significant disadvantage in learning foreign languages (Mathieu, 1961; Napier, 1973).

The foreign language teacher has the primary responsibility for teaching students the target language curriculum. The teaching methods and curriculum used by teachers of foreign languages will vary, depending upon an individual teacher's philosophy, interests, and abilities. Knowing the grammar of a language was once considered to be an adequate qualification to teach a foreign language (Lado, 1964). Presently the emphasis is on the spoken word. Today, students are learning foreign languages through what is referred to as the verbal-active method (Lenard, 1970) or the "oral-aural, aural-oral, audio-oral, audio-lingual, direct, functional, or, if you wish, the natural method" (Mathieu, 1961, p. 269).

The ability to speak the language is a dominant, but certainly not the only, requirement necessary for language teachers. The language teacher must be knowledgeable in teaching and assessment techniques and in the psychology of human learning. In addition, the language teacher must be knowledgeable in linguistics, the language laboratory and other technological aids, teaching machines and programmed learning used in typical language teaching/learning practices, reading, writing, cultural content, and literature (Lado, 1964). Teachers of foreign languages should meet the specific qualifications/standards for membership in the Modern Language Association of America (MLA). MLA is the recognized professional organization for foreign language specialists.

Special Considerations for Visually Handicapped Students

This section discusses the assistance the teacher of the visually handicapped should provide to the teacher of foreign languages who has a visually handicapped student. Learning to speak foreign languages does not pose extraordinary difficulties for the visually handicapped student; however, there may be problems in obtaining written materials, using the phonemic alphabet, and learning to write (Mathieu, 1961; Napier, 1973). For reading, some students will be able to use print, either standard size, large print, or print enlarged through optical or electronic systems, such as optical aids, closed circuit television, or other enlarging systems. (See Chapter 6.) These students will be able to access many of the same, if not all, materials available to their sighted peers.

Other students will require that the material be presented through recordings and/or braille. Many foreign languages use a braille letter by letter transformation, some use just a few contractions, and others "reduce their systems almost to cyphers in which the form of the original text is hardly recognizable" (Mackenzie, 1953, p. 55). Foreign language materials which are transcribed into braille in the United States are done in Grade One braille. Grade One braille is a letter by letter translation and does not utilize contractions (See Chapter 18.) The student must master the alphabet of the foreign language being studied. The braille symbols used for foreign letters which are accented, as in French, Spanish, and Italian, are represented by singular braille symbols. The same braille symbols are used to represent totally different letters or letter combinations in other languages. Examples of some of these are presented in Chart 21.3.

Examination of this chart reveals that the same braille symbol is used to represent the same accented letter in various alphabets. The same symbols represent totally different letters in other languages, such as Polish, Greek, Devanagari, and Swahili. Unaccented letters of the alphabet which are the same in English as they are in the foreign language are represented by the same symbol in the foreign language as they are in English. For example the a, b, c, and d in Afrikaans, Danish, Finnish, Gaelic, German, Portuguese, and Vietnamese are represented by the same symbols as in Standard English Braille.

The teacher of the visually handicapped will need to refer to the Code of Braille Textbook Formats and Techniques (1977) or future editions, for the foreign language alphabets and rules of the braille code. Within this source the alphabets and rules, as they vary from the rules of Standard English Braille, can be found for non-Roman letters, French, German, Greek, Hebrew, Italian, Latin, Russian, and Spanish. For other languages the teacher should use World Braille Usage (Mackenzie, 1953). This publication provides the reader with braille charts which include the braille sign and its print equivalent for foreign language alphabets, contractions, and tone and nasalization indicators. A revision of this resource is expected to be completed by the National Library Service for the Blind and Physically Handicapped, the Library of Congress by 1986-87.

Visually handicapped students should be provided with alphabets in either braille, standard, or large print, for easy referral and study. It is the responsibility of the teacher of the visually handicapped to provide the student with instruction in the recognition of foreign language alphabets, symbols, and accent marks in his reading mode(s) of braille and/or print. Some foreign languages do incorporate the use of contractions. If publications produced in a foreign country are used as supplementary readings, the teacher should instruct the student as to the configurations used to represent the contractions. The low-vision student may require supervised instruction when first learning to read a foreign language, as he is unaccustomed to looking for markings above and below letters and thereby may inadvertently miss them.

Languages vary as to their use of punctuation, capitalization, and other rules of grammar. For example, in German all nouns are capitalized, not just those which are proper names, whereas Hebrew uses no capitalization. Because the French language uses many hyphens and apostrophes, questions regarding syllabication may arise. Basically foreign languages use one of two internationally accepted braille sign systems for punctuation marks, namely Standard English or French (Mackenzie, 1953). Both the teacher of the visually handicapped and the student should make use of the preliminary pages of each volume of the braille edition of books in foreign languages, for it is here that the alphabetic symbols which differ from familiar (Standard English Braille) configurations and other special symbols are found. In addition, any pertinent transcriber's notes which explain necessary variances from print to braille are explained. The preliminary pages of each volume of a brailled text of foreign languages serve as the reader's guide.

Whenever possible the visually handicapped student should be provided with both a hard copy (braille or print) and audio tape edition of the foreign language text. Often a braille edition is not readily available for the student. Teachers of visually handicapped students should begin efforts to obtain or arrange for the transcription of necessary texts and supplementary readings a full semester in advance. Although much emphasis in teaching foreign languages today is placed on the oral-aural method, to be truly literate one needs to be able to read and write the language. Students should be encouraged to find out from the language teacher which specific pages of the text will be used for the next class, so they can bring the appropriate text or braille volume with them to class. This will allow them to take part in reading activities.

Additional Instructional Activities

An important component of any foreign language curriculum is the study of the culture of which the target language is an integral part. Various teaching aids, activities, and field trips may be utilized by the

Chart 21.3   Some foreign language accented letters as presented in braille

Braille Symbol	French	Italian	Spanish	Polish
(braille)	à	à	á	dz or v
(braille)	è	è	é	ź
(braille)	é	---	---	---
(braille)	ÿ	ì	ì	---
(braille)	ù	ù	ú	cz
(braille)	ç	---	ç	ż
(braille)	â	â	---	ą
(braille)	ë	ê	---	ʀ
(braille)	ü	---	ü	dz
(braille)	ô	ô	---	ń
(braille)	í	---	ñ	rz
(braille)	---	ò	ó	---
(braille)	î	î	---	ć
(braille)	û	û	---	---
(braille)	é	---	---	---

language teacher in the process of teaching the target language and culture(s) in which it is used. Some of the teaching aids which may be used include: wall maps and pictures; blackboards, flash cards, charts and overheads; foreign journals, newspapers, magazines, calendars, posters, and bulletin boards; ditto handouts; paintings and sculpture; and films, filmstrips, slides, and television.

Some of the teaching activities might include: games; concerts and dances; cooking; drawing; report writing and tests; construction projects; making of calendars and posters; sending for products and materials; painting and sculpting; learning folk songs and folk dances; celebrating foreign holidays; having pen pals; role playing; mini-dramas; and interviews. Field trips may be made to: department stores; supermarkets; museums; churches; theatres; community bazaars; and ethnic bakeries, restaurants, and communities. Visually handicapped students should also be considered for exchange programs in foreign countries.

A thoughtful review of these teaching aids, activities, and field trips will reveal those which will require some modification(s) for meaningful use by visually handicapped students. For example, the student may need to: have a tactile or large print map of the country or region being studied and simultaneous description of a film being shown; utilize techniques described in Chapter 20 during food preparation or a tape recorder rather than pen and pencil during interviewing processes; tactually examine or utilize a low-vision aid when studying a piece of sculpture; or, use a mobility device when traveling. When preparing typed reports and assignments the use of a typewriter designed for the target language is recommended (Napier, 1973).

The student should be encouraged to constructively and effectively communicate with his language teacher, to discuss options, and the effectiveness of applied modifications. The teacher of the visually handicapped student and the foreign language teacher need to confer regularly with each other to ensure the appropriateness of the learning experiences being provided to the student.

Study questions

1. As an itinerant teacher of blind and visually handicapped students, describe your role and responsibilities to:

   (a) an elementary student who is totally blind and in his first year of studying Spanish as a foreign language; and (b) a secondary student in her third year of studying French as a foreign language who has, within the past three months, become visually impaired and now requires enlarged print for visual reading activities.

2. Identify eight teaching aids which a teacher of foreign languages might use. Four aids should be selected which would be used to teach the language, (e.g., flash cards) and four which would be used to teach about the culture (e.g., film). Identify how you would suggest the teaching aids or their application be adapted for visually handicapped students.

3. You have just observed one of your visually handicapped students in a Russian language class. You have observed that your student participates appropriately in the conversational aspects and responds to the teacher's questions. You also note that the foreign language teacher begins the class with sentences on the board in Russian and English and requests the students verbally translate in unison, while your visually handicapped student, who is unable to read from the chalkboard, sits and listens; that your student does not participate in the reading of passages from the textbook or supplementary readings; and that the teacher routinely dictates a few sentences to be written by the students, and once again your student does not participate. Outline the strategies you would implement with both the teacher and the student to insure your student's full participation in the class activities.

4. You have a college bound student who is a freshman in high school. You are teaching in a small rural high school and there is only one foreign language teacher. This teacher is strongly opposed to having your visually handicapped student in her classroom. Briefly describe how you would approach this situation. Identify whom you would involve and provide a rationale.

5. As a teacher of the blind and visually handicapped in a large urban school district, you have several students, both low vision and blind, who will be enrolled in foreign language studies at the secondary level. You plan a separate in-service training program for the foreign language teachers. They have never taught a visually handicapped student. Write an outline of the content of the in-service program you plan to have with them. Allow yourself a two-hour session. As the foreign language teachers will attend your general in-service training for all school personnel, be specific as to content relevant to foreign language study. The teachers provide instruction in French, Spanish, German, Italian, Russian, and Chinese.

Additional readings

Briggs, B.A. and Tootle, T.N. (1975). *A critical analysis of the Michigan State University Language Laboratory*. East Lansing, Mich.: Michigan State University.

Hester, R.M. (ed.). (1970). *Teaching a living language*. New York, N.Y.: Harper and Row.

Johnson, K. and Murrow, K. (eds.). (1981). *Communication in the classroom*. London, England: Longman.

National Library Service for the Blind and Physically Handicapped (1984) Foreign-language program adds dimension. *News*. Washington, D.C.: The Library of Congress, July-Sept. 15 (3), p. 1

Roy, G.W. (1974). Teaching the blind to read and write Chinese. *Journal of Chinese Teachers Association*, 9(3), 134-136.

THE CREATIVE ARTS
Rona Shaw

This section focuses on developing the creative arts ability of blind and visually handicapped youth. A review of the literature indicates the importance of creativity for cognitive, physical, and psychosocial growth. Problems related to maximizing creativity among visually handicapped students result in great part from the attitudes of sighted persons who believe that this population has built-in limitations in this area. Suggestions are offered to the teacher for working in the areas of art, dance, music, drama, creative writing, and enjoyment of museums. In each area, emphasis is placed on process, flexibility, appropriate time allotment, integration of sensory experience, and attention to developmental needs.

Encouraging the Creative Arts

According to Smith (1964), creativity is defined as "sinking down taps into our past experiences and putting these selected experiences together into new patterns, new ideas, or new products" (p. 8). Kurzhals (1961) writes that creativity is part of all of us and not limited to the talented or the adult. Part of the growth process involves the expression of our innate creativity. Schools have the responsibility to provide an environment where each child can "grow in the ability to express his own thoughts and ideas in his own way and at his own level of development" (Kurzhals, 1961, p. 75). The impairment of blindness should not impose restrictions on the opportunities made available to stimulate creative abilities.

Our educational system is charged with the responsibility of fostering creativity, yet it appears that the opposite occurs. The system, as it exists now, seems to dull the ability of children to wonder, to be surprised, to be creative (Shallcross, 1981; Torrance, 1962; Fromme, 1959). It tends to impose outside ideas or standards on the child, which invalidates his own developing images (Rubin, 1978).

For the child with a visual impairment, as well as for any child, achieving creativity is highly desirable. Progress comes only when one is able to develop, as Smith said, a new pattern, idea, product. Furthermore, the lives of human beings may be enriched by participation in artistic or self-fulfilling activities, and thus it would seem desirable for children to appreciate the arts and try to become creators (Torrance, 1967). The challenge to schools is a great one, for creativity cannot be taught, per se; it can only be developed, and what a teacher must do is set the conditions that are conducive to its development (Smith, 1964).

Fostering Creativity

The single most important factor in fostering creativity in a child is to demonstrate to him that he is of worth in his own right regardless of current condition or behavior, and to demonstrate faith in himself as an individual (Rogers, 1959; Rubin, 1978).

Shallcross (1981) points out that the climate for creative behavior involves three major factors namely, 1) physical—provide a place for storage of materials that are being used; 2) mental—challenge, but don't overwhelm, the child; and 3) emotional—the emphasis is on a supportive atmosphere which is honest and trusting.

Torrance (1977) offers several suggestions for the teacher to utilize in stimulating creativity. He encourages the teacher to respect both unusual questions and unusual ideas and solutions. His approach is one of process, rather than product; provide chances for children to learn, think, and discover without threats of immediate evaluation. He challenges the teacher to provide opportunities for creative behavior by exposing children to experiences which make them more sensitive to environmental stimuli—they should be involved in the sight, sense, touch, and sound of an object.

Importance of Fostering Creativity

When a youngster is aware of a positive attitude on the part of the teacher (or parent or therapist), he is able to sense a climate of both physical and mental safety. The child gradually learns that he can be whatever he is, because he is regarded with worth. The result is a youngster who is less rigid, can discover what it means to be himself, and can try to actualize himself in new and spontaneous ways (Rogers, 1959; Rubin, 1978). The teacher who encourages the creative potential in a child is enabling a child to work toward completion of a project without feeling the pressure of competing against others, or competing to achieve an approved standard. Lowenfeld and Brittain (1964) note that the importance of art goes beyond producing a finished work; rather it is reflective of the cognitive, perceptual, and psychological structure of the child. The art of a youngster demonstrates how he organizes his world.

In an exploratory art program for blind children, Rubin (1975) found that creative expression had a therapeutic effect as it served as an avenue for the expression of important feelings, many related to blindness. She concluded "these blind children were able to utilize the art program to let their feelings go, to move freely and rhythmically, and to experience the pleasure of controlling and creating with materials they could successfully use" (p. 391).

In addition to the creative and therapeutic aspects of the arts, many skills in other areas can be developed. Among these are perceptual, cognitive, motor, social, and affective skills. Art enhances perception by enabling the child to gain experience with concepts of size, shape, distance, color, sameness, difference, texture, temperature, sound, odor, and weight.

The child's cognitive development is furthered by observation and understanding of the properties of various media, as well as problem-solving related to specific projects. Through experimentation with various media the child learns to predict their behavior—for example, to what degree wood can bend and how to mix various colors to yield additional ones.

Gross motor and fine motor skills are strengthened through manipulation of basic materials and tools as well as patterns of movement and rhythm.

Socially, communicating ideas or participating in a group project facilitates interactive skills. Furthermore, seeking approval from parent or teacher for a creation enhances socialization.

Affectively, art enables the child to develop his self-concept. The child is afforded the opportunity to get to know himself by exploring various thoughts and ideas in his creative endeavors. Similarly, the development of self relates to being sensitive to the needs of others; the opportunity to include others in his creative efforts enables the child to define his sense of self. Lowenfeld and Brittan state "aesthetic growth consists of the growth from a chaotic to a harmonious organization of expression in which feeling, perceiving, and thinking are completely integrated" (1964, p. 18).

Creative Arts and the Blind—Traditional Problems

Much of the literature concerning creative arts for blind and visually handicapped persons indicates that it need not differ from that of the sighted. A blind child is deprived of his own creativity if art is approached as an activity that depends only on visual perception (Ancona, 1971; Freund, 1969).

As recently as 1959, however, Von Fieandt (1959) suggested that the quality of art work by those born blind was rather poor. Similarly, Révész (1950) concluded that blind persons are incapable of aesthetic appreciation.

Lisenco (1971) reiterated that a difficulty in achieving success at creative efforts was the demeaning attitude of many sighted persons who perceive blind persons as limited in this area. Cutsforth (1951) argued that blind people produce art work reflective of a different aesthetic environment from sighted people, and that only in the recognition of that nonvisual environment can a work be judged appropriately. He challenged sighted teachers to allow each student to utilize materials in a manner which express the child's relationship with his environment; the value of the activity is reflected in the process, not the product. His work was based on examination of procedures in residential schools for the blind, where he found that much of the art work was visually oriented. "To the teacher the mass of wrought marble about the chiseled figure is drapery. To the blind child it is nothing but mere marble, no matter what he has been taught to call it" (p. 175). He felt that blind people receive such an exaggerated opinion of visual beauty and visual pictorial art that they have no confidence in the validity of their own methods of appreciation. Lisenco (1971) found the same to be true in her work with blind adults.

Rubin (1976) supported Cutsforth and Lisenco in a study using scrap wood sculptures created by totally blind, low vision, and sighted children. The sculptures were judged by other children in all three categories. Results showed an aesthetic quality influenced by associative responses to shape, form, structure, and stability relating to the individual's life experience as well as by an objective standard of beauty.

A concern related to aesthetic appreciation is the controversy over 'art' vs. 'craft' vis-a-vis blind people. Art appears to connote a creative form of expression, such as painting and sculpting; crafts tend to be viewed as the making of things (Coombs, 1967). In the schools, art seems to be given a more important role. There is concern expressed that a blind child's art tends to be more in the realm of crafts, which tend to become rather mechanized, lacking stimulation as creative endeavors (Cutsforth, 1951; Slatoff, 1962). "Once the skill is learned, more by motor than by intellectual or affectual conditioning, the hands can work quite independently of the mind, thus nullifying the reality of the creative and constructive imagination" (Decker, 1960, p. 105). Others disagree, saying there is a fine line between learning the skills of a craft and being creative at it (Anthony, 1969). A teacher may utilize a craft for creativity if he encourages unusual combinations and use of textures, colors, sizes, designs, etc.

Another traditional controversy has concerned the types of media to be used. Haupt (1969) feels that "no one should be asked to create in a medium in which he himself cannot judge the results" (p. 41). This feeling is echoed by many teachers, who frequently rely on clay modeling and ceramics for the majority of art projects for the visually handicapped. However, for a totally blind child, there are many materials which have tactual qualities appropriate for creative art expression. Among these are paper, wood, wire, fiber, papier-mache, and plaster foil reliefs.

Regarding media which traditionally are seen as requiring sight, such as painting and the use of color, several authors feel that these can be satisfying experiences for the blind (Ancona, 1971; Kurzhals, 1961; Lisenco, 1971). Napier (1973), however, points out that the teacher must be careful in selecting creative art activities for the visually handicapped child, especially if the activities are product, not process oriented. Thus, for example, if a blind child is mainstreamed and the class is working with crayons, materials more meaningful should be chosen for him, unless there is no peer competition for a "beautiful" product.

Individual considerations are very important in teaching art to the youngster with a visual impairment. Differential approaches are necessitated by such factors as partial or total loss of vision, age of onset of the impairment, appropriate use of language, social relationships, and orientation to time and space (Ancona, 1971).

Actualizing Creativity Among Blind and Visually Handicapped Pupils

"The ability to give objective form to the creations of the imagination does not depend on the capacity to see and observe things" (Lowenfeld, 1957, p. 270). What it is dependent upon ultimately are the types of experience the artist has with his world (Lowenfeld, 1951). The challenge to the teacher is to establish a climate that affords experiences which foster creative expression. Several authors have suggested specific materials and methods that can lead to success for blind and visually handicapped youngsters.

Art

Judith Rubin, in her book, *Child Art Therapy* (1978), makes specific suggestions that facilitate the conditions for creative growth. She points out that the teacher must consider materials, space, and time, as well as alternative expressive modalities for various individuals who may not be comfortable with, for example, paint or clay. Such a person may need music or drama as an expressive mode. Regarding materials, Rubin suggests that these be readily available for children to use spontaneously and in an unstructured

manner in order to avoid delaying the actualization of a creative impulse. In terms of space, she suggests keeping media and equipment in consistent and predictable places and within reach of the child. This makes the selection of materials possible without the intervention of the teacher. She as well as Lindsay (1972) further suggest space be provided where it is acceptable to mess without fear of disapproval. Time allotments should be often and long enough to allow the child to become involved in the creative process.

These ideas are echoed by Lowenfeld and Brittain (1964), who further note that the teacher must know the physical and psychological needs of the child to foster creative expression. One way of doing this is to become familiar with the stages of art development (see Chart 21.4), and then relate them to the specific child. Permit the child to develop his own technique, and introduce appropriate materials only when the child appears most ready to use them in terms of his own growth and art expression. Another technique that will encourage creativity and simultaneously help build the child's self concept is to ask the child simple questions related to his work, such as "Do you like it? Why? Why not?" Structuring questions in this manner helps the child to appreciate his art and leads to greater sensitivity of emotional, perceptual, and intellectual relationships.

While these factors are important for all children, there are several concerns which need to be considered specific to the visually handicapped youngster.

Haupt (1969) states six points which she feels are important for the totally blind child to achieve success in art experiences. These points are being expanded to include the child with low vision.

1. Know how to help the child use his hands and fingers for their maximum efficiency. By standing (or sitting) behind the child, the teacher can facilitate exploration of objects by placing his hands over the child's and showing the child the various aspects of different objects. With the teacher's fingers as a guide, the child can examine the whole object and analyze its component parts.

2. Understand that it takes time and intense handling to explore objects in depth if clear concepts are to be formed. In the absence, or limitation, of sight, the teacher must be aware that extra time may be necessary to understand objects being examined. Further, as the teacher utilizes the hand over hand technique, accompanying questions will help clarify what is being examined. The child may need to explore objects several times before a clear understanding of it takes place.

3. Use generative questions in order to provoke the spirit of inquiry and stimulate imagination. Ask the child questions that will elicit from the child his thoughts and ideas. For example, as a child examines

Chart 21.4   Summary: Developmental art stages

Summary. Scribbling stage—Two to four years

Characteristics	Human Figure	Space	Color	Design	Motivation Topics	Materials
(1) Disordered. Kinesthetic experience. No control of motions.	None.	None.	No conscious approach. Use of color for mere enjoyment without any intentions.	None.	Through encouragement. Do not interrupt or discourage or divert child from scribbling.	Large black crayon. Smooth paper. Poster paint. Finger paint only for malajusted children. Clay.
(2) Controlled. Repeated motions, establishment of coordination between visual and motor activity. Control of motions. Self-assurance of control through deviations of type of motions.	None.	None, or only kinesthetically.	Same as above.	None.	Same as above.	Same as above.
(3) Naming. Change from kinesthetic to imaginative thinking. Mixing of motions with frequent interruption.	Only imaginatively by the act of naming.	Purely imaginatively.	Color used to distinguish different meanings of scribbling.	None.	In the direction of the child's thinking by continuing the child's story.	Colored crayons. Poster paint. Clay, felt-nibbed pen.

Summary. Preschematic stage—Four to seven years

Characteristics	Human Figure	Space	Color	Design	Motivation Topics	Materials
Discovery of relationship between drawing, thinking, and environment. Change of form symbols because of constant search for definite concept.	Circular motion for head, longitudinal for legs and arms. Head-feet representations develop to more complex form concept. Symbols depending on active knowledge during the act of drawing.	Self as center, with no orderly arrangement of objects in space: "There is a table, there is a door, there is a chair." Also emotional relationships: "This is *my* doll."	No relationship to nature. Color according to emotional appeal.	No conscious approach.	Activating of passive knowledge related mainly to self (body parts).	Crayons, clay, tempera paints (thick), large bristle brushes, large sheets of paper (absorbent).

Summary, Schematic stage—Seven to nine years

Characteristics	Human Figure	Space	Color	Design	Motivation Topics	Materials
Formulation of a definite concept of man and environment.	Definite concept of figure depending on active knowledge and personality, through repetition: schema.	First definite space concept: base line.	Discovery of relationship between color and object; through repetition: color schema.	No conscious design approach.	Best motivation concentrates on action, characterized by we, action, where.	Colored crayons. Colored chalks. Tempera, poster paint.
Self-assurance through repetition of form symbols, schemata.	Deviations expressing experiences can be seen in—(1) Exaggeration of important parts. (2) Neglect or omission of unimportant parts. (3) Change of symbols.	Discovery of being a part of environment: important for cooperation and reading.	Same color for same object.		Topics referring to—(1) Time sequences (journeys, traveling stories). (2) X-ray pictures (inside and outside are emphasized), factory, school, home, etc.	Large paper. Bristle and hair brushes.
In pure schema no intentional experience is expressed, only the thing itself: "the man," "the tree," etc.		Base line expresses— (1) Base. (2) Terrain.	Deviation of color schema shows emotional experience.			Clay: (1) Synthetic (2) Analytic.
Experiences are expressed by deviations from schema.		Deviations from base line express experiences.				
Use of geometric lines.		Subjective space: (1) Folding over (egocentric). (2) Mixed forms for plan and elevation. 3) X-ray pictures. (4) Space-time representations.				

Chart 21.4   Summary: Developmental art stages

Summary. Stage of dawning realism—Nine to eleven years

Characteristics	Human Figure	Space	Color	Design	Motivation Topics	Materials
Gang age. Removal form geometric lines (schema). Lack of cooperation with adults. Greater awareness of the self and of sex differences.	Attention to clothes, (dresses, uniforms), emphasizing difference between girls and boys. Greater stiffness as result of egocentric attitude, and the emphasis on details (clothes, hair, and so forth). Tendency toward realistic lines. Removal from schema.	Removal from baseline expression. Overlapping. Sky comes down to base line. Discovery of plane. Filling in space between base lines. Difficulties in spatial correlations as result of egocentric attitude and lack of cooperation.	Removal from objective stage of color. Emphasis on emotional approach to color. Subjective stage of color. Color is used according to subjective experience.	First conscious approach toward decoration. Acquaintance with materials and their function.	Self-awareness stimulated by characterization of different dresses and suits (professions). Cooperation and overlapping through group work. Subjective cooperation through type of topic: "We are Building a House." Objective cooperation through team work.	Paper cutting. Crayons. Poster paint. Flat, colored chalk. Clay. Papier-mache. Wood. Collage materials. Metal. Prints.

Summary. Pseudo-naturalistic stage—Eleven to thirteen years

Characteristics	Human Figure	Space	Color	Design	Motivation Topics	Materials
Developed intelligence yet unawareness. Naturalistic approach (unconscious). Tendency toward visual- or nonvisual-mindedness. Love for dramatization and action.	Joints. Visual observation of body actions. Proportions. Emphasis on expression by nonvisually minded.	Urge for three-dimensional expression. Diminishing sizes of distant objects. Horizon line (visually minded). Environment only when significant (nonvisually minded).	Changes of color in nature for distance and mood (visually minded). Emotional reaction to color (nonvisually minded).	First conscious approach to stylizing. Symbols for professions. Function of different materials, with related designs.	Dramatic actions in environment. Actions from imagination and posing (with meaning, like scrubbing). Proportions through emphasis on content. Color moods.	Water color. Gouache (water color and tempera). Poster paint. Bristle brush. Hair brush. Clay. Linoleum. Papier-mache. Textiles. Wood.

Summary. Crisis of adolescence—Thirteen to seventeen years

Characteristics	Human Figure	Space	Color	Design	Motivation Topics	Materials
Critical awareness toward environment. Three groups: (1) Visual type: Intermediaries: eyes. Creative concern: environment, appearance. (2) Haptic type: Intermediary: body. Creative concern: self-expression, emotional approach to subjective experiences. (3) In-betweens: Reactions are not definite in either direction. Creative concern: abstract.	Visual type: Emphasis on appearance, proportion. Light and shadow. Depiction of momentary impressions. Naturalistic interpretations of objective validity. Haptic Type: Emphasis on inward expressions. Emotional qualities. Proportion of value. Individual interpretations. Depiction of character.	Visual Type: Perspective representations. Apparent diminution of distant objects. Atmosphere. Appearance Mood. Three-dimensional qualities. Light and shadow. Horizon line. Haptic Type: Perspective of value with relation to the self. Value relationship of objects. Baseline expressions.	Visual Type: Appearance of color in nature. Color reflections. Changing qualities of color in environment, according to distance and mood. Analytic attitude. Impressionistic. Haptic Type: Expressive, subjective meaning of color. Local color when significant. Color changes with emotional and psychological significance.	Type: Aesthetic interpretation of form, balance, and rhythm. Decorative quality of design. Emphasis on harmony. Haptic Type: Emotional design of abstract quality. Functional design. Industrial design.	Visual and haptical stimulations. Environment and figure. Appearance and content. Posing, with interpretations. Sketching. Sculpture. Graphics. Design. Painting. Mural.	Sketching in crayon, oil paint, tempera, conte, watercolor. Easel painting. Mural. Sculpture in clay, plaster, etc. Casting. wood. Metal. Stone. Graphics.

Summary. Adolescent art—Thirteen to seventeen years

Characteristics	Human Figure	Space	Color	Design	Motivation Topics	Materials
Ambition. Energy. Romantic ideals. Introspection. Peer-group pressure. Sexual awakenings.	Action. Participation. Self-identification of empathy. Clothing. Costume. Dance and rhythm.	Visual perspective or perspective of value.	Sophisticated. Not necessarily naturalstic.	As integral part of function. In furniture, clothing, ornament, architecture, home style, site, landscaping, interior decoration). Abstract. Cartoons.	Self, home, community, nature, industry. Explore materials rather than emphasize technical excellence. Develop sensitivity. Excursions.	Any material that contributes to further growth or adult use. All previous materials, plus photography, ceramics, wood (constructing and carving). Natural materials.

Source: V. Lowenfeld & W. Brittain. *Creative and Mental Growth*, 4th Ed. (New York: Macmillan & Co., 1964).

an object, ask him to describe it, to tell whether it looks like anything else he's seen, to tell whether or not he likes it, and why, etc. Avoid questions which result in a yes—no type of response.

4. Use vocabulary that is rich in descriptive terminology and that describes qualities in the "experience realm of his remaining senses." Be conscious of using words which relate to the sound, smell, touch, and, if appropriate, taste of an object. These sensory experiences have a real and rich meaning for the child and will enhance creative ability. Use of visual words, such as color, do not have the same richness of meaning for the totally blind child and will stifle his ability to express himself. For the youngster with limited vision, use of visual words is appropriate, if consideration is given to the child's specific visual needs, that is, the degree of description necessary will reflect the child's field of vision, near and distance vision, color vision, overall blur, etc.

5. Understand the importance of first hand experiences with all objects used in daily life as well as basic geometric forms and their names so that one has the basis for describing newly experienced objects. The importance of interacting with objects cannot be minimized; the child must feel and actively handle, listen, smell, and taste (if appropriate) in order to know. Building in a rich descriptive vocabulary provides the child with the verbal tools he will need to incorporate new and complex objects into his repertoire of experiences.

6. Be aware that many things that sighted people know, blind people can only come to know by the skillful use of analogy (e.g., sky, shadow). There are many experiences which totally blind children cannot enjoy by virtue of their lack of sight. Rather than avoid the words totally (e.g., sky), the teacher should try to convey the concept to the child in terms of what already exists in his world. Thus, for a young child, perhaps picking him up in an outdoor environment and having him hold his arms up and reaching, coupled with an explanation that as far up as anyone could reach, it would feel like that, might start to convey a sense of what the sky is.

Lisenco (1971) reiterates some of the above when he writes that the hands of the blind person are his principal sensing tool. He believes that in order for the senses to develop, like muscles, they need training and exercise. The blind person must learn to use touch flexibly and to combine the information yielded from touch with other sensory input. The blind person needs to be trained to use his hands to explore the environment in a variety of ways: by smoothing, rubbing, tapping, grasping. He should understand that each action differs in the variety and preciseness of information it transmits. The role of the teacher is to help the blind student develop knowledge about kinesthetic and tactile experiences, to arouse potential for creative expression, and to help establish understanding of what things look like to him.

Questions arise concerning the use of media that usually require sight to be "appreciated," like drawing, painting, and the use of color. Opinions vary as to whether or not the blind child should be asked to participate in creating something which he may not be able to appreciate as a finished product, like painting and drawing. Kurzhals (1961) writes that "often for the blind child the fun is not the end product, but in the process. Finding powder paint in a dish, stirring water into the powder to change it into liquid paint, dipping the brush into the paint, smearing it over a clay apple is exciting and fun" (p. 76).

Lisenco (1971) feels that painting can be a satisfying experience for visually handicapped individuals. When only colors and not their boundaries can be discerned, the range of satisfactory choice may be more limited, but collage or three dimensional painting techniques can still be used with the definition of area made tactually. Tactile painting is a possibility. By adding sand or other gritty material to the paint, a different texture for each color can be achieved. For drawing, the use of ballpoint pens or marking wheels on a screenboard can create raised line drawings. The brailler can also be used to create raised outlines in the creation of designs and patterns. The value of using color for the totally blind has been questioned; however, much of the literature states that even if blind children and adults cannot perceive color, they know it exists through language and have associations with it. Jones (1961) suggests that color, texture, and shape be utilized to the maximum in activities for both totally blind children and those with limited vision. This enables the youngster to maximize the sensory input of each quality and yields a more interesting multisensory product.

Feld and Hall (1980) describe an art program for visually handicapped students using a closed circuit television system (CCTV). They found that artistically talented low vision students can benefit from drawing from life objects using a CCTV. Not only did the students' drawing skills improve, but visual efficiency was trained because the students had to attend to details in common objects they may not have noticed before. Success in drawing provided ego boosts and improved the students' confidence in being able to function visually.

In terms of sculpture from a model, it is recommended that a discussion of features be the goal rather than the mere copying of the model (Kewell, 1955). The availability of several models from which to draw similarities and differences will allow the child to develop a product reflective of his own imagination and versatility rather than a product which reflects the teacher's preconceived notions (Napier, 1973).

In a classroom situation the art media selected as suitable for the blind child should be based on the same criteria as for the sighted child with the tactual qualities of the materials being the most important feature. The criteria for selection should be based on chronological age, interest, mental age, physical ability, and behavioral characteristics of the student. Materials should be sturdy and of good quality so children can control and handle them independent of constant adult supervision.

The visually handicapped child, as any student, should be oriented to his surroundings. He should be given a thorough walk through the entire working area and know where necessary materials are located. A well arranged, uncluttered work space with appropriate lighting is important. For the child with low vision special lighting may be required. Color contrasted materials may be useful (white paper on black background). The provision of physical outlines and boundaries within which a child will work and the use of

bowls or trays to contain projects and materials will help reduce mishaps. If a youngster is particularly sensitive to light, such as occurs with aniridia and albinism, provide tinted background, nonglare paper for drawing and painting, instead of white, which would reflect the light more strongly (Lindsay, 1972).

A flexible approach is best when presenting a technique. Permit the low vision or blind child to make suggestions that will enable greater personal productivity and satisfaction. Most of all, allow time for clear explanations and evaluations, and allow the child time to "feel" and/or "see" what is being explained and demonsrated. Give the student time to gain a personal understanding of the project.

If the process, rather than the product, approach is emphasized, then the teacher of the visually handicapped mainstreamed child might suggest projects that are tactually oriented for nonimpaired youngsters. Such an approach affords the normally sighted child new avenues of creative expression. This approach also enables the visually handicapped child to be truly mainstreamed for that particular period of time.

Dance

Art and sculpture are not the only areas which yield creative expression. Another mode is creative dance, which provides the opportunity for individuals to explore and discover their bodies and to express their feelings. At the same time, it allows exploration and discovery of the textures, shapes, space, and sounds in the environment (Joyce, 1973). By its nature, creative dance does not impose predetermined patterns. The movement emanates from the individual, thus avoiding a "right way" and a "wrong way." Establishing rhythm can result from actual body movement, instead of keeping to a set external beat (Chapman & Cramer, 1973; Farley, 1969).

In one program designed to encourage creative dance, Chapman and Cramer (1973) began the training sequence with the entire body lying or sitting on the floor to reduce balance problems and permit greater concentration on movement. They suggest that the teacher help put the child through proper motions until a movement is understood. When participating in an exercise for the first time, the learner might join hands with a partner or stand in a circle with the entire group. To practice balance, the child could hold hands with a partner while lifting one leg. Dalcroze (1934) also encouraged experimentation with space, having children use different body parts in different spatial planes. She provided opportunities for periods of intense concentration for listening to music and then moving with it. Helping children become aware of sound and body rhythms facilitates awareness of the environment and affords greater flexibility in motoric expression of ideas and feelings (King, 1968).

An experimental program of creative dance movement for blind children was conducted by Duehl (1979). In working with congenitally blind eight through ten-year-old children, she found that the dance program not only enhanced large muscle control and balance, but improved movement abilities in general. Dance also increased body image awareness. During the eight week training program, students explored various phases of movement, did creative imitation (crawl like a worm), and analyzed where the movement occurred in the body. Children also moved to a suggested emotion, such as anger, and acted out various descriptive words, such as sleepy.

Beyond a means of expression, creative dance can have an impact on balance, poise, strength, spatial orientation, and independence. Rand (1973) found this to be true of both blind adults and children. During two summers of dance instrucion, she devised sessions which incorporated bending and stretching exercises and activities to limber and tone the muscles. Like Duehl, Rand used various images, superimposing physical interpretations of them to rhythmical phrases. She found that the children were capable of increasingly complex tasks.

Music

The goals and objectives of a music program are very much alike for both sighted and nonsighted youngsters. What differs for the visually handicapped child primarily is methodology. As previously stated, the lack of vision means that learning instruments and reading music must be taken over by the sense of touch. For the young child in a rhythm band, for example, each instrument

must be explored—how it sounds, how it feels. The teacher in such a situation must use other than a visual cue to let different children know when to play (Napier, 1973). Likewise, for older children in a music program, all instruments should be examined and compared.

As with dance, many concepts related to body image and spatial orientation can be achieved through music. Various circle games for young children (Simon

Says, for example) strengthen knowledge of body parts and concepts such as right, left, etc. the inclusion of singing games, stomping, marching, using instruments and personalizing songs are all components of a program which increases self-awareness and social skills in addition to movement skills.

Napier (1973) points out that self expression can be encouraged with music by drawing out ideas, rather than imposing them. She suggests that a teacher should say "Listen to the music, then make your feet do what the music seems to say," rather than "Pretend you are a bear and walk like one" (p. 255). A visually handicapped or blind child may never have seen a bear walk.

Music notation for the child with limited vision can usually be taught through an enlarged staff and notes on both the chalkboard and specially prepared music sheets. The totally blind child uses a braille music code for reading notes, or can make use of the Optacon for this purpose. A recently developed curriculum for music instruction using the Optacon has been tested and is now available (Bruscia & Levinson, 1982). The constraint imposed with either braille or Optacon is the need to memorize prior to playing. Without vision, there is no sight reading of material; similarly the low vision child may not be able to read quickly enough and may have to commit music to memory (Napier, 1973).

For group type activities, participation is possible with little or no modification. For a glee club, lyrics can be typed in large print for the visually handicapped child and his sighted peers, thus minimizing any mainstreaming problems. Lyrics can be made available in braille for the totally blind child. Cues for singing can be audible or tactual instead of visual; the teacher can use a tap as a signal, or a sighted partner can lightly touch the visually handicapped child when it is his turn to participate. The use of a sighted partner can also be helpful for walking on stage or for any other type of procession.

An alternative for studying musical arrangements is the use of prerecorded tapes. This enables study of a particular composition through repeated listening (Napier, 1973).

Music as therapy has recently been applied to visually handicapped children and adults by the Cleveland Society for the Blind (Steele & Crawford, 1982). The program was started in an attempt to provide extra stimulation for those who needed it for learning, a way to reduce mannerisms, improve social skills, and reduce immature behavior. The groups formed by the music therapist emphasized sharing, waiting turns, listening quietly, and following directions—skills important for functioning as a group member. The program is achieving success in these goals, both in school, and, with the inclusion of the parents in the program, at home.

Drama

As with the other creative arts, drama affords children the opportunity for the development of self-concept and social skills. Taking on someone else's role permits a child to externalize internal conflicts that are problematic. Aberrant behavior can often be corrected through the dramatic arts (Lowenfeld, 1971). Watkins (1981) describes a series of workshops in creative dramatics offered to teachers and students at the Georgia Academy for the Blind. She found that the combination of various exercises and activities resulted in growth and development among the children. Some of the activities included two team tug of war, parachute games, pantomime, and drama.

Puppetry for the young child is often an effective means of expression, especially for the withdrawn youngster. The spontaneity and pleasure drawn from an informal classroom puppet show can relieve anxiety by talking through another voice (Napier, 1973).

The use of drama can be used as an avenue for mastering subject matter at the same time it strengthens self-confidence and movement skills. Wagener (1977) found that improvisational type activities, such as television talk shows and situational drama requiring role-play provided a learning environment that was very stimulating. She found that a variety of activities related to a particular time period, such as reading biographies of famous persons, listening to tapes of events, visiting museums, and watching special television programs enriched that period and provided an excellent background for the drama to follow. Children can become immersed in an era via the dramatics, which facilitates a sense of history in a nonthreatening, enjoyable fashion.

Creative Writing

Creative writing provides another avenue for the release of tension through self-expression. It also stimulates original thinking, if that is what is rewarded. The teacher can encourage the child, sighted or non-sighted, to think of ideas that no one else will think of—this tells the child to let his imagination fly. The teacher is communicating to the child that it is legitimate to produce unusual ideas (Torrance, 1977). Evaluation and analysis, rather than grading of such creative endeavors, also serves to encourage use of imagination (Napier, 1973).

Torrance (1977) encourages a purpose to creative writing: assignments should be to communicate something based on incorporation of prior reading. He feels that a purpose to writing will be more helpful than the theme-a-week approach, where children are simply asked to produce a composition each week. If creative writing is to be creative, it must be on-going; a child's urge to write should not be limited to a specified day and time each week. Napier (1973) suggests having a box in the room where children can deposit their writing without disturbing either teacher or class.

Encourage creative expression in the younger child by either writing, brailling, or taping the story or poem. The lack of mechanical skills in the young child should not preclude a creative writing experience. The child will feel proud of his creation and this helps build self-confidence and language skills.

Museums

Despite the concern for wear and/or breakage of precious art work and artifacts, an increasing number of museums is now making certain pieces available for examination by visually handicapped persons. The work of curators and consultants has resulted in many fine touch exhibits and tactile tours throughout the country. For works that are inaccessible, several museums offer models and reproductions. Braille literature and thermoform drawings, while not always satisfactory, are increasingly evident. Many museums offer audio cassettes to guide all persons through exhibits.

The lack of, or limitation of sight, need not deprive a person of the joy of experiencing the creations of people of other times and places. "Museums offer people who have difficulty seeing a range of vision, an independence of imagination, that is a fundamental part of their birthright as human beings" (Kenney, 1983, p. 329).

The foregoing review reveals that teachers of the visually handicapped, as facilitators, can tap a wealth of creative ability among their students. Permitting mess and exploration within structure, allowing frequent and ample time to work on projects, and providing various media encourages self-expression. The visually handicapped child, as a human being, can emerge as a unique individual; the teacher must build a strong foundation for this by providing an environment conducive to creative growth. The definition of who one is begins early on with singing, dancing, and simply smearing.

Study questions

1. According to Shallcross (1981), what are the three major factors involved in establishing a climate of creative behavior?

2. Distinguish between 'art' and 'craft' as applied to stimulating creativity among the blind and visually handicapped school age population.

3. Tell how creative experiences in school can interface with a child's cognitive, physical, social, and emotional growth at a particular grade level.

4. Describe how the six points made by Haupt (1969) can be used to maximize successful art experiences for blind and visually handicapped children and youth.

5. List various materials and equipment and how they would be used to permit totally blind and low vision children to participate in a particular type of art activity.

6. Tell how you would set up a creative arts area in a classroom for blind and visually handicapped children at the elementary level.

Additional readings

Covington, G. (1981). *Let your camera do the seeing—The world's first photography manual for the legally blind.* Washington, D.C.: National Access Center.

Marksberry, M.L. (1963). *Foundations of creativity.* New York, N.Y.: Harper and Row.

Sykes, K., Watson, G., and Menze, R. (1974). *Creative arts and crafts for children with visual handicaps.* Louisville, Ky.: Instructional Materials Reference Center, American Printing House for the Blind.

Torrance, E.P. (1967). Give the devil his dues. In J. Gowan, G. D. and E.P. Torrance, *Creativity and its educational implications.* New York, N.Y.: John Wiley & Sons.

PHYSICAL EDUCATION
Diane Craft

Participation in physical activity is vital to the health and well-being of people of all ages (de Vries, 1980). According to H. Clark and D. Clark (1978), "physically active people are less likely to suffer from chronic disabling conditions" (p. 7). Conversely, physical inactivity may be detrimental to health and well-being. According to Kraus and Raab (1961), physically inactive people are more prone to coronary diseases, ulcers, and many other chronic and disabling conditions. Consequently, participation in physical activities is important if one is to avoid the deleterious effects of physical inactivity (Merriman, 1984).

Despite its proven importance, visually handicapped students have often been excluded or excused from physical education classes despite evidence (Buell, 1975) that they may need it even more than sighted children do. Sighted children learn to move by observing and then imitating others. Because visually handicapped children may not be able to see others move, they cannot learn incidentally by observation. They usually require specific instruction.

Because of its unique contribution to their development, physical education is mandated for all handicapped students under P.L. 94-142, the Education for All Handicapped Children Act of 1975. It is no longer legal to exclude handicapped students from physical education nor is a physician's note excusing the child an option. Many visually handicapped pupils can be accommodated in a regular physical education class with a minimum of modification and expense. When the pupil's needs cannot be met in a regular class, or if additional instruction is required, an adapted program must be developed as it is required by law.

The teacher of the visually handicapped provides technical support to physical education teachers. To provide appropriate assistance, an understanding of physical education in general is necessary.

Scope of Physical Education

Physical education is the development of physical and motor fitness, fundamental motor skills and patterns, and skills in aquatics, dance, and individual and group games and sports (including intramurals and lifetime sports). The scope of physical education is presented in outline form in Chart 21.5. While it addresses all three domains—cognitive, affective, and motor—the unique contribution of physical education is in the motor domain.

Physical education can also contribute to the cognitive and affective domain. The cognitive aspects include understanding the role of regular physical activity in developing fitness and maintaining health, and the knowledge of which specific exercises will develop the desired fitness. The affective aspects include one's attitude toward physical activity and competition, and the interaction of participation in physical activity and self-concept.

Chart 21.5   Scope of physical education

I. Cognitive domain
A. Aptitude (verbal, quantitative)
B. Achievement (knowing, understanding, thinking)

Physical education addresses the cognitive aspects of: activity performance, effects of activity, and factors modifying effects of activity

II. Affective domain
A. Adjustment (PE: self-concept, body image, getting along with others)
B. Temperament (PE: competitive spirit in athletics and other activities)
C. Interest (PE: preferences for various activities)
D. Attitude (PE: attitude toward PE, toward competition, toward girls competing against boys, etc.)
E. Character (PE: sportsmanship)

III. Motor domain
A. Physical fitness—muscular strength, muscular endurance, cardiorespiratory endurance. (The ability to sustain vigorous physical activity.)
B. Motor fitness—muscular strength, muscular endurance, cardiorespiratory endurance, muscular power, speed, agility, flexibility. (The vigor needed to perform motor tasks—running, jumping, kicking, etc.)
C. Motor ability—muscular strength, muscular endurance, cardiorespiratory accuracy, balance, steadiness. (The vigor and skill needed to perform motor tasks.)
D. Motor skill—level of proficiency in a specific task (locomotion—crawling, walking, running, climbing, jumping, rolling, hopping, skipping, sliding; propulsion—throwing, hitting, kicking, pushing, lifting; receiving or absorbing—catching, carrying; balancing—standing, sitting, twisting, bending, stretching, rotating.)
E. Sports skills—shooting baskets, hitting a golf ball, hitting a tennis ball, take-down in wrestling, etc.
F. Sports proficiency—volleyball, softball, football, field hockey, etc.

Physical fitness, the ability to sustain vigorous physical activity, has three components: motor fitness; motor ability; and motor skill.

Motor fitness is the vigor needed to perform motor tasks. In addition to the components of physical fitness, motor fitness includes: muscular power, speed, agility (Corbin & Lindsey, 1979), and flexibility (Baumgartner & Jackson, 1982).

Motor ability, the vigor and skill needed to perform motor tasks includes: coordination, "the ability to use senses together with body parts or to use several body parts together" (Corbin & Lindsey, 1979, p. 190); accuracy; and balance, the ability to maintain the center of gravity over the base of support.

Motor skill is the level of proficiency in specific tasks such as walking, running, throwing, and twisting. Proficiency in motor skill is dependent on a minimum level of physical fitness along with motor fitness and motor ability. Sports skills and sports proficiency are the application of motor skills to a specific sport, e.g., the motor skill of running applied to dribbling downcourt in basketball. The unique contribution of physical education is the development of students skilled in all aspects of the motor domain.

Best Practices in Physical Education

There are wide variations in the physical education curriculum from state to state, district to district, and school to school. Many of these approaches will achieve the goals of physical education. Described below is a summary of the scope of the best practices.

Physical education in kindergarten through second grade emphasizes physical fitness and basic motor skills including running, hopping, skipping, throwing, catching, hitting, and climbing, along with concepts of body image, spatial awareness, directionality, and laterality. A typical first grade class can begin with warm ups and stretches, push-ups, sit-ups, and running for physical fitness followed by instruction in the motor skill of jumping. Practicing the general skill may include negotiating obstacle courses and playing a low organizational game such as Jump the Brook. The class may conclude with a cool-down of stretches and relaxation exercises.

The curriculum in grades three through six emphasizes physical fitness and motor skills in the development of specific sports skills, as shown in Chart 21.6. For example, instruction in jumping may now be in the skills of the jump shot basketball, standing long jump, and the high jump in track and field.

As shown in Chart 21.6, the motor skills and sports skills learned in the elementary grades provide the basis for the later development of sports proficiency in grades seven and above. After grade six there is an increased concern with posture as adolescent students are growing rapidly. In grades nine to twelve the curriculum expands to emphasize proficiency in lifetime and recreational sports such as tennis, hiking, bicycling, and swiming, in which students can participate after school.

Physical Education for Visually Handicapped Students

A sound physical education program for visually handicapped students can develop the physical fitness and motor skills necessary for activities of daily living and orientation and mobility, a more positive self-concept

Chart 21.6   Suggested allocation of specific activities according to grade level

	K	1	2	3	4	5	6
Movement Experiences and Body Mechanics	K	1	2	3	4	5	6
Fundamental movement-locomotor, nonlocomotor	K	1	2	3			
Magic ropes				3	4	5	6
Fundamental movement-manipulative	K	1	2	3	4	5	6
Beanbags	K	1	2	3	4	5	6
Yarn or fleece balls	K	1	2	3			
Playground balls (8½ inch)	K	1	2	3	4	5	6
Small balls (sponge, softball size)				3	4	5	6
Paddles and balls				3	4	5	6
Hoops	K	1	2	3	4	5	6
Jump ropes	K	1	2	3	4	5	6
Parachutes	K	1	2	3	4	5	6
Wands				3	4	5	6
Rhythmics	K	1	2	3	4	5	6
Rope jumping to music				3	4	5	6
Apparatus	K	1	2	3	4	5	6
Bounding boards	K	1	2				
Balance boards	K	1	2	3	4	5	6
Balance beams	K	1	2	3	4	5	6
Benches			2	3	4	5	6
Climbing ropes	K	1	2	3	4	5	6
Climbing frames	K	1	2	3	4	5	6
Individual mats	K	1	2	3			
Jumping boxes	K	1	2	3	4	5	6
Ladders and bars		1	2	3	4	5	6
Stunts and Tumbling	K	1	2	3	4	5	6
Pyramids					4	5	6
Combatives					4	5	6
Simple Games	K	1	2	3	4	5	6
Relays			2	3	4	5	6
Story games, poems, quiet play	K	1	2				
Sports Skills and Activities				3	4	5	6
Basketball				3	4	5	6
Flag football, speedball					4	5	6
Indoor and outdoor hockey					4	5	6
Soccer				3	4	5	6
Softball (mostly skills)				3	4	5	6
Track and field					4	5	6
Volleyball					4	5	6

Source: V.P. Dauer & R.P. Pangray, *Dynamic physical education for elementary school children* (Minneapolis, Minn.: Burgess Publishing Company, 1979).

and sense of personal worth, and sports skills. Certain characteristics of a visual impairment have implications for physical education. Chart 21.7 presents some of these general characteristics which will not of course be found in all blind persons. Degree of vision, age of onset, sex, and personality will alter the characteristics and implications.

Poor posture is a charactertistic of many visually handicapped students. Winnick (1984) suggests that "The lack of sight contributes to poor posture by reducing or eliminating visual stimulation which maintains an erect head position" (p. 5).

Although sighted persons generally have higher fitness levels, some visually handicapped students may approach and even exceed performance levels of their sighted peers (Winnick, 1984). Overall, the less severe the impairment, the higher the fitness and motor performance. The visually handicapped students with higher performance levels and average or above intelligence can generally be mainstreamed into regular physical education classes.

Best Practices in Physical Education for Visually Handicapped Students

The best physical education practices for visually handicapped students are similar to those for non-handicapped students. In any class there is a range in student ability. A teacher who instructs students at both the high and low ends of the range will be able to accommodate visually handicapped students. Individualized, assessment-based instruction is a model which can accommodate a range in student ability. For example, a jump rope unit requires no adaptation. Visually handicapped students can count for others by listening to the sound of the rope striking the floor with each turn. A miss would be heard as an interruption in the rhythm. They can also jump rope independently as it is an intrinsically paced skill which does not require moving through space. In fact, it is often helpful when teaching jumping with a long rope to sighted students to have them jump with their eyes closed so that they concentrate on the rhythm and not be distracted by the turning rope.

Under P.L. 94-142 an Individualized Educational Plan (IEP) must be developed annually for all visually handicapped students with special needs. (See Chapter 12) Physical education should be included in the IEP. The individual assessment-based instructional model presented earlier and the IEP are essentially the same approach. Two assessment instruments have been developed which are appropriate for use with visually handicapped students. One is the *Project UNIQUE Test of Physical Fitness of Sensory and Orthopedically Impaired Youth* developed by Winnick and Short. Test items have been modified for use with blind and low vision students,

10 to 17 years old. Norms developed from a national sample are included.

A second test appropriate for visually handicapped students who have not yet achieved mature patterns in motor skills is the Ohio State University Scale of Intra-Gross Motor Assessment (SIGMA). The SIGMA is a criterion-referenced test in which the student's performance is assigned to one of four developmental

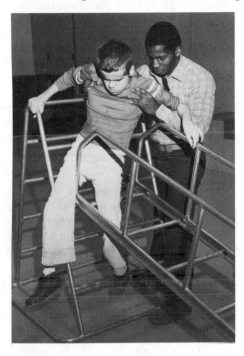

levels for each of the eleven following motor skills: walking, running, stair climbing, jumping, hopping, skipping, throwing, catching, kicking, striking, and ladder climbing. An accompanying curriculum presents teaching strategies for helping students progress from a less to a more mature motor skill pattern. No norms are available and no specific adaptations have been made for use with blind students but it can be useful in teaching any student who has immature motor skills. (See also Chapter 19 for other assessment instruments.)

Using assessment as the basis, appropriate objectives are established and activities are selected which will lead to achievement of the objectives. When necessary, the materials, strategies, and methodologies are adapted as described below.

Materials, Strategies, and Methodological Adaptations Suggested for Teaching Physical Education to Visually Handicapped Students

Organization and consistency are essential with regard to equipment. For example, before a gymnastics unit, it is useful to orient visually handicapped students to the location of the equipment and then avoid rearranging any pieces without first alerting them. Following this suggestion throughout all physical

Chart 21.7   Characteristics of visual impairment

Characteristics of Visual Impairment	*Implications for Physical Education*
Blind students follow the same progression in motor development as sighted children, but tend to lag in motor milestones involving mobility (Winnick, 1984) perhaps because a) "Lack of vision decreases stimulation to move and makes movement more difficult" (Winnick, 1984; Sibod, 1976). b) overprotective parents may discourage a child's natural desire to explore and take risks. Blind, neglected children motorically outperform blind, overprotected children (Winnick, 1984). c) blind children do not have the opportunity to refine motor skills through casual observation of others moving.	Teach motor skills, which sighted peers may already have mastered, such as running, jumping, and throwing
Lack of vision tends to limit mobility (Sherrill, 1976; Hill, 1976).	Teach motor skills which involve moving through space to increase mobility skills
Visually handicapped students, as a group, perform below the physical fitness levels of their sighted peers (Winnick, 1984). The relative performance of blind students on physical fitness varies with the degree of mobility required by a particular test: best performance in flexibility, arm strength, and muscular endurance, and poorest performance in motor skills of throwing.	Emphasize physical fitness activities in which the blind student can fully participate, e.g., jumping rope, swimming
Due to lack of sight it is necessary to use other senses fully (Sherrill, 1976; Barraga, 1964)	Provide an opportunity to practice a variety of movements which may develop kinesthetic sense
Lack of vision can be accompanied by isolation from the sighted community (Sherrill, 1976).	Teach recreational and lifetime sports so that visually handicapped students have the skills to go bowling, dancing, swimming, running, etc. with sighted friends and family
Society holds attitudes that blindness equals helplessness; some blind persons may "learn helplessness."	An opportunity to participate in and master motor skills and sports skills can help "unlearn helplessness" and enhance self-efficacy
Perceptual concepts are learned visually and thus may be delayed in visually handicapped students.	Specifically teach body image, spatial awareness, directionality, laterality, and similar perceptual concepts.
Postural deviations, which can result from holding the head in an unusual position to maximize vision and/or the lack of a visual ideal to emulate, may be present (Sherrill, 1976).	Include corrective exercises to remediate postural deviations and maintain a "normal" appearance
Stereotypical mannerisms, which are repetitious purposeless movements, may be present (Sherrill, 1976).	Provide activities which use large muscle groups to enable "socially appropriate" means for releasing tension thought to be the basis of stereotypic mannerisms
Lack of visual feedback can contribute to the deterioration of motor skills once learned.	Continual follow-up by the physical educator through corrective feedback is needed to maintain motor skills which have been mastered. Many motor skills will be lost without this feedback.
Balance, which in sighted individuals is heavily dependent on vision, may be poor. This may be due to lack of vision or, more likely, to decreased opportunities for regular physical activity through which balancing skills are refined.	Provide activities which promote the development of balance, such as locomotor skills on a floor balance beam; walking a rope placed on the floor; and balancing and hopping on one foot.

education units will enable visually handicapped students to move independently in the gym without fear of injury. To include visually handicapped students during spectator events, assign a student "announcer" who describes a ball game.

When teaching physical education to blind students, follow these guidelines for modifying learning experiences.

Select an activity which does not require modification.
A person with little or no vision can participate in many activities and sports without modification: canoeing and tandem bicycling with a sighted person in the front seat, crew with a sighted coxswain, bowling for a person with tunnel vision, waterskiing using whistle signals, cross country skiing with a sighted partner, tug-of-war and parachute play with young children, folk, modern and square dancing, and wrestling. In fact, visually handicapped wrestlers have a long history of victories against sighted opponents (Buell, 1966). In goalball the visually handicapped students may outperform sighted students because all players are blindfolded (Kearney & Copeland, 1979). A creative teacher will be able to include visually handicapped students in a wide variety of activities and sports.

Modify the rules of the activity.
Many sports have been modified for visually handicapped participants. Minor modifications which do not change the nature of the sport are most desirable. To compensate for mobility and orientation difficulties in baseball, use a larger ball which is hit as it bounces off home plate or use a beeper ball. The first base coach calls to the batter as he runs to the base and modifies track rules to allow visually handicapped runners to follow a guide wire around the inside of the track or run holding a sighted partner's arm above the elbow.

Modify the skill technique.
Swimming is an excellent aerobic sport which does not require vision. Lap swimming is easy once the strokes are learned through auditory and kinesthetic feedback. Lane markers help the swimmer maintain a straight line. Counting the number of strokes required to cross the pool enables a visually handicapped swimmer to slow down before hitting the pool edge in the elementary backstroke, breaststroke, butterfly, and side stroke. The crawl requires no modifications because the head never leads.

Modify the teaching technique.
Perhaps the greatest modification to teaching technique is the addition of verbal and manual manipulation to visual demonstrations. Position visually handicapped students close to the demonstrator so they can see or touch as needed. If the student is adventitiously blind, using visual images in description may be helpful. Both sighted and visually handicapped students benefit from the teacher's use of precise language such as "The racket is held 3-4 inches above your right shoulder" instead of "Hold the racket like this."

Research by Dye (1983) has shown that, for visually handicapped children, kinesthetic feedback is potentially a more efficient method of learning than auditory feedback. These results suggest that teachers should position the child's body correctly when teaching a motor skill to help the student learn.

Modify the environment including space, facilities and equipment.
Brightly colored balls, mats, field markers and goals which contrast with the background will enable visually handicapped students to use any remaining vision. Because the nature of visual limitations vary greatly, it is essential to speak with each visually handicapped student to learn what modifications will be most helpful. Some students can see bright multi-colored objects under strong light best while others need solid colored objects under subdued lights which do not produce glare. In volleyball, use of a beachball makes tracking visually easier and slows the pace of the game. The Freedom Leader is a unique device for running that joins a trained guide and a nonsighted runner while keeping both separated, thus permitting freedom of movement.

In selecting activities to teach visually handicapped students, priority should be given to lifetime sports, such as bowling, hiking, bicycling, swimming, canoeing, sailing, folk, ballroom, square and aerobic dancing, yoga, skiing, and jogging. Many physical educators, recreation specialists, as well as visually handicapped persons themselves have developed approaches to enable visually handicapped youngsters and adults to learn and participate in a wide variety of physical activities.

Frith and Warren (1984) have developed adapted fishing techniques. Several authors have described running and track and field techniques appropriate for visually handicapped persons (Bitby, 1975; Bond, 1975, Sinizin, 1978; Sonka & Bina, 1979).

Skiing, both downhill and cross country, is especially popular with physically active visually handicapped persons (Brennan, 1975; Miller, 1976; Morisbak, 1975). Among the other physical activities and sports that blind and visually handicaps have mastered are archery (Carnochan, 1976), golf (Gosswiller, 1975), sailing (Hale, 1976; Christensen, 1975).

Blind and visually handicapped persons also participate effectively in a wide variety of activities designed to maintain and increase basic physical fitness. Laughlin (1975) described a basic walking-jogging program. Duehl (1979) advocated the use of creative dance movement to improve large muscle control and balance in congenitally blind children. Hatha yoga benefits visually handicapped students both physically and mentally (Krebs, 1979). Koeschke (1977) determined that mime was a beneficial movement technique for both congenitally and adventitiously blind students. Craft (1981) suggests Nautilus equipment for older students.

Multihandicapped students have special physical education needs. One federally funded adaptive program that has been used effectively with visually handicapped students and with multiply handicapped students is *Project I Can*, developed by Janet A. Wessel, Ph.D. of Michigan State University (Wessel, 1976). *I Can* includes resource units that provide assessment, instructional activities, and games. These special education adaptive physical education programs offer the *I Can Primary Skills* package which includes four modules, namely Fundamental Skills, Body Management, Health/Fitness, and Aquatics and the *I Can Sport, Leisure and Recreation Skills* package which includes modules on Team Sports, Dance and Individual Sports, Backyard/Neighborhood Activities, and Outdoor Activities.

In addition, a number of organizations that provide information on physical activities for visually handicapped persons are listed in Appendix G.

Physical Activities for Impaired, Disabled, and Handicapped Individuals is a good general resource (AAHPER, 1976).

Suggestions for Working with the Physical Education Teacher

The teacher of the visually handicapped helps the regular physical education teachers in several ways: 1) by providing a description of the student which covers useful vision; accompanying handicaps such as mental retardation or hearing loss; contraindicated exercises such as contact sports if there is a possibility of detached retinas; information from the child's ophthalmologist or physician; a copy of the child's previous IEP and information.

2) by explaining what the student can and cannot see. It may be especially helpful if the student provides the explanation himself.

3) Together with the physical educator, reviewing the existing program in terms of the student's needs and abilities and discussing possible modifications. Seek the student's input since most visually handicapped students will have already developed some necessary modifications to permit their participation in certain activities.

4) Suggest that the physical educator individually assess the new visually handicapped student's present level of motor performance prior to placement in a physical education class.

5) Once the visually handicapped student is attending physical education class, check with the teacher frequently. Continued support and suggestions may be appreciated.

6) Offer to transcribe print physical education materials into braille, large type, or recorded form.

Occasionally, a blind child may be placed in the physical education class of an uneasy teacher. Try to determine the reason for any reluctance. If extra preparation is needed, work with the principal to

obtain additional time for the teacher. Arranging for the teacher to visit a physical education program in which visually handicapped students are successfully mainstreamed may be useful.

The contribution of physical education to the health and well-being of visually handicapped individuals can be significant. Physical education instruction can help close any gaps in motor performance between visually handicapped and sighted peers who have a greater opportunity for incidental learning to enhance mobility skills and refine the kinesthetic sense. Activities which develop physical fitness, balance, motor skills, body image, and proper body alignment may be especially appropriate, along with sports which promote integration with sighted friends and family.

In educating visually handicapped students in physical education, the easiest aspects to change are the equipment and rules. The most difficult aspects to change are the attitudes which assume that because a person lacks sight he also lacks the ability to participate fully in sports (Sherrill, 1976). The most significant contribution of the teacher of visually handicapped students can be working with others to eliminate these negative attitudes.

Study questions

1. Look through a physical education methods book and select three activities that do not need adaptation. Provide a rationale.
2. Select three activities that need adaptation and describe how you would adapt them.
3. Interview a physical education instructor and find out experiences with teaching a visually handicapped child. If they have not had a visually handicapped pupil, find out what problems they would anticipate.
4. Select a motor skill such as skipping or shooting baskets. List prerequisite skills necessary in order to acquire that skill.
5. Assume that you have lost your sight. Describe how you would continue with or modify your current physical activities.
6. What can you as a teacher of the visually handicapped do to encourage greater participation in physical activities by your student out of school?

Additional readings

Adams, R.; Daniel, A.N.; McCubbins, J.A. and Rullman, L. (1982). *Games, sports, and exercises for the physically handicapped*. Philadelphia, Pa.: Lea and Febinger.

Corbin, C.B. and Lindsey, R. (1979). *Fitness for life*. Glenview, Ill.: Scott, Foresman and Company.

Cordellos, H.C. (1976). *Aquatics recreation for the blind*. Washington, D.C.: American Alliance for Health, Physical Education and Recreation.

Dauer, V.P. and Pangrazi, R.P. (1979). *Dynamic physical education for elementary school children*. Minneapolis, Minn.: Burgess Publishing Company.

Kelly, J.D. (1981). *Recreation programming for visually impaired children and youth*. New York: American Foundation for the Blind, Inc.

National Inconvenienced Sportsman Association. *Teaching the blind to ski*. Carmichael, Calif.: Author.

Sherrill, C. (1976). *Adapted physical education and recreation: A multidisciplinary approach*. Dubuque, Iowa: Wm C Brown.

Sherrill, C., Rainbolt, W., and Eryin, S. (1984). Attitudes of blind persons towards physical education and recreation. *Adapted Physical Activities Quarterly*, **1**(1), pp. 3-11.

CHAPTER 22

Transition to Adulthood

Frank Simpson

This chapter provides a framework that teachers of visually handicapped students can use to integrate career education and career development into curricular and extra-curricular activities from preschool through high school. It emphasizes the holistic nature of the career development process and the collaborative planning needed to accomplish it, and provides, as well, concrete and specific ways to approach it. The chapter also demonstrates how skills learned throughout the school years contribute to the visually handicapped adolescent's successful transition to adulthood.

The years of late adolescence and early adulthood are a time for questioning, for decision-making, and for assumption of new responsibilities. There is a shift or transition from the role of student to that of worker. "Worker" is broadly defined as one who exhibits goal-directed behavior aimed at accomplishing something (Bagley, 1985; Hoyt, 1985). For all youth, disabled or nondisabled, this time of transition is both exciting and stressful.

Blind and visually handicapped youth are faced with many questions during this transition period. They are often asked and ask themselves, "What am I going to do when I finish school?" A more appropriate question would be: "What am I going to do before school is over to prepare for my career?" In addition, teachers, rehabilitation counselors, and parents also have many questions. (See Chart 22.1.) A smooth transition from student to worker requires that youth, parents, teachers, and rehabilitation workers cooperatively seek answers to these questions. Finding answers begins during preschool years and continues throughout the life span; it is referred to as "career development." The process approach is emphasized by several writers.

Bagley (1985) defines it as "the process through which individuals define their work values and create meaning for their activities. It also involves exploration of interests and discovery of potential" (p. 434). Bagley suggests that a more descriptive term for the process is career socialization.

Hoyt (1985) also emphasizes that career development is a process, not a program. It is developmental in nature and includes such components as career awareness; career exploration; career planning; career decision-making; career preparation; career entry; and career progression. Hoyt describes career education as "a fusion of the career development process with the teaching/learning process into the curriculum" (p. 489).

Tennyson, Hansen, Klaurens, and Antholz (1980) emphasize four principles of career development:

1. Career development is a process whereby students continuously assess themselves relative to environmental alternatives and integrate this information into the self-concept; it is the internalization of a personal system of gathering feedback relative to the important aspects of one's life.

2. Career development as a developmental process proceeds from the general to specific at different rates for different people.

3. Each person has the potential for success and satisfaction in many environments and occupations. No single choice or direction is necessarily the "only" choice.

4. Career development emphasizes a need for the individual to gain control over his or her own life and students need to develop skills with which to choose and plan in order to be able to learn how and what to choose relative to a personal value system.

Tennyson et al. (1980) conclude that attention to career development in the school curriculum will benefit not only the individual but society:

• It gives students a clearer understanding of themselves and their roles in the world of work;

Chart 22.1   Questions frequently asked by youth, parents, teachers and rehabilitation counselors.

Questions youth frequently ask:	*Questions parents ask:*	*Questions teachers ask:*	*Questions rehabilitation counselors ask:*
1. What will I do? What do my parents expect me to do?	1. Where do blind and visually handicapped people work?	1. How can the emphasis on work begin at age 16? Isn't that too late since career development should begin very early?	1. Who is responsible for coordinating transitional planning?
2. How do I find out about my vocational aptitudes or abilities?	2. What can our son/daughter do for a living?	2. Can my students benefit from career education programs that have not been designed for visually handicapped students?	2. What do parents, teachers, and students understand about vocational rehabilitation in our state?
3. Should I go to a rehabilitation center?	3. Is the school going to provide vocational training?	3. Where can I find out what experiences, both in the classroom and community, will best prepare my students to be successful in the adult world of work?	3. I am very interested in working with students but where will I find the time since I already have a large caseload?
4. Should I disclose my disability on my job application?	4. When does mobility training begin?	4. How soon can or will a rehabilitation counselor begin work with my students?	4. Should not the schools, both day and residential programs, be providing career/vocational training and guidance?
5. What should I tell an employer about my visual impairment?	5. When is our child assigned a rehabilitation counselor?	5. What do the parents expect me to do in preparing their children for transition?	5. Is there special funding for transitional services?
6. How do I explain my visual impairment to co-workers?	6. Who can help our child find an after-school or summer job?	6. What does the rehabilitation service agency expect me to do in preparing my students for their program?	6. Though transition is a new focus, haven't we been providing these services for some time?
7. How do I explain the nonvisual aids I need to do certain job tasks?	7. We understand the I.E.P. but what is an I.W.R.P.?	7. How can I meet with the rehabilitation agency personnel if my supervisor will not give me released time?	7. How does supportive employment relate to transition?
8. Who will pay for the special equipment I might need?	8. We would like to help during this transition time, but where can we get more information about resources? What are the options?	8. I'm interested, but where do I find time to take on these new responsibilities?	
9. How do I deal with my employer's and co-workers' negative or over-solicitive attitudes?	9. Does transition apply just to employment?	9. How can I get my students into work experience programs like those of their nonhandicapped classmates?	
10. How can I change another person's attitude toward me?	10. Will he/she be able to work in the competitive job market?	10. Is funding available to start a work-experience program?	
	11. What about our multi-handicapped son/daughter who needs a group home?		

Adapted from: F. Simpson, K.M. Huebner, & F. Roberts. *Transition from school to work: Collaborative planning (Training manual)* (New York, N.Y.: American Foundation for the Blind, 1985).

• It promotes an atmosphere of achievement since the value of current studies is associated with future goals and aspirations; and

• It creates an understanding of the relationships among work, leisure, family, and community in formulating life styles.

The concept of career development as a perspective and a process incorporates the realities of a complex world; it acknowledges that adults need no longer define themselves by only the job they do but recognizes the importance of developing meaningful personal, social, and community roles; it fosters respect for each individual's unique career development pattern and unique levels of attainment; it is a humanistic approach; it acknowledges not only the value of individual attainment but also efforts that contribute to the common good of all people; it stresses not only the independent aspects of living and working but the necessary and satisfying interdependent aspects.

Often blind and visually handicapped children and youth receive excellent academic preparation *but* have limited social and career development experiences. Time to think about the future may be limited by the need to devote much effort and energy to meeting the daily demands of school and community activities. In addition, they have neither the time nor the opportunity for after school or summer employment which provides a career exploration experience. The hours that nonhandicapped teenagers often spend in summer or part-time jobs are filled with specialized instruction in orientation and mobility, communication skills, social skills, and remedial academics. The result is that school and preparation for adulthood through work place experiences are totally separate.

This chapter seeks to heighten awareness of the scope and content of career development through a review of milestones to be acquired during the preschool, elementary, middle, and high school/adult years. These milestones are based on a model described by Jones (1984). It provides the individual student with a personalized system for progressively assuming more responsibility, maximizes utilization of significant others in the student's life, and facilitates ongoing clarification of expectations and perceptions. The second part summarizes critical personal skills needed for the transition to adulthood. Finally, for expanded planning efforts to meet the career development needs of all visually handicapped youth in transition from school to work at the community, regional, and state levels, a planning process adapted by the American Foundation for the Blind from Ferrini, Matthews, Foster, and Workman (1980) is described.

A CAREER DEVELOPMENT PROGRAM

The scope of career development in educational programs may be divided into four stages using Brolin's concepts of awareness, exploration, preparation, and placement. (See Chart 22.2.)

Chart 22.2   Scope of career development

Stages	*Age Span*
Awareness Attitudes, information, and self-understanding are basic elements of career awareness. An understanding and appreciation that people make many efforts to produce benefits for themselves and others is developed through awareness.	Entire life
Exploration Through a careful self-examination and understanding of one's unique abilities and needs, the world of work, leisure, social, and recreational interests are explored.	Elementary school years throughout adulthood
Preparation Competencies are developed through training and experiences in daily living skills, personal/social skills, academic instruction, and occupational/vocational preparation.	Middle school years throughout adulthood
Placement Job placement occurs simultaneously with assuming other non-paid adult roles, including leisure, civic, and varied social roles.	High school/college throughout adulthood

Milestones in Career Development

The educational system has the obligation to prepare all students for maximum personal, social, community, and vocational adjustment in these four areas:

Personal Adjustment: Appearance, hygiene, personal mannerisms, and behaviors that contribute to a positive or negative perception of the person by others.

Social Adjustment: The acquisition of those skills that help a person participate as an effective member of a group.

Community Adjustment: Challenges persons meet on entering or re-entering the community such as money management, shopping, and use of community resources.

Vocational Adjustment: The acquisition of those work habits and work skills that facilitate employment in a work setting.

Career development milestones that blind and visually handicapped children and youth should acquire in these four areas in order to make a successful transition from school to adult life are summarized in Chart 22.3. There is considerable overlap among these four areas as well as within the milestones presented in each area. The rate of mastery of related content and skills necessary for developing these milestones will vary and levels of attainment on school completion will also vary. Career development cannot be "taught" as a class, but rather it should be viewed as a process and perspective infused into the school, home, community, and work environments.

A Personalized Career Development System

Career development, as a process, requires a unique approach to meet the individual needs of each blind and visually handicapped student. Many individuals influence the attitudes, perceptions, and expectations of visually handicapped youth. Thus, it is essential that significant others involved in education and rehabilitation clarify their own roles, perceptions, expectations, and contributions relative to each other and to the visually handicapped student. A summary of these ideal roles is included in Chart 22.4.

Overlap in the roles of significant others is evident. For example, parenting and employing also involve aspects of teaching and counseling. In addition, roles change and evolve depending on environmental factors and needs. For example, all four may include nurturing at different times in the career development of the student.

With maturity the student must assume the role as manager of his/her own personal system of career development. This "system" and the resource persons/ significant others will vary with each student. Chart 22.5 outlines suggested actions a student needs to take in order to develop and refine self-awareness. Internalization of these "actions" contributes to taking charge and being one's own career development manager.

Visually handicapped students must recognize that their own career development system is a personal resource for information, ideas, and opportunities. Ideally, students should have the opportunity to invite selected resource persons to meet as a group regarding their career development plans. In reality, this collective meeting may not always be possible; however, the main purpose is to begin developing with each student, as soon as they can play an active role, a personal "vehicle" or method for short- and long-term career development planning. Chart 22.6 outlines steps that might be used in working with an elementary age student who is interested in exploring a career as a veterinarian.

Career development objectives should be included in the Individualized Education Programs (IEP) for students at all ages. As students reach the end of their school careers, they are typically referred to a rehabilitation agency where rehabilitation counselors develop and monitor their Individualized Written Rehabilitation Plans (IWRP). Much of the information included in the IEP can be used in developing the IWRP to provide coordinated, effective services. The IWRP is the basic tool for planning and managing rehabilitation services.

Once an individual has been determined to be eligible for rehabilitation services based on documented existence of a significant visual impairment, need for services and potential for employment, the IWRP is developed. Five kinds of information are included in the IWRP as follows:

1. Long-range Rehabilitation Goal: the realistic vocational placement after services have been provided.
2. Intermediate Rehabilitation Objectives: short term objectives that will lead to attainment of the long-term goal.
3. Specific Rehabilitation Services: counseling, mobility training, medical treatment, vocational training, equipment, etc., needed to attain the objectives.
4. Time Frame for Services: a basic schedule for service delivery and attainment of intermediate rehabilitation objectives.
5. Evaluation: basic criteria used to determine if rehabilitation objectives have been met.

Teachers will note the similarity of these items to those included in an IEP. The contribution of teachers, including regular classroom teachers, to the development of IWRP is essential. Likewise the involvement of local rehabilitation agency personnel as team members in planning each student's IEP, particularly during the high school years, is recommended. These two planning documents are excellent tools for bridging the transition from school to work.

CRITICAL SKILLS FOR TRANSITION

Transition, like career development, is not an isolated event but rather a series of events occurring over time throughout one's life. It is characterized by change and movement. For most people it may involve both feelings of satisfaction and frustration; of comfort with the familiar and fear of the unknown; of belonging and isolation; of competence and incompetence; of hope and despair; and varying degrees and combinations of these feelings. Each individual approaches or avoids transitional events (external aspect) and feelings (internal aspect) in a unique way depending on the level of self-awareness and acceptance; level and scope of coping skills; life experiences; and the spirit of adventure.

Self-Awareness

As development of self-awareness progresses, each student begins to identify personal goals, personal

Chart 22.3   Career development milestones — Pre-school Awareness Level I

Personal Adjustment	Social Adjustment	Community Adjustment	Vocational Adjustment
The Learner: 1. Begins to develop an awareness of self through self identification of physical traits, personal traits, personal likes/dislikes. 2. Begins to understand and accept the value of glasses, mobility aids, various "devices." 3. Begins to understand the need for organizing personal space (room, play area, etc.) 4. Begins to organize personal space. 5. Begins to understand when to ask for assistance. 6. Begins to value appropriate personal appearance. 7. Identifies clothes appropriate for different weather conditions and different social settings such as playground, church, party, etc. 8. Begins, with periodic prompting, to self-correct inappropriate personal behavior and to select, with assistance, more appropriate behavior.	The Learner: 1. Develops an awareness of other people. 2. Acquires knowledge/information from others. 3. Learns to ask appropriate questions in order to gather information. 4. Builds a personal feedback system through significant others in the environment. 5. Learns to offer assistance/help to others. 6. Begins to understand necessary behavior (e.g., waiting for your turn, sharing materials, etc.) 7. Begins to utilize eye contact regardless of visual acuity. 8. Begins to reach beyond the nuclear family to the extended family and immediate neighborhood for social contacts. 9. Begins to identify friends by name.	The Learner: 1. Expands the concept of the community from the *home* to the *neighborhood*. 2. Describes characteristics of the neighborhood when questioned. 3. Begins to understand the concept of money and its use. 4. Begins to understand the concept of time (days, years, hours, minutes, etc.) 5. Begins to use the telephone. 6. Begins to use trailing techniques. 7. Understands and describes the roles of various community helpers. (e.g., fireman, nurse, policeman, etc.)	The Learner: 1. Describes family members' work both at home and on their jobs. 2. Exhibits an understanding of responsibility through describing "things I do to help mommy, daddy, sister," etc." 3. Begins to develop the exchange concept (e.g., for chores completed I receive a special privilege or money for a treat.) 4. Begins to exhibit cooperative/shared efforts with friends to accomplish a group goal or task. 5. Begins to state "what I would like to be when I grow up." 6. Begins to follow multi-step directions. 7. Learns to replicate after demonstration (e.g., "watch me and then you make one"). 8. Begins to distinguish different traits of workers by such factors as "wears a white uniform, carries a mail bag, wears a helmet, etc." 9. Begins to exhibit pride in accomplishment of a task.

Chart 22.3 Career development milestones—Elementary
Awareness level II
Exploration level I

Personal Adjustment	Social Adjustment	Community Adjustment	Vocational Adjustment
The Learner: 1. Continues refining the self concept: a. Identifies personal abilities, not only academic but also social ("people skills"). b. Identifies personal interests. c. Identifies personal achievements. d. begins to describe with assistance how one's abilities and achievements do or do not relate to one's interests. 2. Begins to acquire a sense of personal privacy. 3. Begins to acquire a sense of control of specific aspects of life (e.g., "I can make some choices on my own with the support of others"). 4. Begins to develop, with assistance, a consistent personalized pattern of problem solving/coping. 5. Continues to develop and refine personal management skills. 6. Increases ability to present one's self positively and realistically. 7. Begins to understand how "I can learn most effectively." (Personal, unique learning style.) 8. Describes personal achievements to others reflecting a sense of ownership.	The Learner: 1. Recognizes and describes the unique qualities of individuals. 2. Recognizes the impact of behavior on others. 3. Recognizes different roles (child, student, friend). 4. Describes the qualities associated with friendship (e.g., trust, respect, acceptance, etc.). 5. Recognizes and responds appropriately to emergency situations. 6. Develops and demonstrates respect for the rights and property of others. 7. Begins to differentiate self from others. 8. Begins to understand the concepts of *independent, interdependent,* and *dependent.* 9. Recognizes and demonstrates behavior appropriate in varied settings (home, school, playground, bus, camp, etc.). 10. Begins to recognize the social nuances that facilitate acceptance (e.g., facial distance, listening skills, conversation, closure, etc.).	The Learner: 1. Can describe resources available within the school and immediate neighborhood for recreation/leisure/medical needs. 2. Begins to understand and use locally available transportation services. 3. Can use assistive devices for mobility (low vision aids, cane, etc.) 4. Develops money management skills (concept of saving and basic budgeting). 5. Recognizes possible uses of technology for personal access to information, etc. 6. Demonstrates basic time management skills at school and home in organizing time for chores, leisure, homework, etc. 7. Identifies current issues within the school and community. 8. Begins to understand how different people make different contributions in order for the home, school, and community to function effectively. 9. Recognizes the reason for and observes laws, rules, etc. 10. Begins to recognize that with rights go responsibilities.	The Learner: 1. Continues to develop knowledge about workers one knows outside the family within the school and neighborhood. 2. Begins to identify expectations common to all workers (e.g., getting to work on time, getting along with co-workers, having a neat personal appearance, etc.) 3. Begins to identify skills that may be required in some specific jobs. 4. Identifies self as a worker in varied settings (home, school, club, etc.) 5. Begins recognition and description of the various tasks that are a part of a particular job. 6. Begins to understand how one would learn a task and also how one would teach a task. 7. Begins to recognize the visual demands of various tasks and to decide which can and cannot be done without modification. 8. Begins to recognize sources of career information (people, library, television, etc.) 9. Begins to recognize and identify qualities valued by employers.

9. Demonstrates willingness to take "planned risks" in pursuing goals slightly beyond one's usual boundaries.

10. Describes satisfaction received from giving as well as receiving help and support.

11. Demonstrates skills needed to maintain prosthetic aids.

12. Recognizes and expresses unique medical needs, (e.g., special diet, medications, etc.)

13. Begins to differentiate between feelings that may result from being different and those that result from being treated differently. (Being different is O.K. but being treated differently can be personally devastating.)

Chart 22.3 Career development milestones—Middle school
Awareness level III
Exploration level II
Preparation level I

Personal Adjustment	Social Adjustment	Community Adjustment	Vocational Adjustment
The Learner: 1. Clarifies self-concept: a. Can describe abilities/skills and relate these to preferred social, community, and vocational environments. b. Can identify personal strategies to meet physical and emotional needs. 2. Demonstrates goal setting/planning behavior relating to school activities/actions and community activities/actions to long term personal goals. 3. Refines coping skills (maintains a sense of control of one's life). 4. Differentiates/recognizes the difference between assertive and aggressive behavior. 5. Refines personal problem-solving strategies. 6. Seeks information and develops (with assistance) an understanding of the physical body changes common to all adolescents. 7. Maintains prosthetic devices. 8. Can monitor unique medical needs; (e.g., medication schedule, etc.) 9. Actively seeks environmental supports (resource teacher, readers, aids, appliances, etc.) to maximize learning potential.	The Learner: 1. Develops a personal feedback system to clarify perceptions/ expectations of self (by self) and of others (by others). 2. Begins to recognize environmental barriers (discrimination, prejudice, etc.) which may impact the achievement of goals. 3. Recognizes verbal and nonverbal components in acceptance, praise, rejection, etc. 4. Begins to make decisions relative to one's needs while considering the impact of this decision on significant others in one's life. 5. Refines one's personal "friendship seeking, building, and maintenance" repertoire of skills (language/behavior combination). 6. Develops age-appropriate peer group/referent contacts outside the family/home (a natural support network). 7. Demonstrates active listening skills in various social settings. 8. Recognizes authority and responds appropriately to authority in varied settings. 9. Develops "personal guidelines" for appropriately accepting and refusing assistance.	The Learner: 1. Can locate with assistance resources available within the school and neighborhood for recreation/leisure/medical needs. 2. Plans for travel outside the immediate community and, with assistance, practices orientation and mobility skills in unfamiliar settings. 3. Begins to explore types of housing available within the local community. 4. Refines money management skills. 5. Refines time management skills. 6. Demonstrates awareness of and adherence to school regulations and local laws. 7. Develops an understanding of the interdependence ("connectedness") of various community components.	The Learner: 1. Recognizes the impact of school experience and community experience on future vocational plans/achievement. 2. Begins to understand job clusters/job families. 3. Understands that careers have a specific pattern of preparation, both formal (academic) and informal (experiential). 4. Begins to recognize that adult role models (parents, teachers, siblings) have an impact on one's career choices. 5. Develops ability after gaining information to identify various tasks that are a part of a job (job analysis). 6. Begins to understand the concept of job accommodation and to identify some personal accommodation needs (e.g. applicable technological devices, correct lighting, etc.) 7. Begins to match personal interests and abilities with possible career choices. 8. Increases knowledge base of occupations and careers through reading, observations, and gathering information. 9. Begins to identify job seeking skills.

10. Continues to develop and refine personal management skills.

11. Understands the need to provide information, to project confidence, and to demonstrate competence which will positively influence attitudes of other people towards blindness.

12. Learns strategies to integrate the impairment of blindness into one's self-concept but not as the primary defining trait.

13. Actively seeks opportunities to take "planned risks."

14. Recognizes and incorporates nonverbal aspects of communication into one's personal repertoire.

15. Identifies personal response patterns of behavior to repeated problems/challenges.

16. Describes impact of others' expectations on one's personal goals and expectations.

10. Develops social decision-making skills that include anticipation of consequences of the decision.

11. Seeks opportunities to change the attitudes of other people (proactive approach) while beginning to understand the value in changing stereotypes.

10. Internalizes personal information for use in job seeking (e.g., basic job application and interview information.)

11. Recognizes interdependence of people in the work environment.

12. Develops a personal strategy for involving relevant resource persons in one's career planning process (e.g., school counselor, career development team, etc.)

13. Seeks opportunities for work responsibility in the home, school, and neighborhood.

14. Begins to develop an understanding of the value of work to self and to society (not just monetary but personal and societal).

15. Begins to identify occupational opportunities that are available in the local communities (including resources for the information).

16. Identifies and exhibits positive work habits that generalize to all work settings. (e.g. behavioral aspects, performance aspects, safety aspects, interdependent aspects.)

Chart 22.3   Career development milestones—High school/Adult life
Awareness Level IV
Exploration Level III
Preparation Level II
Placement Level I

Personal Adjustment	Social Adjustment	Community Adjustment	Vocational Adjustment
The Learner:	The Learner:	The Learner:	The Learner:
1. Refines self-concept through reality testing: a. Internalizes an ongoing process of comparing one's actual abilities/aptitudes with one's "imaginary planned for" abilities/aptitudes. b. Internalizes an ongoing process for reducing the distance between one's "real self" and one's "ideal self."	1. Masters nuances of verbal and nonverbal communication. 2. Continues to refine active listening skills. 3. Develops empathic skills (putting oneself in the other person's shoes).	1. Develops independent resource (rehabilitation, training, recreation/leisure, housing, transportation, medical) seeking and accessing skills. 2. Becomes involved in school and community civic activities.	1. Integrates personal values with community experiences into career goals. 2. Determines training needs (academic/vocational/on-the-job) and experiences to achieve chosen career goals.
2. Continues to refine "personal coping skills" across varied situations.	4. Applies reality testing/risk taking in new social situations. 5. Recognizes appropriate qualities/intensities of various relationships across various roles.	3. Demonstrates adequate orientation and mobility skills in both familiar and unfamiliar settings.	3. Increases understanding and knowledge of occupations and varied work settings through involvement in actual after-school/summer work experiences.
3. Begins to integrate and refine how one's personal goals for adult life are an integration of self with the social, community, and vocational environments (an integrated approach).	6. Recognizes/internalizes social (common good/fraternal good) values system and how one's personal values do/do not integrate into this "larger value system."	4. Develops an awareness of civic rights and responsibilities. 5. Differentiates between entitlement and eligibility service programs.	4. Refines knowledge of job clusters/job families. 5. Identifies personal skills that are generalized to a variety of occupations and settings.
4. Refines personal strategies to change the attitudes of other people toward blindness through personal example and advocacy.	7. Develops and refines networking skills and natural support systems.	6. Manages personal finances 7. Develops skills to assess local community relative to one's personal values, goals, and needs.	6. Refines ability to task analyze a variety of jobs. 7. Identifies personal job accommodation needs and actively seeks funds, etc., to secure any assistive/adaptive technology that facilitates employment.
5. Recognizes personal patterns of behavior and develops strategies (self-interventions) to change/intervene in these patterns (e.g., as one becomes an adult and assumes a "new role," coping patterns of childhood are inappropriate.)		8. Identifies personally appropriate future place of residence.	8. Refines job seeking skills in: a. Resume development. b. Employment resources identification; c. Interviewing skills development.

6. Recognizes when one needs outside assistance/intervention to maximize coping and problem solving skills (e.g., as one encounters particularly stressful intrapersonal and/or interpersonal situations, it may be appropriate to seek the professional assistance of a social worker, rehabilitation counselor, etc.).

7. Establishes one's vocational (occupatonal), social, and community goals considering one's own values as primary and the expectation of significant others as secondary/supportive (e.g., as an adult one acknowledges the expectations of significant others but makes choices based on personal needs, goals, and self-expectations.)

8. Mastery of all independent living skills to maximize social, community, and vocational adjustment (including medical management strategies).

9. Internalizes acceptable work habits with special emphasis on responding to supervision and adapting to change.

10. Identifies "promotabilitiy" skills.

11. Acquires and utilizes labor market information from varied resources on a continuing basis.

12. Internalizes the concept of work being a valuable personal experience and social contribution.

Chart 22.4   Ideal roles of significant others in the career development process

Teachers	Parents	Rehabilitative Counselors	Employers
1. Facilitate in the student self-understanding reflected in realistic personal, social, community, and vocational goals.	1. Nurture in the child a sense of personal value and wholeness by ensuring that in all aspects of family and community life there are opportunities to learn, to venture, to try, and to take risks.	1. Provide a habilitation/rehabilitation perspective and comprehensive information relative to the continuum of adult service options.	1. Provide specific information on trends in the local economy and on manpower needs.
2. Provide academic instruction and secure specific skills training/experiences in personal-social skills, daily living skills, and occupational/vocational skills.	2. Provide the child with a perspective and concurrent information that fosters a positive value of work and of leisure within the structure of the home and family.	2. Facilitate the building within the student/youth adult/client of a personal career development plan based on realistic and reasonable expectations.	2. Develop with support of significant others and the student meaningful community/industry-based work experiences.
3. Provide the least restrictive educational environment in which students can develop the confidence to try and to take risks.	3. Assume a leadership role in actively and systematically planning career development with the child and significant others.	3. Facilitate through supportive counseling the student/young adult/client's positive strivings to take charge of his/her career development providing a range of community-based evaluation, training, and placement options.	3. Provide feedback on the relevance and appropriateness of school, community, and family experiences to future occupational success/satisfaction.
4. Facilitate the involvement of other individuals in the career development of students.		4. Assist, through collaborative planning, all significant others and the student to shift from a child-centered to an adult-oriented perspective.	4. Embrace a sensitivity to working with applicants with disabilities as demonstrated in recruitment and employment practices.

Chart 22.5   Ideal role of blind/visually handicapped student as manager of his/her personalized career development system

1. Know and present yourself to significant others in a positive, goal-directed manner through identifying your:
   A. Interests
   B. Abilities
   C. Aptitudes
   D. Experiences
   E. Short and long range goals

2. Clarify the perceptions and expectations significant others hold about you and determine how important it is for you to please these people, such as:
   A. Parents
   B. Teachers
   C. Rehabilitation Counselors
   D. Friends
   E. Others

3. Develop an understanding of your integral "working" dynamics:
   A. How do you solve your problems?
   B. How do you manage your time?
   C. How do you cope with stress?
   D. How do you adjust to change?
   E. How do you deal with disappointment?
   F. How do you deal with success?

4. Identify other persons as possible resources for your immediate and future career development needs, such as:
   A. Blind and visually handicapped adults
   B. Low vision specialists
   C. Mobility specialists
   D. Potential employers
   E. Vocational evaluators
   F. Rehabilitation teacher/independent living instructors

5. Acquire skills you will need to access various adult environments, such as:
   A. Housing
   B. Transportation
   C. Employment
   D. Recreation
   E. Health services
   F. Higher education
   G. Adult education
   H. Financial services

6. Demonstrate to significant others that, with your rights as a young adult, you are assuming responsibility for your behavior and actions.

values, and life styles. A personalized feedback system emerges based on the student's ability to communicate both verbally and nonverbally and to be an active listener. Through individual and peer group discussions, the teacher can foster the development of this most critical skill. Actively encouraging articulate and open communication enables students to assert themselves later in a variety of adult situations. This proactive approach diminishes the likelihood of subsequent passive, helpless behavior and lack of meaningful communication, as participant or as listener. Students are learning at an appropriate age in an appropriate manner to assume control of their own lives.

A school environment that is reality-based utilizing all community resources is essential. To reduce demands or to lower expectations gives visually handicapped students the message that they are less than normal or adequate. To deny the opportunity for risk-taking situations where success or failure may be the outcome is promoting helplessness and dependence. Teachers have the opportunity and the obligation to build confidence and competence; students gain a sense of competence and confidence through age-appropriate responsibilities for self now and in the future.

Understanding the impact of one's behavior on other people enhances the development of meaningful personal and social relationships. This understanding, or the lack of understanding, influences the achievement of future career development in all areas. Few jobs are performed in total isolation and often represent a team effort. Students must learn to be good team members.

Once skills are developed in recognizing and understanding personal behavior patterns, students can begin to develop personal strategies to change their behavior. Behavior that is goal directed is so much different from the helpless, victim role of being controlled by the environment. The process of understanding one's behavior is ongoing. The teacher can foster a classroom environment that provides opportunities for students to observe appropriate role models and seek advice (feedback) from friends and staff. This represents the building of communication loops.

Frequently, individuals have difficulty in distinguishing between assertive and aggressive behavior. Assertive, confident persons are effective in identifying and expressing their feelings while not hurting others or denying their rights. Assertive persons accept the responsibility for their behavior. On the other hand, aggressive people often feel insecure and seek to get their way even at the expense of others.

Through discussion, sentence completion tasks, peer feedback, and training in nonverbal communication skills as described in Chapter 20, teachers can foster assertiveness and assist students in developing an array of verbal and nonverbal communication skills.

Chart 22.6   Steps to follow in a career development system for an elementary student

1. Together with the student, identify from Chart 22.3 a specific aspect (or milestone) of career development based on the student's current level of awareness and need for concrete information and experiences.

2. Together with the student and other classmates, brainstorm possible resources and people who could provide this information and/or experience.

3. Introduce the concept of a career development system to the student by making analogies to teams the student may understand or be familiar with, such as a baseball team. Discuss how a baseball team is a group of people working toward a common goal just as career development resource persons are working toward the common goal of assisting the student as the main person.

4. Assist the student to develop a systematic method of contacting the possible resource persons and to keep a record of contacts. Contacts should be via telephone or in person. Written contacts are usually less effective.

5. Develop a protocol (worksheet) which the student can use to record information gathered.

6. Determine which significant others in the student's environment can assist in networking to or reaching other resources. For example, if the student wants information on a veterinarian career, he or she may know the family's veterinarian but may need the assistance of a parent when he goes to visit.

7. After information is gathered through these methods (telephone calls and visits), provide the student with the opportunity to share the information with other classmates.

8. Discuss with the student what he or she originally thought were the job responsibilities of the veterinarian and if that has changed based on the gathering of more complete information.

9. Based on all information gathered, discuss with the student his or her continued interest in this specific career.

10. With experience in gaining information relative to vocational awareness, introduce another aspect of career development and have the student use this planning approach for gathering information.

Coping Skills

The development of problem management and coping skills is essential if one is to thrive throughout life. Children and youth can learn these necessary skills from parents, teachers, counselors, and other significant persons. The internalization of these skills is a major goal of education and rehabilitation programming. Teachers convey an acceptance of the student's perceptions by:

1. Assisting students to recognize that problems are a matter of perception and perceptions vary from person to person; within the individual at different times in different situations; and across time.

2. Assisting students to define problems in order to limit the complexity of the situation and increase the likelihood of reaching a satisfactory personal solution by setting priorities: those most threatening to physical and mental functioning; students' perceptions of actual and anticipated problems; significant others' perception of actual and anticipated problems; and time factors implicit in "solving" problems.

3. Assisting students (through discussion, reflection and role playing) to develop methods of problem solving, including trial and error problem solving by chance or process of elimination; insight problem solving by solution originally by trial and error and later by insight; and vicarious problem solving by role playing the step-by-step method which should ultimately be used. This method contributes to self-awareness through:

- Recognizing and defining the problem
- Gathering and assessing personal and environmental information
- Developing alternative actions and probable outcomes
- Selecting specific actions and planning implementation
- Implementing action
- Evaluating action and outcomes.

Life Experiences

The student's development of a personal style of problem solving is one of the primary goals teachers can use to promote self-sufficiency. The development of self-knowledge is an ongoing process that occurs over time through varied life experiences. With maturation, the idealized self of childhood approaches the real self of adulthood. An awareness of one's needs, goals, interests, aptitudes, and values facilitates this growth process. Appropriate input from significant others and equal access to opportunities is essential if full potential is to be realized. However, levels of individual achievement and adjustment will vary.

Spirit of Adventure

Children and adolescents who are visually handicapped need to be faced with tasks commensurate with their abilities but they also must be challenged to take risks. With success experiences, they can become self-motivated and gain the confidence needed for the transition to adulthood. Calculated risk taking is necessary in the performance of many tasks being accomplished without vision. Students gain a sense of self-worth and peer acceptance when given the opportunity to perform and accomplish these tasks. To deny this challenge or opportunity implies a lack of confidence. This can reinforce in the child a feeling of being inadequate or different.

"Risk situations" occur at every level of maturation. The unwillingness of parents and educators to help the adolescent "take risks" results in limited goal setting inhibiting the maximum realization of the visually handicapped individual's potential.

Teachers must remember to foster the spirit of adventure that sustains motivation, maintains momentum, and supports hope!

A COLLABORATIVE PLANNING PROCESS TO DEVELOP A TEAM APPROACH

Teachers of visually handicapped youth should become advocates for improving the delivery of services to all visually handicapped pupils in their local educational agency (LEA), region, and state. The activities described in the previous parts focus on what teachers must do for individual pupils to facilitate their transition to adulthood. As advocates, teachers should also work to improve services to all visually handicapped children and youth in their areas. This part presents a framework for collaborative planning on a broader base that will be of benefit to all pupils.

The lack of collaboration and consistent planning is often costly in human terms to individuals in need of services. Duplication of services may result in unnecessary use of already limited funding; programs may compete for particular groups of visually handicapped people to the exclusion of others; handicapped people begin to "slip through the cracks"; referral networks become vague and services difficult to locate. Collaborative planning between and among individuals, agencies, schools, and the business community can assist in avoiding these problems and maintaining existing services as well as expanding their scope and quality.

By bringing together individuals and organizations collaboration fosters:

1. Sharing of school, agency, organizational, parent, and student perspectives;
2. Sharing of information about services currently offered;
3. Identification of critical unmet needs;
4. Identification of new programs or new linkages between existing programs that will meet those needs;

5. Development of long term collaborative agreements among individuals, agencies, schools, and the business community.

Administrative, student, and parent support at the local school district level and support from community-based adult service agencies, business, and industry is needed to effectively implement collaborative planning. The following model is suggested for implementing collaborative planning for successful transition from school to adulthood for all pupils in the LEA, region, or state.

Ten steps are outlined to achieve the goal of developing a collaborative plan to facilitate transition of visually handicapped youth from school to work. It should be noted that this model to develop inter-agency and community collaborative plans differs from the individual career development system for students described earlier.

Step 1
Follow these suggested guidelines for selecting team members.
a. Maintain balance on the team by having the following represented:
• Visually handicapped adults;
• Parents of visually handicapped youth;
• Business firms and associates;
• Private and public schools;
• Public and private rehabilitation agencies; and
• University training programs.
b. Agency, school, and business community representatives need decision-making powers within their organization in order to commit resources. If classroom teachers and rehabiltiation counselors are represented on the team, they need the full support of their administrators to commit resources.
c. Prospective team members need to:
• Commit the time not only to develop a collaborative plan, but to implement it;
• Understand that collaborative planning can assist in overcoming the turf barrier which is often problematic in interagency planning.

Step 2
Once the team is selected, the initial meeting agenda should include the following:
a. Select an impartial team leader who can systematically follow a step-by-step process ensuring that the perspectives of all individuals and agencies are respected;
b. Each team member shares his/her perspectives, services, etc., that impact the transition from school to work;
c. Each team member describes the existence and effectiveness of interagency agreements that currently

facilitate transition. Often these exist on local, regional, and state levels but are not necessarily coordinated.

Step 3
The team should identify transition needs at the local, regional, and/or state level. Some examples of possible needs are as follows:
a. Summer work experiences for visually handicapped youth (local need);
b. Integration of visually handicapped students into vocational education courses (local need);
c. Training of teachers and rehabilitation counselors in job development and modification (local/regional need);
d. Parental involvement in career planning with their visually handicapped adolescent (regional need);
e. Rehabilitation counselor involvement with students at a younger age (state need);
f. State-level transition service agreements between and among special education, vocational education, and vocational rehabilitation (state need).

Step 4
Select three of the transition needs from the list which the team has identified as the highest priority.

Step 5
Based on the three highest priority needs develop a realistic goal for a collaborative transitional plan. The scope of this plan will be determined by the team's focus on local, regional, or state needs. For example, one goal would be to provide quality career development experiences for visually handicapped youth in transition from school to work.

Step 6
Develop a list of strategies that might be used to achieve the identified goal, such as conducting workshops for teachers, rehabilitation counselors, and employers on developing part-time summer employment opportunities; or conducting seminars for students on developing job seeking skills.

Step 7
Identify criteria to used in selecting a preferred strategy; discuss advantages and disadvantages of strategies; and select a strategy to be used to achieve the identified goal. Possible criteria could include:
• Cost to implement each strategy
• Time required to implement each strategy
• Staff available to implement each strategy
• Number of students who will benefit.

Step 8
Identify major tasks necessary to implement the selected strategy, e.g., conducting seminars for students on developing job seeking skills.

Possible Tasks
1. Develop a comprehensive listing of appropriate job seeking skills;
2. Recruit visually handicapped adults who are working to conduct seminars on job-seeking skills;
3. Recruit employers to conduct a workshop on employment practices;
4. Provide students with first-hand experiences in job-seeking skills through involvement in existing after-school or summer work experience programs.

Step 9
Identify the order in which selected tasks are to be accomplished, date of initiation, date of completion, and team member responsibility for completion. Describe how and when team members will communicate with each other and the team leader to monitor progress.

Step 10
Prepare a "master" action plan with the following parts:
• Description of the team, its members, its history, and its overall purpose;
• Statement of the team's program focus with brief rationale;
• Statement of the team's initial strategy with brief rationale;
• Statement of major tasks the team will perform and timetable;
• Projected date for implementing the team's strategy.

Planning together involves the following:
cooperation   coordination
collaboration   commitment
A detailed description of this process is included in Simpson, Huebner, and Roberts (1985) listed in additional readings at the end of this chapter.

CONCLUDING REMARKS
The goal of an appropriate educational program for all pupils including those with visual impairments is to "equip children and youth with life competencies that enable them to love, to work, and to play within the context of an acceptable system of values" consistent with the abilities of each individual (Chapter 13). Achievement of this goal is initiated in the assessment process through the use of appropriate procedures to determine the unique capacities and limitations of the

individual pupil (Chapter 11). Based on the results of this assessment, teachers in collaboration with the parents or primary care-givers develop the IEP (Chapters 12 and 15). Once goals and objectives are identified, and the appropriate placement in the least restrictive environment is determined, teachers implement the curricular and noncurricular activities that will contribute to achieving the goals and objectives (Chapter 21) with particular attention to those specialized areas which are essential for the ultimate adult adjustment of visually handicapped pupils (Chapters 18-20).

In this concluding chapter, the emphasis is placed on helping students develop concepts, acquire skills, and access services *to begin* assuming increased responsibility for determining their unique futures. The ideas and content are presented to challenge teachers to expand their current roles to include the broader role of advocates (Chapter 16); to consider the roles and responsibilities of students, parents, and other professionals in the total educational process through expanding their knowledge base relative to the process of career development which draws together all the components in the educational process to facilitate transition to adulthood. The content should heighten awareness of the value of consistent, collaborative planning; and assist teachers in providing students with opportunities to take risks in learning new skills, developing problem-solving strategies, and internalizing positive personal expectations that maximize personal, social, community, and vocational adjustment as they move into the adult world.

Study questions

1. Interview a visually handicapped student, parent of a visually handicapped student, or teacher at the secondary level about their concerns regarding the transition to the worker role. How do the concerns match with those included in Chart 22.1?

2. Discuss with some of your classmates the evolution of your career plans from your elementary school days to the present. How has your career development differed from that of your classmates?

3. Review the milestones listed in Chart 22.3. Select three that you think should be expanded and present a rationale. What additions to the milestones would you recommend?

4. List resources you used during your own career development. How did you locate them? In what ways did they contribute to your career development?

5. Select three milestones from Chart 22.3 and describe what curricular and noncurricular activities would contribute to the attainment of those milestones.

6. Review Chart 22.4 which describes ideal roles of significant others in the career development process. Using the same format, describe what you experience as typical (rather than ideal) roles. Determine if there is a difference between the described *ideal* and your experienced *real*. Describe what strategies you plan to use to reduce this discrepancy.

7. John is an eight-year-old, totally blind student enrolled in a regular second grade class. John is of average intelligence and is progressing academically on grade level. He is able to find his way around the classroom but has difficulty following directions for errands, such as to the principal's office. He has little awareness about the neighborhood and community in which he lives. His skills in nonverbal communication are poor. He has much trouble taking turns in conversation.

Select three milestones from Chart 22.3 that are appropriate for John and develop an IEP for him utilizing home, classrooms, and community as resources.

8. Tom is an eighteen-year-old of average intelligence in his last year of high school. He plays the piano reasonably well and his mother, a widow, wants him to be a concert pianist. He has no other vocational ambitions. Using Charts 22.5 and 22.6 tell how you would lay out a plan with Tom to assist him in determining whether becoming a concert pianist is a reasonable vocational goal for him.

9. Select from Chart 22.3 one level (e.g., elementary, middle, high school), and tell what content in the school curriculum would contribute to the acquisition of each milestone for blind and visually handicapped pupils at that level.

10. Find out what local and state plans and programs are available for the transition of visually handicapped adolescents into the adult world. Compare the model in your state with that described in this chapter.

Additional readings

Brolin, D.E. (ed.). (1983). *Life centered career education: A competency based program.* (Revised edition). Reston, Va.: Council for Exceptional Children.

Journal of Visual Impairment & Blindness—Special Issue on Career Development. **79**,(10) pp. 433-516.

Roessler, R. and Means, R.L. (1977). *Personal achievement skills training for the visually impaired.* Hot Springs, Ark.: University of Arkansas Hot Springs Rehabilitation Center.

Simpson, F., Huebner, K., and Roberts, F. (1985). *Collaborative planning: Transition from school to work developing your state team: Why and how.* New York, N.Y.: American Foundation for the Blind, Inc.

U.S. Department of Education Office of Special Education and Rehabilitation Services. (1985). *Cooperative programs for transition from school to work.* Washington, D.C.: Author.

APPENDICES

APPENDIX A

Overview of Ocular Diseases and Disorders*

Condition	Affected Area	Cause	Visual Effects	Mode of Detection	Treatment	Prognosis
Achromatopsia (total color blindness)	Retina (cone malformation)	Hereditary	Decreased visual acuity to 20/200, extreme photophobia, and nystagmus. Visual fields are normal.	Color vision screening test and electrodiagnostic tests, especially using the electroretinogram (ERG).	Optical aids, sunglasses, and dim illumination.	Nonprogressive; nystagmus and photophobia reduce with age.
Albinism (total or partial lack of pigment)	Macula (underdeveloped)	Hereditary	Decreased visual acuity (20/200 to 20/70), nystagmus, photophobia, high refractive error, and astigmatism. Visual fields variable and color vision is normal.	Family history and ocular examination.	Painted or pinhole contact lenses, absorptive lenses, optical aids, and dim illumination.	Nonprogressive.
Aniridia	Iris (underdeveloped)	Hereditary	Decreased visual acuity, photophobia, possible nystagmus, cataracts, displaced lens, and underdeveloped retina. Visual fields are normal. Secondary complication: glaucoma, with accompanying constriction of the visual fields, squint, and lens opacification.	Clinical observation of missing iris tissue.	Pin-hole contact lenses, sunglasses, optical aids, and dim illumination.	Milder forms develop slowly, progressive cataracts; severe forms develop glaucoma and corneal opacification.
Cataracts (congenital)	Lens (opacity)	Hereditary, congenital anomalies (rubella, Marfan syndrome,	Decreased visual acuity, blurred vision, nystagmus, squint, photophobia, slight constriction in	Ophthalmoscopy and slit-lamp bio-microscope.	Surgery as early as possible in cases of severe visual impairment.	After surgery, inability to accommodate; problems with glare which are corrected with spec-

Condition	Part of Eye Affected	Etiology	Symptoms	Diagnosis	Treatment	Prognosis/Complications
		Down syndrome), infection or drugs during pregnancy, and severe malnutrition during pregnancy.	the peripheral visual fields is possible, but visual fields are generally normal.			tacles or contact lenses. Complications from surgery: secondary cataracts and detachment of the vitreous or retina.
Cataracts (senile)	Lens (opacity)	Age	Progressively blurred vision; near vision is better than distance vision.	Same as for congenital cataracts.	Surgery, with resultant cataract spectacles, contact lenses, lens implant (IOL, intraocular lens).	Same as for congenital cataracts. Complications from surgery: glaucoma, retinal detachment, hemorrhage of the vitreous, infection. Better candidate for intraocular lens (IOL) implants.
Cataracts (traumatic)	Lens (opacity)	Head injury or metallic foreign body in the eye.	Blurred vision, redness and inflammation of the eye, and decreased visual acuity. Complications: infection, uveitis, retinal detachment, and glaucoma.	Same as for congenital and senile cataracts.	Surgery after inflammation subsides.	Same as for congenital and senile cataracts.
Coloboma	Various parts of the eye may have been deformed, severity depending on when deformity occurred during development.	Hereditary	Decreased visual acuity, nystagmus, strabismus, photophobia, and loss of visual and superior fields. Secondary complication: cataracts. Associated conditions: microphthalmia, polydactyly, and mental retardation.	Fundus examination	Cosmetic contact lenses, sunglasses, and optical aids.	Usually fairly stable.

*Developed by Dr. Jose and Ms. Nance Bauman, O.T., at the Pennsylvania College of Optometry

Condition	Affected Area	Cause	Visual Effects	Mode of Detection	Treatment	Prognosis
Diabetes Mellitus	Retina	Hereditary	Diplopia, inability to accommodate, fluctuating vision, loss of color vision or visual field, refractive error, decreased visual acuity, hemorrhaging of blood vessels in the retina, retinal detachment. Secondary complications: glaucoma and cataracts. Associated conditions: cardiovascular problems, skin problems, and kidney problems.	Ophthalmoscopy; reports of fluctuating vision.	Insulin injections, dietary controls, spectacles, and laser-beam surgery. Various illumination control aids.	Variation in acuity common.
Degenerative Myopia (nearsightedness)	Elongation of the eye; stretching of the posterior of the eye.	Hereditary	Decreased visual acuity in the distance, vitreous floaters, metamorphopsia. Normal visual field unless retina is detached. Secondary complications: retinal detachment and swelling or hemorrhaging of the macula.	Fundus examination.	Prescription correction, preferably contact lenses; optical aids and high illumination.	Unpredictable rate of progression.
Down Syndrome (mongolism)	Various parts of the eye. Associated with a chromosomal abnormality, usually trisomy of chromosome 21.	Hereditary; extra no. 21 chromosome.	Decrease of visual acuity, squint, nystagmus, severe myopia, Brushfield spots, congenital cataracts, and keratoconus. Color vision and visual fields are normal.	Physical appearance. Complete medical work-up.	Depending on patient's intellectual level, optical aids, prescription correction.	Medical problems more severe than usual. Good prognosis.

Disorder	Description	Cause	Symptoms / Associated conditions	Diagnosis	Treatment	Prognosis
Glaucoma (congenital)	Tissues of the eye damaged from increased intraocular pressure.	Hereditary	Associated conditions: mental retardation, cardiac abnormalities, hypotonia, saddle-shaped nose, large protruding tongue, and a short, squat stature.	Tonometry, study of the visual fields, and ophthalmoscopy.	Eye drops; surgery as soon as possible to prevent extensive damage.	With treatment, depends on the innate resistance of the structures of the eye. Blindness if not treated.
Glaucoma (adult)	Same as for congenital glaucoma.	Hereditary or the result of changes in the eye after surgery.	Headaches in front portion of the head, especially in the morning; seeing halos around lights; decreased visual acuity, loss of visual fields, photophobia, and constricted peripheral fields in severe cases.	Same as for congenital glaucoma.	Eye drops, optical aids, sunglasses.	Same as for congenital glaucoma.
Glaucoma (acute attack)	Same as for congenital and adult glaucoma.	Inability of the aqueous to drain.	Nausea, severe redness of the eye, headache, and severe pain.	Same as for congenital and adult glaucoma.	Emergency surgery.	Without emergency surgery, permanent damage to the ocular tissues and loss of visual acuity and peripheral vision.
Histoplasmosis	Macula or periphery (scattered lesions).	Fungus transmitted by spores found in dried excrement of animals.	In the macula: decreased visual acuity, central scotoma, and deficient color vision. In the periphery: scotoma corresponding to the area of lesions.	Ophthalmoscopy.	Optical aids for visual problems; steroids for physical condition.	Can be life threatening if not treated.

Overview of ocular diseases and disorders

Condition	Affected Area	Cause	Visual Effects	Mode of Detection	Treatment	Prognosis
Keratoconus	Cornea (stretched to a cone shape)	Hereditary. Manifested in second decade.	Increased distortion of entire visual field; progressive decrease in visual acuity, especially in the distance. Associated conditions: retinitis pigmentosa, aniridia, Down syndrome, and Marfan syndrome.	Ophthalmoscopy, retinoscopy, keratometry, and slit-lamp biomicroscope.	Hard contact lenses in the early stages; keratoplasty (corneal transplant) as needed.	Without keratoplasty, progressive degenerative thinning of cornea until cornea ruptures and blindness ensues.
Marfan Syndrome (disease of the connective tissues of the body)	Various parts of the eye.	Hereditary	Dislocation of the lens, decreased visual acuity, severe myopia, dislocated or multiple pupil, retinal detachment with accompanying field loss, different-colored eyes, squint, nystagmus, and bluish sclera. Associated conditions: skeletal abnormalities, long, thin fingers and toes, cardio-vascular problems, and muscular under-development.	Medical examination and evaluation.	Optical aids. Surgical or optical management of the dislocated lens.	Vision problems stable; medical problems are more significant.
Retinal Detachment	Retina (portions detach from supporting structure and atrophy)	Numerous, including diabetes, diabetic retinopathy, degenerative myopia, and a blow to the head.	Appearance of flashing lights; sharp, stabbing pain in the eye; visual field loss; micropsia, color defects, and decreased visual acuity if the macula is affected.	Ophthalmoscopy and an internal eye examination.	Laser-beam surgery and cryosurgery, depending on the type and cause of the detachment; optical aids; and usually high illumination.	Guarded.
Retinitis Pigmentosa	Retina (degenerative pigmentary	Hereditary	Decreased visual acuity, photophobia,	Electrodiagnostic testing, especially	Optical aids, prisms. No known medical	Slow, progressive loss in the visual

Disease	Site	Characteristics	Detection	Treatment	Prognosis
condition).		constriction of the visual fields. (loss in the peripheral field), and night blindness. Usher's Syndrome, Laurence-Moon-Biedl Syndrome, and Leber's Syndrome are associated with R.P.	ERG, and ophthalmoscopy.	cure; genetic counseling is essential.	fields that may lead to blindness.
Retinopathy of Prematurity	Retina (growth of blood vessels) and vitreous.	High levels of oxygen administered to premature infants; occasionally found in full-term infants. Decreased visual acuity, severe myopia, scarring, and retinal detachment, with resultant visual field loss and possible blindness. Secondary complications: glaucoma and uveitis.	Ophthalmoscopy.	Optical aids and illumination control devices.	Poor, in severe cases, where further detachments can be expected in third decade.
Rubella	Various parts of the eye.	Virus transmitted to the fetus by the mother during pregnancy. Congenital glaucoma, congenital cataracts, microphthalmia, decreased visual acuity, and constriction of the visual fields. Associated conditions: heart defects, ear defects, and mental retardation.	Ophthalmoscopy, slit-lamp biomicroscope, tonometry, and family history.	Surgery for glaucoma and cataracts, optical aids, establishment of appropriate educational goals.	Poor; post-surgical inflammation.
Toxoplasmosis	Retina, especially macula (lesions)	Intraocular infection caused by Toxoplasma gondii. In congenital type, fetus exposed to organism; in acquired type, through contact with infected animals or ingestion of raw meat. Loss in visual fields corresponding to location of lesion, squint, decreased visual acuity if macula is affected, severe brain damage if congenital.	Ophthalmoscopy.	Optical aids—usually good responses to magnification.	Nonprogressive, although new lesions may develop.

Source: R.T. Jose, *Understanding low vision* (New York: American Foundation for the Blind, Inc., 1984), pp. 9-17.

APPENDIX B

A Glossary of Measurement Terms

This glossary of terms used in educational and psychological measurement is primarily for persons with limited training in measurement, rather than for the specialist. The terms defined are the more common or basic ones which occur in test manuals and educational journals.

academic aptitude   The combination of native and acquired abilities that are needed for school learning; likelihood of success in mastering academic work, as estimated from measures of the necessary abilities. (Also called *scholastic aptitude, school learning ability, academic potential.*)

achievement test   A test that measures the extent to which a person has "achieved" something, acquired certain information, or mastered certain skills—usually as a result of planned instruction or training.

age norms   Originally, values representing typical or average performance for persons of various *age* groups; most current usage refers to sets of complete score interpretive data for appropriate successive age groups. Such norms are generally used in the interpretation of mental ability test scores.

alternate-form reliability   The closeness of correspondence, or correlation, between results on alternate (i.e., equivalent or parallel) forms of a test; thus, a measure of the extent to which the two forms are consistent or reliable in measuring whatever they do measure. The time interval between the two testings must be relatively short so that the examinees themselves are unchanged in the ability being measured. See **reliability, reliability coefficient.**

anecdotal record   A written description of an incident in an individual's behavior that is reported objectively and is considered significant for the understanding of the individual.

aptitude   A combination of abilities and other characteristics, whether native or acquired, that are indicative of an individual's ability to learn or to develop proficiency in some particular area if appropriate education or training is provided. Aptitude tests include those of general academic ability (commonly called mental ability or intelligence tests); those of special abilities, such as verbal, numerical, mechanical, or musical; tests assessing "readiness" for learning; and prognostic tests, which measure both ability and previous learning, and are used to predict future performance—usually in a specific field, such as foreign language, shorthand, or nursing.

arithmetic mean   A kind of average usually referred to as the *mean*. It is obtained by dividing the sum of a set of scores by their number.

average   A general term applied to the various measures of central tendency. The three most widely used averages are the arithmetic mean (mean), the median, and the mode. When the term "average" is used without designation as to type, the most likely assumption is that it is the *arithmetic mean.*

battery   A group of several tests standardized on the same sample population so that results on the several tests are comparable.

ceiling   The upper limit of ability that can be measured by a test. When an individual makes a score which is at or near the highest possible score, it is said that the test has too low a "ceiling" for him; he should be given a higher level of the test.

central tendency   A measure of central tendency provides a single most typical score as representative of a group of scores; the "trend" of a group of measures as indicated by some type of average, usually the *mean* or the *median.*

coefficient of correlation   A measure of the degree of relationship or "going-togetherness" between two sets of measures for the same group of individuals. The correlation coefficient most frequently used in test development and educational research is the Pearson or *product-moment r.* Unless otherwise

Adapted from: Blythe C. Mitchell, *Test Service Notebook, Test Department,* Harcourt Brace Jovanovich, Inc.

specified, "correlation" usually refers to this coefficient, but *rank, biserial, tetrachoric,* and other methods are used in special situations. Correlation coefficients range from .00, denoting a complete absence of relationship, to +1.00, and to −1.00, indicating perfect positive or perfect negative correspondence, respectively. See **correlation.**

concurrent validity   See **validity** (2).

construct validity   See **validity** (3).

content validity   See **validity** (1).

correlation   Relationship or "going-togetherness" between two sets of scores or measures; tendency of one score to vary concomitantly with the other, as the tendency of students of high IQ to be above average in reading ability. The existence of a strong relationship—i.e., a high correlation—between two variables does not necessarily indicate that one has any causal influence on the other. See **coefficient of correlation.**

criterion   A standard by which a test may be judged or evaluated; a set of scores, ratings, etc., that a test is designed to measure, to predict, or to correlate with. See **validity.**

criterion-referenced (content-referenced) test   Terms often used to describe tests designed to provide information on the specific knowledge or skills possessed by a student. Such tests usually cover relatively small units of content and are closely related to instruction. Their scores have meaning in terms of *what* the student knows or can do, rather than in their relation to the scores made by some external reference group.

criterion-related validity   See **validity** (2).

curricular validity   See **validity** (2).

decile   Any one of the nine points (scores) that divide a distribution into ten parts, each containing one-tenth of all the scores or cases; every tenth percentile. The first decile is the 10th percentile, the eighth decile the 80th percentile, etc.

deviation   The amount by which a score differs from some reference value, such as the mean, the norm, or the score on some other test.

diagnostic test   A test used to "diagnose" or analyze; that is, to locate an individual's specific areas of weakness or strength, to determine the nature of his weaknesses or deficiencies, and, wherever possible, to suggest their cause. Such a test yields measures of the components or subparts of some larger body of information or skill. Diagnostic achievement tests are most commonly prepared for the skill subjects.

distribution (frequency distribution)   A tabulation of the scores (or other attributes) of a group of individuals to show the number (frequency) of each score, or of those within the range of each interval.

equivalent form   Any of two or more forms of a test that are closely parallel with respect to the nature of the content and the number and difficulty of the items included, and that will yield very similar average scores and measures of variability for a given group. (Also referred to as *alternate, comparable,* or *parallel* form.)

f   A symbol denoting the *frequency* of a given score or of the scores within an interval grouping.

face validity   See **validity** (1).

grade equivalent (GE)   The grade level for which a given score is the real or estimated average. Grade-equivalent interpretation, most appropriate for elementary level achievement tests, expresses obtained scores in terms of *grade* and *month of grade,* assuming a 10-month school year (e.g., 5.7).

grade norms   Norms based upon the performance of pupils of given grade placement. See **grade equivalent, norms, percentile rank, stanine.**

group test   A test that may be administered to a number of individuals at the same time by one examiner.

individual test   A test that can be administered to only one person at a time, because of the nature of the test and/or the maturity level of the examinees.

intelligence quotient (IQ)   Originally, an index of brightness expressed as the ratio of a person's mental age to his chronological age: MA/CA, multiplied by 100 to eliminate the decimal.

internal consistency   Degree of relationship among the items of a test; consistency in content sampling. See **split-half reliability coefficient.**

inventory   A questionnaire or check list, usually in the form of a self-report, designed to elicit non-intellective information about an individual. Not tests in the usual sense, inventories are most often concerned with personality traits, interests, attitudes, problems, motivation, etc. See **personality test.**

inventory test   An achievement test that attempts to cover rather thoroughly some relatively small unit of specific instruction or training. An inventory test, as the name suggests, is in the nature of a "stock-taking" of an individual's knowledge or skill, and is often administered prior to instruction.

item   A single question or exercise in a test.

item analysis   The process of evaluating single test items in respect to certain characteristics. It usually involves determining the difficulty value and the discriminating power of the item, and often its correlation with some external criterion.

Kuder-Richardson formula(s)   Formulas for estimating the reliability of a test that are based on *inter-item consistency* and require only a single administration of the test. The one most used, formula 20, requires information based on the number of items in the test, the standard deviation of the total score, and the proportion of examinees passing each item. The Kuder-Richardson formulas are not appropriate for use with timed tests.

mastery test   A test designed to determine whether a pupil has mastered a given unit of instruction or a single knowledge or skill; a test giving information on *what* a pupil knows, rather than on how his performance relates to that of some norm-reference group. Such tests are used in computer-assisted instruction, where their results are referred to as content- or criterion-referenced information.

mean (M)   See **arithmetic mean.**

median (Md)   The middle score in a distribution or set of ranked scores; the point (score) that divides the group into two equal parts; the 50th percentile. Half of the scores are below the median and half above it, except when the median itself is one of the obtained scores.

mental age (MA)   The age for which a given score on a mental ability test is average or normal. If the average score made by an unselected group of children 6 years, 10 months of age is 55, then a child making a score of 55 is said to have a mental age of 6—10. Since the mental age unit shrinks with increasing (chronological) age, MAs do not have a uniform interpretation throughout all ages. They are therefore most appropriately used at the early age levels where mental growth is relatively rapid.

modal-age norms   Achievement test norms that are based on the performance of pupils of normal age for their respective grades. Norms derived from such age restricted groups are free from the distorting influence of the scores of underage and overage pupils.

mode   The score or value that occurs most frequently in a distribution.

multiple-choice item   A test item in which the examinee's task is to choose the correct or best answer from several given answers or options.

N   The symbol commonly used to represent the number of cases in a group.

non-verbal test   A test that does not require the use of words in the item or in the response to it. (Oral directions may be included in the formulation of the task.) A test cannot, however, be classified as non-verbal simply because it does not require reading on the part of the examinee. The use of non-verbal tasks cannot completely eliminate the effect of culture.

normal distribution   A distribution of scores or measures that in graphic form has a distinctive bell-shaped appearance. Cases are concentrated near the mean and decrease in frequency, according to a precise mathematical equation, the farther one departs from the mean. *Mean* and *median* are identical.

norms   Statistics that supply a frame of reference by which meaning may be given to obtained test scores. Norms are based upon the actual performance of pupils of various grades or ages in the standardization group for the test. Since they represent average or typical performance, they should not be regarded as standards or as universally desirable levels of attainment. The most common types of norms are deviation IQ, percentile rank, grade equivalent, and stanine. Reference groups are usually those of specified age or grade.

objective test   A test made up of items for which correct responses may be set up in advance; scores are unaffected by the opinion or judgment of the scorer. Objective keys provide for scoring by clerks or by machine. Such a test is contrasted with a "subjective" test, such as the usual essay examination, to which different persons may assign different scores, ratings, or grades.

omnibus test   A test (1) in which items measuring a variety of mental operations are all combined into a single sequence rather than being grouped together by type of operation, and (2) from which only a single score is derived, rather than separate scores for each operation or function. Omnibus tests make for simplicity of administration, since one set of directions and one overall time limit usually suffice. The Elementary, Intermediate, and Advanced tests in the *Otis-Lennon Mental Ability Test* series are omnibus-type tests, as contrasted with the *Kuhlmann Anderson Measure of Academic Potential,* in which the items measuring similar operations occur together, each with its own set of directions. In a *spiral-omnibus* test, the easiest items of each type are presented first, followed by the same succession of item types at a higher difficulty level, and so on in a rising spiral.

predictive validity   See **validity** (2).

profile   A graphic representation of the results on several tests, for either an individual or a group, when the results have been expressed in some uniform or comparable terms (standard scores, percentile ranks, grade equivalents, etc.). The profile method of presentation permits identification of areas of strength or weakness.

prognosis (prognostic) test   A test used to predict future success in a specific subject or field.

projective technique (projective method)   A method of personality study in which the subject responds as he chooses to a series of ambiguous stimuli such as ink blots, pictures, unfinished sentences, etc. It is assumed that under this free-response condition the subject "projects" manifestations of personality characteristics and organization that can, by suitable methods, be scored and interpreted to yield a description of his basic personality structure. The *Rorschach* (ink blot) *Technique,* the *Murray Thematic Apperception Test,* and the *Machover Draw-a-Person Test* are commonly used projective methods.

quartile   One of three points that divide the cases in a distribution into four equal groups. The lower quartile (Q_1), or 25th percentile, sets off the lowest fourth of the group; the middle quartile (Q_2) is the same as the 50th percentile, or median, and divides the second fourth of cases from the third; and the third quartile (Q_3), or 75th percentile, sets off the top fourth.

r   See **coefficient of correlation.**

random sample   A sample of the members of some total population drawn in such a way that every number of the population has an equal chance of being included—that is, in a way that precludes the operation of bias or "selection."

range   For some specified group, the difference between the highest and the lowest obtained score on a test; thus a very rough measure of spread or variability, since it is based upon only two extreme scores. Range is also used in reference to the possible spread of measurement a test provides, which in most instances is the number of items in the test.

raw score   The first quantitative result obtained in scoring a test. Usually the number of right answers, number right minus some fraction of number wrong, time required for performance, number of errors, or similar direct, unconverted, uninterpreted measure.

readiness test   A test that measures the extent to which an individual has achieved a degree of maturity or acquired certain skills or information needed for successfully undertaking some new learning activity. Thus a *reading readiness* test indicates whether a child has reached a developmental stage where he may profitably begin formal reading instruction. *Readiness* tests are classified as *prognostic* tests.

recall item   A type of item that requires the examinee to supply the correct answer from memory or recollection, as contrasted with a *recognition item,* in which he need only identify the correct answer.
   "Columbus discovered America in the year _____" is a *recall* (or *completion)* item. See **recognition item.**

recognition item   An item which requires the examinee to recognize or select the correct answer from among two or more given answers (options).
   Columbus discovered America in
   (a) *1425*   (b) *1492*   (c) *1520*   (d) *1546*
is a *recognition* item.

regression effect   Tendency of a predicted score to be nearer to the mean of its distribution than the score from which it is predicted is to its mean. Because of the effects of regression, students making extremely high or extremely low scores on a test tend to make less extreme scores, i.e., closer to the mean, on a second administration of the same test or on some predicted measure.

reliability   The extent to which a test is consistent in measuring whatever it does measure; dependability, stability, trustworthiness, relative freedom from errors of measurement. Reliability is usually expressed by some form of *reliability coefficient* or by the *standard error of measurement* derived from it.

reliability coefficient   The coefficient of correlation between two forms of a test, between scores on two administrations of the same test, or between halves of a test, properly corrected. The three measure somewhat different aspects of reliability, but all are properly spoken of as reliability coefficients. See **alternate-form reliability, split-half reliability coefficient, test-retest reliability coefficient.**

representative sample   A sample that corresponds to or matches the population of which it is a sample with respect to characteristics important for the purposes under investigation. In an achievement test norm sample, such significant aspects might be the proportion of cases of each sex, from various types of schools, different geographical areas, the several socioeconomic levels, etc.

split-half reliability coefficient   A coefficient of reliability obtained by correlating scores on one half of a test with scores on the other half, and applying the Spearman-Brown formula to adjust for the doubled length of the total test. Generally, but not necessarily, the two halves consist of the odd-numbered and the even-numbered items. Split-half reliability coefficients are sometimes referred to as measures of the *internal consistency* of a test; they involve content sampling only, not stability over time. This type of reliability coefficient is inappropriate for tests in which speed is an important component.

standard deviation (S.D.)   A measure of the variability or dispersion of a distribution of scores. The more the scores cluster around the mean, the smaller the standard deviation. For a normal distribution, approximately two thirds (68.3 percent) of the scores are within the range from one S.D. below the mean to one S.D. above the mean. Computation of the S.D. is based upon the square of the deviation of each score from the mean. The S.D. is sometimes called "sigma" and is represented by the symbol o.

standard error (S.E.)   A statistic providing an estimate of the possible magnitude of "error" present in some obtained measure, whether (1) an *individual* score or (2) some *group* measure, as a mean or a correlation coefficient.

standard score   A general term referring to any of a variety of "transformed" scores, in terms of which raw scores may be expressed for reasons of convenience, comparability, ease of interpretation, etc. The simplest type of standard score, known as a z-score, is an expression of the *deviation* of a score from the mean score of the group *in relation to* the standard deviation of the scores of the group.

standardized test (standard test)   A test designed to provide a systematic sample of individual performance, administered according to prescribed directions, scored in conformance with definite rules, and interpreted in reference to certain normative information.

stanine   One of the steps in a nine-point scale of standard scores. The stanine (short for *standard-nine)* scale has values from 1 to 9, with a mean of 5 and a standard deviation of 2. Each stanine (except 1 and 9) is ½ S.D. in width, with the middle (average) stanine of 5 extending from ¼ S.D. below to ¼ S.D. above the mean.

survey test   A test that measures general achievement in a given area, usually with the connotation that the test is intended to assess group status, rather than to yield precise measures of individual performance.

taxonomy   An embodiment of the principles of classification; a survey, usually in outline form, such as a presentation of the objectives of education.

test-retest reliability coefficient   A type of reliability coefficient obtained by administering the same test a second time, after a short interval, and correlating the two sets of scores. "Same test" was originally understood to mean identical content, i.e., the same form; currently, however, the term "test-retest" is also used to describe the administration of different forms of the same test, in which case this reliability coefficient becomes the same as the alternate-form coefficient. In either case (1) fluctuations over time and in testing situation, and (2) any effect of the first test upon the second are involved. When the time interval between the two testings is considerable, as several months, a test-retest reliability coefficient reflects not only the consistency of measurement provided by the test, but also the stability of the examinee trait being measured.

true score   A score entirely free of error; hence, a hypothetical value that can never be obtained by testing, which always involves some measurement error.

validity   The extent to which a test does the job for which it is used. This definition is more satisfactory than the traditional "extent to which a test measures what it is supposed to measure," since the validity of a test is always specific to the purposes for which the test is used. The term validity, then, has different connotations for various types of tests and, thus, a different kind of validity evidence is appropriate for each.
(1) content, curricular validity. For achievement tests, validity is the extent to which the *content* of the test represents a balanced and adequate sampling of the outcomes (knowledge, skills, etc.) of the course or instructional program it is intended to cover. It is best evidenced by a comparison of the test content with courses of study, instructional materials, and statements of educational goals; and often by analysis of the processes required in making correct responses to the items. *Face validity,* referring to an observation of what a test appears to measure, is a non-technical type of evidence; apparent relevancy is, however, quite desirable.
(2) criterion-related validity. The extent to which scores on the test are in agreement with *(concurrent validity)* or predict *(predictive validity)* some given criterion measure. Predictive validity refers to the accuracy with which an aptitude, prognostic, or readiness test indicates future learning success in some area, as evidenced by correlations between scores on the test and future criterion measures of such success (e.g., the relation of a score on an academic aptitude test administered in high school to grade point average over four years of college). In concurrent validity, no significant time interval elapses between administration of the test being validated and of the criterion measure. Such validity might be evidenced by *concurrent* measures of academic ability and of achievement, by the relation of a new test to one generally accepted as or known to be valid, or by the correlation between scores on a test and criteria measures which are valid but are less objective and more time-consuming to obtain than a test score would be.

(3) construct validity. The extent to which a test measures some relatively abstract psychological trait or construct; applicable in evaluating the validity of tests that have been constructed on the basis of an analysis (often factor analysis) of the nature of the trait and its manifestations. Tests of personality, verbal ability, mechanical aptitude, critical thinking, etc., are validated in terms of their construct and the relation of their scores to pertinent external data.

variability   The spread or dispersion of test scores, best indicated by their standard deviation.

variance   For a distribution, the average of the squared deviations from the means; thus the square of the standard deviation.

APPENDIX C

Suggested Formats for Interviews with Parents and Pupils

INTERVIEW WITH PARENTS

General

    Family members: names, age, grade, occupation

Family History

    Marriage: how long; any separations; previous marriages; if divorced, custody agreement and visiting
             patterns; general tone of marriage

    Mother, Father

        place of birth and where grew up
        family make up
        childhood illnesses, deaths, divorces
        education
        work experience
        aspirations: early and present, satisfaction with progress
        current relationship with extended family
        current health: physical and emotional
        alcohol or drug abuse
        family moves and living arrangements
        family separations when child separated from parents
        familial diseases
        family activities
        sibling(s) age(s), adjustment, and relationship with visually handicapped child
        discipline techniques and consistency

Developmental History

    Pregnancy
        planned or unplanned; parents' attitude when learning of pregnancy
        age of parents and marital status
        mother's health during (vomiting, weight gain, blood pressure problems, swelling, kidneys, etc.)
        complications, such as threatened or voluntary abortions
        parents' emotional state during

    Birth
        if premature, gestation period
        labor and delivery
        complications
        birthweight
        post-partum course
        post-natal difficulties (anoxia, jaundice, etc.)
        any evidence of infection or damage

Development

    infancy: feeding, respiratory, sleep, colic, general mood, responsiveness, sensory deficit, temperament

    milestones: sitting, standing, talking (first word and sentences), walking, toilet training

Medical History
serious illnesses, accidents, head injuries, operations, hospitalizations, convulsions/seizures, allergies, current medications and health status, age at diagnosis of visual impairment; etiology; attitudes when informed, medical treatment, if any

School History

Preschool
    separation difficulties, temper tantrums
    peer relations
    general adjustment

Elementary, Middle, and Senior High
    academic performance
    social: peer relationships, teacher relations
    refusals to attend
    problems or disciplinary actions

Parents' Perceptions
    Father's/Mother's view of their relationship with the child
    Child's current personality
    general view of
    frustration tolerance, anxiety, fears
    what arouses aggression/anger
    general mood, feelings, attitudes
    Child's behavior
    interests, friends
    drug, alcohol, tobacco usage
    police contacts
    suicide, homicide, cruelty to animals
    Child's experiences
    physical assaults (beatings, animal attacks)
    sexual trauma, interests, attitudes and concerns about sex
    Father's/Mother's view of the visually handicapped child; of other siblings
    Father's/Mother's expectations of visually handicapped child; of other siblings

INTERVIEW WITH PUPIL

General conversation: where child lives, interests, hobbies, sports, music, vacations.

Visual impairment: what child knows about it: etiology, etc., how child feels about it

Friends: activities, view of friends, ages of friends, what the child feels parents think of friends

School: likes or dislikes
        subjects of interest
        general attitude towards grades: if poor, why does child think they are
        how does child feel about peers in class and how does child get along with them
        attitudes toward teachers
        problems with teachers

Family: how does child get along with mother, father, each sibling
        worst thing about relationship with each parent
        best thing about relationship with each parent
        which sibling does child get along with best, worst, why
        worries about each parent
        worries about family
        does child think parents' discipline is fair
        where does child think child fits into the family
        if child is adopted and knows this fact: feeling, fantasies regarding natural parents

Affect: how does child feel most of the time
        when trying to fall asleep what thought or fantasies does child often have
        when in a really boring class at school what does child think about and what feelings are associated
        does child sometimes imagine being someplace else or someone else; if so where, who, why, what better
        daydreams, what about
        fears, what makes child angry, sad, happy

APPENDIX D

Publishers of Assessment Instruments

Academic Therapy Publications
28 Commercial Blvd.
Novato, Calif. 94948

American Foundation for the Blind
15 West 16th St.
New York, N.Y. 10011

American Guidance Service
Publishers Building
Circle Pines, Minn. 55014

American Orthopsychiatric Association, Inc.
1775 Broadway
New York, N.Y. 10019

American Printing House for the Blind
1839 Frankfort Ave.
Louisville, Ky. 40206

Bernell Corporation
422 East Monroe St.
South Bend, Ind. 46601

Bobbs-Merrill Educational Publishing Co.
4300 West 62nd St.
Indianapolis, Ind. 46206

Bradley, R.H.
University of Arkansas at Little Rock
33rd & University
Little Rock, Ark. 72204

Callier Center for Communication Disorders
1966 Inwood Road
Dallas, Tex. 75235

Charles E. Merill Publishing Company
Test Division
1300 Alum Creek Dr./Box 508
Columbus, Ohio 43216

Child Psychiatry Research Center
608 South Jackson St.
Louisville, Ky. 40202

Consulting Psychologists Press
577 College Avenue
Palo Alto, Calif. 94306

Curriculum Associates, Inc.
5 Esquire Road
North Billerica, Mass. 01862

Devereux Foundation Press
19 South Waterloo Rd.
Devon, Pa. 19333

Economy Company
P.O. Box 25308
Oklahoma City, Okla. 73125

Educational Products & Training Foundation
P.O. Box 4128
Boise, Idaho: 83704

ERIC Document Reproduction Service
P.O. Box 190
Arlington, Va. 22210

Evaluation Research Associates
P.O. Box 6503 Teall Station
Syracuse, N.Y. 13217

Exceptional Teaching Aids
20102 Woodbine Avenue
Castro Valley, Calif. 94546

Follett Educational Corporation
P.O. Box 5705
Chicago, Ill. 60680

Grune & Stratton, Inc.
757 Third Ave.
New York, N.Y. 10017

**Hahnemann Community Mental Health/
Mental Retardation Center**
314 North Broad St.
Philadelphia, Pa. 19102

Harcourt, Brace & World, Inc.
757 Third Ave.
New York, N.Y. 10017

Houghton Mifflin Company
Test Editorial Offices
P.O. Box 1970
Iowa City, Iowa 52240

Institute of Psychological Research
34 Fleury St. West
Montreal, Quebec J3L 1S9

Jackson County Education Service District
101 West Grape St.
Medford, Oreg. 97501

Kaplan Corporation
600 Jonestown Rd.
Winston-Salem, N.C. 27103

National Association for Visually Handicapped
305 East 24th St.
New York, N.Y. 10010

Nevil Interagency Referral Service
919 Walnut Street
Room 400
Philadelphia, Penn. 19107

New York Association for the Blind
Optical Aids Division
111 East 59th St.
New York, N.Y. 10022

Office of Child Research
Arizona Center for Educational Research and Development
College of Education
University of Arizona
Tucson, Ariz. 85721

Personnel Press
191 Spring St.
Lexington, Mass. 02173

Peterson, D.
39 North Fifth Ave.
Highland Park, N.J. 08904

Psychological Assessment Resource, Inc.
P.O. Box 98
Odessa, Fla. 33556

Psychological Corporation
757 Third Ave.
New York, N.Y. 10017

Publishers Test Service
2500 Garden Rd.
Monterey, Calif. 93940-5380

Scholastic Testing Service
480 Meyer Road
Bensenville, Ill. 60106

Science Research Associates
259 East Erie St.
Chicago, Ill. 60611

Stoelting Company
1350 South Kostner Ave.
Chicago, Ill. 60623

Teachers College Press
525 West 121st St.
New York, N.Y. 10027

Teaching Resources Corporation
100 Boylston St.
Boston, Mass. 02116

University of California
Center for the Study of Visual Impairment
School of Optometry
University of California
Berkeley, Calif. 94720

University of Illinois Press
Urbana, Ill. 61801

Western Psychological Services
12031 Wilshire Boulevard
Los Angeles, Calif. 90025

Competencies of Teachers of Visually Handicapped Learners

Goal 1.0

Teacher Demonstrates Knowledge of Development Patterns in Visually Handicapped Learners

Entry Level of Competency:
Can demonstrate knowledge of normal growth and development including language development from birth to adulthood.
Can demonstrate knowledge of atypical patterns of growth and development.

Knowledge	Skill	Mastery Tasks
The teacher has:	The teacher can:	Proficiency is demonstrated when the teacher can:
1.1 Knowledge of how development can be affected by a visual impairment.	1.1.1 Identify the potential impact of a visual impairment on the child's affective development.	1.1.1.1-1.1.1.8 Produce a written discussion of potential impact, in general terms, with supporting documentation from the literature and practice experiences.
	1.1.2 Identify the potential impact of a visual impairment on the child's language development.	
	1.1.3 Identify the potential impact of a visual impairment on the child's perceptual development.	
	1.1.4 Identify the potential impact of a visual impairment on the child's conceptual development.	
	1.1.5 Identify the potential impact of a visual impairment on the child's motor development.	
	1.1.6 Identify the potential impact of a visual impairment on the child's social development.	
	1.1.7 Identify the potential impact of a visual impairment on the child's general physical health.	
1.2 Knowledge of how variables inherent to visual impairments affect the individual child's development.	1.2.1 Identify the variables inherent to any visual impairment (etiology, age at onset, degree of loss, prognosis).	1.2.1.1 Produce the variables with 100% accuracy on written or oral test.

1.2.2. Identify the interaction of these variables of any visual impairment.

1.2.2.1 Produce a written statement of how various combinations of variables in a particular eye condition interact to produce different functional implications.

1.2.3 Identify and analyze how particular combinations of these variables interface with factors identified in Skills 1.1.1-1.1.7 to enhance or inhibit development.

1.2.3.1 Interpret medical findings and discuss developmental implications from a medical eye report.

1.2.3.2 Describe at least one eye condition that may account for a child's performance from a case study containing developmental and visual functioning information.

1.2.3.3 Describe the potential areas to monitor for development from a case study which describes a child only in terms of ophthalmological variables, age, and present level of functioning.

1.2.3.4 Given 1.2.3.3, recommend instructional strategies as identified in GOAL 5.0 from information in 1.2.3.3.

1.3 Knowledge of the compounding effects of additional handicapping conditions on the individual child.

1.3.1 Identify acceptable definitions of other handicapping conditions.

1.3.1.1 Complete successfully at least one course in general special education or introduction to special education.

1.3.1.2 Describe correctly other handicapping conditions in essay or objective test.

1.3.2 Identify the impact of one or more additional handicaps on the child with visual impairment.

1.3.2.1 Present a case study of a visually handicapped/multiply handicapped child to class, demonstrating knowledge of 1.1, 1.2, and 1.3.

1.3.2.2 Complete practicum experience with multiply handicapped students.

1.3.2.3 Produce a review of literature related to specific combinations of disability (deaf-blind; cerebral palsy and visual motor implications; visual handicaps and learning disabilities; visual development in the severely profoundly handicapped, etc.).

1.3.2.4 Make a list of agencies and organizations serving other disability groups, together with their stated objectives and areas of service.

1.3.2.5 Through an assessment profile for a visually handicapped/multiply handicapped child, produce a written or oral discussion on how the child's development has been affected by the combination of handicapping conditions.

1.4 Knowledge of cultural and environmental factors which may influence the visually handicapped child's overall development.

1.4.1 Identify cultural and environmental factors, including but not limited to, family, peers, neighborhood, furniture fit, lighting, educational placement, opportunities to learn, level of independence, curriculum needs (GOAL 3.0) and instructional strategies (GOAL 5.0).

1.4.1.1 Develop a case study of an individual child and include discussion of cultural and environmental factors.

1.4.1.2 Suggest environmental changes which may enhance the child's development from the case study in 1.4.1.1.

1.5 Knowledge of synthesis and how to apply knowledge demonstrated in GOALS 1.1 to 1.4.

1.5.1 Identify and interpret educational implications of the eye report to parents, school personnel, and other community workers.

1.5.1.1 Orally explain educational implications of all items included in an eye report.

1.5.2 Identify the impact of a visual impairment on child development.

1.5.2.1 Prepare a presentation for parents or community group, using appropriate audio-visual materials.

1.5.2.2 Conduct at least one parent conference on each child during a practicum experience.

1.5.2.3 Develop an inservice on development of the visually handicapped child for (1) regular education teachers (2) preschool handicapped teachers (3) special education teachers of another categorical group.

1.5.3 Utilize knowledge of developmental patterns when demonstrating competence in GOALS 2.0 and 5.0.

1.5.3.1 Develop instructional strategies that address strengths and weaknesses related in an assessment report and a teacher report of the child's performance to the child's visual impairment.

1.5.3.2 Develop a full Individualized Educational Plan for two children in the practicum.

Goal 2.0
Teacher Will Demonstrate the Ability to Assess Visually Handicapped Learners Using a Variety of Informal and Formal Procedures

Entry level of Competency:
Can demonstrate ability to utilize observation and other informal procedures to determine developmental level.
Can demonstrate ability to select, administer, score, interpret, and report findings from a variety of formal assessment instruments.

Knowledge	*Skill*	*Mastery Tasks*
The teacher has:	The teacher can:	Proficiency is demonstrated when the teacher can:
2.1 Knowledge of the educational implications of medical, psychoeducational, and psychological data in the assessment procedure.	2.1.1 Identify assessment information that should be available to the teacher.	2.1.1.1 By means of a series of case studies or assessment profiles, delineate and describe the educational implications and list the modifications required in the learning setting.
		2.1.1.2 Design all learning activities during practicum to meet the individual characteristics of each student with the required task or environmental modifications (See GOAL 5).
	2.1.2 Identify the skill areas of multidisciplinary team members.	2.1.2.1 List areas of expertise of the following: school psychologist, school social worker, speech therapist, occupational therapist, physical therapist, orientation and mobility specialist, low vision specialist.

2.2 Knowledge of formal and informal assessment procedures appropriate for visually handicapped learners, in language, affective, sensory, motor, and perceptual/cognitive areas.		2.1.2.2 Write a referral to one of the professionals listed in 2.1.2.1 for a child with a problem in your practicum.
	2.2.1 Identify types of informal assessment procedures appropriate for visually handicapped learners.	2.2.1.1 Discuss strengths and weaknesses of at least four informal assessment techniques.
		2.2.1.2. Select appropriate informal assessment procedures to generate specified information to answer a specific educational problem.
	2.2.2 Identify a variety of formal assessment procedures and instruments appropriate for visually handicapped learners.	2.2.2.1 Given the essential information, identify one or more formal assessment procedures to generate desired data.
		2.2.2.2 Demonstrate appropriate assessment procedures during the practicum.
		2.2.2.3 Describe and discuss by means of written examination a variety of norm-referenced and criterion-referenced assessment instruments and procedures.
		2.2.2.4 During practicum select, obtain, and modify appropriate norm-referenced and/or criterion-referenced informal assessment instruments which yield significant teaching information.
	2.2.3 Identify from 2.2.2 instruments that typically would be administered by a school psychologist.	2.2.3.1 Describe how you would interpret the needs of the visually handicapped learner to a school psychologist unfamiliar with these learners.
2.3 Knowledge of the selection and adaptation and/or development of assessment procedures and instruments for specific purposes.	2.3.1 Identify instruments for assessing specific skills of visually handicapped learners, including functional vision.	2.3.1.1 Select, adapt, and modify functional reading, math skills, and functional vision instruments appropriate, at the primary, intermediate, and secondary levels in both braille and large type.
		2.3.1.2 Develop an assessment kit and notebook to be used during practicum which includes assessment in-

struments for academic and communication skills, cognitive development, self-concept, O&M, daily living skills, recreation and leisure, vocational and career education, and functional vision.

2.4   Knowledge of procedures for administration and scoring informal and formal assessment instruments for all developmental areas.

2.4.1   Identify observational techniques that should accompany the administration of both formal and informal assessment.

2.4.1.1   List and discuss the various types of observational techniques used both in informal and formal testing. Specify the most significant behaviors to observe.

2.4.1.2   By means of a videotape recorder (VTR), tape a classroom period. List the most significant event observed in the following areas: personal-social development, curriculum adaptations required, learning approach, and interaction.

2.4.2   Identify ways that information resulting from administration of informal assessment data in all developmental skill and curricular areas can be reported.

2.4.2.1   By means of VTR, administer, score and profile a reading skills and math skills assessment (NOTE: 2.4.2 and 2.4.3).

2.4.2.2   Develop comprehensive case studies with a variety of visually handicapped students in the following areas: motor development, perceptual functioning, cognitive operations, social development, communication skills, O&M and DLS, and vocational skills. Tasks demonstrated should include:
—observational techniques
—administering and charting informal assessment techniques
—administering and scoring formal instruments
—analyzing results of formal and informal instruments
—interpreting results of formal and informal instruments
—reporting assessment data
—recording data
—interpreting to concerned others (Note: 2.4.2 to 2.5.3).

		2.4.3 Identify from the test manual procedures for administering and scoring formal assessment instruments for a variety of skill and curricular areas.	2.4.3.1 Select, administer, and score formal assessment instruments designed for a specific purpose.
2.5 Knowledge of methods for analyzing, interpreting, and reporting assessment information.		2.5.1 Identify methods for interpreting assessment data.	2.5.1.1 Demonstrate on an examination the ability to analyze and interpret test data.
			2.5.1.2 Analyze results of informal and formal assessment data given to a variety of visually handicapped learners.
			2.5.1.3 Interpret results of informal and formal assessment data for a variety of visually handicapped learners.
			2.5.1.4 Report results of informal and formal assessment data for a variety of visually handicapped learners.
2.6 Knowledge of appropriate methods to interpret information from the assessment of visually handicapped learners to other school personnel and parents.		2.6.1 Identify a plan to transmit assessment information about visually handicapped learners using a variety of informal and formal procedures.	2.6.1.1 Develop a plan to appropriately record and transmit assessment information.
		2.6.2 Interpret information about assessment results to parents, the student and other school personnel.	2.6.2.1 Interpret results and recommendations to parents, to the student, and to other school personnel.
			2.6.2.2 In a role playing situation explain the results of an assessment to parents.

Goal 3.0
Teacher will Demonstrate the Ability to Select, Design and/or Modify Specialized Curricula for Visually Handicapped Learners
with Varying Degrees of Visual Impairment and at All Developmental Levels

Entry Level of Competency:
Can demonstrate knowledge of curriculum needs and curriculum development for nonhandicapped learners.

Knowledge	Skill	Mastery Tasks
The teacher has:	The teacher can:	Proficiency is demonstrated when the teacher can:
3.1 Knowledge of the area of the specialized curriculum for visually handicapped learners.	3.1.1 Identify the areas of specialized curriculum for the visually handicapped learner.	3.1.1.1 Compile a list of potential specialized curriculum needs for a visually handicapped learner.
3.2 Knowledge of the specialized curriculum in concept development for visually handicapped learners.	3.2.1 Identify instructional modules for visually handicapped learners, such as body image, spatial orientation, directionality, classification, movement seriation, conservation, tactual discrimination, and sensory integration.	3.2.1.1 Given at least two case studies of learners with varying degrees of visual loss, select, design and/or modify instructional modules for concept development.
3.3 Knowledge of communication skills necessary for visually handicapped learners.	3.3.1 Identify a sequential instructional module to meet the specific communication needs of the visually handicapped learner, such as reading, writing, typing, listening, verbal and nonverbal communication.	3.3.1.1 Select, design, and/or modify a sequential instructional module to meet the specific receptive and expressive communication needs of a visually handicapped learner using at least two case studies.
3.4 Knowledge of social and independent living skills necessary for visually handicapped learners.	3.4.1 Identify a sequential instructional module to meet the specific social and/or independent living skills of visually handicapped learners, such as personal hygiene, clothing, human sexuality, food preparation, self-care, financial management, interpersonal relationships, and social interaction with peers.	3.4.1.1 Select, design, and/or modify a daily-living skills module to meet the specific needs of visually handicapped learners using at least two case studies.
		3.4.1.2 Design a module to assist a visually handicapped learner to perform satisfactorily in a social situation with peers.
		3.4.1.3 Design a role playing situation with visually handicapped learners to teach turn-taking in conversation.
3.5 Knowledge of basic orientation and mobility skills and concepts necessary for visually handicapped learners, including body image, spatial concepts, object perception, and movement skills.	3.5.1 Identify a sequential instructional module to teach basic orientation and mobility skills and concepts to a variety of visually handicapped learners, such as sighted guide techniques, orientation, sound localization, protective techniques, direction taking techniques, systematic search patterns, use of optic aids in mobility, map skills, appropriate cane techniques, and use of sensory input in movement.	3.5.1.1 Select, design, and/or modify basic O&M skills and concepts in a module to meet the specific needs of visually handicapped learners in at least two skill areas.

3.6 Knowledge of prevocational and career education skills necessary for visually handicapped learners.

3.6.1 Identify a sequential instructional module to meet the specific prevocational and career education needs of a variety of visually handicapped learners such as: career goals, interpersonal relations, interview techniques, job applications, work experience, career awareness, career exploration, career preparation, and legal aspects of employment.

3.6.1.1 Select, design, and/or modify a prevocational and career education module for visually handicapped learners based on the information from at least two case studies.

3.6.2 Identify information and resources regarding prevocational and career education for visually handicapped learners.

3.6.2.1 Select design, and/or modify a resource list regarding prevocational and career education for visually handicapped learners.

3.6.2.2 Make a referral of a visually handicapped learner to a vocational rehabilitation counselor.

3.7 Knowledge of the relationship of vision to perceptual development and learning.

3.7.1 Identify the degree of efficiency in such ocular-motor skills as tracking, focus, accommodation, and eye-hand coordination in visually handicapped learners.

3.7.1.1 Select, design, and/or modify, given at least two case studies, instructional modules to develop ocular-motor skills.

3.7.2 Identify the sequence of development in visual perceptual learning in normal visual systems.

3.7.2.1 Select, design, and/or modify, an outline in written form of the sequence of development in visual-perceptual learning.

3.7.3 Identify the visual perceptual problems related to impaired vision such as discrimination, recognition, visual closure, part/whole-whole/part relationships, and figure-ground for near and distant vision.

3.7.3.1 Select, design, and/or modify, instructional modules that discuss the problems in visual perception specific to visually handicapped learners.

3.8 Knowledge of auditory and linguistic processes in learning.

3.8.1 Identify the problems and remediations related to auditory processing in visually handicapped learners such as attention, sound localization, ear-hand coordination, auditory memory, etc.

3.8.1.1 Select, design, and/or modify, given at least two case studies, instructional modules that discuss the problems and remediations related to auditory processing in visually handicapped learners.

3.9 Knowledge of the problems and remediations related to language development in visually handicapped learners.

3.9.1 Identify the problems and remediations related to language development in visually handicapped learners such as verbal unreality and echolalia.

3.9.1.1 Design a remedial plan to modify one language problem that may be found in a young preschool visually handicapped learner.

3.9.2 Identify and use basic sign communication systems with multiply handicapped learners.	3.9.1.2 Select, design, and/or modify, given at least two case studies, instructional modules that discuss the problems and remediations related to language development in visually handicapped learners.
	3.9.2.1 Demonstrate the ability to receive and send functional manual signs appropriate for at least three multiply handicapped learners.
3.10 Knowledge of the sequence of development in tactual learning.	
3.10.1 Identify stages of development in tactual learning such as: texture discrimination, shape recognition, familiar objects, topographical, Euclidean and geometric.	3.10.1.1 Select, design, and/or modify, instructional modules utilizing the stages of development in tactual learning.
3.10.2 Identify the uses of tactual learning as an alternative to visual learning and/or enhancement of visual learning.	3.10.2.1 Select, design, and/or modify instructional modules demonstrating how tactual learning development can be an appropriate alternative to visual learning.
3.10.3 Identify specific problems and remediations of tactual learning in visually handicapped learners.	3.10.3.1 Select, design, and/or modify, instructional modules dealing with the specific problems and remediations of tactual learning in visually handicapped learners.
3.11 Knowledge of the sequence of development of gross and fine motor skills.	
3.11.1 Identify sequence of normal development of gross movement and fine motor development.	3.11.1.1 List, in writing, the sequence of normal development of gross and fine motor development.
3.11.2 Identify potential difference and/or variations in the development of gross and fine motor skills for the visually handicapped learner.	3.11.2.1 Select, design, and/or modify instructional modules in gross and fine motor development for the visually handicapped learner.
3.12 Knowledge of play skills necessary for visually handicapped children to maximize their intellectual, emotional, social, and physical development.	
3.12.1 Identify specifics of a child's play behavior as it relates to his/her development.	3.12.1.1 Observe a child's play behavior and discuss how it relates to his/her present stage of development.
3.12.2 Identify programs designed to enhance/teach the visually handicapped child to develop and utilize play skills.	3.12.2.1 Select, design, and/or modify an instructional module to enhance the visually handicapped child's ability to utilize play skills.

Knowledge	Skill	Mastery Tasks
3.13 Knowledge of the values, purposes, and techniques of developing individualized education programs in all curricular areas for visually handicapped learners.		3.12.2.2 Develop a plan of remediation for a visually handicapped learner who is deficient in appropriate play skills.
	3.13.1 Identify components to be included in individualized educational programs based on assessed learning needs.	3.13.1.1 Prepare a written I.E.P. based on a specific visually handicapped learner's assessed learning needs.
	3.13.2 Identify behavioral objectives and task analysis approaches to implement the individualized educational program for visually handicapped learners.	3.13.2.1 Select, design, and/or modify written behavioral objectives and task analysis approaches in an individualized educational program.

Goal 4.0

Teacher will Demonstrate Proficiency in the Operation of Media and Devices Necessary for the Education of the Visually Handicapped Learner

Entry Level of Competency:
Can demonstrate knowledge of a variety of manipulative materials appropriate for use by all children.

Knowledge	Skill	Mastery Tasks
The teacher has:	The teacher can:	Proficiency is demonstrated when the teacher can:
4.1 Knowledge of braille codes and their formats	4.1.1 Read and write Standard English Braille.	4.1.1.1 Successfully pass a course in literary braille with 90% proficiency in Grade II.
		4.1.1.2 Transcribe into Braille Grade II 25 pages with good accuracy.
	4.1.2 Read and write braille mathematics at elementary and secondary levels.	4.1.2.1 Demonstrate proficiency in braille mathematics at the elementary and secondary levels.
	4.1.3 Identify resources for obtaining more advanced information in areas such as foreign language braille, braille music, and computer and scientific notation.	4.1.3.1 Demonstrate basic proficiency in braille codes for foreign language, music, and other technical areas.
		4.1.3.2 List sources for obtaining information about foreign language braille, braille music, and computer and scientific notation.

4.2   Knowledge of techniques for adapting visual formats for tactual readers.

4.2.1   Identify necessary adjustments in printed formats to render them more appropriate for tactile reading.

4.2.1.1   Render a variety of printed formats (a diagram, chart, table, etc.) into forms which can be tactually perceived.

4.3   Knowledge of the criteria to evaluate, adapt and/or design materials for use by visually handicapped readers.

4.3.1   Identify criteria to evaluate print material for specific visually handicapped learners and plan necessary adjustments for ease in reading.

4.3.1.1   Evaluate text, perceptual, and supplementary materials with regard to their visual properties when used with visually handicapped learners.

4.3.1.2   Demonstrate the ability to modify instructional materials for two different visually handicapped learners.

4.4   Knowledge of a variety of mathematical and computational devices suitable for visually handicapped learners.

4.4.1   Identify sources for devices that are available for visually handicapped learners.

4.4.1.1   List devices and their sources currently available and in use by visually handicapped learners.

4.4.1.2   Operate and describe functions of various devices developed specifically for mathematics education of visually handicapped learners such as braille thermometers, rulers, scales, etc.

4.4.1.3   Demonstrate the function of various devices used in mathematics.

4.4.1.4   Demonstrate the use of the abacus in the four basic operations.

4.4.1.5   Add, subtract, multiply, and divide with 100% accuracy on the Cranmer abacus.

4.4.2   Identify ways to modify regular devices for visually handicapped learners.

4.4.2.1   Cite three devices used for mathematics education that can be used by either a visually handicapped or nonhandicapped learner.

4.4.2.2   Adapt various devices used for mathematics education for the nonhandicapped to use for the visually handicapped learner.

4.5 Knowledge of the various listening and recording devices including those with variable speed and compression components, indexing, etc.	4.5.1 Identify from instructional manuals procedures for the care and use of recording and listening equipment.	4.5.1.1 Demonstrate the operation and care of recording and listening equipment.
4.6 Knowledge of writing instruments and devices for tactile and visual learners.	4.6.1 Identify from instructional manuals procedures for operation and care of writing instruments and devices.	4.6.1.1 Operate and care for braillewriters, typewriters, slate and stylus, handwriting devices, raised line drawing kits, etc.
		4.6.1.2 Cite where equipment listed in 4.6.1.1 can be repaired.
		4.6.1.3 Demonstrate appropriate use of these materials/equipment for a variety of educational needs.
4.7 Knowledge of machines and techniques; aids for the production of materials.	4.7.1 Identify procedures for the use and care of technical machines and devices including but not limited to Thermoform, CCTV, Optacon, reading machines, microcomputers.	4.7.1.1 Demonstrate operation and care of equipment used in instructional settings.
4.8 Knowledge of sources and procedures for acquisition of all specialized media and devices.	4.8.1 Identify sources and procedures for acquisition of specialized media and devices.	4.8.1.1 Develop a comprehensive resource file of media and/or devices that may be needed by special learners.
		4.8.1.2 Develop a list of resources for obtaining specialized media and/or devices based upon the unique requirements of the learner.
4.9 Knowledge of influencing factors in the appropriate selection and use of media and equipment necessary for education of visually handicapped learners.	4.9.1 Identify criteria for the selection and use of media and devices necessary for a variety of visually handicapped learners.	4.9.1.1 Outline a plan for the selection and use of media and devices necessary for a variety of visually handicapped learners.
		4.9.1.2 In a practicum situation develop a long range instructional plan that includes the use of media and devices that can be utilized by a variety of visually handicapped learners.
		4.9.1.3 Demonstrate the ability to relate the use of media and devices into a total instructional program which includes a visually handicapped learner.

Goal 5.0

Teacher Will Utilize Instructional Strategies to Facilitate Learning in Visually Handicapped Learners

Entry Level of Competency:
Can demonstrate knowledge of basic learning theory and principles of instruction for learners.
Can demonstrate knowledge of basic principles for the design of instructional strategies for use in all content areas.

Knowledge	Skill	Mastery Tasks
The teacher has:	The teacher can:	Proficiency is demonstrated when the teacher can:
5.1 Knowledge of the application of learning theories to visually handicapped learners.	5.1.1 Identify applicability of general learning theory to visually handicapped learners.	5.1.1.1 Given two or more case studies, provide examples of how a variety of learning theories can be applied to the visually handicapped learner (e.g. Thorndike's Laws of Readiness, Exercise, Effect; Theories of Behaviorism; Gestalt Organization; Functionalism; Purposive Learning; Dewey's Experience; Piaget's stages of cognitive development).
		5.1.1.2 Demonstrate selected uses of the above theories in a. micro-teaching b. practicum.
		5.1.1.3 Document teachers' performance in various skill areas; analyze which learning theories are being used and how.
5.2 Knowledge of basic principles and guidelines for selection and/or development of instructional strategies specific to the needs of visually handicapped learners.	5.2.1 Identify basic principles inherent in instructional strategies specifically for visually handicapped learners.	5.2.1.1 Supply examples in the following areas of how the synthetic/part: whole approach is employed by the visually handicapped student (e.g. low vision training, concept training, academics, orientation and mobility).
		5.2.1.2 Design specific learning environments for individual students, given several case studies (include multiply handicapped and preschool).

5.2.1.3   Select, design and/or modify specific lessons to emphasize a multi-sensory approach for
a. concept development
b. skill acquisition

5.2.1.4   Given child data, determine priorities for children at various developmental and academic levels (include multiply handicapped and preschool).

5.3   Knowledge of basic principles for adaptation of subject areas for visually handicapped learners.

5.3.1   Identify appropriate instructional strategies for teaching subject area content (reading, math, spelling, social studies, science, etc.) to an individual visually handicapped learner; and for a group.

5.3.1.1   Given a practicum setting, demonstrate appropriate instructional strategies for teaching subject area content to an individual visually handicapped learner; to a group.

5.3.1.2   Given several concepts (math, environmental, etc.) analyze which could be effectively adapted, how, and what approaches for teaching the remaining concepts (microscopic, telescopic, dangerous, etc.).

5.3.1.3   Critique commonly used subject matter materials as to appropriateness for three different visually handicapped learners.

5.3.1.4   Adapt highly visual learning activities for meaningful participation by blind and low vision children.

5.3.1.5   Critique and make suggestions for improvement of materials which have been adapted for use with blind and low vison learners.

5.3.1.6   Devise an improved product from above selected materials.

5.3.1.7   Plan a field trip to emphasize specific concepts (science, math, social studies, mobility, low vision, etc.); carry out during practicum; and evaluate.

5.4 Knowledge of principles for selection and/or design of instructional strategies for use in curricular areas of special application to visually handicapped learners.

5.4.1 Identify instructional strategies in special areas such as listening skills, utilization of low vision, daily living skills, typing, motor development, sex education, basic orientation and mobility, concept development, communication skills, vocational and career education, factual learning, play skills.

5.4.1.1 In a practicum setting, demonstrate instructional strategies for each area listed by writing an appropriate IEP based on educational needs of a specific child.

5.4.1.2 Implement selected IEPs during practicum.

5.4.1.3 Provide suggestion for summer/weekend activities for parents to build skills and concepts in each area listed; emphasize natural environments for the activities.

5.4.1.4 Outline assessment needs in the areas listed; carry out selected assessments during practicum; develop a case study (include multiply handicapped and preschool).

5.4.1.5 For the areas of visual efficiency and O&M, outline sequential phases of concepts and skills.

5.4.1.6 From supplied child data, design programs in the above two areas (include multiply handicapped and preschool).

5.4.1.7 Conduct functional assessments in the above two areas during practicum; implement programs based on the results of the assessments.

5.4.1.8 Given several case studies, assign appropriate schedule for a caseload with emphasis on priorities, time, efficiency.

5.4.1.9 Given specific visual conditions, outline influences such conditions may have on reading, use of subject matter, materials/equipment, motor development, as well as on the techniques used to teach these skills.

5.5 Knowledge of procedures for interpretation of basic principles of instructional strategies for visually handicapped learners to other school personnel, parents, and community workers.

5.5.1 Identify procedures for interpretation of basic principles for visually handicapped learners to other school personnel, parents, and community workers.

5.5.1.1 Design a 20-minute audio-visual presentation emphasizing learning similarities and differences between visually handicapped learners and their peers suitable for presentation to

a. regular methods courses
b. regular classroom teachers associated with practicum experiences.

5.5.1.2 Design and implement a role playing exercise involving typical members of an IEP committee meeting.

5.5.1.3 Design a leaflet for orienting the regular classroom teacher and other students to having a visually handicapped learner in class.

5.5.1.4 Prepare a short presentation for PTA or local civic group about educational programs for visually handicapped learners.

5.5.1.5 Describe how to present rights and responsibilities as outlined in P.L. 94-142 to parents.

5.5.1.6 Prepare an outline, including recommended reading, for parents of preschool children.

5.5.1.7 Prepare an outline, including recommended reading, for parents of school aged children and youth.

Goal 6.0

Teacher Can Effectively Utilize Instructional Materials, Media, Devices, etc. Appropriate to the Individual Needs of Visually Handicapped Learners

Entry Level of Competency:
Has knowledge of materials and basic principles for selection of instruction of learners.
Has competence in braille codes—in typing and understanding of the function of instructional media in relation to teacher's own learning theories.

Knowledge	Skill	Mastery Tasks
The teacher has:	The teacher can:	Proficiency is demonstrated when the teacher can:
6.1 Knowledge of basic principles inherent in utilizing of instructional media for visually handicapped learners.	6.1.1 Identify basic media in terms of sensory modalities through which they operate: visual, tactile, auditory, etc.	6.1.1.1 Select media appropriate to a particular child and specify source of the media.
	6.1.2 Identify, evaluate, and select appropriate instructional materials and equipment to enhance learning in content areas, e.g., models for health, sex education, social studies, etc.; tapes; maps.	6.1.2.1 Select and provide a written rationale about one appropriate instructional material in each curriculum area.
		6.1.2.2 In a practicum or teaching setting, assess students' needs and select instructional materials and equipment to meet those needs.
6.2 Knowledge of national, regional, state and local sources for purchase and loan of instructional materials and equipment.	6.2.1 Identify loan sources for a variety of media.	6.2.1.1 Correctly identify at least six major sources which loan media appropriate to visually handicapped learners and correctly describe types of materials available from each.
	6.2.2 Identify sources for specified media especially designed for visually handicapped learners.	6.2.2.1 Describe types of media available from sources to include, but not be limited to: (1) APH, (2) Library of Congress, (3) AFB, (4) Howe Press, (5) other braille presses, (6) distributors of non-prescription optical aids, (7) publishers and distributors of large print books, (8) manufacturers and distributors of technological devices.
6.3 Knowledge of basic principles or development of teacher-made and volunteer produced media.	6.3.1 Identify sources of existing standards for the production of sound, recorded, braille, print, tangible aids, illustrations.	6.3.1.1 Describe standards for the production of sound, recorded, braille, print, tangible aids, and illustrations.

	6.3.2 Identify principles of media development for visually handicapped learner's needs.	6.3.2.1- 6.3.4.1 Describe factors to be considered in media development considering the: (1) needs of the learner, (2) educational placement of the learner, (3) curriculum, and (4) availability of media.
	6.3.3 Identify principles of media development feasible in specific school settings or within given parameters.	
	6.3.4 Identify principles of media development in content areas.	
	6.3.5 Identify and provide direction to volunteers and others in appropriate adaptation and editing of materials.	6.3.5.1 Prepare guidelines for adaptation and editing of materials to be used by volunteers, transcribing groups, or school employed transcribers.
6.4 Knowledge of care, use, and storing procedures for a variety of media for visually handicapped learners.	6.4.1 Identify and describe procedures for proper care, use, and storage of a variety of media for visually handicapped learners.	6.4.1.1 Demonstrate the proper care and storage of media as detailed in owner's manuals.
6.5 Knowledge of methods for instructing others in principles of use of media for visually handicapped learners.	6.5.1 Identify ways of assisting other school personnel, visually handicapped learners, and parents to understand the principles of use of media in their education.	6.5.1.1 Given a student who has not previously used a certain type of instructional equipment, (1) introduce the equipment to the student, (2) demonstrate the appropriate usage of the equipment, and (3) provide opportunities for the visually handicapped learner to apply and evaluate the appropriateness of the opportunities of the equipment for him/her.
		6.5.1.2 Instruct a visually handicapped learner, parents, and school personnel in care, use, and storing of media.
		6.5.2.3 In a practicum setting, demonstrate to learners, parents, classroom teachers, and other school personnel the care, use, and storage of media.
6.6 Knowledge of sources for repair of media for visually handicapped learners.	6.6.1 Identify sources for repair of media for visually handicapped learners.	6.6.1.1 List sources for the maintenance and/or repair of equipment.

Knowledge		Skill		Mastery Tasks	
6.7 Knowledge of standards for media production established by national organization(s) in the field for the visually handicapped.	6.7.1 Identify nationally accepted standards for production of teacher-made or volunteer produced media for visually handicapped learners.		6.7.1.1 Evaluate volunteer produced media against standards established by national organizations.		
			6.7.1.2 Evaluate media produced by peers against national standards.		
			6.7.1.3 Produce media in keeping with national standards in: (1) literary braille, (2) complex braille formats, (3) braille mathematics, (4) large print, (5) recordings.		

Goal 7.0
Teacher Will Demonstrate Ability to Identify and Provide Appropriate Counseling and Guidance Services to Visually Handicapped Learners and Significant Others

Entry Level of Competency:
Has familiarity with general counseling and guidance techniques and services.

Knowledge		Skill		Mastery Tasks	
The teacher has:		The teacher can:		Proficiency is demonstrated when the teacher can:	
7.1 Knowledge of strengths and needs of individual visually handicapped learners during different periods of their school years.		7.1.1 Identify potential strengths and needs of an individual visually handicapped learner.		7.1.1.1 Observe and record from anecdotal records and case studies, strengths and needs of a child's overall adjustment.	
				7.1.1.2 Evaluate during observation the needs and strengths of a particular learner and plan a developmental program based on them.	
				7.1.1.3 Implement a program during a clinical experience at various educational levels.	

Code	Objective	Code	Sub-objective
7.1.2	Identify real and perceived need for guidance services.	7.1.2.1	List needs of specific learners for which the educator is unable to provide guidance and counseling and which should be referred to specified outside counseling services.
7.2	Knowledge of ancillary personnel and services available for visually handicapped learners.		
7.2.1	Identify inter-professional personnel in meeting individual needs of the visually handicapped learner.	7.2.1.1	List individuals and agencies which provide guidance, counseling, and other services to visually handicapped learners.
		7.2.1.2	Present to peers a brief summary of one agency and its services, following an interview or correspondence. Include brochures and other materials provided by the agency.
7.3	Knowledge of methods for communicating guidance-related information to ancillary personnel.		
7.3.1	Identify and communicate with ancillary personnel in meeting individual needs of visually handicapped learners.	7.3.1.1	Prepare a written referral to be sent to one of the services identified in 7.2.1.1
		7.3.1.2	Describe critical information that would be provided preliminary to meeting the ancillary personnel.
7.4	Knowledge of professional ethics involved in dealing with guidance information.		
7.4.1	Identify relevant guidance information in an ethical manner.	7.4.1.1	Explain to peers school regulations regarding confidentiality of records, students' and parents' right to information, and other ethical aspects regarding guidance information.
		7.4.1.2	Utilize 7.3.1.1 above to demonstrate professional ethics as guidance information is shared in a role playing situation.
		7.4.1.3	Prepare a report for presentation to special education personnel and ancillary personnel for a consideration for placement of a particular pupil.

7.5 Knowledge of interviewing techniques.	7.5.1 Identify appropriate techniques for conducting an interview to attain a specific goal.	7.5.1.1 Prepare an outline for an interview, including objectives, questions, and comments to be included, and techniques to be used in description of interviewing.
		7.5.1.2 Role play an interview with another student playing the part of a parent. Evaluate the interview from both perspectives.
7.6 Knowledge of the need for visually handicapped learners to develop positive self-concepts.	7.6.1 Identify ways to help visually handicapped children develop a realistic self-concept.	7.6.1.1 List specific methods of (assessing) determining self-concept in visually handicapped learners.
		7.6.1.2 Evaluate with a formal instrument the self-concept of at least one child in your practicum setting using an appropriate technique for administration and scoring.
7.7 Knowledge of guidance and counseling roles of teachers of visually handicapped learners.	7.7.1 Identify a plan to provide appropriate counseling and guidance services to visually handicapped learners.	7.7.1.1 Analyze case studies for the purpose of determining the role of the teacher in guidance and counseling for visually handicapped children and youth.
		7.7.1.2 Propose a comprehensive guidance and counseling program for visually handicapped learners.
7.8 Knowledge of basic techniques for guidance and counseling.	7.8.1 Identify appropriate guidance and counseling techniques for visually handicapped learners.	7.8.1.1 Confer, during a practicum setting, with others (guidance counselor, regular teacher, parent) in counseling; write a summary of the teacher's role in counseling.

Goal 8.0
Teacher will Demonstrate Ability to Utilize Local, State, and National Legislation, Policy, and Resources to Assist in the Delivery of Services to the Visually Handicapped Learner

Entry level of Competency:
Can demonstrate knowledge of community agencies and services.

Knowledge	Skill	Mastery Tasks
The teacher has:	The teacher can:	Proficiency is demonstrated when the teacher can:
8.1 Knowledge of legislation, policies, and agencies at all levels which affect the visually handicapped learner.	8.1.1 Identify national and state legislation and public policy which affect service delivery.	8.1.1.1 Keep a notebook of national and state professional service sources and policy offices with names of contact persons.
		8.1.1.2 Read state program standards and prepare a written summary of program standards for eligibility, placement, transportation, and instructional and support services required for visually handicapped learners.
		8.1.1.3 Prepare a written summary of various program options available to visually handicapped learners in a given state or district and define the basis for utilization of services of that agency.
	8.1.2 Identify specific type or types of services which each agency provides and the economic basis for the service.	8.1.2.1 Select at least two agencies, one of which is a national organization, if possible. Interview agency personnel, critique tapes of interviews with agency personnel, and/or examine agency literature to determine: a. specific types of service the agency provides b. economic base for that service (source(s) of funds) c. areas to which funds are distributed d. sources of referral and referral procedures e. eligibility for service

f. procedures for evaluation of services.

8.1.3	Identify procedures for implementing legislation and policy.	
	8.1.3.1	Relate three recent acts of legislation or judicial decisions on rights of handicapped persons.
	8.1.3.2	Examine information from appropriate sources and prepare a written summary of any rights specific to the visually handicapped population.
8.1.4	Identify the major resources available through national, state, and local agencies.	
	8.1.4.1	List 25 national, state, and local agencies. Include resources available from each and how to access those resources.
8.1.5	Identify community structures and inter-relationships of agencies.	
	8.1.5.1	Using sources reviewed in 8.1.1.1, document and analyze evidence of participation during a specific time period in civic and political activity within a community.
8.2	Knowledge of resources and services at all levels which serve visually handicapped learners.	
8.2.1	Identify procedures for developing supportive services	
	8.2.1.1	List and describe or prepare a file of national and state volunteer organizations and their services for visually handicapped learners.
	8.2.1.2	Describe volunteer organizations and services available in a specific area.
	8.2.1.3	Describe services considered deficient in a specific area and specify those persons/groups affected by the deficiency.

Goal 9.0
Teacher will Demonstrate Knowledge of and Need for Research with Visually Handicapped Learners

Entry Level of Competency:
Can demonstrate knowledge of nature and needs of visually handicapped children and youth.

Knowledge	Skill	Mastery Tasks
The teacher has:	The teacher can:	Proficiency is demonstrated when the teacher can:
9.1 Knowledge of general theories, concepts, and techniques in research.	9.1.1 Identify basic purposes, concepts, and techniques of research.	9.1.1.1 Describe the role of research as a systematic attempt to provide answers to questions.
		9.1.1.2 Explain how the outcomes of research may eventually improve the teaching-learning process for visually handicapped learners.
		9.1.1.3 Define what is meant by and provide examples from journals of historical, descriptive, and experimental research.
	9.1.2 Identify and use pertinent research information.	9.1.2.1 Describe specific journals, information retrieval systems, and other resources which report research studies relevant to the education of visually handicapped learners.
		9.1.2.2 Select a topic and develop an annotated bibliography about that topic.
	9.1.3 Identify ways to evaluate critically and report accurately on existing research studies.	9.1.3.1 Describe appropriate procedures for obtaining, analyzing, and describing data from single subject and small-N samples and sample selection.
		9.1.3.2 Write a review of the research literature related to any aspect in the education of visually handicapped learners.
		9.1.3.3 Given the format required by a particular funding agency, prepare a brief proposal for a research study.

9.1.4   Identify special issues and considerations in research with visually handicapped learners.

9.1.4.1   Describe a specific population of visually handicapped learners in terms of pertinent variables such as degree of vision, age at onset of visual impairment, number of years in school, etc.

9.1.4.2   Describe the advantages and disadvantages of single subject and small-N samples in research with visually handicapped learners.

9.2   Knowledge of teacher's role in utilizing research in education of visually handicapped learners.

9.2.1   Identify ways in which teachers can apply research findings to education of visually handicapped learners.

9.2.1.1   Interpret and make recommendations for the application of research findings to practice in a specific setting.

9.2.1.2   Identify a specific problem which impinges on the teaching-learning process, and utilize research findings to provide a resolution of the problem.

9.2.1.3   Identify a specific learner and utilize research findings to improve the teacher's understanding of that learner.

9.2.2   Identify the role of the teacher as a member of a team in planning and conducting research.

9.2.2.1   Identify the role of the teacher as a member of a research team.

9.2.2.2   Identify other individuals and/or agencies with whom the teacher may co-operate in planning, conducting, and funding research studies related to visually handicapped learners.

9.2.2.3   Describe the roles performed by each member of a team responsible for conducting co-operative research.

9.3   Knowledge of ethical concerns, current regulations, and professional responsibilities regarding research with human subjects.

9.3.1   Identify ethical considerations in conducting and reporting research with visually handicapped learners.

9.3.1.1   Describe the current policies and guidelines of the school, agency, government, university or other appropriate jurisdiction regarding ethical considerations in research with human subjects.

9.3.1.2 Define the following terms as they relate to research with visually handicpped learners:
—confidentiality
—anonymity
—right to nonparticipation
—parental permission
—experimenter responsibility

9.4 Knowledge of research needs in instruction, technology, and other areas relevant to the education of visually handicapped learners.

9.4.1 Identify research needs regarding instruction, technology, and other areas relevant to the education of visually handicapped learners.

9.4.1.1 Using the products of 9.1.2.1, 9.1.2.2, and 9.1.3.2, prepare a statement of research needs for some segment of the visually handicapped school age population.

9.5 Knowledge necessary to design and disseminate research findings with visually handicapped learners.

9.5.1 Outline a plan for a research study involving visually handicapped learners.

9.5.1.1 Given a specific research problem relating to the education of visually handicapped learners, design a plan for conducting and reporting a research study, either individually or in co-operation with others.

Goal 10.0

Teacher Will Accept Responsibilities of Being a Member of the Teaching Profession and Will Make a Commitment to Improve Services for Visually Handicapped Learners with Varying Degrees of Visual Loss and at All Developmental Levels

Entry Level of Competency:
Can demonstrate knowledge of the teaching profession, its roles and functions.

Knowledge	Skill	Mastery Tasks
The teacher has:	The teacher can:	Proficiency is demonstrated when the teacher can:
10.1 Knowledge of various philosophies regarding the education of visually handicapped learners.	10.1.1 Identify various philosophical and theoretical positions related to education of the visually handicapped learner.	10.1.1.1 Analyze, evaluate, and discuss strengths and weaknesses of programs for the visually handicapped learner, given hypothetical situations.

10.2 Knowledge of attitudes and value systems in various areas and cultures.

10.2.1 Identify various attitude and value systems in different areas and cultures where he/she is or will work.

10.3 Knowledge of attitudes and value systems related to the visually handicapped.

10.3.1 Identify various attitude and value systems related to the visually handicapped.

10.4 Knowledge of one's own professional strengths, weaknesses, values, and attitudes.

10.4.1 Identify personal strengths, weaknesses, anticipated roles, and professional expectations.

10.5 Knowledge of professional responsibilities and interrelationships.

10.5.1 Identify responsibilities to students, school, community, and the education profession.

10.1.1.2 Examine and react to written materials, stated philosophy, and practices of individuals and groups where there are questions of misrepresentation, exploitation, or unethical practices detrimental to visually handicapped persons.

10.1.2.3 Write or present a personal statement of philosophy on the education of the visually handicapped.

10.2.1.1 Describe attitudes and values expressed or implied in interviews with parents, colleagues, school personnel, and society at large.

10.2.1.2 Describe the social and cultural characteristics of the school community.

10.3.1.1 Describe attitudes and values toward the visually handicapped expressed or implied by parents, colleagues, school personnel, the community, and society at large.

10.4.1.1 Discuss 10.4.1 with your advisor or other professional and formulate a plan for your immediate growth.

10.4.1.2 Devise and implement a plan for professional growth based on current and changing needs of the individual and the profession.

10.5.1.1 Submit evidence of membership in professional organizations.

10.5.1.2 Submit evidence of involvement in school and community activities.

10.5.1.3 Demonstrate in practicum settings the ability to work effectively with significant others.

10.5.1.4 Describe the roles of members of the multidisciplinary team and tell how the teacher can participate more effectively as a team member.

10.6 Knowledge of problems, issues, and public policy related to the education of visually handicapped learners.

10.6.1 Identify the dynamics and interaction of public policy, particularly as it relates to education.

10.6.1.1 Summarize major provisions of federal and own individual state legislation pertaining to the visually handicapped.

10.6.1.2 Develop a card file on legislation currently in effect.

10.6.1.3 List sources for legislative information.

10.6.1.4 Attend a civic or legislative group meeting and prepare an analysis of the issues discussed.

10.7 Knowledge of advocacy for the visually handicapped.

10.7.1 Identify the roles and responsibilities of an advocate for the visually handicapped.

10.7.1.1 Make a survey of types of public relations and advocacy roles performed by teachers in the field.

10.7.1.2 In an actual or simulated setting (e.g., IEP meeting or staffing with regular school personnel), perform the role of an advocate for a visually handicapped learner.

APPENDIX F

DVH-CEC Position Paper:
The Role and Function of the Teacher of the Visually Handicapped

Susan Jay Spungin
American Foundation for the Blind

Now more than ever before the field is seeing a need to define the role and function of teachers of the visually handicapped, especially in light of the growing acceptance of the generic special education program models and personnel developed to serve the low prevalence population of visually handicapped children. In order to justify the need for trained teachers in vision to serve these children the field must be very clear as to what is actually meant by "a teacher of the visually handicapped." Consequently, what follows are areas of specialized activities to serve as role guidelines for teachers/consultants of the visually handicapped in community day school programs.

I Assessment and Evaluation
A. Perform functional vision assessments.
B. Obtain and interpret eye/medical reports as they relate to educational environments.
C. Contribute to appropriate portions of the IEP, such as long-term goals, short-term goals, learning style/physical constraints.
D. Recommend appropriate service delivery plans, including physical education, ancillary support services, equipment, time frames.
E. Recommend appropriate specialized evaluations as needed, such as low vision, orientation and mobility, psychological, and adaptive physical education.
F. Confer with special services to aid in evaluation.
G. Assist in determining the eligibility and the appropriate placement of visually handicapped children.
H. Participate in the assessment of each pupil and interpret results to classroom teachers and others.

II Educational and Instructional Strategies:
Learning Environment
A. Assure that the student is trained in the use of, and has available, all devices and technological apparatus useful to the process of academic learning.
B. Assure that the classroom teacher fully under-

Adapted from: *Council for Exceptional Children, Statements of Position* (Reston, Va.: Author, 1980-1981).

stands the unique needs of children with visual losses.
C. Act as a catalyst in developing understanding of a visual loss with sighted children.
D. Interpret adjustments needed in assignments or standards in the regular classroom.
E. Assure that the student has all educational materials in the appropriate media.
F. Consult with the classroom teachers regarding methodology to be used as visually handicapped children are included in classroom learning experiences.
G. Instruct the student in academic subjects and activities requiring adaptation and reinforcement as a direct result of visual impairment.

III Educational and Instructional Strategies:
Unique Curriculum
A. Braille Reading and Writing—It may be necessary for the teacher of the visually handicapped to provide beginning braille reading instruction and to introduce the child to such mechanical aspects of reading as: top of the page, bottom of the page, use of fingers, tracking, etc. Introduction of writing is also the responsibility of the teacher of the visually handicapped. Braille writers and slates and styli are unfamiliar learning tools to the classroom teacher; the classroom teacher should not be expected to master the mechanics of either. The teacher of the visually handicapped will possess the necessary skills in braille mathematics and in braille music, and will provide instruction to students in their use.
B. Handwriting—For the low vision child, certain aspects of handwriting in respect to size and configuration may be the responsibility of the teacher of the visually handicapped. The teaching of signature writing, and, if appropriate, additional handwriting skills to functionally blind children is certainly a responsibility.
C. Typewriting—For most low vision children and functionally blind children typing will be the major means of communication between the child and sighted peers, parents, and teachers. This is a skill which should be carefully and thoroughly taught by the teacher of the visually handicapped as soon as the pupil has sufficient motor skills.
D. Large Print and Optical Aids—It may be necessary for the teacher of the visually handicapped to help

low vision children utilize reading aids in order to fully benefit in the regular classroom.

E. Listening Skills—Both low vision and functionally blind students need to learn good listening skills. Listening becomes extremely important in the secondary grades when print reading assignments become long and laborious. It is necessary for the visually handicapped child to begin a sequential course of study in the development of listening skills as early as possible. The development of listening skills is not confined to the use of an alternate reading system. It is important in mobility, in social conversation, and in interpreting a variety of auditory signals received from the environment.

F. Study Skills—Skimming braille or large print materials, outlining in braille or large print, searching for significant information in recorded materials, and other skills may need to be taught by the teacher of the visually handicapped.

G. Tactual Skills—The development of tactual skills is not confined to the reading of braille. Visually handicapped students should be taught to use their fingers and hands well in order to explore, identify, and appreciate all tangible materials in their environment.

H. Visual Efficiency—This skill underlines achievement in every area for the low vision pupil: academic, psychomotor, self-help, and vocational and social skills. The use of residual vision is one of the most important aspects of the curriculum offered by the teacher of the visually handicapped.

I. Motor Development—The teacher of the visually handicapped must know the potential problem areas in motor development for visually handicapped children. Body image, body in space concepts, visual motor skills, etc., are included in this area.

J. Physical Education—This is often a problem for visually handicapped pupils in public schools. Students must be assisted in understanding and participating in team games. Physical fitness must be stressed.

K. Orientation and Mobility—Much of the orientation and mobility needs of the student are the responsibility of qualified orientation and mobility instructors. The responsibilities of, and the relationship between the teachers of the visually handicapped and the orientation and mobility instructors must be clearly defined. It is possible that the former will assume responsiblity for assuring that students develop in sensory motor, gross, and fine motor skills. Visually handicapped children must be taught to move in space and to be aware of the environment around them. They must learn to use tactual and auditory cues to assist and identify their position in space and the relative position of other persons and objects around them.

L. Concept Development—The teacher of the visually handicapped shares with others the responsiblity for the development of basic concepts by the student.

Future learning is dependent upon the student's thorough understanding and association, discrimination, and relationships.

M. Activities of Daily Living—Thorough knowledge of the activities and techniques of daily living or personal management skills is needed to create independence so that visually handicapped students may become acceptable and personable beings—free of mannerisms, and socially attractive to others. Specific objectives include but are not limited to: a) caring for personal needs; b) developing adequate eating habits; c) mastering the process and routine of dressing and undressing; d) developing a positive self-image.

N. Reasoning—The ability to reason, especially in the abstract, may require specific instruction from the teacher of the visually handicapped. Students may need assistance in the development of decision-making skills, problem solving, and learning to live with occasional frustration and failure.

O. Human Sexuality—Teachers of the visually handicapped, parents, and others share the responsibility for gradual, sequential instruction in human sexuality for visually handicapped students. Because programs in sex education for sighted children assume that much visual information has been previously attained, the visually handicapped pupil may need specific curriculum taught by appropriate, well-prepared professionals.

P. Leisure and Recreation—The teacher of the visually handicapped, parents, and community agencies share a responsibility to expose the student to, and provide learning opportunities in, a wide variety of leisure time activities which have carry-over value to adult life.

IV Guidance and Counseling

A. Guidance and counseling assists visually handicapped students in understanding their attitudes and those of others concerning a visual impairment; in exploring similarities and differences in relation to all children; in becoming socially aware of oneself and environment; in learning acceptable behavior, in encouraging social interactions with peer groups; and in becoming more independent. Parents should be included in this guidance and counseling process.

B. Career education curriculum that has been developed for sighted children may need supplementary instruction from a teacher of the visually handicapped. Career education encompasses four sequential areas: career awareness, career exploration, career preparation, and career placement. Each, in sequence, is dependent upon the other. A curriculum in career education for the visually handicapped may be necessary, and implementation of this curriculum may be the responsibility of the teacher of the visually handicapped. At the career exploration level this could well mean many field trips into the community so that the visually handicapped student will have exposure to people and work situations.

C. Vocational counseling is an integral part of programs designed for visually handicapped students. Career awareness begins on the primary level, continuing with career exploration and orientation on the intermediate and secondary level. The teacher in conjunction with the counselor should involve visually handicapped students and parents in this counseling process. Following the assessment of vocational strengths and weaknesses, the students should participate in work-study experience programs, as appropriate, for career preparation.

D. Social adjustment skills are an integral part of the curriculum and assist the visually handicapped student to blend smoothly into society. Areas that must be emphasized are spatial awareness and orientation, verbal and nonverbal language, self-help skills, socialization processes, interpersonal relations, human sexuality, and real life experiences.

E. Support services to families should include:

1. Interpreting implications of a visual impairment on overall development;

2. Referring to appropriate service providers;

3. Encouraging home involvement in program objectives;

4. Acting as a resource in the field of vision.

V Administration and Supervision

A. Communication with Administrators

1. Pupil information (e.g., visual status, grade level, prototype).

2. Program goals and activities.

3. Program evaluation.

4. Screening and referral procedures.

5. Relationship to other regular and special education programs and support services.

6. Budget funds to include funds for travel time, consultation, instruction, salaries, travel expenses, instructional materials, preparation time, conferences, and benefits.

7. In-service programs by and for teacher/consultants of the visually impaired.

8. Program scheduling to allow adequate time for planning, preparation, reporting, commuting, instruction, and staff conferences.

9. Physical facilities which include instructional settings, offices and storage space.

10. Advocate of students' educational/legal rights and provider of services.

11. Provide input into scheduling of students.

B. Record Keeping

1. Maintain statewide and system-wide student census.

2. Obtain and maintain student medical and optometric reports.

3. Maintain records of pupil assessments, individual educational plans, reviews, and progress reports with signed parental release forms.

4. Maintain material and equipment requests.

C. Casefinding, Student Referral Procedures and Scheduling

1. Act as a vision consultant for system-wide screening, materials, follow-up, and recommendations.

2. Participate in LEA's annual plan for Child Search.

3. Maintain a referral/communication system with nurses and other school staff.

4. Obtain current eye reports and begin notification and assessment.

5. Schedule time for teaching, planning, preparation, travel, and conferences with parents, and relevant school and non-school persons.

6. Maintain records and exchange information about visually handicapped students with appropriate personnel and consistent with school district policies regarding confidentiality.

7. Prepare a master schedule to be given to the supervisor and the principal of the building in which students are served.

8. Work within the framework and policies of the school.

VI School-Community Relations

A. School and Community Involvement—The teacher of the visually handicapped should be prepared to interpret the program to school personnel, board of education, and other groups within the community.

B. Program Liaison

1. Private, state and local agencies and schools

2. Resources within the community

3. Medical specialists

4. Placement transitions

5. Parents

6. Related appropriate specialists

7. Recreation resources

C. Services Development

1. Coordinate ancillary groups and individuals, such as transcribers, recordists, readers for visually handicapped students, counselors, and mobility instructors.

2. Assist in the initiation of new services as well as coordinating existing ones to bring the varied and necessary related services to the educational program.

3. Attend professional meetings (in and out of the district) concerned with the education of visually handicapped students.

4. Keep abreast of new developments in the education of visually handicapped children and youth.

5. Maintain ongoing contact with parents to assure realistic understanding of child's abilities, progress, future goals, community resources, etc.

APPENDIX G

Resources

American Alliance for Health, Physical Education, Recreation and Dance
1900 Association Drive
Reston, Va. 22091
(703) 476-3400

American Association for the Advancement of Science (AAAS)
Project on the Handicapped in Science
Office of Opportunities in Science
1333 H Street, NW
Washington, D.C. 20005
(202) 326-6670

American Blind Bowling Associaton
3500 Terry Drive
Norfolk, Va. 23518
(804) 857-7267

American Camping Association
Bradford Woods
Martinsville, Ind. 46151
(317) 342-8456

American Council of the Blind, Inc.
1211 Connecticut Avenue, NW Suite 506
Washington, D.C. 20036-2775
(202) 393-3666

American Foundation for the Blind
15 West 16th Street
New York, N. Y. 10011
(212) 620-2000

American Printing House for the Blind
1839 Frankfort Avenue
Louisville, Ky. 40206
(502) 895-2405

Association for Education and Rehabilitation of the Blind and Visually Impaired (AERBVI)
206 North Washington Street, Room 320
Alexandria, Va. 22314
(703) 836-6060

Boy Scouts of America
Scouting for the Handicapped Division
1325 Walnut Hill Lane
Irving, Tex. 75038-3039
(214) 659-2127

Center for Multisensory Learning
Lawrence Hall of Science
University of Calif.
Berkeley, California 94720
(415) 642-8941

The Council for Exceptional Children
Division of the Visually Handicapped
1920 Association Drive
Reston, Va. 22091
(703) 620-3660

Girl Scouts of the U.S.A.
Services for Girls with Disabilities
830 Third Avenue
New York, N.Y. 10022
(212) 940-7500

Higher Education and the Handicapped (HEATH) Resource Center
One Dupont Circle
Washington, D.C. 20036
(202) 939-9320

National Association for Disabled Athletes
80 Huguenot Avenue, Suite 11-B
Englewood, N. J. 07631
(201) 569-6627

National Association for Parents of the Visually Impaired, Inc.
P.O. Box 180806
Austin, Tex. 78717
(512) 459-6651; 1-800-225-0227-994610

National Association for Visually Handicapped, Inc.
305 E. 24th Street
New York, N.Y. 10010
(212) 889-3141

National Braille Association
422 Clinton Avenue South
Rochester, N. Y. 14620
(716) 473-0900

National Braille Press
88 Stephen Street
Boston, Mass. 02115
(617) 266-6160

National Federation of the Blind
Parents of Blind Children Division
1800 Johnson Street
Baltimore, Md. 21230
(301) 659-9314

National Handicapped Sports and Recreation Association
P.O. Box 33141, Farragut Station
Washington, D.C. 20033
(202) 783-1441
or
P.O. Box 18664
Capitol Hill Station
Denver, Colo. 80218
(303) 232-4575

National Information Center for Handicapped Children and Youth
Box 1492
Washington, D.C. 20013
(202) 522-3332

National Library Service for the Blind and Physically Handicapped
Library of Congress
1291 Taylor Street, NW
Washington, D.C. 20542
(202) 287-5000

National Science Teachers Association (NSTA)
1742 Connecticut Avenue, NW
Washington, D.C. 20009
(202) 328-5800

National Society to Prevent Blindness
79 Madison Avenue
New York, N.Y. 10016
(212) 684-3505

National Therapeutic Recreation Society
Division of National Recreation and Park
Association, Inc.
3101 Park Center Drive
12th Floor
Alexandria, Va. 22302
(703) 820-3993

Recording for the Blind
20 Roszel Road
Princeton, N. J. 08540
(609) 452-0606

Ski for Light (Handicapped)
1455 W. Lake Street
Minneapolis, Minn. 55408
(612) 827-3232

Special Education Programs
Department of Education
400 Maryland Avenue, SW
Donohoe Building, Room 4918
Washington, D.C. 20202
(202) 732-1265

Special Olympics
1701 K Street, NW
Suite 500
1350 New York Avenue, NW
Washington, D.C. 20005
(202) 628-3630

Vinland National Center
3675 Ihduhapi Road
Loretto, Minn. 55357
(612) 479-3555

APPENDIX <u>H</u>

SAVI Scientific Reasoning Module: Swingers

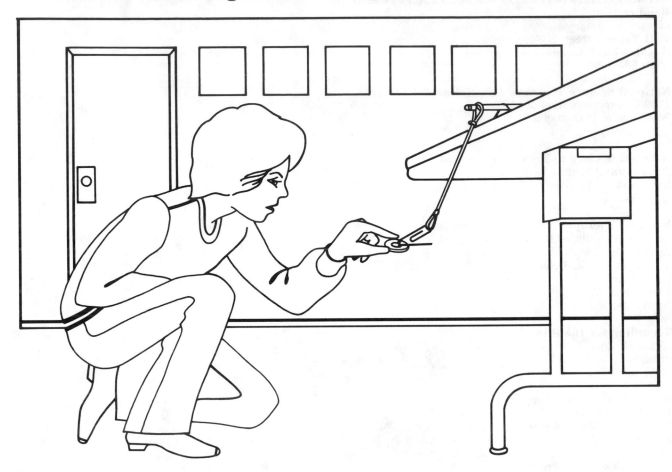

Overview

In Swingers, the students experiment with variables that do and do not affect the behavior of pendulums. After finding that the length of the pendulum is the critical variable that determines the number of swings a pendulum will make in a unit of time, the students graph the results of their experiments. Finally, they use their graph to predict the behavior of additional pendulums.

Background

Remember the unparalled joy you experienced as a little tyke sitting in a swing at the park, going back and forth, back and forth? As long as Dad continued to provide a little push each time you completed a

Source: SAVI, Lawrence Hall of Science, University of California, Berkeley

cycle, the fun went on and on. But if the gentle push stopped, in a minute or so you slowed to a stop.

You were riding on a pendulum. Any mass (weight) suspended on a string, rope, bar, or similar arm that is free to pivot from an anchor point is a pendulum.

When the mass is displaced from its natural resting position (straight down), and released, it swings back and forth, completing each cycle (one complete swing back and forth) in the same length of time as the previous cycle. The distance the mass is displaced from vertical (up to a point) does not affect the length of time it takes for a cycle. The amount of mass at the end of the pendulum does not affect the length of time it takes for a cycle, either. But, the length of the arm (string, bar, etc.) has a great effect on the length of time it takes for a cycle—the longer the arm, the longer it takes for a cycle.

This is a swingin' activity. You and your students should have a lot of fun investigating the variables that govern the behavior of pendulums.

Purpose

In Swingers, the students:
1. Gain more experience with the concept of variable.
2. Record data and use it to make predictions.
3. Conduct experiments with pendulums.

Materials (Supplied for 4 students)
The following is a list of equipment appropriate for all learners (visually impaired, learning disabled, orthopedically disabled, and nondisabled.)

For each student:
3 to 4 steel washers
1 pencil*
For the group:
1 ball of string
1 box of jumbo paper clips
1 number line stick, with hooks* (Optional. See "Anticipating" #6.)
1 watch with a second hand*
1 roll of masking tape*
*Supplied by the teacher.

Anticipating

1. Readiness Skills
a. The students should be able to:
   • count silently to 30.
   • tie knots.
b. The students should be familar with:
   • the terms longer and shorter.
2. Preparing Swingers. Prepare enough identical pendulum strings for each student (or pair of students) to have one. Each string should have a loop at each end, and be 25 to 30 cm long when finished.

The easiest way to get all the strings the same length is to cut 45 cm lengths and tie loops at each end without tightening the loops. When the loops are all tied, run a pencil through all the loops at one end, and a second pencil through all the loops at the other end. Pull all the knots tight at the same time by pulling the two pencils apart.

3. Varying the Lengths of the Strings. Prepare enough pendulum strings of random lengths for each student (or pair) to have one. The lengths should vary from 2 cm to 100 cm or more.

4. Positioning the Swingers. Swingers swing from pencils taped to table tops. Try to position the pencils so that the swinging pendulums won't hit each other or hit the table legs, the students' knees, and so forth.

5. Especially for Blind Students. Blind youngsters can count the swings of the pendulum using either of these methods:
a. Actually hang the pendulum from the student's finger. The finger should then be stabilized by placing the tip on the edge of a table or other convenient surface.

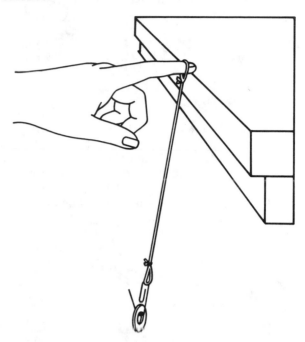

b. Suspend the pendulum from a pencil as described in the activity text. The blind youngster can count swings by pinching onto the pencil right where the string is looped over the pencil.

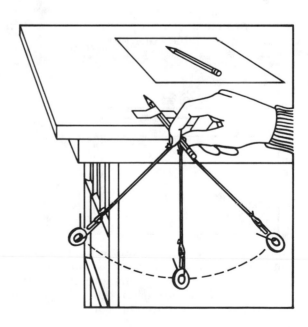

6. Recording Technique. An alternate recording technique can be used if orthopedically disabled students cannot get up to the chalkboard to tape

their pendulums on the number line as described in "Doing the Activity." Simply prepare a stick with evenly spaced hooks (paper clips), numbered from 5 to 30. Rather than taping their pendulums up, the students can hang them on the numbered hook representing the number of swings observed. This transportable number line can then be posted for group discussion.

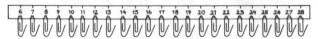

Doing the Activity

1. Introducing Swingers. Distribute the uniform pendulum strings and a jumbo paper clip to each student or pair of students. Ask them to open the paper clip to form a hook, and to hang it on one loop of the string. Then ask the students to hang a washer on the hook. Have them hold the loop at the other end of the string, and show you how they can make the washer swing back and forth.

2. The Swinger Setup. Ask your students how many times they think their swinger will swing in 15 seconds. Suggest using the following method to find out. The youngsters should:
a. Tape a pencil securely to a desk or table so that the pencil sticks over the edge several centimeters.
b. Hang the swinger by the loop from the pencil.
c. Hold the washer straight out parallel to the floor and parallel to the table edge.

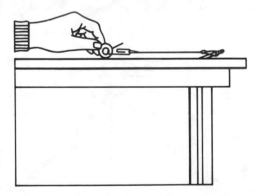

d. At the signal "Go," let go, and count the number of swings until you hear the "Stop" signal. Note: Instruct the students to count complete cycles. That means they should count each time the washer returns to the place closes to where it was released.

3. Counting Swings. Count the number of swings in 15 seconds several times to get the hang of it. Have everyone watch one swinger and count out loud the first time. Then they can practice counting silently.

4. Introducing Variable. Tell the students, "Anything that you can change that might affect the outcome of an experiment is called a variable." Ask the students to think of some variables that might change the number of swings in 15 seconds. Acknowledge their ideas, and then suggest that the students add a second washer to their swinger to see if that variable (weight) will change the number of swings in 15 seconds. Distribute a second washer to the youngsters and ask them to try the experiment.

5. Suggesting another Variable. Instead of releasing the washers straight out (parallel to the floor), have the students release the washers at about a 45° angle. Count swings in 15 seconds to see if this variable makes a difference.

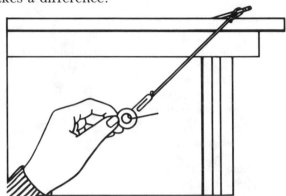

6. Recording the Results. Draw a number line on a chalkboard or on a long piece of paper that you can post about 150 cm from the floor. The numbers should go from 5 to 30, with about 3 or 4 cm between numbers. Then have the students remove one washer from their swinger. Ask each youngster to bring his pendulum up and tape it to the line right under the number that represents the number of times his swinger swings in 15 seconds. The top of the swinger loop should just touch the line. (The swingers should all be in the same spot, as none of

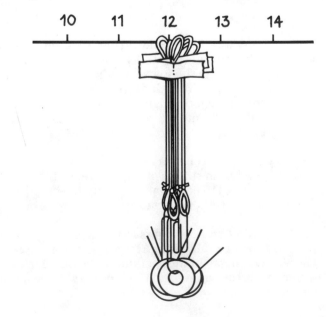

the variables tested so far affect the outcome to a significant degree.)

7. A New Variable. Ask the students if they can think of another variable that might make a difference in the number of swings in 15 seconds. If they don't come up with it, suggest that the length of the string might make a difference. Distribute random-length strings, have the students set them up with a paper clip and 1 washer as before, and then count the number of swings in 15 seconds. The longer swingers will require higher anchor positions from which to swing. Have each student tape his pendulum, as before, under the number that represents the number of swings counted.

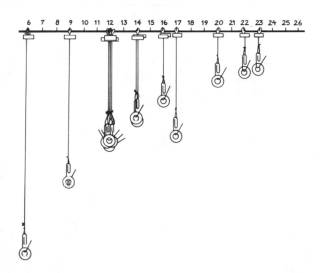

8. Drawing Conclusions. Tell the students that "swingers" are really called pendulums. Ask if anyone has ever seen a pendulum in use before. [Clocks.] Ask the students to look at the pendulums on the number line, and to make a general statement about the relationship between the length of the string and the number of swings a pendulum makes in 15 seconds. [The longer the string, the fewer swings in 15 seconds.] Ask, "What variable made a difference in the number of swings?" [Length.]

9. More Pendulums. Hand out additional strings, and have the students make up pendulums and predict the number of swings they will make in 15 seconds. (Encourage them to go up to the number line to see where the new pendulum "fits in," if they don't do so spontaneously.) Or, give them the ball of string and challenge them to make up a pendulum that will fit into the number line at a place where none is hanging.

These last two activities can help you assess how well your students understand the relationship between the length of the pendulum string and the number of swings, and also how effectively they can use the accrued data.

Follow up (Work with each student individually.)

1. Ask the student, "What variables did we experiment with in this activity?" [Weight, release angle, and string length.] "Which variable(s) made no difference in the number of swings in 15 seconds?" [Weight and angle.] "Which variable(s) did make a difference?" [Length.]

2. Give the student this problem: "Linda has a pendulum 20 cm long, and Sue has a pendulum 40 cm long. Whose pendulum will swing more times in fifteen seconds?" [Linda's.]

3. Have the student cut string, tie knots, and conduct an experiment to verify her answer.

Going Further

1. Ask the youngsters to attach a pendulum to the washer of another pendulum. Have them start the compound pendulum in motion after predicting what will happen.

2. Hang two equal pendulums next to each other. Connect them with a soda straw that has been split a short distance at each end. Start one in motion. What happens?

Language Development

Vocabulary

Pendulum: A mass hung from a fixed point, free to swing to and fro when put into motion.
Variable: Something that can be changed and that might affect the outcome of an experiment or activity.

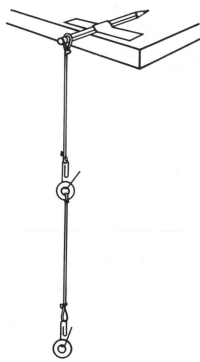

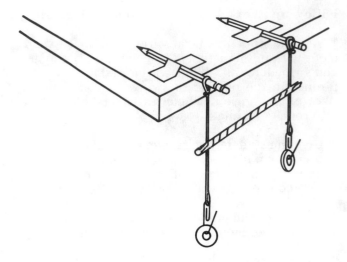

Communication Skills

Oral Language

1. Ask the students to describe the relationship between the length of a pendulum and the number of
times it swings in a unit of time.

2. Swingers is a great activity for peer teaching. Have
one or more students teach the activity to others.
(Teaching younger students is often an effective way
to initiate peer teaching.)

Written Language

1. Have your students make a display poster for the
bulletin board that shows the results of the Swingers
activity. The poster should include:
  • A title.
  • Data display, labelled.
  • A definition of pendulum.
  • A question about pendulums for readers to
    think about, such as, "Do long pendulums swing
    faster or slower than short pendulums?"

2. Pendulums have a prominent place in the history
of timekeeping. Have the students read some of the
history and prepare a report. Some students may
want to include a diagrammatic representation of
clockworks with their report.

General Application Skills

1. Use a swinger to make a simple clock that will let
you accurately time one minute.

2. If possible, bring a pendulum clock to school so
your students can see how the pendulum moves and
investigate the mechanism for adjusting the length
of the pendulum to make the clock go faster or
slower.

REFERENCES

Abel, G.L. (1955). Significant trends affecting the education of blind children. *American Journal of Public Health*, **45** (6), pp. 989-905.

Abel, G.L. (1957). *The growth of the resource room.* New York, N.Y.: American Foundation for the Blind, Inc.

Abel, G.L. (1962). Professional education for teachers of the visually handicapped in a teacher education center. *Education of the Blind*, **7**, pp. 105-112.

Abel, G. L. (1967). Teacher training: Whence and whither bound. *Blindness*, pp. 105-125.

Abrams, F.S. (1982). American immigration policy: How strait the gate. *Law and Contemporary Problems*, **45** (2), pp. 107-162.

Adams, A. C. (1908). The education of the blind child with the seeing child in the public schools. Proceedings, *National Education Association*, pp. 1137-1142.

Adelson, E. (1983). Precursors of early language development in children blind from birth. In A.E. Mills (ed.), *Language acquisition in the blind child: Normal and deficient* (pp. 1-12). San Diego, Calif.: College Hill Press.

Al-Qazzaz, A. (1975). Images of the Arabs in the American social science textbooks. In A. Abu-Laban & A. Zeadey (eds.), *Arabs in America: Myths and realities*. Wilmette, Ill.: Medina University Press International.

Aliotti, N.C. (1977). Alternative assessment strategies in a pluralistic society. *School Psychology Digest*, **6**, pp. 6-12.

Allen, W., Griffith, A., & Shaw, C. (1977). *Orientation and mobility: Behavioral objectives for teaching older adventitiously blinded individuals*. New York, N.Y.: New York Infirmary/Center for Independent Living

American Alliance for Health, Physical Education, and Recreation (AAHPER). (1976). *Physical activities for impaired, disabled and handicapped individuals*. Washington, D.C.: Author.

American Association of Workers for the Blind, Association for the Education of the Visually Handicapped and the National Braille Association. (1973). *The Nemeth code for mathematics and science notation*, 1972 revision. Louisville, Ky.: American Printing House for the Blind.

American Association of Workers for the Blind, Association for the Education of the Visually Handicapped and the National Braille Association. (1973). *Provisional braille for computer notation 1972 as amended by the presentation and outcome of the NBA computer notation workshop, San Francisco, May 1973*. Louisville, Ky.: American Printing House for the Blind.

American Foundation for the Blind, (1953). *Training facilities for the preparation of teachers of blind children in the United States*. New York, N.Y.: Author.

American Foundation for the Blind. (1961). *A teacher education program for those who serve blind children and youth*. New York, N.Y.: Author.

American Foundation for the Blind. (1974). *A step-by-step guide to personal management for blind persons*. New York, N.Y.: Author.

The American Heritage Dictionary: Second college edition. (1982). Boston, Mass.: Houghton Mifflin Co.

American Printing House for the Blind. (1984). *Instructional aids, tools and supplies for the visually handicapped*. Louisville, Ky.: American Printing House for the Blind.

Ancona, R. (1971). The blind child. In Alkema, C. (ed.), *Art for the exceptional* (pp. 81-88). Boulder, Colo.: Pruett Publishing Co.

Anthony, G.M. (1969). Creativity and the visually handicapped. *Education of the Visually Handicapped*, **6** (1), pp. 122-123.

Ardizzone, J. & Scholl, G.T. (1985). Mental retardation. In G.T. Scholl (ed.), *The school psychologist and the exceptional child* (pp. 81-98). Reston, Va.: Council for Exceptional Children.

Aschcroft, S.C., Halliday, C., & Barraga, N.C. (1965). *Study II: Effects of experimental teaching on the visual behavior of children educated as though they had no vision*. Nashville, Tenn.: George Peabody College for Teachers.

Ashcroft, S.C. & Zambone-Ashley, A.M. (1980). Mainstreaming children with visual impairments. *Journal of Research and Development in Education*. **13**(40), pp. 22-36.

Augenstein, L. (1969). *Come, let us play God*. New York, N.Y.: Harper and Row.

Ayres, J.A. (1981). *Sensory integration in the child*. Los Angeles, Calif.: Western Psychological Services.

Ayres, J.A. (1972). *The Ayres space test*. Beverly Hills, Calif.: Western Psychological Services.

Azrin, N.H. & Armstrong, P.M. (1973). The "mini-meal"—A method for teaching eating skills to the profoundly retarded. *Mental Retardation*, **11** (1), pp. 9-11.

Bagley, M. (1985). Service providers assessment of the career development needs of blind and visually impaired students and rehabilitation clients and the resource available to meet those needs. *Journal of Visual Impairment & Blindness*, **79** (10), pp. 434-443.

Bailey, D.B. & Simeonson, R.J. (1984). Critical issues underlying research and intervention with families of young children. *Journal of the Division for Early Childhood*, **9**, pp. 38-48.

Baird, A.S. (1977). Electronic aids: Can they help blind children? *Journal of Visual Impairment & Blindness*, **71** (3), pp. 97-101.

Balthazar, E.E. (1971). *Balthazar scales of adaptive behavior for the profoundly and severely retarded, Section 1*. Champaign, Ill.: Research Press.

Bancroft, N.R. & Bendinelli, L. (1982). Listening comprehension of compressed, accelerated, and normal speech by the visually handicapped. *Journal of Visual Impairment & Blindness*, **76** (6), pp. 235-237.

Bandura, A. (1977). *Social learning theory*. Englewood Cliffs, N.J.: Prentice-Hall.

Baptiste, H.P. & Baptiste, M.L. (n.d.). Multiculturalizing classroom instruction. In C.C. Moody & C.B. Vergon (ed.), *Approaches for achieving a multicultural curriculum* (pp. 10-17). Ann Arbor: Program for Educational Opportunity, The Unversity of Michigan.

Barber, G. A. (1960). Teaching the blind—the resource room approach. *Education*, **80** (6), p. 334.

Barr, R.D., Barth, J.L. & Shermis, S.S. (1977). *Defining the social studies* (Bulletin 51). Arlington, Va.: National Council for the Social Studies.

Barraga, N.C. (1964). *Increased visual behavior in low vision children*. New York, N.Y.: American Foundation for the Blind, Inc.

Barraga, N.C., Collins, M. & Hollis, J. (1977). Development of efficiency in visual functioning: A literature analysis. *Journal of Visual Impairment & Blindness*, **71** (9), pp. 387-391.

Barraga, N.C. & Morris, J.E. (1980). *Source book on low vision*. Louisville, Ky.: American Printing House for the Blind.

Barraga, N.C. (1970). *Teacher's guide for development of visual learning abilities and utilization of low vision*. Louisville, Ky.: American Printing House for the Blind.

Barraga, N.C. (1973). Utilization of sensory-perceptual abilities. In B. Lowenfeld (ed.), *The Visually Handicapped Children in School*. New York, N.Y.: John Day.

Barraga, N.C. (1976). *Visual handicaps and learning*. Belmont, Calif.: Wadsworth.

Barraga, N.C. (1983). *Visual handicaps and learning*. (Rev. ed.) Austin, Tex.: Exceptional Resources.

Barth, J.L. (1982). The development and evaluation of a tactile graphics kit. *Journal of Visual Impairment & Blindness*, **76** (7), pp. 269-273.

Barth, J.L. (1983a). *The development of fundamental skills in tactile graph interpretation: A program for braille readers: Final report* (Project No. 023CH10324, Grant No. G008001878). Louisville, Ky.: American Printing House for the Blind

Barth, J.L. (1983b). Graphic literacy: A neglected area. In J.W. Wiedel (ed.), *Proceedings of the first international symposium on maps and graphics for the visually handicapped* (pp. 9-16). Washington, D.C.: Association of American Geographers.

Barth, J. & Foulke, E. (1979). Preview: A neglected variable in orientation and mobility. *Journal of Visual Impairment & Blindness*, **72** (2), pp. 41-48.

Barth, J.L., Berla, E.P., & Davis, G.L. (1981). *Tactile graphics guidebook*. Louisville, Ky.: American Printing House for the Blind.

Barton, D.D. (1984). Uncharted course: Mothering the blind child. *Journal of Visual Impairment & Blindness*, **78** (2), pp. 66-79.

Barton, L.E. & LaGrow, S.J. (1983). Reducing self-injurious and aggressive behavior in deaf-blind persons through overcorrection. *Journal of Visual Impairment & Blindness*, **77** (9), pp. 421-24.

Bauman, M.K. (1973). The social competency of visually handicapped children. Paper presented at Conference on the Blind Child in Social Interaction: Developing Relationships with Peers and Adults. Unpublished manuscript.

Bauman, M.K. (1974). Blind and partially sighted. In M.V. Wisland (ed.), *Psychoeducational diagnosis of exceptional children* (pp. 159-189). Springfield, Ill.: Charles C Thomas.

Bauman, M.K. & Kropf, C.A. (1979). Psychological tests used with blind and visually handicapped persons. *School Psychology Digest*, **8,** pp. 257-270.

Baumgartner, T.A. & Jackson, A.S. (1982). *Measurement and evaluation in physical education*. Dubuque, Iowa: William C. Brown.

Bayley, N. (1969). *Bayley scales of infant development*. New York, N.Y.: The Psychological Corporation.

Beckett, J. (1985). Comprehensive care for medically vulnerable infants and toddlers: A parent's perspective.

Behavior characteristics progression. (1973). Palo Alto, Calif.: VORT Corporation.

Belcastro, F.B. (1977-78). Use of behavior modification with visually handicapped subjects: A review of the research. *Education of the Visually Handicapped*, **9** (4), pp. 114-118.

Bellamy, G.T., Horner, R.H., & Inman, D.P. (1979). *Vocational habitation of severely retarded adults: A direct service technology*. Baltimore, Md.: University Park Press.

Belliveau, M. (1980). In M. Belliveau, & A. Smith, (eds.), *The interdisciplinary approach to low vision rehabilitation*. New York, N.Y.: American Foundation for the Blind, Inc. and the Rehabilitation Services Administration. (Grant—45-P81535/2-01.)

Bender, D. (1985). *Everyone, everywhere, everyday needs the tools of the trade called living. Home economics/daily living skills assessment*. Nebraska City, Nebr.: Nebraska School for the Visually Handicapped.

Bennett, R.E. (1981). Professional competence and the assessment of exceptional children. *Journal of Special Education*, **15,** pp. 437-446.

Bentzen, B.L. (1980). Orientation aids. In R. Welsh & B. Blasch (eds.), *Foundations of orientation and mobility* (pp. 291-355). New York, N.Y.: American Foundation for the Blind, Inc.

Bentzen, B.L. (1982). Tangible graphic displays in the education of blind persons. In W. Schiff & E. Foulke (eds.), *Tactual perception: A sourcebook*. New York, N.Y.: Cambridge University Press.

Berkson, G. (1973). Animal studies of treatment of impaired young by parents and the social group. Paper presented on The blind child in social interaction: Developing relationships with peers and adults, New York.

Berla, E.P. (1982). Haptic perception of tangible graphic displays. In W. Schiff & E. Foulke (eds.), *Tactual perception: A sourcebook*. New York, N.Y.: Cambridge University Press.

Best, H. (1934). *Blindness and the blind in the United States*. New York, N.Y.: Macmillan.

Best, J. (1963). The need for residential schools. *The New Outlook for the Blind*, **57** (4), pp. 127-130.

Bigge, J.L. (1982). *Teaching individuals with physical and multiple disabilities*. Columbus, Ohio: Charles E. Merrill.

Bina, M. J. (1982). Morale of teachers of visually handicapped: Implications for administrators. *Journal of Visual Impairment & Blindness*, **76** (4), pp. 121-128.

Bishoff, R.W. (1977). The least restrictive educational program: The residential school. *Education of the Visually Handicapped*, **9**(3), pp. 85-91.

Bixby, J. (1975). Marathon. *Dialogue*, **14** (3), pp. 82-85.

Blackhurst, A.E., & Marks, C.H. (1977). Mobility differences between blind children in day school and residential school settings. *Education of the Visually Handicapped*, **9** (3), pp. 85-91.

Blasch, D. (1971). *Orientation and mobility fans out*. Washington, D.C.: American Association of Workers for the Blind.

Blasch, B. (1975). A study of the treatment of blindisms using punishment and positive reinforcement in laboratory and natural settings. Unpublished doctoral dissertation, Michigan State University.

Bledsoe, C.W. (1971). The family of residential schools. *Blindness*, pp. 25-26.

Bleiberg, R. (1970). Is there a need for a specially designed reading series for beginning blind readers? *The New Outlook for the Blind*, **64** (5), pp. 135-138.

Bliss, J.C. & Moore, M.W. (1974). The Optacon reading system. *Education of the Visually Handicapped*, **6** (4), pp. 98-102.

Bloom, B.S. (1964). *Stability and change in human characteristics*. New York, N.Y.: Wiley.

Bloom, L. & Lahey, M. (1978). *Language development and language disorders*. New York, N.Y.: John Wiley.

Boehm, A.E. (1971). *Boehm test of basic concepts: Test manual*. New York, N.Y.: The Psychological Corporation.

Boldt, W. (1969). The development of scientific thinking in blind children and adolescents. *Education of the Visually Handicapped*, **1** (1), pp. 5-11.

Bond, M. (1975). Blind runners "meet" with feet. *The Lion*, **57** (7), pp. 14-16.

Bornstein, M.H. (1976). Infants are trichomats. *Journal of Experimental Child Psychology*, **21,** pp. 425-445.

Bourgeault, S. E. (1960). A discussion of the integrated or resource plan for education of the visually handicapped. *The New Outlook for the Blind*, **54** (4), pp. 153-159.

Bourgeault, S.E., Harley, R.K., & DuBose, R.F. (1977). The model vision project: A conceptual framework for service delivery. *Journal of Visual Impairment & Blindness*, **71** (1), pp. 16-22.

Bower, E.M. (1966). The achievement of competency. In *Mental Health and Learning*. Washington, D.C., Association for Supervision and Curriculum Development.

Bower, T.G. (1977). Blind babies see with their ears. *New Scientist*, **73,** pp. 255-257.

Bower, T.G. (1979). Origins of meaning in perceptual development. In A.D. Pick (ed.) *Perception and its development: A tribute to Eleanor J. Gibson*. New York, N.Y.: John Wiley & Sons.

Bower, T.G. (1977). *A primer of infant development*. San Francisco, Calif.: W.H. Freeman.

Boyer, E.L. (November 11, 1984). The test of growing student diversity. *New York Times*, Section 12, p. 63.

Bradfield, R.H. & Criner, J. (1975). *Classroom interaction analysis*. San Raphael, Calif.: Academic Therapy.

Bradley, R., & Caldwell, B. (1976). Early home environment and changes in mental test performance in children from 6 to 36 months. *Developmental Psychology*, **12,** pp. 93-97.

Bradley, R. & Caldwell, B. (1977). Home observation for measurement for the environment: A validation study of screening efficiency. *American Journal of Mental Deficiency*, **81,** pp. 417-420.

Brambring, M. (1977). [Geographic information for the Blind.] *Zeitschrift fur Experimentelle und Angewandte Psychologie*, **24** (1), 1-20. *(Psychological Abstracts*, 1978, **60,** No. 1605.)

Brasher, B. (1980). The untapped majority. *Education of the Visually Handicapped*, **12** (1), pp. 21-23.

Brazelton, T.B. (1973). *The Brazelton neonatal assessment scale. Clinics in developmental medicine, No. 50*. Philadelphia, Pa.: Lippincott.

Bremer, N.H., Stone, L. C., & Bishop, K. V. (1973). *Skills in spelling, Grade 3.* Cincinnati, Ohio: McCormick-Mathers Publishing Co., Inc.

Brennan, D. (1975). The race for light. *The Lion,* **57** (11), pp. 10-15.

Brewer, G., Dougherty, L., Fleischwar, P., Genensky, S., Kakalik, J., & Walken, L. (1974). *Improving Services for Handicapped Children.* California: Rand.

Bricker, D., Ruder, D., & Vincent, L. (1976). An interview strategy for language-deficient children. In N. Haring & R. Schuefelbusch (eds.), *Teaching special children.* New York, N.Y.: McGraw-Hill.

Briggs, L.J. (1970). Handbook of procedures for the design of instruction. Pittsburgh, Pa.: American Institutes for Research.

Briggs, L.J., Campeau, D.L., Gagne, R.M. & May, M.A. (1967). *Instructional media: A procedure for the design of multi-media instruction, a critical review for research, and suggestions for future research.* Pittsburgh, Pa.: American Institutes for Research.

Brim, Jr., O.G. & Kagan, J. (eds.). (1980). *Constancy and change in human development.* Cambridge, Mass.: Harvard University Press.

Broadhurst, D.D. (1979). *The educator's role in the prevention and treatment of child abuse and neglect.* Washington, D.C.: National Center for Child Abuse and Neglect, Children's Bureau, Administration for Children, Youth and Families, U.S. Department of Health, Education and Welfare.

Brolin, D.E. & Kokaska, C.J. (1979). *Career education for handicapped children and youth.* Columbus, Ohio: Charles E. Merrill.

Bronfenbrenner, M. (1982). Hyphenated Americans: Economic aspects. *Law and Contemporary Problems,* **45** (2), pp. 10-27.

Brothers, R. (1971). Aural study systems for the visually handicapped: Effects of message length. *Education of the Visually Handicapped,* **3** (3), p. 65-70.

Brothers, R. (1972). Arithmetic computation by the blind. *Education of the Visually Handicapped,* **4** (1), pp. 1-8.

Brown, L., Branston, M., Hamre-Nietupski, S., Pumpran, I., Certo, N. & Gruenewald, L. (1979). A strategy for developing chronological age appropriate and functional curriculum content for severely handicapped adolescents and young adults. *Journal of Special Education.* **13**, pp. 81-90.

Bruininks, R.H., Hauber, F.A., & Kudla, M.J. (1980). National survey of community residential facilities: A profile of facilities and residents in 1977. *American Journal of Mental Deficiency,* **84,** pp. 470-478.

Bruner, J. (1977). *Process of education.* Cambridge, Mass.: Harvard University Press.

Bruner, J. (1971). *Toward a theory of instruction.* Cambridge, Mass.: Belknap Press of Harvard University Press, 1971.

Bruner, J.M. & Anglin, J.M. (1973). *Beyond the information given. Studies in the psychology of knowing.* New York, N.Y.: W.W. Norton.

Bruscia, K. & Levinson, S. (1982). Predictive factors in Optacon music reading. *Journal of Visual Impairment & Blindness,* **76** (8), pp. 309-312.

Bryan, D. & Barthman, M. (eds.). (1953). Educating partially seeing children in the public schools. *Exceptional Children,* **19** (7), pp. 269-272, 288.

Bryan, J.H. & Bryan, T.H. (1979). *Exceptional children.* Sherman Oaks, Calif.: Alfred.

Bryant, N.W. (1984). The continuum of services for visually handicapped students. In G.T. Scholl, (ed.) *Quality services for blind and visually handicapped learners: Statements of position* (pp. 15-16). Reston, Va.: Council for Exceptional Children.

Buell, C.E. (1966). *Physical education for blind children.* Springfield, Ill.: Charles C Thomas.

Buell, C.E. (1975). Physical education and recreation for the visually handicapped. In D. Geddes, & W. Burnett, (ed.), *Physical education and recreation for impaired, disabled and handicapped individuals. . .past, present and future.* American Alliance for Health, Physical Education and Recreation. (Grant OEG-0-72-5454-233563. 150-173.)Washington, D.C.: Information and Research Utilization Center.

Buell, C.E. (1982). *Physical education and recreation for the visually handicapped.* Revised edition. Reston, Va.: The American Alliance for Health, Physical Education, Recreation and Dance.

Burkhart, L.J. (1980). *Homemade battery powered toys and educational devices for severely handicapped children.* Millville, Pa.: Author.

Burkhart, L.J. (1982). *More homemade battery devices for severely handicapped children with suggested activities.* Millville, Pa.: Author.

Burlingham, D. (1964). Hearing and its role in the development of the blind. *The Psychoanalytic Study of the Child,* **19,** pp. 95-112. New York, N.Y.: International Universities Press.

Burlingham, D. (1965). Some problems of ego development in blind children. *The Psychoanalytic Study of the Child,* **20,** pp. 194-208. New York, N.Y.: International Universities Press.

Buros, O.K. (ed.). (1972). *The seventh mental measurement yearbook,* 2. Highland Park, N.J.: Gryphon Press.

Buscaglia, L. (1975). *The disabled and their parents: A counseling challenge.* Thorofare, N.J.: Charles B. Slack, Inc.

Bushnell, W.W. (1981). The ontogeny of intermodal relations: Vision and infancy. In R.D. Walk & H.L. Pick (eds.), *Intersensory perception and sensory integration.* New York, N.Y.: Plenum Press.

Butterworth, G. (1981). The origins of auditory-visual proprioception in human development. In R.D. Walk & H.L. Pick (eds.), *Intersensory perception and sensory integration.* New York, N.Y.: Plenum Press.

Caetano, A. & Kaufmann, J. (1975). Reduction of rocking mannerisms in two blind children. *Education of the Visually Handicapped,* **7** (4), pp. 101-105.

Campbell, P.H. (1983). Basic considerations in programming for students with movement difficulties. In M.E. Snell (ed.), *Systematic instruction of the moderately and severely handicapped.* Columbus, Ohio: Charles E. Merrill Publishing Company.

Campbell, P.H. (1977). Daily living skills. In N. Haring (ed.), *Developing individualized education programs for severely handicapped children and youth.* Washington, D.C.: Bureau of Education for the Handicapped, Department of Health, Education, & Welfare.

Cantres, L.A. (1981). Jose P. and the right to bilingual special education. In H. Martinez (ed.), *Special education and the Hispanic child.* ERIC/CUE Urban Diversity Series No. 74. New York, N.Y.: Teachers College, Columbia University.

Carlson, C.I., Scott, M., & Eklund, S.J. (1980). Ecological theory and method for behavioral assessment. *The School Psychology Review,* **9** (1), pp. 75-82.

Carnochan J. (1975-1976). Archery. *St. Dunstan's Review,* pp. 4-6.

Carroll, T. (1961). *Blindness: What it is, what it does and how to live with it.* Boston, Mass.: Little, Brown & Co.

Carroll, J.B. (1963). A model of school learning. *Teachers College Record,* **64** (8), pp. 723-33.

Carroll, J.L. & Rest, J.R. (1982). Moral development. In B.B. Wolman & G. Stricker (eds.), *Handbook of developmental psychology* (pp. 434-451). Englewood Cliffs, N.J.: Prentice Hall.

Carter, K. (1975). The Sonicguide™ and distance vision training. *Optometric Weekly,* pp. 121-126.

Carter, K., Carter, C., & Ferrell, K. (1980). *The implementation of the Sonicguide™ with visually impaired infants and children.* Bensenville, Ill.: Wormald International Sensory Aids Corporation.

Carter, T.P. & Segura, R.D. (1979). *Mexican Americans in school: A decade of change.* New York, N.Y.: College Entrance Examination Board.

Carter, M. & Kelley, J.D. (1981). Recreation programming for visually impaired children. In J.D. Kelley, (ed.), *Recreation programming for visually impaired children and youth.* New York, N.Y.: American Foundation for the Blind, Inc.

Cight, G.P., Cartwright, C.A., & Ward, M.E. (1981). *Educating special learners.* Belmont, Calif.: Wadsworth Publishers.

Casserly, M. (Compiler). (1983). *Statistical profiles of the Great City Schools: 1970-1982*. Washington, D.C.: The Council of Great City Schools.

Cataracts. (1982). Bethesda, Md.: Office of Scientific Reporting, National Eye Institute.

Caton, H.R. (1977). The development and evaluation of a tactile analog to the Boehm test of basic concepts, Form A. *Journal of Visual Impairment & Blindness*, **71** (9), pp. 382-386.

Caton, H.R. (1981). Visual impairments. In A.E. Blackhurst & W.H. Berdine (eds.), *An introduction to special education*. Boston, Mass.: Little, Brown & Co.

Cattell, P. (1940). *The measurement of intelligence of infants and young children*. New York, N.Y.: Johnson Reprint Corporation.

Chabot, M. (1977). *Assessment handbook: Project HAPI*. San Diego, Calif.: San Diego County Superintendent of Schools.

Champion, R. (1979). Mainstreaming—least restrictive environment. *Journal of Visual Impairment & Blindness*, **73** (6), p. 247.

Chandler, L. (1979). Gross and fine motor development. In M.A. Cohen & P.J. Gorss, *The developmental resource* (Vol 1). New York, N.Y.: Grune & Stratton.

Chandler, M. & Boynes, M. (1982). Social-cognitive development. In B.B. Wolman & G. Stricker (eds.), *Handbook of developmental psychology* (pp. 387-402). Englewood Cliffs, N.J.: Prentice Hall.

Chapman, A. & Cramer, M. (1973). *Dance and the blind child*. New York, N.Y.: American Dance Guild, Inc.

Chase, J.B. (1972). *Retrolental fibroplasia and autistic symptomatology*. New York, N.Y.: American Foundation for the Blind, Inc.

Chiago, R.K. (1981). Making education work for the American Indian. *Theory into Practice*, **22** (1), pp. 20-25.

Children's Defense Fund. (1982). *America's children and their families*. Washington, D.C.: Author.

Chinn, P.C. (1979). The exceptional minority child: Issues and some answers. *Exceptional Children*, **45**, pp. 532-36.

Cholden, L.S. (1958). *A psychiatrist works with blindness*. New York, N.Y.: American Foundation for the Blind, Inc.

Chrisholm, B. (1966). Evaluation and treatment. In Seigel, I.M. (ed.), *Posture in the Blind*. Research Series 15. New York, N.Y.: American Foundation for the Blind, Inc.

Christensen, C. (1975). Sailing without sight. *Dialogue*, **14** (2), pp. 77-78.

Chumlea, W.C. (1982). Physical growth in adolescence. In B.B. Wolman & G. Stricker (eds.), *Handbook of developmental psychology* (pp. 471-485). Englewood Cliffs, N.J.: Prentice Hall.

Claiborne, R. (1977). The first Americans. *Time-Life Books*. New York, N.Y.: Holt, Rinehart and Winston.

Clarke, A.M. & Clarke, A.D.B. (1976). *Early experience: Myth and evidence*. New York, N.Y.: Free Press.

Clark, H. & Clark, D. (1978). *Developmental and adapted physical education*, 2nd edition. Englewood Cliffs, N.J.: Prentice-Hall.

Clark, K. (1935). Making normal contacts available for school children. *Teachers Forum*, **8** (2), pp. 31-32, 40.

Cobb, E.S. (1977). Learning through listening: A new approach. *Journal of Visual Impairment & Blindness*, **71**, (5), pp. 206-253.

Code of braille textbook formats techniques. (1977). Louisville, Ky.: American Printing House for the Blind.

Cohen, L.B., DeLoach, J.S. & Strauss, M.S. (1979). Infant visual perception. In J.D. Osofsky (ed.), *Handbook of infant development* (pp. 393-438). New York, N.Y.: John Wiley & Sons.

Coker, G. (1979). A comparison of self-concepts and academic achievement of visually handicapped children enrolled in a regular school and in a residential school. *Education of the Visually Handicapped*, **11** (13), pp. 67-74.

Coleman, C.L. & Weinstock, R.E. (1984). Physically handicapped blind people: Adaptive mobility techniques. *Journal of Visual Impairment & Blindness*, **78**, (3), pp. 113-117.

Colenbrander, A. (1977). Dimensions of visual performance. *Archives of American Academy of Ophthalmology*, **83**, pp. 332-337.

Coles, R. (1967a). Migrants, sharecropper, mountaineers. Vol. II of *Children of Crisis*. Boston, Mass.: Little, Brown & Co.

Coles, R. (1967b). The south goes north. Vol. III of *Children of Crisis*. Boston, Mass.: Little, Brown & Co.

Coles, R. (1977). Eskimos, Chicanos, Indians. Vol. IV of *Children of Crisis*. Boston, Mass.: Little, Brown & Co.

Connolly, A.J., Nachtman, W., & Pritchett, E.M. (1971). *Key math diagnostic arithmetic test*. Circle Pines, Minn.: American Guidance Service.

Connor, F.P., Rusalem, H. & Baker, J. W. (eds.). (1971). *Professional preparation of educators of crippled children: Competency based programming*. A special study institute held December 8-11, New York, N.Y.: Teachers College Press.

Connor, F., Williamson, G. & Siepp, J. (eds.). (1978). *Program guide for infants and toddlers with neuromotor and other developmental disabilities*. New York, N.Y.: Teachers College Press.

Coombs, V.H. (1967). Guidelines for teaching arts and crafts to blind children in the elementary grades. *International Journal for the Education of the Blind*, **16**, pp. 79-83.

Cooper, J.O. (1981). *Measuring behavior* (2nd edition). Columbus, Ohio.: Charles E. Merrill.

Corbin, C.B. & Lindsey, R. (1979). *Fitness for life*. Glenview, Ill.: Scott, Foresman and Company.

Cordasco, F. (1981). Italian Americans: Historical and present perspectives. *Theory into Practice*. **22** (1), pp. 58-62.

Corder, W.O., & Walker, D.L. (1969). The effects of Public Law 89-10, Title VI on programs for visually impaired children. *Education of the Visually Handicapped*, **1** (2), pp. 52-57.

Corn, A. (1977). *Monucular Mac*. New York, N.Y.: National Association for the Visually Handicapped.

Corn, A. (1983). Visual function: A model for individuals with low vision. *Journal of Visual Impairment & Blindness*, **77** (8), pp. 373-377.

Corn, A.L. & Scholl, G.T. (1984). Education of gifted/visually handicapped children. In G.T. Scholl (ed.), *Quality services for blind and visually handicapped learners: Statements of position*. Reston, Va.: Council for Exceptional Children.

Correa, V.I. (1982). Development of reach-grasp behavior in young blind, severely/profoundly retarded children as an effect of a graduated prompting treatment package with noise-making toys. Unpublished doctoral dissertation, George Peabody College.

Correa, V.I., & Hill, E.W. (in preparation). Developmental skills related to O&M.

Corwin, A.F. (1982). The numbers game: Estimates of illegal aliens in the United States, 1970-1981. *Law and Contemporary Problems*, **45** (2), pp. 223-297.

Council for Exceptional Children. (1966). *Professional standards for personnel in the education of exceptional children*. Reston, Va.: Author.

Cowen, E.L., Underberg, R.P., Verillo, R.T., & Benham, F.G. (1961). *Adjustment to visual disability in adolescence*. New York, N.Y.: American Foundation for the Blind, Inc.

Craft, D. (1981). Athletics for visually handicapped participants. *Nautilus Magazine*, **3** (5), pp. 22-23.

Crane, J. (1978). *Sewing*. New York, N.Y.: Center for Independent Living.

Cratty, B.J. (1967). *Developmental sequences of perceptual motor tasks*. Freeport, N.Y.: Educational Activities, Inc.

Cratty, B.J., & Sam, R.S. (1968). *The body-image of blind children*. New York, N.Y.: American Foundation for the Blind, Inc.

Crook, C.K. (1978). Taste perception in the newborn infant. *Infant Behavior and Development*, **1**, pp. 52-69.

Curtis, J. B. (1907). Education of the blind in the Chicago public schools. *Outlook for the Blind*, **1** (2), pp. 35-37.

Curtis, J.B. (1908). Education of the blind in the Chicago public schools. *Outlook for the Blind*, **2**, (1), pp. 48-49.

Cutsforth, T. (1951). *The blind in school and society*. New York, N.Y.: American Foundation for the Blind, Inc.

Dauer, V.P. & Pangray, R.P. (1979). *Dynamic physical education for elementary school children.* Minneapolis, Minn.: Burgess Publishing Co.

DeVries, H. (1980).*Physiology of exercise for physical education and athletics,* 3rd edition. Dubuque, Iowa: Wm C Brown.

DeWeerd, J., & Cole, A. (1976). Handicapped children's early education program. *Exceptional Children, 43,* (3), pp. 155-157.

DHEW (August 23, 1977). *Implementation of Part B of the Education of the Handicapped Act.* Federal Register, 42 (163), 42490.

Dickens, C. (1907). *American notes and pictures from Italy.* New York, N.Y.: E.P. Dutton & Co.

Dickman, I.R. (1975). *Sex education and family life for visually handicapped children and youth: A resource guide.* New York, N.Y.: SIECUS and AFB.

Dickman, I.R. & Gordon, S. (1983). *Getting help for a disabled child: Advice from parents.* Public Affairs Pamphlet No. 615. New York, N.Y.: Public Affairs Committee, Inc.

Diderot, D. (1749). *Lettre sur les aveugles a l'usage de ceux qui voient.* London.

Dobzhansky, T. (1973). *Genetic diversity and human equality.* New York, N.Y.: Basic Books.

Dodds, A.G., Armstrong, J.D., & Shingledecker, C.A. (1981). The Nottingham obstacle detector: Development and evaluation. *Journal of Visual Impairment & Blindness, 75* (5), pp. 203-209.

Doll, E.A. (1953). *A measurement of social competence: A manual for the Vineland Social Maturity Scale.* Educational Test Bureau, Educational Publishers, Inc.

Doll, E.A. (1966). *Preschool attainment record.* Circle Pines, Minn.: American Guidance Service.

Doorlag, D.M., & Doorlag, D.H. (1983). Cassette braille: A new communication tool for blind people. *Journal of Visual Impairment & Blindness, 77* (4), pp. 158-161.

Dreyer, P.H. (1982). Sexuality during adolescence. In B.B. Wolman & G. Stricker (eds.), *Handbook of developmental psychology.* Englewood Cliffs, N.J.: Prentice Hall.

Dronek, M. (1977). *Assessment tool comparison,* Sacramento, Calif.: California State Department of Education, Southwestern Region Deaf-Blind Center.

Dubanoski, R.A., Inaba, M., Gerkewicz, B.A. (1983). Corporal punishment in schools: Myths, problems and alternatives. *Child Abuse and Neglect: The International Journal, 7* (3), pp. 271-278.

DuBose, R.F. (1976). Developmental needs in blind infants. *The New Outlook for the Blind, 70* (2), pp. 49-52.

DuBose, R.F. & Langley, M.B. (1977). *Developmental activities screening inventory.* Boston, Mass.: Teaching Resources.

Dubowitz, L.M., Dubowitz, V., Morante, A., & Verghote, M. (1980). Visual function in the preterm and full-term newborn infant. *Developmental Medicine and Child Neurology, 22,* pp. 465-475.

Duehl, A. (1973). The effect of creative dance movement on large muscle control and balance in congenitally blind children. *Journal of Visual Impairment & Blindness, 73* (4), pp. 127-133.

Duncan, D., Sbardellati, E., Maheady, L. & Sainato, D. (1981). Nondiscriminating assessment of severely physically handicapped individuals. *Journal of the Association for the Severely Handicapped, 6* pp. 17-22.

Dunn, L. & Markwardt, F. (1970). *Peabody individual achievement test.* Circle Pines, Minn.: American Guidance Service.

Dye, L.S. (1983). A study of augmented modes of feedback used by blind children to learn a selected motor task. Unpublished doctoral dissertation, New York University.

Edelman, M.W. (1980). *Portrait of inequality: Black and white children in America.* Washington, D.C.: Children's Defense Fund.

Efron, M. & DuBooff, B.R. (1975). *A vision guide for teachers of deaf-blind children.* Raleigh, N.C.: North Carolina Department of Public Instruction.

Eichel, V.J. (1978). Mannerisms of the blind: A review of the literature. *Journal of Visual Impairment & Blindness, 72* (4), pp. 125-130.

Eichel, V.J. (1979). A taxonomy for mannerisms of blind children. *Journal of Visual Impairment & Blindness, 73* (5), pp. 167-168.

Eisenberg, R.B. (1976). *Auditory competence in early life. The roots of communicative behavior.* Baltimore, Md.: University Park Press.

Elkholy, A. (1974). *The Arab Muslims in the United States: Religion and assimilation.* New Haven, Conn.: College and University Press Associations.

Elkind, D. & Flavell, J.H. (eds.). (1969). *Studies in cognitive development: Essays in honor of Jean Piaget.* New York, N.Y.: Oxford University Press.

Emerick, L. & Hatten, J. (1979). *Diagnosis and evaluation in speech pathology* (2nd edition). Englewood Cliffs, N.J.: Prentice-Hall.

Endo, G.T. & Della-Piana, C.K. (1981). Japanese Americans, pluralism and the model minority myth. *Theory into Practice, 20* (1), pp. 45-51.

Endress, D.T. (1968). Developmental levels and parental attitudes of preschool blind children in Colorado. Unpublished doctoral dissertation, Colorado State College.

Engelmann, S.E. (1967). *The basic concept inventory.* Chicago, Ill.: Follett Educational Corporation.

Enright, K.H. (1953). Education for the blind in the public schools of California. *The New Outlook for the Blind, 47* (10), pp. 6-10.

Erikson, E.H. (1963). *Childhood and society* (2nd ed.). New York, N.Y.: W.W. Norton & Company.

Erikson, E.H. (1968). *Identity: Youth and crisis.* New York, N.Y.: W.W. Norton & Company.

Erikson, E.H. (ed.). (1978). *Adulthood.* New York, N.Y.: W.W. Norton & Company.

Fantz, R. (1974). Pattern discrimination and selective attention as determinants of perceptual development from birth. In A.H. Kidd & J.L. Rivoire (eds.), *Perceptual development in children.* New York, N.Y.: International Press.

Fantz, R.L., Fagan, J.F. & Miranda, S.B. (1975). Early visual selectivity as a function of pattern variables, previous exposure, age from birth, and conceptual and expected cognitive deficits. In L. Cohen & P. Salapatek (eds.), *Infant perception from sensation to cognition.* New York, N.Y.: Academic Press.

Farkas, G.M., Sherick, R.B., Matson, J.C. & Loebig, M. (1981). Social skills training of a blind child through differential reinforcement. *The Behavior Therapist, 4,* pp. 24-26.

Farley, P. (1969). *A teacher's guide to creative dance.* Sydney, Australia: A.H. & A.W. Reed.

Farmer, L.W. (1975). Travel in adverse weather using electronic mobility guidance devices. *The New Outlook for the Blind, 69,* (10), pp. 433-439.

Farmer, L.W. (1980). Mobility devices. In R. Welsh, & B. Blasch (eds.), *Foundations of orientation and mobility.* New York, N.Y.: American Foundation for the Blind, Inc.

Faye, E.E. (1970). *The low-vision patient.* New York, N.Y.: Grune & Stratton.

Faye, E.E. (ed.). (1984). *Clinical low vision.* (2nd edition). Boston: Little, Brown & Co.

Featherstone, H. (1980). *A difference in the family.* New York, N.Y.: Basic Books.

Fein, G.G. (1978). *Child development.* Englewood Cliffs, N.J.: Prentice Hall.

Feld, G.F. & Hall, C.C. (1980). The CCTV as an art tool. *Journal of Visual Impairment & Blindness, 74* (4), pp. 151-153.

Fernandez, M.C. (1983). An analysis of the neuropsychological and behavioral characteristics of visual functioning of the high-risk, premature neonate in the neonatal intensive care unit relative to conceptual age. Unpublished doctoral dissertation, The University of Texas at Austin.

Ferrell, K.A. (1980). Can infants use the Sonicguide™? Two years experience of Project VIEW. *Journal of Visual Impairment & Blindness, 74* (2), pp. 209-220.

Ferrell, K.A. (1980). Orientation and mobility for preschool children: What we have and what we need. *Journal of Visual Impairment & Blindness, 72* (2), pp. 59-66.

Ferrell, K.A. (1984). *Parenting preschoolers: Suggestions for raising young blind and visually impaired children.* New York, N.Y.: American Foundation for the Blind, Inc.

Ferrell, K.A. (1984). A second look at sensory aids in early childhood. *Education of the Visually Handicapped,* 16, (3), pp. 83-101.

Ferrell, K.A. (1984). Visual perceptual performance of visually handicapped infants with and without the use of binaural sensory aids. Doctoral dissertation, University of Pittsburgh, 1983. Dissertation Abstracts International, 44.000. (University Microfilms No. 83-27,684).

Ferrell, K.A. (1985). *Reach out and teach.* New York, N.Y.: American Foundation for the Blind, Inc.

Ferrini, P., Matthews, B.L., Foster, J. & Workman, J. (1980). *The interdependent community: Collaborative planning for handicapped youth (Leader's guide).* Cambridge, Mass.: Technical Education Research Centers.

Fewell, R.R., Langley, M.B., & Roll, A. (1982). Informant versus direct screening: A preliminary comparative study. *Diagnostique,* 7, pp. 163-167.

Fieandt, K. (1966). *The world of perception.* Homewood, Ill.: Dorsey Press.

Fieber, N.M. (1977). Sensorimotor cognitive assessment and curriculum for the multihandicapped child. In *The severely and profoundly handicapped child, Proceedings from the 1977 Statewide Institute for Educators of the Severely and Profoundly Handicapped,* pp. 46-61.

Finn, P.J. (1985). *Helping children learn to read.* New York, N.Y.: Random House.

Finnie, N. (1975). Handling the young cerebral palsied child at home. New York, N.Y.: E.P. Dutton.

Flavell, J.H. (1963). *The developmental psychology of Jean Piaget.* New York, N.Y.: Van Nostrand-Reinhold.

Fletcher, J.F. (1980). Spatial representation in blind children. 1. Development compared to sighted children. *Journal of Visual Impairment & Blindness,* 74 (10), pp. 381-385.

Fletcher, J.F. (1981). Spatial representation in blind children 3. Effects of individual differences. *Journal of Visual Impairment & Blindness,* 75, (2) pp. 46-49.

Flexner, R., & Martin, A. (1978). Sheltered workshops and vocational training settings. In M.E. Snell (ed.), *Systematic instruction of the moderately and severely handicapped.* Columbus, Ohio: Charles E. Merrill.

Florida Association for Education of the Visually Handicapped Survey of Teachers of Visually Handicapped. (1977). Unpublished report.

Folio, M.R. & Fewell, R. (1983). *Peabody developmental scales and activity cards.* Allen, Tex.: DLM-Teaching Resources.

Ford, A., Brown, L., Pumpian, I., Baumgart, D., Schroeder, J., & Loomis, R. (1981). *Strategies for developing individualized recreation/leisure plans for adolescent and young adult severely handicapped students.* Madison, Wis.: Madison Metropolitan School District.

Fortner, E.N. (1945). Oregon state supervisory program for the visually handicapped. *The New Outlook for the Blind,* 39, (1), pp. 3.

Foulke, E., Amsler, C.H., Nolan, C.Y., & Bixler, R.H. (1962). The comprehension of rapid speech by the blind. *Exceptional Children,* 29 (2), pp. 134-141.

Foulke, E. (1968). Listening comprehension as a function of word rate. *Journal of Communication,* 18 (3), pp. 198-206.

Foulke, E. (1971). Nonvisual communication: XI-reading by touch. *Education of the Visually Handicapped,* 3, (2), pp. 55-58.

Foulke, E. (1974). Significance of time-compressed recorded speech for blind readers. In S. Duker (ed.), *Time-compressed speech* (Volume 3). Metuchen, N.J.: Scarecrow Press.

Foulke, E. & Uhde, T. (1975). Do blind children need sex education? *Sex education for the visually handicapped in schools and agencies. . .selected papers.* New York, N.Y.: American Foundation for the Blind, Inc.

Foukle, E. (1981). Impact of science and technology on the early years. *Journal of Visual Impairment & Blindness,* 75, (3), pp. 101-108.

Foxx, R.M. & Azrin, N.H. (1973). *Toilet training the retarded: A rapid program for day and nighttime independent toileting.* Champaign, Ill.: Research Press.

Fraiberg, S., & Freedman, D. (1964). Studies in the ego development of the congenitally blind child. *The psychoanalytic study of the child,* 19, pp. 113-169.

Fraiberg, S., Smith, M., & Adelson, E. (1969). An educational program for blind infants. *Journal of Special Education,* 3, pp. 121-139.

Fraiberg, S. (1977). *Insights from the blind: Comparative studies of blind and sighted infants.* New York, N.Y.: Basic Books, Inc.

Fraiberg, S. (1977). Smiling and stranger reaction in blind infants. In J. Hellmuth (ed.), *Exceptional infant.* New York, N.Y.: Brunner-Mazel.

Fraiberg, S., Smith, M., & Adelson, E. (1966). An educational program for blind infants. *Journal of Special Education,* 3, (2), pp. 121-139.

Frampton, M.E. & Kerney, E. (1953). *The residential school.* New York, N.Y.: Edwin Gould Printery.

Frankenbert, W.K., Dodds, J.B., & Fandal, A.W. (1967). *Denver developmental screening test.* Denver, Colo.: Lodoca.

Franks, F. (1983). Applying educational research to maps and graphics for the visually handicapped. In J.W. Wiedel (ed.), *Proceedings of the first international symposium on maps and graphics for the visually handicapped.* Washington, D.C.: Association of American Geographers.

Franks, F. (1979). The tactile modality in adapting and developing science materials. In H. Hoffman & Ricker (eds.), *Sourcebook, science education and the physically handicapped.* Washington, D.C.: National Science Teachers Association.

Franks, F.L. & Nolan, C.Y. (1970). Development of geographical concepts in blind children. *Education of the Visually Handicapped,* 2, (1), pp. 1-8.

Freund, C. (1969). Teaching art to the blind child integrated with sighted children. *The New Outlook for the Blind,* 63 (7), pp. 205-210.

Freund, E.D. (1970). *Longhand writing for the blind.* Louisville, Ky.: American Printing House for the Blind.

Friedman, G. (1976). Distance low vision aids for primary level school age children. *Journal of Visual Impairment & Blindness,* 70 (3), pp. 376-379.

Friedman, J. & Pasnak, R. (1973). Attainment of classification and concepts by blind and sighted subjects. *Education of the Visually Handicapped,* 5 (2), pp. 55-62.

Friedman, S. (1972). Habituation and recovery of visual response in the alert human newborn. *Journal of Experimental Child Psychology,* 13 (2), pp. 339-349.

Friedrich, O. (August 15, 1983). What do babies know? *Time,* pp. 70-76.

Frith, G.H. & Warren, L.D. (1984). Adapted canoeing for the handicapped. *Teaching Exceptional Children,* pp. 219-221.

Fromm, E. (1959). The creative attitude. In H. Anderson (ed.), *Creativity and its cultivation.* New York, N.Y.: Harper & Row.

Frostig, M. & Horne, D. (1964). *The Frostig program for the development of visual perception: Teachers guide.* Chicago, Ill.: Follett Publishing Co.

Frostig, M., LeFever, W., & Whittlesey, J.R. (1966). *Administration and scoring manual for the Marianne Frostig test of visual perception,* (rev.). Palo Alto, Calif.: Consulting Psychologists Press.

Fuchs, L.H. (1956). Some political aspects of immigration. *Law and Contemporary Problems,* 21 (2), pp. 270-283.

Furth, H.G. (1969). *Piaget and knowledge: Theoretical foundations.* Englewood Cliffs, N.J.: Prentice Hall.

Gadbaw, P.D., Dolan, M.T., & De l'Aune, W.R. (1977). Optacon skill acquisition by blind veterans. *Journal of Visual Impairment & Blindness,* 77 (1), pp. 23-28.

Gagne, R.M. (1977). *Conditions of learning* (3rd edition). New York, N.Y.: Holt, Rinehart & Winston.

Gagne, R.M. & Briggs, L.J. (1974). *Principles of instructional design.* New York, N.Y.: Holt, Rinehart & Winston.

Gallagher, J.J. (1975). *Teaching the gifted child* (2nd edition) Boston, Mass.: Allyn & Bacon.

Gallagher, P.A. & Heim, R.E. (1974). The classroom application of behavior modification principles for multiply handicapped blind students. *The New Outlook for the Blind,* **68** (10), pp. 447-453.

Gaylord-Ross, R.J. (1980). A decision model for the treatment of aberrant behavior in applied settings. In W. Sailor, B. Wilcox, & L. Brown (eds.), *Methods of instruction for severely handicapped students.* Baltimore, Md.: Paul H. Brooks.

Gearhearth, B.R. (1980). *Special Education for the 80s.* St. Louis, Mo.: C.V. Mosby.

Gelbart, S.S., Hoyt, C.S., Jastrebski, G., & Marg, E. (1982). *American Journal of Ophthalmology,* **93,** pp. 615-621.

Geldard, F.A. (1972). *The human senses.* New York, N.Y.: John Wiley & Sons.

Gendel, E.S. (1973). *Sex education of the blind.* Paper presented at Conference on the Blind Child in Social Interaction: Developing Relationships with Peers and Adults, New York.

Genensky, S.M. (1974). *Binoculars: A long ignored aid for the partially sighted.* Santa Monica, Calif.: Rand.

Genshaft, J.L., Dare, N.L., & O'Malley, P.L. (1980). Assessing the visually impaired child: A school psychology view. *Journal of Visual Impairment & Blindness,* **74** (8), pp. 344-350.

Gesell, A. & Ilg, F.L. (1946). *The child from five to ten.* New York, N.Y.: Harper & Brothers.

Gil, R.M. (1981). Puerto Rican mothers' cultural attitudes toward children's problems and toward the use of mental health services. In Martinez, H. (ed.), *Special education and the Hispanic child.* ERIC/CUE Urban Diversity Series, No. 74. New York, N.Y.: Institute for Urban and Minority Education, Teachers College, Columbia University.

Gilbeau, E. (1907). *Histoire de l'institution des jeunes aveugles.* Paris: Belise Freres.

Gilmore, F. (1956). One public school's experiment with blind children. *The New Outlook for the Blind,* **50** (2), pp. 45.

Ginsberg, A.P. (1981). Spatial filtering and vision: Implications for normal and abnormal vision. In L.M. Proenza, J. Enoch, & A. Jampolsky (eds.), *Clinical applications of visual psychophysics.* Cambridge, England: University of Cambridge.

Ginsberg, A.P., Evans, D.W., & Canna, M. (1984). Large-sample norms for contrast sensitivity. *American Journal of Optometry and Physiological Optics,* **61** (2), pp. 80-84.

Ginsburg, H. & Opper, S. (1979). *Piaget's theory of intellectual development* (2nd ed.). Englewood Cliffs, N.J.: Prentice-Hall.

Glaser, R. (1981). The future of testing. *American Psychologist,* **36,** pp. 923-936.

Glass, D.D. (1984). Sexuality and visual impairment. *SIECUS Report,* **12** (5), pp. 1-4.

Glennon, V.J., (eds.). (1981). *The mathematical education of exceptional children and youth: An interdisciplinary approach.* Reston, Va.: National Council of Teachers of Mathematics.

Glidwell, J.C., Kantor, M.B., Smith, L.M. & Steinger, L.A. (1966). Socialization and social structure in the classroom. In L.W. Hoffman & M.L. Hoffman (eds.), *Review of child development research,* Vol. II, New York, N.Y.: Russell Sage Publications.

Gliedman, J. & Roth, W. (1980). *The unexpected minority: Handicapped children in America.* New York, N.Y.: Harcourt Brace Jovanovich.

Goddard, H.H. (1912). *The Kallikak family: A study of the heredity of feeblemindedness.* New York, N.Y.: Macmillan.

Goetz, P.W. (ed.). (1984). *Britannica Book of the Year: 1984.* Chicago, Ill.: Encyclopedia Britannica, Inc.

Gold, M. (1973). Research on the vocational rehabilitation of the retarded: The present and the future. In N. Ellis (ed.), *International review of research in mental retardation* (Vol. 6). New York, N.Y.: Academic Press.

Gold, M.W. (1976). Task analysis of a complex assembly task by the retarded blind. *Exceptional Children,* **43** (2), pp. 78-84.

Goldberg, S. (1982). *Ophthalmology made ridiculously simple.* Miami, Fla.: Medmasters, Inc.

Goldie, D. (1977). The use of the C-5 laser cane by school age children. *Journal of Visual Impairment & Blindness,* **71** (8), pp. 345-348.

Goldish, L.H. & Taylor, H.E. (1974). The Optacon: A valuable device for blind persons. *The New Outlook for the Blind,* **68** (1), p. 2.

Goldstein, H. (1980). *The demography of blindness throughout the world.* New York, N.Y.: American Foundation for the Blind, Inc.

Goodrich, G. & Quillman, R. (1977). Training eccentric viewing. *Journal of Visual Impairment & Blindness,* **71** (9), pp. 377-381.

Goodrich, G. L., Bennett, R.R., Paul, H.S., & Wiley, J.K. (1980). Preliminary report on evaluation of synthetic speech for reading machines. *Journal of Visual Impairment & Blindness,* **74** (1), p. 9.

Goodstein, H.A. (1982). The reliability of criterion-referenced tests and special education: Assumed versus demonstrated. *Journal of Special Education,* **16,** pp. 37-48.

Gorham, K. (1975). A lost generation of parents. *Exceptional Children,* **41** (8), pp. 521-525.

Goswiller, R. (1975). Champions before the tee off. *The Lion,* **58** (5), pp. 20-23.

Gottesman, M.A. (1973). Conservation development in blind children. *Child Development,* **44,** pp. 824-927.

Gottesman, M. (1976). Stage development in blind children: A Piagetian view. *The New Outlook for the Blind.* **70** (3), pp. 94-100.

Graham, M.D. (1966). *Multiply impaired blind children: A national problem.* New York, N.Y.: American Foundation for the Blind, Inc.

Granger, C. & Wehman, P. (1979). Sensory stimulation. In P. Wehman (ed.), *Recreational programming for the developmentally disabled person.* Baltimore, Md.: University Park Press.

Grant, I.L.C. (1966). The challenge of modern day education of blind children and youth. *Braille Monitor,* pp. 35-40.

Grant, W.V. & Eiden, L.J. (1982). *Digest of educational statistics: 1982.* Washington, D.C.: Superintendent of Documents, U.S. Government Printing Office.

Greeley, A.M. & Rossi, P.H. (1972). *The denominational society: A sociological approach to religion in America.* Glenview, Ill.: Scott, Foresman and Co.

Green, J.L. (1981). The Louisiana Cajuns: The quest for identity through education. *Theory into Practice,* **22** (1), pp. 63-69.

Gregory, R.L. (1974). *Concepts and mechanisms of perception.* London: Duckworth.

Griffin, H.C. & Gerber, P.J. (1982). Tactual development and its implications for the education of blind children. *Education of the Visually Handicapped,* **13,** pp. 116-123.

Griffin, H.C. (1981). Motor development in congenitally blind children. *Education of the Visually Handicapped,* **7** (4), pp. 107-111.

Grossman, H. (ed.). (1983). *Classification in mental retardation.* Washington, D.C.: American Association on Mental Deficiency.

Gruber, K. & Moor, P. (eds.). *No place to go.* New York, N.Y.: American Foundation for the Blind, Inc.

Grumpelt, H.R. & Rubin, E. (1972). Speed listening skill by the blind as a function of training. *The Journal of Educational Research,* **65,** pp. 10.

Guerin, G.R. & Maier, A.S. (1983). *Informal assessment in education.* Palo Alto, Calif.: Mayfield Publishing Co.

Guess, D. (1969). The influence of visual and ambulation restrictions on stereotyped behavior. *American Journal of Mental Deficiency,* **70,** pp. 542-547.

Guess, D., Sailor, W., & Baer, D. (1974). To teach language to retarded children. In R.L. Schiefelbusch & L.L. Loyd (eds.), *Language perspective: Acquisition, retardation, and intervention.* Baltimore, Md.: University Park Press.

Guess, D., Sailor, W., & Baer, D. (1976). *Functional speech and language training for the severely handicapped. Part 2: Actions with persons and things.* Lawrence, Kans.: H&H Enterprises.

Guess, D., Sailor, W., & Baer, D. (1977). *Functional speech and language training for the severely handicapped. Part 3: Possession and color.* Lawrence, Kans.: H&H Enterprises.

Guess, D., Sailor, W. & Baer, D. (1978). *Functional speech and language training for the severely handicapped. Part 4: Size, relation & location.* Lawrence, Kans.: H&H Enterprises, Inc.

Guldager, L., Hamill, M., & McGlamery, R. (1983). Group homes for severely multiply handicapped persons with visual problems. *Journal of Visual Impairment & Blindness,* **77** (1), pp. 4-8.

Haith, M.M. & Campos, J.J. (1977). Human Infancy. *Annual Review of Psychology,* **28**, pp. 251-293.

Hale, Robert (1976). A new adventure for the blind: Sailing without sight. *The Lion,* **59** (5), pp. 16-17.

Hall, A. (1981). Mental images and the cognitive development of the congenitally blind. *Journal of Visual Impairment & Blindness,* **75** (7), pp. 281-285.

Hall, A. (1983). Methods of equivalence grouping by the congenitally blind: Implications for education. *Journal of Visual Impairment & Blindness,* **77**, (4), pp. 172-174.

Hall, C.S. (1954). *A primer of Freudian psychology.* New York, N.Y.: World.

Hall, E.T. (1969). *The hidden dimension.* New York, N.Y.: Doubleday & Company.

Hall, R.V. (1975). *Managing behavior. Part 2: Behavior modification—Basic principles.* Lawrence, Kans.: H&H Enterprises.

Hallenbeck, J. (1954). Two essential factors in the development of young blind children. *The New Outlook for the Blind,* **48** (9), pp. 308-315.

Hammer, E. (1982). The development of language in the deaf-blind multihandicapped child: Progression of instructional methods. In D. Tweedie & E.H. Shroyer (eds.), *The multihandicapped hearing impaired.* Washington, D.C.: Gallaudet College Press.

Hanninen, K.A. (1976). The influence of preference of texture on the accuracy of tactile discrimination. *Education of the Visually Handicapped,* **8** (2), pp. 44-52.

Hanninen, K. (1979). *Teaching the visually handicapped* (2nd edition). Detroit, Mich.: Blindness Publications.

Hapeman, L. (1967). Developmental concepts of blind children between the ages of three and six as they relate to orientation and mobility. *The International Journal for the Education of the Blind,* **17** (2), pp. 41-48.

Hapeman, L. (1977). Reservations about the effect of P.L. 94-142 on the education of visually handicapped children. *Education of the Visually Handicapped,* **9** (3), pp. 33-36.

Haring, N. & Billingsley, F. (1984). Systems-change strategies to ensure the future of integration. In N. Certo, N. Haring, & R. York, *Public school integration of severely handicapped students.* Baltimore, Md.: Paul H. Brooks Publishing Company.

Harley, R.K. (1963). *Verbalism among blind children.* (Research Series #10). New York, N.Y.: American Foundation for the Blind, Inc.

Harley, R.K. & Altmeyer, E.A. (1982). Cerebral palsy and associated visual defects. *Education of the Visually Handicapped,* **14** (1), pp. 41-49.

Harley, R.K., Henderson, F.M., & Truan, M.B. (1979). *The teaching of braille reading.* Springfield, Ill.: Charles C Thomas.

Harley, R.K., Wood, T.A., & Merbler, J.B. (1981). *Peabody mobility scales.* Chicago, Ill.: Stoelting Company.

Hart, V. (1980). Environmental orientation and human mobility. In R. Welsh & B. Blasch (eds.), *Foundations of orientation and mobility.* New York, N.Y.: American Foundation of the Blind, Inc.

Hart, V. (1983). Motor development in blind children. In M. Wurster & M.E. Mulholland (eds.), *Help me become everything I can be.* Proceedings of the North American Conference on Visually Handicapped Infants and Young Children. New York, N.Y.: American Foundation for the Blind, Inc.

Hart, V. (1977). The use of many disciplines with the severely and profoundly handicapped. In E. Sontag, J. Smith, & N. Certo (eds.), *Educational programming for the severely and profoundly handicapped.* Reston, Va: Council for Exceptional Children.

Hart, V. & Ferrell, K.A. (1983). *Effects of binaural sensory aids on the development of visual perceptual abiltiies in visually handicapped infants* (Grant No. G008200054). Washington, D.C.: U.S. Department of Education, Special Education Programs.

Hart, V. & Ferrell, K.A. (1985). Cooperative efforts in education of the visually handicapped. In G.T. Scholl (ed.), *Quality services for blind and visually handicapped learners: Statements of position.* Reston, Va.: Division for the Visually Handicapped, Council for Exceptional Children.

Hatfield, E.M. (1975). Why are they blind? *The Sight-Saving Review,* **45** (1), pp. 3-22.

Hathaway, W. (1959). *Education and health of the partially seeing child* (4th edition). New York, N.Y.: Columbia University Press.

Hatlen, P. (1976). Priorities in educational programs for visually handicapped children and youth. *DVH Newsletter.*

Hatwell, Y. (1985). *Piagetian reasoning and the blind.* New York, N.Y.: American Foundation for the Blind, Inc.

Haupt, C. (1969). Creative expression through art. *Education of the Visually Handicapped,* **1** (1), pp. 41-43.

Havighurst, R.J. (1953). *Human development and education.* New York, N.Y.: David McKay.

Havighurst, R.J. (1972). *Developmental tasks and education* (3rd ed.). New York, N.Y.: David McKay.

Hayden, A.M., Morris, K.J. & Bailey, D.B. (1977). *Effectiveness of early education for handicapped children* (Contract No. 300-76-0518). Washington, D.C.: Department of Health, Education, and Welfare, Bureau of Education for the Handicapped.

Hayes, C.S. & Weinhouse, E. (1978). Application of behavior modification to blind children. *Journal of Visual Impairment & Blindness,* **72** (4), pp. 139-146.

Hayes, S.P. (1941). *Contributions to a psychology of blindness.* New York, N.Y.: American Foundation for the Blind, Inc.

Hechinger, G. & Hechinger, F. (1984). *How to raise a street-smart child: The complete parent's guide to safety on the street and at home.* New York, N.Y.: Facts on File Publications.

Head, D.N. (1979). A comparison of self-concept scores for visually impaired adolescents in several class settings. *Education of the Visually Handicapped,* **11** (2), pp. 51-55.

Healy, A. (1983). Cerebral palsy. In Blackman, J.A. (ed.), *Medical aspects of developmental disabilities in children from birth to three.* Iowa: Department of Pediatrics, University Hospital School, The University of Iowa.

Heaney, J.P. (1984). A free and appropriate public education: Has the Supreme Court misinterpreted Congressional intent? *Exceptional Children,* **50** (5), pp. 456-62.

Hebel, D.H. & Weisel, T.N. (1963). Receptive fields of cells in striate cortex of very young visually inexperienced kittens. *Journal of Neurophysiology,* **26**, pp. 994-1002.

Heimbuch, D. (1962). The blind child in the public school. *Ohio Schools,* **40** (2), pp. 12-13.

Helge, D. (1984a). Models for serving rural students with low-incidence handicapping conditions. *Exceptional Children,* **51** (4), pp. 313-324.

Helge, D. (1984b). The state of the art of rural special education. *Exceptional Children,* pp. 294-305.

Henderson, F.M. (1967). The effects of character recognition training on braille reading. Unpublished specialist in education thesis, Nashville, George Peabody College for Teachers.

Henderson, F.M. (1973). Communication skills. In Berthold Lowenfield (ed.), *The visually handicapped child in school* (pp. 218-219). New York, N.Y.: The John Day Co.

Henderson, R.W., Bergan, J.R. & Hurt, M. Jr. (1972). Development and validation of the Henderson Environmental Learning Process Scale. *Journal of Social Psychology,* **88**, pp. 185-196.

Herbers, J. (Nov. 4, 1981). The mood has changed, along with much else. *The New York Times,* Section E, p. 5.

Hicks, S. (1980). Relationship and sexual problems of the visually handicapped. *Sexuality and Disability,* **3** (3).

Higgins, L.C. (1973). *Classification in congenitally blind children.* (Research Series, No. 25). New York: American Foundation for the Blind, Inc.

Higham, J. (1957). American immigration policy in historical perspective. *Law and Contemporary Problems,* 21 (2), pp. 213-235.

Hill, E.W. (1970). The formation of concepts involved in body position in space. *Education of the Visually Handicapped,* 2 (4), pp. 112-114.

Hill, E.W. (1971). The formation of concepts involved in body position in space, Part II. *Education of the Visually Handicapped,* 3 (1), pp. 21-24.

Hill, E.W. (1981). *Hill performance test on selected positional concepts.* Chicago: Stoelting Company.

Hill, E.W. & Ponder, P. (1976). *Orientation and mobility techniques: A guide for the practitioner.* New York, N.Y.: American Foundation for the Blind, Inc.

Hill, E.W. & Blasch, B.B. (1980). Concept development. In R.L. Welsh & B.B. Blasch (eds.), *Foundations of orientation and mobility* (pp. 265-290). New York, N.Y.: American Foundation for the Blind, Inc.

Hill, E.W. & Hill, M.M. (1980). Revision and validation of a test for assessing the spatial conceptual abilities of visually impaired children. *Journal of Visual Impairment & Blindness,* 74 (10), pp. 373-380.

Hill, J. (1982). Vocational training. In L. Sternberg & G. Adams. *Educating severely and profoundly handicapped students.* Rockville, Md: Aspen Systems Corporation.

Hirshoren, A. & Schnittjer, C.J. (1983). Behavior problems in blind children and youth: A prevalence study. *Psychology in the Schools,* 20, pp. 197-201.

Hively, Wells, & Reynolds (eds.) (1975) *Domain-Referenced testing in special education.* Minn.: Leadership Training Institute/Special Education, University of Minnesota.

Hoben, M. & Lindstrom, V. (1980). Evidence of isolation in the mainstream. *Journal of Visual Impairment & Blindness,* 74 (8), pp. 289-292.

Hodapp, R.M. & Mueller, E. (1982). Early social development. In Wolman, B.B. & G. Stricker (eds.). *Handbook of developmental psychology* (pp. 284-300). Englewood Cliffs, N.J.: Prentice-Hall.

Hofstetter, R.R. (1982). Economic underdevelopment and the population explosion: Implications for U.S. immigration policy. *Law and Contemporary Problems,* 45 (2), pp. 55-77.

Holland, L. (1971). How to deal with blindisms. *Long Cane News,* 4 (5), pp. 24-27.

Holman, I.J. & Scholl, G.T. (1982). Competency movement in special education for the visual handicapped: Status and issues. *Educational Horizons,* 60 (3).

Holman, I.J. (1983). Competencies for teachers of the visually handicapped as perceived by administrators. Unpublished doctoral dissertation. The University of Michigan, Ann Arbor, Mich.

Holmes, R.B. (1967). Training residual vision in adolescents educated previously as nonvisual. Unpublished master's thesis, Illinois State University.

Hoshmand, L.T. (1975). "Blindisms": Some observations and propositons. *Education of the Visually Handicapped,* 3, pp. 37-40.

Hoshmand, L.T. (1975). Blindisms: Some observations and propositions. *Education of the Visually Handicapped.* 7 (2), pp. 56-60.

Howe, S.G. (1866). *Address: at the laying of the cornerstone of the New York Institution for the Blind at Batavia* (pp. 165-187). Boston, Mass.: Walker, Fuller & Co.

Howe, S.G. (1840). In *Eighth annual report of the trustees of the Perkins Institution and Massachusetts Asylum for the Blind,* Appendix A. Boston, Mass.: John H. Eastburn.

Howe, S.G. (1851). *Annual report of the trustees of the Perkins Intitution.* Cambridge, Mass.: Metcalf and Co.

Howe, S.G. (1871). In *Proceedings of the second convention of American Instructors of the Blind.* Ind.: Indianapolis Printing and Publishing House.

Hoyt, K. (1985). The concept of career education: Implications for blind/visually impaired persons. *Journal of Visual Impairment & Blindness,* 79 (10), pp. 487-489.

Hubel, D.H. & Wiesel, T.N. (1979). Brain mechanisms of vision. In R.L. Atkinson (ed.), *Mind and behavior.* San Francisco, Calif.: W.H. Freeman, Co.

Huckins, A. (1965). Teaching handwriting to the blind student. *The New Outlook for the Blind,* 59 (2), pp. 63-65.

Hunt, J.M. (1961). *Intelligence and experience.* New York, N.Y.: The Ronald Press Company.

Hyer, R. (1979). Interpersonal behavior of blind and sighted adolescents in public schools and residential schools. Unpublished doctoral dissertation, University of Georgia.

Hyman, I.A. (1980). Corporal punishment in the schools: America's officially sanctioned brand of child abuse. In G.J. Williams & J. Money. (eds.), *Traumatic abuse and neglect of children at home.* (pp. 33-43). Baltimore Md.: The Johns Hopkins University Press.

Igarashi, N. (1971). Ocular autostimulation of preschool blind children. *Bulletin of the Tokyo Metropolitan Rehabilitation Center for the Physically and Mentally Handicapped,* pp. 39-45.

Ilg, F.L. & Ames, L.B. (1955). *Child behavior.* New York, N.Y.: Harper.

Illingworth, W.H. (1910). *History of the education of the blind.* London: Sampson Low, Marston & Co.

Illinois Office of Education. (1974). *A curriculum guide for the development of body and sensory awareness for the visually impaired.* Springfield, Ill.: Author.

Inkster, W. (1977). *Personal management: behavioral objectives for teaching older adventitiously blind individuals.* New York, N.Y.: New York Infirmary/Center for Independent Living.

Introduction to Ophthalmology. American Academy of Ophthalmology. (1980). San Francisco, Calif.: Author.

Irwin, R. B. (1913-1914). Classes for the Blind. *Annual Report to the Board of Education* (pp. 42-46). Cleveland.

Irwin, R.B. (1955). *As I saw it.* New York, N.Y.: American Foundation for the Blind, Inc.

Itinerant teaching service for blind children: Proceedings of a national work session held at Bear Mountain, New York, August 20-24, 1956. (1957). New York, N.Y.: American Foundation for the Blind, Inc.

Jacobson, W. (1979). Complementary travel aids for blind persons: The Sonicguide™ used with a dog guide. *Journal of Visual Impairment & Blindness,* 73 (1), pp. 10-12.

Jaffe, L.L. (1956). The philosophy of our immigration law. *Law and Contemporary Problems,* 21 (2), pp. 358-375.

Jamieson, J.D. (1984). Attitudes of educators toward the handicapped. In R.L. Jones, (ed.), *Attitudes and attitude change in special education* (pp. 206-222). Reston, Va.: Council for Exceptional Children.

Jan, J., Freeman, R., & Scott, E. (1977). *Visual impairment in children and adolescents.* New York, N.Y.: Grune & Stratton.

Jastak, J.F. & Jastak, S. (1965). *Wide range achievement test.* Wilmington, Del.: Guidance Associates.

Jensen, A.R. (1973). *Educability and group differences.* New York, N.Y.: Harper & Row.

Joffe, L.S. & Vaughn, B.E. (1982). Infant-mother attachment: Theory, assessment, and implication for development. In B.B. Wolman & G. Stricker (eds.), *Handbook of developmental psychology.* Englewood Cliffs, N.J.: Prentice-Hall.

Johnson, O.G. (ed.). (1977). *Tests and measurement in child devlopment: Handbook I and II.* San Francisco, Calif.: Jossey-Bass.

Johnson, Y. (1961). *A blind child becomes a member of your class.* New York, N.Y.: American Foundation for the Blind, Inc.

Jones, C.R. (1961). Art for the blind and partially seeing. *Seeing Arts,* 60, pp. 21-22.

Jones, J. W. (1953). Developments in Oregon's program for educating blind children. *Exceptional Children,* 19 (4), pp. 131-134, 142.

Jones, J.W. (1962). Problems in defining and classifying blindness. *The New Outlook for the Blind*, **56,** (4), pp. 115-121.

Jones, J.W. and Collins, A.P. (1966). *Educational programs for visually handicapped children*. Washington, D.C.: U.S. Government Printing Office.

Jones, L. (1984). Career development is a team effort. Unpublished presentation, Honolulu, Hawaii.

Jones, R.L & Gruskin, S. (1984). Attitudes and attitude change in special education. In R.L. Jones, (ed.), *Attitudes and attitude change in special education: Theory and practice* (pp. 1-20). Reston, Va.: Council for Exceptional Children.

Jones, R.L., Lavine, K., & Sheel, J. (1972). Blind children integrated in classrooms with sighted children. *The New Outlook for the Blind*, **66** (3), pp. 75-80.

Jose, R. (1983). *Understanding low vision*. New York, N.Y.: American Foundation for the Blind, Inc.

Joyce, M. (1973). *First steps in teaching creative dance—A handbook for teachers of children K-6th grade*. Palo Alto, Calif.: National Press Books.

Juurmaa, J. (1967). *Ability structure and loss of vision*. New York, N.Y.: American Foundation for the Blind, Inc.

Kagan, J. (1972). Do infants think? *Scientific American*, **226,** pp. 74-82.

Kagan, J. (1984). *The nature of the child*. New York, N.Y.: Basic Books.

Kahn, H.A. & Moorhead, H.B. (1973). *Statistics on blindness in the model reporting area 1969-1970*. DHEW Pub. No. (NIH) 73-427. Washington, D.C.: Superintendent of Documents, U.S. Government Printing Office.

Kang-Ning, C. (1981). Education for Chinese and Indochinese. *Theory into Practice*, **22** (1), pp. 35-44.

Kappan, D. (1971). Orientation and mobility program. Unpublished manuscript, South Dakota Rehabilitation Center for the Blind.

Karnes, M.B. & Teska, J.A. (1975). Children's response to intervention programs. In J.J. Gallagher (ed.), *The application of child development research to exceptional children*. Reston, Va.: Council for Exceptional Children.

Kay, L., Strelow, E.R., & Kay, N. (1977). Electronic spatial senses as training aids for blind children. *Journal of Visual Impairment & Blindness*, **71** (4), pp. 174-175.

Kearney, S. & Copland, R. (1979). Goal ball. *Journal of Physical Education and Recreation*, **2,** pp. 24-26.

Keilbaugh, W.S. (1977). Attitudes of classroom teachers toward their visually handicapped students. *Journal of Visual Impairment & Blindness*, **71** (10), pp. 430-434.

Kekelis, L.S. & Anderson, E.S. (1984). Family communication styles and language development. *Journal of Visual Impairment & Blindness*, **78** (2), pp. 54-65.

Keller, P.W. (1960). Major findings in the past ten years. *Journal of Communication*, **10.**

Kelley, J.D. & Ludwig, I. (1984). *Recreation programming for visually impaired children and youth*. New York, N.Y.: American Foundation for the Blind, Inc.

Kenney, A. (1983). A range of vision: Museum accommodations for visually impaired people. *Journal of Visual Impairment & Blindness*, **77** (7), pp. 325-329.

Kent, D. (1983). Finding a way through the rough years: How blind girls survive adolescence. *Journal of Visual Impairment & Blindness*, **77** (6), pp. 247-249.

Kent, L. (1974). *Language acquisition program for the retarded or multiply impaired*. Champaign, Ill.: Research Press.

Keogh, B.K. (1973). Perceptual and cognitive styles: Implication for special education. *First Review of Special Education*, pp. 83-109.

Kephart, J. & Kephart, C.P. (1973). The Kephart scale. Unpublished manuscript. Florida School for the Deaf and Blind.

Kephart, J., Kephart, C.P., & Schwartz, G.C. (1974). A journey into the world of the blind child. *Exceptional Children*, **40** (6), pp. 421-427.

Kerlinger, F.N. (1973). *Foundations of behavioral research* (2nd ed.). New York, N.Y.: Holt, Rinehart & Winston.

Kershman, S.M. (1976). A hierarchy of tasks in the development of tactual discrimination: Part one. *Education of the Visually Handicapped*, **8** (3), pp. 73-82.

Kershman, S.M. (1982). Part one: The parent competencies. *Education of the Visually Handicapped*, **13,** pp. 98-108.

Kershman, S.M. (1982). The training needs of parents of deaf-blind multihandicapped. Part 2: Factors associated with parental responses. *Education of the Visually Handicapped*, **14,** pp. 4-14.

Kewell, J. (1955). *Sculpture by blind children*. New York, N.Y.: American Foundation for the Blind, Inc.

Kimbrough, J. Huebner, K., & Lowry, L. (1976). *Sensory training: A curriculum guide*. Bridgeville, Pa.: The Greater Pittsburgh Guild for the Blind.

King, S. (1968). *Creative dance experience for learning*. New York, N.Y.: Bruce King Studio.

Kinney, R. (1977). Touch communication. In E. Lowell & C. Rouin, *State of the art: Perspectives on serving deaf-blind children*. Sacramento, Calif.: Southwestern Region Deaf-Blind Center, California State Department of Education.

Kinsella, J. (1965). *Secondary school mathematics*. New York, N.Y.: Center for Applied Research in Education.

Kirby, D., Alter, J., & Scales, P. (1979). *An analysis of U.S. sex education programs and evaluation methods*. Washington, D.C.: U.S. Department of Health, Education and Welfare, Public Health Service Education. Report No. CDC-2021-79-DK-FR.

Kirchner, C. (1983). Special education for visually handicapped children: A critique of data on numbers served and costs. Statistical Brief #23. *Journal of Visual Impairment & Blindness*, **77** (5), pp. 219-23.

Kirchner, C. (1985). *Data on blindness and visual impairment in the U.S.: A resource manual on characteristics, education, employment and service delivery*. New York, N.Y.: American Foundation for the Blind, Inc.

Kirchner, C. & Peterson, R. (1981). Estimates of race-ethnic groups in the U.S. visually impaired and blind population. Statistical Brief #13. *Journal of Visual Impairment & Blindness*, **75** (2), pp. 73-75.

Kirchner, C. & Peterson, R. (1985). Estimates of race-ethnic groups in the U.S. visually impaired. In Kirchner, C. (ed.), *Data on blindness and visual impairment in the U.S.: A resource manual on characteristics, education, employment and service delivery*. New York, N.Y.: American Foundation for the Blind, Inc.

Kirk, S.A. (1958). *Early education of the mentally retarded*. Urbana, Ill.: University of Illinois Press.

Kirk, S.A. & Gallagher, J.J. (1983). *Educating exceptional children*. Boston, Mass.: Houghton-Mifflin.

Kirtley, D.D. (1975). *The psychology of blindness*. Chicago, Ill.: Nelson-Hall.

Kitzhoffer, G.J. (1983). An adaptive approach to teaching the use of the Sonicguide™ with modifications for orthopedic involvement. *Journal of Visual Impairment & Blindness*, **77** (3), pp. 100-102.

Kline, D.F. (1982). *The disabled child and child abuse*. Chicago, Ill.: National Committee on Child Abuse.

Knapp, M.L. (1978). *Nonverbal communication in human interaction*, 2nd Edition. New York, N.Y.: Holt, Rinehart and Winston.

Knight, J. (1972). Mannerisms in the congenitally blind child. *The New Outlook for the Blind*, **66** (9), pp. 297-302.

Koenig, A.J. & Rex, E.J. (1983). Assessment of Optacon reading. A preliminary investigation. *Journal of Visual Impairment & Blindness*, **77** (2), pp. 55-60.

Koestler, F. (1976). *The unseen minority: A social history of blindness in the United States*. New York, N.Y.: David McKay Co.

Kohlberg, L. (1981). *The philosophy of moral development: Moral stages and the idea of justice*. New York, N.Y.: Harper & Row.

Kornsweit, D.K. & Yarnell, G. (1981). Increasing attending to tasks and completion of tasks with an easily-distracted, visually impaired eleven-year-old. *Education of the Visually Handicapped*, **13** (3), pp. 84-90.

Korbin, J.E. (1980). The cross-cultural context of child abuse and neglect. In C.H. Kempe & R.E. Helfer, (eds.), *The Battered Child*, (3rd edition). Chicago, Ill.: The University of Chicago Press.

Kraetch-Heller, G. (1976). Use of the Beery Visual-Motor Integration Test with partially sighted students. *Perceptual and Motor Skills*, **43**, pp. 11-14.

Kraus & Raab (1961). *Hypokinetic disease: Disease produced by lack of exercise*. Springfield, Ill.: Charles C Thomas.

Krebs, C.S. (1979). Hatha yoga for visually impaired students. *Journal of Visual Impairment & Blindness*, **73** (6), pp. 209-216.

Krogman, W.M. (1972). *Child Growth*. Ann Arbor, Mich.: University of Michigan Press.

Krolikowski, W.P. (1981). Poles in America: Maintaining the ties. *Theory into Practice*, **22** (1), pp. 52-57.

Krueger, L.E. & Ward, M.E. (1983). Letter search by braille readers: Implications for instruction. *Journal of Visual Impairment & Blindness*, **77** (1), p. 4.

Kuder, J.F. (1948). *Kuder preference record: Vocational*. Chicago, Ill.: Science Research Associates.

Kurzhals, I.W. (1961). Creating with materials can be of value for young blind children. *International Journal for the Education of the Blind*, **10** (3), pp. 75-79.

La Greca, A.M. & Mesibov, G.B. (1979). Social skills intervention with learning disabled children: Selecting skills and implementing training. *Journal of Clinical Psychology*, **8**, pp. 234-241.

Lado, R. (1964). *Language teaching: A scientific approach*. New York, N.Y.: McGraw-Hill, Inc.

Lairy, G.C. & Harrison-Covello, A. (1973). *The blind child and his parents: Congenital visual defect and the repercussion of family attitudes on the early development of the child* (pp. 1-24). (Research Bulletin, **255**). New York, N.Y.: American Foundation for the Blind, Inc.

Langley, M.B. (1977). Developmental guidelines for teachers and evaluators of multihandicapped children. *An introduction to assessment of severely profoundly handicapped children: Module III*. Austin, Tex.: Education Service Center, Region XIII.

Langley, M.B. (1978). *Assessment of multihandicapped visually impaired children*. Nashville, Tenn.: George Peabody College for Teachers.

Langley, M.B. (1980). *Assessment of multihandicapped, visually impaired children*. Chicago, Ill.: Stoelting Company.

Langley, M.B. (1980). *The teachable moment and the handicapped infant*. Reston, Va.: ERIC Clearinghouse on Handicapped and Gifted Children, Council for Exceptional Children.

Laughlin, S. (1975). A walking-jogging program for blind persons. *The New Outlook for the Blind*, **69** (1), pp. 312-313.

Lazar, I., Hubell, V.R., Murray, H., Bosche, M., & Boyce, J. (1972). *Summary report: The persistence of preschool effects: A long-term follow-up of 14 infant and preschool experiments* (Grant No. 18-76-0784). Washington, D.C.: Department of Health, Education, and Welfare, Administration of Children, Youth and Families.

Lederman, S.J. (1982). The perception of texture by touch. In W. Schiff & E. Foulke (eds.), *Tactual perception: A sourcebook*. New York, N.Y.: Cambridge University Press.

Lemish, P.S. (1981). Hanukah bush: The Jewish experience in America. *Theory into Practice*. **22** (1), pp. 26-34.

Lenard, Y., (1970). Methods and materials, techniques and the teacher. In Hester, R.M. (ed.), *Teaching a living language*. New York, N.Y.: Harper & Row.

Lerner, R.M. & Shea, J.S. (1982). Social behavior in adolescence. In B.B. Wolman & G. Stricker (eds.), *Handbook of developmental psychology*. Englewood Cliffs, N.J.: Prentice-Hall.

Lewis, M. (1983). Research panel on parent-infant relationships. In P.B. Neubauer (Chair). *Infants can't wait*. Training institute conducted by the National Center for Clinical Infant Programs, Washington, D.C.: National Center for Clinical Infants Program.

Liepmann, L. (1973). *Your child's sensory world*. New York, N.Y.: Dial Press.

Lindberg, E. & Garling, T. (1981). Acquisition of locational information about reference points during locomotion: Effects of a concurrent task during learning and test trials. *Umea Psychological Reports*, p. 146.

Lindsay, Z. (1972). *Art and the handicapped*. New York, N.Y.: Van Nostrand Reinhold Co.

Link, H.J. (1980). The Optacon: Its possibilities and limitations. In C.W. Hoehne, J.G. Cull, & R.E. Hardy (eds.), *Ophthalmological considerations in the rehabilitation of the blind*. Springfield, Ill.: Charles C Thomas.

Lisenco, Y. (1071). *Art not by eye*. New York, N.Y.: American Foundation for the Blind, Inc.

Listen & Think (1973). Educational Development Laboratories. Louisville, Ky.: American Printing House for the Blind.

Livneh, H. (1984). On the origins of negative attitudes toward people with disabilities. In Marinelli, R.P. & Dell Ort, A.E., (eds.), *The psychological and social impact of physical disability*. (2nd edition) New York, N.Y.: Springer Publishing Co.

Lockett, T. (ed.) (1978). *An education-training guide to prevocational skills for deaf-blind persons*. Lansing, Mich.: Midwest Regional Center for Services to Deaf Blind Children.

Loeschke, Maravene (1977). Mime: A movement program for the visually handicapped. *Journal of Visual Impairment & Blindness*, **71** (8), pp. 337-345.

Long, E.H. (1984). Funding. In G.T. Scholl (ed.), *Quality services for blind and visually handicapped learners: Statements of position*. Reston, Va.: Council for Exceptional Children.

Longo, J., Rotatori, A.F., Kapperman, G., & Heinze, T. (1981). Procedures used to modify self-injurious behaviors in visually impaired, mentally retarded individuals. *Education of the Visually Handicapped*, **13** (3), pp. 77-83.

Loomis, J. (1877). In *Proceedings of the Convention of the American Association of Instructors of the Blind*. Philadelphia, Pa.: Culbertson Bache.

Lord, F.E. (1969). Development of scales for the measurement of orientation and mobility of young blind children. *Exceptional Children*, **36**, (2), pp. 77-81.

Lowenfeld, B. (1948). Effects of blindness on the cognitive functioning of children. *The Nervous Child*, **7**, pp. 45-54.

Lowenfeld, B. (1956). *Our blind children*. Springfield, Ill.: Charles C Thomas.

Lowenfeld, B. (1956). History and development of specialized education for the blind. *American Association of Workers for the Blind*, pp. 15-21.

Lowenfeld, B. (1959). The blind adolescent in a seeing world. *The New Outlook for the Blind*, **53** (10), pp. 389-395.

Lowenfeld, B. (1964). The blind child as an integral part of the family and community. In B. Lowenfeld, (1981), *Berthold Lowenfeld on blindness and Blind People*. New York, N.Y.: American Foundation for the Blind, Inc.

Lowenfeld, B., Abel, G.L., & Hatlen, P.H. (1969). *Blind children learn to read*. Springfield, Ill.: Charles C Thomas.

Lowenfeld, B. (1975). *The changing status of the blind*. Springfield, Ill.: Charles C Thomas.

Lowenfeld, B. (ed). (1973). *The visually handicapped child in school*. New York, N.Y.: John Day.

Lowenfeld, B. (1971). *Our blind children* (3rd ed.). Springfield, Ill.: Charles C Thomas.

Lowenfeld, B. (1980). Psychological problems of children with severely impaired vision. In Cruickshank, W.M. (ed.). *Psychology of Exceptional Children and Youth* (4th ed.). Englewood Cliffs, N.J.: Prentice-Hall.

Lowenfeld, B. (1981). Effects of blindness on the cognitive functions of children (1948). In Lowenfeld, B. (1981). *Berthold Lowenfeld on blindness and blind people*. New York, N.Y.: American Foundation for the Blind, Inc.

Lowenfeld, V. (1951). Psycho-aesthetic implications of the art of the blind. *Journal of Aesthetics and Art Criticism*, **10** (1), pp. 1-9.

Lowenfeld, V. & Brittain, W.L. (1964). *Creative and mental growth* (4th ed.). New York, N.Y.: Macmillan & Co.

Lowenfeld, V. (1957). *Creative and mental growth.* New York, N.Y.: Macmillan Publishing Co.

Ludel, J. (1978). *Introduction to sensory processes.* San Francisco, Calif.: W.H. Freeman.

Luiselli, J.K. & Michaud, R.L. (1983). Behavioral treatment of aggression and self-injury in developmentally disabled, visually handicapped students. *Journal of Visual Impairment & Blindness,* **77** (8), pp. 388-392.

Luxton, K. & Kelley, J.D. (1981). Foundations and basis of recreation and leisure services for blind and visually impaired children. In Kelley, J.D. (ed.), *Recreation programming for visually impaired children and youth* (pp. 1-14). New York, N.Y.: American Foundation for the Blind, Inc.

Lydon, W.T. & McGraw, M.L. (1973). *Concept development for visually handicapped children.* New York, N.Y.: American Foundation for the Blind, Inc.

MacFarlane, J.A. (1975). Olfaction in the development of social preferences in the human neonate. In M.A. Hofer (ed.), *Parent-infant interaction.* Amsterdam: Elsevier.

Mackenzie, S.C. (1953). *World braille usage.* Paris: UNESCO.

Mackie, R.P. & Cohoe, E. (1956). *Teachers of children who are partially seeing.* Washington, D.C.: U.S. Government Printing Office.

Mackie, R.P. & Dunn, L.M. (1954). *College and university programs for the preparation of teachers of exceptional children.* Washington, D.C.: U.S. Government Printing Office.

Mackie, R.P. & Dunn, L.M. (1955). *Teachers of children who are blind.* U.S. Office of Education, Bulletin No. 10. Washington, D.C.: U.S. Government Printing Office.

MacMillan, D.L. (1982). *Mental retardation in school and society.* Boston, Mass.: Little, Brown & Co.

Mangold, P.N. (1980). *The pleasure of eating for those who are visually impaired.* Castro Valley, Calif.: Exceptional Teaching Aids.

Mangold, S.S. (1977). *The Mangold developmental program of tactile perception and braille letter recognition.* Castro Valley, Calif.: Exceptional Teaching Aids.

Mangold, Sally. (1978). Tactile perception and braille 1—Letter recognition: Effects of developmental teaching. *Journal of Visual Impairment & Blindness,* **72** (7), pp. 259-266.

Marion, R. (1981). *Educators, parents and exceptional children.* Rochelle, Md.: Aspen Publications.

Marks, A. & Marks, R. (1956). *Teaching the blind script-writing by the Marks' method.* New York, N.Y.: American Foundation for the Blind, Inc.

Marland, S. (1972). *Education of the gifted and talented: A report to the Congress of the United States by the U.S. Commissioner of Education.* Washington, D.C.: U.S. Government Printing Office.

Marmolin, H., Nilsson, L., & Smedshammer, H. (1979). The mediated reading process of the partially sighted. *Visible Language,* **12,** p. 2.

Maron, S. (1977). P.L. 94-142 and the residential school—A rebuttal to Dr. Hapeman. *Education of the Visually Handicapped.* **9** (4), pp. 121-122.

Marston, D., Mirkin, P., & Deno, S. (1984). Curriculum-based measurement: An alternative to traditional screening, referral, and identification. *Journal of Special Education.* **10** (2), pp. 100-118.

Martin, P.L. & Houstoun, M.F. (1982). European and American immigration policies. *Law and Contemporary Problems,* **45** (2), pp. 29-54.

Martinez, H. (ed.). (1981). *Special education and the Hispanic child.* ERIC/CUE Urban Diversity Series No. 74. New York, N.Y.: Teachers College, Columbia University.

Martinez, I. & Grayson, D. (1981). Introduction to visual impairment: The process of seeing and its relationship to the provision of recreation services. In Kelley, J.D. (ed.), *Recreation programming for visually impaired children and youth.* New York, N.Y.: American Foundation for the Blind, Inc.

Maslach, C. (1978). Job burnout: How people cope. *Public Welfare,* **36,** pp. 56-88.

Mathieu, G. (1961). A second language means a second sight. *Exceptional Children,* **27** (5), pp. 269-273.

Matsuda, M. M. (1984). A comparative analysis of blind and sighted children's communication skills. *Journal of Visual Impairment & Blindness,* **78** (1), pp. 1-5.

Maxfield, K.E. & Buchholz, S. (1957). *A social maturity scale for blind preschool children: A guide to its use.* New York, N.Y.: American Foundation for the Blind, Inc.

Maxfield, K.E. & Fjeld, H.A. (1942). Social maturity of visually handicapped preschool children. *Child Development,* **13,** pp. 1-27.

Maure, D.R., Mellon, D.R., & Uslan, M.M. (1981). AFB's computerized travel aid: Experimenters wanted. *Journal of Visual Impairment & Blindness,* **73** (9), pp. 380-381.

Mauser, A.J. (1976). *Assessing the learning disabled: Selected instruments.* San Rafael, Calif.: Academic Therapy Publications.

McBride, V.G. (1974). Explorations in rapid reading in braille. *The New Outlook for the Blind,* **68** (1), pp. 8-12.

McBurney, D.H. & Collings, V.B. (1977). *Introduction to sensation/perception.* Englewood Cliffs, N.J.: Prentice Hall.

McClennen, S.E., Hockstra, R.R., & Bryan, J.E. (1980). *Social skills for severely retarded adults.* Champaign, Ill.: Research Press.

McCoy, K. & Leader, L. (1980). Teaching cursive signatures to the blind: A task analysis approach. *Journal of Visual Impairment & Blindness,* **74** (2), pp. 69-71.

McGuinness, R.M. (1970). *A descriptive study of blind children educated in the itinerant teacher, resource room, and special school setting.* (Research Bulletin, #20, pp.1-56). New York, N.Y.: American Foundation for the Blind, Inc.

McKinney, J.P. & Moore, D. (1982). Attitudes and values during adolescence. In B.B. Wolman, & G. Stricker (eds.), *Handbook of developmental psychology.* Englewood, Cliffs, N.J.: Prentice-Hall.

McLoughlin, J. & Lewis, R.B. (1981). *Assessing special students: Strategies and procedures.* Columbus, Ohio: Charles E. Merrill.

McMakin, S.M. (1976). Training in daily living skills and its effects on the self-concept of visually impaired children. Unpublished doctoral dissertation. University of South Carolina.

Melendez D., Melendez, D.C., & Molina, A. (1981). Pluralism and the Hispanic student: Challenge to educators. *Theory into Practice.* **22** (1), pp. 7-12.

Mercer, C.D. & Mercer, A.R. (1981). *Teaching students with learning problems.* Columbus, Ohio: Charles E. Merrill.

Merriman, W.J. (1984). The relationship of socialization, attitude and placement to the degree of participation in physical activity of emotionally disturbed high school students. Unpublished doctoral dissertation, New York University.

Merry, R.V. (1933). *Problems in the education of visually handicapped children.* Cambridge, Mass.: Harvard University Press.

Meyer, G.F. (1925). *Public school training for children with impaired vision.* American Association of Workers for the Blind.

Millar, S. (1981). Crossmodal and intersensory perception and the blind. In R.D. Walk and H.L. Pick (eds.), *Intersensory sensory integration.* New York, N.Y.: Plenum Press.

Miller, B.S. & Miller, W.H. (1976). Extinguishing "blindisms:" A paradigm for intervention. *Education of the Visually Handicapped,* **8** (1), pp. 6-15.

Miller, Oral (1976). Blind skiing: Cross country. *Journey of Physical Education and Recreation,* **47,** pp. 63-64.

Miller, J.W. (1982a). Development of an audio-tutorial system for teaching basic geographic concepts. *Education of the Visually Handicapped,* **13,** pp. 109-115.

Miller, J.W. (1982b). Geography for the blind: Developing audio-tutorial map material. *The Social Studies,* **73,** pp. 263-267.

Miller, P.H. (1983). *Theories of developmental psychology.* San Francisco, Calif.: W.H. Freeman and Company.

Miller, S.E. (1982). Relationship between mobility level and development of positional concepts in visually impaired children. *Journal of Visual Impairment & Blindness,* **76** (5), pp. 149-153.

Miller, W.H. (1984). The role of residential schools for the blind in educating visually handicapped pupils. In G.T. School (ed.), *Quality services for the blind and visually handicapped learners: Statements of position*. Reston, Va: Council for Exceptional Children.

Mills, A.E. (1983). *Language acquisition in the blind child: Normal and deficient*. San Diego, Calif.: College Hill Press.

Mills, R. & Adamschick, D. (1969). The effectiveness of structured sensory training experiences prior to formal orientation and mobility instruction. *Education of the Visually Handicapped*, **1** (1), pp. 14-21.

Miranda, S.B. & Hack, M. (1979). The predictive value of neonatal visual-perceptive behaviors. In T.M. Field, A.M. Sostek, S. Goldbert & H.H. Schuman (eds.), *Infants born at risk: Behavior and development*. New York, N.Y.: Medical and Scientific Books.

Mitchell & Watson, M. (1980). Personal cultural orientations and educational practices. In Baptiste, H.P., Baptiste M.L., & Gollnick, D.M. (eds.), *Multicultural teacher education: Preparing educators to provide educational equity* (pp. 154-176). Washington, D.C.: Commission on Multicultural Education, American Association of Colleges for Teacher Education.

Molfese, D.L., Molfese, V.J. & Carrell, P.L. (1982). Early language development. In Wolman, B.B. & Stricker, G. (eds.), *Handbook of developmental psychology*. Englewood Cliffs, N.J.: Prentice-Hall.

Monbeck, M.E. (1973). *The meaning of blindness: Attitudes toward blindness and blind people*. Bloomington, Ind.: Indiana University Press.

Moore, B. & Hunt, S. (1981). Optacon: A versatile communication tool. *Journal of Visual Impairment & Blindness*, **75** (8), pp. 343-345.

Moore, M.W. (1973). *Professional preparation of teachers of reading with the Optacon*. Pittsburgh, Pa.: University of Pittsburgh Press.

Moore, M.W. & Bliss, J.C. (1975). The Optacon reading system. *Education of the Visually Handicapped*, **7** (2), pp. 33-39.

Moore, M.G., Fredericks, H.D., & Baldwin, V.L. (1981). The long range effects of early childhood education on a trainable mentally retarded population. *Journal for the Division of Early Childhood*, **4**, pp. 94-110.

Moore, M.W. & Peabody, R.L. (1976). *A functional description of the itinerant teachers of visually handicapped children in the Commonwealth of Pennsylvania*. Pittsburgh, Pa.: University of Pittsburgh, Faculty Research Grant.

Moore, S. (1984). The need for programs and services for visually handicapped infants. *Education of the Visually Handicapped*, **16**, pp. 48-57.

Moores, D. (1974). Nonvocal systems of verbal behavior. In R. Schifelbusch & L. Lloyd (eds.), *Language perspectives—Acquisition, retardation, and intervention*. Baltimore, Md.: University Park Press.

Moos, R.H. (1974). *Evaluating treatment environments: A social ecological approach*. New York, N.Y.: Wiley Interscience.

Moos, R.H. (1975). Assessment and impact of social climate. In P. McReynolds (ed.), *Advances in psychological assessment* (Vol. 3) (pp.8-41). San Francisco, Calif.: Jossey-Bass.

Moos, R.H. (1979). *Evaluating educational environments*. San Francisco, Calif.: Jossey-Bass.

Morgan, D.P. (1981). *A primer on individualized education programs for exceptional children*. Reston, Va.: Foundation for Exceptional Children.

Morisbak, I. (1975). Cross country skiing for the blind. A paper presented at the ski-week in connection with the Race for Light in Breckinridge, Colorado, February 14-24, 1975.

Morris, J.E. & Nolan, C.Y. (1970). *Aural study systems for the visually handicapped: Recorded textbook formats and aural study methods: A summary of user opinions: Interim progress report No. 2* (Project No. 8-0046, Grant No. OEG-0-8-080046-2670-[032]). Louisville, Ky.: American Printing House for the Blind.

Morris, J.E., Nolan, C.Y., & Brothers, R.J. (1973). *Aural study systems for the visually handicapped: Field trial of the Aural Study System: Interim progress report No. 10* (Project No. 8-0046, Grant No. OEG-0-8-080046-2670[032]). Louisville, Ky.: American Printing House for the Blind.

Morris, J.E., Nolan, C.Y. & Phelps, B.G. (1973). *Aural study systems for the visually handicapped: Description of the Aural Study System: Interim progress report No. 9* (Project No. 8-0046, Grant No. OEG-08-080046-2670[032]). Louisville, Ky.: American Printing House for the Blind.

Morrison, M. (1974). The other 128 hours a week: Teaching personal management to blind young adults. *The New Outlook for the Blind*, **68** (10), pp. 454-459.

Morrow, H.W. (1979). Nondiscriminatory assessment: Implications for teacher education. *Teacher Education and Special Education*, **2** (4), pp. 59-64.

Morse, J. (1965). Mannerisms, not blindisms: Causation and treatment. *International Journal for the Education of the Blind*, **15** (1), pp. 12-16.

Muldoon, John F. (1980). The burnout syndrome: Caring for yourself. *Journal of Visual Impairment & Blindness*, **75** (4), pp. 112-116.

Mussen, P.H., Conger, J.J., & Kagan, J. (1979). *Child development and personality* (5th ed.). New York, N.Y.: Harper & Row.

Myers, L.J. (1981). The nature of pluralism and the African American case. *Theory into Practice*, **20** (1), pp. 2-6.

Napier, G.D. (1973). Special subject adjustments and skills. In Lowenfeld, B. (ed.), *The visually handicapped child in school*. New York, N.Y.: The John Day Company.

National Alliance of Black School Educators. (1981a). *The development and delivery of instructional services: A commitment to minority handicapped students*. Module V. Washington, D.C.: NABSE.

National Alliance of Black School Educators. (1981b). *Minority handicapped students: Assessment issues and practices*. Module III. Washington, D.C.: NABSE.

National Alliance of Black School Educators. (1981c). *Structuring the learning climate for minority handicapped students*. Module IV. Washington, D.C.: NABSE.

National Alliance of Black School Educators. (1981d). *Valuing the diversity of minority handicapped students*. Module II. Washington, D.C.: NABSE.

National Advisory Council on the Education of Disadvantaged Children. (n.d.). *Special report on Indian education*. Washington, D.C.: Author.

National Committee for Prevention of Child Abuse. (1982). Annual report. Chicago, Ill.: Author.

National Council for Accreditation of Teacher Education. (1979). *Standards for the accreditation of teacher education*. Washington, D.C.: Author.

National Society for the Prevention of Blindness (1956). *Recommended basic course for preparation of teachers of partially seeing children*, **24**, (4).

National Society to Prevent Blindness. (1980). *Vision problems in the U.S.: Data analysis*. New York, N.Y.: Author.

National survey: Social studies education kindergarten-grade 12. (1976). Richmond, Va.: Virginia Department of Education (Division of Secondary Education, History, Government and Geography Service).

Neff, J. (1982). Sexuality education methodology. In Mangold, S.S. (ed.), *A teacher's guide to the special educational needs of blind and visually handicapped children*. New York, N.Y.: American Foundation for the Blind, Inc.

Newcomer, J. (1977). Sonicguide™: Its use with public school children. *Journal of Visual Impairment & Blindness*, **71** (6), pp. 268-271.

Newell, F.W. & Ernest, J.T. (1974). *Ophthalmology: Principles and concepts*. St. Louis, Mo.: C.V. Mosby Company.

Newland, T.E. (1971). *Blind learning aptitude test.* Urbana, Ill.: University of Illinois Press.

Newman, P.R. (1982). The peer group. In B.B. Wolman & G. Stricker (eds.), *Handbook of developmental psychology.* Englewood Cliffs, N.J.: Prentice-Hall.

Nillson, B. (1982). Braille: A medium for everybody? *Journal of Visual Impairment & Blindness,* **76** (5), pp. 197-199.

Noam, G.G., Higgins, R.C., & Goethals, G.W. (1982). Psychoanalytic approaches to developmental psychology. In B.B. Wolman & G. Stricker, (eds.). *Handbook of developmental psychology* (pp. 23-43). Englewood Cliffs, N.J.: Prentice-Hall.

Nolan, C. (1959). Achievement in arithmetic computation; analysis of school differences and identification of areas of low achievement. *International Journal for the Education of the Blind,* **4,** pp. 125-128.

Nolan, C. (1966). Audio materials for the blind. *Audiovisual Instruction,* **2** (9), pp. 124-126.

Nolan, C.Y. (1966). *Reading and listening in learning by the blind: Progress report* (PHS Grant No. NB-04870-4). Louisville, Ky.: American Printing House for the Blind.

Nolan, C.Y. (1983). *Providing educational materials under the 'Act to Promote the Education of the Blind.'* Louisville, Ky.: American Printing House for the Blind.

Nolan, C.Y. & Kederis, C.J. (1960). *Perceptual factors in braille word recognition.* Research Series, #20. New York, N.Y.: American Foundation for the Blind, Inc.

Nolan, C. & Morris, J. (1969). Learning by blind students through active and passive listening. *Exceptional Children,* **36** (3), pp. 173-186.

Nolan, C.Y. & Morris, J.E. (1971). *Improvement of tactual symbols for blind children: Final report* (Project No. 5-0421, Grant No. OEG-32-27-0000-1012). (ERIC Document Reproduction Service No. ED 070 228). Louisville, Ky.: American Printing House for the Blind.

Nolan, C.Y. (ed.). (1976). *Facilitating the education of the visually handicapped through research in communications: Part three, facilitating tactile map reading: Final report* (Grant No. OEG-0-73-0642). Louisville, Ky.: American Printing House for the Blind.

Norris, M., Spaulding, P.J., & Brodie, F.H. (1957). *Blindness in children.* Chicago, Ill.: University of Chicago Press.

Oakland, T. (1981). *Nonbiased assessment.* Minneapolis, Minn.: University of Minnesota School Psychology Inservice Training Network.

O'Brien, R. (1976). *Alive. . .aware. . .a person.* Rockville, Md.: Montgomery County Public Schools.

O'Brien, R. (1976). *A developmental model for early children services with special definition for visually impaired children and their parents.* Rockville, Md.: Montgomery County Public Schools.

O'Brien, R. (1975). Early childhood services for visually impaired children: A model program. *The New Outlook for the Blind,* **69** (5), pp. 201-206.

O'Brien, R. (1973). The integrated resource room for the visually impaired children, *The New Outlook for the Blind,* **67** (8), pp. 363-368.

Ohlsen, R.L., Jr., (1971). New reform in residential schools. *Education of the Visually Handicapped,* **3** (2), pp. 60-62.

Oka, E.I. & Scholl, G.T. (1984). Nontest-based approaches to assessment. In G.T. Scholl, (ed.) (1985), *The school psychologist and the exceptional child.* Reston, Va.: Council for Exceptional Children.

Olson, M. (1975). *The effects of training in rapid reading on the reading rate and comprehension of braille and large print readers.* Ann Arbor, Mich.: University Microfilms International.

Olson, M. (1976). Faster braille reading: Preparation at the reading readiness level. *The New Outlook for the Blind,* **70,** (8), pp. 341-343.

Olson, M. (1982). Staying alive in the field of vision. *DVH Newsletter,* p. 10.

Olson, M.R. (1979). Suggestions for working with the remedial braille reader. *Journal of Visual Impairment & Blindness,* **73** (1), pp. 314-317.

Olson, M.R. & Mangold, S. (1981). *Guidelines and games for teaching efficient braille reading.* New York, N.Y.: American Foundation for the Blind, Inc.

Olson, W.C. (1959). *Child development.* Indianapolis, Ind.: Heath.

Organization for Social and Technical Innovation. (1971). *Blindness and services to the blind in the United States.* Cambridge, Mass.: OSTI, Inc.

Orlansky, M. & Rhyne, J. (1981). Special adaptations necessitated by visual impairments. In J.M. Kauffman & D.P. Hallahan (eds.), *Handbook of special education.* Englewood Cliffs, N.J.: Prentice-Hall.

Orr, D., Friedman, H. & Williams, J. (1965). Trainability of listening comprehension of speeded discourse. *Journal of Educational psychology,* **56.**

Ortiz, C.D. (1981). Training educators to meet the needs of Hispanic exceptional students: A perspective. In H. Martinez, (ed.), *Special education and the Hispanic child.* ERIC/CUE Urban Diversity Series, No. 74. New York, N.Y.: Teachers College, Columbia University.

Ortiz, K.K. (1973). Maternal childbearing attitudes and developmental growth of Rubella deaf-blind children. Doctoral dissertation, University of Southern California, University microfilms 74-936.

Parke, K.L., Shallcross, R., & Anderson, R.J. (1980). Differences in overall behavior between blind and sighted persons during dyadic communication. *Journal of Visual Impairment & Blindness,* **74** (4), pp. 142-146.

Paterson, J.O. (1913). Elements of strengths and weaknesses in educating blind children in schools for the seeing and in schools for the blind. *The New Outlook for the Blind,* **7** (4), pp. 117-122.

Payne, C.R. Multicultural education: A natural way to teach. *Contemporary Education* **54** (2), pp. 98-104.

Payne, J. & Scholl, G.T. (1981). Teaching mathematics to the visually impaired. In V.J. Glennan (ed.), *Mathematical education of exceptional children and youth.* Reston, Va.: National Council of Teachers of Mathematics.

Peiser, I.J. (1978). Vision and learning disabilities. In Wold, R.M. (ed.), *Vision: Its impact on learning.* Seattle, Wash.: Special Child Publications

Peterson, M.L. (1983). The Indo-Chinese refugee child in Iowa: Talking with the teachers. *Contemporary Education* **54** (2), pp. 126-129.

Piaget, J. (1954). *The construction of reality in the child.* New York, N.Y.: Ballantine.

Piaget, J. (1960). *Psychology of intelligence.* Patterson, N.J.: Littlefield-Adams.

Piaget, J. (1963). *The origins of intelligence in children.* New York, N.Y.: W.W. Norton.

Piaget, J. (1970). *Science of education and the psychology of the child.* New York, N.Y.: Orion Press.

Piaget, J. (1973). *The child and reality.* New York, N.Y.: Grossman.

Piaget, J. (1981). *Intelligence and affectivity: Their relationship during child development.* Palo Alto, Calif.: Annual Reviews, Inc.

Piaget, J. & Inhelder, B. (1948). *The child's conception of space.* London: Routledge & Kegan Paul.

Piaget, J. & Inhelder, B. (1969). *The psychology of the child.* New York, N.Y.: Basic Books.

Pick, H.L., Jr. (1961). Research on taste in the Soviet Union. In M.R. Kare & B.P. Halpern (eds.), *Physiological and behavioral aspects of taste.* Chicago, Ill.: University of Chicago Press.

Plisko, V.W. (1983). *The condition of education: Statistical report.* National Center for Education Statistics. Washington, D.C.: U.S. Government Printing Office.

Popham, W.J. (1975). *Educational evaluation.* Englewood Cliffs, N.J.: Prentice-Hall.

Popovich, D. (1981). *Effective educational and behavorial programming for severely and profoundly handicapped students.* Baltimore, Md.: Paul H. Brooks Company.

Porter, J.D. (1981). Appalachians: Adrift in the mainstream. *Theory into Practice,* **22** (1), pp. 13-19.

Poss, D. (1980). Optacon teaching of a bilaterally hand-injured student. *Journal of Visual Impairment & Blindness,* **74** (1), pp. 33-37.

Powell, M.L. (1981). *Assessment and management of developmental changes and problems in children* (2nd Edition). St. Louis, Mo.: The C.V. Mosby Company.

Professional standards in education of exceptional children. (1966). Washington, D.C.: Council for Exceptional Children.

Pulaski, M.A.S. (1980). *Understanding Piaget: An introduction to children's cognitive development.* New York, N.Y.: Harper & Row.

Putnam, P. (1963). *The triumph of the Seeing Eye.* New York, N.Y.: Harper & Row.

Rahn, C.H. (1972). *Home economics guide for visually handicapped students: A five county vocational skills training program for the blind.* Sacramento, Calif.: California State Department of Education.

Ramey, C., Beckman-Bell, P., & Gowan, J. (1980). Infant characteristics and infant caregiver interactions. In J.J. Gallagher (ed.), *New directions for exceptional children: Parents and families of handicapped children.*

Rand, M. (1973). Dance and creative movement for blind persons. *The New Outlook for the Blind,* **67** (2), pp. 90-93.

Randolph, L.G. (1971). Don't rearrange the classroom: Why not? A proposal for meaningful classroom mobility. *The Long Cane News,* **4** (3), pp. 15-22.

Rathbager, J.M. (1969). *Experimental listening curriculum.* Blauvelt, N.Y.: Dominican College of Blauvelt, U.S. Office of Education, Project #6-8477.

Rawlings, B.W. (1983). *The Nebraska survey of sensory impaired children and youth, 1982-83. Final Report.* Washington, D.C.: Gallaudet College.

Révész, G. (1950). *Psychology and art of the blind.* New York, N.Y.: Longmans, Green and Co.

Rex, E.J. (1971). A study of basal readers and experimental supplemental instructional materials for teaching primary reading in braille, Part I. *Education of the Visually Handicapped,* **3** (1), pp. 1-6.

Reynell, J. (1983). *Manual for the Reynell Zinkin Scales.* Windsor, Berks., U.K.: NFER-NELSON Publishing Co., Ltd.

Reynolds, M.C. & Birch, J.W. (1982). *Teaching exceptional children in all America's schools.* Reston, Va.: Council for Exceptional Children.

Rhyne, J.M. (1981). *Curriculum for teaching the visually impaired.* Springfield, Ill.: Charles C Thomas.

Richards, L.E. (ed.). (1909). *Journals and Letters of Samuel G. Howe.* Boston, Mass.: Dana Estes and Co.

Ricser, J.J., Guth, D.A., & Hill, E.W. (1982). Mental processes mediating independent travel: Implications for orientation and mobility. *Journal of Visual Impairment & Blindness,* **76** (7), pp. 213-218.

Riesman, F.K. (1972). *A guide to the diagnostic teaching of arithmetic.* Columbus, Ohio: Charles E. Merrill.

Risley, B.L. (1971). Toward more effective services: Cooperation and coordination as the imperative for relevance, *Education of the Visually Handicapped,* **3** (3), pp. 73-79.

Roades, S., Pisch, L., & Axelrod, S. (1974). Use of behavior modification procedures with visually handicapped students. *Education of the Visually Handicapped,* **6** (1), pp. 19-26.

Robbin, J. (1960). *Louis Braille.* London: Royal National Institute for the Blind.

Roberts, F.R. (1973). F.R. Preparation of Teachers. In B. Lowenfeld, *The visually handicapped child in school.* New York, N.Y.: John Day.

Roberts, T.B. (ed.). (1975). *Four psychologies applied to education: Freudian behavioral humanistic transpersonal.* New York, N.Y.: John Wiley and Sons.

Roessing, L.J. (1982). Functional vision criterion-referenced checklists. In S.S. Mangold, *A teacher's guide to educational needs of blind and visually handicapped children.* New York, N.Y.: American Foundation for the Blind, Inc.

Rogers, C. (1959). Towards a theory of creativity. In H. Anderson, (ed.), *Creativity and its cultivation.* New York, N.Y.: Harper & Row.

Rogow, S. (1980). Language development in blind multihandicapped children: A model of co-active intervention. *Child Care, Health, and Development,* **6,** pp. 301-308.

Rogow, S. & Rodrigues, M. (1977). *Their special needs: An action guide to working with blind residents of mental retardation facilities.* Toronto, Canada: Ministry of Community and Social Services.

Romano, M.D. (1982). Sex and disability. Are they mutually exclusive? In Eisenberg, M. (ed.), *Disabled people as second class citizens.* New York, N.Y.: Springer Publishing Co.

Root, F. (1960). The elementary school meets the blind child. In V.J. Glennon (ed.), *Frontiers of elementary education, VI.* Syracuse, N.Y.: Syracuse University Press.

Rose, S.A. (1981). Lags in the cognitive competence of prematurely born infants. In S.L. Friedman & M. Sigman (eds.), *Preterm birth and psychological development.* New York, N.Y.: Academic Press.

Rose, S.A., Schmidt, K., Riese, M.L. & Bridger, W.H. (1980). Effects of prematurity and early intervention in responsivity of premature and full-term infants. *Child Development,* **50,** pp. 416-425.

Rosenblith, J.F. (1974). Relations between neonatal behaviors and those at eight months. *Developmental Psychology,* **10,** pp. 779-792.

Rosenthal, T.L. & Zimmerman, B.J. (1978). *Social learning and cognition.* New York, N.Y.: Academic Press.

Roy Littlejohn Associates Inc. (1982). *An analysis of the impact of the handicapped children's early education program* (Contract No. 300-81-0661). Washington, D.C. U.S. Department of Education, Special Education Programs.

Rubin, E.J. (1964). Abstract functioning in the blind. New York, N.Y.: American Foundation for the Blind, Inc.

Rubin, J.A. (1975). Through art to affect: Blind children express their feelings. *The New Outlook for the Blind,* **69** (9), pp. 385-391.

Rubin, J.A. (1976). The exploration of a "tactile aesthetic." *The New Outlook for the Blind,* **70** (9), pp. 369-375.

Rubin, J.A. (1978). *Child art therapy.* New York, N.Y.: Van Nostrand Reinhold Co.

Rusalem, H. (1972). *Coping with the unseen environment.* New York, N.Y.: Teachers College Press.

Russell, L. (1975). *Operating instructions for SE Model Path-Sounders.* Cambridge, Mass.: Sensory Aids Evaluation and Development Center, Massachusetts Institute of Technology.

Sadowsky, A.D. (1985). Visual impairment among developmentally disabled clients in California regional centers. *Journal of Visual Impairment & Blindness,* **79** (5), pp. 199-202.

Safir, A. (1983). Personal communication. University of Connecticut Medical School.

Salend, S.J., Michael, R.J., & Taylor, M. (1984). Competencies necessary for instructing migrant handicapped students. *Exceptional children,* **51** (1), pp. 50-55.

Salvia, J. & Ysseldyke, J.E. (1981). *Assessment in special and remedial education.* Boston, Mass.: Houghton Mifflin.

Sandler, A. (1963). Aspects of passivity and ego development in the blind infant. *Psychoanalytic Study of the Child.* **18,** pp. 343-361.

Sanford, A. (1974). *Learning accomplishment profile.* Winston-Salem, N.C.: Kaplan Press.

Scadden, L. (1984). Blindness in the information age: Equality or irony?'' *Journal of Visual Impairment & Blindness*, **78** (9), pp. 394-400.

Scarr, S. (1981). Testing *for* children. *American Psychologist*, **36**, pp. 1159-1166.

Schaeffer, M., Hatcher, R.P., & Barglow, P.D. (1980). Prematurity and infant stimulation: A review of research. *Child Psychiatry and Human Development*, **10**, pp. 197-264.

Schell, G.C. (1981). The young handicapped child: A family perspective. *Topics in Early Childhood Education*, **1** (3), pp. 21-27.

Schiff, W. & Foulke, E. (eds.). (1982). *Tactual perception: A sourcebook*. New York, N.Y.: Cambridge University Press.

Schneider, C., Helfer, R.E., & Hoffmeister, J.K. (1980). Screening for potential to abuse: A review. In C.H. Kempe & R.E. Helfer, (ed.), *The battered child* (3rd ed.). Chicago, Ill.: University of Chicago Press.

Scholl, G.T. (1971). Fringe benefits of accreditation for residential schools. *The New Outlook for the Blind*, **65** (7), pp. 220-223.

Scholl, G.T. (1968). *The principal works with the visually impaired CEC*. Washington, D.C.: National Education Association.

Scholl, G.T. (1975). The psychosocial effects of blindness: Implications for program planning in sex education. In *Sex education for the visually handicapped in schools and agencies. . .Selected papers*. New York, N.Y.: American Foundation for the Blind, Inc.

Scholl, G.T. (1984). The role and function of the school psychologist in special education. In Scholl, G.T. (ed.). (1985). *The school psychologist and the exceptional child* (pp. 3-24). Reston, Va.: Council for Exceptional Children.

Scholl, G.T. (1981). *Self-study and evaluation guide for day school programs for visually handicapped pupils: A guide for program improvement*. Reston, Va.: Council for Exceptional Children.

Scholl, G.T. (1967). Teacher preparation for visually handicapped children: A look into the future. *Special Education in Canada*, **41** (3), pp. 19-26.

Scholl, G.T., Long, E.H., & Tuttle, D.W. (1980). Monitoring program quality: Who and how should it be done? *DVH Newsletter*, **25** (1), pp. 12-18.

Scholl, G.T. & Schnur, R. (1976). *Measures of psychological, vocational, and educational functioning in the blind and visually handicapped*. New York, N.Y.: American Foundation for the Blind, Inc.

Scholl, G.T. & Vaughan, M. (1980). Where have all the children gone? *DVH Newsletter*, **25** (2), pp. 9-10.

Schor, D.P. (1983). Visual impairment. In Blackman, J.A. (ed.), *Medical aspects of developmental disabilities in children birth to three* (pp. 227-231). Iowa City, Iowa: Department of Pediatrics, University Hospital School, The University of Iowa.

Schultz, E. (1968). Programs in daily living skills. In *Association for Education of the Visually Handicapped Forty-Ninth Biennal Conference Proceedings*. Toronto, Canada.

Schulz, P.J. (1980). *How does it feel to be blind?* Los Angeles, Calif.: Muse-Ed.

Schwarz, H. (1956). *Samuel Gridley Howe*. Cambridge, Mass.: Harvard University Press.

Schwarzbeck, C. (1980). Identification of infants at risk for child abuse: Observations and inferences in the examination of the mother-infant dyad. In G.J. Williams & J. Money, (eds.), *Traumatic abuse and neglect of children at home*. Baltimore, Md.: John Hopkins University Press.

Schweinhart, L. & Weikart, D. (1980). *Young children grow up: The effects of the Perry Preschool Program on youths through age 15*. Ypsilanti: Mich.: High/Scope Educational Research Foundation.

Schworm, R.W. (1977). Walking in rhythm, moving in style. *Teaching Exceptional Children*, pp. 52-53.

Scione, M.W. (1978). Electronic sensory aids in a concept development program for congenitally blind young adults. *Journal of Visual Impairment & Blindness*, **72** (3), pp. 88-93.

Scott, J.P. (1962). Critical periods in behavioral development. *Science*, **138**, pp. 949-958.

Scott, R.A. (1969). *The making of blind men: A study of adult socialization*. New York, N.Y.: Russell Sage Foundation.

Scott, R.A. (1969). The socialization of blind children. In D.A. Goslin (ed.), *Handbook of socialization theory and research*. Chicago, Ill.: Rand McNally.

Scott, R.J. (1984). *Teaching and learning in remote schools: A dilemma beyond rural education*. Washington, D.C.: National Information Center for Handicapped Children and Youth.

Seaver, J. & Cartwright, C.A. (1977). A pluralistic foundation for training early childhood professionals. *Curriculum Inquiry*, **7** (4), pp. 305-329.

Sefein, N.A. (1981). Islamic beliefs and practices. *Social Studies*, **72** (4), pp. 158-64.

Seller, M. (1982). Historical perspectives on American immigration policy: Case studies and current implications. *Law and Contemporary Problems*, **45** (2), pp. 137-162.

Selvin, H.D. (1979). Sexuality among the visually handicapped: A beginning. *Sexuality and Disability*, **2** (3), pp. 192-198.

Selvin, H.C. (1981). The Kurzweil Reading Machine: False hopes and realistic expectations. *Journal of Visual Impairment & Blindness*, **75** (2), pp. 76-77.

Sexton, D., Kelley, M.F., & Scott, R. (1982). Comparison of maternal estimates and performance-based assessment scores for young handicapped children. *Diagnostique*, **7**, pp. 168-173.

Shallcross, D.J. (1981). *Teaching creative behavior*. Englewood Cliffs, N. J.: Prentice-Hall.

Sherrill, C. (1976). *Adapted physical education and recreation: A multidisciplinary approach*. Dubuque, Iowa: Wm C Brown.

Sherrill, C., Rainbolt, W. & Ervin, S. (1984). Attitudes of blind persons towards physical education and recreation. *Adapted Physical Activities Quarterly*, **1** (1), pp. 3-11.

Sherrill, C., Rainbolt, W. & Ervin, S. (1984). Physical recreation of blind adults: Present practices and childhood memories. *Journal of Visual Impairment & Blindness*, **78** (8), pp. 367-368.

Siegel, A. & White, S. (1975). The development of spatial representations of large-scale environments. In H. Reese (ed.), *Advances in child development and behavior* (Vol. 10). New York, N.Y.: Academic Press.

Siegel, O. (1982). Personality development in adolescence. In B.B. Wolman & B.B. Stricker, (ed.). *Handbook of developmental psychology*. Englewood Cliffs, N.J.: Prentice-Hall.

Sigelman, C.K., Vengroff, L.P., & Spanhel, C.L. (1984). Disability and the concept of life functions. In R.P. Marinelli & A.E. Dell Orto, (eds.). *The psychological and social impact of phsyical disability (2nd ed.)* New York, N.Y.: Springer Publishing Co.

Silberman, R. & Tripodi, V. (1979). Adaptation of project "I CAN" primary skills physical education program for deaf blind children. *Journal of Visual Impairment & Blindness*, **73** (7), pp. 270-276.

Silberman, R.K. (1981). Assessment and evaluation of visually handicapped students. *Journal of Visual Impairment & Blindness*, **75** (3), pp. 109-114.

Siller, J. (1984). Attitudes toward the physically disabled. In R.L. Jones (ed.), *Attitudes and attitude change in special education: Theory and Practice*. Reston, Va.: Council for Exceptional Children.

Silverstein, R. (1985). The legal necessity for residential schools serving deaf, blind, and multihandicapped sensory-impaired children. Unpublished paper.

Simon, J. (1979). The work performed by houseparents in residential schools for the visually handicapped. *Education of the Visually Handicapped*, **11** (1), pp. 2-8.

Simpkins, K. (1978). Piagetian theory works well with pre-academic children. *Vision-Up News*, **2**, pp. 1-2, 8, 10-11.

Simpkins, K. (1979). Development of the concept of space. *Journal of Visual Impairment & Blindness*, **73** (3), pp. 81-85.

Simpkins, K. & Stephens, B. (1974). Cognitive development of blind subjects. *Proceedings of the 52nd Biennial Conference of the Education of the Visually Handicapped*, pp. 26-38.

Simpson, R.L., Sasso, G.M., and Bump, N. (1982), Modification of manneristic behavior in a visually impaired child via a time-out procedure. *Education of the Visually Handicapped*, 14 (2), pp. 50-55.

Singleton, L.R. (1979). *Social studies for the visually impaired child: MAVIS Sourcebook 4*. Boulder, Colo.: Social Science Education Consortium.

Singleton, L.R. & Leslie, M. (1979). *Resources for teaching social studies in the mainstreamed classroom: MAVIS Sourcebook 6*. Boulder, Colo.: Social Science Education Consortium.

Sinizin, B.G. (1978). Track and field events. *The European Blend*, 7 (3), pp. 2, 6, 8, 10.

Sirvis, B. (1978). Developing IEPs for physically handicapped students: A transdisciplinary viewpoint. *Teaching Exceptional Children*, 10, pp. 78-82.

Sklar, M.J. & Rampulla, J. (1973). Decreasing inappropriate classroom behavior of a multiply handicapped blind student. *Education of the Visually Handicapped*, 5 (3), pp. 71-74.

Skeels, H.M. (1941). A study of the effects of differential stimulation on mentally retarded children: A follow-up report. *American Journal of Mental Deficiency*, 46, pp. 340-350.

Skeels, H.M. (1966). Status of children with contrasting early life experiences. *Monographs of the Society for Research in Child Development*, 31 (Whole No. 105).

Skeels, H.M. & Dye, H.B. (1939). A study of the effects of differential stimulation on mentally retarded children. *Proceedings and addresses of the Sixty-Third Annual Session of the American Association for Mental Deficiency*, 44 (1), pp. 114-136.

Slatoff, H. (1962). Integrated art experiences for blind children. *International Journal for the Education of the Blind*, 12 (1), pp. 17-18.

Sloan, I.J. (1983). *Child abuse: Governing law and legislation*. New York, N.Y.: Occana Publications, Inc.

Sloan, L. & Habel, A. (1973). Problems in providing reading aids for partially sighted children. *American Journal of Ophthalmology*, 75 (6), pp. 1023-1035.

Smith, A.J. & Cote, K.S. (1982). *Look at me: A resource manual for the development of residual vision in multiply impaired children*. Philadelphia, Pa.: Pennsylvania College of Optometry.

Smith, J.A. (1964). *Creativity: Its nature and nurture*. Syracuse, N.Y.: Syracuse University Press.

Smith, M.A., Chetnik, M., & Adelson, E. (1969). Differential assessments of "blindisms." *American Journal of Orthopsychiatry*, 39, pp. 807-817.

Smith, M.M. (1984). *If blindness strikes: Don't strike out—A lively look at living with a visual impairment*. Springfield, Ill.: Charles C Thomas.

Smith, R.P. & Dailey, R.H. (1978). The Sonicguide™: A valuable aid for blind children and infants. *Journal of Visual Impairment & Blindness*, 72 (8), pp. 317-319.

Smith, W.F. (1982). Introduction. *Law and Contemporary Problems*. 45 (2), pp. 3-8.

Smitherman, G. (ed.). (1981). *Black English and the education of black children and youth*. Detroit, Mich.: Wayne State University, Center for Black Studies.

Smits, B.W.G.M. & Mommers, M.J.C. (1976). Differences between blind and sighted children on WISC verbal subtests. *The New Outlook for the Blind*, 70 (6), pp. 240-246.

Snell, M. & Smith, D. (1983). Developing the IEP: Selecting and assessing skills. In M. Snell (ed.), *Systematic instruction of the moderately and severely handicapped*, 2nd edition. Columbus, Ohio: Charles E. Merrill Publishing Co.

Social studies materials adaptations for visually handicapped elementary students: Final report (Grant No. G007701353). (1981). Boulder, Colo.: Social Science Education Consortium.

Somerton-Fair, E. & Turner, K. (1979). *Pennsylvania training model*. Harrisburg, Pa.: Pennsylvania Department of Education.

Sommers, V.S. (1944). *The influence of parental attitudes and social environment on the personality development of the adolescent blind*. New York, N.Y.: American Foundation for the Blind, Inc.

Sonenstein, F.L. & Pittman, K.J. (1984). The availability of sex education in large city schools. *Family Planning Perspectives*. 16 (1), pp. 19-25.

Sonka, J.J. & Bina, M.J. (1978). Cross-country running for visually impaired young adults. *Journal of Visual Impairment & Blindness*, 72 (6), pp. 212-214.

Spengler, J.J. (1956). Some economic aspects of immigration into the United States. *Law and Contemporary Problems*, 21 (2), pp. 236-255.

Spungin, S.J. (1977). *Competency-based curriculum for teachers of the visually handicapped: A national study*. New York, N.Y.: American Foundation for the Blind, Inc.

Spungin, S.J. (1978). Mainstreaming visually handicapped children: Problems and issues. *Journal of Visual Impairment & Blindness*, 72 (10), pp. 422-423.

Spungin, S.J. (1978). Competency-based curriculum: A national survey of teachers. *Journal of Visual Impairment & Blindness*, 73 (5), pp. 163-169.

Spungin, S.J. (1981). *Guidelines for public school programs serving visually handicapped children*. New York, N.Y.: American Foundation for the Blind, Inc.

Spungin, S.J. (1982). The future role of residential schools for visually handicapped children. *Journal of Visual Impairment & Blindness*, 76 (6), pp. 229-233.

Spungin, S.J. (1984). The role and function of the teacher of the visually handicapped. In G.T. Scholl (ed.), *Quality services for blind and visually handicapped learners: Statements of position*. Reston, Va.: Council for Exceptional Children.

Stager, J.D. (1978). Assessing public school programs for visually handicapped students. *Journal of Visual Impairment & Blindness*, 72 (5), pp. 170-172.

Stager, J.D. (1981). *Program assessment guide for public school special education services to visually handicapped students*. West Boylston, Mass.: Massachusetts Department of Education.

Stark, M.L. (1970). Restoration and habilitation of handwriting skills to adults in a rehabilitation center setting. *The New Outlook for the Blind*, 64 (10), pp. 330-339.

State Education Consultants for the Visually Handicapped. (1984). The role and responsibility of the state education consultant for the visually handicapped. In G.T. Scholl (ed.), *Quality services for blind and visually handicapped learners: Statements of position*. Reston, Va.: Council for Exceptional Children.

Stechler, G. & Halton, A. (1982). Prenatal influences on human development. In B.B. Wolman, & G. Stricker, *Handbook of developmental psychology*. Englewood Cliffs, N.J.: Prentice-Hall.

Steele, A. & Crawford, C. (1982). Music therapy for the visually impaired. *Education of the Visually Handicapped*, 14 (2), pp. 56-62.

Stein, H. & Slatt, B. (1985). *The ophthalmic assistant*. St. Louis, Mo.: The C.V. Mosby Co.

Stephens, B. & Grube, C. (1982). Development of Piagetian reasoning in congenitally blind children. *Journal of Visual Impairment & Blindness*, 76 (5), pp. 133-143.

Stephens, B. & Simpkins, K. (1974). *The reasoning, moral judgment and moral conduct of the congenitally blind*. (Report No. H23-3197). Washington, D.C.: Office of Education, Bureau of Education for the Handicapped.

Stepick, A. (1982). Haitian boat people: A study in the conflicting forces shaping U.S. immigration policy. *Law and Contemporary problems*, 45 (2), pp. 163-196.

Stile, S., Cole, J., & Garner, A. (1979). Maximizing parental involvement in programs for exceptional chidlren. Strategies for education and related service personnel. *Journal of the Divisiion for Early Childhood*, 1, pp. 68-82.

Stillman, R. (1978). *Callier-Azusa scale*. Dallas, Tex.: Callier Center for Communication Disorders.

Stock, J.R., Newborg, J., Wnek, L.L., Schneck, E.A., Gabel, J.R. Spurgeon, M.S., & Ray, H.W. (1976). *Evaluation of handicapped children's early education program (HCEEP) final report*. Columbus, Ohio: Batelle Center for Improved Education.

Stocker, C. (1963). A new approach to teaching handwriting to the blind. *The New Outlook for the Blind*, **57** (6), pp. 208-217.

Stocker, C. (1973). *Listening for the visually impaired: A teaching manual*. Springfield, Ill.: Charles C Thomas.

Stocker, C. (1970). Preface to restoration and habilitation of handwriting skills to adults in a rehabilitation setting. *The New Outlook for the Blind*, **64** (10). p. 330.

Stokes, L. (1976). Educational considerations for the child with low vision. In E. Faye, (ed.), *Clinical low vision*. Boston, Mass.: Little, Brown & Co.

Stotland, J. (1984). Relationships of parents to professionals: A challenge to professionals. *Journal of Visual Impairment & Blindness*, **78** (2), pp. 69-74.

Strain, P.S. (1984). Efficacy research with young handicapped children: A critique of the status quo. *Journal of the Division for Early Childhood*, **9** (1), pp. 4-10.

Strazicich, M. (1983). *The school counselor and the migrant student*. Sacramento, Calif.: California State Department of Education.

Strelow, E.R., Kay, N., & Kay, L. (1978). Binaural sensory aid: Case studies of use by two children. *Journal of Visual Impairment & Blindness*, **72** (1), pp. 1-8.

Strohmer, D.C., Grand, S.A., & Purcell, M.J. (1984). Attitudes toward persons with a disability—An examination of demographic factors, social context, and specific disability. *Rehabilitation Psychology*, **29** (3), pp. 131-146.

Struve, N., Cheney, K., & Rudd, C. (1979-1980). Chisenbop for blind math students. *Education of the Visually Handicapped*, **7** (4), pp. 108-112.

Swallow, R., Mangold, S., & Mangold, P. (1978). *Informal assessment of the visually impaired*. New York, N.Y.: American Foundation for the Blind, Inc.

Swallow, R.M. (1981). Fifty assessment instruments commonly used with blind and partially seeing individuals. *Journal of Visual Impairment & Blindness*, **75** (2), pp. 65-72.

Swallow, R.M. & Conner, A. (1982). Aural reading. In S. Mangold (ed.), *A teacher's guide to the special educational needs of blind and visually handicapped children*. New York, N.Y.: American Foundation for the Blind, Inc.

Swanson, H.L. & Watson, B.L. (1982). *Education and psychological assessment of exceptional children*. St. Louis, Mo.: The C.V. Mosby Co.

Tait, P. (1972). The implications of play as it relates to the emotional development of the blind child. *Education of the Visually Handicapped*, **4** (2), pp. 52-54.

Taylor, J.L. (1973). Educational Programs. In B. Lowenfeld (ed), *The visually handicapped child in school* (pp. 165-184). New York, N.Y.: John Day.

Taylor, J.L. (1978). Mainstreaming visually handicapped children and youth: Yesterday, today and tomorrow. Unpublished paper.

Taylor, M.M., Lederman, S.J., & Gibson, R.H. Tactual perception of texture. In E.C. Carterette & M.P. Friedman (eds.), *Handbook of perception: Biology of perceptual systems*. New York, N.Y.: Academic Press.

Taylor, S.E. (1973). *What research says to the teacher: Listening*. Washington, D.C.: National Education Association of the United States.

Telesensory Systems, Inc. (1977). *Optacon training: Teaching guidelines*. Palo Alto, Calif.: Author.

Tennyson, W., Hansen, L., Klaurens, M.K., & Antholz, M.B. (1980). *Career development education: A program approved for teachers and counselors*. Washington, D.C.: National Vocational Guidance Association.

Terzieff, I., Stagg, V., & Ashcroft, S.C. (1982). Increasing reading speed with the Optacon: A pilot study. *Journal of Visual Impairment & Blindness*, **77** (1), pp. 17-22.

Thompson, C. (1950). *Psychoanalysis: Evaluation and development*. New York, N.Y.: Hermitage House.

Thompson, Z.H., & Rainforth, B. (1979). A functional fine motor program for the severely and profoundly retarded. In R. York, & E. Edgar, *Teaching the severely handicapped* (Vol. IV). Seattle, Wash.: American Association for the Education of the Severely/Profoundly Handicapped.

Thomson, J.A. (1983). Cognitive maps and motor programs in visually guided locomotion. *Journal of Experimental Psychology*.

Thurman, D. & Weiss-Kapp, S. (1977). Optacon instruction for the deaf-blind. *Education of the Visually Handicapped*, **9** (2), pp. 47-50.

Tibaudo, L. (1976). *Physical activities for impaired, disabled, and handicapped individuals*. Washington, D.C.: American Alliance for Health, Physical Education and Recreation.

Tillman, M.H. (1967). The performance of blind and sighted children on the Wechsler Intelligence Scale for Children. Study II. *International Journal for the Education for the Blind*, **16,** pp. 65-74.

Tillman, M.H. & Osbourne, R.T. (1969). The performance of blind and sighted children: Interaction effects. *Education of the Visually Handicapped*, **1** (1), pp. 1-4.

Tobin, M.J. (1972). Conservation of substance in the blind and sighted. *British Journal of Education Psychology*, **42** (2), pp. 192-197.

Tooze, D. (1980). *Independence training for visually handicapped children*. Baltimore, Md.: University Park Press.

Torbett, D.S. (1975). A humanistic and futuristic approach to sex education for blind children. *Sex education for the visually handicapped in schools and agencies. . .Selected papers*. New York, N.Y.: American Foundation for the Blind, Inc.

Torrance, E.P. (1962). *Guiding creative talent*. Englewood Cliffs, N.J.: Prentice-Hall.

Torrance, E.P. (1967). Creativity teaching makes a difference. In Gowan, Demos & Torrance, *Creativity and its educational implications*. New York, N.Y.: John Wiley & Sons.

Torrance, E.P. (1977). *Creativity in the classroom*. Washington, D.C.: National Education Association.

Torres, S. (ed.), (1977). *Primer on individualized education programs for handicapped children*. Reston, Va.: Council for Exceptional Children.

Touwen, H.C.L. (1980). The preterm infant in the estrauterine environment: Implications for neurology. *Early Human Development*, **4**, pp. 287-300.

Towner, A.G. (1984). Modifying attitudes toward the handicapped: A review of the literature and methodology. In R.J. Jones (ed.), *Attitudes and attitude change in special education: Theory and practice* (pp. 223-257). Reston, Va.: Council for Exceptional Children.

Tucker, J.A. (1976). *Nontest-based assessment*. Minn.: University of Minnesota National School Psychology Inservice Training Network.

Turnbill, A. (1983). Parent professional interactions. In M. Snell (ed.), *Systematic instruction of the moderately and severely handicapped*. Columbus, Ohio: Charles E. Merrill Publishing Co.

Turnbull, H.R., Turnbull, A.P., & Wheat. (1982). Assumptions about parental participation: A legislative history. *Exceptional Education Quarterly*, **3**, pp. 1-8.

Tuttle, D.W. (1981). Academics are not enough: Techniques of daily living for visually impaired children. *Handbook for teachers of the visually handicapped*. Louisville, Ky.: American Printing House for the Blind.

Tuttle, D.W. (1984). *Self-esteem and adjusting with blindness*. Springfield, Ill.: Charles C Thomas.

Ulrey, G. (1982). Assessment considerations with language impaired children. In G. Ulrey & S.J. Rogers (eds.), *Psychological assessment of handicapped infants and young children* (pp. 123-134). New York, N.Y.: Thieme-Stratton.

Umansky, W. (1983). On families and the revaluing of childhood: A position paper developed for the Association for Childhood Education International, Washington, D.C.

Umsted, R. (1972). Improving braille reading. *The New Outlook for the Blind*, **66** (6), pp. 169-178.

United States Department of Commerce, (1983). *World Population*. Washington, D.C.: United States Department of Commerce: Bureau of the Census.

United States Office of Education. (1975). Programs for education of the handicapped. *Federal Register*, **40** (35).

United States Department of Education. (1983). *Fifth annual report to congress on the implementation of Public Law 94-142: The education for all handicapped children act*. Washington, D.C.: Author.

United States Department of Education, (1984). *Sixth annual report to Congress on the implementation of Public Law 94-142: The education for all handicapped children act*. Washington, D.C.: Author.

United States Department of Health and Human Services, (1981). *National study of the incidence and severity of child abuse and neglect:* Executive Summary. DHHS Pub. No. 81-30329. Washington, D.C.: Author.

Uslan, M.M., Hill, E.W., & Peck, F.A. (in preparation). The identification of preservice O&M competencies.

Uslan, M.M., Peck, F.A., & Kirchner, C. (1981). Demand for orientation and mobility specialist in 1980. *Journal of Visual Impairment & Blindness*, **75** (1), pp. 8-12.

Uzgiris, I. & Hunt, J. McV. (1975). *Assessment in infancy: Ordinal scales of psychological development*. Urbana, Ill.: University of Illinois Press.

Vail, P.L. (1979). *The world of the gifted child*. New York, N.Y.: Random House.

Valvo, A. (1971). *Sight restoration after long-term blindness: The problems and behavior patterns of visual rehabilitation*. New York, N.Y.: American Foundation for the Blind, Inc.

Van Dijk, J. (1965). *The first steps of the deaf/blind child towards language. Proceedings of the conference on the deaf/blind*. Boston, Mass.: Perkins School for the Blind.

Van Etten, G., Arkell, C., & Van Etten, C. (1980). *The severely and profoundly handicapped*. St. Louis, Mo.: The C.V. Mosby Company.

Van Hasselt, V.R., Hersen, M., Kazdin, A.E., Simon, J., & Mastantuono, A.K., (1983). Training blind adolescents in social skills. *Journal of Visual Impairment & Blindness*, **77** (5), pp. 199-203.

van'T Hooft, F. & Heslinga, K. (1975). Sex education of blind children. *Sex education for the visually handicapped in schools and agencies. . .Selected papers*. New york, N.Y.: American Foundation for the Blind, Inc.

Vaughan, D. & Asbury, T. (1980). *General ophthamology*. (9th ed.) Los Altos, Calif.: Lange Medical Publications.

Von Fieandt, K. (1959). Form perception and modeling of patients without sight. *Confina Psychiatrica*, **2**, pp. 205-213.

Vondrack, F.W. & Lerner, R.M. Vocational role development in adolescence. In B.B. Wolman & G. Stricker, *Handbook of developmental psychology* (pp. 602-616). Englewood Cliffs, N.J.: Prentice-Hall.

Wait, W.B. (1871). *Proceedings of the second convention of American Instructors of the Blind*. Indianapolis, Ind.: Indianapolis Printing and Publishing House.

Waldinger, R. (1982). The occupational and economic integration of the new immigrants. *Law and contemporary Problems*, **45** (2), pp. 197-222.

Walk, R.D. & Pick, H.L., Jr. (1981). *Intersensory perception and sensory integration*. New York, N.Y.: Plenum Press.

Walker, J.E. & Shea, T.M. (1976). *Behavior modification: A practical approach for educators*. St. Louis, Mo.: The C.V. Mosby Company.

Wallace, D. (1973). The effect of rapid reading instruction and recognition training on the reading rate and comprehension of adult legally blind print and braille readers. Unpublished doctoral dissertation, Brigham Young University.

Wallace, G. & Larsen, S.C. (1978). *Educational assessment of learning problems: Testing for teaching*. Boston, Mass.: Allyn and Bacon, Inc.

Wardell, K.T. (1976a). Assessment of blind students' conceptual understanding. *The New Outlook for the Blind*, **76** (10), pp. 445-446.

Wardell, K.T. (1976b). Parental assistance in orientation and mobility instruction. *The New Outook for the Blind*, **70** (8), pp. 321-324.

Ware, (1981). Shattered pre-birth dreams and the parental impact of the socio-emotional development of the infant. *Proceedings of the International Symposium of Visually Handicapped Infants and Young People* (pp. 43-52). Watertown, Mass.: Perkins School for the Blind.

Warren, D.H. (1982). The development of haptic perception. In W. Schiff & E. Foulke (eds.), *Tactual perception: A sourcebook*. New York, N.Y.: Cambridge University Press.

Warren, D.H. (1984). *Blindness and early childhood development*. Revised (2nd ed.). New York, N.Y.: American Foundation for the Blind, Inc.

Watkins, K. (1981). A creative dramatics project at the Georgia Academy for the Blind. *Journal of Visual Impairment & Blindness*, **75** (7), pp. 277-280.

Watts, W.A. (1984). Attitude change: Theories and methods. In R.L. Jones (ed.), *Attitudes and attitude change in special education: Theory and practice* (pp. 41-69). Reston, Va.: Council for Exceptional Children.

Webb, L. (n.d.). Cultural pluralism: Curriculum assessment, development, implementation and evaluation. In C.D. Moody & C.B. Vergon (ed.), *Approaches for achieving a multicultural curriculum*. Ann Arbor, Mich.: Program for Educational Opportunity, The University of Michigan.

Webster's New World Dictionary. Second college edition. (1982). New York, N.Y.: Simon and Schuster.

Webster, R. (1976). A concept development program for future mobility training. *The New Outlook for the Blind*, **70** (5), pp. 195-197.

Wechsler, D. (1949). *The Wechsler Intelligence Scale for children*. New York, N.Y.: Psychological Corporation.

Weffer, R. (1981). Factors to be considered when assessing bilingual Hispanic children. In H. Martinez, (ed.), (1981). *Special education and the Hispanic child. ERIC/CUE Urban Diversity Series No. 74*. New York, N.Y.: Teachers College, Columbia University, pp. 19-29.

Wegner, E. (1977). Drama: Key to history for the visually impaired child. *Education of the Visually Handicapped*, **9** (2), pp. 45-47.

Wehrum, M.E. (1977). *Techniques of daily living: A curriculum guide*. Bridgeville, Pa.: The Greater Pittsburgh Guild for the Blind.

Weiner, W.R. (1980). Audition. In R.L. Welsh & B.B. Blasch (eds.), *Foundations of orientation and mobility*. New York, N.Y.: American Foundation for the Blind, Inc.

Weiner, W. & Vopata, A. (1980). Suggested curriculum for distance vision training with optical aids. *Journal of Visual Impairment & Blindness*, **74** (2), pp. 49-56.

Weisfeld. (1982). The nature-nurture issues and the integrating concept of function. In B.B.Wolman & G. Stricker (eds.), *Handbook of developmental psychology*. Englewood Cliffs, N.J.: Prentice-Hall.

Weisgerber, R.A. & Hall, A. (1975). *Environmental sensing skills and behaviors*. Palo Alto, Calif.: American Institute for Research.

Welsh, R.L. & Blasch, B.B. (eds.). (1980). *Foundations of orientation and mobility*. New York, N.Y.: American Foundation for the Blind, Inc.

Welsh, R.L. (1982). *The residential school for the blind as a specialized method of service delivery*. American Association of Workers for the Blind, International Conference, Orlando, Fla.

Wessell, J.A. (1976). *I CAN implementation guide*. Northbrook, Ill.: Hubbard Scientific Company.

Wessell, J.A. (1976). *Final report*. ERIC No. ED 121 039 EC 082 717. Arlington, Va.: ERIC.

Westinghouse Learning Corporation—Ohio University. (1969). *The impact of Head Start on children's cognitive and affective development.* Ohio: Author.

White, B.L. (1975). *The first three years of life.* Englewood Cliffs, N.J.: Prentice-Hall.

White, K.R., Mastropieri, M. & Castro, G. (1984). An analysis of special education early childhood projects approved by Joint Dissemination Review Panel. *Journal of the Division for Early Childhood,* 9 (1), pp. 11-26.

Whitehurst, G.J. (1982). Language development. In B.B. Wolman & G. Stricker (eds.), *Handbook of developmental psychology.* Englewood Cliffs, N.J.: Prentice-Hall.

Whitstock, R.H. (1980). Dog guides. In R.L. Welsh & B.B. Blasch (eds.), *Foundations of orientation and mobility.* New York, N.Y.: American Foundation for the Blind, Inc.

Wiggins, E.S. (1873). *Proceedings of the first meeting of the American Association of Instructors of the Blind.* Boston, Mass.: Rand, Avery & Co.

Wilhelm, J. (1980). *Presentation and demonstration of the Kurzweil Reading Machine.* Boston, Mass.: AEUH/Helen Keller Conference.

Wilkinson, L.C. & Saywitz, K. (1982). Theoretical bases of language and communcation development in preschool children. In M. Lewis & L.T. Taft (eds.), *Developmental disabilities: Theory, assessment and intervention.*

Williams, W., Hamre-Nietupski, S., Pumpian, I., McDaniel-Marx, J., & Wheeler, J. (1978). Teaching social skills. In M. Snell (ed.), *Systematic instruction of the moderately and severely handicapped.* Columbus, Ohio: Charles E. Merrill Publishing Company.

Williams, W.W. (1975). Procedures of task analysis as related to developing instructional programs for the severly handicapped. In L. Brown, T. Crowner, W. Williams, & R. York (eds.), *Madison's alternative to zero exclusion: A book of readings.* Madison, Wis.: Madison Public Schools.

Williams, J.D. (ed.). (1983). *The state of Black Americans: 1983.* New York, N.Y.: National Urban League, Inc.

Willis, D.H. (1979). Relationship between visual acuity, reading mode, and school systems for blind chidlren: A 1979 replication (unpublished paper). Louisville, Ky.: American Printing House, 4, 28.

Willis, D.H. (1979). Relationship between visual acuity, reading mode and school systems for blind students. *Exceptional Children,* 46 (3), pp. 186-191.

Wilson, B. (1968). Religion and the churches in contemporary America. In W.G. McLoughlin & R.N. Bellah (eds.), *Religion in America* (pp. 73-110). Boston, Mass.: Houghton Mifflin Co.

Wilson, J.D., McVeigh, V.M., McMahon, J.F., Bauer, A.M., & Richardson, P.C. (1976). Early intervention: The right to sight. *Education of the Visually Handicapped,* 8 (3), pp. 91-93.

Winkley, W.M. (1971). The geographically deprived. *The New Outlook for the Blind,* 65 (1), pp. 21-24.

Winnick, J.P. (1984). The performance of visually impaired youngsters in physical education activities: Implications for mainstreaming. Mainstreaming: Theory into Practice, Motor Skills Monograph 4 (in press).

Wisland, M.V. (1974). Criterion of selecting tests. In M.V. Wisland, *Psychoeducational diagnosis of exceptional children.* Springfield, Ill.: Charles C Thomas.

Witkin, H.A., Birnaum, J., Lomonaco, S., Lehr, S., & Herman, J.L. (1968). Cognitive patterning in congenitally totally blind children. *Child Development,* 39 (3), pp. 767-786.

Witkin, H.A., Oltman, P.K., Chase, J.B., & Friedman, F. (1971). Cognitive patterning in the blind. In J. Helmuth (ed.), *Cognitive studies—Deficits in cognition.* New York, N.Y.: Brunner-Mazel.

Wixon, K.K. & Peters, C.W. (1983). Reading redefined: A Michigan reading association position paper.

Wood, P. (1980). Cost of services. In C. Garland, N. Stone, J. Swanson, & G. Woodruff (eds.), *Early intervention for children with special needs and their families: Findings and recommendations.* Arlington, Va.: Interact.

Worchel, P. (1951). Space perception and orientation in the blind. *Psychological Monographs,* 65, pp. 1-28.

World Almanac and Book of Facts. (1983). New York, N.Y.: The New York World Telegraph.

Wright, B.A. (1969). *The self-concept.* Lincoln, Nebr.: Unversity of Nebraska Press.

Wuerch, B.B. & Voeltz, L.M. (1982). *Longitudinal leisure skills for severely handicapped learners.* Baltimore, Md.: Paul H. Brooks Publishing Co.

Yao, E.L. (1983). A training program in Asian-American culture for elementary school teachers. *Contemporary Education,* 54 (2), pp. 86-93.

Yarnell, G. & Dodgion-Ensir, B. (1980). Identifying effective reinforcers for a multiply handicapped student. *Education of the Visually Handicapped,* 12 (1), pp. 11-20.

Yeadon, A. (1974). *Toward independence: The use of instructional objectives in teaching daily living skills to the blind.* New York, N.Y.: American Foundation for the Blind, Inc.

Yeadon, A. & Newman, L. (1980). *Housekeeping skills: Self-study course.* New York, N.Y.: Center for Independent Living.

Ysseldyke, J.E. & Salvia, J. (1974). Diagnostic-prescriptive teaching: Two models. *Exceptional Children,* 41 (3), pp. 181-185.

Ysseldyke, J.E. (1979). Issues in psychoeducational assessment. In G. Phye & D.J. Reschly (eds.), *School psychology: Perspectives and issues* (pp. 87-121). New York, N.Y.: Academic Press.

Ysseldyke, J.E., Regan, R., Thurlow, M., & Schwartz, S. (1981). Current assessment practices: The "cattle dip" approach. *Diagnostique,* 6, pp. 16-27.

ABOUT THE AUTHORS

Natalie C. Barraga, Ed.D., is professor emerita at the Program for Visually Handicapped, Department of Special Education, The University of Texas at Austin. She is the author of *Increased Visual Behavior in Low Vision Children, Visual Handicaps and Learning,* and numerous articles and book chapters.

Anne L. Corn, Ed.D., is associate professor and coordinator of Programs in the Education of the Visually Handicapped, Department of Special Education, The University of Texas at Austin. She is co-author of *When You Have a Visually Handicapped Child in Your Classroom: Suggestions for Teachers* and numerous articles and book chapters.

Diane H. Craft, Ph.D., is associate professor and coordinator of special physical education in the Department of Physical Education, State University of New York at Cortland. She has written several articles on physical education and the handicapped.

Linda De Lucchi, M.A., is science curriculum developer at Lawrence Hall of Science, University of California at Berkeley. She is the author of numerous articles and book chapters on science education and the visually handicapped.

Kay Alicyn Ferrell, Ph.D., is national consultant on early childhood at the American Foundation for the Blind. She is the author of *Parenting Preschoolers* and *Reach Out & Teach: Materials for Parents of Visually Handicapped and Multihandicapped Young Children.*

Amanda Hall, Ph.D., is research specialist and low vision services coordinator at the Center for the Study of Visual Impairment, School of Optometry, University of California at Berkeley. She is currently working on the development of assessment scales for visually handicapped children from birth to two years.

Jack Hazekamp, M.Ed., is special education consultant at the California Department of Education and has most recently been responsible for the development of *Guidelines for Programs Serving Visually Impaired Students.* He has been a regular classroom teacher, a teacher of the visually impaired, an orientation and mobility specialist, an administrator, a lecturer at several universities, and a consulting editor for *Education of the Visually Handicapped.*

Toni Heinze, Ed.D., is associate professor of special education at The Northern Illinois University at Dekalb. She has worked with visually handicapped and multihandicapped children as teacher, psychologist, mobility specialist, and is presently a teacher trainer.

Everett W. Hill, Ed.D., is assistant professor of special education at George Peabody College for Teachers at Vanderbilt University. He has taught orientation and mobility to both blind children and adults, was co-author

of *Orientation and Mobility: A Guide for the Practitioner,* and has written a number of articles on concept development of visually handicapped children.

Kathleen Mary Huebner, Ph.D., is national consultant in education at the American Foundation for the Blind. She has taught visually handicapped children in residential and itinerant programs and directed a teacher preparation program at the State University of New York at Geneseo.

Berthold Lowenfeld was superintendent of the California School for the Blind. A pioneering educator, author and advocate for blind and visually impaired children, his books include *Our Blind Children, The Changing Status of the Blind, The Visually Handicapped Child in School,* and *Berthold Lowenfeld on Blindness and Blind People* which is a selection from 40 years of published works, journal articles, and commission reports.

Larry Malone, M.A., is curriculum and training specialist at the Center for Multisensory Learning at the Lawrence Hall of Science, University of California, Berkeley, designing and conducting teacher training courses and computer training classes. He is author and co-author of numerous articles and chapters in books related to science education and the visually handicapped.

June E. Morris, M.A., is director of educational research at the American Printing House for the Blind in which she plays an active role in the ongoing research program addressing symbology, design, and use of tactile graphics.

Myrna Olson, Ed.D., is professor of special education at The University of North Dakota. She is the author of *Guidelines and Games for Teaching Efficient Braille Reading* and several articles and book chapters on blindness.

Ferne K. Roberts, M.S., is coordinator of proposal writing activities at the American Foundation for the Blind. She is a former teacher of visually handicapped pupils, education consultant at the American Foundation for the Blind, and associate professor of special education at Hunter College where she coordinated the teacher preparation program in the area of the visually handicapped.

Pete Rossi, M.A., is supervisor of the George F. Meyer Textbook and Materials Center at the New Jersey Commission for the Blind and Visually Impaired. He is dually certified as a teacher of mathematics on the secondary level and teacher of the visually impaired. He is a former itinerant instructor and has co-authored several publications.

Geraldine T. Scholl, Ph.D., is professor of education in the special education program, School of Education at The University of Michigan and secretary of the board of trustees of the American Foundation for the Blind. She has authored several books including *Measures of Psychological, Vocational, and Educational Functioning in the Blind and*

Visually Handicapped and *The School Psychologist and the Exceptional Child,* and a number of articles in educational journals.

Rona A. Shaw, Ed.D., is associate professor and coordinator of the training program for teachers of the visually impaired at Dominican College in Rockland County of New York and formerly held a similar position at Temple University.

Rosanne K. Silberman, Ed.D., is associate professor of special education at Hunter College and coordinator of the teacher preparation program in the areas of visually handicapped and the severely/ multiply handicapped. She is executive editor of *Education of the Visually Handicapped.*

Frank Simpson, M.Ed., is national consultant on employment at the American Foundation for the Blind where he provides consultation on employment especially in the area of transition from school to work and career development planning.

Susan Jay Spungin, Ed.D., is associate executive director of program services at the American Foundation for the Blind. She is a former itinerant teacher of the visually handicapped. Her publications include *Competency-Based Curriculum for Teachers of the Visually Handicapped* and *Guidelines for Public School Programs Serving Visually Handicapped Children.*

Rose-Marie Swallow, Ed.D., is professor and coordinator of the teacher education program in the visually impaired at California State University, Los Angeles and a former teacher of visually handicapped students. She was co-author of *Informal Assessment of Developmental Skills for Visually Handicapped Students* and several articles related to assessment and teaching strategies, instructional programming, and preschool education.

Julia Holton Todd, M.A., is coordinator of the Ohio Resource Center for Low Incidence and Severely Handicapped, and a former teacher of the mentally retarded and curriculum consultant. She has a long standing interest in technology and the handicapped. She is the author of *The Visually Impaired Student in the Regular Classroom—A Resource Book* and several publications related to instructional materials.

Josephine L. Taylor, D.Sc.Ed., was formerly chief, Special Education Branch, Division of Personnel Preparation of the Bureau of Education for the Handicapped, U.S. Department of Education. She is the recipient of numerous professional awards including the Migel Award and the Mary K. Bauman Award.

Dean W. Tuttle, Ph.D., is professor of special education at the University of Northern Colorado. He is the author of *Self-esteem and Adjusting with Blindness* and has written numerous articles on the education of the visually handicapped.

Marjorie E. Ward, Ph.D., is associate professor at the Department of Human Services Education at The Ohio State University where she coordinates the graduate program for teachers of visually handicapped children. She has had experience working as an itinerant teacher of low vision and blind children and is co-author of *Educating Special Learners.*

INDEX

Education of the Visually Handicapped: A Selective Timeline

by Geraldine T. Scholl, Mary Ellen Mulholland, Alberta Lonergan (continued from inside front cover)

GENERAL | LEGISLATION | PROFESSIONALISM

1935 to 1950

GENERAL

1935 Social Security Act adopts AMA definition of blindness.
1939-1945 World War II.
1940 National Federation of the Blind (NFB) founded.
1941 Growing incidence of retrolental fibroplasia (RLF) noted in infants.
1942 First computer.
1942 Magnetic tape recording.
1942 RLF identified.
1944 Hoover and others develop long-cane mobility techniques at Valley Forge Army Hospital.
1947 Transistor.

LEGISLATION

1937 PL 75-37 provides special postage rates for the blind.
1943 PL 78-113 (The Barden-LaFollette Vocational Rehabilitation Act Amendments of 1943) increases services for the blind.
1949 PL 81-290 permits braillewriters to be mailed at base rate.

PROFESSIONALISM

1935 Columbia University starts year-round program for teachers of the blind at Teachers College.
1938 AAIB sets up teacher certification program.
1943 Hathaway publishes first text for teachers of partially seeing.
1948 Council for Education of the Partially Seeing established.

1951 to 1985

GENERAL

1953 Study links RLF to high oxygen treatment of premature infants.
1957 U.S.S.R. launches first satellites, Sputnik I and II.
1961 American Council of the Blind (ACB) founded.
1961-1977 U.S. involvement in Vietnam.
1962 First U.S. manned spaceflight.
1963 First "Freedom March" on Washington.
1963 John F. Kennedy assassinated.
1963 *The Feminine Mystique* published.
1963 Rubella (German measles) epidemic in pregnant women causes deafness and blindness in babies.
1964 President Johnson launches "The Great Society" human services legislative initiative.
1968 Martin Luther King, Jr. assassinated.
1968 Robert F. Kennedy assassinated.
1968 Helen Keller dies.
1968 National Eye Institute established.
1969 Armstrong first man to walk on moon.
1975 First microcomputer.
1979 American Council for Blind Parents formed by ACB.
1980 National Association of Parents of the Visually Impaired (NAPVI) established.
1984 NFB creates Division of Parents of Blind Children.

LEGISLATION

1952 Pratt-Smoot Act extended to children's books.
1958 PL 85-926 provides funding for personnel preparation in mental retardation.
1961 PL 87-294 authorizes wider distribution of books, instructional materials for blind.
1963 PL 88-164 extends funding for personnel preparation to all handicapped categories.
1963 Rehabilitation Act amendments include recreation.
1964 PL 88-164 Title XI allows universities to create departments for teachers of exceptional children.
1965 PL 89-313 amends Elementary and Secondary Education Act to provide support for education of handicapped in state schools, hospitals.
1966 PL 89-750 requires states to detail needs, priorities and creates bureau to administer federal agencies involved in handicapped education.
1966 PL 89-522 expands talking book services to physically handicapped.
1967 PL 90-170 establishes Bureau of Education for Handicapped, authorizes funds for physical education, recreation.
1968 PL 90-480 mandates elimination of architectural barriers.
1972 PL 92-316 provides free or reduced-rate transportation for attendants for the blind.
1973 PL 93-112 (Rehabilitation Act of 1973) changes law from provision for vocational rehabilitation only to comprehensive rehabilitation, and introduces special projects in recreation. Section 504 prohibits discrimination in programs receiving federal funds.
1974 PL 93-380 (Educational Amendments of 1974) grants handicapped additional rights in public education, physical education, recreation.
1975 PL 94-142 (The Education for All Handicapped Children Act) guarantees free and appropriate public education with special education, related services and individualized education program for each handicapped child.
1976 Vocational education legislation expanded to include handicapped.
1978 PL 95-602 (Rehabilitation Act of 1978) authorizes funds to integrate handicapped into recreation programs and provide rehabilitation for severely handicapped for whom employment may not be primary goal.

PROFESSIONALISM

1951 World Council for the Welfare of the Blind incorporated.
1951 First issue of the *International Journal for the Education of the Blind* published (now *Education of the Visually Handicapped*).
1953 Carroll mounts Gloucester Conference to define mobility instructor's role, training.
1953 U.S. Office of Education issues competency studies for teachers of blind, partially seeing.
1955 Perkins starts first training program for teachers of deaf-blind.
1957 Peabody College for Teachers sets up year-round program for teachers of the blind.
1960 Boston College starts first university program for O&M instructors.
1961 Carroll publishes blindness study.
1966 CEC Project on Professional Standards uses "visually handicapped" to include both blind and partially sighted.
1966 COMSTAC report published.
1967 San Francisco State University, Florida State University, establish first programs to train mobility instructors of children.
1967 National Accreditation Council for Agencies Serving the Blind and Visually Handicapped (NAC) founded.
1968 AAIB becomes Association for Education of the Visually Handicapped (AEVH).
1969 Scott publishes *The Making of Blind Men*.
1973 Lowenfeld publishes *The Visually Handicapped Child in School*.
1977 Spungin publishes competency study.
1978 NSPB changes name to National Society to Prevent Blindness.
1980 Helen Keller Centennial Congress held.
1984 AAWB and AEVH merge to become Association for Education and Rehabilitation of Blind and Visually Impaired (AER).
1985 World Council for the Welfare of the Blind and International Federation of the Blind merge as World Blind Union.

EDUCATIONAL PROGRAMS

1784 Valentin Haüy establishes *Institution des Jeunes Aveugles* (Institution for Blind Youth); the first school for blind children, in Paris.
1791 First school for the blind in England opens in Liverpool.
1829 New England Asylum for the Blind (Perkins) incorporated.
1831 New York Institution for the Blind incorporated.
1832 First students accepted at New England Asylum for the Blind and New York Institution for the Blind.
1833 Pennsylvania Institution for the Instruction of the Blind opens.
1837 Ohio establishes first state residential school.
1837 Laura Bridgman, first deaf-blind child to be educated, admitted to Perkins.

1866 Howe, first Perkins director, expresses concern about segregated education in residential schools.
1872 *On the Blind Walking Alone and of Guides* published.
1880 Helen Keller born in Tuscumbia, Alabama.
1880 Anne Sullivan enters Perkins.
1882 Pennsylvania Institution starts organized kindergarten.
1887 Perkins founds kindergarten for blind babies.
1887 Anne Sullivan begins teaching Helen Keller.
1893 First nursery for neglected blind babies started in Hartford, Connecticut.
1898 First day-school for the blind established in England.

1900 Day school classes established in Chicago.
1904 Helen Keller first deaf-blind person to get college degree.
1909 Irwin organizes braille reading classes in Cleveland public schools.
1909 Ohio appoints first state supervisor of education for visually impaired children.
1910 Arthur Sunshine Home and Kindergarten for Blind Babies opens.
1911 New York State makes education compulsory for the blind.
1913 Boston and Cleveland start classes for partially seeing pupils.
1914 Guyton becomes first blind man in U.S. to hold full professorship in college for sighted students.
1916 Hayes establishes departments of psychological research at Overbrook and Perkins.
1929 The Seeing Eye, first dog guide school in U.S., incorporated.
1930 Hayes-Binet test for blind children developed.
1930 Cutsforth's *The Blind In School and Society* published.

COMMUNICATIONS

1784-1800 Haüy uses raised Roman letters to teach blind students.
1808 Barbier invents *Ecriture Nocturne* (night writing) for use by French soldiers at night.
1829 Louis Braille publishes explanation of his embossed dot code, inspired by Barbier.
1833 Howe publishes first book in "Boston Line" type.
1834 Braille perfects literary braille code.
1836 Taylor devises tangible mathematics apparatus.
1837 Perkins establishes printing plant, later named Howe Memorial Press.
1839 Electrotyping process, for making duplicate plates for relief printing, invented.
1847 Moon Type.

1852 "Boston Line" type accepted form of raised type.
1855 Kentucky sets up printing house for the blind.
1858 Kentucky printing house incorporated as American Printing House for the Blind (APH).
1860 Missouri School for the Blind first institution to use braille in U.S.
1868 New York Point raised type developed at New York Institution for the Blind by Wait.
1871 Stereotype plates for braille production.
1871 First pamphlet on braille music notation published.
1871 AAIB endorses New York Point.
1878 Smith at Perkins develops American raised point system modeled closely on braille, foundation for American braille.
1887 Anne Sullivan gives understanding of language to Helen Keller, aged 7, deaf blind.
1888 International Congress for standardization of braille music notation held at Cologne.
1889 de la Sizaranne founds first major library of braille books at Valentin Haüy Institute, Paris.
1892 Hall and Sieber develop Braillewriter, first mechanical device for writing braille.
1899 Braille shorthand system.

1902 Library and reading room for the blind opens in San Francisco.
1907 Helen Keller, who had to learn four embossed codes, pleads for single code.
1910 Alcorn develops "Tadoma Method" of teaching deaf-blind children.
1912 Optophone translates printed letters to musical tones.
1913 Irwin uses 36 point type in books for partially seeing pupils.
1916 Braille officially adopted in U.S. schools.
1917 The "War of the Dots" ends. Braille code accepted as the universal American standard for the written word.
1918 APH adopts Revised Standard English Braille grade 1½ for textbooks.
1918 Percy invents system of communication with deaf-blind by Morse Code and small hammers which tap fingers of person addressed.
1920 Barr, Stroud and Fournier d'Albe patent first reading machine for the blind, the Optophone.
1923 APH expands tangible apparatus facilities.
1930 Ophthalmologists suggest vision not harmed by use.
1930 National Institute for the Blind introduces high speed rotary press for embossed type.
1931 Library of Congress begins to distribute braille materials and phonograph records to blind readers, in accordance with Pratt-Smoot Act of 1930.
1932 AFB starts development of talking book, a long playing record, and playback machines.
1932 Standard English braille adopted by American and British committees as uniform type.
1933 APH adopts Standard English Braille Grade 2 for junior and senior high school textbooks.

FOUNDATIONS OF EDUCATION for Blind and Visually Handicapped Children and Youth:

THEORY AND PRACTICE

GERALDINE T. SCHOLL
Editor

AMERICAN FOUNDATION FOR THE BLIND, INC.
NEW YORK 1986

FOUNDATIONS OF EDUCATION FOR BLIND
AND VISUALLY HANDICAPPED CHILDREN AND YOUTH: Theory and Practice
copyright © 1986

American Foundation for the Blind, Inc.
15 West 16th St.
New York, N.Y. 10011

Library of Congress Cataloging-in-Publication Data
Main entry under title:

Foundations of education for blind and visually
    handicapped children and youth.

    Includes bibliographies and index.
    1. Blind--Education--Addresses, essays, lectures.
2. Children, Blind--Education--Addresses, essays,
lectures. 3. Visually handicapped--Education--Addresses,
essays, lectures. 4. Visually handicapped children--
Education--Addresses, essays, lectures. I. Scholl,
Geraldine T. II. American Foundation for the Blind.
HV1626.F67 1986   371.91'1   85-31794
ISBN 0-89128-124-X

Graphic Design/Illustration: Mary Williams
Typography: Sauna Trenkle

Printed in the United States of America

Credits:
AFB—Figures 3.10, 19.10, Tables 8.1, 19.2, Appendix A; APH—Chart 21.1; Archives of American Academy of Ophthalmology—Chart 5.1; Aspen Systems Corporation, Germantown, Md.— Table 7.2; Burgess Publishing Co.—Chart 21.5; Council for Exceptional Children—Appendix G; C.V. Mosby—Figure 3.3; Charles E. Merrill—Figure 9.6; Education Service Center, Region XIII—Table 19.6; *Exceptional Children*—Figures 10.2; Table 19.4; Exceptional Resources, Austin, Texas—Chart 5.2; Foundation for Exceptional Children—Figure 12.4; Grune & Stratton, New York—Figures 9.2, 9.4, 9.5; Harcourt Brace Jovanovich—Appendix B; Holt, Rinehart & Winston—Figure 12.8; Macmillan & Co.—Table 21.1; Medmaster, Florida—Figures 3.1, 3.6; Table 3.1; National Council of Teachers of Mathematics—Figure 12.9; National Society to Prevent Blindness—Figure 3.11; Tables 3.2, 3.3, 3.4, 3.5; Ohio Department of Education, Division of Special Education—Figure 12.5; Paul H. Brookes—Figure 9.1; Pennsylvania Department of Education, Bureau of Special Education—Figure 12.3; Reichart Scientific Instruments—Figure 3.2; Lawrence Hall of Science—Appendix H; *Sight-Saving Review* (SSR)—Figure 3.5; Stoelting Company, Chicago, Ill.—Table 19.6; University of Michigan Press—Figures 4.1, 4.2; Wadsworth—Figure 12.6; Willis, D.H.—Tables 3.5, 3.6;

PHOTO CREDITS
AFB—pp. 2,3,5,6,7,9,16; APH—p. 369; Jane Evelyn Atwood, Perkins School for the Blind—p. 401; Jack Bensel, Maryland School for the Blind—pp. 27, 75, 141, 146, 152, 242, 258, 266, 276, 289, 313, 376, 399, 402; Robert Campbell—pp. 24, 155, 157; Janet Charles—pp. 26, 74, 78, 84, 90, 91, 120, 128, 133, 167, 173, 283, 344, 345; Paul Cockerham—p. 289; Joseph Cocozza & Robert Turner of Elwyn Institutes—pp. 233, 217; Columbus Children's Hospital—p. 272; Crissy Cowan—pp. 101, 105, 106; Sally DiMartini—pp. 24, 26, 79, 105, 226, 240, 245, 271, 310, 345, 346, 348; Greg Dorata—pp. 112, 114; Suzie Fitzhugh, Maryland School for the Blind—p. 121; Andrea Helms—348, 355; Steven Mallett—pp. 316, 318, 331, 332, 333, 335; Carol Morton—p. 27; Neldine Nichols, Wisconsin Department of Public Instruction—pp. 73, 141, 304, 380; National Council of Teachers of Mathematics (NCTM)—p. 139; New Mexico School for the Visually Handicapped—pp. 140, 156, 161, 172, 174, 180, 262, 279, 347, 370, 392, 393, 394; Nurion Inc.—p. 320; Geraldine T. Scholl—p. 257; Telesensory Systems— p. 291; Meg Theno, Northern Illinois University—p. 287; Visualtek—p. 291; Wormwald International—p. 288.